ALL COLOR
ENCYCLOPEDIA OF
INTERNATIONAL
COOKING

Contributing writers: Joyce Allen, Vo Bacon, Neville Baker, Joan Barbour, Geraldine Dillon, Betty Dunleavy, Mary Dunne, Len Evans, Margaret Fulton, Jill Graham, Gordon Grimsdale, Leone Harrington, Babette Hayes, Rosemary Hemphill, Wendy Hutton, Ted Maloney, Anne Marshall, Jackie Passmore, Michel Ray, Daniel Reid, Patrick Robinson, Lauma Rungis, Betty Sim, Maurice Tattersall, Johnnie Walker, Phyllis Wright.

Contributing photographers and libraries: Bay Books, Michael Cook, Ben Eriksson, Mary Evans Picture Library, Ray Joyce, John Leung Studio, Reg Morrison, Tony Schmaeling, Nik Wheeler, Weldons Trannie Library.

Published in the United States of America by
The Knapp Press
5900 Wilshire Boulevard
Los Angeles, California 90036

Edited, designed and produced by Lansdowne Press
a division of Kevin Weldon & Associates Pty Limited
372 Eastern Valley Way, Willoughby, NSW 2068, Australia
First published 1988

Designer   Susan Kinealy
Managing Editor   Laurine Croasdale
Editor: Patricia Connell

Copyright © **1988** this selection Kevin Weldon & Associates Pty Limited
Copyright © **1988** Design Kevin Weldon & Associates Pty Limited
Typeset in Australia by Savage Type, Brisbane
Printed in Spain by Cronion S.A. Barcelona
Color separations by Rainbow Graphics, Hong Kong

Library of Congress Cataloging-in-Publication Data

The All color encyclopedia of international cooking

Includes index.
1. Cookery, International.
TX725. A1A36   1988   641.5   88-2681
ISBN 0-89535-207-9

ALL COLOR
ENCYCLOPEDIA OF
INTERNATIONAL
COOKING

Each recipe has a flag to denote its country of origin. However, where the origin is not clear, or the recipe has several sources of origin, a star has been placed alongside. The color of the flag is for reference only.

AUSTRALIA	
AUSTRIA	
BELGIUM	
BURMA	
CANADA	
CHINA	
DENMARK	
EGYPT	
FRANCE	
GERMANY	
GREAT BRITAIN	
GREECE	
HUNGARY	
INDIA	
INDONESIA	
IRELAND	
ITALY	
JAPAN	
KOREA	
MALAYSIA	
MEXICO	
NEW ZEALAND	
NORWAY	
PHILIPPINES	
POLAND	
PORTUGAL	
SINGAPORE	
SPAIN	
SWEDEN	
SWITZERLAND	
THAILAND	
U.S.A.	
U.S.S.R.	
VIETNAM	
INTERNATIONAL	★

CONTENTS

THE EVOLUTION OF WESTERN COOKING	7
CUISINES AROUND THE WORLD	16
COOKING TECHNIQUES	36
SNACKS AND APPETIZERS	38
SOUPS	83
SALADS & SIDE DISHES	103
RICE, PASTA & NOODLES	133
SEAFOOD	166
POULTRY	193
GAME	235
MEAT	256
VEGETARIAN	298
DESSERTS	318
CAKES, COOKIES & TEA BREADS	361
GLOSSARY	386
INDEX	393

Marchetti's illustration of chefs at work in a restaurant kitchen in 1893.

The Evolution of Western Cooking

No one knows exactly when the first chefs appeared. Judging by Belshazzar's feast where, according to the Book of Daniel in the Old Testament, over "a thousand of his lords were fed," one can only assume that some kind of "chef" organized and controlled the cooking.

Equally, one of the first cookbooks, *The Learned Banquet* by Athenaeus, published in the third century A.D., was written in the form of two gourmets discussing their favorite recipes. Although nothing explicit is offered it is reasonable to assume that there were chefs in Athens at the time who were interested in advancing the culinary arts.

Similarly, someone had to be responsible for the food at the vast eating orgies in Imperial Rome, and someone had to prepare the huge quarters of beef, mutton and pork, and the spitted carcasses of wild boar, peacock, roebuck and hedgehog which were a feature of the gluttonous feasts of the Middle Ages.

Why do the cooks and chefs at these ancient feasts fail to get accolades from modern-day gourmets? Firstly, because they were all anonymous — such was the status of cooks in Roman and medieval times. Secondly, because the food they served was almost certainly crude, poorly cooked, and eaten in a rather coarse manner by people, at all levels, who wrenched chunks of meat from the spitted carcasses and ate it not on plates or with knives and forks but with their bare hands. The concept of appreciating the subtleties of food or, as the French gourmet and aphorist Brillat-Savarin puts it, "the intelligent knowledge of whatever concerns man's nourishment," is something that doesn't really enter European eating habits until the Renaissance.

Perhaps the best way to understand the crudity of pre-Renaissance cooking is to note the kinds of dishes described by Guillaume Tirel in his cookbook, *Le Viandier*, written in 1375. At the time of its publication *Le Viandier* was regarded as the definitive book on French culinary arts, yet it relied on bread as a sauce thickener, encouraged the excessive use of spices such as ginger, cinnamon, cloves and nutmeg, and described foods so heavily seasoned that the original taste was all but obliterated.

The great turning point in European cooking occurs when the cooks and chefs of Italy and France came to realize that sauces and spices could be used to subtly complement the taste of a meal, rather than to obliterate the questionable flavor of unrefrigerated foodstuffs.

This revelation seems to have occurred in the period from 1450 to 1500, when the Italian city states were at the height of their power and wealth. It is no accident that the first significant cookbook for nearly a thousand years appeared in 1475 when the Vatican librarian, Bartolomeo de Sacchi, wrote *De Honesta Voluptate* (Concerning Honest Pleasure and Well-being). It is also no accident that the main thrust of the book is an attack on the excessive use of spices and the advocacy of lemon juice, wine and orange juice as suitable flavorings. De Sacchi was also an advocate of fresh fruit as a suitable opening to a meal.

A medieval banquet in progress.

By the beginning of the sixteenth century, Italy had become the center of civilized cuisine. The powerful city states, particularly Rome, Florence and Venice, prided themselves on the quality of their cooks and the quality of the food served to the nobility. Florence even opened up an exclusive school of chefs known as the Company of the Cauldron ("Compagnia del Paiolo"), which had only twelve members at any one time.

The fifteenth century had also seen a systematic move in Italy away from the vast meat consumption of medieval banquets. In their stead came such delicacies as pasta in the form of lasagne and ravioli, and mushrooms, garlic and truffles. There was also an emphasis on the manner in which these new delicacies should be eaten. The practice of munching pieces of meat ripped from a carcass and swilling wine from huge carafes was replaced by eating with utensils of great beauty and sophistication. An observer at the wedding of the Duke of Mantua in the sixteenth century noted, "on a hand-

A fanfare by musicians accompanies the presentation and serving of the meal.

In fairness it should be pointed out that during her life Catherine acquired a terrible reputation as a glutton. She is said to have eaten so much at Mademoiselle Martigue's wedding that she thought she was going to burst.

But there is little doubt that Catherine had a profound impact on French cuisine. Her cooks were experts in the arts of Florentine cookery and as such they introduced to France such new delicacies as truffles, macaroons, aspics, sweetbreads, zabagliones, ice cream, artichoke hearts, broccoli, tiny peas now known as petits pois, liver crepinettes and quenelles of poultry. She also did much to change French eating customs. She saw eating as a refined and civilized activity and thus removed the acrobats and jugglers from the court dining room, while introducing women into what had previously been an all-male sanctuary. She was also active in the introduction of exquisite silver and glassware to the banquet table.

A contemporary observer noted: "the court of Catherine de Medici was a veritable earthly paradise and a school for all the chivalry and flower of France."

Thus Catherine can rightly be seen as the true founder of French cuisine — now universally recognized as the best in the world. She introduced simplicity, new ingredients and sophistication to the tables of France.

Of all human activities, eating is the one we are most conservative about. We resist change and long for our favorite dishes cooked in familiar ways. And so it was in France. Catherine de Medici's Florentine cooks did not change the French nobility's eating habits overnight. In fact, it took the best part of a century before the French were prepared to fully accept the changes brought about by Italian cooking styles. By 1570, the French were acknowledging the need for some refinement at the table and were discussing place settings, the use of the fork, and the skills involved in successfully carving meat.

The French surrender to Italian culinary arts came in 1651 when the first of the great French chefs, François Pierre de La Varenne, published his highly influential *Le Cuisine François*. It is no small irony that La Varenne reputedly learned to cook in the kitchens of Catherine de Medici's cousin, Marie de Medici. Marie was married to Henri IV of France and, like her cousin before her, had been active in promoting Italian cooking in France.

With La Varenne the idea of sauces and spices to kill the taste was finally laid to rest. His emphasis was on mushrooms and butter to enhance the taste of a meal, while he recommended natural meat juices, vinegar and lemon as the most appropriate sauces.

During his life La Varenne became massively wealthy and this wealth allowed him to leave the service of Henri IV and move to the household of the Marquis d'Uxelles. It was here that he created some of his most famous dishes, notably the sauce of mushrooms and shallots (which is known variously

some sideboard was visible a perspective of divers cups, carafes and goblets, and such beautiful vessels of Venetian glass as I think would defy description."

Thus it was that the Italian city states, vastly wealthy from their mercantile trade throughout the Mediterranean, developed a cuisine which in its subtlety and variety was far removed from the crude overeating that was still normal throughout the rest of Europe.

It has become known that the spread of Italian cooking throughout Europe began in earnest when the young Duc d'Orléans (he later became Henri II of France) married the Florentine princess Catherine de Medici. When Henri brought his young wife back to France she, knowing the paucity of good cooking in the country, insisted upon being accompanied by a retinue of some fifty Florentine chefs, waiters and household advisers.

as *duxelles* or *champignons à l'Olivier*) and chicken actually cooked in a bottle to be eaten on the battlefield.

La Varenne is widely recognized as the first great chef of France because of his imaginative culinary flair, his excellent literary style, the organization and richness of detail he brought to *Le Cuisine François,* and the way in which he comprehensively dragged French cooking out of the Middle Ages and set standards to which it still aspires today.

Perhaps La Varenne's greatest admirer was the Sun King, Louis XIV, who had come to power in France in 1643 when he was only four years old. As a huge eater and bon vivant, Louis was enamored of food. He employed over 300 people in the kitchen of his palace at Versailles and was known to consume absolutely vast meals. His sister-in-law once observed him eating "four plates of different soups, an entire pheasant, a partridge, a large plateful of salad, mutton cut up in its juice with garlic, two pieces of ham, a plateful of cakes, and fruits and jams" at one sitting.

In spite of Louis' excessive consumption it was during his reign that the groundwork established by La Varenne came to fruition and France became known as the home of haute cuisine.

The man who came to symbolize the fanaticism and commitment involved in the preparation and serving of French haute cuisine was Henri Vatel. In his early twenties Vatel became maître d'hôtel to the French treasurer, Nicholas Fouquet. In such a position Vatel was responsible for a feast in 1661 in Louis XIV's honor. He managed to organize the preparation and service of a meal which involved some 6000 silver dishes, but instead of being impressed Louis was convinced of Fouquet's corruption and had him jailed. Vatel found himself without a job. A decade later Vatel once again prepared a banquet for Louis but so obsessed was he with the organizational niceties of the meal that he convinced himself he had blundered and committed suicide before the meal was served. Today he stands as a symbol to the importance of organization in the preparation of any meal. Anyone who could use 6000 silver dishes during a meal deserves to be remembered as "the best organized head in the world."

Vatel also symbolizes the low esteem the French aristocracy held for their chefs. Although the aristocrats loved to eat the new creations of their chefs, they rarely acknowledged even their existence. This is brought home by the names of French dishes. Often they are named after aristocrats — *les cailles à la Talleyrand, le pigeonneau Villeroi, les filets de sole Richelieu;* they are never named after the chefs who labored to create them.

In spite of Louis XIV's greed the standards of French cooking continued to improve during his reign so that by the early eighteenth century France was known as the home of fine cooking throughout Europe.

Louis XV and Louis XVI continued the traditions which had emerged during the Sun King's reign. They successfully

The illustration used to decorate the cover of Le Patissier François, published in 1655.

fought against the "quantity versus quality" style of cooking which had persisted during Louis XIV's gluttonous reign, and managed to establish customs of throwing out poorly cooked meals and abandoning the excessive use of sauces.

With such culinary traditions persisting in France it is hardly surprising that 1758 saw the birth of the first admirer of great chefs — the gourmet writer and critic. Grimod de la Reynière was by profession a lawyer, by commitment a connoisseur of food. His great, and very legitimate, claim to fame came in 1803 when he wrote the *Almanach des Gourmands* — the first restaurant guide. He was followed by a man now recognized as the greatest of all gourmet writers — Jean Anthelme Brillat-Savarin.

A classic French presentation of soups as shown in Le Cuisinier Moderne published in 1887.

Even though Brillat-Savarin is not a household name today his aphorism about food, "Tell me what you eat, and I shall tell you what you are," has become world famous.

Like Grimod de la Reynière, Brillat-Savarin was a lawyer who devoted his life to an interest in the joys of eating. His single book on food, *La Physiologie du Goût* (1825), is a masterpiece. In it he raises eating to an art form. Published months before his death, the book distilled a lifetime's fascination with food. Not only did Brillat-Savarin observe, but he had a comment for everything he saw. He praised the consumption of wine but warned against the evils of coffee. "It is the duty of all papas and mamas," he declared, "to forbid their children coffee, unless they wish to have little dried-up machines, stunted and old at the age of twenty. This warning is particularly commended to the Parisians, whose children are not always so strong and healthy as if they had been born in other parts of the country."

Savory dishes illustrated from Mrs Beeton's Cook Book.

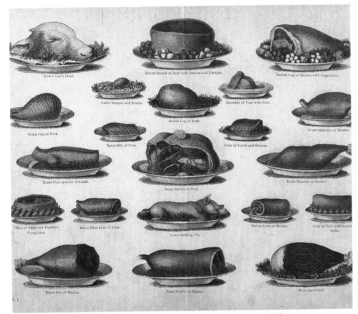

An extract from Mrs Beeton's Cook Book showing prepared meat dishes.

Similarly, he developed a wonderful set of rules for the ideal dinner party. According to Brillat-Savarin the perfect dinner party should have no fewer than twelve people, all of whom have come from different occupational backgrounds but who enjoy similar tastes and interests so that "the odious formalities of introduction can be dispensed with." The dining room should be well-lit and a temperature between 65°F and 68°F should be maintained during the course of the meal. The tablecloth should be "superlatively white." The company should comprise witty men and "women charming but not over prone to flirt." The meal should be organized so there are few dishes, which should be presented slowly and accompanied firstly by "wines of the first quality" followed,

after the meal, by coffees and liqueurs. After the meal the guests should be able to retire to a "withdrawing room large enough to allow a game of cards for those who cannot do without, yet still to leave space for colloquies apart; let the guests be willingly detained by the pleasures of social intercourse and sustained by hope that the evening will not pass without some ulterior joy; let the tea be not too strong, the toast craftily buttered and the punch mixed with all due care; let the retreat begin not earlier than eleven o'clock but by midnight let all be abed."

It was also Brillat-Savarin who recognized the importance of the French Revolution to French cuisine:

The ranks of every profession concerned with the sale or preparation of food, including cooks, caterers, confectioners, pastry cooks, provision merchants and the like, have multiplied in ever-increasing proportions ... New Professions have arisen; that, for example, of the pastry cook — in his domain are biscuits, macaroons, fancy cakes, meringues ... The art of preserving has also become a profession in itself whereby we are enabled to enjoy, at all times of the year, things naturally peculiar to one or other season ... French cookery has annexed dishes of foreign extraction ... A wide variety of vessels, utensils and accessories of every sort has been invented, so that foreigners coming to Paris find many objects on the table the very names of which they know not, nor dare to ask their use.

The Revolution profoundly affected French eating habits. Firstly, as Brillat-Savarin has observed, it created a boom in the culinary arts. Secondly, with the overthrow of the aristocracy, it put thousands of cooks and chefs out of work. And thirdly, the rise of the new bourgeoisie saw the massive introduction of restaurants as popular places for gathering and eating. In 1789 it was estimated that Paris had 100 restaurants; by 1804 this number had increased to somewhere between five and six hundred.

Brillat-Savarin, one of the outstanding chefs in the history of cuisine.

Leave us to our squalid poverty; it is our lot. Die we must as we have lived, penniless. This is the age of quick fortunes. There are splendid opportunities for all who, like thee, have a ready wit.''

Carême's first job was in a restaurant. It was a lucky omen, for he devoted the rest of his life to cooking. By the time he was twelve or thirteen he was apprenticed to the famous Bailly patisserie and it was there that he acquired his love of extravagant design. He wandered Paris soaking up the architecture and then would return to make patisseries which featured classical temples, bridges and rotundas all bound together by dough and spun sugar. In one of his books he went so far as to suggest that ''A pastry-cook of the present day should possess the skill of the architect. The columns that more particularly belong to our style of decoration are the Doric, Ionic and Corinthian.''

A menu from the Splendid Hotel in Châtel-Guyon, France.

The significance of the French Revolution to French cuisine cannot be overemphasized. Brillat-Savarin stands as the chronicler of this extraordinary development and it is impossible now not to recognize that the dishes and the sauces he described in 1825 still form the basis for French cooking today.

The chef who stands like a colossus over nineteenth-century French cuisine was Marie-Antoine Carême. He has rightly been called ''The Architect of French Cooking'' (although there is a pun intended because he had a penchant for converting meals into edifices) and, almost singlehandedly, he was responsible for the French cuisine we know today.

Carême was born in 1784 in Paris. He was the youngest in a family of seventeen. His father was an improverished itinerant stonemason and Carême was ''abandoned'' to seek his fortune when he was either eight or eleven. He reports that his father said to him on their parting, ''Go, go, and fare thee well, my child. The world is large; chances are many.

Carême's rise was meteoric. By the time he was sixteen he was working in the kitchens of the French foreign minister, Charles-Maurice de Talleyrand. Their minds were perfectly attuned. Talleyrand believed in the value of good food to diplomatic negotiation and Carême, while respecting Talleyrand's gastronomic refinement, believed that artful presentation improved the quality of a meal enormously. "A well displayed meal is enhanced one hundred per cent in my eyes," he once wrote.

But Carême was a freelance. After working for Talleyrand he moved on. He worked briefly for Napoleon (he had little time for Napoleon but history has been unable to determine whether this was based on gastronomic considerations or whether it was anger at the fact that fifty of France's greatest chefs had died in 1812 during the retreat from Moscow), then he worked for Tsar Alexander of Russia, George IV of England and finally Baroness Rothschild.

In culinary terms Carême was a renaissance man. Not only was he a master chef and supreme patisserie maker but also he was concerned with the poor conditions chefs and cooks worked in; he philosophized about the role of the chef: "The chef who is a man of routine lacks courage. His life drips away in mediocrity"; he saw architecture as an essential part of food preparation and he wrote some eight books while he continued to work in the great kitchens of Europe.

Carême wrote two important books. *Le Maître d'Hôtel Français* contains a complete menu for every day of the year plus marvelous essays on the vegetables which are available in the various seasons with advice as to how best to use them. His masterpiece is *L'Art de la Cuisine au 19ème Siècle,* which appeared in five volumes, influenced the course of French cooking for the next century, and was as comprehensive as any book on the subject of gastronomy until Prosper Montagné published *Larousse Gastronomique* in 1938.

In spite of Carême's influence the nineteenth century saw a decline in French cooking which was largely brought about by the rise of a middle class with a weakness for stodgy and unimaginative food. It wasn't until the 1890s that the dining tables of France were once again enriched by food prepared with the imagination and art of a Marie-Antoine Carême.

Ironically, as France declined many of its most accomplished cooks emigrated to Britain. It was here that Alexis Soyer, the chef most responsible for popularizing French cooking abroad, spent most of his life.

Soyer was born in Paris in 1809 and trained for four years at the restaurant Chez Grignon. By 1830 he was the second chef at the French Foreign Office but after rebels invaded the kitchens and killed two of the cooks (an enterprising Soyer started singing the Marseillaise during the fighting and was cheered by the rebels) he decided that he'd be safer and happier in England. For seven years he worked for the English aristocracy before being appointed chef at the newly established Reform Club in London.

In 1846 Soyer established a soup kitchen in London's Farringdon Road, and in 1855 he went off to cook for the British Army in the Crimea. He died in 1858 leaving behind not only a wealth of culinary invention but also a series of books which did much to bring French haute cuisine, previously restricted to the wealthy, to the attention of the ordinary person. Among his most famous works were *A Shilling Cookery, Instructions to Military Hospital Cooks* and *The Poor Man's Regenerator*, a spin-off from his major work the *Gastronomic Regenerator*. Soyer did much to demythologize the role of the French chef. He believed that there were no secrets in cooking and actively devoted his life to explaining his recipes to anyone who was interested.

If Soyer was responsible for popularizing French cuisine outside France then it was two men, Georges Auguste Escoffier and César Ritz, who really introduced the concept of French haute cuisine to the fashionable bourgeoisie of England, Europe and America. Escoffier and Ritz made French cuisine the byword of sophisticated living throughout the Western world.

An old advert featuring Liebig's Extract of Beef.

Although Escoffier is equal in importance to Carême and Soyer it is worth remembering that the impetus for his radical rethinking of French cuisine came from Prosper Montagné.

Montagné, while working as a young assistant chef at the Grand Hotel in Monte Carlo, started to question the received wisdom from Carême that architecture and artistry in presentation of food were as important as the cooking of food. It is probable that Montagné's theories would have gone unnoticed had not they been taken up by Escoffier, who was also a chef at the Grand Hotel.

Like the great chefs before him Escoffier came from a humble non-culinary background. Born in 1846, he was the son of a blacksmith. By the age of 13 he was training in a restaurant in Nice and for the next twenty-four years he gained experience in the expensive holiday hotels at Nice, Monte Carlo and Lucerne, at three of the most exclusive restaurants in Paris, and at the Rhine Army Headquarters.

By 1883 Escoffier was working at the Grand Hotel in Monte Carlo which, at the time, was under the management of César Ritz. Ritz and Escoffier formed an informal partnership and over the next thirty years they took their distinctive French style of hotel living and hotel cuisine first to the Savoy Hotel in London (1889), then to the Carlton, then later to the chain of Ritz Hotels which César established in Paris, Rome, Madrid, New York, Budapest, Montreal, Philadelphia and Pittsburgh. As an entrepreneurial duo they were responsible for the concept of the grand Edwardian hotel with magnificent continental cuisine in the dining room.

But Escoffier's contribution was much greater than this. He invented literally thousands of new dishes. In his most famous book, *Le Guide Culinaire* (1921), he listed some 5000 recipes although he freely admitted that they were not all his own creations. He followed it with two equally famous books, *Le Livre des Menus* (1924) and *Ma Cuisine* (1934).

Escoffier was an intellectual rather than a purely intuitive chef. He passed sleepless nights thinking up new dishes to satisfy the demands of his fashionable customers. His approach was orderly and, in his writing, his great distinction lay in having codified almost everything to do with cooking, explaining it meticulously and bringing up to date much that was old-fashioned. He distilled the experience of a century and added to it his own extraordinary flair.

Gourmets and chefs look upon Escoffier with great affection. He was a man who devoted his life to food and the legacy he left is contained in the recognition that the disciplines and subtleties of French cuisine are the most exacting and rewarding in the world.

Escoffier came to haute cuisine with one huge advantage. In 1860 the great French chef Felix Urbain-Dubois had introduced the Russian table service to French cooking, thus giving the French meal an organization it had not previously enjoyed. The Russian table service divided a meal into a series of courses and each course was presented only when the previous one had been consumed and the plates removed. Prior to the introduction of the Russian system the French had been wont to put all courses on the table at the same time. The Russian principle of staggering the courses meant that meals could be served hot, and with some likelihood of them actually being eaten hot.

Thus the combination of Escoffier and the Russian table service resulted in French grande cuisine being the only organized and structured gastronomy in the world.

The trend in French cuisine since Escoffier has been towards greater simplicity with no diminution of standard. Chefs such as Paul Bocuse, Michel Guérard and Roger Vergé have been influential in creating "nouvelle cuisine."

A chef at the Savoy Hotel in 1899.

Cuisines Around the World

China

Chinese cooking as we know it today has evolved from the distinctive regional styles of the provinces. Centuries ago, when the means of preserving and transporting foods were inadequate for a regional exchange of ingredients, the style of cooking was restricted to its place of origin. Therefore, each regional style developed according to its geographic conditions, climate, available ingredients and local customs.

It wasn't until the Sung Dynasty (960–1279 AD) that regional cooking styles began to merge into a national cuisine. Encouraged by the dynasty rulers, methods of growing, preserving, storing and distributing food progressed rapidly. Food and eating became an extension of the Chinese philosophy and were intimately connected with other aspects of Chinese civilization, such as art and medicine. Like Yin and Yang, complementary opposing forces, food and culture were distinct, yet inseparable elements of life in ancient Chinese society.

Fresh produce on display in a typical Chinese market.

The North
Northern-style cuisine embraces the geographical areas of China that lie north of the Yangtse River. The entire northern region is relatively dry and arid compared to the rest of China and this has severely limited the variety of ingredients available for cooking. Dusty, biting winds from Mongolia pervade the northernmost parts of the area, especially around Beijing, and the winters are long and cold.

The most distinctive features native to northern cuisine are the hardy staples, wheat and millet. Millet is perhaps the oldest of all foods in China, predating both rice and wheat. The most common winter dish is millet gruel served with dried bean curd, salted fish, beans or pickled vegetables.

Steaming (zheng), baking (kao) and "explode frying" (bao) are the most popular cooking methods used in the north. One reason for this is the scarcity of cooking fuel and *bao* is by far the fastest cooking method, requiring only 30–90 seconds. To cook *bao* style, oil is heated in a wok until smoking, then all the ingredients are dropped into the deep oil, creating a sound like an explosion, locking in the original flavors and coating the outside surface with the condiments.

The East
The climate of the eastern/coastal region is the mildest in China, rainfall is abundant and the soil is fertile. The region is dominated by the lower Yangtse River and its intricate network of small rivers, lakes and man-made canals. These waterways provide water for irrigation, produce fresh water fish and mollusks, and form extensive transportation networks for harvested foods.

Seafood and freshwater fish form the mainstay of the eastern/coastal menu and fish recipes from this area are among the best in China. Abundant supplies of every type of vegetable are available as well, adding much color and variety to the menu. Meat and poultry are also popular, the favorite choices being pork and chicken.

The eastern/coastal region is one of the most diverse culinary areas of China. Fukien is famous for its rich stews, soups and stocks, as well as congee or rice gruel. Kiangsu has developed the "red stew" to perfection using rock crystal sugar to achieve the light sweetness, shiny colors and smooth textures which characterize this type of dish. Elaborate kitchen preparations, especially very fine, even cutting, are part of the cooking style.

The Central West
The central western culinary region of China includes the provinces and cuisines of Sichuan and Hunan. The cuisines of these regions are the most distinctive in all of China in terms of flavor.

While the climates of Sichuan and Hunan are quite similar, their geographical conditions differ significantly and these differences are reflected in the food. Both provinces are dominated by hot, humid weather. Hunan is a verdant province of fertile soil, abundant rainfall and gentle topography where most ingredients for the Chinese kitchen thrive. Meat, fish and fowl play prominent roles on the Hunan menu and the entire spectrum of the vegetable kingdom is represented as well.

Sichuan, however, is a province of craggy mountains, abrupt, deep valleys and steep, jagged cliffs. The bulk of the province's crops are grown in the broad plains surrounding the capital city of Chengtu. Sichuan cuisine offers less variety of cultivated ingredients than Hunan, but the mountain recesses provide a wide range of medicinal cooking herbs as well as wild game.

Red chilies of the bell pepper (capsicum) family are the king of condiments in this region. Due to the pharmacological effects — they tend to dry out the body and thus balance excess dampness — chilies have been extremely popular in this intensely humid region ever since their introduction from the New World. The native fragrant pepper is also extensively used, as well as garlic, ginger and scallions. Fermented bean paste and chili sauce feature too, giving the dishes a pungent style of their own.

Lush Hunan province produces plenty of meat, fish and fowl for its tables and these rich items are central in the Hunan diet. However, they are rarely, if ever, cooked in the raw state; instead, they are usually cured, marinated, pickled or otherwise processed before cooking.

Local villagers in Luding enjoy lunch at the market place café.

Sichuan has a more limited selection of ingredients for cooking. Most prominent in the kitchen are pork, poultry, legumes, soybean products, nuts of various sorts and wild mountain products, including medicinal herbs and wild game.

Sichuan and Hunan cooking does not emphasize color or appearance; in fact one of its features is its rustic style. However, it is considered to be one of the most nourishing and tasty cuisines in China.

The South

Southern Chinese cooking is the best known in the Western world. The culinary capital of this region, and indeed of all China, is the city of Canton, which boasts more restaurants and original culinary creations than any other Chinese city.

Historically and geographically, the south has been China's rice bowl, since rice thrives in the moist, warm climate and fertile conditions. Its location on the coast also gives access to abundant sources of fresh seafoods from the South China Sea.

Among the main ingredients that commonly appear on the southern menu are fish and crustaceans from the ocean and fish from freshwater ponds and paddies. Poultry is also central to the southern cuisine. From the vegetable kingdom comes an incredible variety of fresh vegetables; the green, leafy varieties with crispy textures are especially favored.

Cantonese food is further renowned for its great variety of snack foods, collectively called *dim sum*. Dim sum is usually eaten for lunch or as a midafternoon snack with pots of strong, fragrant tea. The dishes include stuffed dumplings, delicate pastries, cakes, puddings and cold plates of roasted meats and poultry. Southern-style cuisine is generally considered to be the most highly developed form of Chinese cooking. It is certainly the most diverse. Southern flavors are the least contrived, relying almost entirely on the fresh flavors of the main ingredients.

In China, all members of the family are involved in the preparation of food.

France

In medieval France, both cooking and learning were nurtured within the confines of convents and monasteries. Gradually, literature and cooking emerged from the cloisters and French peasants, who had previously supped on a basic Celtic and Roman cuisine, eagerly adapted the food as it appeared and began to develop it. The geography of each region offered its own contribution in the way of available produce and gradually, over the centuries, a regional cuisine developed.

French cooking as it is known today combines dishes that reflect the varied produce and characteristics of each region. By discovering what each area has to offer, one can begin to understand the diversity and richness of one of the world's most outstanding cuisines. Here some of the better known regions are outlined.

Visited by millions of tourists each year, the Eiffel Tower is a major tourist attraction.

Ile-de-France
The historical center of France, this region is irrigated by three rivers, creating a fertile agricultural basin. Even though many of the old farms and market gardens have been replaced by factories and houses, the area still produces a varied selection of ingredients such as Chantilly cream, Brie cheese and mushrooms. The immediate vicinity of Paris provides the Parisians with their game, game pâtés, fish and crayfish. However, the best known products of the region, which have been copied throughout France, are such pastries as Gâteau Pithiviers and Tarte Tatin.

Normandy
Normandy's northwest coastline produces an abundance of seafood. Eel, sole, turbot, herring and mackerel are caught daily, as are mussels, one of the area's great specialties. Freshwater fish are plentiful and the streams in the south provide trout, salmon, pike and crayfish.

Local pastures are rich grazing areas and the dairy industry makes the best butter and cream in France. Most of France's Camembert is also produced here.

The flat salt marshes by the sea are used for grazing sheep and Normandy is renowned for the salt-flavored lamb and mutton served in its homes and restaurants.

Normandy is the most important apple-growing region in France and cider replaces wine as the local drink and cooking aid. The cider is also distilled to make an apple brandy called Calvados.

Brittany
The westernmost corner of France, Brittany is a rock-bound peninsula surrounded by the Atlantic Ocean on three sides. It has retained many of its ancient traditions and its inhabitants still converse in an ancient Celtic dialect.

Brittany is acclaimed for its lobster, oysters, cockles and sea urchins as well as other crustaceans particular to that area. Sea bass, monkfish, mackerel, sardines and whiting are cooked into hearty soups and stews such as Cotriade.

One of the highlights of a trip to Brittany is a visit to the creperie. There is a wide selection of crepes such as *Crepes Dentelles,* a thin lacy pancake, and *Crêpe de Sarrazin* — a thicker crepe made with buckwheat flour. The best known, however, is *Galette,* a thick griddle-type pancake made with buckwheat flour and filled with ham, cheese and onion.

Burgundy and Lyonnaise
Burgundy is situated in the very heart of France and is renowned for its traditional dishes which incorporate the local wines. One such dish is *Boeuf à la Bourguignonne* (see page 261), a rich beef and baby onion stew cooked in red wine. *Matelote* is another stew incorporating red wine, but

this dish contains a variety of locally caught river fish such as pike and carp. Complementing the wealth of good wines and cassis produced in the area is a variety of soft cheese.

Lyonnaise is considered to be the country's culinary capital and the excellent and varied produce from this area is presented on the tables of some of France's best three-star restaurants.

However, in spite of being home to some of France's greatest chefs, such as Troisgros and Bocuse, many of the restaurants in this region were and still are owned by female chefs, the best known being Mère Fillioux, who ran her famous kitchen after World War I.

Bordeaux

Bordeaux boasts an abundance of fresh and saltwater fish, salt mutton, cheese, fruit and vegetables. Its most acclaimed product, however, is wine.

Centuries ago, when the Romans inhabited the city of Bordeaux, they planted grape vines around the city in all directions. In the 1100s the area was ruled by the English, who popularized the local wines and exported large cargoes back to Britain. The wine continued to grow in popularity and the local cuisine developed alongside it, matching the high quality of the wine.

Provence

In the Middle Ages, when the Romans lived in Provence, they planted olives and vines throughout the sunny rolling hills and used the wild herbs, which grew abundantly, to flavor their food. Provence has an ideal climate for growing any variety of fruit and vegetable; lemon and orange groves dot the hillsides, the air is scented with thyme and rosemary, and the huge salt marshes of the Camargue provide grazing ground for cattle.

The culinary traditions started by the Romans were adapted and refined by the French, who then introduced southern-style cooking to the rest of the country.

Sun umbrellas form a colourful canopy over the outdoor cafés in Avignon.

The province of Nice and the Mediterranean island of Corsica share a tradition of flavorful, colorful cooking. Settled by the Greeks and then the Romans, these areas share the wealth of centuries-old olive vines, pungent herbs, citrus fruit, tomatoes and nuts. Classic dishes from this region include *Salade Niçoise* (see page 123) and *Ratatouille*.

Languedoc

A sunny southern province on the shores of the Mediterranean, Languedoc is most famous for creating *Cassoulet* (see page 262). This dish was also introduced by the Romans and has been refined and improved to its present form. The quality of Cassoulet is taken very seriously and neighboring townships hotly contest the superiority of their recipe.

Languedoc has a good supply of game, sea and freshwater fish, vegetables and fruit. Livestock is also plentiful and includes mountain lamb and mutton, veal, beef and home-grown pigs.

Périgord

Home of the black truffle, the Périgord region forms part of a high plateau in southwest France. The area is surrounded by fertile river valleys whose rivers abound with freshwater crayfish, and the forests grow walnuts and chestnuts. The rich valley region yields a big selection of vegetables and stone fruits. Mushrooms and truffles are also collected in the meadows and alert visitors may spot the secretive buying and selling of truffles in the local market.

Franche-Comté, Savoy and Dauphiné

These scenic mountain regions serve simple but nourishing food, such as fondues and gratin dishes. The original style of cooking reflects the Alpine terrain, evolving from produce that could be found or cultivated in high remote areas. Dishes were created using simple, fresh ingredients that were both nourishing and fortifying for the climate. Swiss and Italian influences are also very much in evidence, with ingredients such as pasta being adopted from their nearby neighbors.

Café society in St Tropez on the Cote d'Azure in South France.

Japan

A sensitivity to and appreciation of nature is expressed in all facets of Japanese life but it is particularly significant in the attitude towards food and the emphasis placed on its presentation. With simplicity and elegance, each ingredient is carefully prepared and served so that the color, texture and characteristic of each dish reflects the season and the beauty of the Japanese countryside.

A grand Tori bridge, one of the many which feature prominently throughout Japan.

History

It is thought that the Japanese were originally immigrants from Siberia or Korea who journeyed across the hostile environment of northern Asia and discovered the fertile islands and temperate climate of Japan.

The settlers' appreciation and reverence for the beauty of their new homeland developed into a cult dedicated to the worship of nature, which became the Shinto religion.

Able to cultivate only a small area of land, the Japanese lived on a simple diet that included rice, fish, vegetables, seaweed and fruit. This was occasionally supplemented by venison, game birds and wild boar. The sacredness of food, which was rarely available in surplus quantities, was highly revered and frequent prayers and offerings were made to the food goddess, Ukemochi-no-kami, for good harvests.

Throughout the centuries the Japanese opened and closed their doors to foreigners. The Chinese were one of the first countries to influence the Japanese and two of their notable contributions were the soybean and green tea. The Portuguese passed on their technique for deep frying, which gradually evolved into *Tempura* (see page 81). Centuries later the Americans arrived, bringing Western technology and a preference for eating meat and poultry that was quickly adapted by the Japanese.

Climatic Influences

The long, narrow strip of islands encompasses a diverse range of climates. The north is snowbound in winter, with a European-type climate, while the south is nearly tropical. As a result of the differing climate and terrain, the produce varies from area to area, giving rise to different cooking traditions and specialties. Be it one-pot dishes and stews from the north, or Zen-inspired temple cuisine from Kyoto, food throughout Japan is a direct indication of the seasonal produce from the surrounding countryside and provides a common thread throughout all Japanese cuisine.

Seasonal Produce

All food served is compatible with the season and each season is heralded with ceremony, as tradition dictates the cookery and food considered suitable to use and serve. On the first day of spring, for example, the Japanese discard all winter clothing, regardless of climate, and don their lighter summer clothes. Thick winter stews are also replaced with lighter dishes displaying young spring vegetables. In summer, chilled dishes are served on a bed of ice cubes and in autumn one would find dishes like wild mushrooms or chestnuts presented on beautiful red and gold leaves.

Produce in Japan is restricted, not just because food is only served in season but because a large portion of the country is steep and mountainous, making it unsuitable for cultivation or development. All remaining land is well utilized, with the majority being used to grow rice.

Rice is more than just a staple food to the Japanese. For centuries it was regarded as a standard of wealth, samurais were paid with it and feudal chiefs were ranked according to their rice yield. To this day, rice is an integral part of the culture and a Japanese person doesn't feel as if he has eaten until his bowl of rice is finished.

Like rice, soybeans play an integral part in Japanese cooking. Three soybean products — soy sauce, tofu (a custard-like bean curd) and miso (fermented soybean paste) — feature prominently in such dishes as soups, breakfast foods, dressings and stews. Tofu's bland flavor is a perfect foil for seasonings and an accompaniment to other ingredients. It can be broiled, fried and steamed and is full of protein.

Seafood is another popular ingredient and Japan has learned to farm the sea bed and shores for a rich selection of fish, seaweeds and shellfish.

Presentation of Meals

A formal meal in Japan, as it is served in a restaurant, is made up of a succession of dishes, each employing a different cooking technique. For example, the meal would commence with clear soup, then raw fish followed by a simmered dish, a broiled dish, a deep fried course, a steamed dish and a dressed salad. It would then end with rice, pickles and possibly a thick miso soup. A home cook would not go to such elaborate lengths, but would prepare a simpler version using a smaller selection of cooking techniques.

A bridge at the Shrine in Miyajama, Hiroshima.

Concern for visual quality is as important in the home as it is in restaurants. The combination of shape, color and texture is also considered to be as important as taste and the Japanese housewife must balance all of these elements within the meal. Each meal is made up of several tiny portions, decoratively arranged on dishes suited to the particular season and arranged on lacquered trays according to certain rules.

Rather than serving a combination of food on one plate, such as meat and vegetables, each ingredient is served individually in order to appreciate each taste separately. Flavoring is kept to a minimum and there are only two flavorings which the Japanese consider essential. These are *dashi*, a stock added to soups and stews which is made of kelp and dried bonito flakes, and *soy sauce*.

Cooking Methods

Cooking methods used are very simple. Rather than changing the texture and color of the ingredients, or concealing them with a sauce, the cooking preserves their original state as much as possible. To achieve this successfully, ingredients must be fresh and of the best quality. Housewives tend to shop daily and slightly old produce is quickly discarded. One of the prerequisites to making fine Japanese food is selecting the best ingredients.

Although the Japanese do not bake or roast food, they do boil, fry, steam and broil in much the same manner as we do in the West.

The subtlety of Japanese food and its attractive appearance can be achieved by learning several basic techniques. Once achieved, the cook has limitless choice in combining seasonal produce, striving for the perfect harmony of texture, color, flavor and arrangement which characterizes Japanese food.

A young Japanese girl in traditional dress feeding doves.

Italy

History

The food enjoyed by the Romans at the peak of the Roman Empire is legendary. Most of us have a Hollywood vision of exotic slaves bearing platters of whole roast peacocks decked in their former glory, wild boars stuffed with herbs and smaller game, pyramids of succulent fruit and honeyed cakes flavored with oriental spices. Yet only the privileged patricians were present at such banquets, which drew on all the produce of the Empire. The average Roman citizen ate foods that were available locally and prepared simply.

A glance at an extract from a household accounts list dating from the Empire tells us that poultry, cereals such as corn and barley, olives, oil, vegetables and fruit were all readily available on the Roman market, although some of them were out of the price range of the poorer Romans. Many Italians today have a small "kitchen garden" in which they grow a few herbs and vegetables. This may well be a practice dating back to the days of the Empire. Taverns selling wine and snack foods such as sausages and olives were common and also within the means of the passersby.

The Roman army, which had fought to establish the Empire, lived mainly on a diet of *pulmentum*, a kind of gruel similar to polenta. The Romans inherited *pulmentum* from the Etruscans, a people who had inhabited Italy before the Latins, the forebears of the Romans. The Etruscans are an enigmatic group but their legacy to the Romans probably included agricultural techniques.

The Romans were quite scientific about the cultivation of grapes, olives and vegetables and the care of livestock. Some of the best writers of the time wrote treatises on farming. They may have adopted this concept from the Greeks, whose culture the Romans greatly admired, and whose agricultural methods were recorded by Hesiod. The importance of agriculture is evident in Italian cookery today, where excellence and freshness of ingredients, particularly herbs and vegetables, are essential.

The arrival of the Moslem Arabs in the eighth century brought a whole new range of foods to Italy: melons, figs, spinach, rice and oranges, to name a few. Four hundred years later the Crusades re-established contact with the Middle East and Italian cookery was revitalized by Arab spices.

Would Italian cooking be so distinctive without pasta? Perhaps it would, but the world's cuisine would be poorer without the variety and richness of Italian sauces — for pasta cannot be served without some sort of sauce or dressing.

In the sixteenth century Italians felt the impact of the discovery of the New World in much the same way as other European countries. Colorful new foods became available. The Italians received some of these enthusiastically and cultivated them to perfection. The supreme example is the tomato. Only tiny when it was first introduced, it became the plump, juicy, indispensable ingredient of hundreds of Italian dishes.

The Italian was one of the earliest of the European cuisines to develop a distinctive style and flavor. It was an influence that Catherine de Medici, the Italian wife of Henry II, introduced to France. However, French cookery evolved to become subtle and elaborate whereas Italian remained basically simple, fresh and exuberant.

Regional Flavors

The Roman Empire imposed a unity on what was most of the known world. Within the Empire, each province was governed individually and each was able to maintain its own

The leaning tower of Pisa.

customs. In Italy itself each city became allied to Rome; it did not become Roman. When the Roman Empire collapsed in the fifth century each region simply continued to develop its own customs, dialect and, of course, culinary habits.

Although today there are ingredients and flavors that are used throughout Italy, each region has its own specialties. So great are the number of these specialties that great tomes could be written simply listing the recipes! Each region also has its own wine industry.

Piedmontese truffles give much of its cookery a distinctive aroma. Truffles only grow wild and can only be unearthed by an experienced truffle hunter, aided by a specially trained dog. Piedmont produces a number of fine cheeses so it is not surprising that *fonduta*, a cheese fondue, is a regional specialty.

Zuppa alla pavese, from Lombardy, was said to have been improvized for Francis I of France when he was passing through the region. Two other well-known products of Lombardy are *panettone*, a leavened Christmas cake made with raisins and candied peel, and gorgonzola cheese, which is not for the faint-hearted.

In Veneto, polenta and fish are popular staple foods. Its capital, Venice, developed a highly sophisticated cuisine when it was the center of the spice trade in Europe, evidenced in the fragrantly spiced *San Daniele* ham.

During the balmy summer months, many Italians frequent the street cafés for light meals and refreshments.

From Liguria comes the sweetly aromatic sauce known as *pesto* (see page 315). *Pesto* is made of fresh basil, garlic, Parmesan cheese and olive oil, ground patiently together with a mortar and pestle (or impatiently in a food processor!).

The cookery of Tuscany is simple yet elegant. A traditional method of cooking beans is in a wine flask on charcoal. *Fritto del mare* is a fried mixture of small fish, baby eels and red mullet. Siena produces a wonderfully rich Christmas cake known as Sienna Christmas cake (see page 383).

Emilia-Romagna is renowned for its mortadella sausage and its *tortellini*, a tiny stuffed and rolled pasta. The city of Parma was the original producer of Parmesan cheese.

In the Marches a fine fish soup known as *brodetto* rivals the French version, *bouillabaise*. Umbria is one of the largest producers of pork and the region also specializes in spit roasts. Neighboring Lazio, wherein lies the capital Rome, is also noted for its pork dishes and the famed *spaghetti alla matriciana*, which has a sauce of tomatoes, peppers, onions and fat salt pork.

Sicilian bakers are noted for their sweet *cannoli* and their buns filled with pork and cheese. On Sardinia the visitor may expect to eat sardines, to which the island has given its name. However, a whole sheep or goat roasted over an aromatic wood fire would be more indicative of local tastes.

The south of Italy, particularly Campania, has some rich agricultural areas. Around Naples, the capital of Campania, are found all the ingredients of one of Italy's greatest exports, the pizza. Especially unique to the area is the white buffalo, whose milk becomes *mozzarella* cheese. Although Naples is credited with the invention of the pizza, Calabrians, further south, consume *pitta*, which is, basically, bread "colored" with tomatoes, sardines, peppers and herbs.

The thriving fishing industry in Genova contributes to the regional cuisine.

Singapore/Malaysia

Centuries after the fall of the Javanese Majapahit Empire, *Singa Pura*, or "Lion City" as it was called, was rediscovered by Sir Stamford Raffles. An official of the East India Company, Raffles proclaimed Singapore the site for "a great commercial empire." His magic words "free trade" began a rush of immigrants, and Chinese traders from nearby Malacca and faraway Manila were soon joined by their countrymen direct from southern China, all in search of a new life and profits.

High rise apartment blocks are an imposing contrast to the small timber homes along the foreshore.

Immigration
Just five years after Raffles stepped ashore, the racial mixture of Chinese, Malays, Buginese, Indians, Europeans, Americans and Arabs was established. Over the past 150 years, this incredible melting pot of people has lived in Singapore, remaining largely within their own ethnic communities yet unconsciously influencing each other and their food.

The Chinese
The Chinese migrants did not form one homogeneous group. Although they came almost exclusively from southern China, they were from different provinces and spoke distinctly different languages. Even their food and eating habits differed.

The Malays
The various Malayan peoples of Singapore had more in common with each other than the Chinese migrants. They were bound by a common faith, Islam, by the Malay language and by centuries of contact. Territorial boundaries in the Malay peninsula and the islands of what is now Indonesia had always been fluid. At various times, groups of people from one area would migrate to another island or state, most of them continuing to work as fishermen or farmers, leaving trade and commerce to the soon-dominant Chinese.

The Indians
Traders were the cornerstone of the Indian community in Singapore, although the majority of Indians prior to 1860 came as soldiers or convicts. The slender, dark-skinned Tamils from Madras state make up just over half of Singapore's Indian population today, with the Malayalee group from Kerala in the southwest of India forming the next largest group. There are also Sri Lankans, Pakistanis, Punjabis, Bengalis and Eurasians, all adding to the cultural contribution of the vast Indian subcontinent.

Culinary Influences
Today it is possible to eat your way around China in Singapore's restaurants. From the mild, sophisticated cuisine of Beijing, with its occasional Mongolian dishes, you can move to the seafoods of the Shanghai region. Heading further south you meet the heavier pork stews of the Teochews and Hokkiens, sample the imaginative bean curd creations of the Hakkas and the chicken rice favorite of the Hainanese, before letting yourself be wooed and won by the internationally acclaimed Cantonese cuisine. Moving west, you can sting your taste buds into new life with the chili-hot, garlic-laden dishes of Sichuan and Hunan.

Life alongside the chili-loving Malays and Indians has resulted in the Chinese liking a touch of heat. Chinese noodle dishes in Singapore are invariably accompanied by a side dish of pickled green chilies, red chili paste is smeared inside popiahs (a type of spring roll) or tossed with fried noodles, and a dish of red chilies pounded with ginger and garlic is served with chicken, rice or steamed crab and prawns. Malay-style curries are served on occasion in many Chinese homes, especially on the second day of the Chinese New Year celebrations — the first day being reserved for all the traditional Chinese favorites.

The gentle, conservative lifestyle of the Malays has given them a reputation for being traditionalists, yet their cuisine shows anything but a resistance to change. What is today regarded as Malay food is the result of centuries of outside influence.

Until adequate roads were constructed during the twentieth century, most Malays lived along the peninsular or island coasts, or at the edge of the wide brown rivers that provided their only means of transport. For more than a thousand years, the coastal Malays dealt with foreign traders and were inevitably influenced by them. Many of the seasonings that are now essential to Malay cuisine, such as fragrant root ginger, pepper, pungent lemon, cardamom and fennel, were introduced by the Arabs and Indians.

Because Malays have traditionally lived near the water, the abundance of fish, shrimp, crabs, squid and all kinds of seafood naturally made them regular items in the daily diet. Fish is still the main source of protein, with chicken second in importance. Rice is the staple of the Malays, though tapioca, sweet potatoes, yams and other tubers that flourish in the tropical climate are cheap and popular. A typical Malay meal consists of plenty of rice with fish, vegetables and sometimes poultry, meat or eggs, served with *sambals*, the savory and often spicy side dishes. Until 1867, Singapore was administered by the East India Company and was regarded as a part of India. If you ate in an Indian home today, you might think that Singapore was still part of India, for alone amongst the people of Singapore, the Indians continue to cook and eat almost exactly as their forebears did, with very little evidence of a century and a half of contact with the Malays, Chinese and Europeans.

A dragon dance through the main streets of Singapore is the highlight of traditional ceremonies.

and such fruits as unripe jack fruit and plantains or cooking bananas. Indians from the lush green coast of Kerala in the southwest happily turn Singapore's plentiful seafood into excellent fish head and crab curries, for which they are renowned, while Indian and Pakistani Muslims specialize in fiery hot mutton curries, rice pilau and biryani and delicious breads.

In spite of the influence from some of the world's best cuisines, a cooking style unique to Singapore has managed to evolve. This is the food of the Nonyas, the Straits Chinese women whose cooking is perhaps the most creative to be found in Singapore. The development of Nonya cuisine is a romantic story. Long before the large-scale immigration of Chinese towards the end of the nineteenth century, a number of Chinese traders settled in Malacca and later in Penang and Singapore. Because of the dearth of Chinese women, these men took Malay wives, and their language, customs and food eventually became a fascinating mixture of Chinese and Malay.

The children of these mixed marriages were known as *Peranakan* or Straits Chinese. Nonya food is prepared using Malay methods and is therefore often time consuming, another factor contributing to its slow demise. Many typically Chinese ingredients such as pork and dried mushrooms take on a totally new flavor when cooked by Nonyas with coconut milk, *asam* (the sour acidic fruit of the tamarind tree), *blacan* (pungent dried shrimp paste), hot red chilies and the aromatic roots and leaves so essential in a Nonya kitchen.

Nonya food is a mixture of Chinese and Malay with Indonesian and Thai overtones. The Indonesian influence isn't surprising, since some Singapore Peranakan families came from Java or Sumatra. Through their willingness to adapt and absorb new ways, the Nonyas have created a unique cuisine that is too good to be allowed to fade into oblivion. Yet perhaps a new Singaporean cuisine is evolving even now and, in years to come, a harmonious combination of Malay, Chinese and Indian cuisines will equal the delights of Nonya food.

The Raffles Hotel in Singapore is famous for its architectural splendor and lavish gardens.

Bound by ancient religious and cultural observations, Singapore's Indians have been slow to change any aspect of their lifestyle, although twentieth-century pressures have forced on many the change to high-rise living.

The Tamils of southeast India brought their unusual vegetables, such as snake gourd and drumsticks (long tree-grown seedpods), to supplement the familiar tropical vegetables and fruit they found growing in their new home. They have retained their superb vegetarian cuisine, creating endlessly varied dishes from all kinds of lentils, dried beans, vegetables

Indonesia

History

Three thousand islands seemingly flung like their famed spice berries across the Equator over some two thousand miles of sea. Rugged mountains, steaming jungles, peaceful cultivated terraces of rice, swaying coconut palms, sun-drenched beaches. The diversity of Indonesia is immediately apparent. Nonetheless, there is a character that is distinctively Indonesian, reflected in its cuisine, its customs and its culture.

The influences that have helped to form the present-day Republic of Indonesia are almost as numerous as the ethnic groups that make up its population. The largest group is Malay, although there are thirteen other major groups and many minorities as well.

Historians have detected an Indian influence on Indonesian life as early as the fifth century AD. This was probably due to trading contacts and a subsequent adaptation of Indian culture. The early presence of Indian culture can be seen in Indonesia's Hindu and Buddhist temples, particularly in Java, and in the performance of Hindu epics such as the Ramayana in drama and shadow plays. Both Indonesian and Indian food tend to be hot and spicy, but their origins could be argued in favor of either cuisine.

Rural workers in Lonbok head home after a day's work.

Arab traders had been purchasing exotic spices and fragrant woods for centuries in Indonesia before the birth of the Islamic religion in the seventh century. The Arabs probably brought other foreign spices and plants to Indonesia. Perhaps ginger and chili were originally imported by this means. As a matter of course, Islam was brought to Indonesia on the same winds as the traders. Moslems are forbidden to eat pork and although Indonesians of other faiths can purchase it readily, recipes for other meats are usually more common.

The Chinese have always been a strong contingent in Indonesia. In Chinese cuisine most foods maintain their recognizable taste and quality and this, too, may have influenced the style of Indonesian cooking. With the arrival of European traders from the fifteenth century onwards, Indonesian life underwent another, largely economic change. The vast majority of native Indonesians continued to work the land while the Chinese became the retailers and traders. As European interest in the spice trade and plantation crops, such as sugar and palm oil, became stronger and more competitive, the control of the East Indies, as they were called, became more important. The Dutch emerged as the controllers so that by the nineteenth century they were the governors. Some historians argue that the period of Dutch rule unified the islands of Indonesia, preparing the way for the modern Republic. Certainly, Indonesian history, culture and geography reflect its national motto: Unity in Diversity.

Selamat Makan!

Rice is the basis of all meals. Rice is to Indonesians what bread and other cereals are to Europeans. There are even four Indonesian words to denote rice: *padi*, which is rice on its stalks; *gabah*, unhulled rice separated from its stalks; *beras*, hulled rice; and *nasi*, cooked rice.

The previous evening's rice may be served for breakfast topped by a fried egg or an omelet cut into strips. Or rice may be served with coconut milk (*santan*) and tropical fruit.

Lunch, which is usually eaten at home, again features rice with meat and vegetables. Between-meal snacks may be rice cakes or fried bananas. At dinner a platter of rice occupies the center of the table and the other side dishes of meat, seafood, poultry, sambals (spicy relishes), vegetables and fresh salads are arranged around it. Dinner is usually finished with fresh fruit (there being an abundant supply in this tropical country) and coffee. Cakes and desserts, in the Western sense, are eaten between meals, if at all.

The influences of India, Arabia and China have helped to produce a cuisine which uses as its flavors chili, curry leaves, lemongrass, turmeric, coriander, cumin, garlic, scallions, coconut milk, tamarind and ginger. Nonetheless, the availability of local ingredients influences the flavor of regional cookery as well. In Java, fresh spices and sugar (grown locally) may be dominant flavors, whereas in Sumatra, which was a great center of trade in early times, the original foreign spices of chili and ginger are more common.

The tropical climate of Indonesia and its rich volcanic soil produce a prolific variety of vegetables and fruit. Many of these can only be cultivated in the tropics and are, seemingly, particularly suitable eating in a tropical climate. Fresh lime juice with iced water and sugar is the perfect refreshment on a sultry afternoon!

Seafood, both fresh and dried, is also consumed in great quantities. Inland lakes, rivers and even rice fields are reliable sources of fish as well. Meat tends to be an expensive item so it is almost always served thinly sliced or cubed. Street vendors cook cubed meat, poultry or fish as saté — hot and spicy and barbecued on the spot. If you intend to cook saté at home on bamboo skewers, soak them in cold water for 30 minutes or so before use to keep the skewers from burning.

A west Sumatran farmer plants rice in the terraced paddy fields.

A colorful array of produce at the local markets in Lonbok.

Indonesian hospitality is a way of life. On a festive occasion, of which there are many, or if guests are present, more food than can be eaten by those partaking of the meal will be served. Wedding feasts, for example, are lavish affairs. Because of the inevitable expense they are classified as one of the three traditional emergencies that justify the sale of family land for cash.

Selamat makan (good eating) is a traditional toast to begin the meal. On similar European occasions wine or other kinds of alcohol are often consumed. However, alcohol is not a traditional addition to the Indonesian banquet. Not only are many Indonesians prohibited from consuming it (being of Moslem faith) but it is generally too expensive for most Indonesians. Fruit juices, tea, coffee or just water are more commonly drunk at meal times.

Indonesians have a natural respect for the forces of nature, so that a small offering of food will often be made to the appropriate deity or supernatural force at a festival. Sometimes a little rice on a banana leaf may be found by a river, a tree or even a crossroads. Perhaps the Indonesians understand something about the sharing of food .

Great Britain

Traditional Fare

Like much of British life, the eating habits and culinary art of this nation are rooted in traditions. These traditions stretch back before the recorded history of Great Britain.

The staples of the British diet have been, for hundreds of years, meat, bread, cheese and ale. "Pete Marsh," an Iron Age man who was buried in peat around two thousand years ago, ate coarse bread, slightly charred and so probably cooked on a fire, for his last meal. For hundreds of years after Pete Marsh's death the peasants of the British Isles tilled the soil in return for their meager diet of bread and meat, supplemented by a few home-grown vegetables and local game and fish.

Lush farmland near Bath.

The Germanic Angles, Saxons and Jutes began to arrive in the fifth century. Their way of life differed little from that of the people they conquered. However, they brought with them the arts of baking, brewing and cheese-making.

The Anglo-Saxons lived in communities dominated by a *thane* or lord. On long winter nights the men would gather in the thane's hall feasting, drinking and story-telling. Game was roasted on spits, and mead (made from fermented honey) or ale flowed from drinking horns passed from man to man because its shape prevented its being placed on a horizontal surface until its contents had been consumed. Perhaps this was the origin of the tradition of passing the port until the bottle has been emptied.

The Norman invaders of the eleventh century did not conquer the traditional eating patterns already established. Nevertheless, the ruling Norman aristocracy brought different and more imaginative cooking techniques with them. These gradually infiltrated the ovens and cooking pots of peasants and town dwellers. The Normans favored lighter breads and pies filled with spiced meats.

It is impossible to say whether or not the Anglo-Saxons were eating pies before the Normans arrived as there are no existing cookery books! There probably never were any, as availability of local ingredients dictated the flavors of prepared food, and very few people would have been able to read them in any case.

The pudding (now a highly evolved English specialty) may have been a development of the steak and kidney pudding. Suet mixed with flour and water was simply wrapped around meat before being boiled. The next step could well have been baking the same mixture of ingredients to produce a pie or a pastie, an envelope of pastry filled with meat and vegetables, usually potatoes.

British eating habits have largely developed from simple country cooking which sustained the farmer and laborer through their daily work. Over the centuries imported flavorings were added to those which were native. The development of the British Empire enriched the table of, firstly, the well-to-do and later, the whole nation. The spices of India and Sri Lanka have invaded almost every home in the form of sauces and condiments such as Worcestershire sauce, a spicy concoction used to douse grilled meat and a favorite at hearty breakfasts of bacon and eggs.

The British have a reputation as a nation of beef eaters. The traditional Sunday roast dinner is almost always beef with Yorkshire pudding, a kind of small batter cake that is cooked in the juices of the roast. Accompaniments for this robust repast are usually roast potatoes, green vegetables (perhaps Brussels sprouts or peas), brown gravy, horseradish sauce and mustard. Dessert may be a steamed pudding served with custard.

Puddings are steamed in a deep bowl standing in a pan of simmering water or wrapped in a floured cloth and boiled. To the basic mixture of flour, butter and eggs may be added fresh or dried fruit and spices. Some puddings are "self-saucing," while others need an additional sauce, cream or custard topping. So much a part of British life is the pudding that the dessert course may be referred to as "pudding."

London's Tower Bridge which crosses the Thames River.

Tea is an institution rather than a tradition in Great Britain. After a somewhat slow introduction in the seventeenth century, due to its expense, it became increasingly popular and cheaper over the next century. By the late eighteenth century it had surpassed ale as a national beverage.

The word "tea" can refer to a cup of the golden beverage itself or to what is virtually a meal in the afternoon or early evening where a tempting array of toast, sandwiches, cakes, potted meats, scones and biscuits are served. An invitation to tea may presage quite a formal occasion. Traditionally, the main meal of the day was eaten at midday and so tea was often eaten as the evening meal.

Teashops opened for business in the late nineteenth century. At first bread was offered for sale with cups of tea. Gradually cakes, scones, meat pies and fried potatoes and other snacks or light meals were introduced.

Picturesque Loch Lomond surrounded by the snowy peaks of Stirling Shire, Scotland.

Country Cooking

Cakes, buns and scones are now part of traditional fare, particularly in the many cozy teashops found in country villages. Those of Devon are especially renowned for "Devonshire Teas" of scones, homemade jam and rich clotted cream.

The English countryside is picturesquely measured out by hedgerows of trees, shrubs and bushes. In summer, these provide a feast of wild fruits, nuts and berries. Many of these are the origin of traditional jellies such as cranberry or redcurrant, served with roasted meat.

A quaint thatched cottage in Newbury, Berkshire.

Scottish specialties include shortbread, black bun (a dark fruit cake encased in pastry), haggis (sheep's stomach stuffed with offal and oatmeal), Dundee marmalade and, of course, oatmeal porridge. The Scottish are intensely proud of their traditional fare and each is surrounded with an almost legendary tale of its origin and development.

The traditional Irish dependence on potatoes dates to the seventeenth century, when they were introduced from the New World. "Irish stew" may consist simply of boiled meat and potatoes, perhaps served with crusty soda bread.

The national emblem of Wales is the leek and it is not surprising that their cookery includes this tasty vegetable. Welsh cuisine, as hearty as that of neighboring England, has sustained generations of coal miners as well as farmers.

Great Britain has an abundant supply of fish in its rivers, lakes and coastal waters. The salmon of Scotland, Irish mackerel and Cornish lobster are all favorites which the British feel need very little additional flavoring.

In most English pubs, both in country villages and in cities, a "ploughman's lunch" will be offered on the menu. This simple meal of bread, cheese, pickled onion and ale reflects very accurately the heritage of Britain's culinary past.

Germany

History

Germany has no natural frontiers on its western or eastern borders. Consequently, Germans have spent much of their history fighting over borders and territories. Until the last century Germany was a group of states, each with its own ruler. After its unification by the Prussian, Bismarck, in 1871, it had a unity which was not geographically based, as is the case with many nations.

Historians have suggested that the popularity of pork in Germany is due to the fact that pigs were a good supply of meat for armies on the move. They were easily bred, easily fed and easily roasted.

The earliest written record of German life is that of the Roman historian Tacitus, who described the various tribes which occupied the area now known as Germany in the first century. Like most people of that time in Europe they lived on gruels, breads, cheese, wild fruit, berries and meat. When the Huns began to move down into Germany during the fourth and fifth centuries the land could not support the increased population. The German tribes, such as the Angles and the Saxons, were forced to find other suitable places in which to live.

The fairy tale Neuschwanstein Castle in southern Bavaria.

Throughout the Middle Ages and the early modern age, German eating habits were based on available food supplies. The poor, particularly in rural areas, ate the same kind of foods that their ancestors had eaten for centuries in the past. However, the well-to-do and upper class feasted on roast poultry, game and meat, spicy pies, marzipan sweets. Imported delicacies included capers, rice, figs, currants, cinnamon, mustard and sugar.

German cookery for the wealthy was strongly influenced by the French, particularly during the eighteenth century. During the next century, as the middle classes became more affluent due to Germany's industrialization, richly flavored food and elegant dinners and table manners were no longer the prerogative of the upper class. World War I brought an end to the old ways of living for the wealthy.

Guten Appetit!

German cookery is traditionally hearty to satisfy the notoriously large German appetites. Many visitors to Germany find German hospitality and food a little overwhelming.

Germans tend to have an early breakfast of bread with butter, honey or jam, sausage, cheese and coffee — not a large breakfast by some standards. However, around 11 a.m. a second breakfast is eaten. During the nineteenth century this was almost a formal meal; even the farmer in his field would stop work for some thick slices of bread and ham, washed down by a glass or two of fortifying *schnaps*, a kind of brandy. Today, second breakfast is usually just a sausage sandwich.

Sheep grazing on the shores of the River Elbe.

The midday meal consists of a number of hot courses. Soup, often brimming with plump dumplings or rich egg noodles, is followed by meat, potatoes and vegetables. Potatoes are consumed in vast quantities and are served boiled, mashed, fried or as pancakes. Sometimes a salad, equally substantial and a course in itself, is served as well.

Late afternoon is a time for *Kaffee mit Kuchen*, or coffee with cakes. This is similar to the English high tea. The Germans are venerable bakers and their cakes, pastries and tarts are mouthwatering temptations. *Konditoreien* are cake and pastry shops that also serve coffee. Some of Germany's *Konditoreien* have been operating for over a century and have not suffered a decline in either standards or reputation. Some may see them as the memory of a more elegant past.

The evening meal is, not surprisingly, a light one and usually cold. Several kinds of bread, cold meats, sausage, cheese and salads are the common elements of this somewhat informal meal.

The American hotdog has its origins in the spicy frankfurters of Germany. Frankfurters are but one of a bewildering array of sausages (hundreds and hundreds of them!) that are found in German delicatessens. The most common fall into half a dozen or so categories.

Salami is made of raw smoked beef and pork. *Fleischwurst* consists of finely chopped meat that is not smoked and is often flavored with garlic. *Blutwurst* is basically dried pig's blood and fat. *Leberwurst* is made of calves' or pigs' liver and is usually spread on bread. *Bockwurst* is a kind of sausage that is heated in water before being served. *Bratwurst* must be grilled or fried before being eaten. Some sausages are flavored with herbs, spices or truffles.

The range of German breads is almost as great. Germans favor the heavier rye breads such as *Graubrot*. *Mischbrot* is a mixture of rye and wheat flours and is usually sold outside Germany as rye bread. *Pumpernickel* is a very dark bread containing whole grains of rye. Its flavor is somewhat sweet and it is usually packaged already sliced very thinly.

An artist captures the beauty of the Bamberg River.

German cheeses include nutty *Emmentaler*, mild *Tilsiter* and strongly flavored *Limburger*. Processed cream cheeses with mushrooms or herbs are favorite spreads for black breads.

The flavors of German food do vary from one region to another although many of the available ingredients are common throughout Germany. Apples are used as a sweetening in potato, pork and other vegetable dishes. These combinations have a bitter-sweet and often salty taste. German cookery also uses a great deal of butter, eggs, pork fat and aromatic flavorings such as caraway.

Cabbage is second only to potatoes as Germany's favorite vegetable. Most of the millions grown each year end up in fermenting vats to become *Sauerkraut*. This has a salty, slightly sour taste and is used everywhere from sophisticated restaurants to snack bars in railway stations. It is cooked with apples or pineapple, beer or wine, and served with just about anything.

Much of Germany is far from the sea so smoked fish is a popular alternative to the fresh variety. Herrings may be served as pickled rollmops or fried and marinated. Germany's rivers provide a good supply of trout and carp. North Sea fish such as flounder and sole are usually cooked very simply and served with butter and lemon.

Another German specialty is goose, which is roasted, stuffed with apples and prunes, or eaten as a smoked delicacy. A popular saying about the prodigious German appetite is that a goose is not enough for two people but a little too much for one!

A printed facade and window boxes decorate this cottage in Munster.

India

India is over one million square miles, approximately one-third the size of America, and is divided into 31 states and territories. It embodies a number of religious faiths, a diversity of terrain and climate, as well as a multitude of regional characteristics and specialties.

Autumnal trees contrast against the rich blue sky in Srinigar, Kashmir.

History
Throughout the centuries India has been subjected to invasions and control by many nations. The Moghuls, who took control in the sixteenth century, made a serious and somewhat successful effort to unite the country. Moghul rulers married Hindu princesses, art and crafts were encouraged and many dishes such as basmati rice pullao, do piaza and pan-fried kebabs, which were served in the royal palaces, were gradually integrated into the everyday cuisine.

Another nation that had a pronounced affect on Indian food was Portugal, which ruled on the west coast for four centuries. The Portuguese not only introduced their own style of cooking but also introduced the chili, which they had brought back from the New World. Nowadays, chilies feature prominently in Indian cooking, but until the Portuguese arrived black peppercorns and mustard seeds were the main pungent ingredients used.

Before India gained independence, it was ruled by 600 semi-independent kingdoms, some of which were ruled by Hindu Maharajas and some by Muslim Nawabs. It had 15 major languages as well as hundreds of minor languages and dialects, and five major faiths. When independence came, the government divided the land into states so each area had its own major language and culture. This also applied to the food, and each region retained and developed its local specialties.

Regional Differences
Each state reflects its own religious beliefs and locally grown produce in the food they eat. For example, people in the south are predominantly Hindu and most Hindus are vegetarians. Eggs, which are considered to be an embryonic form of life, are avoided and in some areas, blood-colored vegetables such as tomatoes and beets are refused. Rice, which grows abundantly in the humid, well-irrigated fields, is eaten as the staple food and locally grown sesame seeds and

Tea, spiced with cardomoms and cinnamon, is served from the samovar.

coconut are ground for use as cooking oil. Coconuts, which are widely available, are well utilized in southern cooking, their milk is added to sauces, the flesh is chopped or ground for some dishes and the shells are used as containers.

Cooking in the south is done largely by steam and a steaming pot is considered essential equipment in all kitchens. This technique is not used much in the north, however, where ingredients are often cooked in a pot sealed with dough and baked slowly over smoldering ashes.

As the traveler makes his way north to the deserts of Rajasthan and the mountainous regions of Kashmir, the change in diet is very marked. Although many people are also vegetarian, the use of meat, particularly lamb and goat (which is similar to our mutton), is much more pronounced.

Ghee or clarified butter, which is used in preference to oil, is used for cooking all meat dishes. Traditionally this was prepared by boiling down large quantities of butter for hours at a time to burn out all impurities. The remaining waxy mass was then strained and could be stored indefinitely without refrigeration. Oil is used to cook vegetables.

Due to the harsh winter climate, much of the produce that is so cheap and plentiful during the summer months is dried and stored for winter.

Vegetable sellers travel the many water ways and lakes in Srinigar to sell their produce.

Spices

In spite of the enormously varied food eaten throughout the country, there are still some similar traditions that are followed by everyone. The combination and use of spices is the major unifying element of Indian food and its distinguishing factor when compared with other world cuisines.

Spices were first recorded in Sanskrit writings 3000 years ago, emphasizing their value as a food preservative and medicine. Nowadays, spices are mainly used for seasoning although their medicinal properties are still valued. Northern people tend to dry the spices grown during summer and store them for use throughout the winter. Spices are pounded in large quantities by either the householder or professional teams of women who travel door to door. These large quantities of basic spice preparations, such as garam masala, are then stored in airtight jars for use during winter.

Generally speaking, the southerners prefer to cook with fresh green spices, which are ground with coconut milk, water, lime juice or vinegar to make a wet masala (spice paste). In the south the masalas vary in consistency, being very liquid to complement the rice, which tends to be a little dry. In the north the sauce is reduced almost to a glaze as this is more practical to eat with their staple, bread.

Curry, the anglicized version of the Tamil word *kari*, is frequently and incorrectly used to describe Indian food. *Kari*, in fact, simply means sauce or a combination of seasonings cooked with vegetables or meat to make a stew-type dish.

Meals

Traditionally, restaurants are not a feature of Indian life and Indian people prefer to entertain or be entertained at home. Meals are served in the same fashion throughout the country. That is, guests and men eat first, then the children and finally the women. Indian women do not see this as submissive behavior. Instead, they regard it as a gesture of graciousness which they, as mistress of the home, choose to extend.

Food is served in *thalis*, shallow round trays on which the entire meal is presented at one time, leaving the individual to eat dishes according to his own preference.

Food is served by the women and it is considered bad manners for people to help themselves. It is also always eaten with the right hand as the left is considered unclean.

At the conclusion of the meal, hands are washed in a bowl that is presented to each person in turn. Then *paan* is served; this is a small roll of betel leaves filled with spices, which is chewed to aid digestion and cleanse the palate. Filling and wrapping the betel leaves is always done by the women and its preparation is considered an art.

The woman's role as a homemaker is one that is highly respected and revered by both men and women throughout India. Her cooking talents are also considered to be equally vital and in some regions the bride stands on a grinding stone during the prenuptial rituals to symbolize her new status as mistress of her own household.

Mexico

History

The discovery of South America by Columbus transformed the lives of both the native Indians and the Europeans who eventually conquered them. Skillful Indian farmers had been growing a wide variety of plants for hundreds, perhaps thousands, of years. These have been added to the world's smorgasbord of food and are almost all now cultivated outside South America. Among these are corn, potatoes, tomatoes, chili, peanuts, beans, avocados, vanilla, sweet potatoes, pineapples, papaya and chocolate.

The Mexican pyramids, surrounded by village ruins reflect the country's ancient civilization.

Mexico is the home of corn. The remains of an ancient wild corn have been found in caves once inhabited by the early Mexicans. Each tiny ear was approximately 1 inch (2.5 cm) long. From these humble beginnings hundreds of varieties were developed: yellow corn, red corn, sweet corn, popcorn and so on.

Corn was the staple of the Mexican diet but it contains less protein and vitamins than wheat. The answer to this problem was provided naturally by beans, which are rich in protein. The ancient Mexicans cultivated corn and beans together. They are still the basis of many Mexicans' diet today. Corn and beans are, in fact, the combination — in *tacos* and *tortillas* — for which Mexican food is renowned.

When the Spanish *conquistadors*, or conquerors, led by Hernando Cortes, arrived in Mexico in the early sixteenth century, they were dazzled by the magnificence of the Aztec capital, Tenochtitlán. From there the Aztecs were ruled by Montezuma, their emperor. Many descriptions of the whitewashed city glistening on Lake Texcoco, its vibrant people, its colorful markets, its monumental temples, its exotic food and, of course, its fabulous treasures, have survived.

A list of foods displayed for the pleasure of Montezuma tells us much about the sophisticated cuisine of the Aztecs: large tortillas, tortillas formed in rolls, white tamales with beans forming a seashell on top, roast turkey hen, roast quail, white fish with yellow chili, squash flowers, turkey with a sauce of red chili, tomato and ground squash seeds — the list goes on and on, finishing with a number of different chocolate delicacies. Of course, most Aztecs would not have had such an array from which to choose. They ate corn, beans and perhaps a little chili.

The Spanish brought their own European foods to the conquered land. Some historians have noted that the import that had the greatest impact was the pig. Not only were pigs an easily husbanded supply of meat, but they also provided the fat that was missing from the Mexican diet. Fat, or lard, meant that food could be fried as well as boiled or roasted. A new range of possible tastes and combinations was opened up. For example, beans could be boiled, mashed and fried slowly to create *frijoles refritos* (refried beans), which are consumed in every home and restaurant right throughout Mexico. Mexicans also readily assimilated garlic, onions, rice and spices such as pepper.

A roadside stand in Can Cun.

A local beach in Can Cun is popular with tourists for its exotic beauty.

Although the pre-conquest diet lacked dairy foods and fat, it included a wonderful array of fruit and vegetables. Avocado is native to Mexico and has been eaten on its own, in or with sauces and as an addition to soups and casseroles for centuries.

The use of some native plants has not spread outside Mexico. The maguey is a large, strong, spiky plant, the sap of which is used to produce a somewhat alcoholic yet nutritious beverage.

Regional Specialties

It is almost impossible to describe Mexican food without a word or two about tortillas, so ubiquitous is their presence. Tortillas are the daily bread of Mexicans and have been so since, at the very least, the beginning of recorded history.

Corn is first heated in a corrosive solution to remove the skins from the kernels, then boiled and mashed before being made into dough for tortillas. Unlike wheat, corn contains no gluten and therefore cannot be made into leavened bread.

Today tortillas are made mechanically. Originally the softened kernels were pounded on a stone *metate* before being deftly shaped by hand into a flat round. Tortillas were then toasted briefly on a hot pottery griddle.

Just about anything, as long as it is not too liquid, can be wrapped in a tortilla, which then becomes a sort of sandwich. Tortillas can also be used shredded in a casserole as *chilaquiles* or dipped in a sauce, fried, filled with beans or some other filling and rolled as *enchiladas*.

In general, Mexican cookery features sauces and casseroles, inherited from the techniques of cooking in the fat-free past. Nonetheless many dishes are fried at some point in their preparation. Many recipes may seem time-consuming even using the convenience of a food processor. To achieve a desired flavor the Mexican gourmet may spend hours chopping, frying, simmering and blending.

Mexico's mountainous terrain encouraged the development of *patrias chicas*, little homelands. These were, and still are, separate communities confined within a particular locality. These regions have evolved distinctive styles of cookery using local ingredients.

The arid northern parts of Mexico often feature a kind of dried beef, called *cecina*. This is prepared with salt, pepper and lemon juice over a number of days. Cheese is used as a melted topping on soups and beans.

In the more tropical, coastal areas of Mexico beef and cheese are used less extensively. Fruit and vegetables are eaten both raw and cooked. Non-sweet bananas, or *plantains*, are often cooked with chili, onions and tomatoes and are a delicious accompaniment to shrimp. The renowned *guacamole* (avocado dip or sauce) is eaten with almost anything or simply with *tortillas*.

Southern Mexican cookery features wonderful *moles* or complicated sauces. Local specialties include squash flowers and crickets, which may be an acquired taste! On the Yucatan peninsula, the home of the ancient Mayan people, the cuisine features seafood and rolled tortillas stuffed with delectable fillings and garnished with perhaps two sauces.

Many Mexican foods have infiltrated and become acceptable to foreign palates but the uninitiated are advised to approach chilis with due respect. The tantalizing aroma of cooked food in Mexican markets has tempted many an unsuspecting enthusiast whose system has not become adjusted, or, some might say, desensitized. Nevertheless, care must be taken when handling fresh chilis so that the oils do not burn the cook's eyes or mouth. After preparing chilis always wash hands thoroughly in soap and water.

A nunnery and church set amongst the lush countryside of Itza.

Cooking Techniques

Bain marie: A large shallow pan half filled with water kept just below boiling point. The bain marie (or water bath) is used to cook delicate dishes such as custards, butter sauces and fish mousses, protecting them from fierce direct heat and preventing boiling, which causes the ingredients to separate and become oily. A *double boiler* can be used in the same fashion as a bain marie. Alternatively, a roasting pan could be used instead.

Bake: To cook food in an oven by dry heat.

Blanch: To cook vegetables briefly in boiling water or to immerse meats (such as variety meats) in cold water and bring to the boil in order to whiten or remove the strong flavor.

Blind bake: To precook an empty pie shell, which is then filled before completing cooking. If the filling does not require cooking, the shell is blind baked until cooked. All shortcrust and puff pastry may be blind baked. The pastry case is often filled with rice or beans to retain shape and distribute heat evenly.

Boil: To cook ingredients such as vegetables, rice, pasta and suet puddings in liquid at boiling point (212F/100C). Sauces, casseroles, syrups and glazes are also boiled to reduce and thicken the liquid.

Braise: To cook poultry, game, fish, meat or vegetables in a small amount of liquid in a closed pan, so the steam produced cooks the food. Sometimes the food is browned first in hot fat, then placed on a bed of chopped vegetables (see Mirepoix, page 390) and cooked over low heat. Often used for tough cuts that require long, gentle cooking in order to tenderize the flesh.

Broil: A quick cooking method using direct radiant heat. Particularly suited for meat, fish and poultry. As cooking is done by direct, intense heat the food is best basted with oil, butter or marinade to retain the moisture.

Browning dish: A shallow ceramic dish with a special tin oxide coating on the underside which absorbs microwave energy when it is preheated without food. The dish is heated for approximately 10 minutes, then the food is placed on the dish and browns as it does under a broiler.

Brûlée: Applying direct heat to the sugar topping of a dessert in order to caramelize it.

Cure: A method of preserving fish, meat or poultry by drying, salting or smoking.

Deep Fry: A method of frying ingredients in a deep pan of hot peanut or vegetable oil to seal the food in a crisp coating. If the food is fried too slowly it does not seal the ingredient but absorbs fat; if it is too hot, it will scorch. The correct temperature varies between 355–390F (180–200C), allowing longer time at a lower temperature for large pieces of food and less time at a higher temperature for smaller pieces or precooked food. A deep fat thermometer is useful for assessing the correct temperature. For best results, strain the oil through a cheesecloth when cold after use.

Drop Lid: A lid used in Japanese cookery, particularly for simmering. As it is made from wood, it floats on top of the simmering liquid, ensuring that the food is completely submerged and evenly cooked. The lid should be moistened before use. A circle of waxed paper or a flat, light lid can be used as an alternative.

Fire Pot: A tabletop cooking device with a tray in the base to contain charcoal, and a funnel-shaped chimney in the center of a moat in which stock is heated for cooking at the table. Guests sit at the table and cook ingredients in the simmering stock. A substitute fire pot can be made with a table top electric hot plate and an attractive saucepan or a fondue pot.

Flambé: To flavor a dish with alcohol which is then ignited to burn off the alcoholic content.

Glaze: Ingredients such as beaten egg, egg white, milk, syrup and jam brushed over sweet or savory ingredients to give a glossy, attractive coating.

Gratin: A thin layer of grated cheese or breadcrumbs sprinkled over a finished dish and browned in an oven or broiler to give a crisp crust.

Marinate: To soak meat, seafood, poultry or game in a mixture of oil, wine, vinegar and flavorings to tenderize and add flavor. Sweet marinades are also used for fruit and dried fruit.

Microwave: A method of cooking by which the microwaves are absorbed into the moisture molecules of food. The molecules vibrate at such a rapid rate that they produce intense heat which cooks the food. Microwaves penetrate all surfaces of the food to a depth of 2in (5cm) and the heat then spreads to the rest of the ingredient or dish. Metal objects and dishes should not be placed in a microwave as they cause sparking and possibly fire. Combination cooking is the use of both microwave and conventional ovens to prepare the dish.

Poach: To cook food in seasoned liquid at simmering point.

Preserve: Maintaining food in an edible condition by refrigerating, freezing, cooking, pickling, crystallizing, bottling, drying or smoking.

Pressure Cooking: A method of cooking food quickly in steam built up under pressure.

Reduce: Boiling a liquid, such as in stocks, stews, curries, sauces and glazes, to evaporate the liquid and intensify the flavor.

Roast: A method of cooking meat, poultry or game over an open flame. Cooking meat in an oven is also referred to as roasting.

Sauté: Term taken from the French verb *sauter* meaning "to jump." The food is browned briskly in hot fat, shaking the pan constantly to turn the food and prevent it burning.

Scald: To pour boiling water over food to clean it, loosen hairs or remove the skin. Do not leave the food in the boiling water or it will start cooking. It is also a term used for heating milk to just below boiling point, to retard souring or infuse it with another flavor.

Simmer: To maintain a liquid just below boiling point.

Steam: To cook food rapidly in steam created by boiling water.

Steamer: A traditional Chinese cooking vessel which consists of several bamboo or aluminum steaming baskets stacked on top of each other. The boiling water in the bottom pan produces steam in the enclosed container and cooks the food placed in the racks above. It is a very healthy cooking method as no fats or oils are required for cooking.

Stew: A broad term used to describe any dish in which meat or poultry is cut into pieces, either browned or not, then cooked slowly in a substantial amount of liquid. It is best suited to the cheaper, tough cuts which benefit from a slow, gentle cooking process. By the end of cooking the liquid should have reduced to a concentrated sauce.

Stir-fry: A quick method of frying in shallow fat. All ingredients must be pre-prepared and cut into small, even-sized pieces. Once the oil is hot, the spices, then the meat and vegetables, starting with the firmest and slowest to cook, are added and cooked while stirring briskly. A wok is the pan most commonly used but a large skillet is a suitable alternative.

Sweat: To cook food gently, e.g. onions, in melted fat until the juices run or until the food has softened slightly.

Wok: An iron, shallow, bowl-shaped cooking vessel traditionally associated with Chinese cooking. The iron distributes heat quickly and, due to its shape, little cooking oil is required. It can be used for stir-frying, braising, poaching, boiling and stewing.

SNACKS & APPETIZERS

A

Apples with Bacon

Serves 4: 4 apples, peeled; 4 slices streaky bacon, thinly sliced

Poach the peeled apples gently in water until they are only just cooked and still firm. Wrap each apple in a slice of bacon, securing with a toothpick, and place them in an ungreased ovenproof dish. Bake in an oven preheated to 350°F (180°C) until they are golden brown. Serve the apples very hot.

Artichoke Hors d'Oeuvre

Serves 4: 4 artichokes; 4 tablespoons (2 oz) butter; 2 tablespoons lemon juice, or ½ cup (4 fl oz) French dressing

Trim the artichokes and wash under cold running water. Cook in boiling, salted water to cover for 30–60 minutes (depending on size), until tender.

Drain the artichokes and serve hot with melted butter and lemon juice mixed together, or chill and serve with French dressing.

To eat artichokes, pull the leaves away with the fingers and dip them into the dressing. The fleshy part of the leaves only is eaten. The heart is eaten last.

Asparagus Cream Canapés ⭐

Makes 48: ¾ cup (6 fl oz) heavy cream; ½ × 11-oz (340-g) can asparagus tips, thoroughly drained and the liquid reserved; 1½ tablespoons cornstarch; salt and black pepper; 2 eggs; 48 precooked puff pastry vol au vents

Mix the cream, 2 tablespoons of the reserved asparagus liquid and the cornstarch together in a jug and season generously with salt and pepper. Microwave on HIGH (100%) for 3 minutes, then stir, adding in the asparagus. Microwave on HIGH (100%) for a further 1–2 minutes.

Break the eggs into custard cups and prick both whites and yolks. Cover and microwave on MEDIUM-HIGH (70%) for about 50 seconds, until the yolks are firm. (Non-carousel ovens: Give eggs a half-turn so they cook evenly.) Let stand for 1 minute, then turn out and chop finely. Stir into the asparagus cream.

If serving immediately, heat the pastry shells on HIGH (100%) on a rack or on a plate covered with two layers of paper towels. Fill and serve. Pastry cases will be crisper if heated conventionally.

The canapes can be filled in advance and reheated on a rack or paper towels until they feel warm underneath. Heating time from room temperature is approximately 1 minute on HIGH (100%) for 12 canapés.

Note: The filling will become much hotter than the pastry or bread canapés.

Asparagus Hollandaise 🟥⬜🟩

Serves 6: 1½ lb (750 g) asparagus
Hollandaise Sauce: ½ cup (4 oz) clarified butter; 4 egg yolks; 2 teaspoons lemon juice; salt

Stand bundles of asparagus in a large saucepan with the tips at the top. Add salt and 2 in (5 cm) of water. Cook for 15 minutes with the lid on tightly. Drain well.

Meanwhile, to make the sauce, put the butter and egg yolks in the top of a double boiler. Place over hot but not boiling water and whisk constantly until the butter and eggs are combined. Slowly pour in the remaining butter, whisking constantly until the sauce is well mixed and thickened. Remove from the heat and keep whisking, add the lemon juice and seasoning, then whisk over heat for a further 2 minutes.

Arrange asparagus on individual plates, keeping all the tips at the same end. Pour hollandaise sauce on tips only and serve immediately.

Note: If the Hollandaise sauce curdles, add 1–2 tablespoons of cold water and whisk until smooth.

Asparagus with Mustard-Flavored Dressing ⚫

Serves 4: 20 asparagus spears; ½ teaspoon English mustard powder; 1 egg yolk; 2 teaspoons light soy sauce

Trim the hard ends off the asparagus. Simmer in plenty of lightly salted water until just cooked but still firm. Drain and hold under cold running water so that the bright green color is retained. Drain again and cut into 1½-in (4-cm) lengths.

Mix the mustard powder with ½ teaspoon cold water, then beat lightly with a wooden spoon into the egg yolk. Add the soy sauce, mix well and put into a bowl. Toss the asparagus very carefully, then divide among individual serving bowls, arranging the asparagus pieces in a pyramid. Serve at room temperature.

Asparagus with Mustard-Flavored Dressing

Asparagus Cream Canapes

Bacon and Date Curls

Avocados with Shrimp

Serves 6: 6 tablespoons oil; 2 tablespoons white wine vinegar; 1 garlic clove, crushed; salt and pepper; 12 oz (375 g) shelled shrimp; 3 avocados

Whisk the oil, vinegar, garlic and seasonings together well in a bowl. Add the shrimp and chill in a refrigerator.

Cut the avocados in half lengthwise and remove the pits. Place shrimp in the cavity, making sure the dressing covers the whole cut area of the avocados to prevent discoloration.

Note: The shrimp may be omitted and other seafood substituted, e.g. crayfish, crab or a mixture of seafoods. The avocados may also be served alone with the dressing covering the whole cut area and an extra spoonful in the cavity.

B

Bacon and Date Curls ★

Makes 12: 2 large slices bacon; 12 fresh pitted dates; 12 whole blanched almonds

Cut the bacon into 12 pieces after removing the rind. Each piece should be large enough to wrap around a date. Press an almond into each date where the pit has been removed. Wrap with a piece of bacon and secure with toothpicks.

Line a plate with a paper towel and arrange the bacon curls on top. Cover with another paper towel. Microwave on HIGH (100%) for 1 minute, then remove the paper. Microwave uncovered for a further 1–2 minutes on HIGH (100%). Stand for 2–3 minutes to crisp before serving.

Baked Avocados

Serves 6: 3 ripe avocados; 4 tablespoons (2 oz) butter; ¼ cup (1 oz) all purpose flour; ¼ teaspoon salt; ½ teaspoon curry powder; 1¼ cups (10 fl oz) milk; 7-oz (220-g) can salmon, tuna or crabmeat; 1½ tablespoons fruit chutney or relish; ⅓ cup (2 oz) grated cheese

Cut the avocados in half and discard the pits. Arrange in a microwave-safe dish and cover with plastic wrap. Set aside.

In a 2–3 cup (16–24 fl oz) capacity jug,

melt the butter on MEDIUM-HIGH (70%) for 1 minute. Stir in the flour, salt and curry powder, then add the milk and stir until smooth. Microwave on HIGH (100%) for 4 minutes, stirring from time to time, until the sauce is smooth and thick.

Drain and flake the fish or crabmeat and mix with three-quarters of the sauce. Fill into the cavities of the avocados and coat with the remaining sauce.

Place 1 teaspoonful of the chutney in the center of each filling, then spread the grated cheese evenly over the top. Microwave uncovered for 7½–8 minutes on MEDIUM-HIGH (70%) until the avocados feel warm underneath and the cheese has melted on top. (Non-carousel ovens: Give the dish a half-turn after 4 minutes.)

Baked Oysters

Serves 4: 24 oysters; 3 tablespoons oil;
3 tablespoons lemon juice; ½ teaspoon salt; freshly ground black pepper; 1 teaspoon dry mustard;
½ teaspoon curry powder; 2 tablespoons (1 oz) butter; 1 cup soft white breadcrumbs

Drain the oysters well. Mix the oil, lemon juice and seasonings in a shallow dish and put the oysters in this marinade. Leave for 30 minutes, turning once.

Melt the butter in a small pan and stir in the breadcrumbs, frying until lightly colored. Remove the oysters from the marinade and drain on paper towels. Roll each oyster in the prepared crumbs and place a single layer on a baking sheet. Bake in an oven preheated to 450°F (230°C) for about 20 minutes, or until puffed and crisp.

Baked Spinach and Cheese

Serves 4: 1½ lb (750 g) fresh spinach leaves;
7 tablespoons (3½ oz) butter; 1 onion, finely chopped; 1 garlic clove, crushed; salt and freshly ground black pepper; ¼ teaspoon nutmeg;
1 teaspoon paprika; 4 oz (125 g) grated Gruyère-type cheese

Blanch the spinach in boiling water for 5 minutes, then drain. Squeeze out all excess water and chop coarsely.

In a saucepan, melt the butter. Fry the onion and garlic until the onion is soft and transparent. Add the spinach and sauté lightly until most of the moisture has evaporated. Season and add nutmeg and paprika.

Grease an ovenproof dish. Sprinkle the bottom and sides with half of the cheese. Spoon the spinach into the dish, level the top and sprinkle with the rest of the cheese. Bake in an oven preheated to 350°F (180°C) for 20–30 minutes until the cheese melts. Serve hot.

Beef in Buddhist Robes

Serves 4-6: Batter: 5 eggs, well beaten; 1 tablespoon cornstarch; 1 tablespoon water; 1 teaspoon vegetable oil; ¾ teaspoon salt; few drops of orange-red food coloring
12 oz (375 g) lean beef, finely ground;
1½ tablespoons finely chopped scallion; 1 teaspoon grated fresh ginger; oil for frying
Seasoning: 1 tablespoon Chinese pepper-salt (see Note); 1 tablespoon light soy sauce; 2 tablespoons water; 1 tablespoon cornstarch
Sealing Paste: 1 egg, well beaten; 1 tablespoon cornstarch; 2 teaspoons water

Beat the batter ingredients together thoroughly, then set aside for 25 minutes. Mix the beef, scallion and ginger with the seasoning ingredients and leave for 20 minutes, then refrigerate for 1 hour.

Wipe out a 9-in (22-cm) diameter omelet pan with an oiled cloth. Pour in one-sixth of the batter and cook on moderate heat until small bubbles appear on the surface and the underside is specked with brown. Lift one corner and carefully turn. Cook

Beef in Buddhist Robes

the other side until firm and very lightly colored. Cook the remaining batter in this way, giving six pancakes.

Mix the sealing paste ingredients together and spread on one side of each pancake when cool. Cover half of the pancakes with a thick layer of beef mixture and press the remaining pancakes on top, pasted sides down.

Cut each into wide slices, then into diamond-shape pieces by cutting diagonally to the first cuts.

Heat shallow oil to moderately hot and fry the pancake slices until golden brown, turning once. Lift out and drain well. Arrange on a bed of shredded lettuce or a paper towel on a serving plate and serve with dips of Chinese pepper-salt and light soy sauce.

Note: To make Chinese pepper-salt, dry-fry 1½ tablespoons Chinese brown peppercorns over low heat for 3 minutes or until aromatic, stirring constantly. Grind to a fine powder, then dry-fry with 1¼ teaspoons salt, mixing constantly. Do not allow the salt to color. Cool, then store in an airtight jar.

Belgian Endive with Mornay Sauce

Serves 4: 2 cups (16 fl oz) milk; ½ onion, chopped;
6 peppercorns; 4 sprigs parsley, chopped; 2 sprigs thyme, chopped; 1 bay leaf; 3 tablespoons (1½ oz) butter; 1¾ oz (50 g) all purpose flour; ½ cup (4 fl oz) meat or fish stock; ½ cup (2 oz) Parmesan cheese, freshly grated; ½ cup (2 oz) grated Gruyère cheese; salt and pepper; 1 teaspoon sugar; juice of ½ lemon; 6–8 Belgian endive (chicory)

Simmer the milk with the onion, peppercorns and herbs for 10 minutes. Strain the milk. Melt the butter in a saucepan, whisk in the flour and cook it for 2–3 minutes. Add the hot milk all at once and whisk vigorously to obtain a smooth sauce. Pour in the stock and simmer for 30 minutes, stirring from time to time. Add the cheese, heat and stir until the cheese dissolves. Season to taste.

In a saucepan, boil some water, add the sugar and lemon juice, drop in endive and boil for 2–3 minutes. Cut the endive into slices ½ in (1-cm) thick and arrange them on the bottom of an ovenproof dish. Pour the sauce over the endive and bake in an oven preheated to 400°F (200°C) until the top browns.

C

Calamari Provençale

Serves 6: 11 oz (345 g) cleaned calamari (squid);
1 green bell pepper; 1 red bell pepper; 3 garlic
cloves, crushed; 1 large onion, chopped;
2 tablespoons olive oil; 2 large tomatoes, coarsely
chopped; 1 bay leaf; 1 teaspoon dried mixed thyme,
oregano and rosemary; 1 tablespoon tomato paste
or powder; 1 cup (8 fl oz) water; salt and black
pepper

Cut the calamari into rings and soak in
cold water. Remove seeds from the peppers
and dice.

Place the garlic, onion and olive oil in a
microwave-safe casserole and cover.
Microwave on HIGH (100%) for 4 minutes, then add the peppers, tomatoes, bay
leaf and herbs and microwave 4 minutes on
HIGH (100%), covered.

Add the tomato paste, water, salt and
pepper to taste. Stir well and microwave,
covered, on HIGH (100%) for 10–12 minutes until the vegetables are very tender.
(Give the dish a half turn after 5 minutes in
a non-carousel oven.)

Add the drained calamari and cover
tightly. Microwave on MEDIUM-HIGH
(70%) for 4–6 minutes until the calamari is
white and cooked through but still tender.
Do not overcook.

Cauliflower-Stuffed Parathas

Serves 4: 2 cups (8 oz) fine whole-wheat flour;
1½ teaspoons salt; ghee
Filling: 2 cups uncooked cauliflower, grated;
1-2 fresh red chilies, seeded and chopped;
2 tablespoons ghee

Sift the flour and salt into a bowl and add
just enough water to make a fairly stiff
dough. Knead with well-greased hands for
at least 8 minutes. Divide into 12 portions
and roll each into a ball with greased
hands. Flatten with the fingers and by
gently stretching until quite large and thin.

Squeeze the cauliflower hard to extract
as much water as possible. Mix the
cauliflower pulp with the chili and fry in
the *ghee* for approximately 3 minutes. Add
salt and leave to cool.

Spread the cauliflower stuffing in the
center of each paratha and fold in four

sides to make square packages. Press over
gently with the rolling pin. Fry on a greased
heavy skillet or a griddle lightly coated with
ghee, until the underside is well colored,
then turn and cook the other side. Spread
on *ghee* or butter generously and cut into
quarters. Serve hot.

Cauliflower-Stuffed Parathas

Cheese and Cayenne Straws

Serves 4: 4 tablespoons (2 oz) butter; ½ cup (2 oz)
all purpose flour; ½ cup (2 oz) grated cheese;
cayenne pepper; salt

Rub the butter, flour and cheese together;
season with cayenne pepper and salt. If the
mixture is too stiff, moisten with a little
water. Roll out and cut into thin strips;
twist strips, or leave straight. Form several
of the strips into circles. Place carefully on
a greased baking sheet and bake in an oven
preheated to 450°F (230°C) until light
brown in color, about 15 minutes. Cool.
Fit the cheese straws in bundles into the
circles.

Cheese Blintzes

Serves 6: Batter: 1 cup (4 oz) whole-wheat flour;
2 tablespoons (1 oz) butter; 3 eggs; 1¼ cups
(10 fl oz) milk
8 oz (250 g) cottage cheese; 2 tablespoons sour
cream; salt and pepper; ¼ teaspoon paprika; pinch
of cayenne pepper; ghee for frying; 1¼ cups
(10 fl oz) sour cream and 1 finely chopped onion for
serving

To make the batter, sift the flour into a
mixing bowl and make a well in the center.
Add the melted butter, eggs and half the
milk and beat until smooth. Stir in the
remaining milk.

To make the filling, mix together the cottage cheese, sour cream and seasonings;
beat well.

Melt a small piece of *ghee* in a small skillet or pancake pan over a fairly high heat.
Pour in 2-3 tablespoons batter, tilting the
pan to coat the bottom evenly. Cook the
pancake until golden brown underneath,
2-3 minutes. Loosen with a spatula, turn
over and cook until the other side is
golden. Turn out carefully and keep warm.

When all the blintzes are cooked, place a
little filling on each, fold the sides over and
roll up. Place in a greased ovenproof dish
and bake in an oven preheated to 450°F
(230°C) for 10 minutes. Serve hot, topped
with sour cream and chopped onion.

Cheese Fritters

Serves 4: ¾ cup (6 fl oz) milk; 3½ tablespoons
(1¾ oz) butter; 1 cup (4 oz) all purpose flour;
4 eggs; salt and pepper; pinch of nutmeg; 1 cup
(4 oz) grated Gruyère cheese; oil for deep frying

In a saucepan, bring the milk and butter to
the boil. Add the flour all at once and stir
vigorously with a wooden spoon until the
pastry comes away from the sides of the
pan. Remove from the heat and beat in the
eggs one at a time, making sure that the
mixture is not too thin. Add salt, pepper
and nutmeg. Cool, then stir in the cheese.
Refrigerate for 1 hour.

Preheat the oil to approximately 350°F
(180°C) and, with a tablespoon, form the
cheese mixture into small balls. Fry the fritters until golden brown and serve them hot
with a piquant tomato sauce (see page 138).

Cheese Mushrooms ★

Serves 4: 6 oz (185 g) fresh mushrooms (approx. 12 medium-size); 1 small onion, finely chopped; 1 slice bacon, diced; 4 tablespoons (2 oz) butter; 1 slice day-old bread; 2 tablespoons feta cheese, crumbled; 1 tablespoon finely chopped parsley; 3 stuffed olives, finely chopped; black pepper

Peel the mushrooms and remove stems. Chop the stems finely and place in a small microwave-safe dish with the onion, bacon and the butter. Microwave uncovered on HIGH (100%) for 3 minutes. Remove and stir well.

Remove the crusts from the bread and place in a food processor or blender. Chop to fine crumbs and stir into the bacon mixture, adding the feta cheese, parsley and olives. Season well with black pepper.

Pile the filling onto the mushroom caps and arrange in circles on two plates. Microwave each plate for 1½–1¾ minutes on HIGH (100%). Serve at once.

Chicken Kebabs ★

Makes 12: 11 oz (345 g) boneless chicken breasts; 2 teaspoons lemon juice; 1 teaspoon mild curry powder; pinch of chili powder or cayenne pepper; ¼ teaspoon salt; oil for deep frying
Batter: 1 cup (4 oz) all purpose flour; 1 cup (8 fl oz) water; ½ teaspoon salt; 1 teaspoon baking powder; ½ teaspoon mild curry powder; ¾ cup (3 oz) dry breadcrumbs

Skin the chicken breasts and rub with a mixture of the lemon juice, curry and chili powder (or cayenne) and the salt. Place on a covered plate and set aside at room temperature for 10 minutes to absorb the flavors.

Cut the chicken meat into 12 strips and thread each strip onto a bamboo or metal skewer. Mix the batter ingredients, except the breadcrumbs, together in a bowl. Spread the crumbs on a plate.

Heat the oil to moderately hot. Dip the chicken into the batter, then coat with crumbs. Deep fry in the oil for about 2½ minutes or until cooked through and golden brown on the surface. Serve hot with wedges of lemon and sweet chutney.

Chicken Liver Pâté de Luxe

Chicken Liver Pâté de Luxe 🇫🇷

Serves 10: 4 tablespoons (2 oz) butter; 1 lb (500 g) chicken livers, skinned and trimmed; 1 large onion, chopped; 2 stalks celery, chopped; 2 garlic cloves, crushed; 3 tablespoons chopped parsley; 1–1¼ teaspoons salt; 1 teaspoon cracked black peppercorns, or ground black pepper; 2 teaspoons dry mustard; ¼ teaspoon ground cloves; ¼ teaspoon ground allspice; ¾ cup (6 fl oz) goose fat or melted butter; 1 teaspoon Tabasco sauce; 2 tablespoons brandy; ½ cup (4 fl oz) melted butter (optional)

Melt the butter in a skillet and when sizzling, add the chicken livers. Cook for 3 minutes only, turning them until they are sealed on all sides. Remove the livers from the pan with a slotted spoon and set aside. Add the onion, celery and garlic to the pan and sauté until softened but not brown.

Transfer the contents of the pan to a blender or food processor and puree. Mix the parsley with the salt, black pepper, mustard and spices in a small bowl, and blend gradually into the pâté. Lastly, blend in the goose fat or butter, Tabasco and brandy.

Turn the mixture out of the blender into a lightly oiled pâté mold or terrine. Level the surface with a spatula and chill for an hour or so before coating the surface with melted butter.

Chicken Livers Creole 🇺🇸

Serves 4-6: 3 tablespoons (1½ oz) butter; 3 tablespoons olive oil; 1 lb (500 g) chicken livers, skinned and trimmed; 2 hot red chili peppers, seeded and finely chopped; 2 garlic cloves, finely chopped; 2 tablespoons water; salt and freshly ground black pepper; 4 large tomatoes, peeled and thickly sliced; 1 tablespoon chopped fresh cilantro

Melt half the butter and oil in a skillet and sauté the livers, chilies and garlic for 2–3 minutes, turning the livers until they are sealed on all sides. Add the water and season with salt and black pepper to taste. Cover and simmer over very low heat while you cook the tomatoes.

Melt the remaining butter and oil in a skillet. Quickly sauté the sliced tomatoes, turning once, until they are just softened. Season to taste, arrange on a heated serving dish and sprinkle with the cilantro. Stir the livers, adjust the seasoning and spoon over the tomatoes. Serve immediately.

Chicken Livers Flambé 🇫🇷

Serves 4: 7 oz (220 g) long grain rice; 2 tablespoons (1 oz) butter; 2 tablespoons vegetable oil; 6 scallions, chopped; 8 oz (250 g) button mushrooms, sliced; 1 lb (500 g) chicken livers, skinned and trimmed; 2 tablespoons golden raisins; salt and freshly ground black pepper; 1 teaspoon Angostura bitters; 2 tablespoons brandy

Boil the rice in salted water until tender. In the meantime, melt the butter and oil in a pan over medium heat. Stir the scallions and mushrooms into the fat and sauté for 2–3 minutes. Add the chicken livers and golden raisins, and turn the livers carefully until sealed on all sides. Lower the heat, season with salt and black pepper to taste and add the bitters. Cover and cook for 5 minutes. Drain the rice and transfer to a shallow heated bowl. Make a well in the center and fill with the liver mixture. Just before serving, warm the brandy, flame and pour over the livers.

Chicken Livers with Avocado

Serves 4: Avocado Sauce: 1 large ripe avocado;
2 teaspoons lemon juice; 2–3 drops of Tabasco
sauce; 2–3 drops of Worcestershire sauce;
2–4 tablespoons cream; salt
2 tablespoons (1 oz) butter; 1 tablespoon vegetable
oil; 1 small garlic clove, crushed; 1 medium-size
onion, quartered and sliced; 12 oz (375 g) chicken
livers, skinned and trimmed; salt and freshly ground
black pepper; pinch of cayenne or red pepper;
2 tablespoons Madeira; 2 tablespoons tomato paste

To make the sauce, peel the avocado and
remove the pit. Cut a small quarter from it
and sprinkle it with the lemon juice to prevent it from discoloring. Set aside to use
for the garnish. Puree the rest of the avocado in a blender or food processor or
mash with a fork until it is very smooth.
Blend with the Tabasco and Worcestershire
sauces and enough cream to give a consistency just heavy enough to fall from the
spoon. Season with salt to taste and set
aside.

Melt the butter and oil in a large skillet.
Add the garlic and onion, and sauté until
the onion is transparent. Add the chicken
livers and cook for about 5–7 minutes,
until they are firm but still slightly pink in
the center. Season to taste with salt, black
pepper and cayenne or red pepper. Fold in
the Madeira and tomato paste. Simmer
very gently for 2–3 minutes, until very hot.

Transfer the chicken livers to a heated
serving dish, spread the sauce along the
center and top with the sliced, reserved
avocado. Serve immediately.

Chicken Livers with Green Peppercorns

Serves 6: 1 lb (500 g) chicken livers; 1 large onion,
finely chopped; 1–2 garlic cloves, crushed;
4 tablespoons (2 oz) butter, preferably unsalted;
½ cup (4 fl oz) tomato puree; 2 tablespoons green
peppercorns, in their liquid; ½ teaspoon salt;
½ teaspoon dried oregano or basil

Rinse the livers and drain well. Cut into
small pieces and set aside. Place the onion,
garlic and butter in a microwave-safe casserole and cover with the lid or plastic
wrap. Microwave on HIGH (100%) for
3–4 minutes.

Add the livers, stirring evenly into the

Chicken Livers with Avocado

onion. Cover and vent one corner. Microwave on MEDIUM (50%) for 5 minutes.
Stir, bringing the livers to the outside of the
dish into the center. Add the tomato puree
and peppercorns, and microwave on
MEDIUM (50%) for a further 6 minutes.
Rearrange the livers again, add the salt and
oregano and microwave a further 7–9 minutes on MEDIUM (50%), stirring once or
twice, until the livers are cooked through
with just a hint of pink in the center.

Chicken Walnut Rolls

Serves 4–6: 8 oz (250 g) boneless chicken breast;
1½ oz (45 g) walnuts, blanched and drained; 4 cups
oil for deep frying; 5 oz (155 g) young bok choy or
broccoli broken into florets; dash of wine; salt;
sugar to taste; 2 tablespoons chicken stock or water;
½ teaspoon white vinegar; 1 teaspoon sesame oil
(optional)
Seasoning A: 1 egg white, beaten; ¼ teaspoon salt;
1 tablespoon cornstarch; 1 tablespoon water

Seasoning B: 2 tablespoons softened lard;
¼ teaspoon grated fresh ginger; 1 tablespoon finely
chopped scallion; ¼ teaspoon crushed garlic
Sauce: ½ cup (4 fl oz) chicken stock; 1 tablespoon
light soy sauce; ¼ teaspoon salt; ½ teaspoon sugar;
¼ teaspoon white pepper; ½ teaspoon cornstarch

Skin the chicken breasts and cut the meat
across the grain into reasonably thin slices,
then flatten gently with the side of a
cleaver. Mix with the seasoning A ingredients and set aside to marinate for 15 minutes. Dry the walnuts and deep fry in fairly
hot oil until lightly colored. Lift out and
drain well. Leave to cool. Place a walnut in
the center of each chicken slice, roll up and
squeeze gently to hold. Toothpicks may be
necessary to secure some of the rolls, but
most should stay in place unaided.

Reheat the deep frying oil to moderate
and fry the chicken walnut rolls until the
meat whitens, about 1 minute. Lift out and
drain well. Pour off all but 2 tablespoons of
the oil and sauté the vegetables for 4 minutes. Add the wine, salt, sugar to taste, and

the chicken stock or cold water. Cook, covered, for a further 1 minute.

Fry the seasoning B ingredients together in another pan, then add the premixed sauce ingredients and bring to the boil. Add the chicken rolls and warm through the sauce. Season with vinegar and sesame oil, if used. Transfer to a warmed serving dish.

Chicken Wings Simmered in Wine

Serves 6–12: 12 chicken wings; 6 large dried black mushrooms, soaked for 25 minutes; ½ cup (4 fl oz) oil or softened lard; 2 tablespoons finely chopped scallion; 1 teaspoon grated fresh ginger; 1 large brown onion, thinly sliced; 2 tablespoons red wine
Seasoning A: 2 tablespoons light soy sauce; 1 teaspoon sugar
Seasoning B/Sauce: 2¼ cups (18 fl oz) chicken stock; 1 tablespoon light soy sauce; 2 teaspoons dark soy sauce; 1¼ teaspoons sugar; ¼ teaspoon salt; 2 tablespoons red wine

Cut off the wing tips and divide each wing into two at the joints. Drain the mushrooms and remove the stems.

Heat half the oil or lard and fry the scallion and ginger on moderately high heat for 1 minute. Add the wings with the seasoning A ingredients and stir-fry on high heat until the seasoning is absorbed into the wings and they turn a red-brown color.

Transfer to a casserole or slow cooker and add the seasoning B/sauce ingredients. Cover and braise for 20 minutes or the equivalent in a slow cooker.

Fry the sliced onion in the remaining oil or lard until well browned. Add the mushrooms and fry briefly, then add to the casserole. Re-cover and braise a further 15 minutes. Stir in the remaining red wine just before serving.

Chicken Wings with Plum Sauce

Serves 6: 6 chicken wings, approx. 1 lb (500 g); 1 tablespoon hoisin sauce or sweet bean paste; 2 teaspoons dry sherry; 1 teaspoon grated fresh ginger; 1 garlic clove, crushed; ¾ teaspoon salt; 1 cup (4 oz) cornstarch; oil for deep frying; 1½ tablespoons Chinese plum sauce

Chicken Wings with Plum Sauce

Remove the wing tips and keep for soup making. Wipe the wings with paper towels and place in a dish. Add the *hoisin* sauce, sherry, ginger, garlic and salt and mix thoroughly, rubbing it evenly into the wings. Leave for 30 minutes to absorb the flavorings, then drain on paper towels and coat thickly with the cornstarch.

Heat the oil to fairly hot, then decrease the heat slightly. Deep fry the wings for about 4½ minutes, turning frequently. Remove with a slotted spoon and arrange on a serving dish. Pour the plum sauce over and serve at once.

Rub sauce into wings.

Deep fry until golden.

Chili con Carne

Serves 6: 1 large onion, finely chopped; 2 garlic cloves, crushed; 2 tablespoons olive oil; 1 lb (500 g) ground beef; 2 tomatoes, finely chopped; 2 tablespoons tomato paste; two 14-oz (440-g) cans red kidney beans; 1 tablespoon Mexican or taco seasoning, or to taste; salt and black pepper

Place the onion, garlic and olive oil in a large casserole. Cover and microwave on HIGH (100%) for 3½ minutes. Add the beef and microwave for 1½ minutes, covered, on HIGH (100%), stir well to break up lumps, then microwave a further 1½ minutes on HIGH (100%). Add the tomatoes, cover and microwave on HIGH (100%) for 4 minutes, then stir in the tomato paste and the kidney beans with their liquid. Add the seasonings, cover and microwave on MEDIUM (50%) for 15–20 minutes, stirring twice.

Chicken Wings Simmered in Wine

Clams in Yellow Bean Sauce

Chili Eggs

Serves 4–6: 6 large eggs; oil for deep frying; 2 medium-size onions, chopped; 2 garlic cloves, chopped; ½-in (1-cm) piece fresh ginger, chopped; 1 teaspoon dried shrimp paste; 1 tablespoon chili powder; 2 fresh red chilies, finely chopped; 2-in (5-cm) stalk lemongrass, finely chopped; 1 teaspoon tamarind; 2 tablespoons boiling water; 2 teaspoons sugar; ¾ teaspoon turmeric; salt and pepper; fresh cilantro leaves

Hard-cook the eggs and place in cold water. When cold, remove the shells and prick the eggs with a fork to allow the seasonings to penetrate. Heat the oil and gently fry the eggs until they are a deep golden color and slightly crisp on the outside. Remove and set aside.

Pour off all but 1 tablespoon of oil and fry the onions, garlic and ginger for 2 minutes. Add the shrimp paste, chili powder, chopped chilies, lemongrass and tamarind mixed with boiling water. Stir over moderate heat for 2 minutes, then add the sugar and turmeric. Stir well. Replace the eggs and cook until the seasonings have dried up and cling to the eggs. Sprinkle on salt and pepper.

Serve the eggs either whole or halved, garnished with sprigs of fresh cilantro.

Clams in Yellow Bean Sauce

Serves 6: 2 lb (1 kg) fresh clams, in the shell; 2 scallions, trimmed and sliced; 2 teaspoons chopped garlic; ¼ cup (2 fl oz) oil
Seasoning/Sauce: ½ cup (4 fl oz) chicken stock; 1½ tablespoons salted yellow bean sauce; 2 teaspoons rice wine or dry sherry; 2 teaspoons sugar; 1 teaspoon cornstarch; 1–2 teaspoons finely chopped fresh red chili; pepper (optional)

Thoroughly wash the clams, brushing the shells with a soft brush. Rinse well in cold water and place in a large wok. Add the scallions, garlic and oil, and cover the pan. Cook over moderate heat, shaking the pan occasionally to encourage the shells to open.

When the shells are open, add the seasoning/sauce ingredients and bring to the boil. Simmer for about 1½ minutes. Discard those shells which have not opened, then transfer the clams and sauce to a serving dish.

Chili Eggs

Crab-Stuffed Cucumber

Serves 4: 2 small cucumbers, 1–1½ in (2.5–4 cm) in diameter; salt; sprigs from a handful of watercress or fresh cilantro; 2½ oz (75 g) crabmeat (preferably fresh); 1 tablespoon shredded pickled red ginger
Dipping Sauce: 2 tablespoons rice vinegar; 2 tablespoons dashi; 1 tablespoon sugar; 1½ teaspoons light soy sauce

Peel the cucumbers lengthwise, leaving an occasional lengthwise strip of skin on for an attractive appearance. Rub the cucumbers with plenty of salt and set aside for 15 minutes. Rinse under running water and pat dry. Cut off and discard the ends of the cucumbers, then use a teaspoon or curved grapefruit knife to scoop the pulp and seeds from the center of each cucumber.

Slit each cucumber lengthwise then hold slightly open to spoon in the stuffing. First lay sprigs of watercress neatly along the length of the cucumber, then arrange half the crabmeat on top and cover with half the shredded ginger. Press the cucumber firmly to seal. Repeat with the other cucumber. If not serving immediately, wrap tightly in plastic wrap and refrigerate.

Just before serving, cut the cucumber into ¾-in (2-cm) rings and arrange on individual dishes.

Make the dipping sauce well in advance. Put all ingredients into a small pan and bring to the boil. Remove from the heat immediately and allow to cool. Pour into individual sauce bowls.

Crisp-Fried Egg Rolls

Crisp-Fried Egg Rolls

Serves 6: Batter: 4 large eggs, well beaten;
1 tablespoon all purpose flour; 1 tablespoon water;
6 cups (1½ liters) oil for deep frying; Chinese
pepper-salt (see page 40)
8 oz (250 g) lean pork, finely shredded; 4 oz (125 g)
fresh beansprouts; 1 medium-size carrot, finely
shredded; 1 small stalk celery, finely shredded;
2 tablespoons softened lard or oil; 12 garlic chives,
sliced
Seasoning A: ½ teaspoon salt; 2 teaspoons rice wine
or dry sherry; 1½ teaspoons cornstarch
Seasoning B: 1½ teaspoons salt; 1 tablespoon
sugar; ¼ teaspoon ground black pepper;
1½ teaspoons sesame oil
Sauce Dip: 2 tablespoons tomato sauce;
1 tablespoon Worcestershire sauce; 2 tablespoons
light soy sauce; 1 teaspoon hot bean paste or chili
sauce; 1½ teaspoons finely chopped garlic;
1 teaspoon sugar

Mix the batter ingredients together thoroughly. Wipe out an omelet pan with an oiled cloth and heat to moderate. Pour in about 2 tablespoons of the batter. Lift the pan and swirl it slowly around so the mixture flows into a thin circle about 7 in (17.5 cm) in diameter. Cook until the sides lift from the pan, then carefully flip over and briefly cook the other side. The pancake should be firm, but not crisp. Remove to a piece of waxed paper. Cook the remaining pancakes, making twelve. Stack between pieces of waxed paper. Leave to cool.

Mix the pork with the seasoning A ingredients and leave for 10 minutes. Blanch the beansprouts, carrot and celery

Crab with Vinegared Dressing

Serves 4: 2 medium-size crabs or 5 oz (155 g) fresh
crabmeat; 1 Japanese cucumber or ½ medium-size
cucumber; ½ teaspoon salt; ¼ cup (2 fl oz) water;
1 teaspoon ginger juice (see page 209)
Sambai-Zu Sauce: ¼ cup (2 fl oz) dashi; ¼ cup
(2 fl oz) rice vinegar; 1 tablespoon light soy sauce;
1½ teaspoons sweet rice wine (mirin)

If using raw crabs, boil in plenty of water for about 10 minutes until cooked. Cool, then extract all the meat from the crab, flake finely and chill.

Slice the Japanese cucumber finely, then sprinkle with salt. Rub with the hands lightly, sprinkle over the water, stir, cover and leave to stand in the refrigerator for about 15 minutes. If using a medium-size cucumber, peel, leaving on a few narrow strips of skin for a more attractive appearance. Cut the cucumber in half lengthwise, then cut each half in thin slices. Treat as for Japanese cucumber.

Make the sambai-zu sauce by combining all ingredients in a small pan and bringing just to the boil. Cool, then combine with ginger juice and chill in the refrigerator.

Before serving, drain the cucumber, rinse quickly with fresh water, then squeeze out the moisture carefully with your hands. The cucumber should be limp. Divide the crab and cucumber equally among 4 small bowls and pour over a little sambai-zu sauce. Serve chilled.

Crab with Vinegared Dressing

separately. Drain well and set aside.

Heat the lard or oil to moderate and stir-fry the shredded pork until white and firm, about 1½ minutes. Add the seasoning B ingredients, the garlic chives and blanched vegetables and stir-fry together for about 2 minutes. Remove and spread on a plate to cool.

Pour the Chinese pepper-salt into several small dishes to use as a dip, or prepare the sauce dip by mixing the ingredients together.

Place a portion of the filling in a sausage shape slightly off center on each pancake. Fold over the closest edge, then fold in the two sides and roll up. Stick the flaps down with a paste made from flour and water.

Heat the deep frying oil to moderately hot and fry the rolls, several at a time, until golden and crisp. Remove and drain well. Arrange on a paper-lined serving plate or on a bed of finely shredded lettuce and serve with the prepared dips.

Crisp-Fried Shrimp with Garlic and Chili

Serves 4: 1¼ lb (625 g) raw shrimp, in the shell;
6 cups (1½ liters) oil for deep frying; 2 scallions,
trimmed and diced; 5–6 garlic cloves, thinly sliced;
1–2 fresh red chili peppers, seeded and sliced;
1 tablespoon rice wine or dry sherry
Seasoning: 1 teaspoon salt or Chinese pepper-salt
(see page 40); ¼ teaspoon ground black pepper
(omit if using pepper-salt)

Thoroughly wash the shrimp and wipe dry. Do not peel. Heat the deep frying oil to fairly hot and fry the whole shrimp until they turn bright pink, about 35 seconds. Remove and drain.

Pour off all but 2½ tablespoons of the oil and stir-fry the scallions, garlic and chili for 1 minute on moderate heat. Return the shrimp and stir-fry briefly, then sizzle the wine onto the sides of the pan and stir in. Add the seasoning ingredients and mix well. Transfer to a serving plate.

Serve the shrimp in their shells, the intention being to first nibble the whole thing to extract the flavor and saltiness on the shell, then to remove the shell and eat the tender shrimp. They may, however, be cooked without the shells. In this instance, do not deep fry but quickly sauté in shallow oil with the other ingredients and serve at once.

Cucumber with Pork Stuffing

Serves 6: 1 large cucumber; 6 oz (185 g) lean pork,
finely ground; 1 large scallion, chopped; 2 slices
fresh ginger, chopped; 2 teaspoons light soy sauce;
¾ teaspoon dry sherry; ¾ teaspoon sugar;
1 teaspoon cornstarch
Sauce: 2 teaspoons light soy sauce; 2 teaspoons
Chinese oyster sauce; 1 teaspoon cornstarch

Wipe the cucumber and remove the ends, then cut into six thick slices. Use a small knife to remove the seed core, making each piece of cucumber into a ring.

Mix the pork with the remaining ingredients and use to fill the cucumber rings. Set on a lightly oiled plate, then place on a rack in a wok. Add water to just below the rack. Cover and steam gently for about 25 minutes.

Drain the liquid from the plate into a clean pan and add the other sauce ingredients. Bring to the boil and stir for about 1 minute, then pour over the cucumbers and serve.

Remove the seed core.　　Fill the rings with the stuffing.

Cucumber with Pork Stuffing

Cucumber Yogurt Dip (Tzatziki)

Makes 2½ cups (20 fl oz): 2 cucumbers, peeled and
seeds removed; salt; ¾ cup (6 fl oz) plain yogurt;
½ cup (4 fl oz) sour cream; ½ garlic clove, crushed;
juice of ½ lemon; ⅛ teaspoon cayenne pepper

Cut the cucumber into pieces 1–2 in (2.5–5 cm) long and puree in a food processor or blender. Place the puree in a colander, sprinkle with salt and let it stand to drain for 20 minutes. Combine the remaining ingredients, add the cucumber puree and season to taste. Refrigerate for 6 hours and serve as a dip.

Curled Shrimp Steamed with Five Shreds

Curled Shrimp Steamed with Five Shreds

Serves 4: 1 lb (500 g) large raw shrimp, in the shell;
1 egg, well beaten; 3 dried black mushrooms,
soaked for 25 minutes; 1½ oz (45 g) canned
bamboo shoots, drained and shredded; 1 oz (30 g)
cooked ham, shredded; 2 scallions, trimmed and
shredded
Seasoning: ⅓ teaspoon salt; 1 teaspoon rice wine or
dry sherry; 1 teaspoon cornstarch
Sauce: ½ cup (4 fl oz) chicken stock; 2 teaspoons
rice wine or dry sherry; 1 teaspoon sesame oil;
½ teaspoon salt; 1 teaspoon cornstarch

Peel the shrimp, leaving the tail section intact, then place shrimp in a dish with the seasoning ingredients and leave for 15 minutes. Reserve the heads.

Wipe out an omelet pan with an oiled cloth and heat to moderate. Pour in the beaten egg and tilt the pan to give a thin, even coating. Cook until firm but not colored underneath, turn and cook the other side. Remove and spread on a board to cool. Roll up and cut into narrow shreds.

Squeeze the water from the mushrooms and remove the stems. Shred the caps.

Cut down the center backs of the shrimp, cutting deep enough to allow the shrimp to be pressed out flat. Remove the dark veins. Make a central slit and pass the tails through this so that the shrimp are curled up.

Arrange the shrimp with their heads in a dish and arrange the shredded ingredients on top. Set the dish on a rack in a steamer and steam over high heat for 5 minutes.

Remove from the steamer and drain any liquid into a pan. Add the premixed sauce ingredients and bring to the boil. Simmer until the sauce thickens, then pour over the shrimp and serve at once.

Curry Puffs

Serves 4: 1 large package flaky or puff pastry, weighing about 14 oz (450 g); 2 tablespoons oil; 1 medium-size red or brown onion, finely chopped; 2 slices fresh ginger, very finely chopped; 2 heaped tablespoons meat curry powder (see below); 8 oz (250 g) ground lean lamb or beef; 1 large ripe tomato, chopped; ½ teaspoon salt, or more to taste; 1 large potato, boiled and cut into ¼-in (5-mm) dice
Meat Curry Powder: 10 oz (300 g) coriander; 2½ oz (75 g) cumin seeds; 2½ oz (75 g) fennel seeds; 2½ oz (75 g) dried red chilies; 1½ oz (45 g) black peppercorns; ½ oz (15 g) cinnamon sticks; 10 whole cardamom pods; 10 whole cloves; 1½ oz (45 g) turmeric

To make the curry powder, dry-fry each spice separately until golden and giving off a pleasant fragrance. Grind the spices together in a coffee grinder, stirring in turmeric last. Combine, then store in an airtight container when cold.

Allow the pastry to thaw to room temperature. Heat the oil and gently fry the onion and ginger, stirring from time to time, until soft. Mix the curry powder with sufficient water to make a stiff paste, then add to the onions and ginger. Fry for 3–4 minutes, then add the meat and fry until it changes color.

Add the chopped tomato and sprinkle with salt, then cover the pan and simmer gently for 10 minutes, stirring from time to

time. Add a tablespoonful or two of water during cooking if the mixture sticks to the base of the pan. Add the diced potato and cook for another minute or two, taste and adjust the seasonings, then leave to cool.

Roll the pastry out very thinly and cut into about 14 squares measuring 3 in (8 cm). Wet two edges of each square with milk, then put in a tablespoon of the cold meat filling. Fold over to make a triangle, press the edges with a fork, and bake in an oven preheated to 425°F (220°C) for 12–15 minutes, until puffed and golden brown. Serve warm.

D

Deep Fried Crabmeat Balls

Serves 6: 10 oz (315 g) crabmeat; 2 oz (60 g) shrimp meat; 1½ oz (45 g) pork fat; 2 egg whites, beaten; 1 tablespoon finely chopped scallion; 1½ teaspoons grated fresh ginger; 6 cups (1½ liters) oil for deep frying; Chinese pepper-salt (see page 40); sweet soy sauce
Seasoning: ½ teaspoon salt; ½ teaspoon sugar; 1 teaspoon rice wine or dry sherry; 1 tablespoon cornstarch

Pulverize the crabmeat, shrimp meat and pork fat in the food processor or by using two cleavers. Add the egg whites, scallion, ginger and combined seasoning, and mix in one direction only, adding ½–1 tablespoon of water to make a smooth paste.

Heat the deep frying oil to moderate. Form the mixture into balls and spoon into the oil. Fry gently until they rise to the surface and color lightly. Lift out with a perforated spoon and drain well.

Serve on a bed of shredded lettuce with accompaniments of pepper-salt and sweet soy sauce.

Deep Fried Garbanzo Balls (Falafels)

Serves 4-6: 1 lb (500 g) dried garbanzo beans, preferably skinless; 4 slices white bread or 1 piece pita bread; cold milk; 2 large onions, grated; 3 garlic cloves, crushed; 1 large bunch fresh parsley, finely chopped; 1½ teaspoons ground cumin; 2 teaspoons ground coriander; 2 tablespoons lemon

juice; salt and cayenne pepper; oil for deep frying; lettuce, tomatoes, onion rings, tahina cream, olive oil

Soak the beans for 24 hours, then drain. Peel off any skins. Soak the bread in the milk until softened, squeeze out as much milk as possible and place the beans, bread, onions and garlic in a mortar or blender. Pound or blend to a smooth paste and add the parsley, cumin, coriander and lemon juice, seasoning generously with salt and cayenne. Pound again until completely smooth and well mixed. This process is best done in a mortar as it would require the addition of water to grind in a blender, thus spoiling the texture of the bean paste.

Form the paste into walnut-size balls and cover with a dampened cloth for about 1 hour.

Heat the oil to fairly hot and deep fry the balls until well colored. To serve, sandwich several in a piece of *pita* bread, adding shredded lettuce, sliced tomato and onion rings and flavoring with *tahina* cream and olive oil. The dish may also be served as an hors d'oeuvre on cocktail sticks with black olives and a *tahina* cream or unflavored yogurt dip.

Deep Fried Fish Fillets with Black Sesame Seed Dressing

Deep Fried Fish Fillets with Black Sesame Seed Dressing

Serves 4: 10 oz (315 g) boneless white fish; 1 cup (4 oz) all purpose flour; 2 eggs, well beaten; 2 oz (60 g) black sesame seeds; 4 cups (1 liter) oil for deep frying; Chinese pepper-salt (see page 40)
Seasoning: ½ teaspoon salt; ¼ teaspoon white pepper; 1 tablespoon rice wine or dry sherry; 2 teaspoons sesame oil; 1 tablespoon finely chopped scallion; 1 tablespoon grated fresh ginger

Cut the fish into slices across the fillets, cutting at a sharp angle so that the slices are about 1 in (2.5 cm) wide. Place in a dish with the seasoning ingredients and leave to marinate for 20 minutes. Drain and coat with flour, then dip into the beaten egg.

Heat the deep frying oil to moderately hot. Dip the fish pieces into the sesame seeds, coating thickly. Deep fry until the fish is cooked through, about 2 minutes. Drain well. Serve with Chinese pepper-salt.

Deep Fried Lentil Savories

Serves 4: 1½ cups black gram dhal; *2-3 fresh green chilies;1 medium-size red or brown onion; 3 slices fresh ginger; 1 sprig curry leaves; 1 teaspoon salt; oil for deep frying*

Soak the *dhal* in cold water overnight. Drain. Grind to a paste with a mortar and pestle or in an electric blender.

Chop the chilies, onion, ginger and curry leaves very finely and mix with the ground *dhal*. Add the salt and stir thoroughly.

Oil your hands before shaping the mixture into small balls. Place on an oiled plate while heating plenty of oil in a skillet. Fry the balls a few at a time, turning as they cook, until golden brown. This will take at least 5 minutes. Drain and serve.

Note: If you are using an electric blender to grind the *dhal*, you will need to add 3-4 tablespoons of water to keep the blades turning. If the resulting mixture is too wet to handle, add a tablespoon or two of rice flour.

Deep Fried Pork and Shrimp Rolls

Serves 4: 12 oz (375 g) lean pork; 8 oz (250 g) raw shrimp; 1 small carrot, grated; 4 shallots, or ½ medium-size red or brown onion, finely chopped; 2-3 scallions, finely chopped; 6 water chestnuts, finely chopped; ½ teaspoon salt; pinch of white pepper; 1 egg, lightly beaten; 1 heaped tablespoon cornstarch; 3 large dried bean curd sheets; oil for deep frying

Chop the pork and peeled shrimp together with a cleaver or put in a blender or food processor until a fine paste results. Simmer the carrot in 2 tablespoons of water for 2 minutes, then add to the pork paste together with all other ingredients except the bean curd sheets and oil. Mix thoroughly.

Wipe the bean curd sheets with a damp cloth and cut into 6-in (15-cm) squares. Put a little of the mixture into the center of each piece of bean curd and roll up firmly into a cigar shape, tucking in the sides. Deep fry in hot oil for about 4-5 minutes. Drain and serve with plum or chili sauce.

Deep Fried Shrimp Puffs

Serves 4: 12 oz (375 g) fresh raw shrimp, in the shell; 6 egg whites; 1¼ tablespoons all purpose flour; 2 tablespoons cornstarch; 1 tablespoon finely chopped cooked ham; 1 tablespoon finely chopped scallion; cornstarch; 4 cups (1 liter) oil for deep frying; Chinese pepper-salt (see page 40)
Seasoning: 2 tablespoons onion and ginger infusion (see Note); ½ teaspoon salt; pinch of white pepper; ½ teaspoon rice wine or dry sherry

Shell the shrimp and cut in half lengthwise, discarding the dark veins. Cut any larger shrimp in half again. Mix with the seasoning ingredients and leave for 10 minutes.

Beat the egg whites to stiff peaks and carefully fold in the flour, cornstarch, chopped ham and scallion.

Heat the oil to moderate. Drain the shrimp, pat dry and coat lightly with cornstarch, shaking off any excess. Dip into the egg white batter, coating thickly. Deep fry several pieces at a time until golden, about 1¼ minutes. Remove from the oil, drain for a minute and lower the shrimp puffs into hot oil again. Deep fry for 30 seconds. Drain and arrange on a serving plate. Sprinkle on pepper-salt or serve in separate dishes for dipping. Serve at once.

Note: To make the onion and ginger infusion, mix 3 finely chopped scallions, 5 thick slices of finely chopped ginger and ½ cup boiling water. Chill until required. Strain the liquid into a screw-top jar and keep for up to 1 week.

Diced Chicken and Cashew Nuts

Serves 4: 8 oz (250 g) boneless chicken; 1½ oz (45 g) raw cashew nuts or peanuts; 2 cups (16 fl oz) oil; 12 snow peas; 12 canned button mushrooms, drained; 4 canned water chestnuts, drained; 1½ oz (45 g) canned bamboo shoots, drained and sliced; 9 oz (280 g) young bok choy or choy sum
Seasoning A: ½ teaspoon salt; ¾ teaspoon sugar; 1 teaspoon light soy sauce; 1 teaspoon rice wine or dry sherry; ½ teaspoon cornstarch
Seasoning B/Sauce: ¼ cup (2 fl oz) chicken stock or water; ½ teaspoon dark soy sauce; ½ teaspoon salt; ¼ teaspoon sugar; pinch of ground black pepper; ½ teaspoon cornstarch

Diced Chicken and Cashew Nuts

Cut the chicken into small cubes and place in a dish with the seasoning A ingredients. Mix well and leave for 20 minutes. Heat the oil to fairly hot and deep fry the cashew nuts for about 2 minutes, until light gold in color. Remove and drain well. Leave to cool. String the snow peas. Cut the mushrooms in half horizontally and cut the water chestnuts into three pieces each, horizontally. Rinse the vegetables well and cut the stems into 2-in (5-cm) lengths.

Heat a wok and add 2 tablespoons of the oil. When smoking hot, add the chicken and stir-fry for 2 minutes. Remove from the pan and add the *bok choy* or *choy sum*. Splash in a little water, cover the pan and cook on fairly high heat, shaking the pan to keep the vegetables turning, for 1½–2 minutes. Add the remaining vegetables and stir-fry for 30–45 seconds. Add the premixed seasoning B/sauce ingredients and simmer briefly, then return the chicken and continue to cook until the sauce thickens. Stir in the cashews and transfer to a serving plate.

Duck and Orange Terrine

Serves 12: 2 lb (1 kg) duck meat, boned and chopped; 2 lb (1 kg) ground pork; 4 eggs; finely grated peel of 2 oranges; salt and freshly ground black pepper; pinch of allspice; ½ cup (4 fl oz) rum

Blend the duck meat, pork, eggs, orange peel, salt, pepper, allspice and rum until they are all well mixed. Transfer to a well-buttered terrine and cover. Stand the terrine in a dish of simmering water and bake in an oven preheated to 350°F (180°C) for 1½ hours. Allow to cool, then chill well before serving.

E

Easy Muffin Pizzas ★

Serves 8: 4 prepared English muffins; 13½-oz (425-g) can tomatoes; 1½ cups (6 oz) grated sharp cheese; ½ cup (2½ oz) sliced stuffed olives; 4-5 slices hot salami (pepperoni) or microwaved crisp bacon or cooked ham; 3 slices canned pineapple, finely chopped

Split the muffins. Arrange cut sides

upwards on one or two plates lined with paper towels.

Chop the tomatoes and spread generously over the muffins with the remaining ingredients. Place the plate on a microwave rack and microwave on HIGH (100%) for approximately 45 seconds per muffin.

Muffin pizzas can be given a crisp base by cooking on a microwave browning (searing) or pizza dish. Preheat for 5 minutes and cook the muffins for approximately 35 seconds each.

Duck and Orange Terrine

Egg Masala

Serves 4-6: 6 large eggs; 2 green chilies; ½-in (1-cm) piece fresh ginger; 2 oz (60 g) shredded coconut; 2 teaspoons cumin seeds; 1 tablespoon coriander seeds; 1 large onion; 2 tablespoons ghee; 1 teaspoon black mustard seeds; 1 teaspoon turmeric; 2 large tomatoes, chopped; 1 cup (8 fl oz) water; tamarind water or lemon juice; salt and pepper

Place the eggs in a pan of cold water and boil for 10 minutes. Cover with cold water and set aside.

Grind the chilies and ginger to a paste, then grind with the coconut, cumin and coriander. Thinly slice the onion and fry in *ghee* until soft. Add the seasoning paste and fry for 2 minutes. Sprinkle on mustard seeds and turmeric, and add the tomatoes and water. Bring to the boil and simmer for 10 minutes. Season to taste with tamarind water or lemon juice, salt and pepper.

Peel the eggs and cut in half lengthwise. Place in the masala sauce and simmer for 3 minutes.

Eggplant Dip

Serves 10-12: 3-4 large eggplants; 1 garlic clove, crushed (or ½ onion, finely chopped); juice of ½-1 lemon (depending on taste); ½ cup (4 fl oz) olive oil; salt

Bake the eggplants in an oven preheated to 400°F (200°C) for 30–40 minutes. Cool and peel. On a cutting board, chop the eggplant flesh very finely. Put into a bowl with the garlic or onion and the lemon juice, stir and gradually add the oil (as in preparing mayonnaise). Season and refrigerate. Serve it as a dip with chunky fresh bread.

Empanaditas

Makes 48: Picadillo Filling: 1 lb (500 g) finely ground beef (or pork); 1 onion, finely chopped; 1 garlic clove, chopped; 2 tablespoons oil; 1 cup canned tomatoes (or 3 tomatoes, skinned and chopped); 1 teaspoon brown sugar; 2 tablespoons cider vinegar; 1 teaspoon cinnamon; pinch of cloves; ½ teaspoon cumin; 1 teaspoon salt; ½ cup (3 oz) seedless raisins, plumped in ⅓ cup (2 fl oz) hot beef or chicken stock; ⅓ cup (2 oz) blanched almonds, finely chopped
1 unbaked 10-in (25-cm) double shortcrust pie shell, using lard and iced water (see page 336)

To make the filling, brown the meat, onion and garlic in the heated oil. Add the remaining ingredients, except the almonds. Simmer for about 30 minutes or until the mixture has thickened. Stir in the almonds.

Chill the pastry, then roll it out on a lightly floured board to ⅛ in (3 mm) thick. Cut the pastry into tiny rounds with a small scone cutter. Place a spoonful of filling on each round and brush the edges with water. Fold the pastry in half and press the edges together firmly. Bake in an oven preheated to 375°F (190°C) for 15–20 minutes until golden.

F

Fish Fritters (Fritto Misto di Mare)

Serves 4: 8 oz (250 g) fish fillets (oily or white); 4 oz (125 g) large raw shrimp; 4 oz (125 g) small raw shrimp; all purpose flour; oil for deep frying; 2 lemons

Skin the fish fillets and cut into small finger-length strips. Dry well on paper towels. Peel the shrimp. Dip the fish strips and shellfish into the flour, then deep fry in hot oil until golden brown and cooked.

Drain well on paper towels. Serve immediately, piled high on a serving plate, accompanied by wedges of lemon.

Fish Pâté

Makes 1 large pâté mold: 3 lb (1.5 kg) fish fillets; 8 eggs; 1 cup (8 fl oz) cream, chilled; ½ cup (4 fl oz) port; 2 tablespoons whisky; 2 tablespoons brandy; salt and white pepper; 2 oz (60 g) fresh peas; 1 red or green bell pepper, finely chopped; 1 garlic clove, crushed; 10 asparagus spears, cooked
Sauce: 2 cups (16 fl oz) mayonnaise; 2 tablespoons whisky; 1 teaspoon mustard; 1 tablespoon dry sherry; 1 tablespoon black caviar; 1 tablespoon red caviar

Lightly poach the fish fillets in some water. Break up the pieces and put them into a large bowl to cool. With a wooden spoon, beat in the eggs one by one. Make sure they are well incorporated with the fish. Continue beating and gradually incorporate the cream, port, whisky and brandy. Season. Gently mix in the peas, chopped pepper and garlic.

In a greased pâté mold, place a layer of the mixture 1 in (2.5 cm) deep. Arrange some of the asparagus spears so they do not touch each other. Place another layer of the fish paste, then more asparagus and repeat until all ingredients have been used, finishing with a layer of fish paste.

Cover the mold with aluminum foil and place in a baking dish almost filled with hot water. Put it in an oven preheated to 350°F (180°C) and cook for 1½ hours or until the pâté has set.

To make the sauce, mix the sauce ingredients together. Cool the pâté, remove from mold and cut into slices. Mask with the sauce and serve the pâté with slices of toast.

Fish Puree

Serves 6: 1 lb (500 g) white fish meat; 2 large eggplants, chopped; 4 fresh red chilies; 8 scallions; 8 sprigs mint; salt or fish sauce; 1 small head lettuce; small bunch of mint; small bunch of fennel; small bunch of daun kesom; small bunch of sweet basil; shredded scallions

In separate saucepans, boil the fish and eggplants until soft. Lift out, reserving the fish stock. Remove the bones from the fish and put the meat into a blender. Skin the eggplants and combine with the fish. Add the chilies, scallions and mint, and blend to a puree. Add enough fish stock to make a smooth creamy sauce, then season with salt or fish sauce to taste.

Wash the lettuce and arrange in a salad bowl with the washed herbs. To serve, spread the fish puree onto a lettuce leaf, add a few sprigs of herbs and a sprinkling of scallions and roll up.

Fish Roe Spread (Taramosaláta)

Makes 1½ cups: 4 oz (125 g) taramá (salted roe of the grey mullet or tuna or smoked roe of cod); 4 slices stale white bread without crust; juice of 1½–2 lemons; 1 small onion, finely grated; 1 clove garlic, crushed; 1 cup (8 fl oz) olive oil

Taste the roe and if too salty, soak it in milk or water for 5–10 minutes. Drain.

Soak the bread in some water for a few minutes and squeeze dry.

Combine all ingredients, except the oil, in a food processor or blender and mix until creamy, then gradually add the oil. If making the spread by hand, mash the ingredients with a fork, then whisk in the olive oil. Serve chilled.

Five Spice and Garlic Spare Ribs

Serves 6: 18 spare ribs (about 1⅓ lb/700 g); 8 cups (2 liters) oil for deep frying; Chinese pepper-salt (see page 40)
Seasoning A: ½ teaspoon salt; 2 teaspoons sugar; ¾ teaspoon five spice powder; 2 teaspoons light soy sauce; 1 teaspoon white vinegar; 2 teaspoons rice wine or dry sherry; 2 tablespoons cornstarch
Seasoning B: 1 tablespoon chopped garlic; 2 tablespoons light soy sauce; 1 tablespoon white vinegar; 1 tablespoon sugar

Cut the ribs into 3-in (7.5-cm) pieces or leave whole as preferred. Place in a dish and add the premixed seasoning A ingredients, rubbing thoroughly over each piece. Leave for 1 hour.

Heat the oil to fairly hot and deep fry the ribs until crisped on the surface and cooked through, about 3 minutes. Remove and retain the oil.

Transfer about 2 tablespoons of the oil to another wok and add the seasoning B ingredients. Cook, stirring on high heat for 1 minute, then remove from the heat.

Five Spice and Garlic Spare Ribs

Reheat the deep frying oil and fry the ribs again briefly, until very crisp. Remove and drain, then add to the sauce and simmer briefly. Transfer to a serving plate and serve with Chinese pepper-salt.

Fried Bean Curd

Serves 6–8: 8 squares soft bean curd; oil for deep frying; 2 tablespoons light soy sauce; 1 tablespoon spiced salt powder

Choose well-drained, fairly firm pieces of bean curd. Wrap the bean curd in a towel, put in a dish and place a flat weight on top. Leave to drain and firm for at least eight hours.

Wipe the bean curd and place several pieces on a large slotted spoon. Heat the oil to smoking point, then lower slightly. Carefully lower the spoon into the oil and leave until the bean curd has cooked to a light golden color. Lift out and drain thoroughly, then transfer to a serving dish. Cook the remaining bean curd pieces and add to the plate. Sprinkle with soy sauce and serve with a dip of spiced salt.

Fried Dried Anchovies with Peanuts

Serves 4: 2½ cups dried anchovies; ¼ cup (2 fl oz) oil; 8 shallots, or 1 medium-size red or brown onion, pounded or grated; ½–1 teaspoon chili powder; ¼ teaspoon turmeric; 2 teaspoons sugar; ½ cup fried or roasted peanuts

Unless you are using very thin, tiny anchovies, you will need to discard the head and dark intestinal tract of each fish. Make sure the anchovies are completely dry by putting them in the sun for an hour (watch for cats) or drying them in a very low oven for about 15 minutes.

Heat the oil in a wok or skillet and gently fry the anchovies until brown and crisp. Drain and set aside. Wipe out the pan and put in another tablespoon oil. Gently fry the shallots, chili powder and turmeric, stirring frequently, until golden and fragrant. Add the anchovies, sugar and peanuts and fry for another minute or two, stirring constantly to amalgamate all ingredients. Cool before serving.

Fried Oysters

Serves 2: 12 oysters; salt and pepper; 1 egg yolk; ¼ cup (2 fl oz) milk; dry breadcrumbs; oil for deep frying; lemon wedges; chopped parsley (garnish)

Remove the oysters from the shell and season with salt and pepper. Mix the egg yolk with milk, dip the oysters into the mixture, then drain and roll in breadcrumbs. Deep fry in hot oil for 2 minutes. Heat the shells in the oven and place the fried oysters in the hot shells. Serve hot with lemon wedges and sprinkled with parsley.

Fried Savory Pies

Makes 16–24: Mushroom Filling: 8 oz (250 g) mushrooms, chopped; 4 tablespoons (2 oz) butter or margarine; 2 teaspoons lemon juice; salt and pepper, to taste; 1 tablespoon finely chopped parsley; 1 tablespoon chopped pimiento; 1 tablespoon chopped chives; 1 cup (8 fl oz) cream; 1 tablespoon cornstarch
1 unbaked 9-in (23-cm) double shortcrust pastry (see page 321); oil for deep frying

To make the filling, sauté the mushrooms in butter until they are crisp. Add the lemon juice, salt, pepper, parsley, pimiento and chives, and heat through. Blend the cream and cornstarch together, then stir in the mushrooms. Bring to the boil, stirring constantly. Reduce the heat and cook for 1–2 minutes. Cool.

Roll out the pastry and cut into 2–3 in (5–7.5 cm) squares or circles. Fill with the mushroom filling. Fold the pastry into triangles or half circles. Seal and crimp the edges, then fry in oil for 3–4 minutes. Drain. Serve hot with a sauce if desired.

Fried Shrimp Balls

Serves 4: 1 thick slice stale white bread; 1 lb (500 g) raw shrimp; (2 oz) 60 g hard pork fat; 4 whole water chestnuts; 1 slice fresh ginger, very finely chopped; ¾ teaspoon salt; 1 egg, separated; oil for deep frying

Remove crusts from the bread and sprinkle with a couple of tablespoons of cold water. Leave to soak.

Shell the shrimp and chop very finely together with the pork fat, until the mix-

ture becomes pastelike. Chop the water chestnuts finely and put into a bowl together with the pork and shrimp paste, ginger, salt and egg yolk. Add the soaked bread and mix all ingredients together thoroughly. If desired, the mixture may be covered and refrigerated for several hours.

Just before the shrimp balls are required, beat the egg white until fairly stiff and add to the mixture. To make the balls, first wet your hands with a little cold water, then take a handful of the mixture and squeeze a small amount (about a heaped teaspoon) between the thumb and forefinger. Pull the ball off with a spoon and drop immediately in hot oil. Fry for 2–3 minutes, tossing the balls around in the oil frequently. Drain and serve with salt and pepper powder (see Note).

Note: To make salt and pepper powder, heat 4 teaspoons salt and 1 teaspoon black peppercorns until salt turns golden. Remove immediately and grind until fine.

Fried Stuffed Chicken Rolls

Serves 4: 8 oz (250 g) boneless chicken breast; 5 oz (155 g) raw peeled shrimp; 1 oz (30 g) pork fat; 1½ tablespoons finely chopped cooked ham; 1 tablespoon finely chopped fresh cilantro; 5 cups (1¼ liters) oil for deep frying
Seasoning A: 1 egg white, beaten; ¼ teaspoon salt; pinch of white pepper; ½ teaspoon baking soda (optional); ½ teaspoon rice wine or dry sherry; 1 tablespoon water
Seasoning B: ¼ teaspoon salt; pinch of white pepper; 1 teaspoon finely chopped scallion; ⅓ teaspoon grated fresh ginger
Sauce: ½ cup (4 fl oz) chicken stock; 2 teaspoons light soy sauce; ⅓ teaspoon salt; ¾ teaspoon cornstarch

Cut the chicken into slices, dust with cornstarch and flatten each slice gently with a rolling pin. Place in a dish and rub with the seasoning A ingredients. Let stand for 10 minutes, then turn and let stand a further 10 minutes.

Grind the shrimp and pork fat together and add the seasoning B ingredients. Lay the chicken pieces out on a floured board and spread the shrimp filling over each. Garnish with a sprinkling of ham and cilantro and roll into cylindrical shapes. Secure the rolls with toothpicks or squeeze gently to hold in shape.

Heat the deep frying oil to moderate and fry several rolls at a time until lightly colored, about 2½ minutes, then return all together and fry for an additional 30 seconds. Drain and arrange on a serving plate.

Pour off all but 2 tablespoons of the oil and reheat. Add the premixed sauce ingredients and bring to the boil. Simmer for 1 minute, then pour over the chicken rolls and serve.

Fried Stuffed Mushrooms ★

Serves 4–6: 12 large soaked dried or fresh mushrooms; ¼ cup (1 oz) all purpose flour; ¼ cup (1 oz) cornstarch; 1 teaspoon baking powder; ½ teaspoon salt; 1 egg; oil for deep frying
Filling: 6 oz (185 g) lean pork; ½ stalk celery, or 1½ oz (45 g) fresh beansprouts; 2 scallions; ½ fresh red chili, seeded; ½-in (1.25-cm) piece fresh ginger; 1 tablespoon hoisin sauce; 1 teaspoon thick soy sauce; 2 teaspoons dry sherry; ½ teaspoon salt; 2 teaspoons cornstarch

Peel and thoroughly wash the fresh mushrooms or remove the stems from dried mushrooms, drain and squeeze out as much water as possible.

To make the filling, mince the pork with the celery, scallions, chili and ginger. If using beansprouts, chop finely and add to the pork mixture. Season with the *hoisin* sauce, soy sauce, sherry and salt, and bind with the cornstarch. Mix well. Spoon into the mushrooms, rounding the tops.

Mix the flour, cornstarch, baking powder and salt with the egg and enough water to make a thick batter. Beat for 1 minute, then leave for 5 minutes. Heat the oil to moderately hot. Coat the stuffed mushrooms lightly with flour and dip into the batter. Deep fry approximately 4 minutes. Drain and serve hot.

G

Galway Oyster Soufflé 🇮🇹

Serves 4: 24 shelled or bottled oysters; juice of ½ lemon; ½ cup (2 oz) fresh breadcrumbs; ½ cup (4 fl oz) cream; 2 egg yolks, lightly beaten; salt and pepper; pinch of mace; 2 egg whites, stiffly beaten

Chop 20 of the oysters and save four for the garnish.

Fried Stuffed Mushrooms

Herbed Oysters

Mix the oyster liquid and lemon juice, then heat and pour it over the breadcrumbs. Stir in the chopped oysters, cream and egg yolks. Season to taste and add the mace, then fold in the egg whites.

Pour the mixture into one large or several individual buttered soufflé dishes. Do not fill them right to the top. Cover with aluminum foil and place in a baking dish filled with hot water. Cover the dish with foil and steam over medium heat for 1 hour for the large dish and 40–45 minutes if using small dishes. To serve, turn them out onto plates and serve hot.

H

Ham Cornets ▮▮

Serves 4: 2 cups mixed, cooked, diced vegetables (green beans, potatoes, carrots, zucchini); 1 cup (8 fl oz) mayonnaise; 1 teaspoon Dijon mustard; ¼ cup (2 fl oz) lemon juice; 8 thin slices lean cooked ham; julienne strips of red bell pepper for garnish

Combine the mixed vegetables with the mayonnaise, Dijon mustard and lemon juice. Divide the mixture and place some on each slice of ham. Roll into cornets. Place the ham cornets close together on a serving dish and garnish with julienne strips of pepper.

Herbed Oysters ▮

Serves 6: 36 large oysters, in the shell; 6 garlic cloves, finely chopped; ½ fresh red chili, seeded and chopped; ½-in (1-cm) piece fresh ginger, grated; 1-in (2.5-cm) piece lemongrass, finely chopped; 1-2 teaspoons chopped fresh basil; 3 tablespoons peanut or vegetable oil; lime juice; fish sauce; salt, sugar and black pepper; chopped fresh fennel (optional)

Remove the oysters from the shells and discard the top shells. Clean the lower shells and set aside.

Blanch the oysters in boiling salted water for 10 seconds. Drain. Grind the garlic with the chili, ginger, lemongrass and the basil and fry in the oil for about 2 minutes on moderate heat. Add the lime juice, fish sauce and seasonings to taste, then mix in the oysters. Cook on low heat until just warmed through, then return to their shells and serve at once with a garnish of chopped fennel, if used.

Herrings in Sour Cream ▬

Serve 4: 6 Matjes herring fillets; 1 cup (8 fl oz) sour cream; juice of 1 lemon or 2 tablespoons white wine vinegar; ½ tablespoon sugar (optional); freshly ground black pepper: 1 apple, peeled, cored and cut into thin slivers; 1 onion, cut into thin slices; 1 tablespoon finely chopped dill

Cut the herring fillets into 1-in (2.5-cm) pieces and arrange them on a serving dish. Mix the sour cream, lemon juice or vinegar and (if desired) the sugar. Add the pepper and let the mixture stand for 10 minutes. Arrange the apple slivers and onion slices in a layer on the herrings. Cover with the cream and sprinkle with dill.

Homemade Tasty Hamburgers

Makes 8: 2 lb (1 kg) ground hamburger beef; 1 medium-size onion, finely chopped; 1 garlic clove, crushed (optional); ½ teaspoon dried mixed herbs; ½–¾ teaspoon salt; freshly ground black pepper; 1 egg, beaten (optional); 8 hamburger buns; pickle, mustard or relish; 1 large onion, finely chopped (optional); 3 tablespoons (1½ oz) butter (optional)

Mix the meat, onion, garlic, herbs, seasoning and beaten egg together thoroughly, then form into eight hamburger patties.

Preheat a large browning (searing) dish for 6 minutes on HIGH (100%). When ready, add about 1 tablespoon of cooking oil and quickly put in the hamburgers. Microwave on HIGH (100%) for 2 minutes, then turn and microwave for 4 minutes, turn again and microwave a final 2 minutes or until done.

Pour the liquid from the dish each time the burgers are turned and rearrange the hamburgers, bringing the ones in the center of the dish to the outside, to ensure they cook evenly.

During standing time, warm the buns, then assemble adding pickle, relish or mustard to taste. If using onion, remove the hamburgers from the dish and drain. Add the butter and onion and cook, uncovered, on HIGH (100%) for 3½–4 minutes, stirring several times.

Honey-Glazed Ham

Serves 4–6: 1½ lb (750 g) Chinese or cured (Smithfield) ham; 2 scallions, trimmed and sliced; 8 slices fresh ginger or 4 oz (125 g) Chinese red dates; 1 cup rock candy (sugar), crushed to a powder; ¼ cup (2 fl oz) sweet rice wine or Japanese mirin (see Note); 1 teaspoon guei hwa sauce (optional); 1½ teaspoons cornstarch

Cut off the ham skin and wash the ham well. Place in a saucepan and cover with cold water. Add the scallions. Bring to the boil, then reduce the heat and simmer for about 35 minutes. Remove and drain well.

Cut the ham into thin slices, then into pieces about 2½ in (7.25 cm) wide.

Boil the red dates, if used, in 2 cups of water for 10 minutes, then drain. Arrange the ham slices, overlapping, in a dish. Place the ginger or dates on top and add one-third of the sugar. Place in a dish and steam for about 20 minutes, then add the remaining sugar and wine and steam for a further 1½ hours. Strain the liquid into a wok and bring to the boil. Top up with water to make at least 1 cupful and thicken with the cornstarch mixed with a little cold water. Stir in the *guei hwa*, if used and simmer briefly. Pour over the ham.

Honey-glazed ham is traditionally served with large steamed buns. The buns are opened at the fold and the sweet ham inserted, sandwich fashion, with the sauce being mopped up with the remains of the bread. Thinly sliced white bread can be substituted.

Note: Sweet or cream sherry can be used in place of sweet rice wine.

Honey-Glazed Ham

Honey-Glazed Shrimp

Serves 4–6: 1¼ lb (625 g) raw small shrimp, shelled; 2 egg whites, beaten; cornstarch; oil for deep frying; 2 tablespoons clear honey; 1 tablespoon preserved ginger in syrup, shredded; 1 tablespoon syrup from preserved ginger; 1 tablespoon thin soy sauce; ½ teaspoon salt; 1 tablespoon vegetable oil; white sesame seeds; 6 noodle baskets (see page 150), optional

Rinse and thoroughly dry the shrimp. Dip into the beaten egg whites, then coat with cornstarch. This is best done by pouring the cornstarch into a plastic bag, adding the shrimp and shaking vigorously. Transfer to a colander to shake off the excess

flour. Heat the oil to fairly hot and deep fry the shrimp for approximately 10 seconds, then drain and set aside.

Pour off the oil and add the remaining ingredients, except the sesame seeds. Mix well and bring to the boil, then reduce the heat and simmer for 1–2 minutes. Add the shrimp and stir in the sauce until well glazed. Add the sesame seeds and transfer the shrimp to the prepared noodle baskets, or serve in small glass dishes.

Hot Anchovy and Garlic Dip

Serves 6: 1 cauliflower, broken into bite-size florets; 12 small button mushrooms; 2 carrots, peeled and cut into thin strips about 2 in (5 cm) long; 1 cucumber, peeled, seeded and cut into thin strips about 2 in (5 cm) long; 1 red and 1 green bell pepper, seeded and cut into thin strips; 4 stalks celery, cut into thin strips about 2 in (5 cm) long; 12 scallions, trimmed to 2 in (5 cm) long; 12 cherry tomatoes; 12 radishes
Sauce: 2 cups (16 fl oz) cream; 4 tablespoons (2 oz) butter; 12 anchovy fillets, finely chopped; 1 garlic clove, crushed

Prepare the vegetables, place them in a bowl of water and refrigerate for 2 hours.

To make the sauce, simmer the cream for 15–20 minutes until reduced to 1 cup. In another saucepan, melt the butter. Add the anchovies, garlic and then the reduced cream. Bring to simmering point but do not boil. Arrange the vegetables on a serving platter with the sauce in an earthenware dish. To eat, dip the vegetables in the sauce.

Hot Pepper Omelet

Serves 4: 6½ oz (200 g) chorizo (spicy pork sausage), sliced; 3–4 tablespoons olive oil; 1 small thin hot red or green pepper, seeded, washed and sliced; 1 teaspoon paprika; 8 eggs; 2 tablespoons water; salt

In a skillet, sauté the sausage in half the oil. Add the peppers and paprika and lightly sauté over low heat for 10 minutes. In a bowl, whip the eggs well with water and salt. If necessary, add more oil to the skillet, then pour in the eggs, stir with a fork and fry until set. Fold it over, divide into quarters and serve.

L

Leeks à la Grecque

Serves 6: 6 medium-size leeks; 1 tablespoon chopped fresh tarragon or 1 teaspoon dried tarragon; 1 tablespoon lemon juice; 1 garlic clove, crushed; 1 tablespoon finely chopped parsley; 1 tomato, skinned and seeded; pinch of thyme; salt and freshly ground black pepper; 1 bay leaf; ¼ cup (2 fl oz) olive oil; 1 cup (8 fl oz) water

Cut the tops off the leeks, leaving 2 in (5 cm) of green tops. Wash thoroughly to remove any grit. If the leeks are large, cut in half lengthwise. Put all ingredients into a heavy-based saucepan or fireproof casserole. (A flat stainless steel or earthenware pan is best.) Cover and bring to the boil. Lower the heat and simmer gently for about 10 minutes until leeks are tender but firm. Allow to cool, then chill.

Lemon Chicken Wings

Serves 6: 2 lb (1 kg) chicken wings; ½ cup (4½ oz) cornstarch; juice and finely grated peel of 1 lemon; 1 tablespoon light soy sauce; 1 tablespoon maple syrup; oil

Trim the tips from the chicken wings. Mix the cornstarch and lemon peel to a paste with the lemon juice, soy sauce and maple syrup. Brush the wings with the paste, arrange on a rack and leave for an hour or so to dry.

Arrange the chicken on baking sheets brushed with oil and bake in an oven preheated to 400°F (200°C) for 20–30 minutes, turning once, until the wings are crisp and well browned.

Lobster with Mustard Sauce

Serves 2: 1½-lb (750-g) live lobster; 2 large scallions, finely chopped; ½ small red bell pepper, shredded; 2 tablespoons (1 oz) butter; 1 tablespoon Cognac; 1 teaspoon mild prepared mustard; ¼ cup (2 fl oz) cream; salt and pepper

Kill the lobster by piercing with a sharp, heavy knife behind the back of the head, between the head and the first section of the shell. Place in a dish and add ½ cup (4 fl oz) water. Cover tightly with plastic wrap. Microwave on HIGH (100%) for 6–9 minutes until the shell has turned bright red and the meat is firm and white.

Remove and let stand while the sauce is prepared.

Place the scallion and pepper in a microwave-safe dish with the butter, cover and microwave on HIGH (100%) for 3 minutes. Add the remaining ingredients, including half of the liquid which has accumulated in the dish in which the lobster was cooked. Cover and microwave on HIGH (100%) for 2–3 minutes.

Remove the head from the lobster and scrape out the yellowish sac. Use a heavy knife to cut the tail in half lengthwise, then cut through the head. Remove the intestinal vein. Place the lobster and head on plates and cover with the sauce. Garnish with lemon and parsley and serve at once.

M

Malaysian-Style Spring Rolls

Serves 4-6: 24 large spring roll wrappers; 24 spinach or small cabbage leaves; 2 tablespoons hoisin sauce, or mashed preserved yellow soybeans; 1 cucumber, cut into julienne strips; oil for deep frying
Filling: 6 oz (185 g) raw baby shrimp, shelled; 6 oz (185 g) boneless chicken, shredded; 2 cups (8 oz) shredded cabbage; 2 medium-size cooked potatoes, diced; 2 garlic cloves, crushed; 6 scallions, chopped; 1-2 fresh red chilies, seeded and shredded; 1-in (2.5-cm) piece fresh ginger, grated; 3-4 tablespoons vegetable oil; 1 tablespoon thin soy sauce; ½ teaspoon salt; ½ teaspoon black pepper; 1½ teaspoons sugar
Sauce: 2 scallions, chopped; 2-3 garlic cloves, crushed; 1-2 fresh red chilies, seeded and chopped; 3 tablespoons thin soy sauce; 4-5 tablespoons white vinegar; sugar

Cover the spring roll wrappers with a damp cloth to prevent them drying out or they may crack when rolled.

To prepare the filling, wash the spinach or cabbage leaves thoroughly and set aside. Wash and devein the shrimp and pat dry with paper towels. Prepare the chicken and vegetables.

Fry the garlic in the vegetable oil for 30 seconds, then add the chicken and fry until it changes color. Add the shrimp and cook until pink, then add all the vegetables and stir on moderate heat for 3–4 minutes. Add the seasonings, cover and simmer on low heat for a further 1½ minutes, shaking the pan occasionally. Spread on a plate.

Leeks à la Grecque

Pound the scallions, garlic and chili for the sauce to a paste and add the remaining sauce ingredients with sugar to taste. Pour into small dip bowls and set aside.

Place a spinach or cabbage leaf in the center of each wrapper and add a large spoonful of the filling, a dash of *hoisin* sauce and some cucumber. Fold the sides in and roll up firmly. The ends can be stuck down after dipping in water or by using a flour and water paste. Heat the oil to fairly hot and fry the rolls, several at a time, until golden and crisp. Drain and serve with the sauce dip.

Malaysian-Style Spring Rolls

Marinated Fish Appetizer

Serves 4: 4 fillets of bream or a similar soft white fish; 2 medium-size tomatoes, diced; 6–8 chives, snipped; 1 fresh red chili, seeded and chopped; fresh lettuce leaves
Marinade: 3–4 tablespoons lime or lemon juice; 3 tablespoons coconut water (see Note); salt and black pepper; sugar

Skin the fish and cut into narrow strips. Mix the marinade ingredients, adding the salt, pepper and sugar to taste, and pour over the fish. Cover with plastic wrap and marinate overnight or for at least 8 hours in a cool place.

Mix the drained fish with the diced tomato, chives and chili. Wash the lettuce leaves, shake off any excess water and use to line individual appetizer dishes or a salad bowl. Mound the fish on top and serve at once.

Note: If necessary, omit the coconut water and add 1–2 tablespoons thick coconut milk when mixing the fish with the tomato, chives and chili. Do not add the coconut milk to the marinade.

Marinated Salmon (Gravlax)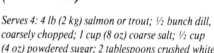

Serves 4: 4 lb (2 kg) salmon or trout; ½ bunch dill, coarsely chopped; 1 cup (8 oz) coarse salt; ½ cup (4 oz) powdered sugar; 2 tablespoons crushed white peppercorns; ¼ cup (2 fl oz) brandy; ¼ cup (2 fl oz) vegetable oil
Mustard Sauce: 1 cup (8 fl oz) mayonnaise; 1 teaspoon hot mustard; 1–2 tablespoons marinade from the fish; 2 tablespoons finely chopped dill

Fillet the fish, removing all bones. Place one fillet skin side down in a glass or glazed earthenware dish. Sprinkle the fillet with the dill. Mix the salt and sugar together and sprinkle it over the fish. Finally pour over the brandy mixed with the oil. Place the second fillet on top. Cover with aluminum foil and a rectangular flat board or plate. Put some weights on top and refrigerate for 2–3 days.

To make the mustard sauce, mix all the ingredients together and put the sauce into a bowl or sauce boat.

Wipe the fillets clean, slice thinly and serve with the sauce.

Masala Shrimp

Serves 4 as a main course, 6 as an appetizer: 12 large raw shrimp in the shell, approx. 1½ lb (750 g); 1 teaspoon crushed garlic; 1 tablespoon finely chopped parsley; 1 tablespoon garam masala, or mild curry powder; ½ teaspoon salt; 1½ tablespoons butter; 1½ tablespoons cooking oil; ½ cup (4 fl oz) heavy cream; salt and black pepper

Masala Shrimp

mix it to a smooth consistency, cook for 2–3 minutes and season. Add the fish paste to the sauce.

Melt the gelatin in a little water, mix it into the hot wine and stir it into the fish mixture. Mix in the cream and season to taste but take care not to oversalt it as the haddock is already salty. Fold in the egg whites.

Spoon the mixture into individual molds or one large one. Refrigerate for a few hours. Turn out the mousse and serve with a salad and buttered toast.

Mushrooms à la Grecque

Serves 4: 2 cups button mushrooms; 2 tablespoons olive oil; 2 tablespoons lemon juice; 1 large tomato, skinned and chopped; 1 bay leaf; sprig thyme; 1 teaspoon coriander seeds, crushed; salt and pepper

Wash and dry the mushrooms. Slice them if large. Put all the ingredients except the mushrooms into a saucepan and bring to the boil. Add the mushrooms and simmer for 6–7 minutes. Place in a shallow serving dish, allow to cool, chill and serve.

Mussels with Garlic (Moules à la Provençale)

Serves 6: 72 mussels; 16 tablespoons (8 oz) butter; salt and pepper; 2 garlic cloves, finely chopped; 2 tablespoons chopped parsley; fine dry breadcrumbs

Scrub the mussels well and wash under cold running water. Steam open the mussels by shaking them in a deep pan over a high flame for 3–5 minutes. Discard any unopened shells.

Keep the mussels in half shells and arrange on a platter. Melt the butter, then add the salt, pepper, garlic and parsley. Drizzle the butter over the mussels, then sprinkle with breadcrumbs and broil under a preheated hot broiler until brown. Serve at once.

Peel the shrimp, leaving the tails intact. Slit each one open down the center back and remove the vein. Mix the garlic, parsley, *garam masala* and salt together and press a portion of this into the opening of each shrimp.

Heat the butter and oil together in a skillet and sauté the shrimp, turning several times, until cooked through, about 6 minutes. Transfer to a serving plate.

Pour the cream into the pan and bring to a rapid boil, stirring to incorporate any spices and herbs remaining in the pan. Add salt and pepper to taste and spoon the sauce over the shrimp. Serve at once with saffron rice.

Mousse of Smoked Haddock

Serves 6: 2 large smoked haddock fillets; 1 tablespoon butter; 1 tablespoon all purpose flour; ⅔ cup (5 fl oz) hot milk; pinch of salt and pepper; ⅔ cup (5 fl oz) cream; ⅔ cup (5 fl oz) dry white wine, heated; 2 teaspoons gelatin; 2 egg whites, stiffly beaten; salt and pepper

Simmer the fish in water until the flesh is soft and cooked. Remove the skin and bones. In a grinder, blender or food processor, blend the flesh to a paste.

To make a béchamel sauce, melt the butter, stir in the flour and cook without browning for 2 minutes. Add the milk and

N

Nachos

Serves 6: 6½-oz (200-g) package corn chips; 3 cups (12 oz) grated cheese; Mexican seasoning or hot paprika

Divide the corn chips among six plates and spread the cheese evenly over them. Dust lightly with the seasoning. Microwave each plate on MEDIUM-HIGH (70%) for 1–1¼ minutes until the cheese has melted and is beginning to bubble. Serve each plate at once.

Note: Experiment with tasty variations by adding sliced, stuffed olives, chopped jalapeño chilies or diced hot salami (pepperoni).

Nachos

Nori-Wrapped Shrimp

Makes 12: 12 large raw shrimp; 2 teaspoons light soy sauce; 2 teaspoons sweet rice wine (mirin); 3–4 sheets dried laver seaweed (nori)

Peel the shrimp, discarding the head, tail and shell. Slit down the back with a sharp knife and remove the dark intestinal vein. Sprinkle with soy sauce and *mirin*, and leave aside for 20 minutes. Cut the *nori* into strips the length of each shrimp and 2 in (5 cm) wide.

Just before cooking, wrap each shrimp tightly in a strip of *nori*, wetting the inside of one end and pressing to seal. Insert a skewer through each shrimp, lengthwise. Cook the shrimp under a preheated broiler for 2 minutes on each side until the *nori* turns shiny and the shrimp are cooked. Cut each shrimp into 2–3 pieces lengthwise, remove the skewers and serve immediately.

O

Omelet Arnold Bennett

Serves 2: 8 oz (250 g) smoked cod; milk; 3 eggs; salt and pepper; 1 oz (30 g) grated cheese, for broiling
Cheese Sauce: 1½ tablespoons butter; 1½ tablespoons all purpose flour; 1¼ cups (10 fl oz) milk; 2 oz (60 g) grated cheese; ½ teaspoon Dijon mustard

Put the fish into an ovenproof dish and barely cover with a mixture of milk and water. Bake in an oven preheated to 375°F (190°C) for 15–20 minutes, or until it yields easily to a fork. Drain well. (This liquid is too salty for the sauce.) Flake the fish finely with a fork and remove any bones or skin. Set aside.

To make the white sauce, melt the butter in a pan, then stir in the flour. Cook stirring until foaming but not brown, then add the milk, whisking until smooth. Bring to the boil, then simmer for several minutes. Spoon into a heatproof bowl and cover the surface with a circle of damp waxed paper, to prevent a skin forming. Put the bowl in a saucepan of warm water and place over a low heat.

Warm the omelet pan, beat the eggs with salt and pepper and combine with the flaked fish. Cook the omelet as usual. When just set, do not fold, but slide onto a hot plate and place in an oven preheated to 200°F (100°C) for a few minutes to keep warm.

Remove the sauce from the heat and beat in grated cheese. Add the Dijon mustard, blend well and spoon the sauce over the omelet. Sprinkle with the remaining cheese and brown quickly under a hot broiler. Serve piping hot.

Onion Pie

Serves 4–6: 3 tablespoons oil; 1 lb 3 oz (600 g) onions, finely chopped; 3 oz (90 g) fatty bacon, chopped; 4 eggs; 2 egg whites, beaten stiff; salt and freshly ground pepper; puff pastry, sufficient to make 2 crusts for a 9-in (23-cm) pie dish; egg wash to glaze

Nori-Wrapped Shrimp

Heat the oil in a skillet and sauté the onions and bacon until the onions are soft. Remove from the heat and incorporate the 4 eggs, lightly beaten, and the egg whites, together with some salt and pepper.

Grease a 9-in (23-cm) pie dish and line it with puff pastry. Pour the mixture into the pie and cover with a pastry lid. Brush the lid with egg wash.

Bake in an oven preheated to 375°F (190°C) for 45 minutes. The pie may be served either hot or cold.

Orecchiette with Avocado

Serves 6-8: 1 quantity fresh pasta (see page 101); 2 teaspoons fresh lime juice; salt and freshly ground black pepper; 1 small red chili, seeded; 2 small onions, roughly chopped; 1 garlic clove, roughly chopped; 1 ripe tomato; 1 teaspoon brown or raw sugar; pinch of nutmeg; ½ cup (4 fl oz) cream; ½ cup (4 fl oz) milk

To make the orecchiette, roll the pasta dough into long sausage-like shapes, about the thickness of your thumb. Cut crosswise into discs about ⅛ in (3 mm) thick. Using the tip of your forefinger, push in the middle of each disc so it becomes hollow. It should resemble an ear shape.

Cook in salted boiling water until al dente, then drain and cool.

Remove the pits from the avocados, scoop out the pulp and put into the bowl of a food processor or blender. Add the lime juice, salt and plenty of pepper, chopped chili, onions and garlic. Add the tomato which has been peeled, seeded and put through a food mill or sieve. Sprinkle in the sugar and nutmeg, and blend. While blending, pour in the cream in a continuous stream and blend for a short time, then add the milk a little at a time, stopping when the sauce is creamy.

There will appear to be a considerable quantity of sauce for the orecchiette, but this is how it should be. Rinse the pasta briefly under cold water, drain, then serve with sauce.

Onion Pie

Orecchiette with Olive Pulp

Orecchiette with Olive Pulp

Serves 4-6: ½ quantity pasta dough (see page 101); 3-4 sprigs parsley, chopped; 1 garlic clove, crushed; 4 tablespoons (2 oz) butter; ½ beef bouillon cube; ¾ teaspoon anchovy paste; ½ tablespoon olive

pulp (obtainable in some specialty shops in jars, and called polpoliva), or use the flesh of 5 good-size black or green olives, put through a food mill with a teaspoon of best quality green olive oil; 5 green olives; 1 tablespoon cream; ¼ cup (2 fl oz) brandy; 3½ oz (100 g) Gorgonzola cheese; 2 oz (60 g) Parmesan cheese, freshly grated

Knead the dough, whether by passing it through a machine or by hand, then roll it into long, sausage-like shapes about the thickness of your thumb. Cut crosswise with a knife into discs about ⅛ in (3 mm) thick. Using the round end of a small table knife, or the tip of your forefinger, push down in the middle of each disc so that it becomes hollow and takes on the typical ear shape of orecchiette. Boil the orecchiette in boiling salted water until al dente. Drain and keep hot.

To make the sauce, in a heavy-based skillet, fry the parsley and garlic lightly in the butter. Crumble the bouillon cube into the pan, add the anchovy paste, olive pulp and the flesh of the green olives cut into very small pieces.

Stir in the cream and the brandy and cook over a low heat until the sauce thickens, then melt in the Gorgonzola. Mix together gently, add the orecchiette and stir until the sauce is well distributed. Sprinkle with Parmesan and serve immediately.

Oysters Mornay ★

Serves 2: 12 oysters; salt and pepper; ⅔ cup (5 fl oz) Mornay Sauce (see page 109); Parmesan cheese

Choose large flat oysters. Sprinkle with salt and pepper and place under a hot broiler for 1 minute. Spread over sufficient mornay sauce to cover each oyster. Sprinkle with Parmesan cheese and bake in an oven preheated to 450°F (230°C) 5-10 minutes or until golden brown. Serve immediately.

Oysters Opera ★

Serves 4: 4 dozen fresh oysters on the shell; 5½-oz (170-g) can crabmeat, drained and flaked; 1 cup (8 fl oz) Béchamel Sauce (see page 144); paprika; ½ cup (2 oz) grated Cheddar cheese

Arrange one dozen oysters on each plate. A bed of rock (sea) salt holds the oysters in

Orecchiette with Avocado (see page 61)

place and retains the heat. If preferred, the salt can be preheated in the microwave on HIGH (100%) for 2 minutes per plate.

Place 1 teaspoon of crabmeat and 1–2 teaspoons of sauce over each oyster. Dust lightly with paprika and cover with a sprinkling of grated cheese. Microwave on MEDIUM-HIGH (70%) for 1–2 minutes.

P

Pearls Hiding in a Crab

Serves 4-6: 1¼-lb (625-g) fresh crab; 6 canned quail or pigeon eggs, drained; ½ cup (4 fl oz) chicken stock; 1 egg white
Seasoning: ¾ teaspoon salt; ¼ teaspoon white pepper; 1 teaspoon rice wine or dry sherry; 2 teaspoons cold water; 2 teaspoons cornstarch

Place the crab in a dish and steam over rapidly boiling water for 12–15 minutes. Lift out and leave until cool enough to handle, then remove the top shell and discard the inedible parts. Lift out the meat and flake finely. Clean the shell thoroughly, rubbing with salt. Rinse well.

Break open the legs and extract the meat, or leave intact to decorate the dish.

Place the quail eggs in a small saucepan with the stock and bring to the boil. Add the seasoning ingredients and simmer briefly, then add the flaked crabmeat and heat until the sauce thickens. Place the lower part of the crab shell on a bed of shredded lettuce on a serving plate and

Pearls Hiding in a Crab

Oysters Opera

arrange the legs in place around it. Pile the crab and egg mixture into the shell and set the top shell in place.

Beat the egg white until it forms soft peaks. Heat a small saucepan of lightly salted water to a rolling boil and add the beaten egg. Cook until set and firm, then place in front of the crab to resemble bubbles exuding from its mouth. Serve at once.

Persian Carpet Eggs (Sherried Eggs) ★

Serves 6: peel of 1 orange; 12 eggs; ¾ cup (6 fl oz) dry sherry (fino); ¼ cup (2 fl oz) Grand Marnier; 2 tablespoons tomato paste; ½ cup (4 fl oz) cream; 2 pinches saffron; ½ teaspoon paprika; 4 tablespoons (2 oz) butter

Slice the orange peel very finely. Put all ingredients except the butter into a mixing bowl and whisk until evenly combined.

Heat the butter in a large saucepan, pour in the mixture and cook over a low heat, stirring occasionally, until the eggs are cooked. Serve with white wine.

Pickled Fish

Serves 6: 1 cup (8 fl oz) olive oil; 2 lb (1 kg) white fish fillets; 3 onions, sliced and separated into rings; 2-4 garlic cloves (according to taste), crushed; 3 carrots, coarsely grated; 4 sprigs parsley, chopped; 3 bay leaves; 1 teaspoon paprika; ¼ teaspoon chili powder or dash of Tabasco sauce; 1½ teaspoons salt; freshly ground black pepper; 1 cup (8 fl oz) white wine vinegar

Heat half of the oil and fry the fish fillets. When they are cooked, remove the skin and any bones, and break them up with a fork into large flakes.

Heat the rest of the oil and sauté the onion rings until soft and transparent. Add the rest of the ingredients and cook for 5 minutes. Check the seasoning. Arrange the fish in a glass or ceramic dish and pour the hot marinade over it. Cover the dish and refrigerate for 2 days. Serve with sautéed potatoes.

Pigeon Pâté with Chinese Herbs Steamed in Soup Ramekins

Serves 4–6: 1¼ lb (625 g) pigeon breast meat; 1½ scallions, trimmed and diced; 3 slices fresh ginger, shredded; 1¾ tablespoons rice wine or dry sherry; 6 slices dan guei (see Note)
Seasoning: 2 egg whites, well beaten; ¾ teaspoon salt; ¼ teaspoon ground black pepper; ½ teaspoon sugar; 1 teaspoon rice wine or dry sherry; 1 tablespoon oil; 2 teaspoons cornstarch

Pulverize the pigeon meat in a food processor. Add the seasoning ingredients and mix thoroughly. Divide among six bamboo containers or ramekins, pushing the paste to the bottom of the cup. Divide the scallions, ginger, wine and *dan guei* among the cups and fill each with water.

Set on a rack in a steamer and steam over high heat until the pigeon pâté is cooked, about 30 minutes. Serve in the containers.

Note: Dan guei is a dried pungent herb said to have beneficial and highly nutritious qualities. It is often used in poultry dishes in China and gives a mildly medicinal taste. It is available in specialist Chinese food or drug stores.

Pineapple Boats

Serves 4: 2 medium-size pineapples, halved; 2 tablespoons (1 oz) butter; 1 tablespoon vegetable oil; 2 stalks celery, sliced; 1 garlic clove, crushed; 2 oz (60 g) button mushrooms, sliced; 1 small tomato, peeled, seeded and chopped; 1 canned pimiento, drained and chopped; 1 teaspoon cornstarch; 2 tablespoons dry sherry; 1 lb (500 g) cubed cooked turkey; salt and freshly ground black pepper; 2 tablespoons finely snipped chives

Twist the spiked stalks from the pineapples and save a few of the leaves for decoration. Halve the pineapples, then cut away and discard the hard core. Carefully scoop out the flesh, leaving a ½-in (1-cm) shell. Do this over a shallow dish to catch the pineapple juice. Dice the fruit and set aside.

Melt the butter and oil in a saucepan and fry the celery over low heat until it begins to soften. Add the garlic, mushrooms, tomato, pimiento and the pineapple juice. Cover and simmer for 3–4 minutes.

Mix the cornstarch to a smooth paste with the sherry and stir into the vegetable mixture with the diced pineapple and the turkey. Season with salt and black pepper to taste and simmer for 2 minutes longer. Put the pineapple shells on a baking sheet, divide the turkey mixture among them and bake in an oven preheated to 350°F (180°C) for 15–20 minutes.

Arrange on a heated serving dish, garnish with the chives and decorate with the reserved pineapple leaves.

Pineapple Boats

Pizza Slice

Serves 6–8: 1¾ cups (7 oz) all purpose flour; 1½ teaspoons baking powder; ¾ teaspoon salt; ½ teaspoon baking soda; 2 tablespoons (1 oz) butter or margarine; ½ cup (2 oz) cornmeal (polenta); ¾ cup (6 fl oz) milk
Sauce: 1 tablespoon olive oil; 1 onion, finely chopped; 1 lb (500 g) finely ground lean beef; 1 garlic clove, chopped; ½ teaspoon chili powder; ½ teaspoon oregano; 15-oz (470-g) can peeled whole tomatoes; 1 cup (8 fl oz) beef consommé (beef stock); 1 tablespoon tomato paste; salt and pepper, to taste
Topping: 2–3 tomatoes; 1 onion; 4 oz (125 g) Cheddar cheese; 2 oz (60 g) mozzarella cheese; paprika; salt and pepper; 2 tablespoons parsley for garnish

Sift the flour, baking powder, salt and soda together in a bowl. Rub in the butter until the mixture resembles breadcrumbs. Add

the cornmeal and blend in, then stir in the milk to form a firm dough. Roll out on a lightly floured board. Knead 8–10 times. Roll out to 12-in (30-cm) circle and press onto a 12-in (30-cm) pizza dish.

To make the sauce, heat the oil and sauté the onion and meat until the onion is tender and the meat golden brown. Add the garlic, chili powder and oregano. Cook for 1 minute. Add the chopped tomatoes. Stir in the consommé, tomato paste, salt and pepper. Bring to the boil and simmer for 30 minutes, stirring occasionally until the sauce is thick. Spread the sauce over the pastry base.

Meanwhile, to prepare the topping, thinly slice the tomatoes and onion. Grate the cheeses and lightly toss together. Cover the top of the sauce with tomatoes and onions. Sprinkle with the cheese, paprika, salt and pepper. Bake in an oven preheated to 400°F (200°C) for 15–20 minutes or until the base is cooked and browned and the top bubbling. Sprinkle with parsley to serve.

Pork Liver Terrine

Serves 8: 1 lb (500 g) pork liver; 8 oz (250 g) veal tenderloin; 8 oz (250 g) fresh lard; 1 onion, chopped; parsley; 4¼ cups (8 oz) fresh breadcrumbs, which have been soaked in cold milk and squeezed dry; salt and freshly ground black pepper; 2 tablespoons brandy; 3 eggs; thin strips of lard to line the terrine; sprig of thyme and bay leaf

Grind the pork liver, veal, lard, onion, parsley and breadcrumbs to a paste in a food processor or food mill. Season with salt and pepper. Add the brandy and eggs and mix together well.

Line a terrine with the thin strips of lard and fill with the mixture. Cover the top with the lard and arrange the sprigs of thyme and the bay leaf decoratively on top. Cover the terrine, stand it in a dish of hot water and bake in an oven preheated to 350°F (180°C) for 1¼ hours. Remove from the oven and cool for 30 minutes. Place a 2-lb (1-kg) weight on top of the terrine, and leave it to set in the refrigerator overnight before serving.

Pork-Stuffed Oranges

Serves 6: 6 large oranges; 1½ tablespoons oil;
8 garlic cloves, chopped; 6 scallions, finely chopped;
1-2 fresh red chilies, chopped; 1 heaped tablespoon
roasted peanuts, crushed; 1¼ lb (625 g) lean pork,
ground; 1 teaspoon dried shrimp paste; 2 teaspoons
light soy sauce; 1½ teaspoons ground coriander;
1½ teaspoons salt; ½ teaspoon white pepper;
1 teaspoon sugar; oil; 6 sprigs of mint

Cut the oranges in half and scoop out most
of the flesh, leaving ½-in (1-cm) layer
attached to the skin.

Heat the oil and sauté the garlic and
scallions for 2 minutes. Add the chili and
peanuts, and cook for a further 2 minutes,
stirring frequently. Stir in the ground pork,
shrimp paste, soy sauce, coriander, salt,
pepper and sugar. Cook, stirring occasionally, on moderate heat or until the meat is
cooked through.

Stuff the mixture into the oranges, pressing it in firmly. Round off the tops and
place the oranges in a large baking pan or
ovenproof tray. Brush with a little oil.
Bake in an oven preheated to 350°F
(180°C) for 15 minutes, brushing with a
little more oil during cooking. Serve two
orange halves on each plate, decorating
each pair with a sprig of mint.

Pork Wontons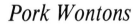

Makes 36: 36 fresh or frozen wonton wrappers; 8 oz
(250 g) pork fillet (tenderloin); 4 oz (125 g) raw
peeled shrimp; 1½ oz (45 g) pork fat; 2 oz (60 g)
canned water chestnuts, drained and finely diced;
1 scallion, finely chopped; 1 tablespoon finely
chopped fresh cilantro; 6 cups (1½ liters) oil for
deep frying
Seasoning: 1½ teaspoons salt; ¼ teaspoon white
pepper; 2 teaspoons sugar; 2 teaspoons light soy
sauce; 2 teaspoons cornstarch

Prepare the wonton wrappers and cover
with a damp cloth until needed. If using
frozen wrappers, remove from the freezer
about 3 hours before using.

Grind the pork fillet, shrimp and pork
fat together and add the chestnuts,
scallion, cilantro and the seasonings. Mix
thoroughly and chill for 1 hour.

Place a spoonful of the mixture in each
wonton wrapper. Pull the edges up around
the filling, forcing it into a ball shape just
slightly off-center. Brush the three corners
closest to the filling with water and press

This shape forms the classic goldfish shape.

Alternatively, pinch together above the filling and flare out corners.

them together. Fold over the filling and
pinch onto the base of the final corner,
completely sealing in the filling. Fold the
final corner up and outward in a petal
shape. The resultant wonton is the classic
goldfish shape.

A simpler shape is to gather the four corners together, then run the fingers from the
tips down to the filling. Pinch together
above the filling, then flare the corners outwards.

Heat the oil to moderately hot and deep
fry several wontons until light golden
brown, about 2 minutes. Drain. Repeat.

Serve with dips of light soy sauce, chili
sauce or sweet and sour sauce.

Note: Use unfried wontons in soup and
soup-noodle dishes. They may be frozen
before cooking and require only a brief
thawing before deep frying or using in
soup.

Quiche Lorraine

Q
Quiche Lorraine

Serves 4-6: shortcrust pastry for an 8-in (20-cm) pie
(see page 321); 4 egg yolks plus 1 whole egg, beaten;
1¼ cups (10 fl oz) cream; salt and freshly ground
black pepper; grated nutmeg; 4 oz (125 g) bacon, in
one piece; 2 tablespoons (1 oz) butter; 4 oz (125 g)
Gruyère cheese, diced

Line a tart or quiche dish with the pastry.
Prick the bottom with a fork, brush with a
little beaten egg and bake blind in an oven
preheated to 375°F (190°C) for 15 minutes.

Whisk the egg yolks in a bowl. Add the
cream and whisk until thick and lemon
colored. Season to taste with salt, pepper
and nutmeg. Cut the bacon into thin strips
and remove the rind, then blanch in boiling
water for 3 minutes. Melt the butter in a
small pan and sauté the bacon gently until
golden. Arrange the diced bacon and
cheese in the pastry case. Pour over the
cream and egg mixture, and bake for about
30 minutes or until golden brown on top.
Serve immediately.

R
Rainbow Beef in Lettuce Leaves

Serves 4: 5 oz (155 g) beef fillet (tenderloin); 2 oz
(60 g) canned bamboo shoots, drained; 2 oz (60 g)
fresh celery; 1 small carrot; 1 small green bell
pepper; 1 fresh red chili pepper; 3 dried black
mushrooms, soaked for 25 minutes; 1½ oz (45 g)
rice vermicelli; 6 cups (1½ liters) oil for deep frying;
12 fresh lettuce leaf cups
Seasoning: ¼ teaspoon salt; ½ teaspoon sugar;
1 teaspoon light soy sauce; 1 teaspoon rice wine or
dry sherry; 1½ teaspoons vegetable oil;
1 tablespoon cold water; 1 teaspoon cornstarch

Thinly slice the beef, then cut into fine
shreds. Place in a dish with the seasoning
ingredients, mix well and leave for 1 hour.
Cut the vegetables into fine shreds.

Heat the oil to smoking point. Break the
rice vermicelli into small pieces and place in
a frying basket. Deep fry for about 20
seconds until it expands and turns crisp.
Drain and place on a serving plate.

Pour off all but 2½ tablespoons of the oil

and fry the meat until it changes color, then push to one side of the wok and add the shredded vegetables. Stir-fry until softened but still crisp, about 2 minutes, then stir in the beef and spoon onto the rice vermicelli.

Wash the lettuce leaves and place on a serving plate. Serve with the beef. To eat, spoon a portion of the meat, vegetables and noodles into the lettuce leaf and roll up. *Hoisin* or plum sauce can be served as a dip.

Rice-Stuffed Grape Leaves (Dolmadakia)

Makes 36: ⅔ cup (5 fl oz) olive oil; 3 large onions, finely chopped; 6 scallions, finely chopped; 1 teaspoon salt; freshly ground black pepper; 2 tablespoons pine nuts; ¾ cup (150 g) rice; 1 tablespoon finely chopped dill; ½ bunch parsley, finely chopped; 1 teaspoon finely chopped mint; juice of ½ lemon; 1 cup (8 fl oz) water; 36 grape leaves; parsley stalks; lemon wedges; parsley sprigs

In half of the olive oil, sauté the onions and scallions until they are soft and transparent. Add the salt, pepper, pine nuts and rice. Cook for 10 minutes, stirring from time to time. Add the dill, parsley, mint, lemon juice and the water, cover the saucepan and simmer for approximately 10 minutes, until the water has been absorbed. Season if necessary.

Spread the grape leaves with the dull side up and place a teaspoon of stuffing on each leaf. First fold the stalk end of the leaf over the stuffing, then the right-hand side, followed by the left-hand side. Finally, starting with the stalk end, roll the grape leaf firmly into a cylindrical shape. Squeeze it gently in the palm of your hand to keep it intact.

Place the parsley stalks on the bottom of the saucepan and arrange the stuffed grape leaves in layers on top of them. Weight them down with an inverted plate.

Combine the remaining olive oil, 2 tablespoons of lemon juice and enough water to barely cover the plate. Cover the pan, bring slowly to the boil and simmer gently for 1½ hours. When cooked, cool for 2–3 hours or overnight Serve at room temperature or slightly chilled.

Rainbow Beef in Lettuce Leaves

Rice-Stuffed Vine Leaves (Dolmadakia)

Rillettes of Pork

Serves 12: 2 lb (1 kg) fat belly pork; salt; 2 garlic cloves, crushed; bouquet garni; ⅔ cup (5 fl oz) water; pepper

Ask your butcher to prepare the belly pork without rind and bones. Rub the meat well with salt and leave to stand for 4 hours. Cut into ½ × 1-in (1 × 2.5-cm) pieces and place in a cast iron casserole with the garlic and bouquet garni. Add the water, season with pepper and cook in an oven preheated to 250°F (120°C) for 4 hours.

Drain the meat and reserve the fat. Place the meat in a mixing bowl and beat slowly with an electric mixer until the meat fibers separate. Pack the meat loosely in jars and fill with the reserved fat. Cool, then cover with aluminum foil.

Serve the rillettes in large slices on individual plates with lightly toasted (unbuttered) brown bread on which to spread it.

Note: It is impractical to make very small quantities of rillettes, but the surplus not required for the meal can be stored in the refrigerator. Remove several hours before serving.

Rollmop Salad

Serves 6: 4 rollmops; ⅔ cup (5 fl oz) salad dressing or sour cream; 1 teaspoon sugar; ¼ teaspoon dry mustard; 1 tablespoon white wine; salt and pepper; 2 large boiled potatoes; 1 small cooked beet; few crisp lettuce leaves; 1 red apple, cut into cubes; 4 dill pickles, sliced; 6 scallions

Cut the rollmops into strips. Mix the salad dressing with the sugar, mustard and wine and season to taste with salt and pepper. Dice the potatoes and beet, and fold into the dressing. Place the lettuce on a flat platter with the potato and beet, then top with the rollmops. Arrange the apple cubes, slices of dill pickles and finely sliced scallion around the side.

Russian Herring

Serves 4: 8 fillets pickled herring or mullet; ½ cup finely chopped onion; 1 large dill pickle; 1 cup (8 fl oz) mayonnaise; scant ½ cup (4 fl oz) lemon juice; 2 tablespoons tomato paste; ¼ cup black caviar

Place the fillets of pickled herring on a board with the skin sides down. Put 1 tablespoon of the chopped onion on each fillet and roll up tightly. Slice the dill pickle into eight thick slices. Place a rolled fillet of herring on each slice of dill pickle and put onto a serving dish. Mix the mayonnaise with the lemon juice and tomato paste and spoon over each rolled fillet. Top with caviar and chill before serving.

Russian Oysters

Serves 2: 12 oysters; 3 tablespoons finely chopped onion or chives; 1 hard-cooked egg; 2 oz (60 g) black caviar

Arrange the oysters on a bed of ice, then sprinkle with the chopped onion or chives. Separate the egg white from the yolk, finely chop the egg white, sieve the egg yolk and sprinkle over the oysters. Top the oysters with black caviar and serve immediately.

Note: Only the freshest oysters should be used for this recipe.

S

Salmon with Horseradish Cream

Serves 4: 1 cup (8 fl oz) heavy cream, whipped; 1 tablespoon prepared horseradish; 1 tablespoon vinegar or juice of 1 lemon; ½ teaspoon sugar; salt and freshly ground black pepper; 1 teaspoon gelatin, dissolved in ¼ cup (2 fl oz) hot water, cooled; 12 slices smoked salmon; 2 sprigs parsley, finely chopped

Combine all ingredients except the smoked salmon and parsley. Form the salmon slices into cones and with a teaspoon or piping bag, fill the cones with the cream. Arrange the cones on a serving platter and refrigerate for 2 hours or until the cream hardens. Serve chilled, sprinkled with parsley.

Samosas

Makes 30–36: 1 cup (4 oz) all purpose flour; ½ teaspoon salt; 1 tablespoon ghee or butter; 3–4 tablespoons lukewarm water; oil for deep frying
Filling: 2 tablespoons (1 oz) ghee or butter; 1 small onion, finely chopped; 2 sweet green chilies, seeded and finely chopped; 2 garlic cloves, crushed; 1-in (2.5-cm) piece of fresh ginger, peeled and grated; ½ teaspoon ground bird's eye chili; ½ teaspoon turmeric; 12 oz (375 g) ground raw chicken; 2 teaspoons garam masala; juice and finely grated peel of ½ lemon; salt

Sift the flour with the ½ teaspoon of salt into a mixing bowl. Rub in the *ghee* or butter and mix to a dough with the lukewarm water. Turn onto a lightly floured board and knead until the dough is elastic and shiny. Set aside while you are making the filling.

Melt the *ghee* or butter in a skillet and fry the onion, chilies, garlic and ginger over moderate heat until the onion is the color of pale straw. Sprinkle with the chili powder and turmeric and mix together. Stir the chicken into the pan, breaking up any lumps with a fork and turning until it is lightly colored. Cook over low heat until most of the moisture in the pan has evaporated. Add the *garam masala*, lemon juice and peel, mixing all the ingredients thoroughly. Season to taste with salt and put the mixture aside to cool.

Divide the dough into 12–15 pieces and roll each to a 4-in (10-cm) circle. Cut each circle in half and put a little of the filling on one side of each piece of pastry. Fold into a roughly shaped triangle, pinching to seal (use a little water on the edges only if necessary). Flatten each samosa slightly and set aside until ready to cook.

Preheat the oil to 375°F (190°C) and deep fry the samosas for 2–3 minutes. Drain on paper towels and serve while very crisp.

Sardine Hors d'Oeuvre

Serves 4: two 3¾-oz (110-g) cans sardines; 1 onion; 2 eggs, hard-cooked; 2 teaspoons capers; 1 lemon

Arrange the sardines in a shallow serving dish. Slice the onion into thin rings and chop the hard-cooked eggs coarsely. Sprinkle the onion rings, chopped eggs and capers over the sardines. Serve with wedges of lemon.

Satay Scallops

Satay Scallops

Serves 6: 12 oz (375 g) fresh scallops; 3 thick slices fresh pineapple, cut into cubes; 2 tablespoons (1 oz) butter, melted; ¾ cup (6 fl oz) prepared satay sauce; ¼ cup (2 fl oz) thick coconut milk or cream

Soak 12 bamboo skewers in water for 1 hour, then drain and dry. Rub with vegetable oil.

Thread scallops and pineapple alternately onto the skewers. Brush the kebabs with melted butter. Microwave on MEDIUM-HIGH (70%), covered with plastic wrap or damp paper towel, or cook on a preheated microwave browning dish on MEDIUM-HIGH (70%) for 4 minutes, turning once or twice.

Mix the satay sauce with the coconut milk or cream in a dish or jug. Cover and microwave on HIGH (100%) for 1 minute.

Trim the scallops.   Brush with the melted butter.

Saucy Chicken Turnovers

Makes 6-8 turnovers: Pastry: 2½ cups (10 oz) all purpose flour; ½ teaspoon salt; ⅛ teaspoon cream of tartar; 8 tablespoons (4 oz) butter; 3 tablespoons lard, cut into pieces; ½ cup (4 fl oz) iced water 1⅓ cups cooked and chopped chicken; 3 oz (85 g) canned mushrooms, drained and chopped; 2 tablespoons chopped pimento; 2 tablespoons chopped parsley; 2 tablespoons chopped scallions; ½ oz (¼ cup) fresh breadcrumbs; salt and pepper to taste; 1 egg white; Mornay Sauce (see page 109)

To make the pastry, sift the flour, salt and cream of tartar into a bowl. Cut the butter

into small pieces and quickly rub with the fingertips until the mixture resembles meal. Add the iced water. Toss until the mixture is blended and form it into a ball. Knead lightly with the heel of the hand and add the lard, blending it evenly through the dough. Form dough into a ball. Chill at least 1 hour.

Preheat the oven to 400°F (200°C). In a bowl, mix the chicken, mushrooms, pimento, parsley, scallions, breadcrumbs, salt and pepper.

On a lightly floured board, roll the pastry to ⅛ in (3 mm) thick and cut into 6-in (15-cm) circles. Spoon the chicken mixture onto the center of each. Brush the edges of the pastry with egg white, then fold each pastry circle in half. With a floured fork, press the edges to seal. Cut slits in the top of each with a sharp knife. Bake for 30 minutes or until golden. Serve with Mornay Sauce.

Savory Crab Dip

Makes 24-36 canapes: 5½-oz (170-g) can crabmeat; 1 small onion, finely chopped; ¼ teaspoon grated fresh ginger; ½ garlic clove, crushed; 4 tablespoons (2 oz) butter; 1 tablespoon all purpose flour; ½ cup (4 fl oz) milk; salt and black pepper; cayenne pepper or chili sauce; lemon juice

Drain and flake the crabmeat. Place the onion, ginger, garlic and butter in a small dish or jug and microwave, covered with plastic wrap, on HIGH (100%) for 3 minutes.

Stir in the flour, then whisk in the milk until the mixture is smooth. Microwave on HIGH (100%) for 1½ minutes, then add the crabmeat, seasonings and lemon juice to taste. Warm through briefly on MEDIUM-HIGH (70%) or serve cold.

Scallops in Pernod

Serves 4: 1 lb (500 g) fresh scallops; 2 tablespoons (1 oz) butter; 1 small onion, chopped; 1 tablespoon all purpose flour; ¼ teaspoon powdered saffron or turmeric; ½ cup (4 fl oz) dry white wine; ½ cup (4 fl oz) light cream; 1½ tablespoons Pernod; salt; lemon juice; chopped parsley

Wash the scallops. Place them in a pan with water to cover and bring quickly to the boil. Drain, cover with cold water and when cool, lift out and drain thoroughly.

Heat the butter until bubbling and sauté the scallops until they turn white and firm, then remove and keep warm.

Add the chopped onion and sauté until transparent, then sprinkle over the flour and add the saffron or turmeric and cook briefly before adding the wine. Stir well, then simmer until thickened and reduced. Add the cream and mix well, then add the Pernod with salt and lemon juice to taste. Return the scallops and gently heat through in the sauce. Serve on a bed of white rice with chopped parsley.

Quickly bring water to a boil.   Mix scallops into sauce.

Scallop Puffs ★

Makes 36: 5 oz (155 g) fresh scallops; 4 oz (125 g) canned button mushrooms, drained; 2 tablespoons butter; 1 tablespoon grated onion; ½ garlic clove, crushed; ¼ teaspoon fennel seeds, crushed; 2½ tablespoons all purpose flour; ⅓ cup (2½ fl oz) milk; ½ teaspoon dry mustard; 2 teaspoons lemon juice; 6 oz (185 g) frozen puff pastry; 3 tablespoons milk; oil for deep frying

Finely chop the scallops and mushrooms. Sauté in the butter with the onion, garlic and fennel seeds for about 2 minutes. Sprinkle over the flour and continue cooking until lightly colored.

Heat the milk with the mustard in a small saucepan. Pour into the scallop mixture and stir on moderate heat until thick and smooth, about 5 minutes, stirring constantly. Remove from the heat, add the lemon juice and leave to cool.

Roll out the pastry fairly thinly and cut into 36 rounds using a 1¼-in (3-cm) circular cutter. Roll each pastry out individually until very thin and almost transparent. Place a spoonful of the filling in the center of each pastry and fold over to form crescents. Pinch the edges together, using a little milk or beaten egg to stick them down, if needed.

Heat the oil to moderately hot and deep fry the puffs, several at a time, until golden and well expanded. Drain well on paper towels and serve hot.

Savory Crab Dip

Scallops in Pernod

Scallops with Cream (Coquilles Saint Jacques à la Crême)

Serves 2: 2 tablespoons (1 oz) butter; 1 oz (30 g) button mushrooms, sliced; ¼ cup (2 fl oz) dry white wine; 4 oz (125 g) scallops; ¼ cup (2 fl oz) cream; pinch of cayenne pepper; salt and pepper; 1 oz (30 g) Parmesan cheese; lemon slices and parsley sprigs for garnish

Melt the butter in a saucepan, add the mushrooms and cook until the wine has reduced by half. Add the scallops and simmer for 2 minutes. Add the cream, cayenne pepper, salt and pepper to taste. Reheat gently and place in scallop shells. Sprinkle with Parmesan cheese and broil under a hot broiler until golden brown. Serve immediately garnished with lemon and parsley sprigs.

Scrambled Eggs Parsi Style

Serves 4: 6 large eggs; salt and black pepper; pinch of turmeric; 1 large onion; 1 green chili; 3 tablespoons fresh cilantro leaves; 3 tablespoons ghee; 1 fresh red chili, thinly sliced

Beat the eggs lightly with salt, pepper and turmeric. Mince or finely chop the onion, chili and cilantro. Heat the *ghee* in a skillet and add the chopped ingredients to the pan, then fry for 3 minutes on moderate heat. Reduce the heat slightly and pour in the beaten egg.

Cook, stirring frequently, until the egg is just set. Check seasoning, then garnish with thinly sliced chili and serve with fresh buttered toast.

Seafood Cocktail

Serves 6: Cocktail Sauce: ¼ cup mayonnaise; 3 tablespoons tomato paste; 1 teaspoon Worcestershire sauce; 1 teaspoon lemon juice; few drops Tabasco sauce; pinch of paprika; ¼ cup heavy cream
12 oz (375 g) mixture shelled shrimp, crayfish, oysters and crab; lemon for garnish; lettuce

To make the cocktail sauce, mix the mayonnaise, tomato paste, Worcestershire sauce, lemon juice, Tabasco sauce and paprika. Whip the cream lightly and fold into the sauce.

Shred the lettuce very finely and put into cocktail glasses. Combine the seafood lightly with the sauce and pile onto the lettuce. Garnish with a small slice of lemon.

Semolina Crisps

Serves 4-6: ½ cup (3 oz) fine semolina; ½ cup (2 oz) all purpose flour; 1-2 tablespoons chickpea flour; salt; water; oil or ghee for deep frying

Dry-fry the semolina, then sift the flour over and add the chickpea flour and a pinch of salt. Work in enough water to make a soft dough and knead for approximately 8 minutes. Cover with a damp cloth and leave for 30 minutes for the semolina to soften.

Break off marble-size pieces of the dough and roll out with a greased rolling pin on a greased surface, into rounds as thin as possible. Cover with a damp cloth until all are done.

Shredded Beef with Bamboo Shoots

Heat the oil to fairly hot, then reduce the heat slightly. Deep fry the crisps, several at a time, splashing with the oil and pushing under the surface to encourage them to expand. Turn once only and cook until golden and crisp. Drain well. They will soften quickly, so serve as soon as possible on a warmed plate.

Shredded Beef with Bamboo Shoots

Serves 4: 8 oz (250 g) beef fillet (tenderloin); 1½ oz (45 g) canned bamboo shoots, drained; 1 medium-size carrot, peeled (see Note); 3 garlic chives; 1-2 fresh red chili peppers; 3 slices fresh ginger; 1½ cups (12 fl oz) oil for deep frying; ½ teaspoon black pepper; ¾ teaspoon sesame oil
Seasoning A: ½ teaspoon salt; 1 tablespoon light soy sauce; 2 teaspoons dark soy sauce; 2 teaspoons rice wine or dry sherry; 2 teaspoons sesame oil; 2 teaspoons ginger wine or ginger juice
Seasoning B/Sauce: 2 tablespoons light soy sauce; 1 teaspoon white vinegar; ½ teaspoon rice wine or dry sherry; 1½ teaspoons sugar; ½ teaspoon cornstarch

Freeze the beef briefly, then cut into paper-thin slices across the grain, then into long narrow shreds. Place in a dish with the seasoning A ingredients. Mix well and leave for 20 minutes.

Cut the bamboo shoots, carrot, chives, chili peppers and ginger into long narrow shreds and set aside.

Heat the oil in a wok and fry the beef shreds in a frying basket for 45 seconds. Remove and drain well. Pour off all but 2½ tablespoons of the oil and stir-fry the shredded ingredients for about 1½ minutes, then return the beef. Sizzle the soy sauce onto the sides of the pan and add the remaining seasoning B/sauce ingredients. Stir on high heat until the liquid has been almost completely absorbed, then transfer to a serving plate and season with the pepper and sesame oil, stirring lightly.

Note: Shredded green or red bell pepper can be used in place of carrot.

Shredded Pork in Sesame Pouches

Shredded Pork in Sesame Pouches

Serves 4: 12 oz (375 g) pork leg (fresh ham); 1 tablespoon dark soy sauce; 2 oz (60 g) Sichuan preserved vegetable or salted mustard root (see Note); ¼ cup (2 fl oz) oil; 6 pieces sesame pocket bread or pita bread
Seasoning: 2 teaspoons sugar (or to taste); 1 tablespoon rice wine or dry sherry

Thinly slice the pork across the grain, then cut into very fine short shreds. Place in a dish and add the soy sauce. Mix well and leave for 20 minutes. Soak the preserved vegetables in cold water for 20 minutes, then drain and squeeze out as much water as possible. Cut into fine shreds.

Heat the oil and stir-fry the pork until it changes color, about 1 minute. Add the preserved vegetables and fry for 1 minute, then stir in the seasoning ingredients and mix well. Cook for about 4 minutes on fairly high heat, stirring continually.

Warm the bread in the oven, cut in half and arrange on a plate. Serve with the shredded pork. To eat, a portion of the meat is stuffed into the "pocket" of the bread and eaten like a sandwich.

Note: Finely shredded dry bean curd is often added to this dish and may be substituted for the preserved or salted vegetable.

Shrimp Brochettes with Dill Mayonnaise

Serves 6: 1 lb (500 g) raw shrimp in the shell; ½ cup (4 fl oz) mayonnaise; ⅓ cup (2½ fl oz) sour cream; 1 teaspoon dried dill; ½ teaspoon dill seeds; 2 tablespoon grated cucumber; salt

Place the shrimp in a microwave-safe dish and cover with a double thickness of wet paper towel. Microwave on HIGH (100%) for 5–6 minutes until the shrimp are pink. (Non-carousel ovens: Give dish a half-turn.) They will be still slightly underdone but will complete cooking during 4–5 minutes standing time.

Mix the remaining ingredients together to make a dipping sauce. Peel the shrimp and thread onto bamboo skewers. Cover and leave to cool. Serve on fresh lettuce leaves with other salad ingredients and the sauce.

Shrimp Brochettes with Dill Mayonnaise

Shrimp Fritters

Serves 2–4: 2 eggs, beaten; 1 teaspoon baking powder; ⅔ cup (2½ oz) all purpose flour; salt and pepper; 3 scallions, finely chopped; 8 oz (250 g) peeled raw shrimp, finely chopped; oil for deep frying

Make a batter with the eggs, baking powder and flour. Season with salt and pepper and stir in the chopped scallions and shrimp. Beat thoroughly.

Heat the oil in a shallow pan and fry spoonfuls of the batter until golden brown and cooked through. Drain on paper towels and serve either hot or cold.

Shrimp in Garlic Butter

Serves 4: 1 lb (500 g) peeled, cooked shrimp; 1½ cups (12 oz) butter; 1 whole head of garlic, peeled and finely chopped; 8 scallions, chopped; ¾ cup (1½ oz) finely chopped parsley; salt and black pepper; lemon wedges

Rinse the shrimp and drain thoroughly. Dry by spreading on and blotting with a paper towel.

Cut the butter into cubes and divide between four dishes, together with the garlic and scallions. Cover and microwave on MEDIUM-HIGH (70%) for about 4 minutes. Add the shrimp, parsley, salt and pepper and cover. Microwave on MEDIUM-HIGH (70%) for 3 minutes. Stir and microwave on MEDIUM-HIGH (70%) for a further 2 minutes or until the butter is bubbling. Serve at once.

Shrimp Toast

Makes 12: 8 oz (250 g) raw shrimp meat; ¾ cup (1½ oz) fresh white breadcrumbs; 1 egg white, beaten; 1½ teaspoons lemon juice; ¾ teaspoon salt; 1 teaspoon cornstarch; 6 slices fresh white bread; 1 egg, beaten; 1 tablespoon white sesame seeds; oil for deep frying

Finely grind the shrimp meat and mix with the breadcrumbs, egg white, lemon juice, salt and cornstarch, working to a smooth paste.

Remove the crusts from the bread and cut each slice in half. Brush one side of each piece with beaten egg and cover with a thick layer of the shrimp paste, smooth-

ing the edges with the back of a spoon dipped in cold water. Brush the tops with more beaten egg and sprinkle over a few sesame seeds.

Heat the oil to moderately hot. Deep fry the shrimp toasts, several at a time and fillings downwards, until golden and crisp, about 1¼ minutes. Turn and cook the other side, then drain well on crumpled absorbent paper before serving.

Brush with beaten egg.

Deep fry until golden.

Shrimp with Yogurt Dressing

Serves 4: 11 oz (345 g) cooked shrimp, peeled; 1 cup (8 fl oz) light yogurt; 1 tablespoon mayonnaise; 1 tablespoon tomato sauce; salt and freshly ground black pepper; 1 teaspoon prepared horseradish; ½ teaspoon sugar; 1 tablespoon brandy

Divide the shrimp into four portions. To make the sauce, combine all the remaining

ingredients. Arrange the shrimp on individual plates and serve the sauce separately.

Sichuan Shrimp in Chili Oil Sauce

Serves 4: 1 lb (500 g) medium-size raw peeled shrimp; 4 cups (1 liter) oil for deep frying; 2 tablespoons chopped leeks; 1 tablespoon finely chopped ginger; 1 teaspoon sesame oil; 1 tablespoon chili oil
Seasoning A: 1 egg white, beaten; 1 teaspoon salt; 1½ teaspoons ginger wine; 1½ tablespoons cornstarch
Seasoning B/Sauce: 2 tablespoons tomato ketchup; ½ teaspoon salt; 1 teaspoon sugar; ¼ cup (2 fl oz) chicken stock; 1 teaspoon cornstarch

Wash the shrimp and cut in half lengthwise. Place in a dish with the seasoning A ingredients, mix well and leave for 20 minutes. Heat the oil to moderately hot and deep fry the shrimp in a basket for about 45 seconds. Remove and drain well.

Pour off all but 2 tablespoons of the oil and fry the leeks and ginger for 30 seconds. Add the sesame and chili oil and stir-fry for 1–2 seconds, then add the premixed seasoning B/sauce ingredients and bring to the boil. Return the shrimp and stir in the sauce until warmed through.

Transfer to a serving plate and garnish with chopped fresh cilantro or scallions.

Shrimp Toast

Sichuan Shrimp in Chili Oil Sauce

Sliced Cucumber Stuffed with Shrimp and Pork

Serves 4: 2 large cucumbers; 2 oz (60 g) fresh shrimp meat, ground; 6 oz (185 g) fatty pork, finely ground; 1 tablespoon finely chopped scallion; 1 teaspoon grated fresh ginger; cornstarch; 2 cups (16 fl oz) oil
Seasoning A: 1 egg white, beaten; 2 teaspoons light soy sauce; 1 teaspoon rice wine or dry sherry; ¼ teaspoon salt; ¾ teaspoon sugar
Seasoning B/Sauce: ¾ cup (6 fl oz) chicken stock; 1 tablespoon light soy sauce; ½ teaspoon rice wine or dry sherry; 1 teaspoon salt; ¾ teaspoon sugar

Cut the cucumbers into 1½-in (4-cm) pieces without peeling and use a sharp paring knife to trim away the seed cores. Mix the shrimp, pork, scallion and ginger with the seasoning A ingredients, kneading to a smooth paste. Dust the cucumber rings with the cornstarch and fill with the prepared stuffing. Smooth the edges and coat lightly all over with cornstarch.

Heat the shallow oil to moderate and fry the cucumbers on both sides until golden brown, about 3 minutes. Drain well.

Bring the seasoning B/sauce ingredients to the boil in another pan. Add the stuffed cucumbers and simmer, covered, for 20 minutes. Remove the lid and continue to

cook until the cucumber is tender and the sauce well reduced.

Transfer the cucumbers to a serving plate. Reheat the sauce and adjust the seasonings. Thicken, if preferred, with a thin solution of cornstarch and cold water. Pour over the cucumbers and serve.

Sliced Cucumber Stuffed with Shrimp and Pork

Smoked Fish Salad ★

Serves 4: 1 cooking apple, peeled, cored and diced; 1 fresh cucumber, peeled, seeded and diced; 1 dill pickle, diced; 4 oz (125 g) shelled cooked peas; 4 oz (125 g) button mushrooms, finely sliced; 4 fillets smoked fish, cut into pieces; ½ cup (4 fl oz) mayonnaise or ½ cup (4 fl oz) French dressing made with lemon juice; 3 sprigs dill, finely chopped for garnish

Mix all the ingredients, garnish with the dill and serve in a salad bowl.

Smoked Salmon Feuilletés ★

Serves 4: 1 x 12-oz (375-g) package frozen puff pastry: 4 oz (125 g) smoked salmon; ½ teaspoon dried dill; 1 egg; 2 teaspoons capers; ¼ cup (2 fl oz) sour cream; 1 recipe Mousseline Sauce (see page 192)

Divide the pastry crosswise into 3 even-sized pieces, and roll each out on a lightly floured board to a rectangle about 8 x 9 in (20 x 23 cm). Stack together, trim the sides square and cut into 4 even-sized pieces. Place the 4 top sheets on a cookie sheet. Cut the smoked salmon into squares slightly smaller than the pastry and place a piece of each, adding a sprinkling of the dill tips.

Beat the eggs well and brush around the edge of each piece of pastry. Cover each one with a second pastry sheet and add any remaining smoked salmon. Finely chop the capers and stir into the sour cream, beating lightly. Spread over the second layer of pastry, leaving a wide border. Brush the border with beaten egg and top with the 4 final sheets of pastry. Pinh the edges together, using a pastry wheel or fork, and brush the top with egg. Use pastry scraps to cut out fish-shaped decorations, position on top and brush with egg. Chill for about 30 minutes before baking.

Bake in an oven preheated to 425°F (210°C) for about 15 minutes until well puffed and golden on top.

Microwave the Mousseline Sauce, using 2 tablespoons lemon juice and adding plenty of freshly ground black pepper.

Transfer the feuilletés to warmed plates. Spoon Mousseline Sauce over the top and garnish with sprigs of fresh dill or fennel and lemon slices.

Smoked Salmon Feuilletes

Smoked Trout

Serves 4: 4 whole smoked trout; 4 large lettuce leaves; 4 lemon wedges; 2 tomatoes, cut into wedges; 1¼ cups (10 fl oz) heavy cream, whipped; 1 oz (30 g) grated horseradish; mustard and cress for garnish

Skin the trout and place on the lettuce leaves. Garnish with the lemon and tomato wedges. Mix the cream and horseradish and serve separately. Decorate with mustard and cress.

Snails in Burgundy Sauce

Serves 4: 4 dozen snails (if canned snails are being used, only the ingredients for Burgundy Butter are needed); 1 cup (7 oz) rock salt; 1 cup (8 fl oz) wine vinegar; ½ cup (2 oz) all purpose flour; bouquet garni; generous pinch thyme; salt and white pepper Stock: 1 bottle white Burgundy; 3 cups (24 fl oz) chicken stock; 2 carrots, finely chopped; 2 onions, finely chopped Burgundy Butter: 1½ cups (12 oz) butter; 2 tablespoons finely chopped parsley; 3 garlic cloves, crushed; 1 tablespoon very finely chopped scallions; 1 tablespoon salt; freshly ground black pepper to taste

Remove the hard covering which seals the snail in the shell, then wash thoroughly under running water. Leave them for 2 hours in a good amount of water with the rock salt, vinegar and flour. Wash the snails again.

Blanch the snails in a large saucepan of boiling water for 5 minutes, then drain and run under cold water. Take each snail out of its shell and cut off the back part at the end of its body. Put the snails into a large, clean saucepan with the white wine and the stock. The liquid should completely cover the snails. Add the carrots, onions, bouquet garni, thyme, salt and pepper, and simmer over a very low heat for about 4 hours. Leave the snails to cool in the liquid. Drain.

To prepare the Burgundy Butter, combine the butter, parsley, garlic, scallions, salt and pepper, and work together with a fork to obtain a smooth paste. Press a nut of butter into each shell, add a well-drained snail and another nut of the butter, smoothing off with the flat of a knife, so that the butter is level with the shell. Arrange the snails on special snail dishes or an ovenproof serving dish. Heat for a few minutes in an oven preheated to 325°F (160°C) without letting the butter boil. Serve immediately with very fresh French bread to soak up the butter.

Spiced Oysters

Serves 4: 2 tablespoons oil; 8 scallions, finely chopped; 4 garlic cloves, chopped; 1-in (2.5-cm) piece fresh ginger, chopped; 1 tablespoon dried shrimp paste; 3 oz (90 g) salted fish, soaked and ground; 2 tablespoons sugar, or to taste; 2 teaspoons fish sauce or light soy sauce; ½ teaspoon white pepper; 1½ teaspoons chili powder; 1 heaped tablespoon chopped fresh cilantro leaves; ¾ cup (6 fl oz) water; 4 dozen very small or 2 dozen medium-size oysters; cornstarch; lemon juice; lemon wedges

Heat the oil and sauté the scallions, garlic and ginger for 3 minutes. Mix the shrimp paste with the ground salted fish, sugar, fish or soy sauce, pepper and chili powder. Add to the pan and sauté for 2 minutes. Stir in the chopped cilantro leaves and water, then simmer on moderate heat for 2 minutes. Add the oysters and cook for 5 minutes. Thicken the sauce with a little cornstarch, if necessary.

Spoon into a serving dish and sprinkle over lemon juice to taste. Surround with lemon wedges.

Spicy Chickpeas

Serves 4: 1¼ cups dried chickpeas; 1 fresh green chili, halved lengthwise; 2 tablespoons ghee or oil; 1 medium-size onion, grated; ½ teaspoon cumin; 2 cardamom pods; 2 teaspoons ground coriander; 4 cloves; 1-in (2.5-cm) stick cinnamon; 1-in (2.5-cm) piece fresh ginger; 6 garlic cloves; ½–1 teaspoon chili powder; 2 medium-size tomatoes, skinned and chopped; salt; fresh cilantro leaves for garnish

Wash the chickpeas thoroughly and discard any grit. Cover with unsalted water and soak overnight. Put the chickpeas into a large saucepan of fresh, unsalted water, then add the green chili and simmer until the chickpeas are tender. Drain and reserve the cooking liquid.

Heat the *ghee* and gently fry the onion until soft. Grind the whole spices. Chop the ginger and garlic very finely, and add to the onion. Fry for 2–3 minutes, then add the ground spices and chili powder, and fry for another minute. Add the tomatoes and continue cooking, stirring frequently, until they soften and blend with the onion and spices. Put in the drained chickpeas and cook gently for 10 minutes, adding a little of the cooking liquid every few minutes until ¾ cup has been used. Season to taste with salt. Serve sprinkled with cilantro leaves.

Spicy Corn Fritters

Makes 24: 14 oz (440 g) frozen or canned corn kernels; 1 medium-size onion, grated; ⅓ cup (1½ oz) all purpose flour; 1½ tablespoons cornstarch; 2 teaspoons baking powder; ¾ teaspoon chili sauce or powder; 1 teaspoon salt; pinch of ground black pepper; 1 egg, beaten

Thaw frozen corn or drain the canned corn, then place in a food processor or blender and crush lightly. Add the onion, after draining thoroughly. Add the flour, cornstarch, baking powder, chili and seasoning. Mix well, then add the egg. The mixture should be quite moist, yet thick

Mix prepared corn into the egg-chili mixture.

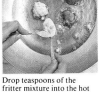
Drop teaspoons of the fritter mixture into the hot oil.

enough to hold together in the oil. Leave for 10–15 minutes.

Heat about 1½ in (4 cm) oil to fairly hot. Drop in teaspoons of the mixture and leave to cook until crisp and golden. Reduce the heat after the first few minutes to ensure that the fritters cook through before becoming too brown on the outside. Drain on crumpled absorbent paper and serve hot or warm. Hot chili sauce, soy sauce or chutney are ideal accompaniments.

Spinach Cheese Puffs

Makes 40 puffs: 1 lb (500 g) filo pastry; 14 tablespoons (7 oz) melted butter
Filling: ½ cup (4 fl oz) olive oil; 6 scallions, chopped; 2 lb (1 kg) fresh spinach, washed, drained and finely chopped, or 1 lb (500 g) frozen chopped spinach, defrosted; 1 lb (500 g) feta cheese, finely crumbled; 9½ oz (300 g) cream cheese; 3 sprigs parsley, finely chopped; freshly ground black pepper; 1 teaspoon chopped dill; 6 eggs, well beaten

Lightly fry the scallions in the oil, add the spinach and sauté until the moisture evaporates.

In a bowl, combine the feta, cream cheese, parsley, pepper, dill and eggs. Add the spinach and onions. Mix well.

Cut the leaves of the filo pastry lengthwise into three equal strips. Cover them with a damp tea towel so that the sheets do not dry out. One strip will be required per puff. Lay out one strip and brush it with melted butter. Fold in half and brush it again with butter. Place a teaspoonful of the mixture on the end of the strip. Fold a corner of pastry over the filling and continue folding until the pastry has been used. Place the triangles on a buttered baking pan, brush tops with melted butter and bake in an oven preheated to 400°F (200°C) for 12–15 minutes until they are plump, crisp and golden. Serve hot.

Spicy Chickpeas

Spring Rolls

*Makes 18: 6 oz (185 g) boneless chicken;
2 teaspoons light soy sauce; 2 teaspoons dry sherry;
¼ teaspoon salt; ¼ teaspoon sugar; ¼ red bell
pepper; 2½ oz (75 g) canned sliced bamboo shoots,
drained; 1 medium-sized carrot, peeled; 2½ oz
(75 g) fresh beansprouts; 2 cabbage or spinach
leaves; oil for deep frying; 2 shallots, shredded;
1 slice fresh ginger, shredded; 1 package 8-in
(20-cm) frozen spring roll wrappers
Sauce: ¾ teaspoon salt; 1 teaspoon sugar;
2 teaspoons light soy sauce; 2 teaspoons cornstarch;
1 tablespoon cold water*

Thinly slice the chicken, then cut into narrow shreds. Place in a dish and add the soy sauce, sherry, salt and sugar, mix well and leave for 20 minutes.

Remove the stem, seeds and inner ribs from the pepper. Shred the pepper, bamboo shoots and carrot into julienne (matchstick) strips. Rinse and thoroughly drain the beansprouts. Finely shred the cabbage or spinach leaves.

Heat about 2 tablespoons of oil and stir-fry the chicken until white. Remove and keep warm. Add the vegetables, shallots and ginger to the pan, and stir-fry until tender. Return the chicken and add the premixed sauce ingredients. Simmer, stirring until there is no liquid in the bottom of the pan, then transfer to a plate to cool.

Thaw the spring roll wrappers under a cloth, then separate and keep covered. To wrap, place a portion of the filling in the center of each wrapper. Fold over one corner and shape the filling into a roll, fold in the two sides, then roll up tightly. Dip the end in water and stick down. If the water is not effective in sticking down the ends, make a paste by boiling 1 tablespoon of cornstarch with about ⅓ cup (2½ fl oz) of water and brush this on.

Heat the oil and deep fry several rolls at a time in moderately hot oil for about 3 minutes. Drain on crumpled absorbent paper and keep warm while the remainder are being cooked. Serve hot with sweet and sour sauce or dips of light soy and chili sauces.

Squid and Kiwi Fruit Salad

*Seves 4: 8 oz (250 g) squid; 1 tablespoon light soy
sauce; 2 tablespoons lemon juice; 2 kiwi fruit*

Clean the squid, discarding the head and tentacles. Peel off the mottled skin, then cut the squid in half lengthwise. Drop the squid into boiling water and leave for just 10 seconds. Remove immediately, drain and cut across into strips ¼ in (5 mm) wide. Combine the soy sauce and lemon juice in a bowl, then toss in the squid.

Peel the kiwi fruit and cut in half lengthwise. Cut each half crosswise into slices about ¼ in (5 mm) thick. Arrange each sliced half on an individual serving dish. Remove the squid from the sauce, drain and divide equally. Arrange neatly on the dish with the kiwi fruit and serve.

Steamed Asparagus on Egg Custard

*Serves 4: 10-oz (315-g) can asparagus spears,
drained; 8 eggs; 1 tablespoon shredded cooked ham
Seasoning: ¾ teaspoon salt; 2 tablespoons chicken
stock
Sauce: ¾ cup (6 fl oz) chicken stock; ½ teaspoon
rice wine or dry sherry; ¼ teaspoon salt;
½ teaspoon cornstarch*

Soak the asparagus in cold water for 10 minutes. Drain well. Discard three egg yolks and beat the remaining eggs and whites together, adding the seasoning ingredients.

Pour into an oiled dish and set on a rack in a steamer. Steam over rapidly boiling water for 10 minutes. Arrange the well-drained asparagus on top and steam for a few more minutes until set.

In a wok or saucepan, boil the sauce ingredients together until thickened. Pour over the egg and garnish with the ham.

Steamed Shrimp Canton

*Serves 2: 1 lb (500 g) raw shrimp in the shell
Dipping Sauce: 1 tablespoon oil; 1 teaspoon sesame
oil; ¼ cup (2 fl oz) light soy sauce; pinch of salt;*

*1 scallion, finely chopped; 3 slices fresh ginger,
chopped; 1 fresh chili, chopped*

Place the shrimp in a dish and cover with a double thickness of wet paper towel. Microwave on HIGH (100%) for 5–6 minutes until the shrimp are pink. (Non-carousel ovens: Give dish a half-turn after 3 minutes.) They should be almost cooked through, but will complete cooking during standing time of 4–5 minutes. Do not overcook.

Mix the sauce ingredients together in a small dish. Serve the hot shrimp with the dipping sauce.

Steamed Stuffed Chicken Wings

*Serves 4–6: 12 chicken wings, lower joints only;
3 cups (24 fl oz) oil for deep frying; 1½ oz (45 g)
chicken or cooked ham; 3 dried black mushrooms,
soaked for 25 minutes; 1½ oz (45 g) canned
bamboo shoots, drained; 6 stems bok choy or fresh
mustard greens; cornstarch
Seasoning A: 1 tablespoon dark soy sauce;
1 teaspoon rice wine or dry sherry
Seasoning B: ¼ teaspoon salt; ⅓ teaspoon sugar;
pinch of white pepper*

Using a sharp small-bladed knife, remove the two thin bones from the wings. Rub with the seasoning A ingredients and leave for 10 minutes. Heat the oil to smoking point and deep fry the wings for 20 seconds. Remove and drain well.

Cut the ham, mushrooms and bamboo shoots into matchstick-size pieces, after removing the mushroom stems and squeezing out excess water. Spoon several pieces into each wing where the bones have been removed. Arrange the stuffed wings on an oiled plate and set on a rack in a steamer. Cover tightly and steam over gently boiling water for 40 minutes.

Stir-fry the *bok choy* or mustard green in 2 tablespoons of oil, adding the seasoning A ingredients and the liquid that has accumulated in the dish containing the wings. Simmer until the vegetables are tender but retaining crispness.

Arrange the chicken wings on a plate and surround with the vegetables. Thicken the sauce with a thin paste of cornstarch and cold water, if necessary, and pour over the wings. Serve at once.

Spring Rolls

Stuffed Artichokes

Serves 6: 6 artichokes; salt; water; 6 garlic cloves, peeled; 6 tablespoons olive oil
Stuffing: 1½ cups (6 oz) fine dry breadcrumbs; 1½ cups (5½ oz) grated Parmesan cheese; ¼ cup finely chopped parsley; salt and freshly ground black pepper

Trim the artichokes by cutting off the tips of each leaf with scissors. Cut the stems. Parboil the artichokes for 10 minutes in salted water. Drain. Remove the center choke from each artichoke.

To prepare the stuffing, mix together the breadcrumbs, Parmesan, parsley, salt and pepper. Push the leaves of the artichoke apart and insert the stuffing in between the leaves. On top of each artichoke place 1 garlic clove.

Put the artichokes into a casserole dish, add water to a depth of approximately ½ in (2 cm) and pour 1 tablespoon of olive oil over each artichoke. Cover the dish and bake in an oven preheated to 375°F (190°C) for 45 minutes or until the leaves easily pull away from the artichoke base. Before serving, remove the garlic clove.

Stuffed Chilies

Serves 4: 12 fresh red or green chilies; 3 oz (90 g) fatty pork, finely ground; 2 oz (60 g) raw shrimp meat, ground; 1 garlic clove, crushed; 1 sprig fresh cilantro, including stem and root; 2 teaspoons fish sauce or thin soy sauce; ½ teaspoon salt; ¼ teaspoon black pepper; 1 tablespoon crushed roasted peanuts; oil for deep frying; 3 eggs (optional)
Batter: ½ cup (2 oz) all purpose flour; 1 egg; pinch salt

Make a slit down one side of each chili and use a sharp knife to cut away the seed cores. Mix the minced pork and shrimp meat together. Grind the garlic, cilantro, fish or soy sauce, salt, pepper and peanuts together and fry in 1 tablespoon oil until fragrant. Add the pork and shrimp mixture and fry, stirring continually, until it changes color. Press the filling into the slits of the chilies, filling plumply.

Mix the batter ingredients with enough water to make a thickish batter. Heat the oil to fairly hot. Dip the chilies into the batter and deep fry until crisp and golden. Drain.

Beat the eggs, if used, until smooth.

Pour into a piping bag fitted with a narrow plain nozzle. Wipe out a fairly large Teflon-lined pan or omelet pan with an oiled cloth and heat until warm. Drizzle the egg into the pan in a lacy pattern until the base of the pan is covered with a thin openweave layer. Cook until just firm, turn and cook the other side. The egg will make three nets. Cut each into quarters and use to wrap the chilies.

Stuffed Crab Claws

Serves 4: 12 large crab claws, meat intact; 12 oz (375 g) raw peeled shrimp; 1¼ cups fresh breadcrumbs; 2 eggs, well beaten; cornstarch; ⅓ cup toasted white sesame seeds; 6 cups (1½ liters) oil for deep frying
Seasoning: 2 egg whites, beaten; ¼ teaspoon salt; ¼ teaspoon white pepper; ⅓ teaspoon dry mustard; 1½ teaspoons lemon juice

Break away the shell from the top of the claw, leaving the meat attached to the central tendon and the claw. Pulverize the shrimp in a food processor, then add the breadcrumbs and seasoning ingredients and mix to a smooth paste. Add a very little water if the mixture is dry. Dust the crabmeat with cornstarch and press on a coating of the shrimp mixture, forming a ball shape around the crabmeat and smoothing around so that only the tip of the claw shows. Dust very lightly with cornstarch, then brush with beaten egg and dip the ends of the stuffed crab claws into the sesame seeds.

Heat the oil to moderately hot and deep fry the crab claws, several at a time, to a golden brown, 2½–3 minutes. Drain well.

Arrange on a bed of shredded lettuce and serve with dips of light soy sauce and Chinese pepper-salt (see page 40).

Steamed Stuffed Chicken Wings (see page 76)

Stuffed Crab Claws

Stuffed Eggs with Mushrooms ★

Serves 6: 14 eggs; 8 oz (250 g) button mushrooms; ²⁄₃ cup (5½ fl oz) mayonnaise; 6 anchovy fillets, chopped; 1 tablespoons finely chopped scallion; salt and pepper; 2 oz (60 g) red caviar for garnish

Boil the eggs for 10 minutes, stirring occasionally to set the yolks in the center. Plunge into cold water and shell when cold. Poach the mushrooms in salted water for 5 minutes, then drain and cool. Select 12 well-shaped mushrooms for decoration and chop the remaining mushrooms finely. Cut 12 eggs in half lengthwise and carefully remove the yolks. Chop the 2 remaining eggs finely. Mix the egg yolks, chopped eggs, mayonnaise, anchovies, scallion, chopped mushrooms, salt and pepper to taste. Spoon the mixture into the egg halves. Place the stuffed eggs on a serving platter and top with the reserved mushrooms. Garnish with red caviar if desired and serve.

Note: Canned button mushrooms may be used instead of fresh mushrooms.

Stuffed Mushroom Caps ★

Serves 6: 6 large mushrooms; 6 tablespoons (3 oz) butter; red bell pepper strips for garnish
Stuffing: 2 tablespoons (1 oz) butter; 1 small onion, finely chopped; 2 tablespoons chopped red bell pepper; ¼–½ cup chopped cooked ham; 2 tablespoons chopped parsley; salt and pepper; 1½ cups fresh white breadcrumbs; ²⁄₃ cup Béchamel Sauce (see page 144)

Prepare the mushrooms and remove the stalks. Chop the stalks finely and reserve for the stuffing. Arrange the mushroom caps in a greased baking dish, dot with butter, and bake in an oven preheated to 350°F (180°C) for 10 minutes.

To make the stuffing, melt the butter in a small saucepan, add the onion and cook until soft but not brown. Add the pepper, ham, parsley, salt and pepper, chopped mushroom stalks and breadcrumbs. Mix thoroughly and bind together with the béchamel sauce.

Remove the mushrooms from the oven and cover each one with the prepared stuffing. Return to the oven and bake for a further 15 minutes or until the mushrooms are tender. Serve hot, garnished with red pepper strips.

Stuffed Crab Shells ▬

Serves 4-6: 6 small raw crabs; 3½ oz (100 g) pork, ground; 4 scallions, chopped; 1–2 fresh red chilies, finely chopped; ½-in (2-cm) piece fresh ginger, chopped; 2 garlic cloves, crushed; 3½ oz (100 g) fresh mushrooms, chopped; 1 teaspoon salt; ¼ teaspoon white pepper; 3 eggs; 2 tablespoons all purpose flour; cornstarch; oil for deep frying; 5 oz (155 g) lettuce, shredded

Drop the crabs into plenty of boiling water and cook for 5–6 minutes. Lift out, put under cold water to cool, then break the shells open underneath. Scoop out the meat and discard the inedible parts. Shred the crabmeat and set aside. Clean the shells by brushing gently, then rinse with warm, salted water. Dry carefully. Crack open the legs and claws to extract the meat.

Mix the crabmeat with the minced pork, scallions, chilies and ginger. Blend in the garlic and mushrooms, season with salt and pepper and bind with 2 beaten eggs and the flour.

Fill the crab shells with the prepared mixture, press down firmly and round off. Coat the top of the mixture with cornstarch and brush with the remaining egg, lightly beaten. Heat 3 in (8 cm) oil in a large skillet and deep fry the stuffed crab shells, several at a time, for 4–5 minutes. Drain well, allow to cool slightly, then arrange on a bed of lettuce to serve.

Carefully break away the top of the shell, leaving the meat attached to the central tendon and claw.

Dust the crabmeat with cornstarch, then press the shrimp mixture around the crabmeat to form a ball.

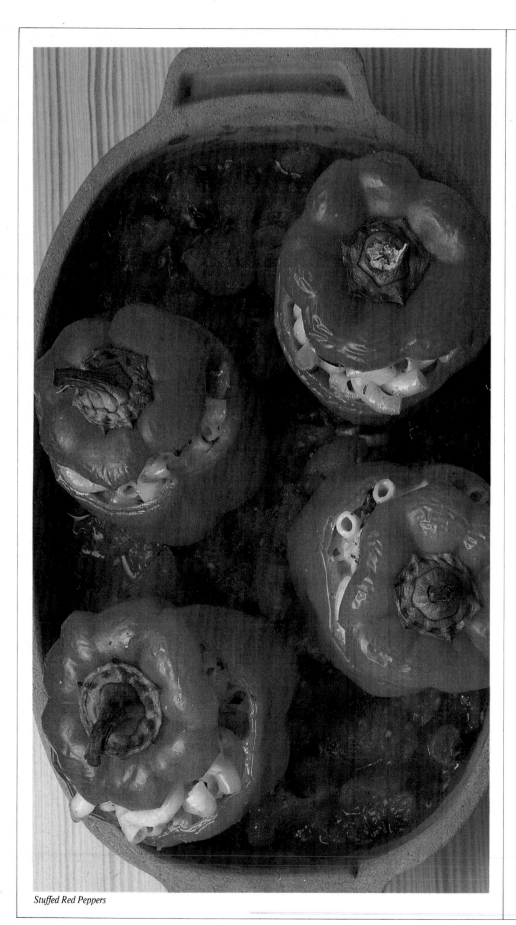

Stuffed Red Peppers

Stuffed Red Peppers

*Serves 4–6: 12 large red chili peppers
4 oz (125 g) lean pork, finely chopped; 1½ oz (45 g)
raw peeled shrimp, chopped; cornstarch; 1¼ cup
(10 fl oz) oil; 1 tablespoon fermented black beans,
washed and chopped; 1 tablespoon finely chopped
scallion; ½ teaspoon finely chopped fresh ginger;
½ teaspoon finely chopped garlic
Seasoning A: ⅓ teaspoon salt; ½ teaspoon sugar;
¼ teaspoon ground black pepper; 1 tablespoon
cornstarch
Seasoning B/Sauce: ⅓ cup chicken stock or cold
water; 1 tablespoon light soy sauce; ¼ teaspoon
salt; ¼ teaspoon sugar*

Cut the chilies along one side and press
open. Trim away the stem and remove the
seed core and the inner white ribs. Mix the
pork and shrimp with the seasoning A
ingredients, working to a smooth paste.
Lightly coat the inside of the chili with
cornstarch and fill generously with the pork
mixture. Dip the whole stuffed chilies into
the cornstarch.

Heat the oil to smoking point and fry the
chilies, filling side downwards, until
golden, turning once. Remove and drain
off all but 2½ tablespoons of the oil. Add
the black beans, scallion, ginger and garlic,
and stir-fry on moderate heat for 1 minute,
then pour in the premixed seasoning
B/sauce ingredients and bring to the boil.
Reduce the heat to low. Return the chilies
and simmer, covered, for about 5 minutes.
Serve hot.

Stuffed Zucchini ★

*Serves 4: 1 lb (500 g) zucchini; ¾ cup (6 fl oz)
French dressing; 4 garlic cloves, finely chopped;
1 onion, thinly sliced; 1 cup (8 fl oz) mayonnaise;
1 tablespoon lemon juice; 2 tomatoes, skinned;
chopped parsley and chives for garnish*

Wash the zucchini and remove the stalks,
then boil in salted water for 15 minutes or
until tender. Drain, slice lengthwise and
place cut side up on a serving platter. Pour
over the French dressing and sprinkle with
the chopped garlic and slices of onion.

Cover tightly with aluminum foil and
marinate in the refrigerator for 5–6 hours.
Drain off excess dressing. Mix the mayonnaise with the lemon juice and spoon onto
each zucchini. Decorate with segments of
tomato, sprinkle with chopped parsley and
chives, and serve.

Tempura

T

Tahina Cream Dip

Serves 4-6: ½ cup (4 fl oz) tahina paste; ½ cup (4 fl oz) lemon juice; ½ cup (4 fl oz) unflavored yogurt; 1-2 garlic cloves, crushed; finely chopped parsley; hard-cooked egg; black olives; olive oil

Blend the tahina paste with the lemon juice, yogurt and garlic, adding about half a cup of water and a pinch of salt. Add more cold water as the paste stiffens and blend to a creamy consistency. Stir in the chopped parsley or use as a garnish. Pour into saucers and decorate with sliced egg, the black olives and a swirl of olive oil. Serve with wedges of pita bread.

Tempura

Serves 6-8 as an appetizer, 4 as a main course: 1 green or red bell pepper; 1 small sweet potato; 1 large onion; 8 scallions; 8 green beans; 3 fillets sea perch or similar (approx. 9 oz/280 g); 3 fresh squid (approx. 4 oz/125 g); 8 medium-size raw shrimp, (approx. 12 oz/375 g); 2 teaspoons dry sherry or ginger wine; pinch of salt; oil for deep frying
Batter: 2 cups (8 oz) all purpose flour; ½ cup (2 oz) cornstarch; 2 medium-size eggs, beaten; 2 cups (16 fl oz) water
Sauce: 1 cup (8 fl oz) dashi (see Note); ½ cup (4 fl oz) light soy sauce; ½ cup (4 fl oz) sweet sherry; 2 tablespoons finely grated white radish or Japanese daikon

Trim away the seed core, stem and inner ribs of the pepper and cut it into small squares. Peel and slice the sweet potato and onion. Trim the scallions and beans but leave whole. Cut the fish into fingers and

the squid into rings. Devein the prawns and marinate with the sherry or wine and the salt. Arrange the vegetables and seafood attractively on a large platter.

Beat the batter ingredients together. The batter should be the consistency of lightly whipped cream. Do not overbeat, as tiny lumps are acceptable in a *tempura* batter.

Mix the sauce ingredients together and pour into a small bowl for each guest.

When ready to serve, heat the oil to hot. Dip the ingredients into the batter and deep fry until crisp and cooked through. Cook each different ingredient separately and serve directly onto your guests' plates. The sauce is used as a dip.

Note: If *dashi* cannot be found at a specialist Chinese or Japanese food supplier, substitute chicken stock made with a bouillon cube or powder and add about ¼ cup of orange juice to give an equally tasty sauce.

Terrine of Duckling with Orange

Serves 12: 2 lb (1 kg) duck meat, boned and chopped; 2 lb (1 kg) ground pork; 4 eggs; finely grated peel of 2 oranges; salt and freshly ground black pepper; pinch of allspice; ½ cup (4 fl oz) rum

Blend the duck meat, pork, eggs, orange peel, salt, pepper, allspice and rum until they are all well mixed. Transfer to a well-buttered terrine dish and cover. Stand the terrine in a dish of simmering water and bake in an oven preheated to 350°F (180°C) for 1½ hours. Cool, then chill well before serving.

V

Vegetable Pork Rolls

Serves 4-6: 1 tablespoon oil; 1 small onion, chopped; 4 garlic cloves, crushed; ¼ lb (125 g) green beans, sliced; 2 small carrots, grated; 5 oz (155 g) cabbage, shredded finely; 1 small sweet potato, peeled and grated, or 3 oz (90 g) thinly sliced palm hearts; 5 oz (150 g) pork, finely diced; ¼ cup (2 fl oz) water; 3 oz (90 g) raw shrimp, peeled and finely diced; light soy sauce; salt and pepper
Wrappers: 10 oz (315 g) all purpose flour; 5 oz (155 g) rice flour; 1 tablespoon salt; 1 tablespoon oil; 3 cups (24 fl oz) water; 2 eggs; 24 lettuce leaves
Sauce: 4 tablespoons brown sugar; 1½ tablespoons cornstarch; 1½ tablespoons dark soy sauce; 1 teaspoon salt; 2 cups (16 fl oz) beef stock; 4 garlic cloves, crushed

To prepare the wrappers, sift the flour, rice flour and salt into a bowl. Beat in the oil, water and eggs, and beat for 2 minutes. Leave to stand for 1 hour.

To prepare the filling, heat the oil and fry the onion and garlic until soft. Add all vegetables and sauté for 2 minutes, then add the pork and stir on moderate heat for 6 minutes. Pour in the water, cover and cook for 3 minutes.

Remove the lid, add the shrimp and season with soy sauce, salt and pepper to taste. Simmer, stirring until the liquid has evaporated and the ingredients are cooked through. Allow to cool before using.

To prepare the sauce, mix the sugar, cornstarch, soy sauce and salt in a small saucepan. Pour in the stock and bring to a rapid boil. Cook over high heat, stirring

frequently, until the sauce thickens.

Add the garlic to the sauce. Stir in and simmer for a further 2 minutes. Pour into one or two small sauce dishes.

To cook the wrappers, heat a well-oiled omelet pan and rub the base with a paper towel. Pour in just enough prepared batter to thinly coat the pan, swirling so it spreads as evenly as possible. Cook the pancake on moderate heat until it can be easily lifted. Lift and turn. Cook the other side to a light golden color. Cook all batter and stack the prepared pancakes between pieces of greaseproof paper.

Wash the lettuce leaves and dry thoroughly. Line each pancake with a lettuce leaf. Spoon on a generous amount of the filling and roll up. Serve with the sauce.

Vine (Grape) Leaf Fritters

Serves 4-6: fresh young vine leaves or vacuum packed vine leaves; juice and finely grated peel of 1 lemon; 1 teaspoon dried oregano; 1 teaspoon salt; 3 tablespoons dry white wine; oil for deep-frying; cayenne or red pepper
Savory Coating Batter: 4 oz (125 g) all purpose flour; 2 tablespoons vegetable oil or butter; ¾ cup (6 fl oz) lukewarm water; ¼ teaspoon salt; ½ teaspoon onion powder; 2 egg whites, stiffly beaten

Lay the vine leaves in a shallow dish. Mix the lemon juice and peel with the oregano, salt and wine, then pour it over the leaves. Marinate for 2-3 hours.

To make the batter, sift the flour into a bowl. Make a well in the center and pour in the oil, water, salt and onion powder. Whisk until the batter is smooth. Leave to stand for 30 minutes, then, just before using, fold in the stiffly beaten egg whites.

Preheat the oil to 365°F (185°C). A small teaspoon of the finished batter dropped into the fat should sizzle and crisp in 45 seconds when the fat is at the correct temperature.

Drain the vine leaves, pat dry on paper towels and dip into the batter. Deep-fry until crisp and golden, drain. on paper towels and sprinkle lightly with cayenne or red pepper before serving.

W

Whitebait Fritters

Serves 4-6: 1 egg; ½ cup (4 fl oz) milk; ⅔ cup (2¾ oz) all purpose flour; salt and pepper; 1 cup whitebait; lard or oil for deep frying; lemon for garnish

Beat the egg and blend with the milk. Sift the flour with the salt and the pepper into a mixing bowl. Whisk the liquid into the flour to form a smooth batter. It should be the consistency of heavy cream. (The quantity of flour or milk may be adjusted slightly to get the required consistency.) Cover the batter and allow to stand while preparing the whitebait.

Put the whitebait into a sieve, run cold water through them and leave to drain well. Mix the drained whitebait with the batter when ready to cook.

Heat the lard or oil in a skillet until very hot. Drop the mixture from a tablespoon into the hot fat and cook quickly until golden, then turn and cook the other side. Drain on paper towels and keep warm while cooking remainder of mixture. Serve hot with slices of lemon.

Y

Yogurt Balls

Serves 6-8: 4 cups (1 liter) natural yogurt; 1 teaspoon lemon juice; 2 teaspoons salt; olive oil; paprika; lettuce leaves; black olives

Line a strainer with cheesecloth and set over a drip tray. Mix the yogurt, lemon juice and salt, and pour into the strainer. Leave overnight to form into solid curds.

Squeeze the cloth to extract as much liquid as possible, then shape the curds into marble-size balls. Dip into olive oil, then roll in paprika and serve cold on lettuce leaves with black olives.

Note: The cheese balls can also be deep fried. Coat first with beaten egg, then roll in all purpose flour and fry very quickly in fairly hot oil until crisped on the surface. Sprinkle on paprika before serving on cocktail sticks.

SOUPS

A

Abalone Soup

Serves 4: 1 tablespoon oil; 1 garlic clove, very finely chopped; 2 slices fresh ginger, very finely chopped; 2½ cups (20 fl oz) mild pork or chicken stock; 3 dried black mushrooms, soaked and shredded; 1½ oz (50 g) lean pork, shredded; ½ teaspoon Chinese rice wine or dry sherry; salt and white pepper to taste; 8 oz (250 g) canned abalone, sliced; 2 lettuce leaves, torn into small pieces; 1 scallion, thinly sliced, for garnish

Heat the oil in a saucepan and gently fry the garlic and ginger until golden. Add the stock, mushrooms, pork, wine and seasonings, and simmer gently for 30 minutes.

Just before serving, put in the abalone and lettuce. Return to the boil and serve immediately, sprinkled with the scallion.

Note: Prolonged cooking will make the abalone shoe-leather tough!

Almond Soup

Serves 4-6: 1 cup (5 oz) shelled blanched almonds; 5 cups (1¼ liters) milk; 1 onion, finely chopped; 1 celery heart, finely chopped; 2 tablespoons (1 oz) butter; 1 tablespoon all purpose flour; cayenne pepper, ground mace and salt to taste; ½ cup (2 oz) toasted almond slivers

Put the almonds through the fine blade of a food grinder. Simmer in 2 cups of milk with the onion and celery. Make a roux of butter and flour, then add the remaining milk gradually. Mix this into the almonds and milk, and cook in a double boiler, stirring, until the thickness of cream soup. Season with cayenne pepper, mace and salt. Top each portion with toasted almond slivers. Serve hot or well chilled.

Asparagus and Crabmeat Soup

Serves 4-6: 4 cups (1 liter) chicken or fish stock; 2 teaspoons fish sauce; ¼ teaspoon white pepper; 9 spears canned asparagus, drained; 6 oz (185 g) shredded crabmeat; 3 egg whites; 2 scallions and fresh red and green chili for garnish

Bring the stock to the boil, then season with fish sauce and white pepper. Cut the asparagus into 2½-in (6-cm) pieces and add to the stock with the crabmeat. Simmer on low heat for 2 minutes.

Beat the egg whites lightly and stir into the soup. The egg should form white threads in the soup. Cook for another minute. Garnish with chopped scallions and shredded chili.

B

Barley Soup

Serves 6-8: 2 parsnips, peeled and finely diced; 3½ oz (100 g) finely chopped celery; 2 large potatoes, peeled and finely diced; 2 leeks, white part only, finely sliced; 2 celery leaves, chopped;

Birds' Nest Soup with Quail Eggs

4-5 cabbage leaves, chopped; 1 veal knuckle; 1 tablespoon melted butter; 3 oz (90 g) barley; 8 cups (2 liters) meat stock; salt and freshly ground pepper; 1 onion spiked with 6 cloves; 3½ oz (100 g) smoked bacon; 10 oz (300 g) smoked pork neck; 7 oz (200 g) smoked beef; 1 egg yolk; ⅓ cup (3 fl oz) cream

In a saucepan, combine the vegetables, veal knuckle and butter. Lightly sauté the mixture, then add the barley and sauté for a few minutes longer. Pour in the stock and add the onion, bacon, pork and beef. Bring to the boil over low heat, then simmer for 2½ hours.

Remove the onion and all the meat. First remove the veal from the bone and, together with the other meat, cut into small dice. Return the diced meat to the broth.

Beat the yolk with the cream and mix it into the soup. Heat, but do not boil. Check the seasoning and serve.

Birds' Nest Soup with Quail Eggs

Serves 4: 4 oz (125 g) prepared birds' nests; 6 cups (1½ liters) chicken stock; 1-2 teaspoons light soy sauce; 1 teaspoon salt; ¼ teaspoon white pepper; 6 oz (185 g) spinach, watercress or other green vegetables; 1 teaspoon cornstarch; 2 egg whites; 12 poached or boiled quail eggs (see Note)

Soak the birds' nests for 4-5 hours in cold water. Pick out the debris with tweezers, then rinse well and drain. Pour into a saucepan, cover with water and bring to the boil. Cook for 2 minutes, then drain. Rinse with cold water.

Return the birds' nests to the saucepan and pour in the chicken stock. Season with the light soy sauce and salt and pepper. Bring to the boil, then reduce heat and simmer for 5 minutes. Add the vegetables and boil until softened.

Beat the egg whites and slowly pour into the soup. They will form into white threads. Do not stir until the egg sets. Add the poached or boiled eggs and heat through before serving.

Note: To poach the quail eggs wipe twelve small soy sauce dishes out with oiled paper and break an egg into each. Place in a steamer and cook until set, about 2½ minutes. To boil, put into a saucepan of cold water and bring to the boil. Cook for 3-5 minutes, then drain and cover with cold water.

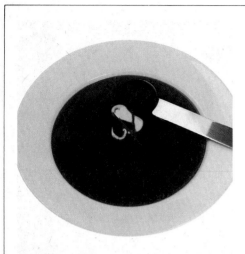

Borsch

Borsch

Serves 8: 2 large brown onions, sliced; 3 oz (90 g) beef dripping; 4 lb (2 kg) stew meat; salt and pepper; good pinch of mixed herbs; 1 bay leaf; sprig of thyme; 8 tablespoons (4 oz) butter; 2 large carrots; 1 leek; 1 turnip; 1 medium-size cabbage; 4 large tomatoes, skinned and chopped; 3 large fresh raw beets; ⅔ cup (5 fl oz) sour cream

Brown the sliced onions in hot beef dripping in a large saucepan. Cut the beef into 2-in (5-cm) cubes, discarding as much fat as possible, then add to the browned onions and quickly sear on all sides, adding a little more dripping if necessary, but try to use as little fat as possible. Add the salt, pepper, mixed herbs, bay leaf and sprig of thyme. Cover with water about ½ in (1 cm) above meat. Bring to the boil, skimming off all froth that rises to the surface, then simmer for 2 hours or until the meat is tender.

Melt butter in another large saucepan. Cut the carrots, leek and turnip into ¼-in (5-mm) slices and add to the sizzling butter. Stir for 2 minutes, then add the shredded cabbage and tomatoes. Simmer uncovered for 10 minutes. Lift the cooked meat out of the stock and add to the fried vegetables. Strain the stock and add it to the meat and vegetables. Simmer for 2 hours.

Shred the beets with a coarse grater and add 3 minutes before you are ready to serve the soup and reheat. Taste and adjust the seasoning if necessary. Add the sour cream and serve hot with an additional fluff of sour cream if desired.

Note: To make Borsch Consommé, strain the soup before adding the grated beets.

C

Cabbage Soup

Serves 6: 2 pig's trotters; 2 calf's knuckles; 1 ham bone; 6 cups (1½ liters) water; 2 tablespoons vinegar; 1 lb (500 g) white cabbage, roughly chopped; 8 oz (250 g) parsnip, sliced; 8 oz (250 g) potatoes, peeled and cut into small dice; ½ teaspoon caraway seeds, crushed; salt and freshly ground black pepper; 1 cup (8 fl oz) sour cream; 3 sprigs parsley, finely chopped

Put the trotters, knuckles and ham bone into a large saucepan, add the water and bring to the boil. Simmer for 2 hours.

Half-fill a separate saucepan with water and bring it to the boil. Add the vinegar and cabbage and cook for 2 minutes. Drain and set aside.

Remove the trotters, knuckles and ham bone from the stock, then cool and skim off all the fat. Cut all the meat off the bones, chop it and set aside.

To the stock, add the cabbage, parsnip and potatoes, and simmer for 30 minutes. Add the caraway seeds, salt, pepper and chopped meat, then stir in the sour cream and serve sprinkled with parsley.

Capri Fish Soup

Serves 4-6: 3 tablespoons olive oil; 2 onions, thinly sliced; 3 stalks celery, chopped; 2 garlic cloves, crushed; 1 teaspoon each fresh marjoram, thyme and basil; 2 lb (1 kg) tomatoes, peeled and chopped; 1 teaspoon grated lemon peel; freshly ground black pepper; 1 cup (8 fl oz) dry white wine; 1 cup (8 fl oz) water; 8 oz (250 g) octopus, chopped; 2 lb (1 kg) mussels, scrubbed; 8 shrimp, uncooked; 12 thick slices fresh tuna, or any fish steaks; 4-6 slices bread, fried in butter

In a saucepan, heat the oil and add the onions, celery and garlic. Sauté for 5 minutes. Add the herbs, tomatoes, lemon peel and black pepper. Cook for a few minutes. Pour in the wine and simmer, covered, until the tomatoes have reduced to a pulp. Add the water and simmer for a further 3 minutes. Stir in the octopus and cook on low heat for 20-30 minutes or until tender. Add the mussels and cook until the shells open, then mix in the shrimp. Cook for 3-5 minutes, then peel and reserve. Finally, stir in the fish, cook for 5 minutes then return the shrimp to the pan. Season and serve with slices of fried bread.

Carrot Soup ★

Serves 4: 12 oz (375 g) carrots, chopped; 3 oz (100 g) turnips, chopped; 3 oz (100 g) onions, chopped; 2 stalks celery, chopped; 4 oz (125 g) potatoes, peeled and diced; 1¾ oz (50 g) chopped ham; 2 tablespoons (1 oz) butter; 1 teaspoon tomato paste; 5 cups (1¼ liters) chicken stock; 3 sprigs fresh herbs, chopped; salt and freshly ground pepper; ⅔ cup (5 fl oz) cream; chopped watercress (garnish)

Sauté the vegetables and ham in the hot butter. Add the tomato paste, stock, herbs, salt and pepper, then simmer for 1½ hours. Cool and rub through a sieve or puree in a food processor or blender. Heat the puree, add the cream and serve garnished with watercress.

Cheese Pasta in Broth, Bologna-Style

Serves 4: 6 oz (185 g) all purpose flour; 1 egg; 2 teaspoons oil; 3 oz (90 g) Parmesan cheese, freshly grated; salt; water
Broth: 6 bouillon cubes or equivalent in granules; 6 cups (1½ liters) water; 1 small carrot, roughly chopped; 1 small onion, roughly chopped; 1 stalk celery, roughly chopped; bouquet garni of oregano, thyme, parsley and bay leaf; salt and freshly ground black pepper; ¼ cup (2 fl oz) dry sherry

To make the pasta, put the flour on a board, make a well in the center and add the egg, oil, cheese and salt. Combine and knead until the dough is smooth and elastic, adding more water if required. The dough should be quite dry. Roll the dough into a ball, cover in plastic wrap and leave for at least 20 minutes before grating into the broth.

Meanwhile, dissolve the bouillon cubes or granules in the boiling water, add the roughly chopped vegetables and the bouquet garni. Add a little salt and a generous grind of pepper and simmer, covered, for about 20 minutes. Strain to produce a clear broth and bring back to the boil.

Using the widest slots on your grater, grate the cheese pasta. Sprinkle on a little flour and toss it through the gratings by hand now and then, to keep them separate and dry. As soon as they are ready, drop the gratings into the boiling broth for 1-2 minutes. Allow the soup to stand off the stove for a couple of minutes before adding the sherry, then serve.

Chicken and Leek Soup

Serves 4-6: 5 oz (155 g) chicken breast; 3 cups light chicken stock or water; 2 Japanese leeks, or 1 leek; 1 tablespoon light soy sauce; 1½ teaspoons salt; 2 teaspoons sake; 2 teaspoons sugar; juice of 1 lemon; 6 very thin, small pieces of lemon or tangerine peel for garnish

Poach the chicken in stock or water until tender. Remove and cut the chicken into very small dice, discarding any bones. Strain the stock and return to the pot with the chicken. Wash the leeks and slice into ½-in (1-cm) pieces. Add to the pot.

Mix the soy sauce, salt, *sake*, sugar and lemon juice and pour into the soup. Simmer until the leek is cooked through but not too soft. Pour the soup into six bowls, add a twist of peel to each and serve.

Chicken Consommé

Serves 4-6: 4-6 cups (1-1½ liters) jellied chicken stock, strained; 2 eggs; salt and white pepper; 3 tablespoons dry sherry; 1 ripe avocado

Put the stock into a fairly large saucepan. Separate the eggs (store the yolks covered in water for other use), crush the shells and add to the stock. Beat the whites until just foamy, then pour into the stock and set the pan over moderate heat. Whisk the stock constantly until it comes to the boil. By rotating the whisk toward you, counterclockwise, the eggs will be more thoroughly pushed through the stock.

Reduce the heat as soon as the stock boils and stop whisking. Simmer for 2 minutes. The egg whites will coagulate and rise to the surface. Remove from the heat, make a hole in the froth and spoon the consommé through a closely woven cloth (a scalded linen tea-towel will do). Allow the clarified stock to drip through without disturbing the egg filter.

Reheat the clear soup, season with salt and pepper to taste and add the sherry. Peel the avocado and cut the flesh into thin slices. Put the avocado into a heated tureen and pour the very hot soup over.

Note: To serve cold, leave a little of the stock until quite cold. If it sets firmly, clarify as described above; if not, add ¼-½ teaspoon of agar agar or gelatin before clarifying. Cool the clarified soup before adding the avocado.

Clockwise from top; Chicken and Leek Soup, Clam Soup (see page 86) and Miso Soup (see page 94).

Chicken Consommé

Chicken Soup

Serves 6: 1 chicken, about 3 lb (1.5 kg); 3 bay leaves; 2 tablespoons finely chopped herbs (fresh thyme, oregano or marjoram); salt and freshly ground black pepper; 2 tablespoons (1 oz) butter; 3 carrots, chopped; ½ bunch celery, chopped; 3 potatoes, diced; 2 leeks (white part only), thinly sliced; 10 oz (300 g) fresh or frozen peas; 6 slices toasted bread; ½ cup (2 oz) freshly grated Parmesan cheese

Put the chicken into a saucepan with enough water to cover. Add the bay leaves, herbs, salt and pepper. Bring slowly to the boil and simmer for 1 hour. Skim the surface.

Heat the butter and sauté all the vegetables except the peas, then add them to the chicken. Simmer for a further 30 minutes, then add the peas. (If raw, simmer for 10 minutes; if deep-frozen, cook for 3 minutes only.) Remove the chicken and take the meat off the bone, keeping it in fairly large pieces. Return the meat to the saucepan. Heat gently and serve with the toasted croutons and grated cheese.

Clear Soup with Shrimp and Mushrooms

Clam Soup

Serves 4: 12 raw clams, in shells; 6 scallions or 2 Japanese leeks; 6 dried Japanese mushrooms, soaked in cold water for 30 minutes; 3 cups dashi; 2-in (5-cm) piece fresh ginger, shredded; 1 teaspoon light soy sauce; 2 teaspoons mirin or sake; 2 oz (60 g) soft bean curd, diced

Steam the clams over a pot of boiling water to open the shells. Remove the beards and wash the clams in salted water. Loosen from the shell but do not remove. Clean the scallions or Japanese leeks and shred finely. Remove the stems from the mushrooms and slice into 2–4 pieces, or leave whole and cut a cross into each cap.

Bring the stock to a rapid boil. Add the mushrooms and ginger and boil for 2 minutes. Season with soy sauce and *mirin* or *sake*. Add the diced bean curd and clams, simmer for 2 minutes, then remove from the heat. Pour into soup bowls and garnish with shredded scallions or Japanese leeks.

Note: Crab pieces may be used instead of clams.

Cock-a-Leekie

Clear Soup with Shrimp and Mushroom

Serves 4: 4 medium-size raw shrimp; 4 small fresh or dried shiitake mushrooms; 4 sprigs of watercress; 3 cups (24 fl oz) dashi; salt to taste; 2 teaspoons light soy sauce; 1 teaspoon sake

Peel the shrimp, discarding the head and shell but leaving the tail intact. Cut deeply along the back of each shrimp (but taking care not to cut right through) and remove the black intestinal vein. Carefully press open each shrimp by putting it on a board and pressing gently with the flat blade of a knife.

Bring a small pan of salted water to the boil. Sprinkle each shrimp with a little cornstarch, shaking to remove any excess, then simmer the shrimp for 2–3 minutes until they are just cooked. Remove from the heat, plunge into cold water to cool, then drain and keep aside.

If using dried mushrooms, prepare ahead of time by soaking in a pan with plenty of warm water for 1 hour. Add 1 tablespoon light soy sauce and ½ teaspoon sugar and simmer the mushrooms, uncovered, for 20–30 minutes until tender. Remove the mushrooms from the cooking liquid, discard the stems and set aside. If using fresh *shiitake*, cut a notch in the cap of each mushroom and remove the stems. Set aside.

Just before the soup is required, arrange 1 shrimp and a sprig of watercress in each soup bowl. Bring the *dashi* to the boil, add the fresh or cooked dried mushrooms and simmer gently for 3 minutes. Add salt to taste, then the soy sauce and *sake*. Put 1 cooked mushroom into each bowl, then carefully ladle in the soup, taking care not to disturb the arrangement of the shrimp, watercress and mushroom. Cover and serve immediately.

Cock-a-Leekie

Serves 4-6: 1 boiling fowl, untrussed; 2 slices bacon, coarsely chopped; 4 leeks, split and cut into 1-in (2.5-cm) lengths; 6-7 cups (1½-1¾ liters) chicken or veal stock; salt and freshly ground black pepper; 4 parsley sprigs; 12 prunes, pitted and roughly chopped

Put the fowl and the bacon into a large saucepan with the leeks and enough stock to cover the bird. Season lightly with salt and pepper and bring slowly to the boil. Reduce the heat, cover and simmer until the chicken is falling from the bones.

Remove the chicken from the stock, discard the skin and bones and chop the meat. Return the meat to the soup with the prunes. Adjust the seasoning and simmer for 15 minutes longer.

Coconut Milk Soup

Serves 4: 1 tablespoon oil; ½ teaspoon brown mustard seed; ½ teaspoon fennel; 2 sprigs curry leaves; 1-2 fresh red chilies, sliced; 1-2 fresh green chilies, sliced; 8 shallots, or 1 medium-size red or brown onion, finely sliced; 2 cups thin coconut milk; ½ teaspoon turmeric; 1 medium-size potato, diced; 4 oz (125 g) white fish, diced, or small raw shrimp, peeled; ½ cup thick coconut milk; ½ teaspoon salt; lime or lemon juice to taste

Heat the oil in a heavy-based saucepan and gently fry the mustard seed, fennel, curry leaves, chilies and shallots until golden. Add the thin coconut milk and turmeric. Bring gently to the boil, stirring constantly. Simmer uncovered for 5 minutes, then add the potato and cook a further 5 minutes. Put in the fish or shrimp and continue to simmer for another few minutes until cooked.

Add the thick coconut milk and salt, and stir over low heat until the soup thickens. Just before serving, squeeze in the lime or lemon juice.

Consommé with Dumplings

Serves 8: 1 lb (500 g) veal, finely ground; 12 oz (375 g) spinach, cooked and pureed; 2 oz (60 g) beef marrow, mashed; 1 cup (4 oz) freshly grated Parmesan cheese; 1 cup (4 oz) fine dry breadcrumbs; 3 tablespoons (1½ oz) softened butter; 5 eggs; pinch of nutmeg; salt and freshly ground black pepper; 6 cups (1.5 liters) beef consommé

Put all the ingredients except the consommé into a food processor and puree to a very fine paste. Spoon the mixture into a colander and press it through holes into the simmering consommé. Boil lightly for 5 minutes and serve with extra grated Parmesan cheese.

Cream of Leek Soup

Serves 8: 1¼ lb (625 g) leeks, washed well; 4 tablespoons (2 oz) butter; 12 oz (375 g) celery, chopped; 7½ cups (1.75 liters) lamb or chicken stock; 1 oz (30 g) parsley, finely chopped; 2 oz (60 g) diced cooked chicken or lamb (optional); salt and pepper; ⅔ cup (5 fl oz) cream

Slice the leeks thinly and reserve some of the green slices for garnish. Melt the butter and cook the leeks and celery over gentle heat in a large, covered pan until soft but not brown. Add the stock, bring to the boil and simmer for 1 hour, skimming if necessary.

Puree the soup in a blender, return it to the pan and add the parsley, reserved leek slices and diced meat. Season with salt and pepper. Add the cream and reheat the soup without allowing it to boil.

Cream of Lentil Soup

Serves 4: ½ cup (3 oz) lentils, soaked; ½-¾ cup (2-3 oz) sliced carrots; ½ cup (2 oz) chopped onions; ½ cup (2 oz) sliced celery; 2 cups (8 fl oz) water; 2 chicken bouillon cubes; 2 tablespoons (1 oz) butter; 1 tablespoon all purpose flour; 2 cups (16 fl oz) milk; 2 oz (60 g) bacon, cooked and crumbled

Put the lentils and vegetables into a medium-size saucepan with a tight-fitting lid. Add the water and simmer for 15 minutes. Add the bouillon cubes and simmer 10–15 minutes longer, or until the lentils are soft and the carrots just tender. Cool.

Puree the mixture in an electric blender or press through a sieve. Melt the butter, add the flour, then the milk in three portions. Stir well and boil between additions. Gradually add the hot pureed vegetables to the hot sauce, stirring constantly. Heat to boiling point. Dilute with more milk if desired, then adjust the seasoning. Serve immediately topped with crumbled bacon.

Note: Replace some of the butter with bacon fat if desired.

Curried Cauliflower and Zucchini Soup

Cucumber Soup

Serves 4: 1 large cucumber; 4 cups (1 liter) chicken stock or water; ¼ cup (1 oz) chopped scallions; ½ garlic clove, finely chopped; 2 tablespoons (1 oz) butter; ¼ cup (1 oz) all purpose flour; 1 teaspoon chopped fresh marjoram; 1 teaspoon chopped fresh thyme; 1 teaspoon chopped fresh basil; salt and freshly ground black pepper; pinch of nutmeg; ½ cup (4 fl oz) cream; ¼ cup sour cream; fresh dill, finely chopped

Peel the cucumber and save the skins. Cut the cucumber lengthwise and with a tablespoon, remove and reserve the seeds. In a saucepan, cook the peelings and seeds in the chicken stock or water for approximately 45 minutes.

Cut the cucumber into slices. Sauté the cucumber with the scallions and garlic in the butter and sprinkle with the flour. Strain the stock over the sautéed cucumber and scallions. Add the marjoram, thyme, basil, salt and pepper, and simmer for approximately 10 minutes. Add the cream and heat it but do not boil. Cool the soup and refrigerate for 3 hours. Serve in individual soup bowls with a tablespoon of sour cream and a sprinkling of dill.

Curried Cauliflower and Zucchini Soup ★

Serves 8: 5 lb (2½ kg) fresh or frozen cauliflower; 1 large onion, finely chopped; 1 garlic clove, crushed (optional); 3-4 thin slices fresh ginger, finely chopped; 3 cups (24 fl oz) chicken stock; 1 large zucchini; 6 tablespoons (3 oz) unsalted butter; 2-2½ teaspoons curry powder; 1-1½ cups (8-12 fl oz) heavy cream; salt and black pepper; cayenne pepper

Cut the cauliflower into small florets and place in a large casserole with the onion, garlic, ginger and 1 cup (8 fl oz) of the stock. Cover and microwave on HIGH (100%) for 25-30 minutes, stirring several times during cooking.

Transfer all but 1½ cups of the vegetables to a food processor in batches and process to a smooth puree. Set aside. Finely chop the remaining cauliflower.

Peel the zucchini lengthwise and shred this peel and flesh into a fine julienne. Discard the central seed core. Place the shredded zucchini in another dish or casserole with the butter and curry powder and microwave on HIGH (100%) for 2 min-

Cut the cauliflower into small florets.

Sprinkle the curry powder over the shredded zucchini.

utes. Add the pureed cauliflower and the remaining ingredients. Warm through for about 25 minutes on MEDIUM (50%), covered and vented. (Non-carousel ovens: Give dish a half-turn twice.)

For extra color, add finely chopped parsley and/or snipped chives just before serving.

D

Duck Soup with Water Chestnuts

Serves 4-6: 12 oz (375 g) duck, boned; 1 set duck giblets (optional); 4-in (10-cm) stalk lemongrass; 8 cups water; 2 tablespoons oil; 3 small red onions or 6 shallots, chopped; 1-2 garlic cloves, chopped; 2½ teaspoons ground coriander; ½ teaspoon ground cumin; ½ teaspoon white pepper; 5 oz (155 g) canned water chestnuts, drained and sliced; 1 tablespoon fish sauce; fresh cilantro leaves, chopped

Chop the duck into 1-in (2.5-cm) cubes. Place the meat, giblets and lemongrass into a large saucepan and pour over the water. Bring to the boil, cover and cook for 1 hour. Strain the soup, reserving the meat and stock. Discard the lemongrass and giblets.

Heat the oil and fry the onions and garlic for 2 minutes, then add the coriander, cumin and pepper. Fry for 2 minutes, stirring constantly. Add the duck and fry on high heat until the meat is well browned. Toss in sliced water chestnuts and season with fish sauce. Brown slightly, then pour in the reserved stock after skimming off fat. Bring to the boil, then reduce the heat and simmer for 10 minutes. Garnish with chopped cilantro before serving.

E

Egg Flower Soup

Serves 4-6: ½ teaspoon fresh ginger juice (see page 209); 4-6 sprigs of watercress or 2 finely chopped scallions; 4 cups (1 liter) dashi or fresh chicken stock; salt to taste; 1 teaspoon light soy sauce; 1 teaspoon sake; 2 teaspoons cornstarch; 2 tablespoons cold water; 2 eggs

Have the ginger juice and decorative greens ready before you begin this dish. Heat the *dashi* and add the salt, soy sauce and *sake*, tasting and adjusting the seasonings if desired. Mix the cornstarch and water, and add to the hot (but not boiling) soup. Stir for 30 seconds until smooth and clear.

Beat the eggs thoroughly and slowly pour in a thin spiral over the soup. Do not stir it immediately but allow the eggs to start to set; this should take 15-30 seconds. Stir the soup gently for about 1 minute so that the egg separates into threads.

Add the ginger juice and watercress or scallions, stir for a few seconds, then serve immediately.

Egg Flower Soup

Egg-Lemon Soup

Serves 6: 6 cups (1½ liters) chicken stock; 2¼ oz (65 g) short grain rice; 4 eggs, well beaten; juice of 1-2 lemons; salt and pepper; 2 tablespoons finely chopped fresh mint for garnish

Bring the stock to the boil, add the rice and simmer for 15 minutes. Combine the beaten eggs, lemon juice, salt and pepper. Add a ladle of the hot stock to the eggs, whisking constantly. Remove the soup from the heat and, while whisking constantly, slowly add the egg mixture to it. Adjust the seasoning. Serve hot sprinkled with the mint.

F

French Onion Soup

Serves 8: 4 lb (2 kg) beef stew meat; 12 cups (3 liters) water; 2 brown onions; ½ bunch celery, coarsely chopped; salt and pepper; 8 tablespoons (4 oz) butter; 1½ lb (750 g) white onions, thinly sliced; melba toast (see Note); 12 oz (375 g) Cheddar cheese, freshly grated

Remove as much fat as possible from the beef and place in a large, covered saucepan with the cold water. Bring to the boil, skimming off any froth that rises to the surface. Reduce the heat and simmer continuously for 1 hour. Cool, then refrigerate until the fat sets on top. Remove the surface fat and strain the stock. Return to the saucepan, add the sliced brown onions, celery, salt and pepper, and simmer for a further 3 hours. Strain the stock, then discard the vegetables and return to a clean pan.

Melt the butter in a saucepan, add the sliced white onions, cover and sauté over low heat until the onions become soft and golden. Stir occasionally with a wooden spoon to prevent sticking as there must not be the tiniest hint of burn. Add the sautéed onions to the stock and simmer continuously for 1 hour.

Cover the base of individual soup bowls with the thinnest possible slices of melba toast. Sprinkle half the freshly grated cheese over the toast. Pour the soup carefully into the dishes, so that the cheese-covered toast floats gently to surface. Sprinkle the remaining cheese over the soup. Place in an oven preheated to 375°F (190°C) for 10 minutes or until cheese turns to a deep golden crust without burning. Serve piping hot.

Note: To make melba toast, remove crusts and slice white bread very thinly, then dry in a 300°F (150°C) oven, until crisp and golden.

G

Garlic Soup

Serves 6: ½ cup (4 fl oz) oil; 4-5 garlic cloves, finely chopped; 8 oz (250 g) stale white bread, no crust, coarsely crumbled; 1 teaspoon paprika; salt; 1 pinch cayenne pepper; 4 cups (1 liter) water; 3 ripe tomatoes, peeled and coarsely chopped; 2 eggs, lightly beaten; 2 sprigs parsley, finely chopped, for garnish

Heat the oil in a saucepan, add the garlic and sauté until soft but not brown. Add the bread and cook over moderate heat until light golden but do not brown. Add the paprika, salt, cayenne, water and tomatoes, then simmer for 30 minutes over low heat.

With a wooden spoon, beat the soup until the bread disintegrates. While beating, add the eggs. Simmer for a few moments but do not boil. The soup should be highly seasoned. If necessary, add more cayenne and salt. Garnish with parsley and serve.

H

Hearty Vegetable Soup

Serves 6: 4 oz (125 g) boneless chicken; 2 small carrots; 6-in (15-cm) piece of giant white radish (daikon); 2 cups sliced bamboo shoots; 6 fresh shiitake or button mushrooms; 6 small new potatoes; 1 cake thin deep fried bean curd; 5 cups (1¼ liters) dashi or fresh chicken stock; salt to taste; 1 tablespoon light soy sauce; 2 tablespoons cornstarch; 2 tablespoons cold water

Cut the chicken into ¾-in (2-cm) square pieces, leaving on any skin. Peel the carrots and scrape the daikon. Cut both into uneven wedges. Rinse the bamboo shoots thoroughly under running water and drain. Wipe the mushrooms, remove the stalks and if using shiitake, cut into quarters. Peel the potatoes and cut in half. Pour boiling water over the deep fried bean curd to remove the oil, then cut into 1-in (2.5-cm) squares.

Put the dashi or chicken stock into a large pan and add all the vegetables, chicken and bean curd squares. Bring to the boil, then simmer gently until the vegetables are tender; this should take about 20 minutes. Season to taste with soy sauce and salt. Mix the cornstarch and water to a paste, then stir into the hot soup. Keep stirring until the soup has cleared and thickened very slightly, then serve immediately in large soup bowls.

Hot Sour Soup

Serves 4: ½ cup yellow lentils; 3 cups (24 fl oz) water; ¼ teaspoon cumin; ½ teaspoon black peppercorns; pinch of turmeric; ½ teaspoon salt, or more to taste; 2-3 garlic cloves, unpeeled and lightly crushed; 1 ripe tomato, skinned and crushed; pea-sized chunk of asafoetida; 2 teaspoons tamarind, soaked in ¼ cup water and strained
Final addition: 1 tablespoon oil; ½ teaspoon brown mustard seed; 2 shallots, or ¼ red or brown onion, finely sliced; 1 sprig curry leaves; 1 dried red chili, broken into ½-in (1-cm) pieces

Wash the lentils thoroughly and soak in cold water to cover for 1 hour. Drain the lentils and put into a saucepan with 3 cups of water, then simmer for 30 minutes. Drain off the water and keep, then discard the lentils.

Grind the cumin and black pepper together and put in a saucepan with the lentil water and all other ingredients (except the "final addition"). Bring to the boil and simmer gently for 10 minutes, stirring from time to time to make sure the asafoetida has dissolved.

To prepare the "final addition," heat the oil in a small pan and fry the mustard seed for 30 seconds. Add all other ingredients and fry gently, stirring frequently, until the dried chili turns brown. Add the fried ingredients to the saucepan, taking care as the oil will sizzle when it meets the hot soup. Bring back to the boil and serve immediately.

I

Iced Vegetable Soup

Serves 4-6: 3 tablespoons stale white breadcrumbs; 1-2 garlic cloves, crushed; 1 tablespoon wine vinegar; 1 tablespoon olive oil; 1 green or red bell pepper, seeded and chopped; 1 onion, chopped; 4 tomatoes, peeled and chopped; 1 cucumber,

Hearty Vegetable Soup

peeled, seeded and chopped; 8 almonds, finely crushed; iced water; salt and finely ground white pepper
Garnishes: 1 large cucumber, peeled, seeded and diced; 1 green and 1 red bell pepper, seeded and cut into small squares; 2 tomatoes, peeled and cut into small dice; 1 onion, finely chopped; 2 hard-cooked eggs, chopped; 2 slices stale white bread, cut into small dice

Combine all soup ingredients except the almonds, water, salt and pepper. Soak and refrigerate for 1 hour. Puree in a blender or food processor. Add the almonds, salt, pepper and enough iced water to dilute to a desired consistency. Refrigerate for 3–4 hours before serving.

Arrange each of the garnishes in a separate dish and serve the soup in chilled bowls. Each diner adds garnishes selected according to individual taste.

Irish Potato Soup

Serves 6: 2 lb (1 kg) potatoes, peeled and diced; 2 large onions, sliced; 6 tablespoons (3 oz) butter; 5 cups (1¼ liters) water; 3 tablespoons mixture of finely chopped parsley, thyme and sage; salt; freshly ground pepper; 1¼ cups (10 fl oz) milk; 2 tablespoons cream and 2 tablespoons chopped chives or mint for garnish

Sauté the potatoes and onions in the butter for approximately 15 minutes but do not brown. Place in a large saucepan, add the water, herbs, salt and pepper, and simmer for approximately 30 minutes or until the vegetables are tender. Remove from the heat and allow to cool.

In a blender or food processor, puree the mixture. Transfer to the saucepan, add the milk and bring to the boil. Serve hot, garnished with cream and the chopped chives or mint.

L

Lentil Soup

Serves 6–8: 1 lb (500 g) lentils; 10 cups (2½ liters) beef stock or water; ½ cup (4 fl oz) olive oil; 2 stalks celery, finely chopped; 1 carrot, chopped; 2 large onions, finely chopped; 3 sprigs parsley, finely chopped; 2 garlic cloves, crushed; 2 tablespoons tomato paste; 2 bay leaves; 1 teaspoon dried oregano; 2 tablespoons wine vinegar; salt and freshly ground black pepper

Place the lentils in a saucepan, pour in the beef stock or water and bring to the boil. Take off the heat and soak for 30 minutes.

In a large skillet, heat the oil and sauté the celery, carrot, onions, parsley and garlic for 10–15 minutes. Mix in the tomato paste, bay leaves, oregano and vinegar. Sauté for a further 5 minutes. Add this mixture to the lentils, season to taste and simmer over low heat for 45 minutes or until the lentils are tender. Serve with chunky fresh bread.

M

Minestrone

Serves 6–8: 4 tablespoons olive oil; 2 onions, finely chopped; 3 small garlic cloves, chopped; 3 oz (90 g) bacon, chopped; 1 tablespoon butter; 3 tomatoes, peeled, seeded and roughly chopped (or substitute canned); ¾ cup (6 fl oz) dry red wine; 8 cups (2 liters) beef stock; 8 oz (250 g) dried white beans, soaked overnight; 6–8 basil leaves, finely chopped; 2 tablespoons finely chopped parsley; 1 large carrot, diced; 1 large potato, peeled and diced; 4 spinach leaves, chopped; 2 small zucchini, diced; 1 stalk celery, chopped; ½ small white cabbage, thinly sliced; 3 oz (90 g) small pasta shapes (conchigliette, farfallette, even alphabet pasta for the children); salt and freshly ground black pepper; 6 tablespoons Parmesan cheese, freshly grated

In a large heavy-based saucepan, heat 3 tablespoons of the oil and gently sauté the onions and garlic until the onions are golden. Add the bacon and cook until the fat becomes transparent. Put in the butter and when it melts, add the tomatoes and the wine. Simmer for a few minutes, then pour in the stock and bring to the boil.

Drain the cold water from the beans and add them to the pan, together with the basil and the parsley. Reduce the heat and simmer gently for about 1½ hours. Add the carrot and potato, and return to the heat for 20 minutes or so. Now put in the spinach leaves, zucchini, celery, cabbage, the pasta, a good pinch of salt and several grinds of black pepper. Cook until the pasta is al dente — the vegetables should be ready at the same time.

At the last moment, stir in half the Parmesan and the remaining 1 tablespoon olive oil. Serve at once with the rest of the Parmesan and plenty of crusty whole-grain bread and butter.

Pour the wine over the sauteed onion and bacon.

Add all the vegetables and continue cooking until the pasta is al dente.

Minestrone with Pesto

Minestrone with Pesto

Serves 6–8: 8 cups (2 liters) water; 4 tablespoons olive oil (or substitute vegetable or corn oil, but the flavor will not be quite as authentic); 5 oz (155 g) dried beans — borlotti, red kidney or white (or substitute canned or fresh); 2 medium-size potatoes, peeled and diced; 3 ripe tomatoes, peeled, seeded and roughly chopped; 2 carrots, finely chopped; 2 small onions, finely chopped; 1 leek, finely chopped (if not available, use 1 extra onion); 3 oz (90 g) pumpkin, peeled and chopped; 3 stalks celery, finely chopped; salt and pepper; 6–8 basil leaves, chopped (or 1 tablespoon chopped parsley); 4 oz (125 g) small pasta shapes (conchigliette, farfallette etc.); 1 generous tablespoon pesto sauce (see page 315); ¼ cup (1 oz) Parmesan cheese, freshly grated; 1 tablespoon pecorino or Romano cheese, freshly grated (or 1 extra tablespoon Parmesan)

Bring the water to a boil in a large heavy saucepan and add 3 tablespoons of the oil. Now add the beans, potatoes, tomatoes, carrots, onions, leek, pumpkin and celery. Season to taste and bring back to the boil, then reduce the heat and simmer, covered, for about 1 hour. Add the basil, re-cover and simmer for about 1 hour longer. The liquid should have thickened but the vegetables should not be mushy.

Put the pasta into the soup until al dente. The time will depend on which type of pasta you use. At the last moment, add the extra 1 tablespoon of olive oil and the pesto sauce. Stir quickly, then serve at once with the grated cheeses mixed together.

Note: If using dried beans, soak 12 hours in water and drain. If using canned, drain. If fresh, shell.

Minestrone

Miso Soup

Serves 4–6: 1 piece dried kelp (kombu) *1 in (2.5 cm) square (optional); 2¾ cups dashi; 3½ oz (100 g) diced chicken or fish; 2½ oz (75 g) diced bean curd; ¼ cup white* miso *paste; 2 teaspoons sugar; 4 scallions, finely chopped; 6 sprigs watercress*

Put the kelp into a large pot with the stock and bring to the boil. Add the chicken and boil for 5 minutes. Remove the kelp and discard, then add the diced bean curd. If fish is used instead of chicken, add at this time and simmer for 2 minutes.

Scoop out ½ cup of the hot stock and blend with the *miso* and sugar, then stir into the soup. Simmer for 4 minutes. Serve in covered lacquered soup bowls, garnished with shredded scallions and a sprig of watercress.

Mulligatawny Soup 🇬🇧

Serves 4–8: 1 small boiling fowl, cut into serving portions; 1 medium-size onion, quartered; 1 small carrot, cut into chunks; 1 stalk celery, quartered; 1 teaspoon salt; 2 parsley sprigs or ½ teaspoon dried parsley; 2 thyme sprigs or ½ teaspoon dried thyme; 2 tarragon sprigs or ½ teaspoon dried tarragon; 2 small bay leaves; 3 slices bacon, chopped; 1 tablespoon ghee or butter; 1 tart cooking apple, peeled, cored and chopped; 3 medium-size tomatoes, peeled, seeded and chopped; 1 tablespoon curry powder; ¼ cup (1 oz) all purpose flour; cayenne or red pepper; salt; ⅓ cup (3 fl oz) cream

Put the fowl into a large pan with the vegetables and salt. Tie the parsley, thyme and tarragon together in a piece of cheesecloth and add to the pan with the bay leaves. Cover with cold water and bring slowly to the boil, removing scum from the surface if necessary. Reduce the heat and simmer until the meat is tender. Remove the chicken from the pan and leave to cool. Strain the stock into a large jug and discard the vegetables and herbs.

Sauté the bacon in the same pan until the fat starts to run, adding the *ghee* or butter if more fat is needed. Stir in the apple and tomatoes and cook for 1–2 minutes, turning to coat well with the fat. Sprinkle with the curry powder and flour, mixing thoroughly. Gradually add the reserved stock, stirring constantly between additions, until the soup is smooth and thick (a little more or less stock can be added to produce the consistency you prefer). Simmer the soup very gently for 10–15 minutes.

Remove and discard the skin and bones of the cooled chicken, cut the meat into strips or cubes, add to the soup and heat through. Add cayenne or red pepper and salt to taste, bring to the boil, then remove from the heat immediately. Stir in the cream and transfer the soup to a heated tureen.

Mussel Soup

Serves 4: 2 lb (1 kg) mussels in the shell; ¼ cup (2 fl oz) water; 3 slices bacon, finely chopped; 2 onions, chopped; 1 stalk celery, chopped; 3 potatoes, peeled and diced; salt and freshly ground black pepper; 2 cups (16 fl oz) milk

Thoroughly clean the mussels and place them in a large saucepan with the water. Cover and cook briefly until the shells open. Discard any mussels that do not open. Take the mussels out of the shells and chop them coarsely.

In a heavy-based skillet, fry the bacon. Add the onions and celery and sauté lightly. Add the potatoes, salt and pepper and the remainder of the mussel cooking liquid. Cook for 15–20 minutes or until the potatoes are tender. Stir in the milk and the chopped mussels. Heat through and serve.

N

Neapolitan Clam Soup

Serves 4: 48 clams (mussels or cockles may be used); 2 cups (16 fl oz) dry white wine; 1 leek (the white part only), chopped; 1 onion, chopped; 1 garlic clove, crushed; 2 tablespoons olive oil; 4 cups (1 liter) fish stock; 1 large tomato, peeled and chopped; 1 teaspoon fresh chopped marjoram; 3–4 leaves of celery, chopped; 4 large croutons, fried in butter

Put the clams into a saucepan, pour in the wine and gently cook until the clams open. Drain, save the liquid and remove the shells. Discard any unopened shells.

Sauté the leek, onion and garlic in the oil, then add the liquid from the clams and the fish stock. Stir in the tomato, marjoram and celery leaves. Simmer for 10 minutes, stir in the clams and serve hot, poured over the croutons.

Noodles in a Pot

Serves 4: 10 oz (300 g) dried udon noodles; 5 oz (150 g) boneless chicken; 4 raw shrimp; 1 Japanese fish cake (kamaboko); 4 fresh shiitake mushrooms; 4 scallions; 4 cups (1 liter) noodle soup (kakejiru); 4 eggs; seven spice mixture (shichimi), optional

Bring at least 6 cups (1½ liters) of unsalted water to the boil and add the noodles slowly. Stir to keep the noodles from sticking. When the water returns to the boil, add 1 cup (8 fl oz) of cold water and bring to the boil again. Simmer until they are almost cooked but still firm. Pour into a sieve or colander and hold under cold running water to cool. Drain well and divide the noodles among four casserole dishes.

Cut the chicken, leaving on any skin, into strips about ½ in (1 cm) wide and 1 in (2.5 cm) long. Peel the shrimp, discarding the heads and shells, and cut each down the back to remove the black intestinal vein. Cut the fish cake into ¼-in (5-mm) slices. Remove the stalks from the fresh *shiitake* mushrooms. Cut scallions, including green tops, into 1½-in (4-cm) slices. Arrange all these ingredients, except for the chicken, on top of the cooked noodles.

Bring the noodle soup almost to the boil in a large pan and add the chicken. Simmer for 1 minute, then carefully ladle over the noodles. Put each casserole over direct heat and bring to simmering point. Cook for just 2 minutes, then using the back of a spoon, make a hollow in the center of each pile of noodles. Gently break in an egg and continue cooking the noodles for another couple of minutes or until the egg white is beginning to set. Put the casseroles onto individual plates and take to the table. The egg will continue to cook in the stored heat of the casserole. When eaten, the white should be set but the yolk still liquid. Each diner sprinkles seven spice mixture if liked.

O

Onion and Fennel Soup

Serves 4: 6 tablespoons (3 oz) butter; 4 medium-size onions, finely sliced; ¼ cup (2 fl oz) brandy; ¼ cup (1 oz) all purpose flour; 6 cups (1½ liters) beef broth; freshly ground black pepper; 4 oz (125 g) conchigliette; ½ cup fennel leaves, loosely packed

Choose a heavy-based saucepan that will hold the broth later. Heat the butter until it froths, then add the onions. Fry gently until turning golden, then add the brandy, which will begin to evaporate quite quickly. When it has reduced to less than half, sprinkle the flour over and cook on a low heat for 3 minutes, stirring constantly.

Warm the broth and pour it gradually into the pan with the brandy, still stirring. Season with several grinds of pepper, cover and simmer for 25–30 minutes.

Uncover the pan, bring to the boil and add the conchigliette. After 5 minutes, add the fennel leaves which have been stripped from the top stalks of the plant. Cook a further 3–4 minutes, or until the pasta is al dente, and serve.

P

Pasta and Bean Soup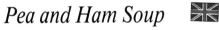

Serves 6: 7 oz (220 g) dried borlotti beans; 1½ oz (45 g) ham or prosciutto, finely chopped; 1 stalk celery, finely chopped; 1 garlic clove, finely chopped; 1 small onion, finely chopped; 1 tablespoon olive oil (or substitute corn or vegetable oil); 1 tablespoon finely chopped parsley; 1 tablespoon finely chopped fresh basil (or use double quantity of parsley); 3½ oz (100 g) tomatoes, peeled and roughly chopped; 2 medium-size potatoes (optional); 2 beef bouillon cubes; freshly ground black pepper; 8 oz (250 g) tagliatelle, linguine or trenette; Parmesan cheese, freshly grated; extra olive oil

Soak the beans in cold water for 12 hours or more, then drain and put in a pan with the ham, celery, garlic, onion, oil, parsley, basil and tomatoes together with 8 cups (2 liters) cold water. If you wish the soup to be even thicker, add the potatoes at this stage; otherwise, omit. Bring to the boil, then dissolve the bouillon cubes, add a generous grind of pepper and simmer gently for 1½ hours or until the beans are soft.

Remove half the beans with a slotted spoon and the potatoes (if used) and mash or puree briefly in a food processor. Return to the pan.

Bring the liquid to the boil, add the pasta cut in 3-in (7.5-cm) lengths and cook until al dente.

Leave the soup off the heat for 1–2 minutes and as you serve, add 1 teaspoon oil to each bowl. Have the grated Parmesan ready for the guests to sprinkle on after they have stirred the oil through the bowl of soup. The soup should be thick.

Pea and Ham Soup

Serves 6–8: 1 large ham bone; 12-oz (375-g) package split peas, lentils or dried soup mix (lentils, red beans, etc.); 1 large onion, chopped; 1 bay leaf; 8 cups (2 liters) water; ½ teaspoon dried mixed herbs; salt and black pepper

Place the ham bone in a large microwave-safe casserole and add the remaining ingredients. Cover and microwave on HIGH (100%) for 10 minutes, then on MEDIUM (50%) for about 1 hour, stirring occasionally. Scrape the meat from the bone and discard the bone. Check the seasoning and serve hot with buttered fresh bread.

Pea and Pork Rib Soup

Serves 8: 1 lb (500 g) pork ribs, soaked overnight in water; 2 tablespoons (1 oz) butter; 4 oz (125 g) onions, chopped; 4 oz (125 g) carrots, diced; 2 oz (60 g) celery, diced; 1 lb (500 g) dried split peas; salt and pepper

Put the ribs into a large pan and cover with 10 cups (2½ liters) water. Bring to the boil and simmer for 1 hour.

Melt the butter in a pan and sauté the onions, carrots and celery until softened but not brown. Add the peas and cook for a further 2–3 minutes, stirring well.

Combine the pea mixture with the stock and ribs, season, bring to the boil and simmer for 2–3 hours. Skim when necessary. Remove the ribs and put the soup through a blender. Return the soup to the rinsed out pan, add the ribs and reheat.

Pasta and Bean Soup

Pea Soup with Sour Cream

Serves 4–6: 8 oz (250 g) fresh shelled peas; 2 cups (16 fl oz) chicken stock; 6 tablespoons (3 oz) butter, softened; 2 tablespoons all purpose flour; 1 egg yolk; ½ cup (4 fl oz) sour cream; salt and freshly ground black pepper; 4 slices white bread, cubed; 2 tablespoons chopped chives

Cook the peas in the stock for 10–15 minutes or until soft. Rub them through a sieve, or puree in a food processor or blender. Make a paste with half the butter, the flour, egg yolk and sour cream. Mix the pea puree and the paste together and heat but do not boil. Season. Make croutons by frying the bread cubes in the remaining butter until golden. Serve the soup hot with the croutons and sprinkled with chives.

Pistou Soup

Serves 6–8: 4 oz (125 g) dried white beans; 4 oz (125 g) dried kidney beans; 8 oz (250 g) green beans, cut in half; 1 large onion, chopped; 8 oz (250 g) carrots, chopped; 8 oz (250 g) zucchini, chopped; 8 oz (250 g) tomatoes, peeled and chopped; 8 oz (250 g) small noodles; 2 garlic cloves; 1½ tablespoons fresh basil; 2 tablespoons olive oil; salt

Soak the white haricot beans and red kidney beans in water for 2–3 hours. Drain.

Put the chopped beans, onion, carrots, zucchini and tomatoes into a large saucepan. Add the dried beans and cover with plenty of salted water. Bring to the boil and simmer for 1½ hours.

Add the noodles to the simmering stock and continue cooking for a further 5–10 minutes.

While the soup is cooking, crush the garlic in a mortar with plenty of green basil leaves. Add the olive oil to the mortar and mix to a paste.

When the vegetables are cooked, add a scoop of the hot soup to the garlic, basil and oil paste. Mix well and return to the soup. Bring to the boil and serve, accompanied by rounds of French bread, olive oil and some grated cheese.

Pork, Shrimp and Crab Ball Soup

Pork, Shrimp and Crab Ball Soup

Serves 4: Meatballs: 8 oz (250 g) lean pork; 4 oz (125 g) raw shrimp, shelled, or white fish; 4 oz (125 g) crabmeat, finely shredded; 2 dried black mushrooms, soaked and finely shredded; 1 tablespoon grated carrot, boiled for 1 minute; 1 scallion, finely sliced; 1 egg; 1 teaspoon cornstarch; ½ teaspoon salt; white pepper to taste
Soup: 2 garlic cloves, finely sliced; 1 tablespoon oil; 5 cups (1¼ liters) chicken stock; 1 cup finely shredded bamboo shoot; salt to taste
Garnish: fried onion flakes (see page 151); fried sliced garlic; fresh cilantro leaves

Chop the pork and shrimp together until finely minced. Combine with crabmeat and other meatball ingredients. Mix well and set aside while preparing the soup.

Fry the garlic gently in oil until golden. Remove and keep aside for garnish. Pour out the oil if the stock is already oily. Add the chicken stock and bamboo shoot to the oil in which the garlic was fried and simmer for 15 minutes.

Shape the pork mixture into balls about 1 in (2.5 cm) in diameter. Drop into the simmering stock and cook for 10–15 minutes. Serve in a large bowl decorated with garnish ingredients.

Pumpkin Soup

Serves 8: 4 tablespoons (2 oz) butter; 1 large white onion, finely chopped; 2½ cups (20 fl oz) chicken stock or water and chicken bouillon cube; 1 lb (500 g) pumpkin; 2½ cups (20 fl oz) hot milk; pinch of allspice; salt and pepper; chopped parsley and croutons for garnish

Melt 2 tablespoons (1 oz) butter in a large saucepan and gently fry the onion for 10 minutes or until soft. Add the chicken stock and bring to the boil.

Peel the pumpkin and cut into 2-in (5-cm) chunks, add to the stock and simmer until tender, about 30 minutes. Cool. Rub through a sieve or puree in an electric blender. Return to the pan, add the hot milk, allspice, salt and pepper to taste and heat gently. Serve in a tureen with 2 tablespoons (1 oz) butter stirred in at last minute and lightly sprinkle with chopped parsley. Serve with croûtons.

R

Ravioli in Chicken Broth

Serves 4: 4 lb (2 kg) boiling fowl; 1 large onion, coarsely chopped; 1 large carrot, coarsely chopped; 2 stalks celery, coarsely chopped; 1 tablespoon tomato paste; 4–5 sprigs parsley; salt and freshly ground black pepper; half quantity pasta (see page 101); additional chopped parsley for garnish
Stuffing: 2 chicken breasts; salt and freshly ground black pepper; 1 egg; 4 oz (125 g) ricotta or cottage cheese; pinch of allspice

Place the cleaned fowl in a large, heavy saucepan, add the onion, carrot, celery, tomato paste and parsley with water to cover. Bring to the boil. Season, then cover the pan and simmer over a low heat for about 2 hours, or until the flesh is tender.

Remove the bird and set aside for use in the stuffing for the ravioli. Use a cheesecloth or very fine strainer to remove the vegetables and parsley from the broth.

To make the stuffing, process the cooked chicken breasts, seasoning, egg, ricotta cheese and allspice until well blended. Reserve.

To make the ravioli, divide the pasta into 2–3 parts and roll one of them into a long thin strip. With a pastry wheel, cut a sheet

Pumpkin Soup

Seafood Chowder

into 3-in (7-cm) strips. Place teaspoons of stuffing in a row about one finger's width apart on the lower half of the strip. Fold the upper half over the lower and firmly press it down so the edges around the stuffing are sealed. Cut with a pastry wheel into squares. Continue until all ingredients have been used.

Cook the ravioli in 6 cups (1½ liters) of the chicken broth until al dente and serve the soup with a garnish of chopped parsley.

Rich Corn Soup

Serves 4: 1 chicken drumstick; 4 cups (1 liter) water; 1 chicken bouillon cube; 1-lb (440-g) can creamed corn; 2 dried black mushrooms, soaked and shredded; 1 teaspoon light soy sauce; 2 scallions, finely sliced; salt and white pepper, to taste; 2 tablespoons cornstarch; ¼ cup (2 fl oz) cold water; 1 oz (30 g) cooked crabmeat (optional); 1 egg, lightly beaten

Boil the chicken drumstick in water until tender. Reserve the water. Remove the chicken and finely shred the meat. Add the bouillon cube to the water and simmer until thoroughly dissolved. Add the corn, mushrooms, soy sauce and half the scallion. Simmer for 2–3 minutes, then add the salt and plenty of white pepper to taste. Thicken with cornstarch mixed with water and simmer for 2 minutes.

Add the chicken and crabmeat, and heat through. Just before serving, add the beaten egg, stirring constantly. Serve sprinkled with the remaining scallion.

S

Seafood Chowder

Serves 4: 3 cups (24 fl oz) milk; 1 scallion, finely chopped; 1½ tablespoons cornstarch; 1 fish stock cube or bouillon powder; large pinch of garlic salt; 4 oz (125 g) white fish fillets, cubed; 6 fresh scallops; 6 fresh oysters; 5 fl oz (150 ml) light cream; 2 eggs, lightly beaten

Pour the milk into a large microwave-safe jug and add the scallion, cornstarch, fish stock and garlic salt. Microwave uncovered on HIGH (100%) for 3 minutes, then stir well and microwave a further 3–4 minutes on HIGH (100%) until thickened.

Add the fish and scallops and stir in lightly. Microwave for 2–2½ minutes on MEDIUM (50%), then add the oysters and microwave on MEDIUM (50%) a final 1 minute.

Stir in the cream and eggs and reheat on HIGH 100% for 1 minute before serving.

Sichuan Sour Hot Soup

Serves 4: 1 oz (30 g) pork, shredded, 1 oz (30 g) chicken breast, shredded; 2 teaspoons peanut oil; 2 heaped tablespoons cloud ear fungus, soaked; 4 large dried black mushrooms, soaked and shredded; 3½ oz (100 g) soft bean curd, diced; 3 cups (24 fl oz) chicken stock; 1 teaspoon light soy sauce; 1 teaspoon Chinese rice wine or dry sherry; 1 teaspoon sesame oil; 2–3 teaspoons malt vinegar; ¼–½ teaspoon chili oil (optional); salt to taste; 1 tablespoon cornstarch, mixed with ¼ cup water; 1 egg, lightly beaten; white pepper; scallion, finely chopped

Fry the pork and chicken gently in peanut oil until they change color. Add the soaked and drained fungus and mushrooms, stirring well. Mix the bean curd and stock, and

simmer for 10 minutes. Add all the seasonings up to the salt and simmer for 3 minutes more. Thicken with the cornstarch mixture.

Just before serving, stir in the beaten egg, sprinkle very liberally with white pepper and garnish with the scallion.

Soup Under a Hat ★

Serves 4–6: 4 oz (125 g) frozen or prepared puff pastry; 1 egg, beaten
Meatballs: 1 lb (500 g) lean pork; 2 scallions, white parts only; 1 garlic clove; 1 slice fresh ginger; 3 sprigs fresh cilantro or parsley; 1 egg; ¼ cup (2 fl oz) water; ½ teaspoon salt; pinch of freshly ground black pepper
Soup: 1–2 scallions; 1 medium-size carrot, peeled; 4 Chinese dried black mushrooms; 1½ oz (45 g) canned or fresh bamboo shoots; 2–3 slices fresh ginger; 4 cups (1 liter) water or chicken stock; chicken bouillon cubes (optional); salt to taste; 1 tablespoon soy sauce

Thaw the pastry, cover and set aside.

Cut the pork into cubes and place in a food processor with the remaining meatball ingredients. Process to a smooth paste, then remove and set aside.

Soup Under a Hat

Cut the scallions and carrot into 1¾-in (4-cm) lengths, then shred finely lengthwise. Place the mushrooms in 1 cup (8 fl oz) of cold water and microwave on HIGH (100%) for 1 minute, then set aside to cool. Drain and shred the bamboo shoots and ginger.

Pour the water with bouillon cubes, or the chicken stock, into a deep microwave-safe casserole and cover. Microwave on HIGH (100%) for 10 minutes. Add the salt, soy sauce, carrots and ginger and microwave on HIGH (100%) a further minute.

Drain the mushrooms, reserving the liquid. Remove the stems and cut the caps into fine shreds.

Using wet hands, form the meat mixture into about 18 meatballs. Place in the stock with the mushrooms and reserved liquid. Microwave on HIGH (100%), covered, for 4 minutes. Add the shredded vegetables and pepper to taste.

Brush the rim of the casserole and about ⅔ in (2 cm) down the outside of the dish generously with beaten egg. Roll out the pastry and cut it to fit the casserole, leaving an overhang. Place on top and press firmly all around the edge. Brush the top with beaten egg. Use the pastry scraps to cut out decorations, place in position and brush with the egg. Bake in an oven preheated to 425°F (210°C) for about 15 minutes until the pastry is well risen and golden on top. Serve at once.

Brush the rim of the casserole generously with beaten egg.

Lay the pastry over the dish and cut to fit.

Sour Shrimp Soup

Serves 6: 1 lemon or lime; 6 cups (1½ liters) fish or chicken stock; 4 lemon or lime leaves (or 1 lemon peel); 2 stalks lemongrass, each cut into 4 pieces; 2 garlic cloves, crushed; 2 fresh red chilies, finely chopped; 1 tablespoon fish sauce; 2 teaspoons ground coriander; 1 tablespoon chili powder (or to taste); 2 teaspoons salt; ½ teaspoon white pepper; 1½ lb (750 g) medium-size shrimp; lemon or lime juice; 6 scallions, finely chopped

Tarator Soup

Slice the lemon or lime into quarters. Combine all ingredients except the shrimp, lemon or lime juice and scallions in a tabletop cooker or a large saucepan and bring to a rapid boil. Cook for 10 minutes on moderate heat, then take to the table, bring to the boil again and cook for a further 10 minutes.

Add the whole shrimp, unpeeled, and cook for 7 minutes. Squeeze in lemon or lime juice to taste and garnish with scallions.

T

Tarator Soup

Serves 8: 2 cucumbers; ¾ cup (6 fl oz) French dressing; 5 cups (1¼ liters) yogurt; 2 tablespoons chopped mint; salt and white pepper

Peel the cucumbers and cut the flesh into very small dice. Combine the French dressing and yogurt, then add the diced cucumber and chopped mint. Season to taste with salt and pepper. Chill thoroughly before serving.

Tomato Soup ★

Serves 6: 6 large tomatoes; 2 medium-size onions, finely chopped; 4 tablespoons (2 oz) unsalted butter; 1 bay leaf; ½ teaspoon dried mixed herbs; 1 teaspoon salt; 1 teaspoon sugar; freshly ground black pepper; 2 cups (16 fl oz) chicken stock; ½ cup (4 fl oz) heavy cream

Place the tomatoes in a dish, cover with plastic wrap and microwave on HIGH (100%) for 3–4 minutes until the skin bursts and can be peeled off. Chop the tomatoes, discarding seeds if preferred.

Place the onions and butter in a microwave-safe casserole, cover and microwave on HIGH (100%) for 3 minutes, add the tomatoes and re-cover. Microwave on MEDIUM-HIGH (70%) for 15 minutes, then add the bay leaf, herbs, salt, sugar and pepper. Microwave a further 10–12 minutes on MEDIUM-HIGH (70%).

Cover with plastic wrap.

Discard the skins.

(Non-carousel ovens: Give the dish a half-turn twice.) Transfer to a food processor and puree until smooth. Add the chicken stock and microwave on HIGH (100%) for 5-6 minutes until boiling.

Stir in the cream and reheat on HIGH (100%) for 1½-2 minutes before serving.

Tortellini in Broth

Serves 4: 3 lb (1½ kg) beef bones; 1 lb (500 g) inexpensive meat such as chuck steak, coarsely chopped; 1 large onion, coarsely chopped; 1 tomato, coarsely chopped; 3 stalks celery, coarsely chopped; 1 large carrot, coarsely chopped; 1 tablespoon finely chopped oregano; 1 tablespoon tomato paste; 1 small bunch parsley; 20 cups (5 liters) water; 2 teaspoons salt; 2 teaspoons scallion, finely sliced, or 1 heaped tablespoon finely chopped chives for garnish; 1 quantity stuffing (see page 96)
Pasta: 1 lb (500 g) all purpose flour; 4 eggs; 2 tablespoons oil, 1 teaspoon salt

Place the bones and meat in a large, heavy-based pan. Add the onion, tomato, celery, carrot, oregano and tomato paste, then the parsley in small sprigs and pour in the water. Bring to the boil, add the salt, cover and simmer gently for about 3 hours, skimming the top to remove the fat and froth that rise to the surface.

Remove the bones and use a cheesecloth or very fine strainer to extract the meat, vegetables and herbs. The result should be a clear, rich, brownish broth. Because this recipe will yield about 12 cups (3 liters) you may wish to refrigerate or freeze some. Allow the broth you intend to reserve to cool naturally before transferring to a container with a tight lid.

To make the pasta, sift the flour, make a well in the centre and add the egg, oil and salt. Combine, then knead until the dough is smooth and elastic, adding a little water if it is dry or flour if it is too moist. Roll the dough into a ball, cover in plastic wrap and refrigerate for 20 minutes.

Divide the dough into quarters and roll each piece out as thinly as possible into a rectangle. Cut into 2 in (5 cm) circles and place a spoonful of prepared stuffing in the center. Brush the edges with water and fold circles in half. Curve the circles into a ring shape and pinch ends together. Leave for a few minutes to dry out.

Heat 6 cups (1½ liters) of meat broth in a large saucepan and cook the tortellini until al dente (check at least once to make sure you do not overcook). Just before

Tomato Soup

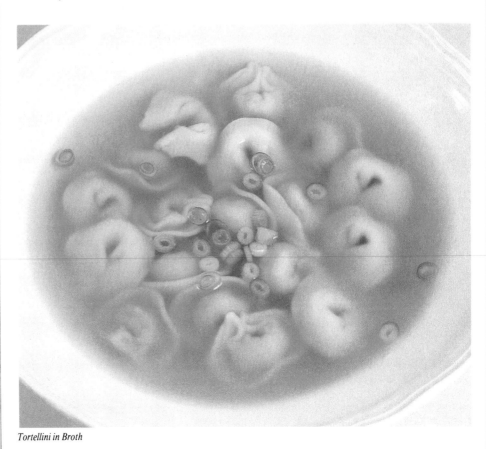
Tortellini in Broth

Watercress Soup

W

Watercress Soup

Serves 4: 2 tablespoons (1 oz) butter; 1 small onion, finely chopped; 1 small leek, finely chopped; 1 bunch watercress, washed; 2½ cups (20 fl oz) chicken or veal stock; 8 oz (250 g) potatoes, peeled and sliced; salt and pepper; ¼ cup (2 fl oz) cream

Melt the butter in a saucepan and sauté the onion and leek without browning. Chop the watercress, reserving a few leaves for the garnish. Add the chopped watercress to the onion and leek and cook for a few minutes. Pour in the stock and add the potatoes, salt and pepper. Simmer for 30 minutes.

Pass the soup through a coarse strainer or puree in a blender. Return to the rinsed-out pan and add the cream. Reheat gently, being careful that it doesn't boil. Pour into warm soup bowls, float the reserved watercress leaves on top and serve.

serving, add the scallions. Serve with Parmesan cheese and have the pepper grinder handy.

Note: For a quicker variation, the rectangles of pasta can be cut into wide strips to make tagliatelle or thinner noodles for vermicelli. The noodles are cooked in the broth before serving. Any left over pasta can be stored in the refrigerator in plastic wrap for several days.

Tuscan Bean Soup

Serves 4: 1 lb (500 g) white dried beans; 6 cups (1½ liters) water or beef stock; salt and freshly ground black pepper; 2 tablespoons olive oil; 1-2 garlic cloves, crushed; ¼ cup chopped parsley

Wash the dried beans and soak them in the water or stock overnight. Gently simmer the beans in the same water or stock for approximately 3 hours or until they are soft. When cooked, put half the beans in a food processor and puree them until they are fine in texture. If a processor is not available, rub them through a sieve. Return the pureed beans to the saucepan and season.

In hot olive oil, lightly fry the garlic and the parsley. Stir this mixture into the soup and serve hot with crusty bread.

V

Vietnamese Noodle Soup

Serves 4-6: 14 cups (3½ liters) water; 4 lb (2 kg) beef shank or rib bones; 1½ lb (750 g) flank steak; 3 scallions; 2-in (5-cm) piece fresh ginger; 1 teaspoon black peppercorns; salt or fish sauce; 1 lb (500 g) beansprouts; 1 lb (500 g) hor fun noodles; 3 scallions; fish sauce; chili sauce; fresh cilantro leaves or chilies, chopped

Pour the water into a large pan and add the bones and cubed flank steak. Trim the scallions, slice the ginger and add to pan with the peppercorns. Cover and simmer for 5 hours on moderately low heat. Season to taste with salt or fish sauce.

Discard the beef bones, lift out the meat and tear into shreds. Drop the beansprouts into boiling stock for 1 minute to soften, then lift out and drain well. Place the noodles in the stock and cook until softened, then remove with a slotted spoon. Trim and slice the scallions finely.

Place a portion of shredded beef, beansprouts, noodles and scallions into each soup bowl. Add a ladleful of the rich soup stock. Serve the fish sauce, chili sauce and bowl of chopped fresh cilantro leaves or chili on the side.

Won Ton Soup

Serves 4: 4 oz (125 g) won ton wrappers (fresh or frozen); 4 oz (125 g) lean pork; 2 oz (60 g) raw shrimp; 1 scallion, including green top; ½ teaspoon salt; ½ teaspoon light soy sauce; pinch of white pepper; 1 dried black mushroom, soaked and finely shredded
Soup: 6 cups (1½ liters) chicken stock; few drops of sesame oil; 1 scallion, finely sliced

Prepare the dumplings first. If using frozen *won ton* wrappers, allow to thaw. Chop the pork and shrimp together very finely, or mix in the food processor to a very fine texture. Add the seasonings and mushroom, mixing to blend thoroughly. Make the dumplings one at a time. Take one wrapper and moisten each corner with a wet finger, then put about ½ teaspoon of filling into the center of each wrapper. Gather up the corners and press the edges firmly together to seal. This should make around 40 dumplings.

Bring a large saucepan full of lightly salted water to the boil. Add the dumplings and simmer, uncovered, for 7 minutes. Drain and put into a serving bowl.

Heat the chicken stock. Add a few drops of sesame oil and pour the soup over the dumplings. Sprinkle with the scallion and serve immediately.

SALADS & SIDE DISHES

A

Artichoke Heart Salad ■■

Serves 6: 2 cups watercress sprigs; 1 small firm lettuce, washed; 15 oz (450 g) canned artichoke hearts, chilled; ½ cup (2 oz) salted almonds, chopped; 6 scallions, sliced; ¼ teaspoon dry mustard; pinch of sugar; ½ cup (4 fl oz) French dressing, made with red wine vinegar

Trim the watercress, tear the lettuce into bite-size pieces and place both in a chilled salad bowl. Add the drained artichoke hearts, almonds and scallions. Add the mustard and sugar to the French dressing and shake well. Drizzle over the salad, roll with clean hands, or toss gently until evenly coated.

Assorted Sautéed Vegetables in Cream Sauce

Serves 4-6: 2 small cucumbers; 6 dried black mushrooms, soaked for 25 minutes; 2 medium-size carrots, sliced; 2 oz (60 g) sweet white turnips, peeled and cubed; 4 cups (1 liter) chicken stock; ⅓ cup (2½ fl oz) oil; 1½ oz (45 g) canned bamboo shoots, drained and sliced; 6 cubes deep fried bean curd, soaked for 10 minutes (optional); 1 tablespoon rendered chicken fat (optional) Seasoning/Sauce: ¾ cup (6 fl oz) chicken stock; 1 tablespoon light soy sauce; ¾ teaspoon salt; ½ teaspoon sugar; 1 teaspoon cornstarch

Cut the cucumber into sticks about 2 in (5 cm) long and discard the seeds but do not peel. Drain the mushrooms and remove the stems. Parboil the cucumbers, mushrooms, carrots and turnips in the chicken stock for 5 minutes and drain well.

Heat the oil in a wok and sauté all the vegetables together for 2 minutes. Add the

Assorted Vegetables with Bean Curd Skin

bean curd, if used, after squeezing out any excess water. Fry for 2 minutes, then pour in the premixed seasoning/sauce ingredients and bring to the boil. Simmer for 1 minute, stir in the chicken fat, if used, and transfer to a serving plate.

Assorted Vegetables with Bean Curd Skin ■■

Serves 4: 2 oz (60 g) dried rolled bean curd skin; 3 cups (24 fl oz) oil for deep frying; 3 dried gluten balls; 6 dried black mushrooms, soaked for 25 minutes; ¾ oz (20 g) dried lily buds, soaked for 25 minutes; ¾ oz (20 g) dried wood ear fungus, soaked for 25 minutes; 4 oz (125 g) young bok choy; 1 oz (30 g) canned bamboo shoots, drained and sliced; 1½ oz (45 g) dried lotus seeds, steamed to soften; 1½ tablespoons light soy sauce; 1 teaspoon

sesame oil (optional); 1 teaspoon cornstarch Seasoning/Sauce: 1½ cups (12 fl oz) chicken stock or water; 1 teaspoon salt

Fry the bean curd skin in smoking hot oil until crisp and bubbling on the surface, about 20 seconds. Drain and cut into 2-in (5-cm) pieces, then soak with the gluten balls in cold water until softened.

Drain the soaked ingredients, remove the mushroom stems and cut the "wood ears" into smaller pieces. Thoroughly wash the *bok choy* and cut each piece lengthwise into quarters.

Pour off all but 3 tablespoons of the oil and stir-fry all the vegetables together for 2 minutes, then add the seasoning/sauce ingredients and bring to the boil. Cover and simmer for 10 minutes, add the soy sauce and sesame oil, if used, and thicken the sauce with a paste of cornstarch and cold water. Serve.

Avocado Mousse Salad

Serves 6: 1 large or 2 small avocados, well ripened, peeled and pitted; 1 small onion, grated; 1 teaspoon salt; freshly ground black pepper; few drops Worcestershire sauce; 1 tablespoon gelatin; ½ cup (4 fl oz) cold water; ¼ cup (2 fl oz) boiling water; ¼ cup (2 fl oz) heavy cream, whipped; ¼ cup (2 fl oz) mayonnaise; lettuce leaves; 4–6 radish roses or 2 tomatoes for garnish

Puree the avocado, onion, salt, pepper and Worcestershire sauce in blender or food processor. Soften the gelatin in ⅓ cup cold water. Add the boiling water and stir until dissolved. Stir in the remaining cold water, then cool. When the gelatin mixture is the consistency of egg white, gradually fold in the whipped cream, mayonnaise and avocado mixture. Pour into a mold, previously rinsed with cold water, then chill until set. Invert and unmold onto a chilled plate lined with lettuce leaves. Garnish with radish roses or wedges of tomato. Serve with melba toast (see page 90).

B

Baked Chive Potatoes

Serves 4: 4 large well-shaped potatoes; 2 tablespoons (1 oz) butter or margarine; 1 tablespoon rich milk or cream; salt and freshly ground pepper; 2 tablespoons chopped chives; ¼ cup grated cheese

Scrub the potatoes and place on the middle shelf of an oven preheated to 375°F (190°C) for approximately 1 hour, or until soft in the center when pierced with a skewer. Halve the potatoes and carefully scoop out all the white flesh. Mash this to a cream in a mixing bowl with the butter, milk, salt and pepper. Add the chives and fill the potato shells with the mixture. Top with grated cheese, return to the oven and bake for a further 15 minutes, or until the cheese has melted. Serve hot.

Batter-Dipped Vegetables

Serves 4: 2 cups (8 oz) chickpea flour; 1 teaspoon baking powder; ½–1 teaspoon chili powder; 1 teaspoon salt; 1 fresh green chili, seeded and very finely chopped; 1 egg, lightly beaten; juice of ½ lemon; warm water to mix; oil for deep frying
Vegetables: use a mixture of any of the following — ¼-in (5-mm)-thick slices of eggplant, potato or sweet potato; small pieces of cauliflower; onion rings; small whole okra (ladies' fingers); whole beet greens or spinach leaves; green beans; rings of green bell pepper

To make the batter, mix all dry ingredients, then add the egg, lemon juice and sufficient warm water to make a thick batter.

Wash and dry the vegetables. Heat the oil in a large skillet. Dip the vegetables one at a time into the batter and deep fry, a few at a time, until just turning golden. Remove and drain. Allow time for the oil to reheat before adding the next batch of vegetables.

Just before serving, heat the oil until it is very hot and deep fry the vegetables a second time for 30 seconds until brown on both sides. Although this second frying is not essential, it makes the vegetables more crisp.

Bavarian Potato Salad

Serves 6–8: 1½–2 lb (750 g–1 kg) new potatoes; 2 onions, finely chopped
Dressing: ½ cup (4 fl oz) oil; 3 tablespoons lemon juice; salt and freshly ground black pepper; ½ teaspoon sugar
Optional additions of which one or several may be used: 1 tablespoon chopped borage, basil, tarragon, parsley, chives; 1–2 apples, peeled and finely chopped; 1–2 pickles, finely chopped

Boil the potatoes, making sure that they are not too soft. Cool, then peel. Cut the potatoes into slices and place them in a mixing bowl with the chopped onions. Prepare the dressing by vigorously mixing all the ingredients together. While the potatoes are still warm, pour the dressing over and mix them gently. Serve at room temperature.

Bean and Beet Salad

Serves 6: 2 lb (1 kg) fresh green beans; salt; ½ cup (4 fl oz) white wine vinegar; ½ cup (4 fl oz) olive oil; ½ teaspoon salt; freshly ground black pepper; 1 lb (500 g) fresh, small beets; 1 tablespoon sugar; ½ cup (4 fl oz) vinegar; 4 cloves; 1 small head lettuce, washed

Trim and string the beans. Blanch in ½ in (1 cm) boiling salted water. Drain while the beans are still green and crisp, then arrange in a shallow bowl. Shake the vinegar and oil together, season with salt and pepper, and pour over the beans while still hot. Chill 1 hour.

Boil the beets in water to cover, with the sugar, until tender. Drain and reserve ½ cup cooking water. Remove the outer skin from the beets, arrange in a shallow dish and cool. Boil the vinegar, reserved beet cooking water and cloves for 5 minutes and pour over the beets. Chill in the refrigerator.

Arrange the lettuce leaves in a large salad bowl. Place the beans in the center. Drain the beets and arrange around the beans. Pour any excess dressing from the beans over the lettuce and serve immediately.

Bean Curd Cakes with Fresh Cilantro and Soy Sauce

Serves 4: 6 squares soft bean curd; 1 large bunch fresh cilantro
Sauce: 2 tablespoons light soy sauce; 1 tablespoon dark soy sauce; 1½ tablespoons vegetable oil; 1 tablespoon water; 1–2 teaspoons sesame oil; 1½ teaspoons sugar

Separately wrap each square of bean curd in a piece of clean cheesecloth. Place in a dish and set on a rack in a steamer. Steam over rapidly boiling water for 15 minutes, then remove from the heat. Unwrap and place on a serving plate. Garnish with the well-washed fresh cilantro.

Mix the sauce ingredients together in a wok and bring to the boil. Pour over the bean curd and serve at once.

Bean Curd in Spicy Coconut Milk Gravy

Serves 4: Spice Paste: 1 stalk lemongrass; 1 thick slice lengkuas; *6-8 fresh red chilies; 10-12 shallots or 2 small red or brown onions; 1 teaspoon dried shrimp paste*
6 pieces hard bean curd; 3 tablespoons oil; 8 oz (250 g) raw shrimp, peeled; 1 teaspoon salt; 1 cup (8 fl oz) thin coconut milk; 2 fragrant lime leaves or young citrus leaves (optional); ½ cup (4 fl oz) thick coconut milk

Prepare the spice paste first. Cut all ingredients except the dried shrimp paste into small pieces, then grind everything to a fine paste with a mortar and pestle or blender. If using a blender or food processor, add a little of the oil to keep the blades turning.

Wipe the bean curd dry and cut each piece into 3-4 thick slices. Set aside. Heat the oil in a skillet and fry the spice paste gently for about 5 minutes. Put in the shrimp, stir for a moment or two, then add the salt and thin coconut milk a little at a time. Bring the coconut milk to the boil, stirring all the time, then simmer for 1 minute before adding the bean curd and lime leaves (if used). Simmer for 10 minutes, then add the thick coconut milk and cook for a couple of minutes to allow the gravy to thicken. Serve with rice.

Bean Curd, Mushrooms and Vegetables Simmered in an Earthenware Crock

Serves 4-6: 3 squares soft bean curd; 1½ oz (45 g) golden mushrooms (see Note); 6 dried black mushrooms, soaked for 25 minutes; ½ cup (4 fl oz) oil or softened lard; 1 oz (30 g) canned bamboo shoots, drained and shredded; 1 oz (30 g) cooked chicken breast, shredded; 1 oz (30 g) cooked ham, shredded; 7 cups (1¾ liters) chicken stock; 6 Chinese cabbage hearts, young bok choy or kale; 1 tablespoon rendered chicken fat (optional)
Seasoning: 1 tablespoon rice wine; 1¾ teaspoons salt; ½ teaspoon ground black pepper

Cut the bean curd into small diamond-shaped pieces and soak in hot water for 10 minutes. Drain the golden mushrooms and rinse in cold water. Squeeze the water from

Bean Curd, Mushrooms and Vegetables Simmered in an Earthenware Crock

Belgique Salad Bowl (top) and Avocado Mousse Salad

the soaked mushrooms, remove the stems and slice finely.

Heat half the oil or lard in a wok and fry the golden mushrooms, black mushrooms and bamboo shoots for 1 minute. Add the chicken and ham and fry briefly, then add the chicken stock and the seasoning

ingredients and bring to the boil. Simmer for 1 minute, then transfer to a flameproof casserole. Add the bean curd and cover tightly. Simmer for 15 minutes on very low heat.

Fry the washed vegetable hearts in the remaining oil or lard for 2 minutes, then add to the crock and simmer for a few minutes more. Check the seasoning, adding the chicken fat, if used. Serve in the crock.

Note: Golden mushrooms have minute golden caps on long, thin golden stems. They are sold in cans or jars where Chinese or Japanese foods are available. If unobtainable, substitute with thinly sliced button mushrooms.

Beet and Endive Salad

Serves 4: 2 medium-size beets, cooked and diced; 3 endives, sliced; 1 cooking apple, peeled, cored and finely diced; 1 small onion, finely chopped; 2 tablespoons prepared horseradish; 2 egg yolks; juice of 1 lemon; 3 tablespoons sour cream; ½ teaspoon mustard; 1 teaspoon sugar (optional); salt and freshly ground black pepper; 3 tablespoons oil; chopped parsley for garnish

In a bowl, mix the beets, endives, apple, onion and horseradish. In a mixing bowl, combine the egg yolks, lemon juice, sour cream, mustard, sugar, salt and pepper. Whisk for 5 minutes then, while still mixing, gradually whisk in the oil. Pour the dressing over the salad and serve garnished with parsley.

Belgique Spinach Bowl

Serves 4: 2 cups spinach, finely shredded; 2 tablespoons finely chopped parsley; 3 oranges; 2 red skinned apples; ¼ cup (2 fl oz) French dressing, made with lemon juice

Toss the spinach and parsley in a chilled salad bowl. Peel the oranges and remove the pith, then cut between the membranes into segments with a sharp serrated knife. Peel, core and slice the apples into rings. Just before serving, combine the fruits with greens in a salad bowl, pour over the French dressing, toss lightly and serve immediately.

Braised Belgian Endive

Serves 4: 2 teaspoons butter; 4 medium-size heads of Belgian endive, trimmed; juice of 1 small lemon; 2 tablespoons dry white wine; ½ teaspoon salt; freshly ground black pepper

Spread the butter over the base of a shallow roasting dish. Arrange the Belgian endive in the dish and pour the lemon juice and wine over. Sprinkle with the salt and black pepper to taste. Cover the dish with aluminum foil and bake in an oven preheated to 350°F (180°C) for 35–40 minutes, or until just tender.

Braised Black Mushrooms

Serves 4: 16 large thick dried black mushrooms; 2 tablespoons oil; 4 garlic cloves, very finely chopped; 3 slices fresh ginger, very finely chopped; 1½ tablespoons light soy sauce; 1 tablespoon dark soy sauce; ½ teaspoon sesame oil

Rinse the mushrooms thoroughly, then soak in plenty of hot water for 10–15 minutes. Strain, reserving the soaking liquid. Remove the stems.

Heat the oil in a casserole and gently fry the garlic and ginger until golden. Add the drained mushrooms and fry, stirring frequently, for a couple of minutes. Cover with soaking liquid and put in the light and dark soy sauce. Cover tightly and simmer over very low heat for 2 hours, checking occasionally to make sure the liquid does not dry out, adding a little water if necessary. Sprinkle with sesame oil just before serving.

Braised Cabbage with Bacon Pieces

Serves 6–8: 1 tablespoon oil; 2 tablespoons (1 oz) butter; 1 large onion, thinly sliced; 8 oz (250 g) bacon, cut into cubes; ½ cabbage, chopped; 1 garlic clove, crushed; salt and pepper; 3 tablespoons dry white wine

In a heavy-based saucepan, heat the oil and butter and gently fry the onion without letting it color. Add the bacon cubes and cook gently for 5 minutes, then gently fry the cabbage, stirring so it does not stick.

Add the garlic, salt and pepper and continue to cook, stirring all the time. Pour in the wine and simmer gently until the cabbage is tender but still crisp. Serve immediately.

Braised Celery

Serves 4: 1 bunch celery; 3 tablespoons (1½ oz) butter; ¼ cup (1 oz) all purpose flour; 1¼ cups (10 fl oz) chicken stock or water and chicken bouillon cube; salt and pepper

Wash the celery well, removing the leaves, and divide into neat pieces about 3 in (7.5 cm) in length. Heat 2 tablespoons of the butter in a saucepan and toss the celery in it for 5–10 minutes, until slightly brown on the outside. Remove the celery and keep warm.

Melt the remaining butter in the pan and remove from the heat. Stir in the flour, then gradually add the stock. Return to the heat and bring to a boil, stirring continuously, then cook for about 5 minutes or until thick. Add salt and pepper to taste. Return the celery to the pan and cook over a very low heat, with the lid on, for approximately 1 hour.

Braised Eggplant with Onions and Tomatoes

Serves 6: 3 long eggplants each weighing 1 lb (500 g); salt; ½ cup (4 fl oz) olive oil; 4 onions, cut in half and sliced; 2 garlic cloves; 5 large firm ripe tomatoes, peeled and chopped or 2 cups (500 g) drained canned tomatoes, chopped; 4 sprigs parsley, chopped; freshly ground black pepper; juice of 1 lemon; 1 teaspoon sugar; ½ cup (4 fl oz) water; 3 sprigs parsley, chopped for garnish

Cut off the stem and peel each eggplant lengthwise, leaving alternate strips of skin about 1 in (2.5 cm) wide. Cut each eggplant in half. Into the cut side, make 3–4 long incisions and sprinkle these sides with salt. Place them, salted side down, in a shallow dish, pour in enough water to cover and let stand for 30 minutes.

Heat half the oil over low heat and fry the onions and garlic until soft and transparent. In a bowl, combine the onions and garlic, tomatoes and parsley. Season to taste. Remove the eggplant from the water,

squeeze the pieces gently and dry them with a paper towel.

Using an oven dish or casserole large enough to contain the eggplant in one layer, fry them lightly on both sides in the remaining oil. Arrange them with the cut side up and force the onion–tomato mixture into the cuts; heap the rest in equal amounts on each. Sprinkle each eggplant with the lemon juice and sugar and spoon some of the oil on top. Add ½ cup of water to the dish, bring to the boil, then reduce the heat, cover and simmer for 1 hour, basting occasionally with the cooking juices. If necessary, add more water. To serve, spoon the cooking juices over them and garnish with parsley.

Braised Fennel

Serves 4: 4 tablespoons (2 oz) butter; 2 large or 4 small bulbs of fennel, trimmed and quartered; ⅓ cup (2½ fl oz) water; salt and pepper

Melt the butter and sauté the fennel quickly until lightly browned on all sides. Lower the heat, add the water and cover. Simmer until the fennel is just tender. Season to taste and serve hot or chilled.

Braised Pumpkin

Serves 4–6: 1¼ lb (625 g) pumpkin; 3 garlic cloves; 3 dried chilies, soaked; 1 medium-size onion; 1 large onion; 2 tablespoons ghee; 1 teaspoon salt; ¼ teaspoon black pepper; 1 teaspoon tamarind; 2 tablespoons boiling water; ¾ cup (6 fl oz) water; 1 tablespoon chopped fresh cilantro

Peel and slice the pumpkin. Grind the garlic, chilies and medium onion to a paste. Slice the large onion thinly and fry in *ghee* until soft. Add the pumpkin pieces and fry until lightly colored, then add the seasoning paste and stir on moderate heat for 2 minutes.

Season with salt, pepper and tamarind mixed with boiling water. Cover with water and bring to the boil. Simmer, uncovered, until the pumpkin is tender, allowing most of the liquid to evaporate. Adjust the seasonings, adding a little sugar if necessary. Garnish with chopped cilantro.

Broad Beans, Bacon and Sausage

Serves 4: 5 tablespoons (2½ oz) lard; 1 onion, finely sliced; 1 garlic clove, crushed; 1 sprig cilantro or parsley, chopped; 2 slices bacon, chopped; 8 oz (250 g) chorizo (spicy pork sausage), chopped; 1 tablespoon sugar; salt; 1 lb (500 g) fresh broad beans; 1-2 cups (8-16 fl oz) stock

In a casserole, heat the lard and sauté the onion and garlic until the onion is soft and transparent. Add the cilantro or parsley, bacon, sausage, sugar, salt, beans and enough stock to cover. Cover the casserole and simmer for approximately 1 hour or until the beans are cooked.

Broccoli in Foaming Lemon Butter ★

Serves 6: 1 lb (500 g) fresh broccoli; 4 tablespoons (2 oz) butter; salt and black pepper; juice of 1 large lemon

Cut the broccoli into florets, peel and trim the stems, then cut a deep cross in the base of each stem for even cooking. Rinse well in cold water.

Place the broccoli in a microwave-safe dish with a fitted lid and add 1 tablespoon of water. Arrange the broccoli with the stems pointing outwards. Cover the dish and microwave on HIGH (100%) for 5 minutes. Drain and leave in the dish.

In a one-cup measure, melt the butter on MEDIUM HIGH (70%) for 1½ minutes. Add salt and pepper and strained lemon juice, and microwave on HIGH (100%) for a further minute until bubbling briskly. Transfer the broccoli to a dish and pour over the butter.

Broccoli with Sesame Seeds ●

Serves 4-6: 10 oz (315 g) broccoli; 2 cups (16 fl oz) light dashi; ½ teaspoon light soy sauce; pinch of sugar; 2 teaspoons black sesame seeds

Cut the broccoli into small florets. Bring the *dashi* to the boil and add the broccoli. Simmer until just cooked but still firm. Reserve 1 tablespoon of the cooking liquid and discard the rest. Put the broccoli into a colander under cold running water to stop the cooking and maintain its color. Drain well and put in a bowl.

Combine the reserved cooking liquid with soy sauce and sugar, mixing well to dissolve the sugar. Pour over the broccoli, mix well and leave at room temperature until serving time. Toast the sesame seeds in a dry pan over low heat for about 3 minutes, shaking to toast the seeds evenly. Pour into a dish and cool.

Serve the broccoli sprinkled with sesame seeds.

Broiled Vegetables ▬

Serves 4-6: 4 red bell peppers, cut in half and seeded; 4 small eggplants, whole; 4 tomatoes, whole; 4 onions, whole; 1 cup (8 fl oz) olive oil; 1 sprig parsley, finely chopped; 1 garlic clove, crushed; salt and freshly ground black pepper

Preheat the broiler and broil the vegetables until they are blackened all round, then cool.

To make the dressing, combine the oil, parsley, garlic, salt and pepper in a screw-top jar and shake well.

Peel the broiled vegetables, cut them into strips, pour the dressing over and serve them with broiled or roasted meats.

Note: This can also be served as a first course with aioli sauce.

Brussels Sprouts with Chestnuts 🇬🇧

Serves 4-6: 12 dried chestnuts, soaked in cold water for 1 hour; salt; 24 small Brussels sprouts; 2 teaspoons butter; freshly ground black pepper

Drain the chestnuts and cook in lightly salted water until tender; drain. Steam or boil the sprouts until just tender, then drain. Shake the chestnuts and sprouts with the butter in a saucepan, season to taste, and serve very hot.

Variation:
Cook the sprouts and sauté 3 tablespoons of slivered almonds in butter. Toss the drained sprouts and almonds together and season with a little freshly grated nutmeg.

Broccoli in Foaming Lemon Butter

Burmese Cucumber and Shrimp Salad

Serves 4: 2 medium-size cucumbers, peeled; 1 lb (500 g) boiled shrimp, peeled; 6 scallions or 1 medium-size onion, thinly sliced; 3 garlic cloves, crushed; ¼ cup (2 fl oz) vegetable or peanut oil; 1-2 fresh red chilies, seeded and shredded; 1¼ teaspoons turmeric; 1½ teaspoons salt; lime juice; fish sauce; ½ fresh lettuce or 2 cups shredded cabbage; 1½ tablespoons crushed roasted peanuts for garnish

Cut the cucumbers into sticks, discarding the seed cores. Mix the cucumber and shrimp in a bowl and set aside.

Sauté the scallions and garlic in the oil until softened. Add the chili, turmeric, salt and plenty of lime juice and fish sauce. Stir well, then remove from the heat and pour it over the cucumber and shrimp. Toss to evenly distribute the seasoned dressing.

Arrange the washed lettuce leaves or the shredded cabbage in a salad bowl and mound the cucumber and shrimp on top. Garnish with the peanuts and serve slightly chilled.

C

Cabbage in Coconut Milk

Serves 4: 1 tablespoon oil; 4 shallots, or ½ medium-size red or brown onion, finely sliced; 1 garlic clove, finely sliced; 1-2 fresh red chilies, sliced; 2 cups (16 fl oz) thin coconut milk; ½ medium-size cabbage, coarsely shredded; 1 heaped tablespoon dried shrimp, soaked; ½ cup (4 fl oz) thick coconut milk; ½ teaspoon salt

Heat the oil in a skillet and gently fry the shallots, garlic and chilies for 2-3 minutes until they soften. Do not allow to brown. Add the thin coconut milk and bring to the boil, stirring all the time. Put in the cabbage and dried shrimp, and simmer gently with the pan uncovered until the cabbage is cooked. Add the thick coconut milk and salt, and cook for another couple of minutes.

Note: This method can also be used to cook green beans, spinach, pumpkin or zucchini.

Burmese Cucumber and Shrimp Salad

Cabbage Medley

Serves 4-6: 2 tablespoons (1 oz) butter; 1 tablespoon vegetable oil; 1 large onion, thinly sliced; 2 medium-size tart cooking apples, peeled, cored and diced; ½ teaspoon celery seed; 2 medium-size tomatoes, peeled, seeded and sliced; 1 medium-size firm white cabbage (not Savoy), thickly shredded; salt and freshly ground black pepper; ½ cup (4 fl oz) natural yogurt or sour cream

Melt the butter and oil in a large saucepan. When the fat is just sizzling, add the onion and cook until transparent. Stir the apples, celery seed, tomatoes and cabbage into the pan and mix thoroughly until all the ingredients are lightly coated with the fat. Season lightly with salt and black pepper. Cover and simmer over moderate heat for 10 minutes, stirring from time to time.

Remove the lid and turn the mixture with a fork until most of the liquid has evaporated and the cabbage is just tender. Add the yogurt or sour cream, stir into the cabbage and adjust the seasoning before transferring to a heated serving dish.

Caesar Salad

Serves 6: Dressing: 1 garlic clove, cut; 1 teaspoon salt; ¾ teaspoon freshly ground black pepper; ¼ teaspoon dry mustard; ¼ teaspoon sugar; 1 teaspoon fresh lemon juice; 4 anchovy fillets; 2 tablespoons tarragon vinegar; ½ cup (4 fl oz) olive oil; 1 egg
2 hearts of lettuce; 2 garlic cloves, thinly sliced; ¼ cup (2 fl oz) olive oil; 1 cup croutons; 2 tablespoons finely chopped parsley; 2 tablespoons Parmesan cheese, freshly grated

To make the dressing, rub the salad bowl with the cut clove of garlic. Add the salt, pepper, mustard, sugar, lemon juice and anchovy fillets, then mash until smooth. Add the vinegar, oil and egg, and stir well until blended.

To make the salad, tear the prepared lettuce into small pieces. Cover the garlic with olive oil and leave for at least 30 minutes (overnight if possible). Use garlic-flavored oil to fry the croutons until golden on all sides. Drain on paper towels.

Stir the dressing into a salad bowl, put the lettuce on top and sprinkle with the parsley. Roll the salad gently from the bottom of the bowl so that the dressing coats the lettuce evenly. Sprinkle crisp croutons and Parmesan cheese over and serve immediately.

Cardamom Glazed Sweet Potatoes

Serves 4: 1 lb (500 g) sweet potatoes; juice and grated peel of 1 orange; 1 tablespoon honey; 1 white onion, thinly sliced; salt; 2 teaspoons ground cardamom seed; 4 tablespoons (2 oz) butter or margarine; 2 tablespoons breadcrumbs

Wash and peel the potatoes, then slice thinly. Mix the orange juice, grated peel and honey together. Arrange the potato slices and onion rings in a greased ovenproof dish, pour over the orange and honey mixture and sprinkle with salt and cardamom. Dot with the butter, then sprinkle with breadcrumbs. Bake in an oven preheated to 375°F (190°C) for 45 minutes. Serve hot.

Carrot and Daikon Salad

Serves 4-6: about 6 in (15 cm) giant white radish (daikon); 1 medium-size carrot; ½ teaspoon salt; 2 tablespoons rice vinegar; 2 tablespoons dashi; 2 teaspoons sugar

Peel the *daikon* and carrot and shred or grate coarsely. You should finish up with about 2 cups (3 oz) of *daikon* and 1 cup (1½ oz) of carrot. Sprinkle the vegetables with salt, toss together in a bowl and leave for 30 minutes. Squeeze out the liquid that will have accumulated and transfer the *daikon* and carrot to another bowl. Combine the vinegar, *dashi* and sugar in a pan and bring just to the boil. Remove from the heat and cool before using.

Toss the cooled dressing with the vegetables and allow to stand for at least 30 minutes before serving. Any leftover salad can be kept for several days in refrigerator.

Carrot and Daikon Salad

Carrot and Water Chestnut Timbales

Serves 6: 1 lb (500 g) carrots (2 medium-size large carrots); 2 tablespoons (1 oz) butter; ¾ cup (6 fl oz) milk; 3 oz (75 g) canned water chestnuts, drained; 1 small scallion; 2 large eggs; 2 tablespoons heavy cream; pinch of grated nutmeg; salt and white pepper

Finely grate the carrots and place in a microwave-safe covered dish. Add the butter and milk, cover and microwave on HIGH (100%) for 8 minutes, stirring once or twice.

Thinly slice the water chestnuts, reserving one for decoration. Finely chop the scallion. Beat the eggs and cream together, adding the seasonings and nutmeg.

Transfer the carrot and cooking liquid to a blender or food processor and process until fairly smooth. Add the egg mixture and the chopped scallion and process briefly. Stir in the water chestnuts.

Wipe out six custard cups or teacups with an oiled cloth and place a disc of water chestnut and a small sprig of parsley or sliver of green scallion top in the bottom of each. Divide the mixture evenly between the cups and cover each loosely with a piece of plastic wrap. Arrange around the outer edge of the carousel, keeping the cups at an even distance from each other.

Microwave on MEDIUM-HIGH (70%) for 4 minutes, then give each cup a half turn to bring the inside edges to the outer side. Microwave on MEDIUM-HIGH (70%) for a further 3–4 minutes. Let stand for 6–7 minutes before turning out. They can be reheated on MEDIUM (50%) if prepared in advance.

Carrots Vichy

Serves 4: 1 lb (500 g) even-size carrots; ⅔ cup (5 fl oz) water; 2 tablespoons (1 oz) butter; salt and pepper; 1 teaspoon sugar; chopped parsley; freshly ground black pepper

Wash and prepare the carrots, then cut into very thin rounds. Put into a pan with the water and add the butter, seasoning and sugar. Press a piece of buttered paper down onto the carrots, cover the pan and cook gently until tender, about 20 minutes. By this time the liquid will have disappeared and the carrots will cook gently in the butter and become lightly browned. Sprinkle with parsley and freshly ground black pepper and serve.

Casserole of Peppers

Serves 4: 4 large bell peppers; ¼ cup (2 fl oz) olive oil; 3 large onions, sliced; 10 oz (315 g) tomatoes, quartered and seeded; 2 tablespoons white wine vinegar; salt; 2 oz (60 g) green olives, pitted and sliced

Quarter the peppers and remove the seeds. In a skillet, heat the oil and brown the onions, then add the tomatoes and the peppers. When all the vegetables are brown, sprinkle with the vinegar. Add the salt and after cooking for 10 minutes, add the olives. Mix well and when the peppers are cooked, but not too soft, transfer to a serving plate.

Cauliflower Cheese

Serves 6: 1 head cauliflower (about 1¾ lb/825 g) Cheese Sauce: 1½ tablespoons butter; 1½ tablespoons all purpose flour; 1⅓ cups (10½ fl oz) milk; ¼ teaspoon prepared mustard; ½ teaspoon salt; pinch of black pepper; pinch of grated nutmeg; 1½ cups (6 oz) loosely packed grated cheese; paprika

Trim the base from the cauliflower and cut a deep cross in the stem. Rinse the cauliflower thoroughly under running cold water, then place in a plastic bag and tie the top with a strip of plastic. Pierce in two places near the top. Set the bag in a microwave-safe dish and microwave on HIGH (100%) for 5 minutes. Turn the cauliflower and microwave on HIGH (100%) for a further 4–5 minutes. Remove from the oven and leave in the bag.

In a jug, melt the butter on MEDIUM-HIGH (70%) for 1½ minutes. Stir in the flour and cook on HIGH (100%) for about 30 seconds. Add the milk and seasonings, stir thoroughly, then return to the oven and microwave on HIGH (100%) for 2 minutes. Remove and stir thoroughly, then return to the oven to microwave on HIGH (100%) for a further 2 minutes.

Stir in 1 cup (4 oz) of the cheese and beat until the sauce is smooth. Avoid further cooking at this stage or the cheese will become overcooked and rubbery when the assembled dish is cooked.

Drain the cauliflower and transfer to a microwave-safe serving dish. Spoon the sauce over the cauliflower, masking it evenly. Top with the remaining cheese and sprinkle on a generous amount of paprika. Microwave on MEDIUM-HIGH (70%) for 2 minutes, or until heated through and the cheese has melted.

Cauliflower Masala

Serves 4: 1 lb (500 g) cauliflower; 3 tablespoons ghee or oil; ½ teaspoon brown mustard seed; ½ teaspoon cumin; pinch fenugreek; ½ teaspoon turmeric; 3 slices fresh ginger, very finely chopped; 2 garlic cloves, finely chopped; 1 medium-size onion, finely sliced; 1 large tomato, chopped; 1 fresh green chili, sliced; ½ teaspoon salt; few grindings black pepper

Separate the cauliflower into florets and set aside.

Heat the *ghee* or oil and fry the mustard seed until it starts popping. Add the cumin, fenugreek, turmeric, ginger, garlic and onion. Cook gently, stirring frequently, for 3–4 minutes until the onion turns golden. Add the cauliflower and fry for a couple of minutes, stirring well to coat it with the spices. Add the tomato, chili, salt and pepper, and cook gently until the tomato softens. Cover the pan and cook gently, stirring from time to time, until the cauliflower is tender.

Chapati (Unleavened Bread)

Serves 4: 2 cups (8 oz) fine whole-wheat flour; about ½ cup (4 fl oz) warm water; 2 teaspoons softened ghee or butter (optional)

Mix the flour and water together to make a reasonably stiff dough. The amount of water required varies slightly with the quality of the flour and the humidity of the climate. Be careful to keep the dough soft but not sticky, adding a little more flour if necessary to achieve this. Add the butter or *ghee*, if using, and knead the dough on a lightly floured board for 10 minutes.

Roll the dough into a ball and put in a greased plastic bag or cover with a damp towel and leave for at least 1 hour. The dough can even be left in the refrigerator overnight, provided it is properly wrapped.

Knead the dough for another 3–5 minutes, then break off pieces the size of a golf ball. Flatten each ball with the hands; then, using a rolling pin, roll out into thin circles about 8 in (20 cm) in diameter.

Heat a griddle or heavy iron skillet until very hot. Cook the *chapati* for about 1 minute until brown spots appear on the underside. Turn and cook on the other side, pressing the top of the *chapati* with a clean towel to help make air bubbles form and keep light. As each *chapati* is cooked, wrap in a clean cloth to keep warm while the rest are cooking. Serve hot with curries, *dhal* or vegetables.

Chinese Cabbage with Pork or Shrimp

Serves 4: ½ Chinese celery cabbage; 2 tablespoons oil or lard; 1 garlic clove, finely chopped; 4 shallots or ½ medium-size red or brown onion, finely sliced; 2 oz (60 g) pork, shredded, or raw shrimp, peeled; 2 tablespoons water or chicken stock; ¼ teaspoon salt; 1 teaspoon light soy sauce

Wash the cabbage and cut it into 1½-in (4-cm) pieces, keeping the stalks separate from the leafy part.

Heat the oil or lard in a skillet and gently fry the garlic and shallots until soft. Add the pork or shrimp and fry quickly for a couple of minutes until they change color. Put in the cabbage stalks and stir-fry for 2 minutes, then add the leafy part and stir-fry a further 2 minutes. Sprinkle over the water or stock, salt and soy sauce. Cover the pan and simmer the cabbage for another 2–3 minutes until cooked.

Chinese-Style Vegetable Platter

Serves 4: 1 zucchini, thinly sliced; 1 medium-size carrot, peeled and thinly sliced; 3 oz (90 g) broccoli florets; 2½ oz (75 g) canned bamboo shoots, drained; 1 tablespoon vegetable oil; 1 large scallion, trimmed and shredded; 2½ oz (75 g) canned button mushrooms, drained; ½ teaspoon grated fresh ginger; ½ cup (4 fl oz) chicken stock; 1 tablespoon cornstarch; 2 teaspoons light soy sauce; pinch each of salt, pepper and sugar

Prepare the zucchini and carrot. Cut the broccoli into small florets and cut a cross in the base of the stems to ensure even cooking. Cut larger pieces of bamboo shoot in half.

Pour the oil into a vegetable dish with a lid and add the zucchini, carrot and scallion. Cover and microwave on HIGH (100%) for 2 minutes, then add the broccoli and bamboo shoots and microwave on HIGH (100%) for a further 2 minutes. Add the mushrooms.

Mix the chicken stock, cornstarch, soy sauce and seasonings together and pour over the vegetables. Cover and microwave on HIGH (100%) for 2–2½ minutes. Serve at once.

Chinese Style Vegetable Platter

Coleslaw

Serves 6: Sour Cream Dressing: 2 teaspoons all purpose flour; 2 teaspoons sugar; 1 teaspoon dry mustard; 1 teaspoon salt; pinch of cayenne pepper; 1 egg yolk; ⅓ cup (2½ fl oz) cider vinegar; 2 tablespoons (1 oz) butter; ½ cup (4 fl oz) sour cream, whipped
1 large pineapple or 2 small pineapples; 3 cups cabbage, shredded; 2 carrots, grated; 10 scallions, finely sliced; 3 red apples, unpeeled and diced; 1 tablespoon lemon juice; salt and freshly ground black pepper; ¾ cup sliced celery; 1 onion, finely chopped (optional); sour cream dressing or mayonnaise

To make the sour cream dressing, combine the flour, sugar, mustard, salt and cayenne pepper in the top of a double boiler. Beat the egg yolk and cider vinegar and add to double boiler. Cook over hot water for 7–8 minutes, stirring constantly. Stir in the melted butter and leave to cool. Fold the mixture into the sour cream.

Cut the pineapple in half lengthwise. Remove the flesh from the skins, reserve the shell and dice the pineapple. Combine the pineapple, cabbage, carrots and scallions. Prepare the apples and sprinkle with the lemon juice. Add the apples to the cabbage with salt, pepper, celery and onion. Toss gently to combine. Add sufficient sour cream dressing to coat. Chill. Spoon the coleslaw into the pineapple shells, then serve.

Cracked Wheat and Parsley Salad (Tabbouleh)

Serves 4–6: 8 oz (250 g) burghul (cracked wheat); 2 scallions, chopped; 1 very large bunch fresh parsley, finely chopped; 1 tablespoon chopped fresh mint (stems removed); 1 large ripe tomato, finely chopped; 4–5 tablespoons olive oil; 4–5 tablespoons lemon juice; salt and black pepper; 12 canned vine leaves, drained or fresh lettuce leaves

Soak the cracked wheat overnight to soften. Drain and leave in a warm oven for about 30 minutes to dry and expand. Crush lightly with the scallions and transfer to a mixing bowl.

Add the remaining salad ingredients, with salt and pepper to taste. Mix well.

Pour boiling water over the vine leaves, if used, and soak for 10 minutes. Drain, rinse in cold water and drain again. Arrange the vine leaves or lettuce leaves in a salad bowl and mound the salad on top. Garnish with sliced hard-cooked egg, black olives, sliced tomato and sliced cucumber.

Creamed Cauliflower

Serves 4–6: 1 cauliflower; salt; 1 egg yolk; 3 tablespoons cream; white pepper

Separate the leaves from the cauliflower, trim away the tough stalks and chop the leaves coarsely. Set aside. Divide the cauliflower into small sprigs, discarding the thickest parts of the stems. Boil with a little salt and barely enough water to cover until they are very tender but not falling apart. Drain and set aside.

Wash the leaves thoroughly and put into a saucepan with a little salt and about ³/₄ cup (6 fl oz) of boiling water. Cook until the leaves are just tender. While they are cooking, mash the sprigs until quite smooth. Over gentle heat, beat the egg yolk into the puree. Add the cream and season with salt and pepper to taste. Keep hot.

Drain the leaves, chop lightly and adjust the seasoning. To serve, arrange the creamed cauliflower in the center of a heated dish and surround with the leaves.

Creamed, Scalloped Potatoes with Rosemary

Serves 4: 2 lb (1 kg) potatoes, peeled and very thinly sliced; 2 garlic cloves, finely chopped; 1 teaspoon crushed dried rosemary; 4 tablespoons (2 oz) softened butter; 1 cup (8 fl oz) cream; salt and black pepper

Layer the potatoes in a microwave-safe dish with the garlic and rosemary. Drizzle over the butter, then add the cream. Season generously with pepper, leaving the salt until the dish has been cooked. Cover with plastic wrap and vent.

Microwave on MEDIUM (70%) for 25–30 minutes. (Give the dish several half-turns if using a non-carousel oven.) Leave to stand for 3–4 minutes before serving.

Creamed Spinach

Serves 4–6: approx. 2 lb (1 kg) spinach or beet greens; 2 tablespoons (1 oz) butter; salt; approx. 3 tablespoons cream; white pepper

Wash the whole spinach leaves or beet greens in several changes of water. Strip away and discard any coarse stalks. Chop the leaves roughly. Put the leaves into a large pan with only the water that clings to them. Add the butter and sprinkle very lightly with salt. Cover and cook over gentle heat for 7–10 minutes, until the spinach is wilted and soft. Strain out any excess liquid.

Puree the spinach in a blender or food processor and add enough cream to give the spinach a rich consistency. Season with more salt if necessary and pepper to taste. Reheat just before serving.

Creamed White Beans

Serves 6: 1 lb (500 g) dried white beans, soaked overnight; 4 tablespoons (2 oz) butter; 1¼ cups (10 fl oz) cream; salt and pepper

Place the beans in a saucepan, cover with cold water and bring to the boil. Simmer slowly for 2–2½ hours or until tender. Drain. Return beans to the pan and add the butter and cream. Simmer gently until thickened, stirring occasionally. Season to taste and serve.

Creamed, Scalloped Potatoes with Rosemary

Crisp Zucchini or Eggplant Slices

Serves 4: 1 large zucchini, or 1–2 long thin eggplants; salt and pepper; 1 cup (4 oz) all purpose flour; oil for deep frying; 2 tablespoons Parmesan cheese, freshly grated

Thinly slice the vegetables without peeling and spread on a board or tray. Sprinkle generously with salt and leave for 1 hour. The salt will draw off the bitter juices.

Rinse the vegetables thoroughly, then dry on a cloth. Season the flour with salt and pepper and coat the vegetables.

Heat the oil to fairly hot, then deep fry the vegetables in two or three batches until crisp and golden. Drain and transfer to a serving dish, sprinkle the cheese over and serve at once.

Thinly slice the vegetables diagonally.

Sprinkle with salt to degorge.

Crisp Zucchini or Eggplant Slices

Cucumber and Wakame Salad

Serves 4: 4 small Japanese cucumbers (about 5 in/ 12 cm in length) or 1 medium-size cucumber; 1 tablespoon salt; 1¾ oz (50 g) salted or dried wakame seaweed; 2 tablespoons rice vinegar; 1 tablespoon light soy sauce; 1 teaspoon superfine sugar

If using a medium-size cucumber, peel lengthwise, leaving on some strips of skin for a decorative appearance. Cut the cucumber in half lengthwise, discard the seeds and cut the flesh at an angle crosswise into thin slices. Sprinkle with salt and refrigerate for 30 minutes.

If using salted *wakame*, soak in cold water for 5 minutes, then rinse and drain. If using dried *wakame*, soak for 20 minutes, then drain. Remove any tough central ribs from the *wakame* if this has not already been done. Simmer the soaked, dried *wakame* for 5 minutes, then drain, plunge in cold water to cool and drain again. Salted *wakame* will not need this treatment. Cut the *wakame* into 3-in (8-cm) lengths and put into a bowl.

Combine the rice vinegar, soy sauce and sugar, stirring well to dissolve the sugar. Just before serving, spoon a little of this dressing over the *wakame* and toss well. Divide the *wakame* between four small bowls. Rinse the cucumbers, gently squeeze out the water and divide among the bowls. Spoon a little of the dressing over the cucumbers and serve.

Cucumber with Yogurt

Serves 4: 1 cucumber, peeled and sliced; 1 teaspoon salt; 1 tablespoon cold water; ½ cup (4 fl oz) yogurt; 2 shallots or ¼ medium-size red or brown onion, very finely sliced; 2 teaspoons finely chopped mint or fresh cilantro leaves; few seedless raisins or golden raisins (optional); ¼ teaspoon garam masala

Spinkle the sliced cucumber with salt and water, and refrigerate for 30 minutes. Drain and squeeze out all moisture. Combine with the yogurt, shallots, mint and raisins. Put in a serving dish with the *garam masala* sprinkled on top.

E
Eggplant Braised with Soybean Paste

Serves 4: 12 oz (375 g) eggplant; 2 teaspoons salt; 2 cups (16 fl oz) oil for deep frying; 2 tablespoons finely chopped scallion; 1¼ teaspoons grated fresh ginger; 1½ teaspoons crushed garlic; 1¼ tablespoons soybean paste (or hot bean paste, if preferred); sesame oil
Seasoning/Sauce: ½ cup (4 fl oz) chicken stock; 1 tablespoon light soy sauce; 1 tablespoon rice wine or dry sherry; 1 tablespoon sugar

Wash the eggplant, removing the skin if preferred, and cut into 1-in (2.5-cm) cubes. Sprinkle the salt over, cover with a plate and leave, weighted lightly, for 45 minutes. Rinse in cold water and pat dry.

Deep fry the eggplant in moderately hot oil until brown. Drain and pour off all but 2 tablespoons oil.

Sauté the scallion, ginger and garlic for 1 minute, add the bean paste and cook a further 1 minute, stirring constantly.

Pour in the premixed seasoning/sauce ingredients and bring to the boil. Return the eggplant to the pan, reduce the heat and cook, covered, until the eggplant is tender and the sauce has been absorbed. Stir in a dash of sesame oil.

Eggplant with Dried Shrimp Topping

Serves 6–8: 4 medium-size eggplants, long green variety if possible; ½ cup (4 fl oz) oil; ¼ cup dried shrimp, soaked; 4–6 shallots or 1 small red or brown onion; 2 garlic cloves; 1 teaspoon chili powder; 2 teaspoons vinegar; 2 teaspoons sugar; ¼ teaspoon salt

Wipe the eggplants but do not peel. Cut in half lengthwise and fry in hot oil for a few minutes on either side, until soft. Drain and set aside. Pound the soaked dried shrimp until fine and set aside. Pound the shallots and garlic together.

Add enough oil to the pan in which the eggplant was fried to make ¼ cup. Heat the oil, then gently fry the shallots, garlic and chili powder for 1 minute. Add the dried shrimp, vinegar, sugar and salt. Cook for a few minutes until golden brown, then spread a little of this mixture over each of the fried eggplant halves. Serve warm.

F

Fennel Peas

Serves 4-6: 3 tablespoons (1½ oz) butter; 2 large bulbs of fennel, trimmed and thickly sliced; 12 oz (375 g) shelled peas; 2 tablespoons white wine or water; salt and freshly ground black pepper

Melt the butter in a saucepan and sauté the fennel over moderate heat until lightly browned but still crisp. Reduce the heat, add the peas and wine and cover. Simmer for 10 minutes. Season with salt and a generous amount of pepper. Serve hot or chilled.

Note: If using fresh peas, as opposed to frozen, blanch them in boiling water for 3-4 minutes, strain, and add to the fennel. Frozen peas, if very hard, should be dipped into cold water to separate them.

French Fried Cauliflower

Serves 6: Sauce: 2 tablespoons (1 oz) butter; ¼ cup (1 oz) all purpose flour; 1¼ cups (10 fl oz) milk; salt and pepper
1 medium-size cauliflower; ½ cup (2 oz) all purpose flour; 1 egg yolk; salt and pepper; ⅓ cup (2½ fl oz) warm water; 1 teaspoon butter; 2 egg whites; oil for deep frying; parsley sprigs for garnish

To make the sauce, melt the butter in a small saucepan, remove from the heat and whisk in the flour. Stir until smooth. Add the milk and blend until smooth. Return to the heat, stirring constantly until boiling, then cook for 2 minutes. Season with salt and pepper.

Break the cauliflower into florets and cut a slit in the stems. Place in a saucepan with a little boiling salted water. Bring back to a boil, then simmer for 7-10 minutes, until barely cooked. Drain and cool.

Dip the cold cauliflower pieces into the hot white sauce and cool. Make a batter with the sifted flour, egg yolk, salt, pepper and warm water. Stir in the melted butter and the stiffly beaten egg whites. Dip the sauce-covered cauliflower into the batter and deep fry until golden brown. Drain and serve garnished with parsley sprigs.

Fresh Celery with Creamy Mustard Sauce

Serves 4: 4 stalks fresh celery; ½ teaspoon salt
Sauce: ½ cup (4 fl oz) chicken stock or water; 1 tablespoon evaporated milk; 2 tablespoons vegetable oil; 1-1½ teaspoons dry mustard; ½ teaspoon salt; ½ teaspoon sugar; 1¼ teaspoons cornstarch

String the celery and cut into 2-in (5-cm) pieces, then cut each piece lengthwise into 2-3 sticks. Blanch in boiling salted water for 1 minute, then drain and refresh with cold water. Drain again and arrange on a serving plate.

Pour the premixed sauce ingredients into a pan and bring to the boil. Simmer until thickened, then pour over the vegetables and serve at once.

Fried Bean Curd and Scallions

Serves 4: 3 squares hard bean curd; 20 scallions; 3 tablespoons oil; ½ teaspoon salt; 2 tablespoons light soy sauce

Pat the bean curd dry and cut into cubes ½ in (1 cm) square. Cut the scallions, including the green tops, into 1-in (2.5-cm) lengths.

Heat the oil in a skillet until very hot and fry the bean curd, stirring occasionally, for a couple of minutes until crisp and golden. Add the scallions and fry for another couple of minutes, stirring occasionally. Put in the salt and soy sauce and cook another minute. Serve immediately.

Fried Bean Curd Squares

Serves 4: 3 green chilies; 1 fresh red chili; 1 garlic clove; 2 tablespoons brown sugar; 1 tablespoon dark soy sauce; 1 tablespoon white wine vinegar; 1 teaspoon cumin, ground; ½ cup (4 fl oz) water; 5 oz (155 g) roasted peanuts, crushed; salt; 6 squares hard bean curd; 2 oz (60 g) beansprouts; 1 small cucumber; peanut oil

Chop the chilies and garlic finely, then mix with the brown sugar, soy sauce, vinegar, cumin and cold water. Stir in the crushed

peanuts and add the salt. Cook on moderate heat for 10 minutes, stirring frequently. Keep warm while the bean curd is prepared.

Cut the bean curd squares into 3 slices, horizontally. Heat ½ in (1 cm) oil and carefully lower in several bean curd squares. Fry for 3-4 minutes. Transfer to a serving plate and keep warm.

Wash and dry the cucumber, rub with salt and shred or grate. Remove the roots and tops from the beansprouts and scald with boiling water. Arrange a little shredded cucumber and several beansprouts on top of each bean curd slice. Reheat the sauce and spoon a little onto each bean curd square before serving.

Fried Beansprouts

Serves 4: 8 oz (250 g) beansprouts; 2 tablespoons oil; 1 garlic clove, lightly crushed; 4 slices fresh ginger; 1 teaspoon light soy sauce; ¼ teaspoon salt; 2 scallions, cut in 1-in (2.5-cm) lengths

Wash the beansprouts, then drain thoroughly and pinch off any brown straggly tails.

Heat the oil in a skillet and fry the garlic until golden, then discard. Fry the beansprouts and ginger in garlic-flavored oil over high heat, tossing constantly, for 1 minute. Add the soy sauce, salt and scallions and continue to stir-fry for another minute. The beansprouts should still be slightly crisp.

Fried Cauliflower

Serves 4: 1 small cauliflower; salt; oil for deep frying; ¼ cup (1 oz) all purpose flour; 2 eggs, beaten; 1 cup (4 oz) dry breadcrumbs; freshly ground black pepper

Break the cauliflower into small sprigs and trim away the tough stalks. Bring quickly to the boil in lightly salted water, then simmer for 5 minutes. Drain, refresh under cold running water and drain thoroughly.

Preheat the oil to 325°F (160°C). Dust the cauliflower with the flour, dip in the egg and roll lightly in the breadcrumbs. Deep fry until crisp and golden. Drain on paper towels and sprinkle with salt and black pepper before serving.

Fried Eggplant with Sesame Seed Dressing

*Serves 4: 2 eggplants 4–5 in (10–12 cm) long, or
1 medium-size eggplant; 2–4 tablespoons oil;
1 tablespoon white sesame seeds; 1 tablespoon dark
soy sauce; ½ teaspoon superfine sugar*

Cut small unpeeled eggplants in half lengthwise and score about ¼ in (5 mm) deep in a diagonal pattern with the point of a sharp knife. If using a medium-size eggplant, do not peel but cut crosswise in 1-in (2.5-cm) slices. Score one side of each slice.

Heat the oil in a heavy-based skillet and fry the eggplant, cut side down if using halved eggplant. Fry over moderate heat until golden brown. Turn and continue cooking until the eggplant is tender but not too soft. Remove from the pan and drain on a paper towel.

Toast the sesame seeds in a dry pan over low heat, stirring frequently until they turn golden brown. Grind to a paste while still hot, using a mortar and pestle or electric grinder. Combine this paste with the soy sauce and sugar, mixing well to dissolve the sugar. Spoon over the surface of the eggplant, pressing it in well. Cut the eggplant into bite-size portions and reassemble on individual serving plates.

Fried Potato Bread (Puri)

*Serves 4: 8 oz (250 g) potatoes; 2 cups (8 oz) all
purpose flour; 2 teaspoons salt; 6–7 tablespoons
warm water; oil for deep frying*

Peel the potatoes and boil until tender. Drain well, then put back into dry saucepan over very low heat for a couple of minutes to allow them to dry out thoroughly. Mash well and leave to cool.

Sift the flour and salt into a bowl, then add the mashed potatoes. Mix with a wooden spoon and add the water, a little at a time, until a firm dough forms. Flour your hands and a board or table and knead the dough thoroughly for 10 minutes. Roll the dough into a ball, cover and leave to stand for at least 30 minutes. (The dough can be stored in the refrigerator for several hours, if wrapped well in plastic.)

Divide the dough into 16 pieces, roll each piece into a small ball, then flatten with the hands into a circle. Roll each piece out

Fried Eggplant with Sesame Seed Dressing

carefully until it is about 6 in (15 cm) in diameter.

Heat the oil until very hot. Put in one *puri* and immediately start spooning or flicking oil over the top side so that it puffs up. As soon as the *puri* is golden on the underside, flip it over and cook for another moment or two until the second side is golden. Drain and serve hot with curries, *dhal* or vegetables.

Fried Salted Cabbage

*Serves 4: 10 oz (300 g) salted cabbage; 2 pieces hard
bean curd (optional); ½ cup (4 fl oz) oil; 2 garlic
cloves, very finely chopped; 3½ oz (100 g) belly
pork, very finely sliced; 2 teaspoons sugar;
1 teaspoon thick black soy sauce; 1–2 fresh red
chilies, cut in lengthwise strips; white pepper*

Soak salted cabbage in cold water, changing the water two or three times, for about 1 hour. Rinse and squeeze thoroughly to remove all moisture, then chop finely.

Cut the bean curd into small cubes. Heat the oil in a skillet and fry the bean curd, stirring occasionally, until crisp and golden brown. Remove from the pan and drain.

Pour out all but 1 tablespoon of oil from the skillet. Heat, then add the garlic. Fry for just 15 seconds, then add the pork and stir-fry for 2 minutes. Add the cabbage and continue to stir-fry for another 5 minutes. Sprinkle over the sugar and soy sauce, and add the chili and fried bean curd. Cook for another 2 minutes. Sprinkle with white pepper and serve.

G
Game Chips

*Serves 4–6: 4–6 medium-size potatoes, peeled and
thinly sliced; oil for deep frying; salt*

Cover the sliced potatoes with iced water and soak for 20–30 minutes before deep frying.

Preheat the oil to 375°F (190°C). Dry the potatoes and fry, a few at a time, for 2–3 minutes. Drain on paper towels.

Shortly before serving, fry the chips again until crisp and golden. Drain and sprinkle lightly with salt. Serve in a shallow dish or basket.

Note: Double-frying the chips means that you can do the first cooking early in the day and finish them when needed.

Glazed Onions

*Serves 4: 1 lb (500 g) small onions; 2 tablespoons
(1 oz) butter; 1 teaspoon sugar; salt and pepper*

Peel the onions and blanch for 5–7 minutes, drain well. Put into a saucepan with the butter, sugar and seasoning. Cook gently with a lid on, shaking and stirring from time to time until the onions become tender and well glazed, 7–10 minutes. Care must be taken that the cooking is slow or the sugar will burn. Serve hot.

Glazed Turnips

*Serves 4: 4–8 turnips, peeled; ½ teaspoon salt;
2 tablespoons (1 oz) butter; 2 tablespoons (1 oz)
brown sugar, mixed with ¼ teaspoon ground
nutmeg*

Quarter or halve the turnips according to size. Cover with water, add the salt and bring to the boil. Cook for 5 minutes and drain.

Melt the butter in a baking dish, add the parboiled turnips and turn until lightly coated with the butter. Sprinkle evenly with the brown sugar and nutmeg and bake just below the center of an oven preheated to 425°F (220°C) for 25–30 minutes.

Note: Glazed turnips are a delicious accompaniment to roast duck, chicken or goose.

Gold Coast Salad

Serves 4: 4 young, tender spinach leaves; 1 lb (500 g) cooked shrimp, shelled and deveined; ½ cup (4 fl oz) French dressing; 3 oranges, peeled; 1 lb (500 g) roast pork, sliced; 1 fresh, ripe pineapple, peeled; 8 oz (250 g) cream style cottage cheese; 2 tablespoons flaked macadamia or Brazil nuts, toasted

Line 1 large or 4 individual platters with torn spinach leaves, chop the remaining leaves and pile in the center. Marinate the shrimp in French dressing for 30 minutes. Cut the oranges into slices or segments, cut the sliced pork into strips and toss together. Remove the "eyes" from the pineapple and cut into 12 slices, then remove the inner core. Drain the shrimp with a slotted spoon and arrange in an outer circle around the sliced spinach leaves. Pile the pork and oranges on top of the leaves in the center. Garnish the platter with pineapple slices topped with scoops of cottage cheese and sprinkle with flaked, toasted nuts. Serve with mayonnaise.

Greek Salad

Serves 6: 3 firm ripe tomatoes, cut into wedges; 2 cucumbers, peeled and sliced; 3 green bell peppers, seeded and cut into strips; 2 onions, roughly chopped; 6 fillets of anchovies; 12 Kalamata olives; 8 oz (250 g) feta cheese, cut into ¾-in (1.5-cm) cubes
Dressing: ½ cup (4 fl oz) olive oil; ⅓ cup (3 fl oz) white or red wine vinegar; 1 garlic clove, crushed; 2 tablespoons finely chopped dill; 1 teaspoon fresh (or dried) oregano; ½ teaspoon salt; freshly ground black pepper

Combine all the vegetables in a salad bowl.
  To prepare the dressing, combine the ingredients in a watertight screw-top jar, shake vigorously and taste for seasoning. Pour the dressing over the salad and toss. Arrange the anchovies and olives on top and sprinkle with the feta.

Greek White Beans

Serves 4: ½ cup (4 fl oz) olive oil; 8 oz (250 g) dry white beans; 1 garlic clove, crushed; 2 bay leaves; 2 sprigs thyme, chopped; 1 tablespoon tomato paste; juice of 1 lemon; 1 onion, sliced into rings; salt and freshly ground black pepper

Gold Coast Salad

Greek Salad

Soak the beans in water overnight.

In a saucepan, heat the oil and add the strained beans. Simmer over low heat for 10 minutes, then add the garlic, bay leaves, thyme, tomato paste and enough boiling water to cover the beans by 1 in (2.5 cm). Cook over low heat for 3 hours, then add the lemon juice, onion, salt and pepper. Serve at room temperature.

Green Bean Sambal

Serves 4: 8 shallots or 1 medium-size red or brown onion; 3 fresh red chilies; ½ teaspoon dried shrimp paste; 4 candlenuts or macadamias; 1 tablespoon oil; 8 oz (250 g) green beans, cut in 1-in (2.5-cm) lengths; 1½ cups (12 fl oz) coconut milk; ½ teaspoon salt; 8 raw shrimp, peeled, or 1 tablespoon dried shrimp, soaked

Grind the shallots, chilies, dried shrimp paste and candlenuts until fine. Heat the oil and fry the ground ingredients for 3–4 minutes. Add the beans and fry for a minute, then put in the coconut milk, salt and dried shrimp. If using raw shrimp, do not add yet.

Simmer, with the pan uncovered, until the beans are almost cooked. If using raw shrimp, add and simmer for another 3 minutes.

Green Beans with Sesame and Miso

Serves 4: 8 oz (250 g) green beans; salt; 1 tablespoon white sesame seeds; 2 teaspoons superfine sugar; 1 tablespoon sake; 1 tablespoon red miso

Top and tail the beans and remove any strings. Cook whole in plenty of lightly salted boiling water until just tender. Cool under running water, drain, then cut into 1½-in (4-cm) lengths.

Toast the sesame seeds in a dry pan over low heat until golden brown, stirring and taking care they do not burn. While the seeds are still hot, grind in a mortar and pestle or blender until they form a paste. Add the sugar and mix well. Heat the *sake* in a pan until it just comes to the boil, then mix into the sesame paste together with the red *miso*.

Toss the beans with this sauce while it is still warm, coating thoroughly.

Green Beans with Sesame and Miso

Green Beans with Tomatoes

Serves 6: 1½ lb (750 g) fresh green beans; 1 teaspoon salt; ¼ cup (2 fl oz) olive oil; 2 onions, finely chopped; ½ garlic clove, crushed; 6 fresh ripe tomatoes, peeled and chopped; 2 teaspoons red or white wine vinegar; 1 teaspoon dried or 2 teaspoons fresh oregano, chopped; 1 teaspoon dried or 2 teaspoons fresh marjoram, chopped; salt and freshly ground black pepper

Top and tail and, if necessary, string the beans.

Bring a large pan of water to the boil, add the salt and beans and blanch for 8 minutes or until just tender. Drain the beans and rinse under cold running water.

In a skillet, heat the oil and lightly fry the onions and garlic until the onions are soft and transparent. Add the tomatoes, vinegar, oregano and marjoram, and simmer for 10 minutes. Add the beans and simmer for a further 5 minutes. Season with salt and pepper, and serve hot as a vegetable with a meat dish.

Green Papaya Salad

Serves 4–6: 8 oz (250 g) hard green papaya; 4 oz (125 g) green beans; 2 medium-size tomatoes; ¼ cup (2 fl oz) thick coconut milk; 2 tablespoons fish sauce or light soy sauce; 2 garlic cloves, crushed; 2 tablespoons roasted peanuts, crushed

Peel the papaya, grate and cover with cold water. Remove strings from the beans and cut into 1-in (2.5-cm) lengths. Cook in slightly salted water until just tender. Drain and refresh with cold water. Put the tomatoes into boiling water, count to seven, then lift out and peel. Cut into thin wedges. Drain the papaya.

Arrange the papaya, beans and tomato wedges in a salad bowl. Mix the coconut milk with the fish sauce or soy sauce and stir in the crushed garlic. Pour onto the salad and toss a little. Sprinkle over the crushed peanuts. Garnish, if desired, with sprigs of fresh cilantro.

Green Salad ★

Serves 6–8: 1 garlic clove, cut in half; ½ head iceberg lettuce; 1 romaine lettuce; 4 young spinach leaves; 3 Belgian endive (optional); 1 green bell pepper; 1½ cups sliced celery
Green Goddess Dressing: 6 anchovy fillets; ¼ cup finely chopped green scallion tops; ¼ cup finely chopped parsley; ¼ cup finely snipped chives; ¼ cup (2 fl oz) tarragon vinegar; 1 cup (8 fl oz) mayonnaise; mustard; salt and freshly ground black pepper

Rub the salad bowl with garlic. Tear the prepared lettuces and spinach into bite-size pieces and put into a salad bowl. If using Belgian endive, separate the leaves, trim the stem ends, wash, dry and crisp. Cut into 1-in (2.5-cm) pieces. Quarter the pepper, remove the seeds and membrane, and cut into thin strips. Add the celery to the bowl and toss all together. Cover and chill.

To make the dressing, chop the anchovy fillets finely and add the scallion tops, parsley and chives. Add the tarragon vinegar, mayonnaise and mustard, and mix well. Add salt and pepper to taste. Blend well, cover and seal. Chill for several hours, or overnight, to blend flavors.

When ready to serve, add half the Green Goddess Dressing to the salad, then toss gently and thoroughly. Serve the remaining dressing in a small, chilled bowl.

H

Herring and Apple Salad

Serves 4: ½ cup (4 fl oz) sour cream; 1 tablespoon vinegar or juice of 1 lemon; freshly ground black pepper; 1 teaspoon prepared horseradish; 4 Matjes herring fillets, cut into 1-in (2.5-cm) pieces; 2 small onions, thinly sliced; 1 firm apple, peeled, quartered, cored and thinly sliced; lettuce leaves; 1 egg, hard-cooked and sliced; 1 green or red bell pepper, halved, seeded and cut into strips

In a bowl, combine the sour cream, vinegar or lemon juice, pepper and horseradish. To this dressing, add the herrings, onions and apple, and mix gently together. Refrigerate for 2–3 hours.

To serve, divide the salad into 4 portions, heap onto 4 lettuce leaves and garnish with slices of hard-cooked egg and pepper strips.

Hot Bean Salad ★

Serves 4: 3 slices bacon; 1 medium-size onion; 4 oz (125 g) white beans, cooked; 4 oz (125 g) green beans, cooked; 1 red or green bell pepper

Cut the bacon into pieces and microwave in a dish on HIGH (100%) uncovered for 3 minutes. Remove the bacon. Cook the onion, covered, in the bacon fat on HIGH (100%) for 3 minutes. Add the white beans, green beans and the pepper cut into small pieces. Return the bacon to the dish and cover. Microwave on HIGH (100%) for 3 minutes. Dress with a sharp vinaigrette.

I

Indonesian Salad (Gado Gado)

Serves 4: waxy potatoes, boiled and sliced; cabbage, shredded and steamed; long beans or green beans, cut into 1½-in (4-cm) lengths, steamed; beansprouts, scalded; hard bean curd, deep fried and sliced; cucumber, skin left on, sliced diagonally; hard-cooked eggs, sliced
Gado Gado Sauce: 8 fresh red chilies; 1 teaspoon dried shrimp paste; 2 tablespoons oil; 8 shallots or 1 medium-size onion, finely sliced; 1½ cups (12 fl oz) coconut milk; ½ cup peanuts, roasted and coarsely crushed, or ½ cup crunchy peanut butter; 1–2 teaspoons palm or brown sugar; ¼ cup (2 fl oz) tamarind water (see page 392); salt to taste

Cook the vegetables until slightly crisp, varying the amounts to suit the number of people. Arrange the vegetables and other salad ingredients on a platter.

To make the sauce, pound chilies and dried shrimp paste together until finely ground. Heat the oil in a saucepan and fry the shallots gently until soft. Add the pounded mixture and fry, stirring occasionally for 4–5 minutes. Gradually add the coconut milk, then add the remaining ingredients and simmer for 3 minutes or until the sauce thickens. When the sauce is at room temperature, pour over the salad and serve.

Clockwise from top: Turnips with Pimiento Cream Sauce (see page 132), Jacket Baked Potatoes and Parsnips in Orange Sauce (see page 120)

J

Jacket Baked Potatoes ★

Serves 4-6: 4-6 medium-size potatoes

Put the washed and dried potatoes onto a baking sheet and cook just above the center of an oven preheated to 425°F (220°C) for 45–60 minutes, until the skin is crisp but the potato yields to the touch.

Cut a cross on top, squeeze open and serve with any of the following dressings: butter and seasoning; sour cream and chopped herbs; finely grated cheese; equal quantities of cream cheese and chopped shrimp, mixed.

Indonesian Salad (Gado Gado)

Leeks in Tomato and Parsley Sauce

L

Leeks in Tomato and Parsley Sauce 🇮🇹

Serves 4–6: 6 fresh leeks; 1 medium-size onion, sliced; 2 tablespoons olive oil; 1 large tomato, chopped; 1 tablespoon tomato paste, puree or sauce; ¼ cup chopped parsley; ¾ cup (6 fl oz) water; salt and black pepper; lemon juice

Remove the coarse outer leaves from the leeks and trim off the root, cutting from two sides to form a point. Split the white parts down the center. This preparation makes it easier to clean the leeks. Wash thoroughly in cold water and drain.

Sauté the onion in the oil until transparent, then add the tomato and sauté until softened. Stir in the tomato paste, half the parsley and add the water. Bring to the boil, cover the pan and simmer for 7–8 minutes.

Add the leeks, cover again and simmer gently until the leeks are tender, about 20 minutes. Add the salt, pepper and lemon juice to taste, then stir in the remaining parsley. Serve hot or well chilled.

M

Marinated Zucchini 🇮🇹

Serves 4: 8 large firm zucchini, sliced; 1 cup (8 fl oz) olive oil; 2–4 cups (16–32 fl oz) vinegar; salt; 1 tablespoon finely chopped red chili

Brown the zucchini a few at a time in the oil, then place in a dish (not aluminum). Heat sufficient vinegar to cover the zucchini, then add the salt and chili to taste. When the vinegar boils, pour it over the zucchini. Allow to cool, place in a glass jar and preserve for serving.

Masala Potato with Okra 🇮🇳

Serves 4–6: 2 large potatoes; 8 oz (250 g) okra; 3 green chilies; 1 tablespoon fresh cilantro leaves; 1 large onion; 1 large tomato; 2 garlic cloves; ½-in (1-cm) piece fresh ginger; 2 tablespoons ghee; 2 teaspoons chat masala (see below); ½ teaspoon turmeric powder; 1 cup (8 fl oz) water; sugar; salt Chat Masala: 1 oz (30 g) cumin seeds; 1 tablespoon salt; pinch asafoetida; 1 tablespoon chili powder;

2 tablespoons dried green mango powder (amchur); 1 tablespoon crushed dried mint; 2 teaspoons powdered ginger

To make the *chat masala*, lightly toast the cumin with salt and asafoetida. Grind all ingredients to a fine powder and pour into a jar with a tight-fitting lid.

Peel the potatoes and cut into 1-in (2.5-cm) cubes. Wash the okra and remove the stems, then slit lengthwise. Cut the green chilies into thin slices, removing the seeds for a milder taste. Chop the cilantro and slice the onion and tomato. Crush the garlic and shred the ginger.

Heat the *ghee* and fry the sliced onion for 2 minutes, then add garlic and ginger and fry for a further 2 minutes. Sprinkle over the *chat masala* and turmeric and stir on high heat for 1 minute.

Add the potatoes and okra and pour the water over. Add the chopped cilantro leaves and tomato. Season to taste with sugar and salt and bring to the boil. Reduce the heat and simmer until the potatoes and okra are tender. Serve with the sauce or cook until the liquid has almost evaporated.

Minced Bean Curd Cake with Spinach

Serves 4: 4 squares soft bean curd; 1½ tablespoons finely chopped cooked ham; 3 oz (90 g) fresh young spinach leaves (collard greens), chopped; chicken stock
Seasoning A: ¾ teaspoon salt; ¼ teaspoon white pepper; 5 egg whites, well beaten; ⅓ cup cornstarch
Seasoning B/Sauce: 1 cup (8 fl oz) chicken stock; 2 teaspoons rice wine or dry sherry; ⅓ teaspoon salt; ¼ teaspoon ground black pepper

Mash the bean curd with a fork and mix in the seasoning A ingredients. Grease a round baking tin with lard or oil and pour in the bean curd mixture. Sprinkle the chopped ham on top and set on a rack in a steamer. Steam over high heat for 6–8 minutes or until set. Slide the bean curd cake from the tin into a dish of cold chicken stock.

Heat the wok and add the seasoning B ingredients and the spinach. Simmer for 1 minute, then add the bean curd cake and simmer gently on low heat for 5 minutes or until the bean curd and spinach are both tender. Transfer the spinach to a serving plate and thicken the sauce around the bean curd cake with a paste of cornstarch and cold water. Simmer until thickened, then slide the cake and sauce onto the spinach. Serve at once.

Note: The bean curd cake may crumble at the edges but should remain intact as a soft textured mound.

Miso Potatoes

Serves 4: 4 medium-size potatoes; 2 cups (16 fl oz) dashi; 3 tablespoons red miso or 4½ tablespoons white miso; 12 snow peas or 8 green beans

Peel the potatoes and quarter. Boil in salted water for 5 minutes, then drain. Put 1½ cups (12 fl oz) of *dashi* into a pan and mix the remainder with the *miso*, then push it through a sieve into the rest of the *dashi*.

Bring the *dashi* and *miso* just to the boil, add the parboiled potatoes and cover with a drop lid or saucer. Simmer very gently for about 15 minutes or until the potatoes are soft but not falling apart.

While the potatoes are simmering, boil the snow peas or beans (if using the latter, cut diagonally into 1½-in (4-cm) lengths) in lightly salted water until just cooked. Drain, cool under running water and drain again.

To serve, put 4 pieces of potato in each serving dish, add a couple of tablespoons of the hot stock and garnish with the snow peas or beans. Serve hot.

Mixed Vegetable Dish

Serves 4: 2 tablespoons cloud ear fungus; 2–3 sticks dried bean curd twists, cut in 1-in (2.5-cm) pieces; 15–20 dried lily buds; 4–6 dried black mushrooms; 1 oz (30 g) cellophane noodles; 1 tablespoon oil; 3 garlic cloves, very finely chopped; 2 slices fresh ginger, very finely chopped; 1 teaspoon salted soybeans, mashed; 3½ oz (100 g) lean pork, shredded; 1 cup soaking liquid (see method); 2 teaspoons light soy sauce; ½ teaspoon salt; white pepper; ½ small cabbage, sliced; 2 oz (60 g) raw shrimp (optional); 1 piece bamboo shoot (about 3½ oz/100 g), sliced; 2 teaspoons cornstarch mixed with ¼ cup water; 2 scallions, finely sliced; 1 piece hard bean curd, deep fried and cut in strips

Rinse the cloud ear fungus thoroughly, then put in a bowl with dried bean curd twists, lily buds and mushrooms. Cover with warm water and leave to soak for 15 minutes. Soak the noodles in hot water for

10 minutes, then cut with scissors into small pieces. When the dried ingredients have finished soaking, reserve 1 cup of the liquid. Drain thoroughly, then remove the stems from the dried mushrooms and cut the caps in half.

Heat the oil and gently fry the garlic and ginger for 30 seconds, then put in the salted soy beans and fry for another 30 seconds. Add the pork and cook, stirring frequently, for a couple of minutes, until the meat changes color. Add the soaking liquid, soy sauce, salt, pepper and all dried ingredients except the noodles. Cover the pan and simmer for 15 minutes.

Add the cabbage, bamboo shoot and shrimp (if using) to the pan. Stir well and continue cooking until the cabbage is tender, about 10 minutes. Thicken with the cornstarch mixture. Stir in the noodles, chopped scallions and bean curd and serve.

N
Naan
(Leavened Bread)

Serves 4: 2 cups (8 oz) all purpose flour; 1 teaspoon baking powder; ½ teaspoon salt; ¼ cup plain yogurt; 1 tablespoon oil; 1 egg, lightly beaten; 1 tablespoon ghee or butter, melted; sprinkle of black cumin seeds (optional); few slivered almonds (optional)

Sift the flour, baking powder and salt into a bowl and stir in the yogurt, oil and egg. Add a little warm water if necessary to make a pliable, reasonably soft dough. Knead on a board for 5 minutes, then cover with a floured cloth and leave in a warm place for 3 hours.

Knead the bread for a minute or two, then divide into six pieces. Using your hands, pull each piece of dough into a teardrop shape about 8 in (20 cm) long. Heat a metal griddle or heavy-based skillet and put a *naan* on to cook. Leave for about 2 minutes, then turn and cook for another two minutes until golden brown and slightly puffed.

Brush each *naan* on one side with a little melted *ghee* or butter and sprinkle with a few black cumin seeds and almond flakes, if using. Put under a preheated broiler for about 2 minutes. Serve warm with *tandoori* chicken or any dishes with gravy.

Northumbrian Leek Pudding

Serves 6: 3½ lb (1.75 kg) suet pastry (see page 259); 2½ lb (1.25 kg) leeks, cleaned and chopped; 8 tablespoons (4 oz) butter; salt and freshly ground pepper

Line a 3-pt (1.5-l) pudding basin with three-quarters of the suet pastry. Fill the

Miso Potatoes

119

basin with leeks, dot with butter and season with salt and pepper. Cover with the rest of the pastry, secure with aluminum foil and place in a saucepan half-filled with water. Cover and steam for 2 hours. Traditionally, this is served with stews.

O

Okra Salad

Serves 4: 8 oz (250 g) young okra; ½ teaspoon horseradish powder (wasabi); 2 tablespoons dark soy sauce; 1 tablespoon sweet rice wine (mirin); 2 teaspoons dried bonito flakes (hana-katsuo)

Put the whole okra into boiling, salted water and boil over high heat for 3 minutes. Drain, cool under running water, then remove the stem ends. Slice each pod diagonally into 1-in (2.5-cm) lengths.

Mix the horseradish powder to a paste with a little cold water, then combine with the soy sauce and *mirin*. Just before serving the okra, either at room temperature or chilled, divide between four serving dishes and spoon a little of the sauce over each portion. Sprinkle each serving with ½ teaspoon of dried bonito flakes and serve.

Omelet Roll

Serves 4: 6 eggs; 6 tablespoons dashi fish stock; 2 teaspoons sweet sherry; ½ teaspoon salt; 1½ tablespoons sugar; 2 teaspoons cornstarch (optional); vegetable oil

Beat all the ingredients, except the vegetable oil, together. Heat a square skillet and wipe with an oiled cloth. Pour in a thin layer of the egg and cook over moderate heat. Roll up and push to one side of the pan. Add a little more oil and repeat the process, wrapping this omelet layer around the first roll. Progress in this way until all the batter has been used and the roll is quite plump. Transfer to a clean piece of muslin and squeeze into a firm square or round shaped loaf. Cut into slices and serve warm or cold with rice or vegetables.

'Pearl' Balls

Onion and Tomato Salad

Serves 4: 2 large red or brown onions, very finely sliced; 2 tablespoons lemon juice; ½ teaspoon salt; ½ teaspoon sugar; 1 tomato, sliced; ½ fresh green chili, seeded and sliced (optional); 1 tablespoon chopped fresh cilantro leaves

Combine the onions with the lemon juice and salt, and set aside for at least 1 hour. Just before serving, add all other ingredients, toss thoroughly and serve.

P

Parsnips in Orange Sauce

Serves 4-6: 2 tablespoons (1 oz) butter; 1 teaspoon

honey; ¼ teaspoon cinnamon; 2 teaspoons finely grated orange peel; 1½ cups (14 fl oz) orange juice; 1 lb (500 g) young parsnips, peeled and cut into small wedges; 1 tablespoon all purpose flour; salt; 1 orange, thinly sliced

Melt half the butter with the honey in a saucepan set over low heat. Add the cinnamon and the orange peel, stir well and add the orange juice. Raise the heat and bring the mixture to the boil. Add the parsnips, reduce the heat and cover. Simmer for 25–30 minutes or until the parsnips are just tender. Lift the parsnips from the pan with a slotted spoon and set aside.

Work the flour into the remaining tablespoons of butter and add in small pieces to the sauce, whisking between each addition, until the sauce has thickened enough to coat the parsnips lightly. Adjust the seasoning and return the parsnips to the pan, turning in the sauce until hot. Serve in a heated dish, garnished with the sliced orange.

'Pearl' Balls

Serves 4: 8 oz (250 g) lean pork, finely ground;
6 canned water chestnuts, chopped; ½ oz (15 g)
dried shrimp, soaked for 1 hour (optional);
1 tablespoon finely chopped scallion; 1 teaspoon
finely chopped fresh ginger; 1 cup long grain raw
glutinous rice, soaked for 2 hours
Seasoning: 1 tablespoon light soy sauce; 2 teaspoons
rice wine or dry sherry; ¼ teaspoon salt;
½ teaspoon sugar; ¼ teaspoon black pepper;
1¼ tablespoons cornstarch

Mix the pork and water chestnuts with the
seasoning ingredients. Drain and finely
chop the dried shrimp, if used, and mix
into the pork with the scallion and ginger.
Knead to a smooth paste, squeezing continually through the fingers until
thoroughly mixed and sticky.

Use wet hands to roll the mixture into 24
balls. Drain the rice thoroughly and spread
on a plate. Roll each ball in the rice until
thickly coated with rice grains. Arrange on
a lightly oiled plate and set on a rack in a
steamer. Leave a little space between each
ball to allow the rice to expand.

Steam over rapidly boiling water for
about 30 minutes until the rice is transparent and tender and the pork cooked
through. Serve on the same plate with a
garnish of fresh cilantro and dips of light
soy and chili sauces.

Pease Pudding

Serves 4-6: 8 oz (250 g) yellow split peas; 4 cups
(1 liter) stock made from ham or bacon bones,
heated; salt and freshly ground black pepper

Place the peas in a cheesecloth bag
allowing plenty of room for them to swell
up. Put the bag into the pan of hot stock
and leave to soak for 3 hours.

Bring the stock and bag of peas to the
boil, then simmer for 45 minutes or until
the peas are soft. Remove the peas from
the bag and place in a bowl, then beat with
a wooden spoon until creamy. Reheat for
a few minutes over low heat and serve
immediately with salted meat.

Pock-Marked Mama's Bean Curd

Serves 4-6: 4 squares soft bean curd; 1 small leek;
⅓ cup (2½ fl oz) oil; 7 oz (210 g) lean beef, finely
ground; 1 tablespoon fermented black beans, finely
chopped; 2 teaspoons hot bean paste; 2 teaspoons
crushed garlic; 2 teaspoons finely chopped fresh
ginger; 1 teaspoon finely chopped fresh red chili
pepper or chili sauce; 1 teaspoon Chinese brown
peppercorn powder
Seasoning: 1½ tablespoons light soy sauce;
1 tablespoon rice wine or dry sherry; ½ teaspoon
salt; 1½ teaspoons sugar; 1 cup (8 fl oz) chicken
stock or water; 1 tablespoon cornstarch

Cut the bean curd into ½-in (1-cm) cubes
and soak in hot water until needed. Trim
and shred the leek. Heat the oil and stir-fry
the beef until lightly colored, then add the
leek and stir-fry a further 30 seconds. Add
the chopped black beans, the bean paste,
garlic, ginger and chili pepper or chili sauce
and stir-fry for a further 30 seconds, then
add the premixed seasoning ingredients and
bring to the boil. Simmer for 1 minute.

Drain the bean curd then add it to the
sauce, reduce the heat and simmer until the
sauce is well reduced and the flavor
thoroughly permeates the bean curd.
Transfer to a serving dish and season with
the pepper.

Portuguese Cucumber

Serves 4-6: 4 small cucumbers, peeled and quartered
lengthwise; 2 tablespoons (1 oz) butter;
2 tablespoons vegetable oil; 2 medium-size onions,
finely chopped; 1 garlic clove, crushed; 2 tomatoes,
peeled, seeded, and coarsely chopped; 2 teaspoons
tomato paste; juice of ½ lemon; ½ teaspoon dried
oregano; salt and freshly ground black pepper

Remove the seeds and cut the cucumbers
into 1-in (2.5-cm) lengths. Cover with boiling water and blanch for 5 minutes. Drain
and refresh under cold running water. Set
aside.

Melt the butter and oil in a skillet and
sauté the onions over a fairly high heat
until lightly browned but still crisp. Reduce
the heat and add the garlic, tomatoes and
tomato paste. Cook for 2-3 minutes, until
the vegetables are hot but not mushy. Stir
in the lemon juice and cucumbers, cook
gently for 1-2 minutes, then season with
the oregano and salt and black pepper to
taste.

Potato Cakes

Serves 4: 8 oz (250 g) cooked, cold potatoes;
1 tablespoon butter, melted; ½ teaspoon salt;
½ cup (2 oz) all purpose flour or fine oatmeal;
½ teaspoon baking powder

Mash the potatoes and add the butter and
salt. Work in as much flour mixed with
baking powder as you need to make a pliable dough. Roll the dough out thinly, cut
in rounds with a bread and butter plate,
then mark into quarters. Prick with a fork
and cook on a hot griddle for 5 minutes
each side. Serve with plenty of butter.

Potato Cheese Puff

Serves 4-6: 1½ lb (750 g) potatoes, peeled and cut
into small chunks; ½ teaspoon salt; 3 eggs,
separated; 1-2 tablespoons butter; 4 oz (125 g)
grated Cheddar cheese; 1 small onion, very finely
chopped; 1 small green bell pepper, very finely
chopped; ½ teaspoon celery salt; white pepper;
½ teaspoon Hungarian paprika

Cover the potatoes with water, add the salt
and boil until tender. Drain and transfer to
a mixing bowl.

Mash the potatoes and beat the egg yolks
in, one at a time, until thoroughly combined. Beat in 1 tablespoon of the butter
with the cheese, onion, green pepper, celery salt and white pepper to taste. Add the
remaining butter only if the mixture is very
stiff.

Whisk the egg whites until stiff, then fold
into the potato mixture. Spoon carefully
into an oiled baking dish. Sprinkle with the
paprika and bake in an oven preheated to
400°F (200°C) for 25-30 minutes, or until
golden.

Potatoes and Cheese au Gratin (Gratin Dauphinois)

Serves 4-6: 1 garlic clove; 2 lb (1 kg) potatoes,
peeled and finely sliced; salt and freshly ground
black pepper; 8 oz (250 g) grated cheese; 1 cup
(8 fl oz) milk; 1 egg; pinch of nutmeg; knob of
butter

Rub a deep ovenproof dish with a garlic
clove, then butter well.

Line the bottom of the dish with a layer of potatoes. Add some salt, pepper and a sprinkling of cheese; repeat the layers of potatoes, salt, pepper and cheese. Beat the egg and milk together, then pour over the potatoes until almost but not quite covered. Finish with grated nutmeg and cheese and dot with butter. Bake in an oven preheated to 350°F (180°C) for about 1 hour or until the potatoes are cooked and the top is golden.

Potato Cutlets

Serves 4: 1 lb (500 g) potatoes; ½ teaspoon salt; white pepper; 1 scallion, finely sliced; 6 shallots, finely sliced and fried until golden, or 2 tablespoons fried onion flakes (see page 151); 1 egg, beaten; oil for deep frying

Boil the potatoes whole. Cool slightly, peel, then mash roughly. Add the salt, pepper, scallion, fried shallots or onion flakes, and stir to mix well. Leave the mixture until cold, then form into eight round balls. Flatten the balls to a thickness of 1 in (2.5 cm), dip into beaten egg and deep fry in very hot oil for about 2-3 minutes. Drain and serve.

Potatoes Sautéed with Onions

Serves 6: 2 lb (1 kg) potatoes; 10 tablespoons (5 oz) butter; 4 onions, finely sliced; salt and pepper

Peel and slice the potatoes thinly and dry them well. Melt 6 tablespoons (3 oz) of the butter in a heavy-based skillet. Fry the potatoes over medium heat, turning them regularly until they are golden brown and evenly cooked.

In a separate pan, melt the remaining butter and gently fry the onions until they are golden brown. Add the onions to the potatoes and continue cooking, shaking the pan so that the potatoes and onions are well mixed. When they are both cooked, season with salt and freshly ground black pepper.

Pumpkin and Long Bean Curry

Serves 4: 10 shallots or 1 large red or brown onion; 2 fresh red chilies; ½ teaspoon dried shrimp paste; 1½ tablespoons oil; 1 heaped tablespoon dried shrimp, soaked; 1¾ cups (14 fl oz) coconut milk; ½ teaspoon salt; 12 oz (375 g) pumpkin, peeled and cut into chunks; 5 oz (150 g) long beans, cut in 1½-in (4-cm) pieces

Grind the shallots, chilies and shrimp paste together until fine. Heat the oil in a skillet and gently fry the ground ingredients for 3-4 minutes, stirring frequently. Add the dried shrimp and fry for 2 minutes. Put in the coconut milk and salt, and bring to the boil, stirring constantly. Add the pumpkin and beans, and simmer uncovered until cooked.

Pureed Potatoes and Apples with Black Pudding

Serves 4: 4 large potatoes, peeled and diced; 3 cooking apples, peeled, cored and quartered; salt and freshly ground black pepper; 1 tablespoon sugar; 5 tablespoons (2½ oz) butter; 1 lb (500 g) blood sausage (black pudding)

In a saucepan, cook the potatoes in boiling salted water for 15 minutes or until tender. Drain off most of the water and add the apples. Cook until tender. Mash the potato and apple mixture and season with the salt and pepper. Add the sugar and 4 tablespoons (2 oz) of the butter. Slice the sausage and fry in the remaining butter until brown on each side. To serve, arrange the fried slices of sausage over the mashed potato and apple mixture.

R

Radish Balls with Scallops in Cream Sauce

Serves 4: 12 oz (375 g) peeled giant white (icicle) radishes, sweet white turnips or about 24 small red radishes, peeled; 1½ teaspoons salt; 4 pieces (1 oz/30 g) dried scallops, soaked for 2 hours;

2 cups (16 fl oz) chicken stock; 1 thick slice fresh ginger, bruised; 2 slices fresh ginger, shredded; ⅓ cup (2½ fl oz) oil or softened lard; 1 tablespoon rendered chicken fat
Seasoning/Sauce: ¾ teaspoon salt; ½ teaspoon sugar; 1 teaspoon rice wine or dry sherry

Wash the radishes or turnips and use a melon scoop to form into balls. Boil in salted water to cover for 10 minutes. Drain well. Simmer the drained scallops in the chicken stock with the slice of ginger for 1 hour or until completely tender. Drain and reserve the liquid. Shred the scallops by rubbing gently between forefinger and thumb.

Heat the oil or lard in a wok and fry the vegetable balls with the shredded ginger for 1½ minutes. Add the shredded scallop and fry briefly, then pour in the reserved stock mixed with the seasoning/sauce ingredients and bring to the boil.

Thicken with a paste of 1 tablespoon cornstarch mixed with 1 tablespoon cold water and stir in the chicken fat.

Red Cabbage and Apples

Serves 4-6: 3 tablespoons (1½ oz) butter; 1-1½ lb (500-750 g) red cabbage, shredded; juice of 1 lemon; 2 apples, peeled and diced; 2 tablespoons redcurrant jelly; 2 cloves; 2 tablespoons beef stock

In a heavy-based casserole, melt the butter. Add the cabbage and pour over the lemon juice — this will help to preserve the color. Add the apples, redcurrant jelly, cloves and beef stock. Mix all the ingredients together and simmer for 10-20 minutes. The cabbage should not be overcooked.

Roti Paratha

Serves 4: 2 cups (8 oz) all purpose flour; 1 scant teaspoon salt; ⅓-½ cup (2½-4 fl oz) warm water; 7 tablespoons (3½ oz) melted ghee or butter

Sift the flour and salt and add sufficient water to make a soft dough. Knead thoroughly for 5 minutes. Add 2 teaspoons of melted *ghee* and continue kneading for a further 5 minutes. Roll the dough into a ball and put in a greased plastic bag or cover with a damp cloth. Leave in a warm place for 30 minutes.

Divide the dough into 12 pieces and roll into balls. Flatten each ball into a circle with your hands, then roll out as thinly as possible with a rolling pin. Spread each circle with 1 teaspoon *ghee* and fold in three crosswise. Spread the surface with a little more *ghee* and fold in three lengthwise. Cover with greased plastic and leave for 10 minutes. If you wish, the dough can be left for several hours provided it is well covered.

Press each piece of dough into a circle with your hands, then roll out to about 8 in (20 cm) in diameter. Heat a metal griddle or heavy iron skillet and put in 1 teaspoon of *ghee*. Put in a *paratha* and pour a little more melted *ghee* around the edges as it cooks to help make it puff up. When the underside is evenly golden, turn it over and cook another 30 seconds until golden. Serve hot.

S

Salade Niçoise

Serves 4–6: 15 oz (470 g) canned salmon or tuna, drained; 12 oz (375 g) fresh green beans; good pinch of ground coriander; 8 oz (250 g) small new potatoes; 1 cucumber; 4 tomatoes, skinned and sliced; 4 oz (125 g) black olives; 2 oz (60 g) canned flat anchovy fillets
Herb Dressing: 3 tablespoons olive oil; 1 tablespoon lemon juice; 2 tablespoons each finely chopped parsley and chives; good pinch of thyme, crumbled; ½ garlic clove; ¼ teaspoon salt; pinch of sugar; freshly ground black pepper

Break the salmon into chunks, arrange in a chilled glass bowl, cover and chill. Cook the beans whole, cool and slice diagonally into ½-in (1-cm) pieces. Lay on top of the salmon and sprinkle with the coriander. Cook the new potatoes, peel and slice. Peel, score and thinly slice the cucumber, arrange in a bowl, sprinkle with salt, and leave for 30 minutes, pressing with a weight to remove any excess water. Layer the potatoes, drained cucumber and tomatoes on top of the beans. Garnish with the black olives and anchovy fillets.

To make the herb dressing, combine the oil, lemon juice, parsley, chives and thyme. Crush the garlic with the salt, add to the oil mixture and season with sugar and pepper to taste. Shake or beat well, then trickle over the salad.

Salt Broiled Shiitake Mushrooms

Salt Broiled Shiitake Mushrooms

Serves 4: 12 large, fresh shiitake or other mushrooms; salt
Dipping Sauce: 3 tablespoons dark soy sauce; 3 tablespoons lemon juice; ½ teaspoon sweet rice wine (mirin)

Cut the stems off the mushrooms and discard. Sprinkle both sides lightly with salt, then put under a very hot broiler or over charcoal and cook for about 2 minutes on either side, putting the underside towards the heat first.

Cut each mushroom into 2–3 pieces and divide between individual serving dishes. Serve hot with the dipping sauce which is prepared by combining all ingredients.

Sautéed Broccoli ★

Serves 4–6: 2 lb (1 kg) broccoli; salt; 4 tablespoons (2 oz) butter; freshly ground black pepper

Trim the larger leaves from the broccoli stalks (if they are really fresh they can be cooked as you would spinach). Cut the tough ends from the stems and discard them.

Bring a pan of water to the boil, add 1 teaspoon of salt and plunge the broccoli in. Cook for 7 minutes, slightly less if the stalks are very thin. Drain the broccoli and cool slightly before slicing into 1-in (2.5-cm) lengths.

Melt the butter in a skillet until foaming. Add the sliced broccoli and sauté quickly for 3–4 minutes. Adjust the seasoning and serve very hot.

Sautéed Fresh Choy Sum

Serves 4–6: 1¼ lb (625 g) fresh young choy sum (see Note); 2 tablespoons oil; 2 tablespoons rendered chicken fat or lard; ¼ teaspoon salt; ½ teaspoon sugar; 1½ teaspoons rice wine or dry sherry

Trim off any wilted leaves and cut the *choy sum* into 2-in (5-cm) pieces. Peel the thick skin from the lower section of the stems, if preferred. Simmer in boiling water for 2 minutes, then drain.

Heat the oil and chicken fat or lard in a wok and add the salt and sugar. Sauté the vegetables on moderate heat for 2 minutes or until tender, then sizzle the wine onto the sides of the pan, stir in and serve.

Note: Any fresh seasonal green vegetable can be used if *choy sum* is not in season.

Sautéed Mushrooms ★

Serves 6: 1 lb (500 g) fresh small mushrooms; 6 tablespoons (3 oz) butter; 2 teaspoons lemon juice; salt and black pepper; 1 teaspoon grated lemon peel; 2 tablespoons fresh (soft) brown breadcrumbs (see Note); 1 tablespoon chopped parsley

Wipe over the mushrooms and trim the stalks. Heat the butter and when foaming, add the mushrooms. Sauté the mushrooms on moderate heat until tender. Sprinkle the lemon juice over and season to taste with salt and freshly ground black pepper.

Mix the lemon peel with the breadcrumbs and parsley. Transfer the mushrooms to a serving plate and sauté the crumb mixture in the remaining butter for 1–2 minutes, then sprinkle over the mushrooms and serve at once.

Note: Make fresh (soft) breadcrumbs by placing day-old bread (crusts removed) in a blender or food processor and chopping briskly.

Sevillian Salad

Serves 8: 6 red or green bell peppers, cut in half and seeded; 4 cups (20 oz) cooked rice; 4 onions, finely sliced; 6 tomatoes, peeled and each cut into 8 segments; 6½ oz (200 g) green olives, may be pitted if preferred; ½ cup (4 fl oz) olive oil; 2 tablespoons vinegar; 1 garlic clove, crushed; salt and freshly ground black pepper

Place the pepper halves, skin side up, under a preheated broiler until the skin blackens. Cool, then remove the skin. Cut the peppers into strips.

Put the rice on the bottom of a serving dish and arrange the pepper strips, onions, tomatoes and olives on top.

In a screw-top jar, make a dressing from the oil, vinegar, garlic, salt and pepper. Shake well and pour over the salad.

Sicilian Ratatouille

Serves 6: 2 lb (1 kg) eggplant, cut into cubes; salt; 1 lb (500 g) onions, sliced; ½ cup (4 fl oz) olive oil; 1 lb (500 g) tomatoes, peeled, seeded and chopped; 2 tablespoons capers, washed; 3 oz (90 g) celery stalks, roughly chopped; ½ cup (2½ oz) pitted olives; ½ cup (4 fl oz) white wine vinegar; 1 tablespoon sugar

Arrange the eggplant on a rack or in a sieve. Sprinkle with salt and leave for 1–2

hours until the liquid has completely drained off.

Sauté the onions in half the oil and when golden brown, add the tomatoes, capers, celery and olives. Brown all these ingredients and remove the pan from the heat.

Lightly squeeze any remaining liquid from the eggplant and dry the pieces in a cloth. In the remaining oil in a separate pan, fry the eggplant and when brown, drain off the oil and add the eggplant to the above mixture. Add the vinegar and sprinkle with sugar. Mix well and continue cooking over a low heat until most of the liquid has evaporated.

Simple Dhal Stew

Serves 4: 1 cup yellow or red lentils; 1½ tablespoons ghee or oil; 1 teaspoon brown mustard seeds; 1 medium-size red or brown onion, sliced; 2 garlic cloves, finely chopped; 2 slices fresh ginger, finely chopped; 2 sprigs curry leaves (optional); ½ teaspoon turmeric powder; 1 teaspoon garam masala; 2–2½ cups (16–20 fl oz) water; 1 teaspoon salt

Wash the lentils thoroughly and leave them to soak while preparing other ingredients. Heat the *ghee* and gently fry the mustard seeds until they pop. Add the onion, garlic, ginger and curry leaves and fry until the onion is soft and golden. Sprinkle in the

turmeric and *garam masala*. Stir thoroughly, then add the lentils, well drained, and stir over low heat for a couple of minutes until all the *ghee* has been absorbed. Add the water and salt, and simmer until the lentils are soft.

Snow Peas, Mushrooms and Bamboo Shoots

Serves 4: 6 dried black mushrooms; 1 tablespoon oil; 1 garlic clove, lightly crushed; large chunk bamboo shoot weighing about 4 oz (125 g), sliced; 8 oz (250 g) snow peas, strings removed; ½ teaspoon salt; ½ teaspoon sugar

Rinse the mushrooms and soak in hot water for 30 minutes. Drain and reserve the soaking liquid; discard the mushroom stems and cut the caps in half.

Heat the oil in a skillet and fry the garlic until golden. Discard the garlic and raise the heat. Stir-fry the mushrooms for a few seconds, then add the sliced bamboo shoot and stir-fry for another few seconds. Add the snow peas and continue to stir-fry over high heat for 1–2 minutes. Put in 4 tablespoons of the mushroom soaking liquid, salt and sugar.

Continue to cook, stirring constantly, for about 2 minutes, until all the liquid has evaporated and the vegetables are cooked but still firm. Serve immediately.

Sour Cabbage with Caraway Seeds

Serves 4-6: 1 lb (500 g) white cabbage; 2 tablespoons (1 oz) butter; ½ teaspoon caraway seeds; 6 black peppercorns, lightly crushed; 2 tablespoons white vinegar; salt

Finely shred the cabbage and place in a microwave-safe covered dish.

In a jug, melt the butter for 1½ minutes on MEDIUM-HIGH (70%). Add the caraway seeds and crushed peppercorns, then pour evenly over the cabbage. Sprinkle over the vinegar and toss thoroughly.

Cover the dish and microwave on HIGH (100%) for 4 minutes. Toss the cabbage, then microwave on HIGH (100%) for a further 3 minutes. Sprinkle over salt to taste and leave covered until ready to serve.

Note: This makes a delicious accompaniment to pork or chicken dishes.

Simple Dhal Stew

Sour Cabbage with Walnuts

Serves 4-6: 1 lb (500 g) white cabbage;
2 tablespoons (1 oz) butter; 5 black peppercorns;
2 tablespoons chopped walnuts; 2 tablespoons white
vinegar; 2½ teaspoons sugar; salt

Rinse, dry and finely shred the cabbage. Heat the butter in a skillet, then add the lightly crushed peppercorns and the walnuts. Sauté for 1 minute, then add the cabbage and toss until evenly coated with the butter. Sauté, stirring, for about 5 minutes until almost tender.

Add the vinegar mixed with the sugar and continue to cook and stir until the liquid has evaporated. Add salt to taste and serve.

Sour Cabbage with Walnuts

Southern Indian Cabbage

Serves 4: 2 tablespoons oil; 1 teaspoon brown
mustard seeds; 1-2 fresh green chilies, sliced;
4-6 shallots, or 1 small red or brown onion, very
finely sliced; 2 sprigs curry leaves; 1 teaspoon black
gram dhal; 1 lb (500 g) cabbage, coarsely shredded;
¼ teaspoon sugar; 1 teaspoon salt; ¼ cup (2 fl oz)
water; 3 tablespoons freshly grated coconut

Heat the oil in a skillet and put in the mustard seeds. As soon as they start popping, add the chilies, shallots, curry leaves and *dhal*. Fry, stirring frequently, for 3-4 minutes. Add the cabbage and fry, stirring to mix thoroughly, for 1 minute. Add the sugar, salt and water. Cover the skillet and simmer gently for about 10 minutes or until the cabbage is almost soft. Remove the lid, increase the heat and cook rapidly to evaporate any liquid. Stir in the coconut and serve at room temperature.

Spaghetti Salad

Serves 4: 4 ripe tomatoes; 12 oz (375 g) spaghetti;
4 black olives, pitted and quartered; 1 large garlic
clove, crushed; 12 basil leaves, roughly chopped (or
1 generous tablespoon chopped parsley); ¼ cup
(2 fl oz) good quality olive oil; salt and pepper

Plunge the tomatoes into boiling water until the skins split, then remove and peel. Cut into segments and set aside to cool thoroughly.

Meanwhile, cook the spaghetti in plenty of boiling, salted water to which a little oil has been added. When al dente, run under cold water to stop cooking, then drain. Place in a serving bowl.

In a smaller bowl, put the tomatoes, olives, garlic, basil, oil and salt and pepper to taste. Toss lightly, then add to the pasta and toss again. Cover the bowl with plastic wrap and refrigerate for 15-45 minutes.

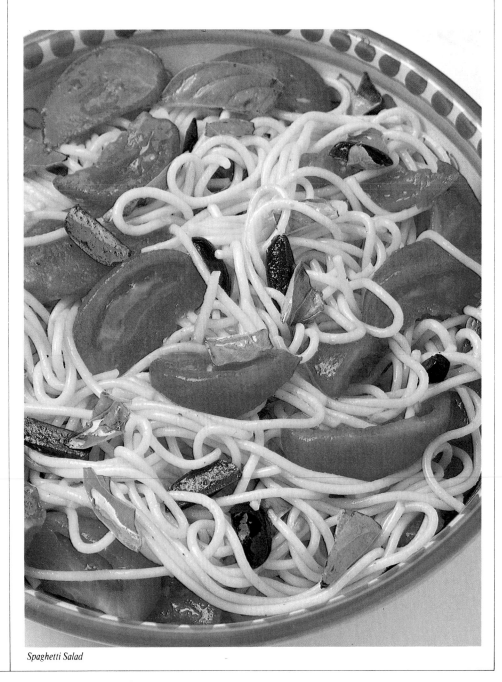

Spaghetti Salad

Spanish Corn

Serves 4: 2 tablespoons olive oil; corn stripped from 4 corn cobs (about 2 cups); 2 tablespoons all purpose flour; salt; cayenne pepper; ¼–½ teaspoon chili powder (optional); 1 cup (4 oz) grated Parmesan cheese; 1 onion, finely chopped; 12 olives, pitted and roughly chopped; 1 garlic clove, crushed; 4–6 tomatoes, peeled and finely chopped

In a saucepan, combine the oil, corn, flour, salt, cayenne and chili powder if using and cook over low heat for 10 minutes, stirring constantly. Add the cheese, onion, olives, garlic and tomatoes. Pour into a small casserole and bake in an oven preheated to 350°F (180°C) for 30–40 minutes.

Spiced Cabbage

Serves 6: 1 lb (500 g) Chinese (celery) cabbage; 1 tablespoon salt; 1½-in (4-cm) piece fresh ginger; 2½ tablespoons oil; ¼ cup (2 fl oz) Chinese brown vinegar; 1 tablespoon sugar; 1 teaspoon chili oil, or chili flakes soaked in oil

Wash the cabbage thoroughly and separate the leaves. Cut into 2-in (5-cm) squares and place in a glass dish. Add the salt and toss lightly, then cover with plastic wrap and leave for 4 hours. Peel and finely shred the ginger and add to the cabbage.

Heat the oil until warm and add the remaining ingredients. Pour over the cabbage, toss thoroughly and leave for a further 4 hours.

Note: Spiced Cabbage keeps for up to a week in the refrigerator, tightly covered with plastic wrap.

Spiced Pineapple

Serves 4: 1 medium-size half-ripe pineapple, peeled and "eyes" removed; water; 1 heaped teaspoon turmeric; ¼ cup oil; 2 medium-size red or brown onions, finely sliced; 1 whole star anise; 2-in (5-cm) stick cinnamon; 6 cardamom pods, slit and bruised; 8 cloves; 4 garlic cloves, very finely chopped; 2-in (5-cm) piece fresh ginger, very finely chopped; 1 cup (8 fl oz) water; 1 teaspoon salt; 1½ tablespoons sugar, or more to taste; 2–3 red chilies, sliced in half lengthwise

Cut the pineapple lengthwise in four and remove the core. Cut each piece in half crosswise. Put the pineapple, enough water to cover it, and turmeric powder into a saucepan and simmer uncovered for 10 minutes. Drain the pineapple and discard the liquid.

Heat the oil and fry the onions and whole spices for 2 minutes. Add the garlic and ginger, and fry for another 2 minutes. Put in the water, salt and sugar, and boil rapidly for 2 minutes. Add the chili and pineapple and simmer for 2 minutes more. Taste and adjust the seasoning if necessary. The flavor should be hot and sour with a touch of sweetness.

Spicy Bean Curd Salad

Serves 4: 4–5 large pieces hard bean curd; oil for deep frying; 1 small cucumber; 5 oz (150 g) beansprouts
Sauce: 2–3 fresh red chilies; 4 shallots or ½ medium-size red or brown onion; 2 tablespoons palm sugar or brown sugar; 4 heaped tablespoons crunchy peanut butter; 1 tablespoon thick black soy sauce; ¼ cup (2 fl oz) tamarind water (see page 392); salt to taste; ¼ cup water

Wipe the bean curd dry with a paper towel and deep fry in hot oil for 4–5 minutes until golden brown. Drain, then cut into thick slices. Leave to cool.

Prepare the sauce by grinding together the chilies and shallots. Add the palm sugar and pound to mix, then combine with all other ingredients. If using an electric blender or food processor, grind the chilies and shallots with just a little of the water until fine. Add all other ingredients and blend for a few seconds. Put the sauce into a bowl.

Scrape the skin of the cucumber with a fork, rub with a little salt, rinse, then slice finely. Blanch the beansprouts in boiling water for 30 seconds, drain, run cold water over to refresh, then drain thoroughly. To serve the salad, arrange the cucumber slices on a large platter. Put the sliced bean curd on top and scatter the beansprouts over the bean curd. Pour over the sauce and serve immediately.

Spicy Cucumber Dish

Serves 4: Sambal: 3 tablespoons dried shrimp; 1 teaspoon dried shrimp paste, broiled; 2 fresh red chilies; 2 tablespoons Chinese lime juice or juice from half-ripe kumquat or lemon; 1–2 teaspoons sugar; ½ teaspoon salt
2 medium-size cucumbers; 5 oz (150 g) belly pork, boiled in one piece and sliced, or 1 chicken liver and 1 chicken gizzard, boiled and sliced

Prepare the *sambal* mixture first. Soak the dried shrimp in hot water for 10 minutes, then pound coarsely and set aside. Make sure the dried shrimp paste is thoroughly broiled on both sides, then pound with the chilies. Add the shrimp, pound a little, then mix in all other *sambal* ingredients. Taste, adding more sugar and lime juice if desired. Keep aside in a covered container.

To remove any bitterness from the cucumber, cut ½ in (1 cm) off the top. Take the cut top portion of the cucumber and rub it in a circular motion for 30 seconds over the cut surface of the rest of the cucumber. A white "scum" will accumulate on both cut surfaces. Discard the cut top portion. Cut another ½ in (1 cm) off the top of the rest of the cucumber and discard this also. Repeat the procedure with the other cucumber. Do not peel the cucumbers but cut in half lengthwise, then cut across diagonally in pieces about 1 in (2.5 cm) wide.

Just before serving, combine the cucumber, pork or chicken liver and gizzard, and *sambal* ingredients. Serve immediately ·

Spinach Egg Puffs

Serves 6: 1 lb (500 g) fresh spinach or collard greens; 8 egg whites; ½ teaspoon salt; 2 tablespoons all purpose flour; 1 tablespoon cornstarch; 6 cups (1½ liters) oil for deep frying; Chinese pepper-salt

Thoroughly wash the spinach and squeeze out as much water as possible. Spread on kitchen towels and leave to dry, then cut into pieces about 2 in (5 cm) long.

Beat the egg whites to stiff peaks, then gently fold in the salt, flour, and cornstarch. Heat the oil to moderate. Dip small bundles of the spinach into the egg batter, coating thickly, then deep fry until golden and cooked through, about 2½ minutes.

Drain well and sprinkle generously with pepper-salt before serving.

Spinach with Bean Curd Dressing

Serves 4: 10 oz (315 g) fresh spinach; 5 oz (155 g) "silken" bean curd; 2 tablespoons white sesame

Spiced Pineapple

seeds; ¾ teaspoon salt; 1 tablespoon superfine sugar

If using Japanese spinach, which is sold with the fine stems still joined together at the root end, do not cut but wash and drain. For other types, tie so that the stems lie together and the leaves lie together. Cook in a large pan of boiling salted water for 2–3 minutes until the spinach is just cooked. Remove from the boiling water and hold under cold running water to retain the color. Drain well, then cut into 1½-in (4-cm) lengths.

Drain the bean curd and mash finely with a fork. Toast the sesame seeds in a dry pan over low heat, stirring constantly, until golden brown. Grind to an oily paste while still warm using a mortar and pestle or electric spice grinder. Mix the sesame seed paste with the bean curd, salt and sugar, stirring well to make a smooth, creamy dressing. Add the spinach, toss lightly, then serve at room temperature.

Spinach with Cottage Cheese

Serves 6–8: 3 lb (1.5 kg) fresh spinach or 1 lb (500 g) frozen spinach; 3 tablespoons ghee; 6 oz (185 g) prepared paneer (see Note); 1 garlic clove; ½-in (1-cm) piece fresh ginger; 1 tablespoon chopped fresh cilantro (optional); ½ teaspoon chili powder; ¼ teaspoon freshly grated nutmeg; ½ cup (4 fl oz) heavy cream; salt and pepper

Wash the fresh spinach in several changes of cold water and shake out all excess liquid. Shred the spinach and simmer with 1 tablespoon *ghee* and a very little water until completely tender. If using frozen spinach, place the unthawed block in a pan with 1 tablespoon *ghee*, cover and simmer until thawed. Remove the lid and cook until most of the liquid has evaporated.

Cut the *paneer* into 1-in (2.5-cm) cubes. Grind the garlic, ginger and cilantro (if used) to a paste and add the chili and nutmeg. Heat the remaining *ghee* and fry the seasoning paste for 2 minutes. Add the *paneer* cubes, and fry until lightly colored, then put in the spinach and heat through. Stir in the cream and check seasoning. Heat through before serving.

For a smoother sauce, blend the spinach and cream in a blender before adding to the pan to heat.

Spicy Cucumber Dish (see page 126)

Steamed Broccoli with Crabmeat Sauce

Note: To make *paneer*, pour 4 cups (2 pints) yogurt into a cheesecloth bag and suspend for at least 3½ hours or until all liquid has drained off. Pour thick curds into a square pan and place a heavy weight on top. Leave overnight to harden.

Steamed Broccoli with Crabmeat Sauce

Serves 6: 1 lb (500 g) fresh broccoli, trimmed and cut into florets; ¼ cup (2 fl oz) oil; 2 oz (60 g) fresh crabmeat; 1½ tablespoons chopped scallion; ⅓ teaspoon grated fresh ginger; 2 teaspoons rice wine or dry sherry; 2 egg whites, well beaten; chopped cooked ham (optional)
Seasoning A: 1 teaspoon salt; pinch of white pepper; ½ teaspoon sugar; 1 teaspoon rice wine or dry sherry; ¾ cup (6 fl oz) chicken stock
Seasoning B/Sauce: ¾ cup (6 fl oz) chicken stock; ½ teaspoon salt; pinch of white pepper; ½ teaspoon sugar; 1 teaspoon cornstarch

Wash the broccoli and drain well. Heat the oil in a wok and sauté the broccoli on moderate heat for 2 minutes, then remove and drain well. Transfer to a dish and add the seasoning A ingredients and steam over rapidly boiling water for 10 minutes. Remove, drain and arrange on a serving plate.

Reheat the wok and sauté the crabmeat with the scallion and ginger for 1 minute. Sizzle the wine onto the sides of the pan, then add the premixed seasoning B/sauce ingredients and bring to the boil.

Remove from the heat and drizzle in the beaten egg whites, allowing to set in the sauce before stirring. Check the seasonings and pour over the broccoli. Garnish with the chopped ham, if used, and serve.

Straw Mushrooms in Crab Sauce

Serves 6: 1 large can (1 lb/500 g) straw mushrooms; 2½ oz (75 g) fresh or canned crabmeat; 8 oz (250 g) romaine lettuce; 2 teaspoons oil; ¾ cup (6 fl oz) chicken stock; ½ teaspoon light soy sauce; pinch sugar; ¼ teaspoon sesame oil; white pepper to taste; 1 tablespoon cornstarch mixed with ¼ cup (2 fl oz) water

Drain the straw mushrooms and cut each one in half lengthwise. Flake the crabmeat

and set aside. Drop the lettuce leaves into a pan full of boiling salted water with a little oil added and cook for 2 minutes only. Drain and put on a serving dish.

Heat the oil and gently fry the mushrooms, stirring constantly for 1 minute. Add all the remaining ingredients except the cornstarch mixture and crabmeat, and simmer for 3 minutes. Mix in the crabmeat, then thicken with cornstarch. Pour over the arranged lettuce leaves and serve.

Stuffed Dried Mushrooms with Broccoli

Serves 4-6: 12 large dried black mushrooms; 2 cups (16 fl oz) warm water; 1 tablespoon oil; 2 garlic cloves, smashed and chopped; ½ chicken bouillon cube; 2 teaspoons cornstarch; 1 tablespoon cold water; 8 oz (250 g) fresh or frozen broccoli
Filling: 8 oz (250 g) raw shrimp; 3½ oz (100 g) fresh or canned crabmeat; 3 water chestnuts; 1 tablespoon finely diced hard pork fat; ½ teaspoon salt; white pepper

Rinse the mushrooms in cold water, then leave to soak in 2 cups of warm water for about 2 hours. Drain, reserving the soaking liquid. Discard the mushroom stems and squeeze the mushrooms dry.

Heat the oil in a saucepan and gently fry the garlic for about 15 seconds. Raise the heat and add the mushrooms. Stir-fry for 1 minute, then add the mushroom soaking liquid and bouillon cube. Simmer very gently for about 1 hour or until the mushrooms are tender, then remove from the cooking liquid and drain. Thicken the cooking liquid with 1 teaspoon cornstarch mixed with cold water and set this sauce aside.

While the mushrooms are simmering, prepare the filling. Peel the shrimp, flake the crabmeat and peel the water chestnuts. If you have a food processor, put the water chestnuts and pork fat in and blend for about 30 seconds until a rough paste results. Add the shrimp, crabmeat, salt and pepper and process for another few seconds. If you do not have a processor, chop all filling ingredients together with a cleaver to get a fine paste.

When the cooked, drained mushrooms have cooled sufficiently to handle, sprinkle the inside of each cap with a little cornstarch. Press on some of the filling, mounding it slightly. If desired, the mushrooms can now be stored in the refrigerator

for several hours and the dish finalized just before the meal.

Put the stuffed mushrooms into an enamel plate or low-sided bowl and steam for 20 minutes. Cook the broccoli until it is just tender. Arrange the mushrooms in the center of a serving platter. Pour any liquid that has accumulated in the steaming plate into the prepared sauce, reheat and pour over the mushrooms. Arrange the broccoli around the edge of the serving platter, sprinkle the mushrooms with a little white pepper and serve immediately.

Stuffed Mushroom Caps

Stuffed Mushroom Caps ★

Serves 6: 6 large mushrooms; 6 tablespoons (3 oz) butter; red pepper strips, to garnish
For stuffing: 2 tablespoons (1 oz) butter; 1 small onion, finely chopped; 1 tablespoon chopped red pepper; 2-4 oz (60-120 g) chopped cooked ham; 1 tablespoon chopped parsley; salt and pepper; 1½ cups soft white breadcrumbs; ½ cup (4 fl oz) béchamel sauce (see page 144)

Remove the mushroom stalks and chop finely. Reserve for the stuffing. Arrange the mushroom caps in a greased baking dish, dot with the butter and bake in an oven preheated to 350°F (180°C) for 10 minutes.

Meanwhile make the stuffing: melt the butter in a small saucepan, add the onion and sauté until soft but not brown. Add the red pepper, ham, parsley, salt and pepper, chopped mushroom stalks and breadcrumbs. Mix thoroughly and bind together with the béchamel sauce.

Remove the mushrooms from the oven and spoon the prepared stuffing onto each cap. Return to the oven and bake for a further 15 minutes or until the mushrooms are tender. Serve hot, garnished with red pepper strips.

Stuffed Onions

Serves 4: 8 large onions, peeled; ½ cup (3 oz) rice; 2 cups (16 fl oz) stock or water; 2 garlic cloves, crushed; 2 red or green bell peppers, chopped; 2 tablespoons olive oil; 2 hard-cooked eggs, finely chopped; salt and freshly ground black pepper; ½ cup (1 oz) fresh breadcrumbs; 2 tablespoons (1 oz) butter, softened

Cut the top third off each onion and set aside. In a saucepan, boil some water, add the onions and cook for 1 minute. Take out the center of each onion, leaving an outer casing of 2–3 layers. Set the centers aside.

Boil the rice in 1 cup of stock for 15 minutes. Finely chop the tops and centers of the onions and, together with the garlic, add to the rice. Sauté the chopped peppers in the oil for 15 minutes. Add the peppers to the rice, then add the chopped eggs and season.

Stuff the onion casings and place them in a baking dish. Add the remaining stock, cover the dish and bake in an oven preheated to 350°F (180°C) for 45 minutes. Remove the cover, sprinkle the onions with breadcrumbs, turn the oven up to 400°F (200°C) and bake for a further 15 minutes or until the breadcrumbs turn brown.

Stuffed Tomatoes

Serves 4: 8 large firm tomatoes; 1 tablespoon sugar; salt; 3 tablespoons olive oil; 1 large onion, finely chopped; 1 garlic clove, crushed; 1 lb (500 g) ground beef or lamb; 1 teaspoon salt; freshly ground black pepper; ¼ cup (2 oz) long grain rice, parboiled; ½ teaspoon dried mint or 2 sprigs fresh mint, chopped; ½ cup (4 fl oz) dry red wine; ¼ cup (1 oz) dry breadcrumbs; 2 tablespoons grated Kefalotíri or Parmesan cheese; 2 cups fresh tomato sauce (see page 138)

Cut a slice off the top of each tomato and save it for use later as a lid. With a tea-

spoon, scoop out the pulp, chop it and save for use in the stuffing. Sprinkle the inside of the tomatoes with sugar and salt and place them upside down on a rack to drain.

In a large skillet, heat the oil and sauté the onion and garlic until the onion is soft and transparent. Add the ground meat and mix well with the back of a fork until it is broken up. Fry until brown. Add the reserved tomato pulp, salt, pepper, rice, mint and wine. Simmer over low heat for 20 minutes, stirring occasionally. Add more wine or water if the mixture gets too dry. Remove from the heat and cool.

With a teaspoon, fill the tomatoes with the mixture. Sprinkle the top with breadcrumbs and cheese and cover with the tomato lids. Place the tomatoes in a baking dish and pour the tomato sauce around them. Bake in an oven preheated to 350°F (180°C) for 15–20 minutes; occasionally remove the caps and baste with the sauce. Serve hot or lukewarm with the sauce poured over the tomatoes.

Swabian Noodles (Spätzle)

Serves 4-6: 2½ cups (10 oz) all purpose flour; ½ teaspoon salt; 2 eggs, beaten; ½ cup (4 fl oz) water

In a bowl, combine the flour and salt. Add the eggs and ¼ cup (2 fl oz) of the water. Mix until the dough is stiff. Continue adding water until it comes away easily from the sides of the bowl. Knead the dough for several minutes until it is smooth, then let it stand for 30 minutes.

Flour a pastry board and roll out to the desired thickness, approximately ⅛ in (4 mm). With a sharp knife, cut the dough into thin slivers and poach them in a saucepan of boiling salted water. Do not put too many slivers in the saucepan at one time because they will stick. Poach for approximately 5 minutes until they rise to the surface. Remove them with a slotted spoon or drain them in a colander. Serve hot tossed in butter as a side dish in soup.

Swabian Sauerkraut

Serves 6: 3 apples, peeled and diced; 1 onion, sliced; 2 tablespoons lard; ½ teaspoon crushed juniper berries; 1 teaspoon sugar; 2 lb (1 kg) fresh

sauerkraut, rinsed and drained; 2 tablespoons all purpose flour; 2 cups (16 fl oz) dry white wine; ½ teaspoon salt; freshly ground black pepper

Sauté the apples and onion in the lard until light brown. Add the juniper berries, sugar and sauerkraut. Cover and simmer for 30 minutes. Add the flour and stir in well, then add the wine, salt and pepper. Continue simmering for approximately 1 hour or until the sauerkraut is tender.

Swedish Hash

Serves 4-6: 6 potatoes, cooked in their jackets, peeled and cut into small dice; 4 tablespoons (2 oz) butter; 2 cups diced, fried or boiled leftover meat; 3 onions, chopped; 1 cup diced ham; salt and freshly ground pepper; 4 sprigs parsley, chopped; sliced pickled beets; 4-6 egg yolks or fried eggs

Fry the potatoes in the butter until golden brown. Put them in a casserole and keep warm. In the same butter, fry the meat, then add it to the potatoes.

If necessary add more butter, sauté the onions and put them into the casserole. Add the ham, salt and pepper. Mix all the ingredients together and heat for a few minutes. Transfer to a heated serving platter and sprinkle with parsley. Serve with pickled beets and either raw egg yolks (which each person mixes into their portion) or fried eggs.

Sweet Pepper Salad ★

Serves 4-6: 1 green bell pepper; 1 red bell pepper; 2 cups (1-pt) cream-style cottage cheese; 3 tablespoons finely chopped parsley; ¼ cup finely chopped chives or scallions; ¼ cup chopped pimiento; salt and freshly ground white pepper; 1 head lettuce; ½ cup (4 fl oz) French dressing

Wash and dry the peppers. Cut a slice from each stem end. Remove the seeds and membrane. Combine the cottage cheese, parsley, chives, pimiento, salt and pepper. Spoon into the pepper shells. Wrap in clear plastic and chill overnight, or for at least 1 hour.

With a very sharp knife, slice the peppers into ¼-in (5-mm) thick slices. Tear the prepared lettuce leaves into an open, shallow bowl and toss with French dressing. Arrange the pepper slices lightly on top. Serve at once.

Swiss Fried Potatoes (Rösti)

Serves 6: 6 large potatoes; 4 tablespoons (2 oz) butter or 2 tablespoons (1 oz) butter and 2 tablespoons (1 oz) lard; 1 onion, finely chopped, or 2 oz (60 g) bacon (optional); salt and pepper

Scrub the potatoes and boil in their skins until barely tender, drain and peel immediately. Cut into thin slices.

Heat the butter (or mixture of butter and lard, which gives the best results) in a heavy skillet, add the potato slices and the onion or bacon (if used) and season with salt and pepper. Fry over a high heat, turning the potatoes occasionally to brown on all sides. Lower the heat, press the potatoes firmly into the pan and fry slowly for a few minutes until a golden crust forms underneath. Cover and cook gently until tender, about 5–10 minutes. To serve, turn onto a plate so that brown crust is uppermost. Serve at once.

T

Three Kinds of Mushrooms

Serves 4–6: 6 dried black mushrooms, soaked for 25 minutes; ½ fresh lettuce, well washed; ½ cup (4 fl oz) oil; half × 10-oz (315-g) can straw mushrooms, drained; half × 10-oz (315-g) can button mushrooms, drained
Seasoning/Sauce A: ½ cup (4 fl oz) chicken stock; 2 teaspoons rice wine or dry sherry; 1 tablespoon softened lard or oil; ½ teaspoon salt; ½ teaspoon sugar; 1½ tablespoons oyster sauce; 1 teaspoon cornstarch
Seasoning/Sauce B: ¼ cup (2 fl oz) chicken stock; 1¼ tablespoons light soy sauce; 1 teaspoon rice wine or dry sherry; ⅓ teaspoon salt; ¼ teaspoon ground black pepper; 1 teaspoon cornstarch; 1 tablespoon rendered chicken fat
Seasoning/Sauce C: ¼ cup (2 fl oz) chicken stock; ⅓ teaspoon salt; ¼ teaspoon sugar; ¼ teaspoon ground black pepper; 1 teaspoon cornstarch; 1 tablespoon evaporated milk

Drain the black mushrooms and squeeze out the water. Remove the stems and place the mushrooms in a dish with the seasoning/sauce A ingredients, except the oyster sauce and cornstarch. Steam for 25 minutes.

Three Kinds of Mushrooms

Dip the lettuce into lightly salted boiling water with 1 tablespoon oil added, and cook for 45 seconds. Remove, drain well and arrange on a large oval serving plate.

Heat one-third of the oil and stir-fry the straw mushrooms for 1 minute. Add the seasoning/sauce B ingredients, except the chicken fat, and simmer until the sauce thickens. Add the chicken fat and stir thoroughly, then transfer to one side of the serving plate.

Heat another third of the oil and stir-fry the button mushrooms for 30 seconds. Add the premixed seasoning/sauce C ingredients, except the evaporated milk, and simmer until the sauce thickens. Stir in the evaporated milk and heat through briefly. Transfer to the other side of the serving plate.

Heat the remaining oil and stir-fry the drained black mushrooms for 1 minute. Add ¼ cup of the reserved steaming liquid, stir in the cornstarch and bring to the boil. Simmer until thickened, then add the oyster sauce. Arrange in the center of the serving plate and serve.

Tomatoes in Cream Sauce

Serves 4–6: 1 lb (500 g) firm ripe tomatoes; 1 tablespoon cornstarch; ¼ cup (2 fl oz) milk; 2 teaspoons rendered chicken fat (optional)

Seasoning: ¾ teaspoon salt; 2 teaspoons rice wine or dry sherry; ¾ teaspoon sugar; ½ cup (4 fl oz) chicken stock

Scald the tomatoes in boiling water for 8 seconds, drain and peel. Cut into quarters. Simmer in a wok with the seasoning ingredients until softened, about 4 minutes, then thicken the sauce with the cornstarch mixed with milk. Add the chicken fat, if used, and serve.

Trieste Potato Cake

Serves 4–6: 3½ lb (1.75 kg) potatoes; salt; 3 oz (90 g) bacon, finely chopped; 2 tablespoons (1 oz) butter; 2 tablespoons olive oil; 1 onion, thinly sliced; ½ cup (4 fl oz) beef stock

Boil the potatoes in salted water until they are tender. Drain, peel and cut them into slices. Lightly sauté the bacon in the butter and oil, add the onion and sauté until golden brown. Add the potatoes, season and add the beef stock. With the back of a fork, crush the potatoes roughly. Over a low heat, cook the potatoes until the underside is brown. Slide the potato cake onto a plate and reverse the sides. Fry again, adding more butter if necessary, until the second side is brown and crisp.

Turnips with Pimiento Cream Sauce ★

Serves 4: 8 small or 4 medium-size turnips, trimmed and peeled; 1 tablespoon butter; 1 quantity of Bechamel Sauce (see page 144); 1 pimiento; 1 teaspoon tomato paste; 2 tablespoons cream; salt and freshly ground pepper

Rub the turnips lightly with the butter and steam over simmering water until tender.

Prepare the bechamel sauce, then stir in the pureed pimiento, tomato paste and cream. Season to taste with salt and pepper. Arrange the cooked turnips in a heated serving dish and coat with the sauce.

Tuscan French Beans

Serves 6: 2 tablespoons (1 oz) butter; ¼ cup dry breadcrumbs; ½ teaspoon paprika; 3 tablespoons grated Parmesan cheese; 1 lb (500 g) French beans, cooked; 1 teaspoon butter; salt and pepper

Melt 2 tablespoons (1 oz) butter in a small pan, add the crumbs and stir over medium heat until a light golden brown. Blend in the paprika. Remove from the heat, add the Parmesan cheese and toss until blended.

To the hot, cooked green beans, add 1 teaspoon butter and seasonings. Top with the breadcrumb mixture.

V

Vegetables with Yogurt

Serves 6: 1½ lb (750 g) mixed vegetables; 4 fresh green chilies, halved lengthwise; 1 teaspoon salt; ¼ teaspoon turmeric; ¼ teaspoon cumin; 1 cup freshly grated coconut or ⅔ cup shredded coconut; 4-6 shallots or 1 small red or brown onion; ½ cup (4 fl oz) plain yogurt

Cut the vegetables into cubes or shreds, then combine with the chilies, salt, turmeric and cumin. Add just enough water to prevent the vegetables from drying out and cook in a covered pan until just cooked. Remove the lid and evaporate any liquid that may be left in the pan.

Pound the freshly grated coconut and shallots together, then add with the yogurt

to the cooked vegetables. Mix well, then serve. If using shredded coconut, mix with the yogurt before preparing and cooking the vegetables to allow the coconut to soften.

Note: Use any of the following vegetables, either on their own or in combination: zucchini, chayote, cabbage, okra, green beans, potatoes.

W

Watercress Salad

Serves 6: 6 cups watercress; 1 small head lettuce; 1 garlic clove, cut; ½ cup (4 fl oz) olive oil; 3 tablespoons vermouth; salt and freshly ground white pepper; pinch of sugar; 1-1½ teaspoons lemon juice

Wash and dry the watercress and break into neat sprigs. Wash and dry the lettuce. Lightly pack both the greens into plastic bags, seal and crisp in the refrigerator until serving time.

Rub the salad bowl with garlic. Add the watercress and tear the lettuce into the bowl. Combine the oil and vermouth with salt, pepper, sugar and lemon juice to taste in a screw-top jar and shake until well blended. Pour over the greens and mix thoroughly until each leaf is glistening. Serve immediately.

Welsh Onion Cake

Serves 6: 2 lb (1 kg) potatoes, peeled and sliced; 8 oz (250 g) onions, finely chopped; 6 tablespoons (3 oz) butter, melted; salt and freshly ground pepper

Grease a 7-in (18-cm) soufflé dish. Arrange a layer of potatoes on the bottom and then a layer of onions, dot with butter and sprinkle with salt and pepper. Repeat the layers, finishing with potatoes. Brush with butter and bake in an oven preheated to 375°F (190°C) for 1-1¼ hours. Turn out and serve hot.

Wild Rice

Serves 4: 4½ oz (140 g) wild rice; 3 cups (24 fl oz) hot chicken stock; 2 tablespoons (1 oz) butter; 1 tablespoon vegetable oil; 1 large onion, chopped; 1 small garlic clove, crushed; 1 medium-size bulb of fennel, trimmed and chopped, or 2 stalks celery, thinly sliced; 6 oz (185 g) mushrooms, sliced; ½ teaspoon dried mixed herbs; salt and freshly ground black pepper

Wash the rice thoroughly under cold running water. Drain and stir into the hot chicken stock. When the stock boils, reduce the heat and cover. Simmer until the grains are tender and most of the stock has been absorbed, about 30 minutes.

While the rice is cooking, melt the butter and oil and fry the onion, garlic and fennel or celery until softened but not browned. Add the mushrooms and cook for 1-2 minutes, until they begin to soften. Sprinkle with the herbs and season with salt and black pepper to taste. Drain the rice and fork together with the vegetables. Adjust the seasoning and serve hot or chilled.

Z

Zucchini Provençale

Serves 6: 6 zucchini; 1 small onion, chopped; 4 tablespoons (2 oz) butter; 1 lb (500 g) tomatoes; 3 oz (90 g) grated cheese; salt and pepper

Cut the zucchini into 2-in (5-cm) slices and sauté, with the onion, in heated butter for 10-15 minutes. Skin the tomatoes, cut into 1-in (2.5-cm) slices and add to the pan with the zucchini. Cook for a few minutes.

Grease an ovenproof dish and arrange a layer of tomatoes, followed by a layer of zucchini, in the dish. Sprinkle between layers with grated cheese, salt and pepper. Finish with a layer of tomatoes, sprinkling with cheese. Bake in an oven preheated to 375°F (190°C) for 45 minutes.

RICE, PASTA & NOODLES

A

Anchovies with Broccoli and Fettuccine

Serves 4: ¼ cup (2 fl oz) olive or corn oil; 4 anchovy fillets, very finely chopped; 1 small red chili, seeded; 1 small onion, finely chopped; 1 lb (500 g) broccoli; salt; 2 oz (60 g) pine nuts, chopped and roasted; 12 oz (375 g) fettuccine; 2 tablespoons (1 oz) butter; 2 oz (60 g) pecorino cheese, freshly grated (or substitute Parmesan)

Heat the oil in a large, heavy-based skillet and add the anchovies. Mash the anchovies in the pan until they combine with the oil, then add the chili, cut into three or four pieces, and the onion. Sauté for a few minutes until the onion turns transparent. Set aside.

Remove the large stems from the broccoli, separate the florets and cook them in a little lightly salted boiling water until just tender. Drain and add to the skillet. Add the pine nuts, increase the heat to high and toss for 1–2 minutes. Reduce the heat to low and simmer for a further 10 minutes. Remove all the chili pieces and discard.

Meanwhile, cook the fettuccine in a large pan of salted boiling water until al dente. Drain briefly, so that some of the water is still clinging to the pasta strips, and transfer to a preheated serving dish.

Melt the butter, then add the contents of the skillet, toss the fettuccine gently and sprinkle with the cheese.

Note: For a better flavor, pine nuts can be roasted in an oven preheated to 350°F (180°C) for a few minutes.

Anchovies with Broccoli and Fettuccine

Asparagus with Tomato-Flavored Tagliatelle

Serves 4: 1 lb (500 g) fresh asparagus; 2 tablespoons (1 oz) butter; 2 tablespoons olive or corn oil; 1 garlic clove; 1 lb (500 g) canned, peeled tomatoes, finely chopped; ½ cup (4 fl oz) cream; salt and freshly ground black pepper; 1 quantity tomato-flavored tagliatelle (see Note); 2 oz (60 g) Parmesan cheese, freshly grated

Wash the asparagus and cut off the bottom third of each stalk and discard. Cut the top portions into ¾-in (2-cm) lengths and steam to half-cooked, about 4 minutes.

Heat the butter and oil in a skillet and add the garlic. Crush the garlic in the pan with the back of a spoon and cook until it is just turning light brown. Remove. Add the asparagus and sauté for 5 minutes, then add the tomatoes with the juice from the can. Simmer for a further 15 minutes over a low heat, stirring occasionally but taking care not to break the asparagus pieces. Add the cream, a pinch of salt and a grind or two of pepper. Simmer, stirring, for 3 minutes, or until the sauce has begun to thicken.

Meanwhile, cook the tagliatelle in plenty of boiling, salted water until al dente. Drain, then transfer to a preheated serving dish. Pour the sauce over, toss well, sprinkle with Parmesan and serve.

Note: To make tomato-flavored pasta, mix 2–3 tablespoons of tomato paste into the basic dough recipe (see page 101). Well-reduced and strained Fresh Tomato Sauce (see page 138) can also be used.

B

Bacon and Broccoli Pasta Pie

Serves 6–10: 12oz (375 g) bacon; 12oz (375g) broccoli florets (fresh or frozen); 6oz (185g) mozzarella cheese, grated; 5oz (155g) Parmesan cheese, freshly grated; 6 large eggs or 7 medium-size, lightly beaten; ½ teaspoon salt; freshly ground pepper; 1 recipe fresh pasta (see page 101); 2 cups (16 fl oz) fresh Tomato Sauce (see page 138), put through a food mill

Remove the bacon rind, then dice and fry in a large, heavy-based skillet to taste. If there is an excessive amount of bacon fat, drain off a little.

Remove any stalks from the broccoli and cut the florets into small buds, about the size of a walnut. Steam or boil in a minimum of salted water, until they are tender but with some bite left in them. Drain and add to the skillet with the bacon.

Add the mozzarella and the Parmesan to the pan, together with the eggs, the salt and pepper. Mix gently to distribute the bacon and the broccoli evenly through the filling.

Roll out the pasta dough into thin strips and cut into large rectangles about 14 × 4 in (36 × 10 cm). Do not worry if you cannot achieve these lengths; it is quite easy to overlap the strips.

Cook the strips in boiling, salted water for 1½ minutes. The pasta will continue cooking in the pie later. Plunge the strips briefly into cold water, then spread on tea towels and dry. They will have less tendency to stick to the cotton surface if you dampen the towels very slightly.

Butter a round casserole dish, about 9 in (23 cm) in diameter and 2½–3 in (7–8 cm) deep. Lay the pasta across the bottom of the dish and up and over the sides, starting in the middle and working outward in both directions. The bottom and sides should be completely covered with pasta.

Spoon in half the filling, then place another layer of pasta on top. Spread the rest of the filling over and cover with the remaining pasta. Moisten with water or a little of the beaten egg to make a perfect seal. Trim around the rim of the casserole dish and cover with aluminum foil. Place in a preheated oven at 400°F (200°C) and bake for 45–50 minutes.

Allow to stand for 30 minutes, then invert the casserole onto a large plate.

Note: Commercially made Lasagne can also be used in this recipe.

Balinese Noodles with Chicken in Coconut Sauce

Serves 6: 9 cups (2¼ liters) water; 3 lb (1.5 kg) chicken; 1 tablespoon ground coriander; 1 heaped teaspoon cumin seeds; 1½ teaspoons grated fresh turmeric, or ½ teaspoon turmeric powder; 1-in (2.5-cm) piece fresh ginger, shredded; 3 garlic cloves, crushed; 6 scallions, chopped; 4 candlenuts, ground; 1 teaspoon dried shrimp paste;

Balinese Noodles with Chicken in Coconut Sauce

*3 tablespoons coconut or vegetable oil; 4 oz (125 g) peeled raw shrimp; 1 lemon, quartered; 4-in (10-cm) stalk lemongrass; 2 lemon leaves (optional); 1¼ cups (10 fl oz) thick coconut milk; salt and pepper; 1 lb (500 g) thin rice vermicelli
Garnishes: Shrimp Fritters (see page 72); dry fried onion flakes (see page 151); scallion, chopped; celery leaves, chopped; fresh basil leaves (optional); fresh cilantro or mint leaves; hard-cooked egg, sliced*

Pour the water into a large saucepan and add the cleaned chicken. Simmer for 1½ hours, then remove the chicken, drain and set aside. When cool, shred the meat. Continue boiling the stock until it has reduced to 6 cups. Set aside.

Pound the seasonings from coriander to shrimp paste to a paste and fry in the hot coconut or vegetable oil for 3 minutes, stirring constantly. Add the shrimp and fry briefly, then mix into the reserved chicken stock. Add the lemon, lemongrass and lemon leaves (if used), and bring to the boil. Reduce the heat and simmer the soup for 10 minutes, then discard the lemon. Pour in the coconut milk and season to taste with salt and pepper. Keep warm while the garnishes are prepared.

Cover the vermicelli with boiling water and leave to soften, then drain. Prepare all other garnishes and arrange on a serving plate. Divide the vermicelli among six large bowls and add a generous serving of coconut soup and shredded chicken. Serve the garnishes separately to be added to taste.

Beef and Broccoli on Ribbon Noodles

*Serves 4: 3 oz (90 g) beef fillet (tenderloin); 1 teaspoon light soy sauce; 1 teaspoon dry sherry; 1 teaspoon vegetable oil; 1 teaspoon cornstarch; ½ teaspoon sugar; pinch of white pepper; 3 oz (90 g) broccoli florets; 2 scallions, shredded; 2 slices fresh ginger, shredded; 12 oz (375 g) fresh rice ribbon noodles; oil
Sauce: ¾ cup (6 fl oz) chicken stock; 2–3 teaspoons Chinese oyster sauce; 1 teaspoon dark soy sauce (mushroom soy); 1 teaspoon dry sherry; ¾ teaspoon sugar; 2 teaspoons cornstarch*

Cut the beef into paper-thin slices, then into strips and place in a dish with the soy sauce, sherry, oil, cornstarch, sugar and pepper. Mix well and leave for 20 minutes.

Rinse the broccoli and drain well. Prepare the scallions and ginger. Pour boiling water over the noodles and stir gently to separate.

In a small jug, mix together all the sauce ingredients except the cornstarch. Make a paste with a little of the mixture and the cornstarch, then add it to the sauce and set aside.

Heat a skillet and add about ¼ cup (2 fl oz) of oil. Stir-fry the beef on high heat until lightly colored, then remove. Add the vegetables and stir-fry for about 2 minutes, then remove.

Mix in the noodles and stir-fry in the oil remaining until lightly colored, about 4 minutes. Transfer to a serving plate.

Return the vetetables to the pan and pour in the sauce. Bring to the boil, stirring. Return the meat and heat through, then pour over the noodles and serve at once.

Note: Put the beef into the freezer until it is firm to make it easier to slice thinly.

Beef and Broccoli on Ribbon Noodles

Black Risotto

Serves 4: 2 lb (1 kg) cuttlefish; ½ cup (4 fl oz) olive oil; ½ onion, finely chopped; 1 garlic clove, peeled; ¼ cup chopped parsley; ½ cup (4 fl oz) dry white wine; 1½ cups (9 oz) rice; 2 tablespoons tomato puree; 3-4 cups (24-32 fl oz) fish stock; salt and pepper

Remove the ink bag from the cuttlefish and reserve it. Cut the cuttlefish into short lengths.

In a casserole, sauté the onion and garlic in the hot oil. Remove the garlic when it is brown. Add the parsley and cuttlefish, and sauté it for 10-15 minutes. Pour in the wine and add the ink. Sauté for a further 5 minutes. Stir in the rice. Add the tomato puree, then add the boiling fish stock, a spoonful at a time, until the rice is completely cooked. Season to taste before serving.

Broccoli and Mushroom Lasagne

Serves 6-8: 1 tablespoon olive oil; 1 teaspoon salt; 7 oz (220 g) lasagne, preferably green; 12 oz (375 g) broccoli florets; 12 oz (375 g) fresh mushrooms; 1 large onion, finely chopped; 2 garlic cloves, crushed; 4 tablespoons (2 oz) butter; 2 oz (60 g) grated sharp cheese; 2 tablespoons grated Parmesan cheese
White Sauce: 3½ cups (28 fl oz) milk; ½ cup (2 oz) cornstarch; 1 teaspoon nutmeg; 1¼ teaspoons salt; freshly ground black pepper
Cheese Sauce: 2 cups (16 fl oz) milk; ¼ cup (1 oz) cornstarch; pinch each of salt, pepper, nutmeg; 4 oz (125 g) grated sharp cheese

In a large casserole, microwave 8 cups (2 liters) of the hottest tap water for 10 minutes, covered, on HIGH (100%). Add the oil, salt and pasta and microwave for 12 minutes on HIGH (100%). Remove from the oven, let stand 6-8 minutes, then drain and cover with cold water.

Cut each broccoli floret into smaller sprigs and rinse with cold water. Place in a covered vegetable dish and microwave on HIGH (100%) for 3 minutes. Shake the dish to rearrange the broccoli, then microwave on HIGH (100%) a further 3 minutes. Set aside.

Wipe the mushrooms, then slice thinly. In a covered vegetable dish, microwave the onion and garlic with the butter for 3 minutes on HIGH (100%), then add the mushrooms and microwave on HIGH (100%) a further 4 minutes. Set aside.

In a very large microwave-safe jug or dish, mix the white sauce ingredients. Microwave on HIGH (100%) for 4 minutes, whisk well and microwave on HIGH (100%) a further 4 minutes. Whisk again and microwave a final 4 minutes on HIGH (100%).

Cook the cheese sauce ingredients, except the grated cheese, for 3 minutes on HIGH (100%), whisk and repeat a further 3 minutes, then whisk well and stir in the cheese.

In a large casserole, layer half the pasta, half the mushrooms, half the white sauce and half the broccoli, then repeat these layers. Spread the cheese sauce over the top of the dish and reheat, partially covered, on MEDIUM (50%) for about 15 minutes. Arrange the grated cheese over the top and sprinkle on the Parmesan. Reheat and serve.

Buttered Saffron Rice with Cashew Nuts

Serves 6: 3¼ cups (26 fl oz) hottest tap water; 1 teaspoon salt; ⅓ teaspoon powdered saffron; 4-6 tablespoons (2-3 oz) butter; 2 cups (10 oz) long grain rice; 2 oz (60 g) raw cashew nuts; 1 tablespoon chopped parsley

Pour the water into a large casserole, cover and microwave on HIGH (100%) for 7 minutes. Add the salt, saffron, half the butter and the rice. Stir well. Microwave on MEDIUM-HIGH (70%) for 8 minutes, then stir well. Cover and microwave on MEDIUM-HIGH (70%) for a further 6-8 minutes until the water has been absorbed and the rice is tender. Remove from the oven. Place a double thickness of paper towels over the rice and replace the lid. Stand for 5 minutes.

In a small dish, microwave the cashew nuts in the remaining butter for 2½-3 minutes on HIGH (100%), stirring occasionally. Stir the nuts lightly into the rice with a fork and add the parsley, or use to garnish.

C

Calabrian Lasagne

Serves 6: Tomato Sauce: ¼ cup olive oil; 4 oz (125 g) fresh Italian sweet sausage, peeled and chopped; 4 oz (125 g) fresh Italian hot sausage, peeled and chopped; 2 teaspoons chopped fresh basil; 2 garlic cloves, crushed; salt and freshly ground pepper; ¼ cup tomato paste; 4 cups tomato puree
1 lb (500 g) lasagne; 2 cups (1 lb) ricotta or cottage cheese, crumbled; 1½ cups (7 oz) roughly grated mozzarella cheese; 12 oz (375 g) fresh mushrooms, sliced; 4 tablespoons (2 oz) butter; ½ cup (1 oz) grated Parmesan or Romano cheese

To make the tomato sauce, heat the oil in a saucepan; add the two types of sausage, the basil, garlic, salt and pepper. Sauté for 3-5 minutes, then add the tomato paste and tomato puree. Simmer the sauce uncovered until it is fairly thick.

Boil the lasagne in a large saucepan of salted water a few at a time to prevent sticking. Remove the cooked pieces and plunge them into cold water.

Oil a baking dish, place a layer of

lasagne in the dish, then a layer of ricotta mixed with the mozzarella. Top with a layer of mushrooms which have been sautéed in the butter. Over the mushrooms pour a layer of tomato sauce. Repeat the above, finishing with a layer of tomato sauce. Sprinkle the top with grated cheese and bake in oven preheated to 400°F (200°C) for 30 minutes. Serve very hot.

Cannelloni with Beef Filling and Tomato Sauce

Serves 4–6: Filling: 3 tablespoons (1½ oz) butter; 12 oz (375 g) lean beef round, ground twice; 1 tablespoon oil; 1 medium-size onion, finely chopped; 2 garlic cloves, finely chopped; ½ stalk celery, finely chopped; 2 tablespoons finely chopped parsley; 8 oz (250 g) fresh spinach, cooked, or 6 oz (180 g) frozen chopped spinach; 1 tablespoon butter; 1½ oz (45 g) chicken livers, chopped; 1½ oz (45 g) Parmesan cheese, freshly grated; 1 tablespoon cream; 1 egg, lightly beaten; 1 egg yolk, lightly beaten; salt and freshly ground black pepper
12 oz (350 g) cannelloni; 1 quantity fresh Tomato Sauce (see page 138); 1 quantity Béchamel Sauce (see page 144); 1½ oz (45 g) Parmesan cheese, freshly grated; 2 tablespoons (1 oz) butter, diced

Cannelloni with Beef Filling and Tomato Sauce

To make the filling, melt 3 tablespoons (1½ oz) butter in a large skillet, add the beef and sauté until it is lightly browned, stirring all the time. Transfer to a large mixing bowl. Put the oil in the same pan, add the onion, garlic, celery and parsley and sauté until the onion is soft and golden. Add the cooked and drained spinach and cook for a further 4 minutes or until all liquid has evaporated. Transfer the contents of the pan to a bowl and mix thoroughly with the meat.

Use the same pan to heat the extra butter. Gently sauté the chicken livers until they change color, 1–2 minutes. Add them to the bowl, together with the Parmesan cheese and the cream. Fold the egg and egg yolk into the mixture, then season to taste with salt and pepper. Set aside to cool.

Stuff the cannelloni with the filling. Butter a large, shallow dish and spread a thin layer of the tomato sauce on the bottom. Carefully place the cannelloni on top of this layer, then pour the béchamel sauce over the pasta. Spread the rest of the tomato sauce on top, sprinkle with the extra Parmesan cheese and dot with small pieces of the extra butter.

Bake in an oven preheated to 475°F (240°C) for 15–20 minutes, or until the top has browned lightly, then serve.

Cheese and Macaroni Stuffed Peppers

Serves 4: 4 large bell peppers or 6 small; 1 tablespoon olive oil; 1 large onion, finely sliced; 1 garlic clove, finely sliced; 2 eggs, lightly beaten; 1 teaspoon finely chopped fresh oregano (or ½ teaspoon dried); 1 generous tablespoon chopped parsley; 1 oz (30 g) pecorino cheese, freshly grated (or substitute Parmesan); 2 oz (60 g) mozzarella cheese; 6 black olives, pitted; 4 oz (125 g) canned tuna fish in oil; 2 anchovy fillets; salt and freshly ground black pepper; 4 oz (125 g) small elbow macaroni; 2 cups (16 fl oz) fresh Tomato Sauce, unstrained (see page 138)

Wash the peppers and slice off the top third, keeping it in one piece. Carefully scoop out the seeds. Set aside.

Heat the oil in a medium-size skillet and sauté the onion and garlic until the onion

is soft and golden. Remove from the heat and transfer to a mixing bowl. Add the eggs, oregano, parsley, the pecorino cheese and the diced mozzarella. Chop the olives into four. Drain and flake the tuna, chop the anchovies into small pieces and add all these to the pan. Season to taste with a little salt and pepper. Mix together and let stand.

Cook the macaroni in boiling, salted water, until just al dente. Drain, and combine with the rest of the stuffing. While the macaroni is cooking, heat the tomato sauce in a small pan.

Using butter or oil, grease a small casserole dish, fill the peppers with the stuffing, replace the tops and stand upright, slightly apart, in the dish. (If they do not stand easily, carefully cut the rounded ends to give a flat surface). Pour the tomato sauce around the peppers, cover and bake in an oven preheated to 400°F (200°C) for 20 minutes, then take off the cover and cook for 15 minutes more at a slightly lower temperature.

Serve with a spoonful or two of the tomato sauce surrounding each pepper.

Chicken Rice Cake

Serves 4: 1½ cups (9 oz) glutinous rice (see Note); 1 cup (8 fl oz) thick coconut milk; 1 teaspoon salt; 2-in (5-cm) cinnamon stick; 1 lb (500 g) boneless chicken; 1 large onion, chopped; 3 garlic cloves, crushed; ½-in (1-cm) piece fresh ginger, grated; 2 tablespoons vegetable oil; 1 teaspoon coriander seeds, toasted; ½ teaspoon cumin seeds, toasted; ½ teaspoon turmeric; ½ cup (4 fl oz) thick coconut milk; 2-in (5-cm) piece lemongrass, chopped; 2 tablespoons ground almonds or peanuts; ¾ teaspoon salt; ¼ teaspoon black pepper; 2 tablespoons (1 oz) melted butter

Soak the rice in water to cover for 4 hours. Drain well, transfer to a saucepan and add the coconut milk and enough water to cover the rice by 1½ in (4 cm). Add the salt and cinnamon stick and bring to the boil, reduce the heat and simmer until the rice has softened and absorbed the water. Pour half into a square, well-greased baking pan and leave to cool.

Dice the chicken. Fry the chopped onion, garlic and ginger in the oil until soft. Grind the spices and add to the pan. Fry briefly, then add the diced chicken. Cook until it changes color, then pour in the coconut milk and add the lemongrass, ground almonds or peanuts, salt and pepper. Simmer until the liquid is well reduced, pour over the rice and spread the remaining rice evenly on top. Press down gently and smooth the top. Cover with aluminum foil pierced in several places.

Cook in an oven preheated to 400°F (200°C) for 30 minutes. Remove the foil and pour the butter over. Raise the heat and cook for a further 8–10 minutes. Cut into squares and serve hot or cold.

Note: Long grain rice can be used, but add water to only 1 in (2.5 cm) above the level of the rice when cooking.

Coconut Rice

Serves 4: ¾ lb (375 g) long grain rice; ½ cup (4 fl oz) thick coconut milk; 2¼ cups (18 fl oz) thin coconut milk; 2 teaspoons salt; 2 eggs; dried salted whitebait; sliced onion or onion sambal; sliced cucumber

Wash the rice and pour into a saucepan with the thick coconut milk. Cook over moderate heat for 10 minutes, stirring frequently. Pour in the thin coconut milk, add the salt and cover. Bring to the boil, reduce the heat and cook until the rice is tender and coconut milk has been absorbed.

Beat the eggs and pour into a very lightly oiled pan. Swirl the pan to make the omelet as thin as possible. Cook until firm, then remove and leave to cool. Shred finely.

Wash the salt fish and dry thoroughly, then fry in hot oil until very crisp. Drain well. Spoon the cooked rice into a serving bowl and garnish with the fried salt fish and shredded omelet. Arrange the sliced onion and cucumber around the rice and serve the onion sambal in a separate dish.

Cold Turkey Pilaf

Cold Turkey Pilaf ⭐

Serves 8–10: 10–11 lb (5–5.5 kg) turkey; salt; goose fat or butter; white pepper; 2 tomatoes, quartered (optional); 2 kiwi fruit, sliced (optional)
Pilaf: 3 tablespoons (1½ oz) butter; 2 medium-size onions, chopped; 1 red bell pepper, seeded and diced; 2 oz (60 g) pine nuts; 1 tablespoon finely chopped cilantro or parsley; 13½ oz (425 g) cooked long grain rice; salt and pepper

Season the turkey inside with salt, fold the wings neatly under the body and tie the legs together. Put the bird on a rack set over a roasting dish. Brush liberally with goose fat or butter, season with pepper and roast just below the center of an oven preheated to 500°F (260°C) for 15 minutes.

Reduce the temperature to 325°F (160°C), cover the thighs and breast loosely with aluminum foil and cook for 2½–2¾ hours, until the juices run clear when a thigh is pierced with a skewer. Baste the bird every 20 minutes during the cooking time and remove the foil for the last 30 minutes. While the turkey is cooking, make the pilaf.

Melt the butter in a saucepan and sauté the onions until golden. Add the pepper and nuts and cook over low heat until the pepper has softened. Stir in the cilantro and rice, mix thoroughly and season well with salt and pepper. Remove from the heat and cool before chilling.

Remove the cooked turkey from the oven and leave to cool. Insert a sharp, pointed knife into the flesh at the end of the breastbone. Cut away the meat in a wide circle from the point of the breast to the front of the second wing joint. Repeat on the other side of the bird. Remove and discard the skin, chop the meat finely and mix with the pilaf.

When the turkey is quite cold, put it on a large serving platter and spoon the pilaf into the cavity. Garnish with the tomatoes and kiwi fruit.

Compressed Rice Cakes

Serves 4: 2 cups (12 oz) short grain rice; 2½ cups (20 fl oz) water; banana leaf or aluminum foil; oil for greasing

Boil the rice in lightly salted water until cooked. While the rice is cooking, choose a rectangular dish that will hold the rice to a depth of about 1 in (2.5 cm) when spread. A dish roughly equivalent to 10 × 14 in (25 × 35 cm) should be adequate. Cut two pieces of banana leaf to fit into the bottom of this dish. Lightly oil the dish and both pieces of banana leaf, then place one piece of leaf on the bottom of the dish.

As soon as the rice is cooked, spoon it into the lined dish, pressing it in firmly and smoothing the top with the back of an oiled spoon. Place the second banana leaf on top of the rice and press firmly with your hands to compress the rice as much as possible. Place weights on top of the banana leaf and leave at room temperature for several hours until firmly set. Cut with a wet knife into 2-in (5-cm) squares. Serve with satay (see page 292).

Cracked Wheat Pilaf ★

Serves 4–6: 2 tablespoons (1 oz) butter; 1 large stalk celery, finely chopped; 1 medium-size onion, finely chopped; 3 oz (90 g) golden raisins; 7 oz (220 g) cracked wheat (bulgur); 2 cups (16 fl oz) chicken stock; salt and freshly ground black pepper; 1 oz (30 g) coarsely chopped pistachios

Melt the butter in a flameproof casserole over moderate heat. Add the celery, onion, and golden raisins and cook until the onion is transparent. Mix the cracked wheat into the pan and stir until the grains are coated with the butter and very lightly browned. Add the chicken stock, stir and bring to the boil. Reduce the heat, season with salt and black pepper and cover. Simmer very gently for 20–30 minutes, until most of the liquid has been absorbed, stirring occasionally.

Remove the lid to finish cooking the pilaf and fork through the mixture once or twice, to prevent it from sticking and to keep it fluffy. Adjust the seasoning and sprinkle with the pistachios before serving.

F

Farfalle with Broccoli Sauce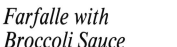

Serves 4: 1 bunch of broccoli; 2 garlic cloves, very finely chopped; 1 tablespoon olive or corn oil; ½ cup (4 fl oz) cream; salt and freshly ground black pepper; 12 oz (350 g) farfalle or macaroni; paprika; Parmesan cheese, freshly grated

Cook the broccoli in the minimum amount of lightly salted, boiling water until it is cooked but still firm, about 4–5 minutes. Set aside ½ cup (4 fl oz) of the cooking water. Also reserve a few of the small broccoli florets, refresh them in cold water and set aside.

Cook the garlic in the oil until just turning golden. Add the broccoli, cut into small pieces, and toss gently for a few minutes. Put the contents of the pan, together with the reserved broccoli water, into a blender and blend for a few seconds. Pour this puree back into the pan and add the cream. Bring to a gentle simmer, season and cook over a low heat until the sauce is smooth. Meanwhile, cook the farfalle in boiling, salted water until al dente. Drain.

Divide the reserved broccoli florets into small segments and plunge them into boiling water for a minute or two to reheat them. Pour the sauce over the farfalle, decorate with the broccoli florets and dust lightly with paprika. Serve the grated Parmesan on the side.

Fettuccine alla Carbonara

Serves 4: 8 oz (250 g) bacon; 4 tablespoons (2 oz) butter; 1 whole egg, beaten; 3 egg yolks, beaten; 6 tablespoons cream (or use ½ cream, ½ milk); 4 oz (125 g) Parmesan cheese, freshly grated; freshly ground black pepper; 1 lb (500 g) fettuccine

Remove the rind from the bacon and cut into thin strips. Fry in the melted butter in a large skillet until well cooked, then remove from the heat. Combine the beaten eggs in a bowl, stir in the cream and half the grated cheese, then add a generous grind of black pepper. Set aside.

Cook the fettuccine in plenty of boiling salted water and drain well. Place the skillet with the bacon back on the heat for a moment or two, then add the fettuccine, stirring thoroughly to distribute the bacon strips evenly through the pasta. Take the skillet off the heat again, leave for a few moments only, then quickly stir in the egg mixture, which will cook to a creamy sauce in the hot fettuccine. Serve immediately, with the rest of the Parmesan cheese on the side.

Note: This carbonara sauce is sometimes enlivened with either just a sprinkle of dried red pepper, crumbled, or a few tiny strips of fresh chili pepper, seeded. This is added to the skillet just as the bacon is cooked.

Fettuccine and Olive Sauce

Serves 4: 12 large black olives; ½ small red chili, seeds removed; 1 tablespoon capers; ½ cup (4 fl oz) olive oil; 1 medium-size onion, finely chopped; 2 garlic cloves, crushed; 12 oz (375 g) fettuccine; 1 lb (500 g) ripe tomatoes, or 1 can tomatoes; ½ teaspoon dried oregano or 2 teaspoons chopped fresh oregano leaves

Pit and chop the olives. In a glass or ceramic bowl, marinate the olives, chili and

capers in most of the olive oil for an hour or so. Meanwhile, gently sauté the onion and garlic in the small remaining amount of oil until golden. Cook the fettuccine in boiling salted water until al dente.

Peel, seed and chop the tomatoes, if fresh, or sieve the canned tomatoes. Now, turn all the ingredients into a pan and simmer over moderate to high heat until the mixture thickens slightly and darkens. Remove the chili. Pour over the al dente pasta and serve at once.

Note: If preparing the sauce in advance, remove the chili before storing.

Fettuccine with Bacon and Mushrooms

Serves 4: 2 slices lean bacon; 2 oz (60 g) fresh mushrooms; 8 tablespoons (4 oz) butter; 2 oz (375 g) fettuccine; 3 oz (90 g) Parmesan cheese, freshly grated; freshly ground black pepper

Remove the rind from the bacon, cut into small pieces and fry in a heavy-based skillet until nearly cooked. Set aside. In the same pan, cook the sliced mushrooms in 6 tablespoons (3 oz) of the butter, return the bacon to the pan and cook a little longer. Keep on low heat.

Meanwhile, cook the fettuccine in boiling salted water until al dente. Drain well, sprinkle with the Parmesan, mix in the remaining butter and stir gently to make sure the fettuccine is evenly covered. Now add the bacon, mushrooms and pepper, mix through the pasta and serve with a little extra Parmesan on the side.

Fettuccine with Lobster or Crayfish

*Serves 4: Fresh Tomato Sauce: 2½ tablespoons olive oil; 4 oz (125 g) onion, finely chopped; 1 stalk celery, finely chopped; 2 lb (1 kg) very ripe fresh tomatoes or canned Italian tomatoes, roughly chopped; 2 tablespoons tomato paste; 1 bay leaf; 6–8 fresh basil leaves, chopped or 1 teaspoon dried; salt and freshly ground black pepper
1 cooked lobster, enough to provide 7–8 oz (220–250 g) flesh; 2 tablespoons all purpose flour; 2 tablespoons (1 oz) butter; ¼ cup corn oil; ½ cup (4 fl oz) Cognac; ¾ cup (6 fl oz) cream; 1 teaspoon rock salt (or ½ teaspoon table salt); ½ teaspoon dried chili powder, or 1 small chili pepper, finely*

Fettuccine with Lobster or Crayfish

Fettuccine with Prosciutto

Serves 4: 4 oz (125 g) prosciutto; 3 tablespoons (1½ oz) butter; 12 oz (375 g) fettuccine; freshly ground black pepper; 2½ oz (75 g) Parmesan cheese, freshly grated

Cut the prosciutto into small pieces. Melt the butter in a large skillet over a low heat, add the prosciutto and just warm it.

Cook fettuccine in boiling salted water until al dente and drain. Immediately transfer it to the skillet. Toss gently, still over a very low heat, and when you have the ham mixed nicely through the pasta, sprinkle over 1½ oz (45 g) of the Parmesan and the pepper. Toss again to coat the fettuccine strands well, and serve immediately. Serve the rest of the Parmesan cheese separately.

Fried Fresh Rice-Flour Noodles

Serves 6: 3½ oz (100 g) hard pork fat; 4 garlic cloves, very finely chopped; 2 fresh red chilies, pounded; 6½ oz (200 g) lean pork, shredded; 12 oz (375 g) raw shrimp, peeled; 6½ oz (200 g) squid (optional); 1 tablespoon light soy sauce; 1 tablespoon dark soy sauce; 2 teaspoons oyster sauce; ½ teaspoon salt; pepper to taste; 8 oz (250 g) beansprouts; 2 lb (1 kg) fresh rice-flour noodles cut in strips ½ in (1 cm) wide; fresh red chili, sliced; fresh cilantro leaves

Cut the pork fat into ½-in (1-cm) dice and put into a dry skillet over medium heat until the lard runs out and the pieces of fat turn golden and crisp. Remove the crisp pieces of fat and leave 3 tablespoons of lard in the skillet.

Fry the garlic and chili gently in the lard until the garlic starts to turn golden. Raise the heat, add the pork and stir-fry for 2 minutes. Put in the shrimp and squid, and stir-fry for another 2 minutes. Add the sauces, salt, pepper and beansprouts. Mix well and stir-fry for just 2 minutes.

Add the noodles, previously scalded with boiling water and drained, and stir-fry for 2-3 minutes to heat through. Stir in the fried fat crisps and serve on a large platter, garnished with chili and cilantro.

Note: Oil can be used instead of lard, and the fat crisps omitted, but the dish will lack its characteristic flavor.

chopped; 12 oz (375 g) fettuccine; 3 cups (24 fl oz) Fresh Tomato Sauce; parsley

To make the tomato sauce, heat the oil in a heavy-based pan and sauté the onion and celery. When the onion is golden, add the tomatoes, tomato paste, bay leaf, basil, salt and pepper. Bring to the boil, reduce the heat and simmer uncovered, stirring occasionally, for 45 minutes or until thickened.

Remove as much flesh as possible from the body and claws of the lobster, reserving the legs for decoration. Sprinkle the flour over the flesh, and toss to make sure it is well distributed.

In a large, heavy-based skillet, heat the butter and oil together. Turn the heat up high and add the lobster pieces to the pan. Agitate the pan to make sure the flour cooks on all sides. This should take no more than 1 minute. Add a little more butter if needed and turn the heat to very low. Simmer for 3-4 minutes, tossing the flesh gently all the while. Remove from the heat and add the Cognac and the cream. Sprinkle over the salt and the chili and return to a low heat. Meanwhile, cook the fettuccine in boiling salted water until al dente.

Mix the tomato sauce into the lobster and add the well-drained fettuccine. Serve in a preheated bowl with the lobster arranged on top. Garnish with parsley.

Note: The tomato sauce can be pureed or sieved for a finer sauce.

Fried Hokkien Noodles

Serves 6-8: 1 lb (500 g) fresh yellow noodles; 8 oz (250 g) raw shrimp; 3 tablespoons oil; 1 cup (8 fl oz) water; 8 oz (250 g) boiled pork belly or pancetta; 8 oz (250 g) beansprouts; 8-10 garlic cloves, pounded; 2 eggs, lightly beaten; salt and pepper, to taste
Garnish: 1-2 fresh red chilies, thinly sliced lengthwise; 2 scallions, cut in 1-in (2.5-cm) lengths; few stalks young celery, finely chopped

Put the noodles into a bowl and pour over boiling water to cover. Stand for 1 minute, then drain and set aside.

Peel the shrimp, keeping the shells and heads. Heat 1 tablespoon of oil in a saucepan and fry the shells and heads, stirring constantly, for 1 minute. Add the water and bring to the boil. Cover the pan and simmer for 5 minutes, then pour through a sieve and discard the shells. Simmer the shrimp in this stock until cooked. Strain and reserve the stock.

Slice the pork finely. Rinse the beansprouts and discard any black husks. Heat the remaining 2 tablespoons of oil in a large skillet and fry the garlic gently until golden to flavor the oil. Discard the garlic.

Raise the heat and when the oil is really hot, pour in the beaten eggs. Stir constantly for 1 minute, then add the noodles, beansprouts and ½ cup of the shrimp stock. Cook over high heat for 1 minute, stirring constantly, then add the pork, shrimp and salt and pepper to taste. Stir-fry for another 2-3 minutes, adding more shrimp stock if the noodles appear to be sticking. Serve on a platter with garnish ingredients.

Fried Rice

Serves 8-10: 2 oz (60 g) raw peeled shrimp; ½ teaspoon salt; 1½ teaspoons cornstarch; 1 teaspoon ginger wine (see Note); ⅓ cup softened lard or oil; 2 eggs, well beaten; 2 oz (60 g) roast pork or cooked ham, diced; 2 oz (60 g) green peas, cooked; 2 tablespoons finely chopped scallion; 4 cups cooked short grain rice; fresh red chili powder or sprigs of cilantro for garnish
Seasoning: 2 teaspoons salt; ½ teaspoon sugar; 1 tablespoon light soy sauce; ¾ teaspoon dark soy sauce; ¼ teaspoon ground black pepper

Devein the shrimp with a toothpick and rub with the salt and cornstarch, then rinse

well. Wipe dry with paper towels, then rub with the ginger wine.

Heat a very little lard or oil in a wok or skillet and add the beaten eggs, tilting the pan so that the egg forms into a thin pancake over the entire bottom of the pan. Cook until lightly colored and firm underneath, then turn and briefly cook the other side. Remove and leave to cool, then shred finely.

Reheat the wok and add the remaining oil. Stir-fry the shrimp, pork or ham, peas and scallion together for 2 minutes. Add the seasoning ingredients and fry briefly, then add the rice and stir-fry on moderate heat until each grain is coated with the seasonings and the other ingredients are evenly distributed.

Stir in half the shredded egg and transfer to a serving plate. Garnish with the remaining egg and a few shreds of fresh red chili pepper or sprigs of fresh cilantro.

Note: To make ginger wine, mix ¼ cup rice wine or dry sherry with 2 tablespoons of grated fresh ginger. This will keep for many weeks. Commercial brands of ginger wine can also be used.

Fried Rice Noodles

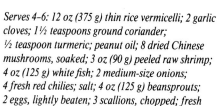

Serves 4-6: 12 oz (375 g) thin rice vermicelli; 2 garlic cloves; 1½ teaspoons ground coriander; ½ teaspoon turmeric; peanut oil; 8 dried Chinese mushrooms, soaked; 3 oz (90 g) peeled raw shrimp; 4 oz (125 g) white fish; 2 medium-size onions; 4 fresh red chilies; salt; 4 oz (125 g) beansprouts; 2 eggs, lightly beaten; 3 scallions, chopped; fresh cilantro sprigs

Soak the noodles in cold water for 5 minutes, then drop into boiling water and steep for about 6-10 minutes until soft. Drain well and rinse in cold water.

Crush the garlic and make into a paste with the coriander and turmeric. Heat 1 tablespoon of oil in a wok or skillet and fry the seasoning paste for 2 minutes.

Remove the mushroom stems and slice the mushrooms thinly. Chop the shrimp and fish into small dice and add to the pan together with the mushrooms. Fry on moderate heat for 4 minutes. Remove from the pan and keep warm.

Add 2 tablespoons oil to the pan and fry the sliced onions and chilies. Add the noodles, season with salt and stir thoroughly. Scatter the beansprouts on top and cook, covered, for 1 minute. Mix the beansprouts into the noodles and remove

from the pan. Pour in the beaten egg, swirling the pan to make a very thin omelet. Cook until set, then remove and cool slightly. Shred.

Reheat the noodles, adding half the shrimp and mushrooms and half of the shredded egg to the pan. Lift onto a flat serving dish and garnish with the remaining shrimp and mushrooms. Top with shredded egg, chopped scallions and cilantro sprigs.

Fried Thai Noodles

Serves 6-8: 5 oz (155 g) chicken meat; 2 oz (60 g) chicken livers; 2½ oz (75 g) Chinese roast pork; 2 oz (60 g) cabbage or Chinese cabbage; 2 squares hard bean curd (optional); 2 oz (60 g) canned bamboo shoots; vegetable oil; 2 lb (1 kg) fresh Chinese egg noodles, parboiled; ½-in (1-cm) piece fresh ginger, chopped; 2 garlic cloves, crushed; 6 scallions, chopped; 2 fresh red chilies, thinly sliced; 2 oz (60 g) beansprouts; 2½ oz (75 g) raw shrimp, peeled; 4 Chinese dried mushrooms, soaked in cold water for ½ hour; 1 tablespoon fish sauce; 1½ teaspoons chili powder; 1 teaspoon salt; ½ cup chicken stock; 2 teaspoons cornstarch

Chop the chicken, livers and pork into ½-in (1-cm) dice. Wash and chop the cabbage and shake out the water. Cut the bean curd into ¼-in (5-mm) dice. Drain the bamboo shoots and slice thinly.

Heat 2 tablespoons of oil and stir-fry the noodles for 3-4 minutes, then transfer to a warmed plate. Add the ginger and garlic to the pan and cook for 1 minute. Add the scallions, sliced chilies, beansprouts and shrimp, and sauté for 2 minutes. Remove and keep warm. Heat a little more oil and sauté the cabbage, bamboo shoots, drained mushrooms and bean curd for 2 minutes.

In another pan, fry the meat until lightly colored, then season with fish sauce, chili powder and salt. Pour over the stock, bring to the boil and cook for 5 minutes or until the meat is tender. Thicken the gravy with cornstarch mixed with a little cold water. Pour the meat over the vegetables, adding the beansprouts and shrimp. Mix well, then spoon over the noodles. Serve with Chinese brown vinegar or chopped chili mixed with soy sauce.

Note: Prepare half the above amount if served with other dishes.

Fried Wheat Noodles

Serves 4: 8 oz (250 g) dried wheat noodles; 3 tablespoons oil; 1 slice fresh ginger, very finely chopped; 1–2 garlic cloves, very finely chopped; 6–8 shallots, or 1 medium-size red or brown onion, sliced; 3½ oz (100 g) raw shrimp; 2–3 dried black mushrooms, soaked and shredded; small bunch Chinese mustard greens or 4 leaves beet greens; 3½ oz (100 g) red barbecued pork, sliced; 1 tablespoon light soy sauce

Cook the noodles in plenty of rapidly boiling water for 2–3 minutes, separating the strands with a chopstick or fork. Drain and toss with 1 tablespoon of the oil to prevent the noodles sticking together. Spread out and leave aside.

Heat the remaining oil in a skillet and gently fry the ginger, garlic and shallots until soft and golden. Add the shrimp and mushrooms, and cook, stirring, until the shrimp turn pink. Tear the vegetable leaves into small pieces and add to the pan. Cook for 2–3 minutes, then add the meat and heat through for 30 seconds.

Raise the heat and add the noodles. Cook for 1 minute, stirring constantly. Pour over the soy sauce and serve immediately. The dish can be garnished with sliced red chili and scallion, and served with a chili *sambal* (see page 185).

G

Ginger Rice

Serves 6–8: 2 cups (12 oz) short grain white rice; 1 teaspoon salt; 1 large onion, coarsely chopped; 2-in (5-cm) piece fresh ginger, coarsely chopped; 3 cups (24 fl oz) hottest tap water; 4 tablespoons (2 oz) unsalted butter

Put the rice and salt into a large casserole. Place the onion and ginger in a food processor or blender. Puree, then transfer to a clean cloth and squeeze to remove as much liquid as possible. Add this to the rice with the water. Cover and microwave on HIGH (100%) for 14–16 minutes, stirring twice. When ready, remove from the oven and place a double thickness of paper towel over the rice. Cover and let stand for 6–8 minutes. Stir in the butter and serve.

For variety, add 1–2 finely chopped scallions and very fine slivers of fresh ginger. Serve with oriental poultry, fish or vegetable dishes.

Note: To make a delicious quick meal, add small cubes of boneless chicken or pork to the rice after 6–7 minutes and add florets of broccoli in the last 4–5 minutes. Increase cooking time by about 6 minutes, or until the meat and rice are both tender and the liquid has been completely absorbed. Garnish with fine julienne strips of red pepper.

Goose Liver Pilaf

Serves 4: 6 tablespoons (3 oz) butter; 1 tablespoon olive oil or vegetable oil; 1 large onion, halved and sliced; 8 oz (250 g) goose livers, trimmed and cut into ½-in (1-cm) slices; 10 scallions, white and green parts, cut into ½-in (1-cm) lengths; 2 oz (60 g) pine nuts; 1½ oz (45 g) seedless raisins; 4 oz (125 g) dried apricots, chopped; 1½ teaspoons salt, or to taste; ½ teaspoon freshly ground black pepper; 13 oz

Goose Liver Pilaf

Ginger Rice

(410 g) long grain rice; 1 teaspoon sugar; 2 teaspoons lemon juice; 2 teaspoons tomato paste; 1 teaspoon dried dill; 2½ cups (20 fl oz) water or chicken stock

Melt one-third of the butter with the oil in a large skillet. Add the onion and fry gently until transparent. Add the livers and turn in the fat until they are just sealed. Stir in the scallions, half of the pine nuts, the raisins, apricots, salt and black pepper, mixing thoroughly. Cook for 2 minutes longer and remove from the heat.

Melt the remaining butter in a large flameproof casserole over moderate heat and add the rice, stirring until the grains are well coated. Cook until the rice changes color and begins to look milky white. Stir in the liver mixture and all the remaining ingredients except for the rest of the pine nuts. Bring to the boil, then reduce the heat until the stock is barely simmering. Cover and cook for 20 minutes or until the rice is tender and the liquid has been absorbed. When cooked, fork through the rice to separate the grains.

While the pilaf is cooking, sauté the remaining pine nuts in a little butter until golden. To serve, adjust the seasoning, pile the mixture onto a heated serving dish and garnish with the pine nuts.

Note: Any leftover pilaf can be frozen and used as a stuffing for roast goose or chicken.

Green Lasagne in the Emilia-Romagna style

Serves 6: Ragù: 6 tablespoons (3 oz) butter; 2 medium-size onions; 1 stalk celery; 1 medium-size carrot; 3 oz (90 g) prosciutto or bacon with fat; 1 lb (500 g) ground lean beef round (or 1½ lb (750 g) if you prefer a very meaty sauce); ⅔ cup (5 fl oz) dry wine, red or white; 2 cans (1 lb each) peeled tomatoes, seeded; 2 tablespoons tomato paste; 1 tablespoon finely chopped fresh oregano, or 2 teaspoons dried; salt and freshly ground black pepper
Béchamel: 4 tablespoons (2 oz) butter; ½ cup (2 oz) all purpose flour; 2 cups (16 fl oz) milk; 1 oz (30 g) Parmesan cheese, freshly grated; 3 oz (90 g) additional freshly grated Parmesan for sprinkling between each layer
Green Pasta: 4 cups (1 lb) all purpose flour, unsifted; 3 eggs (or 4 if they are small); 2 tablespoons corn or peanut oil; ¾ teaspoon salt; 4 oz (125 g) cooked weight of finely chopped, or lightly pureed, spinach

To make the ragù, melt the butter in a large heavy-based saucepan and add the finely chopped vegetables. Cook over moderate heat until the onions are golden. Add the prosciutto, also finely chopped, and cook a further 3–4 minutes.

Add the beef and cook until sealed, increase the heat, pour in the wine and keep simmering strongly until more than half the wine has evaporated. Stir in the tomatoes, lower the heat and stir in the tomato paste. Bring up to a simmer, then season with the oregano, a good pinch of salt and a very generous grind of pepper. Simmer for 45 minutes, uncovered, adding a little water if the ragù appears too dry.

Meanwhile prepare the béchamel. Melt the butter in a heavy-based saucepan, add the flour and stir until it is well combined. Cook for 4–5 minutes over low heat, making sure the roux does not burn. Warm the milk and pour it into the pan all at once, whisking to ensure a smooth texture. Continue cooking over very low heat, stirring occasionally, until the sauce is the consistency of cream. Melt in the Parmesan. If the béchamel becomes too thick, add more milk.

To make the pasta, make a well in the center of the flour and add the eggs, oil, salt and spinach. Use no water, as the moisture of the spinach will be more than enough. Have extra flour ready in case the dough is too sticky. Gradually incorporate the flour into the ingredients.

Knead the dough until smooth and elastic, then roll and cut into rectangular sheets about 6 in (15 cm) by 2 in (5 cm). Set over a rack to allow the pieces to dry, keeping them apart.

When the ragù has only 10 minutes of cooking time left, cook 4–5 pasta sheets at a time in boiling, salted water. Boil the pasta for no more than half a minute, then drop them into a sink full of cold water. If you leave them in the boiling water too long they will break up or stick together. Lay the sheets out on clean tea towels to dry until needed.

Layer the lasagne, slightly overlapping, in the base of a well-buttered dish. Spread over a layer of the ragù and then the béchamel, sprinkle with Parmesan cheese and repeat until the dish is full. Finish with a layer of pasta, the remains of the sauce, a good sprinkle of Parmesan, then dot with small pieces of butter. Cook in an oven preheated to 375°F (190°C) for 35 minutes and serve with a crisp green salad.

H

Herbed Rice Molds

Serves 4: 1¾ cups (14 fl oz) hottest tap water; ¾ teaspoon salt; 1 cup (6 oz) short grain white rice; 3 tablespoons (1½ oz) butter; 1 scallion, chopped; 1½ tablespoons chopped parsley; 2–3 teaspoons chopped fresh herbs, or ½–¾ teaspoon dried herbs

Pour the water into a large casserole, add the salt and microwave, covered, on HIGH (100%) for 5 minutes. Add the rice, stir well and microwave on HIGH (100%), uncovered, for 12–14 minutes, stirring twice. Cover the dish for the final 3 minutes of cooking. Remove from oven and cover the rice with a double thickness of paper towel. Cover and let stand for 5 minutes.

In a small dish, microwave the butter for 1 minute on MEDIUM (50%). Add the scallion and herbs, and cover with vented plastic wrap. Microwave on HIGH (100%) for 1 minute, then stir into the rice. Press the rice into four lightly oiled custard cups or other suitable molds and turn out quickly onto dinner plates if serving warm, or refrigerate until firm if serving cold.

To make an attractive centerpiece for a hot or cold meal or buffet, prepare a double quantity of the above recipe and press into a lightly oiled microwave ring cake dish. Turn out and serve warm, or chill and serve cold. The center may be filled with watercress or vegetables.

Hokkien Fried Noodles

Serves 6–8: 8 cups (2 liters) chicken stock; 2 lb (1 kg) fresh thick egg noodles or 12 oz (375 g) spaghetti; 2½ tablespoons peanut oil; 1 medium-size onion, finely chopped; 4 garlic cloves, minced; 2 tablespoons dried shrimp, soaked overnight; 6 oz (185 g) small peeled raw shrimp; 8 oz (250 g) beansprouts; 2 teaspoons chili powder; salt and pepper; 1 fresh red chili, shredded; 4 oz (125 g) cooked shrimp, chopped; 2 hard-cooked eggs
Sauce: 2 medium-size onions; 2 tablespoons oil; 3½ oz (100 g) raw shrimp, finely chopped; 2 squares soft bean curd, diced; 1½ cups chicken or fish stock; 1–2 fresh red chilies, chopped; dark soy sauce to taste; salt and pepper; 1 teaspoon cornstarch

Bring the chicken stock to the boil and drop in the noodles. Cook for about 8 minutes until tender but not soft. Drain and spread on a tray to cool and dry.

Prepare the sauce. Fry the chopped onions in oil for 2 minutes, then add the chopped shrimp and diced bean curd and cook on moderate heat for 3–4 minutes. Pour in the chicken or fish stock and add the chopped chili. Bring to the boil, lower the heat and cook for 10 minutes. Season with soy sauce, salt and pepper. Thicken with cornstarch mixed with a little cold water, stirring until the sauce thickens and clears. Set aside and keep warm.

Heat the oil in a skillet or wok and fry the chopped onion and garlic until golden, then add the drained dried shrimp and fresh shrimp, both finely chopped. Sauté for 3 minutes before adding the noodles and beansprouts. Sauté for a further 3 minutes, then stir in the chili powder and salt and pepper to taste.

Arrange the noodles on a large serving plate, garnish with shredded chili and cooked shrimp and arrange the sliced boiled eggs around the edge of the plate. Reheat the sauce and serve separately or pour over the noodles just before serving.

Note: Hokkien Fried Noodles can be served as a main course or as a side dish, using half the ingredients.

I

Indian Fried Noodles

Serves 4: 1 lb (500 g) fresh yellow egg noodles; ½ cup (4 fl oz) oil; 1 square hard bean curd, cut into small dice; 1 medium-size red or brown onion, chopped; 1 medium-size tomato, finely chopped; 2 tablespoons coarsely chopped coarse chives or scallion; 1 sprig curry leaves, finely chopped; 2 tablespoons tomato sauce; 1 tablespoon chili sauce; 2 teaspoons light soy sauce; 2 eggs, lightly beaten; 1 boiled potato, skinned and cut into small dice; 1 fresh green chili, sliced

Rinse the noodles in warm water, drain and set aside. Heat the oil in a skillet and fry the bean curd until golden brown. Drain and set aside. Cook the onion in the same oil for 2–3 minutes, until soft, then add the drained noodles, tomato, chives, curry leaves and the three sauces. Simmer over gentle heat, stirring frequently, for 3–4 minutes.

Pour over the beaten egg and leave to set for about 45 seconds before stirring to mix it in well with the noodles. Add the potato and bean curd, stir, cook for another 30 seconds and put on a large serving dish. Garnish with green chili and serve with additional tomato and chili sauce to be added according to taste.

Indonesian Fried Rice (Nasi Goreng)

Serves 4: 4½ cups (1⅛ liter) chicken stock; 2 teaspoons tamarind; 11 oz (345 g) rice; 3 medium-size onions; 4 garlic cloves; 1 tablespoon oil; 1 large tomato, sliced; 1½ teaspoons dried shrimp paste; 2 teaspoons chili powder; 3½ oz (100 g) lean beef, shredded; salt and white pepper; 1 stalk celery, sliced; 1 fresh red chili, finely chopped; 2 eggs; dry fried onion flakes (see page 151)

Bring the stock to the boil and add the tamarind and well-washed rice. Boil for 12–15 minutes, or until the rice is tender but not too soft. Drain, rinse in cold water and set aside to cool. Break up the tamarind and stir well to mix into the rice.

Peel and slice the onions and garlic, then fry in hot oil until soft. Add the tomato, shrimp paste and chili powder and cook for 2 minutes. Put in the beef and season with salt and pepper. Sauté for 3–4 minutes, stirring frequently. Add the sliced celery and chopped chili and cook for a further 2 minutes. Remove and set aside.

Wipe out the pan and oil lightly. Beat the eggs and pour into the pan. Cook in a thin omelet until set, then break up with a fork and add to the cooked beef mixture.

Add 2 tablespoons of oil to the pan and stir-fry the rice for 5 minutes. Stir in the cooked mixture and season with salt and pepper and a little soy sauce if desired. Garnish with fried onion flakes.

L

Lasagne Ferrara Style

Serves 4: 1 onion, chopped; 1 carrot, chopped; 1 stalk celery, chopped; 3 tablespoons (1½ oz) butter; 1 cup (5 oz) prosciutto, chopped; 8 oz (250 g) beef, ground; 1 cup (8 fl oz) dry white wine; 2½ cups (1¼ lb) canned peeled tomatoes, chopped; salt and freshly ground black pepper; 12 oz (375 g) lasagne noodles; 1½ cups (6 oz) grated Parmesan cheese
Béchamel Sauce: 2 tablespoons (1 oz) butter;

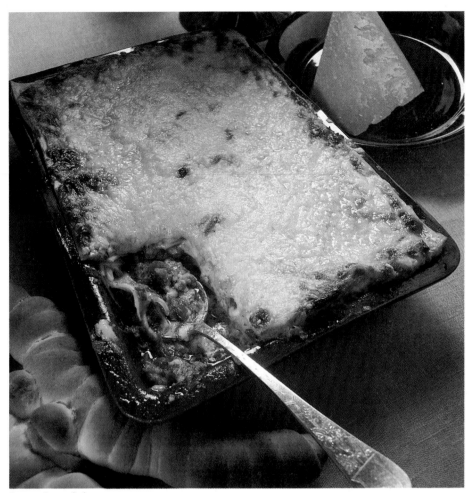
Lasagne Ferrara Style

2 tablespoons all purpose flour; 1½–2 cups (12–16 fl oz) hot milk; ¼ teaspoon nutmeg

Sauté the onion, carrot and celery in the butter, add the prosciutto and cook for 6 minutes. Add the ground beef and brown, stirring constantly, then pour in the wine and cook until it has almost completely evaporated. Mix in the tomatoes, season, lower the heat and simmer for 1 hour. If too much of the liquid evaporates, add some water.

Cook the lasagne in plenty of salted boiling water and when still quite firm, remove it from the heat and rinse it in cold water.

To make the béchamel, melt the butter in a saucepan, add the flour and cook, stirring constantly, for 5 minutes. Whisk in the hot milk and simmer for 10–15 minutes, stirring occasionally. Season and add the nutmeg.

Grease an ovenproof dish and arrange alternate layers of lasagne, meat sauce and

béchamel, sprinkled with some of the Parmesan. Finish with a layer of béchamel sprinkled with the rest of the cheese. Bake in an oven preheated to 400°F (200°C) for 30–45 minutes.

Lasagne with Mushroom Sauce

Serves 4: 6 tablespoons (3 oz) butter; 1 small onion, finely chopped; 1 garlic clove, finely chopped; 1 lb (500 g) canned peeled tomatoes; pinch dried oregano; 2 tablespoons finely chopped parsley; 8 oz (250 g) mushrooms, coarsely sliced; salt and freshly ground black pepper; 12 oz (375 g) lasagne; Parmesan cheese, freshly grated

Heat 2 tablespoons (1 oz) of the butter in a heavy-based pan and fry the onion and garlic until the onion is golden and soft.

An Italian variation of Greek meatballs (see p. 269) using tomato and basil.

Drain the excess liquid from the can of tomatoes and chop them into small pieces. Add them to the pan along with the oregano and parsley, and bring just to the boil. Add the mushrooms and simmer, uncovered, for a further 25–30 minutes. Add the salt and pepper. The sauce should now be quite thick. Keep warm until required.

Meanwhile, cook the lasagne in ample boiling, salted water. When it reaches the al dente stage, drain thoroughly and return to the cooking pan. Add the remaining butter and toss the pasta as it melts. Transfer the lasagne to a preheated serving dish, pour the sauce over and serve with the Parmesan cheese on the side.

Lasagne with Veal and Pork

Serves 6: 1 quantity pasta dough (see page 101)
Ragù: 5 tablespoons (2½ oz) butter; 1 medium-size onion, finely chopped; 1 medium-size carrot, finely chopped; 1 stalk celery, finely chopped; 1 lb (500 g) lean pork and veal, twice ground together; 1 lb (500 g) canned peeled tomatoes, or fresh tomatoes, scalded, peeled, seeded and chopped; 1 tablespoon tomato paste; 3 basil leaves (optional);
1 tablespoon chopped parsley; sprig of oregano, finely chopped; ½ teaspoon dried thyme or 1 teaspoon fresh thyme, finely chopped; salt and freshly ground black pepper
Béchamel Sauce: 4 tablespoons (2 oz) butter; ½ cup (2 oz) all purpose flour; 2 cups (16 fl oz) milk; 1 oz (30 g) Parmesan cheese, freshly grated; 5 oz (155 g) additional freshly grated Parmesan cheese for sprinkling between each layer

To make the ragù, melt the butter in a medium-size saucepan and sauté the onion, carrot and celery. Cook over a moderate heat until the onion is golden. Add the meat and brown evenly.

Put the canned tomatoes through a food mill and add to the pan together with the tomato paste, all the herbs, a good pinch of salt and the pepper. Simmer over moderate heat, uncovered, for 30–40 minutes, stirring now and then.

Meanwhile, prepare the béchamel. In a heavy-based saucepan, melt the butter and add the flour, stirring until absorbed. Cook for 4–5 minutes over a gentle heat, making sure the roux does not burn. Meanwhile, warm the milk, then pour it into the pan, whisking to make sure it is very smooth. Simmer for 20 minutes over a very low heat and when it has thickened to a creamy consistency, add the Parmesan.

Roll out the pasta and cut the sheets into rectangles approximately 6 × 2 in (15 × 5 cm).

Drop 4–5 pieces of lasagne at a time into a pan of boiling, salted water for no more than 1 minute, then lift them carefully and drop into a sink full of cold water. Lay them out on clean tea towels to dry until required.

Place a layer of lasagne in the bottom of a well-buttered, shallow dish, overlapping the strips slightly. Spread a layer of béchamel over it, then a thin layer of the meat sauce. Sprinkle with a light dusting of grated Parmesan. Repeat this process until you have used all the sauce. Place a final layer of lasagne on top, sprinkle with Parmesan and dot with small knobs of butter. Cook in an oven preheated to 400°F (200°C) for 35 minutes.

Linguine with Squid

Serves 4: 1 lb (500 g) squid; 1 lb (500 g) canned peeled tomatoes; 1 teaspoon finely chopped cilantro; 1 teaspoon finely chopped parsley; 2 garlic cloves; ½ small red chili (optional); ¼ cup (2 fl oz) olive oil; salt and freshly ground black pepper; 1 lb (500 g) linguine (or fettuccine)

Clean the squid thoroughly and cut into small strips. Chop the tomatoes roughly in their juice and pour the entire contents of the can into a heavy-based pan with a tight-fitting lid. Add the squid, cilantro and parsley. Cut the garlic cloves into four slivers, crush them gently and add to the pan with the chili (if desired) and the olive oil. Next add a pinch of salt and a good grind of black pepper.

Bring the sauce to simmering point, then cover tightly with the lid, reduce the heat and simmer slowly for 30 minutes or more. The exact cooking time will depend on the squid. Check every now and then, both for tenderness and to make sure that the mixture is not sticking to the bottom of the pot. When the sauce is ready, remove the slivers of garlic.

Cook the linguine in plenty of boiling, salted water until al dente, drain and mix with the sauce. Serve immediately.

Note: If possible use extra vergine olive oil. This is the purest oil available and has the best flavor.

Lasagne with Veal and Pork

Linguine with Squid

Lotus Rice

Lotus Rice

Serves 8–10: 1 fresh or dried lotus leaf; 6 oz (185 g) boneless chicken breast, diced; 4 oz (125 g) roast duck or pork, diced; 4 oz (125 g) raw peeled shrimp, or 2 tablespoons soaked, dried shrimp; 3 oz (90 g) canned straw mushrooms or button mushrooms, drained and diced, or use 4 dried black mushrooms, soaked and diced; 2½ tablespoons softened lard or oil; 1½ tablespoons finely chopped scallion; ½ teaspoon grated fresh ginger; 1¾ teaspoons salt; 1 tablespoon light soy sauce; 2 teaspoons sesame oil (optional); ¼ teaspoon ground black pepper; 4 cups cooked white rice

Soak the dried lotus leaf or blanch the fresh leaf until softened, then squeeze out the water and brush the underside with oil.

Stir-fry the chicken, duck or pork, shrimp and mushrooms in the lard or oil for 2 minutes, then add the scallion and ginger, and cook briefly. Add the salt, soy sauce, sesame oil, if used, and the black pepper, then mix in the rice. Stir thoroughly on moderate heat until evenly blended.

Place the lotus leaf in a wide bowl and pile the rice onto it. Fold in the sides to enclose the rice completely, then invert the parcel so the folds are underneath. Set the bowl on a rack in a steamer and steam over high heat for 15–20 minutes.

Serve hot with the top of the leaf parcel cut open to give access to the rice. If preferred, wrap the rice in smaller individual parcels.

Note: This dish may also be made with steamed glutinous rice. It is a popular dish in dim sum restaurants and makes a delicious alternative to plain white rice at dinner.

M

Macaroni and Eggplant Pie

Serves 4: 1 lb (500 g) eggplant; salt; oil for frying; flour for coating eggplant; 2 eggs; 2 oz (60 g) all purpose flour; 2 tablespoons (1 oz) butter; salt and freshly ground black pepper; 2 cups (16 fl oz) milk or 1½ cups (12 fl oz) milk and ½ cup (4 fl oz) chicken stock if available; 2 oz (60 g) Parmesan cheese, freshly grated; 2 oz (60 g) lean ham, diced; 3 oz (90 g) cooked chicken, diced; 6 oz (185 g) macaroni; 2 or 3 tomatoes, depending on size, very thinly sliced; 8 oz (250 g) mozzarella cheese;

1½ tablespoons finely chopped parsley; 8 fresh basil leaves, finely chopped

Wash the eggplant, cut off the tops and bottoms, but do not peel. Cut into slices about ¼ in (5 mm) thick (or even thinner if you can manage it easily) and sprinkle freely with salt. Leave for 45 minutes or more to degorge. Dry the slices with paper towels and fry in oil until tender, about 3 minutes on each side. Pat dry with paper towels to absorb the excess oil, flour the slices lightly, then dip in the lightly beaten eggs and fry again until they turn golden. Drain on paper towels.

Meanwhile, make a béchamel. Melt the butter in a heavy-based saucepan, then add the flour, stirring with a wooden spoon. Cook over a low heat for 3 minutes, then season to taste. Warm the milk and add to the butter and flour, whisking until the sauce is smooth, and a little thinner than a normal béchamel (if it is too thick, add more milk). Add the Parmesan and stir again; the cheese will thicken the sauce, which should now be the consistency of heavy cream. Add the ham and the cooked chicken to the béchamel. At the same time, cook the macaroni in plenty of boiling salted water until just al dente, drain well and combine with the béchamel.

Butter an 8 × 3-in (20 × 8-cm) deep ovenproof dish. Place one circle of eggplant in the center, and arrange slightly overlapping circles around it, like the petals on a daisy. They should extend up the sides of the dish. Cut enough circles in half to extend the lining of eggplant almost to the top of the dish, making sure there is enough eggplant to cover the dish. Spoon a good thick layer of the béchamel and macaroni mixture into the bottom of the casserole, then cover it with a layer of tomatoes and dot with one-third of the diced mozzarella. Sprinkle over half of the parsley and basil, then add a second generous layer of the béchamel and macaroni, another of tomatoes, mozzarella, parsley and basil and a final thin layer of the sauce and macaroni. Dot with the remaining mozzarella, then cover with the rest of the eggplant, pressing the sides and top together gently to seal the pie. Sprinkle over the remaining ½ oz (15 g) of Parmesan and cover with aluminum foil. Bake in an oven preheated to 375°F (190°C) for 30 minutes.

Leave the pie in a warm place for 4–5 minutes, then invert onto a serving plate and cut into slices as you would a cake.

Macaroni and Eggplant Pie

Macaroni and Pork Pie

Macaroni and Pork Pie

Serves 6–8: Pork Marinade: 10 oz (315 g) lean pork loin; 1 sprig oregano or ½ teaspoon dried oregano; 1 sprig rosemary or ½ teaspoon dried rosemary; 1 garlic clove, crushed; 1 scant teaspoon raw sugar; 1 tablespoon dry white wine; 1 tablespoon vinegar; salt and freshly ground black pepper
Pastry: 12 oz (375 g) all purpose flour; 13 tablespoons (6½ oz) butter, chopped; 1 egg, lightly beaten; pinch of salt; ½ cup (4 fl oz) cold white wine
Filling: 6 tablespoons (3 oz) butter; 1 onion, chopped; ½ cup (4 fl oz) dry white wine; 6 oz (185 g) mushrooms; 1 teaspoon finely chopped fennel (see Note); 1 generous tablespoon chopped parsley; 4 ripe tomatoes, peeled, seeded and chopped; salt and freshly ground black pepper; 12 oz (375 g) macaroni or other hollow pasta
Béchamel Sauce: 6 tablespoons (3 oz) butter; 3 oz (90 g) all purpose flour; 3 cups (24 fl oz) milk, warmed

To prepare the marinade, trim any fat off the pork and chop it very finely. Put it into a container with an airtight lid and add the oregano, rosemary and garlic. Sprinkle the sugar over these, then pour over the wine and the vinegar and add the salt and pepper. Marinate, covered, in the refrigerator for 12–24 hours. Shake the container every so often. Strain the marinated pork and discard the liquid.

To make the pastry, put the flour into a food processor or blender, add the butter, then use an "on-off" motion to mix until crumbly. Add the egg and salt, then the wine, a little at a time, until the dough begins to form into a ball. It should not be too dry. Turn the dough out onto a floured surface and divide into two-thirds and one-third. Cover with plastic wrap and leave for at least 1 hour.

To make the filling, heat 3 tablespoons (1½ oz) butter in a small pan, add the onion and cook until golden. Add the marinated pork and simmer for a few minutes, then pour in the wine and return to a simmer. When the liquid has reduced by half, lower the heat and cook slowly for 5 minutes.

Meanwhile, sauté the sliced mushrooms in the remaining butter in a large skillet. After 2–3 minutes, lower the heat and add the marinated pork, onion and wine mixture, the fennel and parsley and tomatoes. Season to taste with salt and pepper and simmer for 10–12 minutes.

Cook the macaroni for 5–6 minutes in plenty of boiling salted water. It should still be firm. Drain well, transfer to the meat mixture, mix gently and put on one side.

To prepare the béchamel, melt the butter in a heavy-based pan, add the flour and stir until absorbed. Cook for 4–5 minutes, taking care that the roux does not burn. Pour in the warm milk and whisk until smooth, then cook over very low heat, stirring occasionally until it is the consistency of cream. Combine the béchamel with the macaroni and meat mixture in the skillet.

Roll out the 2 balls of pastry dough on a floured board to form two circles, one about 14 in (36 cm) and the other about 11 in (28 cm) across. Butter a round 9-in (23-cm) baking dish, or a cake pan with a removable base. Line it with the larger pastry circle. Pour the mixture from the skillet into the pie shell, then cover with the smaller circle, pinch the edges closely together all round and brush with lightly beaten egg. Use any leftover pastry pieces to decorate the top and brush these also with egg. Make a few air holes in the pastry top with a skewer.

Bake in an oven preheated to 425°F (220°C) for 40–45 minutes or until the pastry is gold in color. Transfer the pie to a warmed serving plate and cut into wedges at the table.

Note: If fennel is unavailable, double the amount of parsley.

Macaroni with Cheese and Ham

Serves 4: 8 oz (250 g) macaroni; 2½ cups (20 fl oz) milk; ½ teaspoon chicken stock granules; 1 teaspoon salt; pinch each of dry mustard and nutmeg; ¼ teaspoon pepper; 1 bay leaf; 3 tablespoons cornstarch; 8 oz (250 g) grated mozzarella cheese; 4 oz (125 g) lean ham; paprika for garnish

Cook the macaroni and set aside in a colander to drain.

Pour the milk into a large microwave-safe jug and add the remaining ingredients, except the cheese, ham and paprika. Stir until the cornstarch is well mixed, then microwave on HIGH (100%) for about 8 minutes, stirring 3–4 times. Add the cheese and ham. Stir in but do not microwave.

Pour half the pasta into a heatproof serving dish and cover with half the sauce. Stir in lightly. Add the remaining pasta and cover with the remaining sauce, again stirring it in lightly. Sprinkle lightly with paprika or leave the top plain as preferred. Reheat for 6 minutes on MEDIUM–HIGH (70%), uncovered. If preparing in advance, preheat for 15 minutes on MEDIUM (50%), covered for the first 10 minutes.

If you have a browning element, reheat for half the time, then brown the top with the element on HIGH (100%).

Macaroni with Cheese and Ham

Macaroni Shells with Clam Sauce

Serves 4–6: 8 oz (250 g) macaroni shells; ¼ cup (2 fl oz) olive oil; 2 garlic cloves, crushed; ¼ cup (2 fl oz) water; 1½ teaspoons chopped parsley; ½ teaspoon salt; ¼ teaspoon dried oregano; dash of pepper; 1 cup clams (one 8 oz (250 g) can), whole or minced, with liquid; 4 tablespoons (2 oz) butter

Cook the macaroni in a big pan of boiling salted water until al dente, then drain and keep hot in a covered pan.

Heat the oil in a skillet, then add the garlic and cook until golden. Slowly stir in the water. Add the parsley, salt, oregano, pepper and clams with their liquid. Mix well. Melt and add the butter in small quantities. Pour the clam sauce over the shells and serve.

Note: Gnocchi (see page 308) may be used instead of macaroni shells. Other shellfish may be used with the clams.

Mushroom and Bacon Topping for Pasta ★

Serves 2: 4 oz (125 g) fresh mushrooms, thinly sliced; 1½ slices bacon, shredded; 6 tablespoons (3 oz) butter, cut into small cubes; 2 tablespoons finely chopped parsley; ¾ cup (6 fl oz) cream; salt and black pepper

Place the mushrooms, bacon and butter in a covered vegetable dish and microwave on HIGH (100%) for 4 minutes. Add the parsley, cream and seasoning. Microwave on HIGH (100%) for 3 minutes. Pour over the pasta and reheat on MEDIUM (50%).

Pour the cream over.

N

Noodle Baskets

Makes 6: 5 cakes of thin egg noodles, approx. 8 oz (250 g); oil for deep frying

Soak the noodles in cold water until they separate. Drain very thoroughly by spreading on several layers of paper towels and covering with more paper.

Select two wire strainers, one slightly larger than the other. Dip them in deep oil, then shake to remove most of the oil. Divide the noodles into six equal portions. Line the larger strainer with a portion of the noodles and press the smaller strainer inside to form the noodles into a nest or basket shape.

Heat the oil to hot. Place the strainers in the oil, holding the two handles firmly together. Cook for about 2 minutes until the smaller basket can be lifted out without disturbing the noodles, then continue to cook until golden and crisp. Lift out, drain well, then invert onto absorbent paper. Tap the bottom of the strainer to release the basket. Leave to drain upside down until needed.

Unused noodle baskets can be stored in an airtight container and warmed in a moderate oven when needed. To use, stand the baskets on a plate and surround with parsley or celery leaves. Fill with the prepared dish and serve.

Line the large strainer with noodles.

Press the small strainer inside to form a basket shape.

Noodles with Clams

Serves 6: ½ cup (4 fl oz) oil; 1 garlic clove, crushed; 2 onions, chopped; 2 red or green bell peppers, seeded and roughly chopped; 2 tomatoes, peeled and chopped; 2 sprigs parsley, chopped; 2 lb (1 kg) clams; 2 cups (16 fl oz) water; 10 oz (300 g) spaghetti; ¼ teaspoon saffron; salt and freshly ground black pepper

Heat the oil in a saucepan and sauté the garlic, onions, peppers, tomatoes and

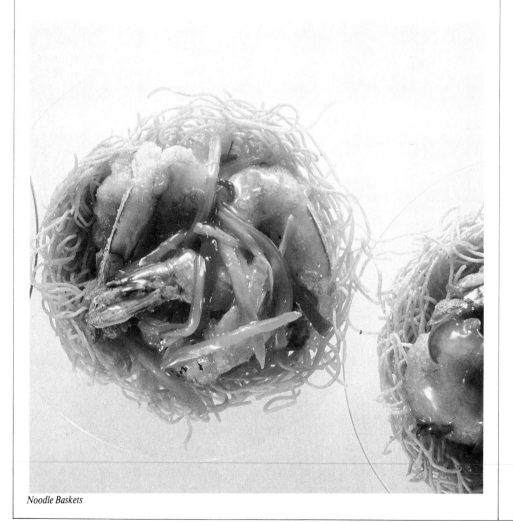

Noodle Baskets

Mushroom and Bacon Topping for Pasta

thickening agent. Heat the gravy through thoroughly.

If using fresh noodles, scald in boiling water for 1 minute, then drain thoroughly. If using dried noodles, boil as directed on the package until just cooked, then drain.

To serve, put some of the noodles and beansprouts into the bottom of large individual bowls and pour the gravy over. Garnish with the listed items. Alternatively, if you have a very large deep bowl, it can be served in this, with diners helping themselves.

Note: Slice the onions so they are paper-thin and evenly cut, then fry in deep hot oil until golden. Cook slowly so all the moisture is cooked out. Alternatively, placed dried onion flakes in a wire mesh ladle and deep fry for a couple of seconds.

Nori-Rolled Sushi

Makes 16 pieces: 2 sheets dried laver (nori); *4 dried black mushrooms* (shiitake); *½ cup (4 fl oz)* dashi; *2 tablespoons light soy sauce; 1 tablespoon sweet rice wine* (mirin); *2 teaspoons sugar; ½ oz (15 g) strips of dried gourd* (kampyo); *¼ cup water; 2 teaspoons salt; 1½ cups (12 fl oz)* dashi; *3 tablespoons dark soy sauce; 1 teaspoon sugar; 1 Japanese cucumber or ½ regular Western cucumber; approximately 2½ cups (12 oz) basic sushi (see page 159)*
Dipping Sauce: ¼ cup light soy sauce; 1 tablespoon sweet rice wine (mirin).

Toast the *nori* by passing it briefly through a flame. Place it on a bamboo mat with the shorter side facing you, ready for the rice and other ingredients.

Soak the dried mushrooms in hot water for 30 minutes, discard the stems and cut the caps into strips about ¼ in (5 mm) wide. Simmer in ½ cup (4 fl oz) *dashi*, 2 tablespoons light soy sauce, 1 tablespoon *mirin* and 2 teaspoons sugar until the mushrooms are soft and most of the liquid has been absorbed. This should take about 20 minutes. Drain off any liquid and cool to room temperature.

Rub the strips of dried gourd in the water with the salt, then rinse well and simmer in water until soft. Drain and put into a pan with 1½ cups (12 fl oz) *dashi*, dark soy sauce and sugar. Simmer the dried gourd strips for a further 15 minutes, then drain and cool to room temperature.

If using Japanese cucumber, do not peel or seed, but cut into very fine strips about 4 in (10 cm) long. With other cucumbers,

parsley until onions are soft and transparent.

Place the clams in a separate saucepan, add the water, cover and heat until the clams open. Discard any shells that do not open. Strain the water into the saucepan with the onion mixture, adding more if necessary. Bring this to the boil, add the noodles and cook until al dente. Add the clams and saffron and season to taste. Serve hot with fresh crusty bread.

Noodles with Meat and Rich Sauce

Serves 6–8: 1 lb (500 g) beef round in one piece; 1 stalk celery with leaves; 1 teaspoon salt; freshly ground black pepper; cold water; 1 lb (500 g) fresh egg noodles or 8 oz (250 g) dried wheat noodles; 8 oz (250 g) beansprouts, scalded.
Gravy: 8–12 dried red chilies, soaked; 3 candlenuts or macadamias; 8–10 shallots or 1½ medium-size red or brown onions; 3 slices lengkuas;
2 tablespoons oil; 2 teaspoons coriander, freshly ground; 2 teaspoons salted soy beans, mashed; ½ cup mashed boiled sweet potato
Garnish: 2 scallions, finely chopped; fried onion flakes (see Note); celery leaves; 1 fresh green and 1 fresh red chili, sliced; 3 pieces hard bean curd, deep fried and sliced; 3–4 Chinese limes, halved, or 1 lemon cut in wedges

Put the beef into a saucepan with the celery, salt and pepper. Pour in just enough water to cover, then simmer gently until cooked. Dice the meat and reserve 2 cups of beef stock.

To prepare the gravy, grind the chilies, candlenuts, shallots and *lengkuas* together and fry in oil in a deep pan for 3–5 minutes. Add the cilantro and cook for another minute before putting in the salted soy beans. Fry gently for another couple of minutes, then add the diced beef. Mix thoroughly, then add the sweet potato. Slowly add the stock, stirring well to incorporate the sweet potato, which acts as a

151

peel, discard the seeds and cut into fine strips as for Japanese cucumber.

Have ready a small bowl of water mixed with a tablespoonful of rice vinegar for moistening your hands as you work with the sushi. Spread half the prepared sushi evenly over the sheet of toasted *nori*, taking it to the edge closest to you and spreading it right to the sides. Leave about 1 in (2.5 cm) of the end furthest away from you uncovered.

Arrange half of the cooked dried mushrooms, strips of gourd and cucumber strips carefully across the rice, about one-third of the way up. Lift up the sheet of *nori* closest to you with both hands and carefully push down the ingredients. Raise the end of the bamboo mat to enclose the roll and roll it up to meet the far end of the sheet of *nori*. Press lightly on the rolled up bamboo mat for about 30 seconds, then unroll onto a cutting board. Use a very sharp knife to cut the *nori* roll into 8 equal pieces.

Repeat the procedure with the remaining sheet of *nori* and other ingredients. Serve with slices of pickled ginger and the combined ingredients for the dipping sauce.

Note: Thin strips of omelet, flaked canned tuna, strips of raw tuna or lightly cooked shrimp can also be added as fillings.

Lift up the sheet of nori and push down the ingredients.

Cut the roll into 8 equal pieces.

Nori-Rolled Sushi

Paella

O

Oven-Baked Thin Spaghetti with Spinach

Serves 4: 8 oz (250 g) frozen chopped spinach, or 1 lb (500 g) fresh; salt; 4 anchovy fillets, chopped; 4 oz (125 g) canned tuna fish in oil; 2 tablespoons finely chopped parsley; 2 small garlic cloves, crushed; 2 teaspoons dried basil; 1/3 cup (2½ fl oz) olive oil; 1 tablespoon pine nuts, finely chopped; 1 lb (500 g) spaghettini; dried breadcrumbs

Cook the spinach in a small amount of salted water, then drain, reserving the cooking water.

Puree the spinach in a blender or food processor and place in a bowl. Put the anchovies and flaked tuna into the bowl, together with the parsley. Add the garlic and the dried basil.

Heat the oil in a pan and add the contents of the bowl. Fry gently, while stirring, for a few minutes, then add the pine nuts. After a further 3 minutes correct the consistency of the sauce with a little of the spinach water; it should be thin enough to pour easily.

Boil the spaghettini in a large pan of salted boiling water for 4 minutes only, then drain thoroughly. Place a layer in the bottom of a lightly buttered shallow casserole dish, pour half the sauce over, then add another layer of spaghettini followed by a second layer of sauce. Sprinkle with breadcrumbs and bake in an oven preheated to 200°C (400°F).

When the breadcrumbs are brown, after about 15–20 minutes, remove and serve. Red, ripe tomato halves look and taste wonderful with this simple pie.

P

Paella

Serves 6: 3 cups (1 lb) raw long grain rice; ½ cup (4 fl oz) olive oil; 1/3 teaspoon saffron; 1½ teaspoons salt; 3 chorizo sausages; 2 large slices bacon or 2 slices raw smoked ham; 1 medium-size onion, chopped; 6 oz (185 g) boneless chicken; 6 oz (185 g) fish fillets; 6 large raw shrimp in the shell; 12 pitted black olives; 6 cups (1.5 liters) chicken stock or water; 1 green bell pepper; 1 red bell pepper; ½ cup frozen green peas, thawed; 12 clams or mussels, in the shell; 1 medium-size sand crab, approx. 10 oz (315 g)

Place the rice in a large skillet or wok with the olive oil, saffron and salt, and sauté until the rice turns a light golden color. Add the sliced chorizo sausage, diced bacon or ham and the onion, and continue

Add the chorizo, bacon or ham and onion.

Add the shrimp.

Pour in the chicken stock or water.

Garnish with mussels and crab.

to sauté, stirring continually, until the bacon begins to crisp and the onion is lightly colored.

Cut the chicken and fish into cubes. Add to the pan with the shrimp, washed but not shelled, and the olives. Add about 5½ cups chicken stock or water and bring briskly to the boil, stirring. Reduce the heat, cover the pan and simmer very gently.

Remove stems, seeds and inner ribs from the peppers and cut them into small squares. Add to the rice, together with the peas, scrubbed clams or mussels and the crab, which has been cut into large pieces and inedible parts removed. Re-cover the pan and simmer for a further 8–10 minutes until the rice and all ingredients are tender.

Stir so that the meat and vegetables are evenly distributed in the rice.

Pasta and Vegetable Ring with Cream of Chicken Filling

Serves 4–6: 3 oz (90 g) linguine or fettuccine; 4 asparagus spears; ¼ of a red bell pepper or ¼ of a firm, red tomato; ¼ of a green bell pepper or ½ stalk celery; 2 tablespoons green peas; 5 large egg yolks; 3 slices white bread; 1½ cups (12 fl oz) milk; 4 tablespoons (2 oz) butter, diced; 3 oz (90 g) pecorino or Parmesan cheese, grated; 3 oz (90 g) fontina or Gruyère cheese, finely chopped; salt and freshly ground black pepper; 6–8 fresh basil leaves (or use parsley sprigs)
Creamed Chicken: 2 chicken breasts; 4 tablespoons (2 oz) butter; 2 oz (60 g) all purpose flour; pinch of dried sage; pinch of dried thyme; pinch of dried oregano; 1½ cups (12 fl oz) milk, warmed

Break the pasta into approximately 1½-in (3.5-cm) lengths and cook in boiling, salted water until al dente. Run under cold water to stop the cooking process, drain.

Cut the coarse part of the stalks from the asparagus spears, then cut the spears into ¾-in (2-cm) lengths. Place all the vegetables, including the green peas, in a small saucepan with very little boiling water and cook for 3–4 minutes, then drain.

Beat the egg yolks in a big mixing bowl. Remove the crusts from the bread and put it in a saucepan with the milk. Heat slowly to boiling point, then add to the eggs. Add the butter and let it melt through, then add the cheese. Add the strained vegetables and the precooked pasta. Season to taste with salt and pepper and mix gently, so as not to break the vegetables.

Butter a 10-in (25-cm) ring mold thoroughly and arrange the basil leaves around the bottom, pressing them into the butter. Carefully pour in the pasta and vegetable mixture without disturbing the basil and bake the mold in an oven preheated to 350°F (180°C) for approximately 45 minutes. Check to see if it is cooked by inserting a skewer into the center; if it comes out clean, the mold is ready. Leave to stand for a few minutes before inverting it onto a wide, flat plate.

Meantime, poach the chicken breasts in water, remove the skin and any bone, and chop into bite-size pieces. Make a roux by heating the butter in a saucepan, and adding the flour mixed with the herbs and seasonings. Cook over low heat for 3–4 minutes, then whisk in the milk all at once. Whisk into a smooth sauce and cook, stirring from time to time, until it is rich and creamy. Add the chicken pieces and mix through. Pile the chicken mixture in the center of the hot pasta mold and serve.

Potato Gnocchi with Beef Sauce

Serves 4: 1 tablespoon corn oil; 2 lb (1 kg) lean beef in one piece (sirloin or top round is best); 1 onion, finely chopped; 3 garlic cloves, crushed; 1 small red chili, cut into small pieces; 1 stalk celery, chopped; 1 scallion, chopped; 4 mushrooms, thinly sliced; 2 large ripe tomatoes, roughly chopped; ½ teaspoon ground coriander; ½ teaspoon dried basil; 1 tablespoon chopped parsley; salt and freshly ground black pepper; 1½ cups (12 fl oz) red wine; ¾ cup (6 fl oz) beef stock (use bouillon cube if desired); 1 recipe potato gnocchi (see page 308)

Heat the oil in a heavy-based casserole and brown the beef on all sides, then remove and set aside.

Add the onion, garlic and chili, and sauté until the onion is golden. Do not allow the garlic to brown. Add the celery, scallion, mushrooms and tomatoes to the pot, together with the herbs, a teaspoon of salt and plenty of black pepper. Cook the tomatoes and mushrooms for a few minutes, then pour in the wine and the beef stock. Bring to simmering point and return the beef to the pot. Depending on how you like your beef cooked, it will need to simmer, tightly covered, for between 50–70 minutes.

Transfer the beef to a low oven and keep warm. With the lid off, boil the sauce over high heat for 8–10 minutes until reduced and thickened, stirring often.

When the sauce is almost ready, reduce the heat to low and begin cooking the gnocchi in boiling, salted water. The moment they are cooked, drain them well, pour the sauce over and serve.

Carve the meat at the table and serve with seasonal vegetables.

Q

Quick Seafood Sauce for Pasta ★

Serves 2: 1 medium-size onion, finely chopped; 1½ tablespoons olive oil; 1 large tomato, peeled and chopped; 2–3 garlic cloves, chopped; 1 bay leaf; ¼ teaspoon each oregano, thyme and mixed herbs; 1 tablespoon tomato paste; ½ cup (4 fl oz) cream; 4 oz (125 g) peeled baby shrimp or canned mixed seafood; salt and pepper; 12 oz (350 g) spaghetti, cooked

Place the onion, oil, tomato and garlic in a covered vegetable dish and microwave on HIGH (100%) for 5 minutes. Add the herbs, tomato paste and cream, and microwave on MEDIUM (50%) for 4 minutes. Add the seafood, salt and pepper, pour over the pasta and reheat on MEDIUM (50%).

R

Ravioli Stuffed with Fish and Ricotta Cheese

*Serves 6: Stuffing: 1 lb (500 g) white, firm non-fatty fish, broiled; 1 bunch borage; 1 small bunch fresh herbs such as oregano or marjoram, finely chopped; 3½ oz (100 g) ricotta cheese; 1 cup (4 oz) grated Parmesan cheese; 2 whole eggs; ¼ teaspoon salt; freshly ground black pepper
5 scant cups (1 lb 3½ oz) all purpose flour; ¾ cup (6 fl oz) water; ½ cup (2 oz) Parmesan cheese, freshly grated*

To make the stuffing, remove all bones from the fish and mince it very finely. Wash the borage and the herbs, remove the leaves and blanch them in a little water for 3–4 minutes. Drain thoroughly, squeeze out all excess water and mince them very finely. In a bowl, combine the minced fish, borage and herbs. Add the rest of the stuffing ingredients and blend together thoroughly to a very fine paste.

To make the pasta, place the flour on a wooden board and form a well. Add the salt to the lukewarm water and carefully mix into the flour to make a flexible dough. Work the pasta vigorously for approximately 15 minutes. Roll into a ball and chill for 20 minutes.

Divide the pasta into 2–3 parts and roll one into a thin sheet. With a pastry wheel, cut the sheet into 3-in (7-cm) wide strips. With a teaspoon, spoon the stuffing approximately one finger's width apart on the lower half of the strip. Fold the upper half of the strip over the lower and firmly press it down so the edges around the stuffing are sealed. With the pastry wheel, cut the strip into individual ravioli. Repeat the above with the remaining pasta.

In a large saucepan, boil a generous amount of salted water and add the ravioli, a few at a time. Boil for approximately 15 minutes. Serve sprinkled with grated Parmesan cheese.

Rice Cooked in Coconut Milk

Serves 4: 2 cups (12 oz) long grain rice; 2½ cups (20 fl oz) coconut milk; 1 teaspoon salt; 1 pandan leaf (optional)

Wash the rice thoroughly, drain and set aside. Bring the coconut milk slowly to the boil, stirring constantly. Add the rice, salt and *pandan* leaf, stir, then simmer with the saucepan lid slightly ajar until all the liquid has evaporated. Cover the saucepan tightly, turn off the heat and allow to stand for 5 minutes. Turn on the heat as low as possible and cook for about 20 minutes. Fluff up the rice with a fork, cover the saucepan and leave to stand at the back of the stove until needed. Take great care during cooking or the bottom of the rice will burn.

Rice with Pork, Tomatoes and Peppers

Serves 4-6: ½ cup (4 fl oz) olive oil; 2 lb (1 kg) lean pork shoulder, cut into 1-in (2.5-cm) cubes; 2 garlic cloves, peeled; 1 lb (500 g) ripe tomatoes, peeled and chopped; 6 red or green bell peppers, seeded and cut into strips; ½ teaspoon saffron; 4 sprigs parsley, finely chopped; 5 cups (1¼ liters) water; 2 cups (12 oz) short grain rice; salt and freshly ground black pepper

Heat the oil in a heavy-based casserole and brown the pork. Remove it and set aside. In the oil, brown the whole garlic cloves, remove and set aside. Add the tomatoes and pepper strips to the oil and cook over low heat. In a mortar or food processor, crush the fried garlic cloves together with the saffron and parsley.

Return the pork and garlic–parsley mixture to the casserole. Add 1 cup (8 fl oz) water, cover and simmer over medium heat for 20 minutes. Stir in the rice and cook for 2–3 minutes. Add 4 cups (1 liter) water, or enough to cover the rice. Season. Cover the casserole and place it in an oven preheated to 350°F (180°C) for 30 minutes or until the meat is tender. Serve with a piquant green salad.

Rich Noodle Soup with Seafood

*Serves 6: 8 oz (250 g) fine-fleshed fish such as wolf herring or Spanish mackerel; ½ teaspoon salt; white pepper; 1 teaspoon cornstarch; 2 tablespoons water; 12 oz (375 g) raw shrimp, in shells if possible; 2 cups (16 fl oz) water; 1½ lb (750 g) fresh laksa noodles or 13 oz (400 g) Chinese rice vermicelli; 6½ oz (200 g) beansprouts, scalded; several sprigs of mint, finely chopped; ½ small cucumber, peeled and cut in matchsticks
Gravy: 4–6 dried red chilies, soaked; 1 stalk lemongrass or substitute; 8 shallots or 1 medium-size red or brown onion; 4 slices lengkuas; ½ in (1 cm) fresh turmeric or 1 teaspoon turmeric powder; 4 candlenuts or macadamias; ½ teaspoon dried shrimp paste (blacan); 4 tablespoons oil; 2 teaspoons coriander, freshly ground; 2 heaped tablespoons dried shrimp, soaked and pounded; 3 cups (24 fl oz) thin coconut milk; ½ cup (4 fl oz) thick coconut milk; 1 teaspoon salt*

To make the fish balls, scrape off all the fish flesh and blend until finely mashed. Add the salt, pepper, cornstarch and 2 tablespoons water. Shape into small balls and keep in the refrigerator until needed.

Put the shrimp and water into a saucepan, bring to the boil, simmer 2 minutes and strain. Keep the stock aside. Peel the shrimp and reserve. Boil the *laksa* noodles in boiling water for 3 minutes and set aside.

To prepare the gravy, pound or grind the first seven ingredients finely, adding about 1½ tablespoons of oil during grinding if using a blender or electric food processor. Mix in the coriander. Heat the remaining oil in a large skillet and gently fry the ground ingredients, stirring frequently, for 4–5 minutes.

Add the pounded dried shrimp and fry a further 2 minutes. Pour in the thin coconut milk and reserved shrimp stock and bring to the boil, stirring constantly. When simmering, add the fish balls and simmer for 5 minutes. Add the thick coconut milk and salt and simmer until the gravy thickens.

To serve, put a few noodles into six deep bowls. Put some beansprouts on top, then pour over the gravy. Garnish with the shrimp, chopped herbs and cucumber. Serve with extra pounded fresh red chilies, if liked.

Rich Noodle Soup with Seafood

S

Shrimp Pilaf

Serves 4: 8 cups (2 liters) water; 1 stalk celery, chopped; 1 carrot, chopped; 2 onions, chopped; 6 peppercorns; 3 bay leaves; ½ teaspoon chopped oregano; 16–24 raw shrimp, depending on size; 2 tablespoons olive oil; ½ garlic clove, crushed; 3 ripe tomatoes, peeled and chopped; 2 tablespoons tomato puree; 1 green bell pepper, seeded and roughly chopped; 1 cup (6 oz) long grain rice; 4 cups shrimp stock (see below); salt and freshly ground black pepper; 12 olives for garnish; grated Kefalotíri or Parmesan cheese (optional)

In a large saucepan, using all the water, simmer the celery, carrot, one of the chopped onions, peppercorns, bay leaves and oregano for 30 minutes.

In the meantime, peel the uncooked shrimp, putting the shells and heads aside. With a sharp knife, make an incision in the back of the shrimp and remove the veins. Rinse the shrimp under cold water and cut each into 2–3 pieces. Set aside.

Add the shrimp shells and heads to the vegetables in the saucepan. Mix well together, then cover and simmer gently for 20 minutes. Remove from the heat and let

it cool for 20–30 minutes. Strain the stock. Reserve.

Heat the oil and sauté the second chopped onion and the garlic until the onion is soft and transparent. Add the tomatoes, tomato puree and green pepper. Cook for 5 minutes. Stir in the rice. Add four cups of strained heated shrimp stock. Season. Cover the saucepan, reduce the heat to low and simmer for 20 minutes without taking off the lid. Stir in the chopped shrimp, cover the saucepan and continue to simmer for 5 minutes. Take off the heat and let stand for 10 minutes. Taste and season if necessary. Serve garnished with black olives and if desired, sprinkled with grated Kefalotíri or Parmesan cheese.

Shrimp Rice

Serves 4–6: 12 oz (375 g) long grain rice; 1 large onion; ¼ cup ghee; 2 garlic cloves; 1-in (2.5-cm) piece fresh ginger; 8 oz (250 g) raw shrimp, peeled; ½ teaspoon ground black pepper; 3 cloves; 2-in (5-cm) cinnamon stick; 2 green cardamoms, crushed; 1 teaspoon salt; ¼ cup (2 fl oz) thick coconut milk or heavy cream; 1 bay leaf; fresh mint or cilantro leaves and red or green chili, sliced, for garnish

Wash the rice and soak in cold water for 40 minutes. Drain well. Slice the onion thinly and fry in *ghee* until soft. Add the minced garlic and ginger and fry for 1 minute, then put in the shrimp and cook until pink. Add the rice and stir on moderate heat until all grains are well coated with the *ghee*. Add the pepper, cloves, cinnamon, cardamoms, salt and coconut milk or cream. Pour in enough water to reach 1¼ in (3 cm) above the level of the rice. Add the bay leaf. Cover and bring to the boil, then reduce the heat and cook until the rice is tender and liquid has been absorbed.

Stir the rice well, cover and place in a warm oven for 15 minutes. Garnish with mint or cilantro leaves and sliced chili.

Siamese-Style Noodles in Spicy Gravy

Serves 6–8: Spice paste: 10 dried red chilies, soaked; 12 shallots or 2 small red or brown onions; 1 stalk lemongrass or substitute; 1 teaspoon dried shrimp paste; 3 tablespoons oil; 2 heaped tablespoons salted soy beans, lightly crushed; 1 teaspoon salt; 1 tablespoon sugar
Gravy: 5 cups (1¼ liters) thin coconut milk; 1 heaped tablespoon dried tamarind; ½ cup (4 fl oz) warm water
1 lb (500 g) Chinese rice vermicelli; oil for deep frying; 2 cakes hard bean curd; 1 lb (500 g) beansprouts; 12 oz (375 g) cooked shrimp, peeled; 1 cup coarse chives, garlic chives or scallions, chopped in 1-in (2.5-cm) lengths; 3 hard-cooked eggs, peeled and quartered; 6–8 Chinese limes, halved, or 2 limes or lemons, quartered

Prepare the spice paste first. Grind the chilies, shallots, lemongrass and dried shrimp paste together to make a paste. Heat the oil in a skillet and gently fry the spice paste for 3–4 minutes. Add the salted soy beans and cook for 1 minute, stirring all the time. Sprinkle in the salt and sugar, and continue frying for another minute. Remove half this mixture to use in making the gravy. Set aside the skillet with the remaining mixture.

To make the gravy, put half the fried spice paste into a large saucepan and add the coconut milk. Bring to the boil, stirring all the time, then add the dried tamarind which has been soaked in warm water and strained. Simmer for 2–3 minutes, stirring all the time, then set aside.

Soak the rice vermicelli in boiling water for 1 minute, then drain and set aside. Heat the oil in a pan and deep fry the bean curd for 3–4 minutes, turning so that it is golden brown on both sides. Drain and slice coarsely. Have all other ingredients prepared and set on a plate for easy assembly of the dish.

Just before serving, heat the spice mixture left in the skillet, then add the beansprouts and cook over high heat, stirring constantly, for just 1 minute. Add half the cooked shrimp and half the chopped chives. Cook for about 30 seconds, stirring constantly, then add the rice vermicelli a little at a time, stirring vigorously to mix well with other ingredients. When all the vermicelli has been added and thoroughly heated, put into a large serving dish. Scatter the remaining shrimp and coarse chives on top. Arrange the eggs, fried bean curd and limes around the edge of the plate. Serve the gravy separately in a deep bowl. The noodles should be put into individual bowls by each diner and plenty of gravy added; the lime juice should be squeezed over the top.

Simple Noodle Dish

Serves 2: 4 cups (1 liter) water; 4–6 stalks Chinese mustard greens or any other leafy green vegetable; 2 packets individual-serving ramen noodles; 1 teaspoon peanut oil; 2 teaspoons sesame oil; 2 teaspoons black soy sauce; 2 teaspoons chili sauce; any of the following: slices of red barbecued pork; shredded cooked chicken; braised black mushrooms; cooked shrimp

Heat the water and simmer the green vegetable until just tender. Drain and reserve the water. Soak the noodles in the vegetable water for the time specified on the noodle package, then drain.

Combine the peanut and sesame oils, soy sauce and chili sauce and toss in a large bowl with the noodles. Serve garnished with the vegetable and other ingredients.

Spaghetti alla Bolognese

Serves 4: 1 medium-size onion; 1 stalk celery; 1 small carrot; 4 oz (125 g) bacon, including fat; 4 tablespoons (2 oz) butter; 4 oz (250 g) finely ground beef; salt and freshly ground pepper; pinch of ground nutmeg or 1 whole clove; a few leaves of oregano, chopped, or ½ teaspoon dried oregano; ½ cup (4 fl oz) dry white wine; 1 cup (8 fl oz) beef stock; 2 generous tablespoons tomato paste; 12 oz (375 g) spaghetti; 2 chicken livers, finely chopped; ½ cup (4 fl oz) heavy cream; Parmesan cheese, freshly grated

Chop the onion, celery, carrot and bacon very finely, then sauté in the butter over moderate heat in a large, heavy-based pan until the onion is soft and translucent. Add the beef and cook until the meat changes color.

Season well with salt and black pepper, nutmeg or clove and oregano, and increase the heat before pouring in the wine. Bring to the boil, stirring constantly, and continue cooking until the wine has almost entirely evaporated. Add the stock and tomato paste and simmer for 35–40 minutes over low heat. Stir frequently.

When the sauce has been simmering for some 25–30 minutes, cook the spaghetti in a large pan of boiling salted water until al dente. Drain. Add the chicken livers and the cream to the sauce. Mix the spaghetti and sauce well and serve sprinkled with Parmesan.

Spaghetti alla Bolognese

Spaghetti Sabatini-Style

Serves 4: 2 tablespoons oil; 4 oz (125 g) bacon, finely chopped; 1 onion, finely chopped; 2 teaspoons grated fresh ginger; 2 cups (16 fl oz) Fresh Tomato Sauce (see page 138); 12 basil leaves, chopped; 2 oz (60 g) Parmesan cheese, freshly grated; 1 egg, lightly beaten; 12 oz (375 g) spaghetti

In a heavy-based saucepan, heat the oil and fry the bacon until it is cooked but not crisp. Next, sauté the onion until it is almost golden, then add the ginger and the tomato sauce, and cook until well heated. Add the basil, then sprinkle in half the Parmesan cheese. When it has melted into the sauce, remove from the heat and stir in the egg.

Cook the spaghetti in boiling, salted water until al dente. Drain well, then combine with the sauce. Serve with the remaining Parmesan.

Spaghetti with Clams

Serves 4: 6–8 baby clams in their shells, per person (or substitute canned baby clams, with some of their liquid); 2 large garlic cloves, sliced into thin slivers; 3 tablespoons oil; 1 lb (500 g) spaghetti; ½ teaspoon dried chili powder, or 1 small, dried red chili, crumbled; ½ cup (4 fl oz) hot water; ½ cup (4 fl oz) dry white wine; salt; 4 tablespoons (2 oz) butter rolled in plenty of chopped parsley

If using fresh clams, clean them thoroughly in cold water. Place the garlic in a large pan with the oil and cook until it turns brown around the edges. Put the clams into the pan, cover, increase the heat and toss in the oil until they open. (If using canned clams, just add to the pan and allow time for them to warm through — too much cooking will make them tough.) Discard any shells which have not opened.

Cook the spaghetti in boiling, salted water until al dente. Drain and keep hot. Sprinkle the chili over the clams, then add the water, wine and a pinch of salt. When the water is nearly boiling, throw in the butter and parsley and bring to a fast boil, tossing gently all the while. Remove the garlic and immediately combine the sauce with the spaghetti. Serve at once.

Note: It is quite permissible to use other shellfish, but they should not be too strongly flavored.

Spaghetti Sabatini-Style

Spaghetti with Clams, Scallops and Anchovies

Serves 4: 12 oz (375 g) scallops, fresh, or frozen and thawed; ¼ cup oil; 1 medium-size onion, finely chopped; 3 garlic cloves, finely chopped; 2 very small, dried red chilies (or 1 small fresh red chili, or pinch of chili powder); salt and freshly ground black pepper; ¼ cup (2 fl oz) dry white wine; 8 oz (250 g) canned peeled tomatoes; 1 generous tablespoon tomato paste; 2 teaspoons chopped fresh basil (see Note); 1 teaspoon chopped fresh oregano; 2 tablespoons chopped parsley; 5 oz (55 g) canned baby clams; 4 anchovy fillets, boned and finely chopped; 12 capers; 1 lb (500 g) spaghetti

Wash the scallops carefully and slice into discs, about three from each scallop. Set aside.

Heat the oil in a heavy-based skillet, add the onion and garlic, and cook until golden and soft. Add the chilies and season to taste. Cook a further 2–3 minutes, then pour in the wine and simmer gently for 5 minutes.

Chop the tomatoes and add them to the pan, together with the tomato paste and herbs. Simmer for 10 minutes or until the tomatoes are quite soft. There should be enough liquid from the oil, wine and tomato juice to poach the scallop pieces on a gentle heat, just until they lose their transparent look, about 3 minutes.

Add the clams with most of the liquid, reduce the heat and simmer for 3 minutes. Now put in the anchovies and the capers and cook just a couple of minutes longer. The sauce should be liquid enough to coat the pasta easily. If it is too thick, thin with a little fish stock, if available, or simply add water.

Cook the spaghetti in boiling salted water until al dente. Drain well. Serve with the sauce poured over.

Note: Dried herbs may be used to substitute for the basil and oregano, but the flavor will not be quite the same.

Spaghetti with Clams, Scallops and Anchovies

Spaghetti with Mussels and White Wine

Spaghetti with Mussels and White Wine

Serves 4: 24 medium-size mussels; 2 scallions, finely chopped; 8 tablespoons (4 oz) butter; 3 strips of lemongrass (or use the peel of half a lemon and 2 tablespoons lemon juice); 1 bay leaf; 1 tablespoon finely chopped fresh oregano; 1 tablespoon chopped parsley; 1 cup (8 fl oz) dry white wine; 12 oz (375 g) spaghetti

The mussels must be completely free of any extraneous matter clinging to the shells so a good scrubbing in cold water is essential.

Put the scallions into a large, heavy-based saucepan or deep casserole dish, together with 4 tablespoons (2 oz) of the butter. Cook gently for 3–4 minutes, then add the lemongrass, bay leaf, oregano, parsley and the wine. Bring just to the boil, then drop in the mussels, cover tightly and reduce to a simmer. After 5 minutes, check to see that all the mussels have opened. If not, re-cover and simmer a little longer. Discard any shells that will not open.

Remove the opened mussels from the pan, stack on a plate and put in a low oven. Reduce the liquid at a fast boil until little more than half remains. Add the remaining butter and cook on high heat for 2 minutes more.

Cook the spaghetti in boiling salted water until al dente. Drain, then stir in the mussels. Pour the liquid evenly over and toss lightly. Decorate with a teaspoon or two of additional chopped oregano and parsley if desired.

Spaghetti with Tomatoes, Cheese and Bacon

Serves 4: 1 medium-size onion, cut in half and sliced; 1 stalk celery, finely sliced; 1 small carrot, finely chopped; 1 garlic clove, crushed; 2 slices bacon, cut into fine strips; ¼ cup (2 fl oz) olive oil; ⅔ cup (5½ fl oz) dry white wine; 4 ripe fresh tomatoes or canned tomatoes, finely chopped; 1 tablespoon tomato puree; salt and freshly ground black pepper; 12 oz (375 g) spaghetti; 5 oz (155 g) pecorino cheese, grated; 6½ oz (200 g) mozzarella or fresh ricotta cheese, diced or crumbled; 1 teaspoon dried oregano

Lightly brown the vegetables and bacon in the oil. Add the wine and cook until it has almost evaporated. Add the tomatoes and tomato puree and season with salt and pep-

per. Cook this mixture until thick, stirring occasionally.

Cook the spaghetti in a large pan of salted boiling water until cooked but still firm. Drain the spaghetti, then add the vegetable mixture and one tablespoon of pecorino. To serve, spoon the spaghetti into a bowl and sprinkle it with mozzarella or ricotta and oregano. Serve the rest of the pecorino separately.

Spaghetti with Tuna and Mushroom Sauce

Spaghetti with Tuna and Mushroom Sauce

Serves 4–6: 5 oz (155 g) fresh mushrooms, sliced, or 1½ oz (45 g) dried mushrooms; 3 tablespoons oil; 1 small onion, finely chopped; 1 garlic clove, finely chopped; 1 slice bacon, finely chopped; freshly ground black pepper; 1 chicken bouillon cube; 1 cup (8 fl oz) water; 1 lb (500 g) spaghetti; 7-oz (200-g) can tuna in oil; ½ cup (4 fl oz) cream; Parmesan cheese, freshly grated

If using dried mushrooms, soak them in tepid water for 15–20 minutes.

Heat the oil in a skillet and cook the onion, garlic and bacon until the onion is golden. Season the mushrooms generously with black pepper and add them to the pan. Toss over a moderate heat for a few moments, then add the bouillon cube which has been dissolved in a cup of boiling water.

Cook the spaghetti in boiling, salted water until al dente. Drain and keep warm.

Simmer the sauce for 8 minutes, then add the tuna which has been broken into

flakes or small pieces. Stir in the cream and cook just until the sauce thickens, no more than 2–3 minutes. Pour over the spaghetti, mix it through gently and serve with Parmesan on the side.

Spit-Roasted Chicken with Piquant Rice

Serves 4: 1 chicken, about 3 lb (1.5 kg); salt and freshly ground black pepper; 2 tablespoons olive oil; 2 cups (12 oz) rice
Peverada Sauce: 4 oz (125 g) chicken livers, chopped; 4 anchovy fillets, chopped; 1 garlic clove, crushed; 4 oz (125 g) pickled green peppers, chopped; ¼ cup (2 fl oz) olive oil; salt and freshly ground black pepper; 2 tablespoons chopped parsley; ¼ cup (2 fl oz) chicken stock; juice of 1 lemon; 1 tablespoon white wine vinegar

Rub the chicken inside and out with salt and pepper, and smear the outside with the oil. Place it in an oven preheated to 375°F (190°C) and spit-roast for 1¼–1½ hours. Baste frequently with the pan juices.

To make the sauce, sauté the chicken livers, anchovies, garlic and green peppers in hot oil, then add the seasoning and the parsley. Gradually pour in the stock and simmer for 20 minutes. Add the lemon juice and vinegar. Meanwhile, boil the rice in salted water until tender.

To serve, mix the peverada sauce into the rice. Serve the chicken carved into pieces surrounded by the rice.

Note: Guinea fowl can be used in place of chicken.

Sushi Rice Cakes

Makes 36: 4 cups (1½ lb) short grain rice; 4½ cups (1⅛ liters) water; 1 cup (8 fl oz) rice vinegar; 1¼ tablespoons salt; 1½ tablespoons sugar
Toppings: raw fish fillets (tuna, trout, mackerel, bream, etc); raw clams, steamed open; raw shrimp, blanched; Omelet Roll (see page 120); powdered horseradish or ginger; salt and sugar

Soak the rice in cold water for about 3 hours. Drain very well. Bring the water to the boil and pour in the rice. When it returns to the boil, cover and turn the heat down very low. Simmer until the water has been completely absorbed into the rice. At this stage the rice will still be quite firm, but should not be hard.

Transfer to a bowl and pour in the pre-mixed vinegar, salt and sugar. Fan the rice and stir carefully during this process. Cover and set aside.

Cut the fish into thin slices approximately 2 × 1 in (5 × 2 cm). Rinse the clams in salted water and drain the shrimp. Mash two or three shrimp with a pinch of salt and sugar and set this paste aside.

Cut the omelet roll into ¼-in (5-mm) slices. Mix the horseradish or ginger powder with water to make a thin paste.

With wet hands, mold the rice into oval-shaped cakes the size of the prepared toppings. Smear on some of the horseradish or ginger paste and press on a piece of fish, several clams or a slice of the omelet roll. Spread the shrimp paste on the underside of the shrimp and press one onto each of the remaining rice cakes.

Arrange the cakes on wooden platters and garnish attractively with shredded ginger, lemon peel, grated radish or carrot and shredded lettuce. Serve with thin soy sauce and more of the horseradish or ginger paste in small bowls for dipping.

T

Tagliatelle with Gorgonzola

Serves 4: 8 tablespoons (4 oz) butter; 4 oz (125 g) Gorgonzola; ⅓ cup (2½ fl oz) cream; 12 oz (375 g) tagliatelle or fettuccine; 1 oz (30 g) Parmesan cheese, freshly grated; freshly ground black pepper (optional)

Melt the butter in a small heavy-based saucepan, add the Gorgonzola, breaking it up gently with a wooden spoon, then pour in the cream and stir constantly until the sauce has a smooth, velvety texture.

Cook the tagliatelle in plenty of boiling, lightly salted water until al dente, drain thoroughly and turn into a warmed bowl. Sprinkle over the Parmesan cheese and a little black pepper and toss quickly but carefully to melt the Parmesan through the pasta. Now combine the cheese sauce with the tagliatelle and serve it at once.

Note: The precise amount of cream can only be decided by the creaminess of the cheese, which will change with the quality of the Gorgonzola. Aim for a thick but still liquid sauce that pours slowly from a spoon.

Tagliatelle with Prosciutto and Mushrooms

Serves 4: 12 oz (375 g) mushrooms; 8 tablespoons (4 oz) butter; ½ teaspoon dried tarragon; ½ teaspoon dried sage; 1 large, ripe tomato; ¾ cup (6 fl oz) cream; 4 oz (125 g) prosciutto; 2 tablespoons chopped parsley; salt and freshly ground black pepper; 12 oz (350 g) tagliatelle; 3 oz (90 g) Parmesan cheese, freshly grated

Thinly slice the mushrooms and sauté them in the butter in a large pan. Crumble the two herbs in your fingers and sprinkle them on top. Toss as you cook for about 7–8

Sushi Rice Cakes

minutes, over moderate heat, making sure the butter does not burn.

Add the skinned and seeded tomato, pour in the cream and stir briefly, then add the prosciutto cut into bite-size pieces. Add the parsley and season to taste with a little salt and pepper. Bring this mixture to a boil, and stir now and then until the sauce thickens.

Cook the tagliatelle in boiling salted water until al dente, then drain. Tip it into the pan with the sauce, toss gently, and serve with the Parmesan cheese for individual sprinkling.

Tagliolini with Baby Shrimp

Serves 4: 12 oz (375 g) small shrimp, cooked; ¼ cup lemon juice; ¼ cup (2 fl oz) dry white wine; ½ cup (4 fl oz) olive oil; 2 garlic cloves, crushed; 3-4 tablespoons finely chopped parsley; 1 teaspoon salt; freshly ground black pepper; 12 oz (375 g) tagliolini

Shell and devein the shrimp. It is a good idea to dry them off a little with a paper towel — they will absorb the marinade better.

Whisk together all the other ingredients, except the tagliolini, in a shallow dish and leave the shrimp to marinate for 45 minutes or so.

Cook the tagliolini in plenty of boiling salted water for 3 minutes or until al dente. Check a strand or two frequently, as it passes the point of no return quite quickly.

Drain the tagliolini thoroughly and place in a preheated serving bowl. Pour the sauce over the pasta and toss gently, making sure the strands are well covered.

Tagliatelle with Gorgonzola

Tagliolini with Baby Shrimp

Tagliolini with Caviar

Serves 4: 12 oz (375 g) tagliolini or vermicelli; 4 tablespoons (2 oz) butter; ⅓ cup (2½ fl oz) cream; 1 small jar of black lumpfish roe or caviar; 1 teaspoon onion juice; 1 teaspoon lemon juice; 2 tablespoons finely chopped parsley

Cook the pasta in a large pan of boiling salted water until just al dente. Drain well. Cut the butter into the hot pasta and pour in the cream as the butter melts through. Add all but a little of the caviar, the onion and lemon juices and the parsley. Combine all these ingredients making sure the pasta is well coated with the sauce. Serve with the remaining caviar dotted over the top of the serving dish.

Tagliolini with Orange and Tomato Sauce

Serves 4: 1½ lb (750 g) fresh, ripe tomatoes, peeled and seeded; 1 tablespoon tomato paste; 2 tablespoons finely chopped chives; 2 sprigs orange thyme (or substitute English thyme); 1 small sprig rosemary; 12 large basil leaves; 1 scant tablespoon pine nuts; 1 garlic clove; pinch of chili powder; 1 tablespoon orange juice; 2 teaspoons grated orange peel; salt; ½ cup (4 fl oz) olive oil; 12 oz (350 g) tagliolini; Parmesan cheese, freshly grated

Chop the tomatoes roughly and combine in a food processor with the tomato paste, the chives and other herbs, the pine nuts, garlic, chili powder, orange juice and peel, and a pinch of salt. Whisk until fairly

Tagliolini with Caviar (see page 161)

smooth, then drizzle in the oil. The result should be a creamy sauce, free of lumps.

Boil the tagliolini in a pan of boiling salted water until al dente, then run briefly under cold water to cool slightly.

Reserve 4 teaspoons of the sauce and mix the rest through the tagliolini in a fresh bowl. Serve on individual plates with a teaspoon of the sauce on top of each and a decoration of small pieces of basil leaf or feathers of fennel tops. Serve with Parmesan cheese.

Tomato Pilaf

Serves 4: 2 large, ripe tomatoes, peeled and chopped; 4 tablespoons (2 oz) butter; 1 teaspoon salt; freshly ground black pepper; 1¾ cups (14 fl oz) beef stock; 1 tablespoon tomato puree; 1 generous cup (7 oz) rice; 3 tablespoons (1½ oz) melted butter

In a heavy-based saucepan, cook the tomatoes, butter, salt, pepper, beef stock and tomato puree until reduced to approximately 2 cups (16 fl oz). Add the rice, stir in well, cover and simmer for about 20 minutes, until the liquid has been absorbed and the rice is tender but not too soft. Add the melted butter and stir it in with a fork. Cover the saucepan with a tea towel and let stand for 20 minutes before serving.

Tomatoes and Tuna Fish with Rigatoni

Serves 4-6: 2 garlic cloves; 3 tablespoons oil; 2 anchovy fillets, finely chopped; 7-oz (220-g) can tuna in oil; 6 good-size ripe tomatoes, peeled and roughly chopped; 12 black olives, pitted and quartered; 1 tablespoon chopped basil leaves (or substitute good pinch of oregano powder, not dried basil); freshly ground black pepper; 1 lb (500 g) rigatoni or macaroni

Crush the garlic and sauté in the oil until it turns light brown. Remove, then add the anchovies. Drain the oil from the tuna and add to the skillet in fine flakes. Cook over medium heat for 5 minutes, stirring to make sure it doesn't stick to the pan.

Add the tomatoes, olives and basil. Season with pepper and simmer for 15–20 minutes.

While the sauce is cooking, boil the pasta in plenty of salted boiling water, drain and transfer to a heated serving dish. Pour the sauce over the top of the pasta and serve.

Trenette with Fish Sauce

Serves 4: ½ cup (4 fl oz) olive oil; 1 small red chili; 1 medium-size onion, chopped; 3 garlic cloves, very finely chopped; ½ green bell pepper, cut into narrow strips; 2 tablespoons tomato paste; 1 lb (500 g) canned, peeled tomatoes, coarsely chopped; 1 leek, cleaned and thinly sliced (use all the white portion and about 1 in (2.5 cm) of the green); 1 generous tablespoon chopped parsley; 2 tablespoons chopped fennel, feathers and small top stalks; ½ teaspoon salt; freshly ground black pepper; 1 cup (8 fl oz) dry white wine; 1 small squid, cut into rings; 8 oz (250 g) firm, white fish fillets; 6 oz (185 g) red fish fillets (or increase quantity of white fish); 4 oz (125 g) fresh scallops; 8 raw shrimp; 8 small to medium-size mussels; 8 oz (250 g) baby clams in their shells, or 4 oz (125 g) canned baby clams; 12 oz (350 g) trenette or fettuccine

Heat the oil in a heavy-based skillet with a lid. Sauté the chili until the pod turns brown and crisp, then add the onion, garlic and the pepper and remove the chili. Stir in the tomato paste, then add the can of tomatoes and the leek. Mix in the parsley, fennel, salt and several grinds of black pepper. Lastly, pour in the white wine. Simmer, covered, for 20 minutes, or longer if possible.

When the basic sauce is ready, add the squid and cook for 10 minutes or so. Add the fish, treating it gently so that it does not break up and disintegrate through the sauce. Put in the scallops and the shrimp with the body shell removed but tails left on. Simmer for a further 8–10 minutes before carefully pouring off about two-thirds of the sauce into another pan.

Throw the scrubbed mussels and clams into this second pan, cover and toss over fairly high heat until they open. Remove and return to the main pan, throwing away any that have failed to open. Simmer on a low heat until reduced and thickened.

Meanwhile, boil the trenette in boiling, salted water until al dente. Drain, then combine with the sauce.

Tomatoes and Tuna Fish with Rigatoni

Trenette with Fresh Tomato, Garlic, Basil and Oil Sauce

Serves 4: 8 ripe tomatoes; 2 garlic cloves, finely chopped; 12 fresh basil leaves, finely chopped; 5 tablespoons best quality olive oil; Parmesan cheese, freshly grated; salt and pepper; 12 oz (350 g) trenette or fettuccine

Scald the tomatoes, peel and chop, then put through a sieve or food mill. Add the garlic, basil, olive oil and Parmesan to taste. Season with salt and pepper and mix all the ingredients well. Place this mixture in a bowl in the refrigerator for 2–3 hours.

To serve, cook the trenette in boiling salted water until al dente. Drain and turn into a heavy-based saucepan or casserole dish in which half the sauce has been heating gently. Arrange the pasta on individual plates and cover with the remainder of the sauce.

Trenette with Potatoes and Beans

Serves 4: 2 medium-size potatoes; 3 oz (90 g) green beans; 12 oz (350 g) trenette or fettuccine; Pesto Sauce (see page 315); Parmesan cheese, freshly grated

Peel the potatoes and cut them into shoe-string pieces. Cook in boiling salted water, but do not overcook; they should not be soft and mushy. Drain well and dry on paper towels. Keep them warm in the oven until needed.

String the beans and slice them diagonally into approximately 1½-in (4-cm) lengths. Using just enough water to cover the beans, bring to the boil, salt and cook until tender but still with some "bite" in them.

Cook the trenette until al dente. Drain briefly, allowing some liquid to remain on the pasta. Transfer most of the pesto sauce to the bottom of a preheated serving dish, add the potatoes, beans and trenette and mix together well. Serve with some pesto sauce on top of each bowl and allow plenty of Parmesan for sprinkling.

Trenette with Seafood Sauce

Trenette with Seafood Sauce

Serves 4: ¾ cup (6 fl oz) dry white wine; 4 oz (125 g) baby clams in their shells, or use canned clams; 12 small mussels in their shells; 4 oz (125 g) fresh, uncooked small shrimp; freshly ground black pepper; chili sauce; 2 garlic cloves, crushed; ⅓ cup (2½ fl oz) oil (olive oil is best); ½ tablespoon finely chopped fresh oregano, or ½ teaspoon dried; 1 tablespoon finely chopped parsley; ½ tablespoon finely chopped fresh cilantro; ¼ cup (60 ml) brandy; 4 oz (125 g) squid; 1 cup (8 fl oz) fresh Tomato Sauce (see page 138); 8 oz (250 g) any firm, boneless white fish; salt; 12 oz (350 g) trenette or fettuccine; 8 tablespoons (4 oz) parsley butter

Heat ¼ cup (2 fl oz) of the wine in a large skillet. Add the cleaned clams and mussels, then the shrimp in their shells. Grind in plenty of black pepper, add a few drops of chili sauce and increase the heat to boiling point, stirring all the time. When the shells of the clams and mussels have all opened, remove them and the shrimp from the pan and set aside. Continue cooking the liquid until it has reduced by about one-third. Meanwhile, shell the clams, mussels and shrimp, then pass the reduced liquid through a fine cloth to remove all traces of grit. Set aside.

In a separate pan, fry the garlic in the oil until it is golden, then remove and discard. Add the oregano, parsley and cilantro, the other ½ cup (4 fl oz) of wine and the brandy. Simmer for 2 minutes, then add the squid and simmer for a further 4 minutes, stirring constantly to prevent burning.

Meanwhile, cook the trenette in a large pan of salted, boiling water until al dente. Drain and keep warm.

Pour in the tomato sauce, bring to the boil, then add the reserved, strained liquid and the white fish, cut into bite-size pieces. Just before the fish is cooked, add the shellfish and shrimp to the pan and give them time to heat through. Taste and add salt if necessary. Combine the sauce with the trenette.

Serve with a knob of parsley butter on top of each bowl and decorate with a leaf or two of cilantro or oregano or both.

Tuna and Spiral Pasta Casserole ★

Serves 6–8: 8-oz (250-g) package frozen spinach; 6–8 medium-size eggs; 2 stalks celery, finely chopped; 1 large onion, finely chopped; 4–6 tablespoons (2–3 oz) butter; 1 cup (8 fl oz) milk; 1 cup (8 fl oz) water; 2 fish bouillon cubes, crumbled (optional); 2½ tablespoons (¾ oz) cornstarch; salt and black pepper; 1 tablespoon lemon juice; 13½-oz (425-g) can tuna, drained; 8 oz (250 g) spiral pasta (or use elbows/bows, etc.), cooked

Defrost the spinach in its box for 8 minutes, then transfer to a plastic strainer and set aside.

Break the eggs into small cups or muffin dishes and prick yolks and whites. Cover and microwave on MEDIUM-HIGH (70%) for 4–6 minutes until the yolks are just firm. Set aside.

Place the celery, onion and butter in a large microwave-safe jug and cover. Microwave on HIGH (100%) for 5 minutes. Add the milk, water and bouillon cubes if used, and microwave on HIGH (100%), uncovered for 5 minutes stirring once. Blend the cornstarch with a little cold water, stir into the sauce and mix well. Microwave a further 3 minutes, stirring once or twice, on HIGH (100%). Add the salt, pepper and lemon juice to taste and the tuna.

Lightly grease a large casserole, put in one-third of the pasta, cover with half the well drained spinach and one-third of the sauce. Repeat with another layer of pasta and spinach.

Remove the eggs from their cups and arrange over the casserole. Top with a further one-third of the sauce followed by a further layer of pasta and sauce.

For extra flavor and color, dust the top lightly with paprika or microwave seasoning/coloring salt or powder. Reheat, covered, on MEDIUM-HIGH (70%) for 12 minutes. (Non-carousel ovens: Give the dish several half-turns.) The top can be removed halfway through reheating so the surface will dry out, making it crisp.

Turmeric Rice

Serves 4: 2 cups glutinous rice; 1 in (2.5 cm) fresh turmeric or 1 teaspoon turmeric powder; boiling water; banana leaf or pandan *leaves; ½ teaspoon salt; ½ cup (4 fl oz) thick coconut milk*

Wash the rice thoroughly and put into a glass or china bowl. Pound the fresh turmeric and extract the juice, then add it to the rice and pour over boiling water to cover. Allow the rice to stand for at least 10 hours, preferably overnight.

Drain the soaking liquid from the rice and rinse well. Line a bamboo or metal steamer with a banana leaf and spread the rice on top. Pour over boiling water and steam for 5 minutes. Uncover the rice, make several holes in it using a chopstick (this is to allow the steam to circulate more easily), then cover and steam again for at least 45 minutes. Check to see if the rice is tender, then put into a bowl, stir in the salt and coconut milk and return to the steamer for another 5 minutes.

V

Venetian Rice and Peas

Serves 4: 1 onion, chopped; 2 oz (60 g) ham, chopped; 3 tablespoons (1½ oz) butter; 12 oz (375 g) shelled peas; 3 cups (24 fl oz) chicken stock or meat stock; 2 cups (12 oz) rice; ¼ cup (1 oz) grated Parmesan cheese

Sauté the onion and the ham in half the butter. Add the peas, mix them well with

the butter, then add 1 cup of the stock or water. When it starts to boil, add the rice and another cup of liquid. As it is absorbed, add more liquid. This will take approximately 12–15 minutes. Limit the stirring to a minimum so that the peas are not squashed. The final result should not be too liquid as the dish is meant to be eaten with a fork. When the rice is cooked, stir in the rest of the butter and the cheese. Serve more Parmesan separately.

Vinegared Rice Salad

Tuna and Spiral Pasta Casserole

Vinegared Rice Salad

Serves 6: 1 quantity of basic sushi (see page 159); 6 dried shiitake *mushrooms; 1½ cups (12 fl oz) dashi; 3 tablespoons light soy sauce; 3 tablespoons mirin; 1 small carrot; 1 section fresh or canned lotus root; 18 snow peas or 1 cup cooked green peas; 7 oz (200 g) small raw shrimp; 3 medium-size squid (optional); 2 eggs; 1 heaped tablespoon shredded pickled ginger*

Have the sushi rice prepared but do not refrigerate. Soak the dried mushrooms in hot water for 30 minutes, then drain and discard the stems. Combine the *dashi*, soy sauce and *mirin* in a pan and simmer the mushrooms for at least 30 minutes or until tender. Leave the liquid in the pan, remove the mushrooms and cut into shreds. Cut the carrot into thin slices and simmer in the mushroom liquid until just tender. Remove the carrot slices with a slotted spoon and hold in a colander under cold running water for a minute or two. Drain and set aside. Cut the lotus root in ¼-in (5-mm) slices and simmer in the same liquid until tender, then drain and cool as for the carrot. Repeat this process if using snow peas. Keep the remaining cooking liquid.

Drop the shrimp into boiling water and simmer for just 2 minutes. Cool under running water, drain, then peel and discard the heads, tails and shells.

Remove the reddish brown skin from the squid and cut off the triangular "wings" at the base. Cut the bodies in half lengthwise, then score diagonal lines about ¼ in (5 mm) apart into the flesh, taking care not to cut right through. Cut into 1½-in (4-cm) lengths and drop into boiling water for just 10 seconds. Remove and immediately plunge into cold water, then drain. The pieces of squid will curl and the scored outside resemble little pine cones.

Beat the eggs together lightly with a pinch of salt and cook in a very thin layer in a lightly oiled pan until just set. Cook on one side only. Turn out onto a board, cool, then slice very finely.

Put the sushi rice into a large bowl and gently toss in all the prepared ingredients as well as the shredded, pickled ginger. Moisten with 2 tablespoons of the reserved cooking liquid. Although this can be prepared ahead of time, it should not be refrigerated.

SEAFOOD

A

American Lobster

Serves 4–6: 2 live lobsters, about 2 lb (1 kg) each; 8 tablespoons (4 oz) butter; ½ cup (4 fl oz) olive oil; 1 carrot, finely chopped; 1 small onion, finely chopped; 2 scallions, finely chopped; 2 garlic cloves, finely chopped; 1 cup (8 fl oz) dry white wine; ¼ cup (2 fl oz) brandy, warmed; 1 cup (8 oz) canned tomatoes; 2 tablespoons tomato paste; 1 bay leaf; ½ cup (4 fl oz) fish stock or dry white wine; salt and freshly ground black pepper; 1 tablespoon butter; 1 tablespoon all purpose flour; juice of ½ lemon; pinch of cayenne pepper; finely chopped fresh parsley, chives and tarragon

Drop the live lobsters into boiling salted water and boil for 25 minutes, then cool under running water. Working over a shallow bowl to catch the juices, break off and crack the claws and cut each lobster tail into thick slices. Cut the body shells in half and discard the intestinal tube. Reserve the coral and all the juices.

Put 3 tablespoons of butter and 3 tablespoons of oil into a heavy-based skillet. Gently fry the lobster pieces for 5 minutes, stirring occasionally. Reserve.

In another skillet with a lid, heat the rest of the butter and oil. Gently fry the chopped carrot, onion, scallions and garlic until the onion is transparent. Place the lobster pieces on top of the vegetables. Pour over the wine and simmer for 3 minutes. Add the warmed brandy and ignite. Add the tomatoes, tomato paste, bay leaf, lobster liquids, fish stock and salt and pepper. Cover and simmer for 15 minutes. Remove the lobster pieces and keep warm.

Cream 1 tablespoon of butter with 1 tablespoon flour. Blend the coral into the butter and flour. Stir into the sauce and simmer until thickened. Strain the sauce. Flavor it to taste with lemon juice, salt, pepper and cayenne. Add the lobster pieces and cooking juices and heat through. Just before serving, sprinkle with finely chopped parsley, chives and tarragon.

B

Baked Crab

Serves 4: 4 crabs; 2 leeks; 3 sprigs parsley, chopped; 4 onions, finely chopped; ¼ cup (2 fl oz) olive oil; 2 carrots, finely chopped; 1 garlic clove, crushed; 1 tablespoon tomato paste; 1 cup (8 fl oz) brandy; salt and freshly ground black pepper; 4 tablespoons (2 oz) butter, softened; ½ cup (2 oz) breadcrumbs

Cook the crabs in salted water with the green part of the leeks, the parsley and half the chopped onions for 10 minutes. Cool in the water. Reserve the stock. Open the crab and take out the meat. Set the meat aside and reserve the shells.

Heat the oil in a skillet, and sauté the remaining chopped onions, the finely chopped white of the leeks, the carrots and garlic until the onions are soft and transparent. Add the tomato paste and the crab meat. Heat the brandy and pour it flaming into the mixture. Pour in some crab stock to moisten the mixture, then cook over low heat for 5 minutes. Season.

Fill the shells with the vegetable mixture. Mix the butter and breadcrumbs and sprinkle over the top. Place under a preheated broiler and brown the top. Serve in the shells.

Baked Fish with Creamed Tomato Sauce

Serves 6: 1½ lb (750 g) snapper, bream or other meaty fish; 3 tablespoons ghee or clarified butter; 1¼ teaspoons fenugreek, ground; 4 garlic cloves, crushed; 1-in (2.5-cm) piece fresh ginger, minced; 1 tablespoon coriander, ground; 2 teaspoons cumin, ground; 1½ teaspoons chili powder; ¾ teaspoon turmeric; 6 medium-size tomatoes, peeled; ¾ cup (6 fl oz) fish stock or water; ½ cup (4 fl oz) heavy cream; ¼ cup (2 fl oz) plain yogurt; salt and black pepper; lemon juice

Clean the fish, remove the scales and clip the fins. Wipe dry.

Heat the *ghee* in a small saucepan. Fry the fenugreek, garlic and ginger for 3 minutes, then add the coriander, cumin, chili and turmeric. Fry for 2 minutes more, stirring frequently.

Chop the tomatoes finely and add to the pan with stock or water. Cover and simmer until the sauce is thick and creamy, then add the cream and yogurt and season to taste with salt and black pepper. Keep warm.

Sprinkle the fish with salt, pepper and lemon juice and place in a lightly oiled ovenproof dish. Cover with aluminum foil and bake in an oven preheated to 400°F (200°C) for 15 minutes. Remove the foil and cook for a further 5 minutes. Pour the hot sauce over and return to the oven for 5 minutes before serving.

Baked Fish with Creamed Tomato Sauce

Baked Fish with Port

Serves 4: 2 tablespoons olive oil; 2 onions, finely chopped; 1 garlic clove, crushed; 4 tomatoes, peeled, seeded and finely chopped; 2 sprigs thyme, finely chopped; ½ cup (4 fl oz) port; salt and freshly ground black pepper; 4 plate-size snapper or other white-fleshed fish

Heat the oil and sauté the onions and garlic until the onions are soft, then add the tomatoes, thyme, port and seasoning. Place the fish in a greased baking dish, pour the sauce over and bake in an oven preheated to 350°F (180°C) for 30 minutes. Serve the fish masked with the sauce.

Baked Jewfish

Serves 4: 4 onions, sliced; 3 lb (1.5 kg) jewfish (halibut); salt and freshly ground black pepper; 1 garlic clove, crushed; 1 cup (8 fl oz) dry white wine; 1 tablespoon vinegar; 2 tomatoes, peeled and sliced; 2 bay leaves; 4 cooked, sliced potatoes; 3 tablespoons olive oil

Place half of the onion slices on the bottom of a buttered ovenproof dish. Put the fish into the dish and sprinkle with salt, pepper, garlic, wine and vinegar. Cover with the remaining onion slices, tomatoes and bay leaves. Arrange the potato slices around the fish. Sprinkle with olive oil and bake in an oven preheated to 400°F (200°C) for 45 minutes or until the fish can be flaked at the thickest part. Occasionally baste with the cooking juices.

Baked Stuffed Fish

Serves 6: 1 × 3-lb (1½-kg) snapper or pearl perch (sea bass, etc.); 1 stalk celery, finely chopped; 1 onion, finely chopped; 1 slice bacon, chopped; 2 tablespoons (1 oz) unsalted butter; 5 large mushrooms, finely chopped; 1 cup (1 oz) beansprouts, chopped; ¼ cup (5 oz) frozen peas; 1 cup (5 oz) cooked rice; 1 egg; ½ teaspoon fennel seeds, lightly crushed; 1 recipe fresh Tomato Sauce (see page 138)

Clean and scale the fish. Use a sharp knife to remove the backbone completely.

Place the celery, onion and bacon in a microwave-safe dish with the butter. Cover and microwave on HIGH (100%) for 3 minutes. Add the mushrooms to the celery together with the beansprouts and peas. Cover again and microwave on HIGH (100%) for 4 minutes, stirring half way. Remove from the oven and add the rice, egg and seasoning. Cool.

Fill the fish with the prepared mixture and place in a large oven bag. Set on a dish. Spread a thin layer of tomato sauce over the fish, pierce the bag in several places on the top and secure the opening of the bag with a strip of plastic wrap. Microwave on HIGH (100%) for 16–20 minutes, until the fish can be flaked at the thickest part. (Non-carousel ovens: Give the dish a quarter-turn every 4 minutes.)

Drain the liquid from the dish (reserve for stock) and spread the remaining sauce over the fish. Bake on HIGH (100%) a further 3–4 minutes until the sauce is well heated. Slide out of the bag without disturbing the sauce, garnish with lemon slices and parsley, and serve.

Clean and scale the fish.   Remove the backbone completely.

Baked Stuffed Fish

Barbecued Whole Fish

Clean and scale the fish.   Cover with marinade inside and out.

Barbecued Whole Fish

Serves 4: 1 whole fish, about 2 lb (1 kg), such as sea perch, snapper, bream or grouper; 1 medium-size red or brown onion; 1 garlic clove; 1 slice lengkuas; 2 stalks lemongrass; 1–2 teaspoons chili powder; ¼ cup (2 fl oz) oil; ½ cup (4 fl oz) thick coconut milk; juice of 1 Chinese lime or ½ lemon; 1 teaspoon salt; 1 teaspoon sugar; pinch of turmeric; 1 fragrant lime leaf or young citrus leaf (optional)

Clean and scale the fish. Pound the onion, garlic, *lengkuas* and lemongrass until fine, then mix in the chili powder. Rub a third of this mixture over the fish, inside and out, and leave to stand while preparing the sauce.

Heat the oil and gently fry the remaining pounded mixture for 3–5 minutes. Add the coconut milk and all other ingredients and cook, stirring constantly, until the sauce thickens.

Cook the fish on a greased grill over a charcoal fire or in a large skillet, basting frequently with the sauce. Serve on a platter with the remaining sauce poured over.

Bouillabaisse

Serves 6–8: 6 tablespoons olive oil; 2 medium-size onions, finely chopped; 1 leek, chopped; ½ stalk fennel, chopped; 2 medium-size tomatoes, peeled, seeded and chopped; 3 garlic cloves, crushed; generous sprig of thyme; 1 bay leaf; 1 stalk celery, chopped; 12 cups (3 liters) white wine fish stock; salt and freshly ground black pepper; 1 teaspoon powdered saffron; 3½ lb (1.75 kg) coarse-fleshed fish, such as cod, mullet, mackerel etc.; 3½ lb (1.75 kg) fine-fleshed fish, such as snapper, whiting, sole, John Dory etc.; garlic-flavored croutons Rouille: 4 garlic cloves, crushed; 1 red chili, chopped; 2 egg yolks; 6 tablespoons olive oil

Heat 4 tablespoons of the olive oil in a large flameproof casserole dish or fish kettle. Add the onions, leek and fennel, and sauté gently over very low heat until the onion is tender but not browned. Add the tomatoes, garlic, thyme, bay leaf and celery, and sauté for a few minutes longer.

Remove the heads from the fish, clean and trim them. Add the fish stock to the vegetables. Season with salt and freshly ground black pepper and the saffron. Bring to the boil, then simmer for 30 minutes. Add the coarse-fleshed fish and cook over brisk heat for 6 minutes, then add the remaining fish and boil for 6 minutes more. Take great care not to overcook the fish. Lift out the fish with a slotted spoon and put into a large warmed serving bowl. Sprinkle with the remaining oil.

To make the rouille, crush the garlic with the chili in a mortar or blend in a food processor. Add the egg yolks and whisk in the oil as for a mayonnaise. Season to taste with salt and freshly ground black pepper. Finish by whisking in a tablespoon of the hot fish broth.

To serve, transfer the fish to a large preheated dish. Pour the stock into a soup tureen. Serve the fish and soup together. The croutons are spread with the rouille and dropped into the broth.

C

Cantonese New Year Salad

Serves 4: 5 oz (150 g) fish fillets (herring, if possible); 8 oz (250 g) carrot; 4 oz (125 g) giant white radish; 4 oz (125 g) sweet potato; 3–4 fragrant lime leaves or young citrus leaves; 3 thin slices fresh ginger, finely shredded; 1 tablespoon pickled red ginger, finely shredded; 1 tablespoon candied melon rind or orange peel; 2 heaped tablespoons shredded mixed pickles: leeks, green papaya and melon
Sauce: 2 teaspoons sugar; ¼ teaspoon five spice powder; ½ teaspoon salt; 1½ tablespoons Chinese lime juice or lime or lemon juice; 2 tablespoons dry-roasted crushed peanuts; 2 teaspoons lightly toasted sesame seeds

Rinse the fish fillets in salty water, then hang to dry for about 4 hours. Chill until firm, then cut into very thin slices. Grate the carrot, white radish and sweet potato into long, very thin shreds (less than half the thickness of a matchstick), then mix with the shredded lime leaves. Put onto a plate with all other salad ingredients, including the fish.

It is considered essential for good luck in the coming year for everyone eating the salad to help stir it, so final preparation is done at the table. Have all the individual sauce items ready, then put the first four sauce ingredients into a large bowl or deep platter. Stir to dissolve, then put in the peanuts and sesame seeds and add the salad ingredients a little at a time. Everyone should help stir the salad with his or her chopsticks. Serve immediately .

Chili-Fried Shrimp

Serves 4: 1 lb (500 g) raw shrimp; 12–15 dried red chilies, soaked; 10 shallots or 1 large red or brown onion; 3 garlic cloves; 2 slices fresh ginger; ½ teaspoon dried shrimp paste; 2 tablespoons oil; 1 large red or brown onion, thinly sliced; 1 tomato, quartered; 1 teaspoon sugar; 1 teaspoon salt; 1 heaped tablespoon dried tamarind, soaked in ½ cup water and strained

Peel the shrimp and set aside. Grind the chilies, shallots, garlic, ginger and dried shrimp paste finely. Heat the oil in a skillet and gently fry the ground ingredients for 3–5 minutes until they smell fragrant. Add the shrimp and fry, stirring constantly, for 1–2 minutes until they change color. Add all other ingredients and simmer gently, uncovered, for 3–5 minutes until the shrimp are cooked.

Chili Shrimp in Coconut Milk

Serves 4: (1 lb) 500 g raw shrimp; 8–10 shallots or 1½ medium-size red or brown onions; 8–12 fresh red chilies; 2 slices lengkuas; 4 candlenuts or macadamias; ½ teaspoon dried shrimp paste; 2 tablespoons oil; 1 cup (8 fl oz) coconut milk; ½ teaspoon salt; ¼ cup (2 fl oz) tamarind water (see page 392); 2 stalks lemongrass, bruised, or substitute

Wash and peel the shrimp. Dry and set aside.

Grind the shallots, chilies, *lengkuas*, candlenuts and dried shrimp paste finely. Heat the oil, then gently fry the ground ingredients for 3–5 minutes, until cooked and fragrant. Add the shrimp and fry for 1 minute, stirring constantly. Put in the coconut milk, salt, tamarind water and

Chili Fried Shrimp

lemongrass, and bring slowly to the boil, stirring. Simmer gently, uncovered, until the coconut milk thickens and the shrimp are cooked.

Note: Some cooks add a cake of finely diced bean curd with the shrimp.

Clams with Sausage and Ham

Serves 4: 3 tablespoons oil; 4 onions, sliced; 1 garlic clove, crushed; 1 teaspoon paprika; dash of hot pepper sauce, to taste; freshly ground black pepper; 2 tomatoes, peeled, seeded and finely chopped; 3½ oz (100 g) smoked ham or prosciutto, chopped; 3½ oz (100 g) chorizo (spicy pork sausage), chopped; ½ cup (4 fl oz) dry white wine; 2 sprigs parsley, finely chopped; 36 clams or mussels, washed

Heat the oil in a casserole and sauté the onions and garlic until the onions are soft and transparent. Add the paprika, pepper sauce, pepper, tomatoes, ham, chorizo sausage, wine and parsley, and simmer for 10 minutes. Place the clams or mussels on top, cover tightly and simmer over medium heat for 8–10 minutes or until all the shellfish open. Discard any unopened shells. Serve immediately.

Cod with Olives and Tomatoes

Serves 4: ¾ cup (6 fl oz) olive oil; 2 onions, finely chopped; 4 tomatoes, peeled and chopped; salt and pepper; 13 oz (400 g) dried and salted cod, soaked overnight and rinsed; 3½ oz (100 g) black olives, pitted

Heat the oil in a casserole, brown the onions, add the tomatoes, season to taste and simmer for 15 minutes. Add the cod, simmer for 10 minutes more, then remove from heat and let stand for 1 hour. Stir in the olives and refrigerate for 2–3 hours before serving.

Cod with Potatoes, Onions and Black Olives

Serves 6: 1½ lb (750 g) dried salt cod; 6 boiling potatoes; 1¼ cups (10 fl oz) olive oil; 4 onions, sliced; 1 garlic clove, crushed; 24 black olives; 6 hard-cooked eggs, cut into quarters; 2 sprigs parsley, finely chopped

Soak the cod in cold water for 12 hours, changing the water several times. Drain the cod and rinse under running water, then put into a saucepan, cover with water and simmer over low heat for 1 hour. Drain, remove the skin and bones and, with a fork, flake into pieces. Set aside.

Boil the potatoes, then peel and slice. Set aside.

In a skillet, heat the oil and sauté the onions and garlic. Grease a casserole and arrange two layers each of potatoes, cod, onions and olives.

Bake in an oven preheated to 350°F (180°C) for 20 minutes or until brown. Serve garnished with eggs and parsley.

Corn, Chicken and Clam Pie

Serves 6–8: 2 tablespoons (1 oz) butter; 8 oz (250 g) very small white onions; 1 stalk celery, finely chopped; ⅓ cup (1½ oz) all purpose flour; 1 teaspoon salt; ¼ teaspoon dried basil; ¼ teaspoon cumin; 2 cups canned clams, undrained; 1 cup (8 fl oz) rich chicken stock; 1 cup (8 fl oz) light cream; 12-oz (340-g) can whole kernel corn, well drained; 1 large cooked chicken, shredded (about 3 cups meat); 2 hard-cooked eggs, coarsely chopped; ¼ cup canned pimiento, chopped; ¼ cup (2 fl oz) sherry or white wine; 1 unbaked 9-in (23-cm) shortcrust pie shell (see page 319)

In a large skillet, heat the butter and sauté the onions and celery. Stir in the flour, salt, basil and cumin. Gradually stir in the clams, stock and cream. Add the corn and chicken and bring to the boil. Simmer for 10 minutes, stirring occasionally.

Spoon into a casserole. Stir in the remaining ingredients and cover the top with pastry. Bake in an oven preheated to 400°F (200°C) for about 30 minutes or until the crust is golden brown.

Cornish Lobsters

Serves 4: 1 small onion chopped; 1 cup (8 fl oz) water; 1 cup (8 fl oz) white wine vinegar; bouquet garni, consisting of 1 sprig fresh thyme, 3 sprigs fresh parsley and 1 bay leaf tied up with string; salt and pepper; 2 live lobsters
Sauce: 2 tablespoons (1 oz) butter; 1 small tin anchovy fillets, drained and chopped; 1 cup (8 fl oz) white wine; 1 tablespoon lemon juice or white wine vinegar; pinch of grated nutmeg; pinch of ground mace; pepper; ¼ cup (½ oz) fresh breadcrumbs

Put the onion, water, vinegar, bouquet garni and salt and pepper into a pan and bring it to the boil. Simmer for 5 minutes.

Wash the lobsters and roast them on a spit in an oven preheated to 350°F (180°C) or in a baking dish for 30 minutes, basting frequently with the above mixture.

Meanwhile, make the sauce. Melt the butter in a pan and add the anchovies, mashing them well with a wooden spoon. Add the wine, lemon juice, nutmeg, mace and pepper, and simmer, stirring occasionally, for 5 minutes. Stir in the breadcrumbs and simmer for a few minutes longer. Remove the lobsters from the oven, split them in half, remove the intestines, crack the claws and serve with the hot sauce.

Note: If you do not wish to cook the lobsters while alive, pierce the brain with a skewer to kill them quickly, fill the hole with butter and then cook as above.

Coulibiac

Serves 6: 1 large onion, finely chopped; 2 tablespoons (1 oz) butter; 6½ oz (200 g) fresh mushrooms, finely chopped; 6½-oz (220-g) can salmon, drained and flaked; 1 cup (5 oz) cooked white rice; 2 tablespoons seedless raisins, chopped; 2–3 tablespoons grated lemon peel; 2 tablespoons lemon juice; 1 egg; salt and black pepper; 12-oz (375-g) package frozen puff pastry, defrosted; 1 egg, lightly beaten

Place the onion and butter in a microwave-safe covered dish and microwave on HIGH (100%) for 3 minutes. Add the mushrooms, cover and vent. Microwave for 2 minutes on HIGH (100%). Mix with the remaining ingredients except the pastry and beaten egg, then cool.

Roll one-third of the pastry into a rectangular shape. Place on a baking sheet, cut out the shape of a large fish and pile the filling in the pastry, leaving a narrow border all around. Brush the border with the beaten egg.

Roll out the remaining pastry and cover the filling. Press around the edges following the shape of the fish. Cut with a sharp knife to give a clean edge. Use a teaspoon to mark the design of scales and fins and make several diagonal slashes across the top. Brush the top of the pastry with the remaining beaten egg.

Bake in a convection oven preheated to 410°F (210°C) for 15 minutes and then 25–30 minutes on 360°F (180°C) until puffed and golden brown.

Crab Hotpot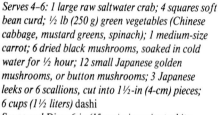

Serves 4–6: 1 large raw saltwater crab; 4 squares soft bean curd; ½ lb (250 g) green vegetables (Chinese cabbage, mustard greens, spinach); 1 medium-size carrot; 6 dried black mushrooms, soaked in cold water for ½ hour; 12 small Japanese golden mushrooms, or button mushrooms; 3 Japanese leeks or 6 scallions, cut into 1½-in (4-cm) pieces; 6 cups (1½ liters) dashi
Sauce and Dips: 6-in (15-cm) piece giant white radish; 1 fresh red chili; 1 large onion; 1 teaspoon salt; ⅔ cup (5 fl oz) lemon juice; ⅔ cup (5 fl oz) dashi; ⅓ cup (2½ fl oz) light soy sauce

Clean the crab and remove any inedible parts, then rinse and chop into several large pieces, leaving the legs attached to the body pieces.

Slice the bean curd into 3–4 pieces. Wash the green vegetables, shake out the water and chop roughly. Scrape the carrot and slice thinly or cut into decorative shapes with a vegetable cutter. Drain the dried mushrooms, discard the stems and cut a cross on the top of each with a sharp knife.

Heat the stock in a large flameproof casserole, put in all the vegetables and crab pieces and simmer for 7 minutes. Add the bean curd. Set over a portable fire on the table and continue to simmer until ready to set.

To make the sauce, mince together the radish and chili and place in a bowl. To make the first dip, mince the onion, then mix the salt and spoon into a bowl. For the second dip, heat the remaining ingredients slightly, cool, then pour into a bowl. Serve the dishes separately with the hotpot.

Crab Mornay

Serves 6: 1 lb (500 g) frozen crabmeat; 1 large scallion, diced; 1 medium-size carrot, peeled and diced; ¼–⅓ red bell pepper, trimmed and diced; ⅔ cup (2 oz) frozen peas; 4 tablespoons (2 oz) butter, diced; 3 tablespoons all purpose flour; 2 cups (16 fl oz) milk; 2 fish stock cubes; pinch of dried dill; salt and black pepper; 2½ oz (75 g) canned button mushrooms, drained and chopped; 1 cup (4 oz) grated cheese

Place the block of crabmeat in its plastic wrapping in a dish and microwave on DEFROST (30%) for 20 minutes, turning twice and flexing the bag to break up the block as soon as it begins to soften. Remove from the microwave when the crab still feels very cold and allow to thaw completely.

Place the scallion, carrot, pepper and peas in a dish and add the butter. Cover and microwave on HIGH (100%) for 4½ minutes. Remove the vegetables with a slotted spoon and set aside. Add the flour to the butter and stir well, then add the milk, stock cubes, dill and seasonings. Mix thoroughly. Microwave for 9 minutes on HIGH (100%), stirring every 3 minutes.

Add the vegetables, mushrooms and drained crabmeat and mix well with the sauce. Cover with plastic wrap and microwave on MEDIUM (50%) for 5 minutes. Spread the grated cheese over the dish and microwave, uncovered, a final 2 minutes on MEDIUM (50%). Serve hot.

Crab Quiche

Serves 6–8: 1 cup flaked crabmeat; 1 cup (4 oz) finely diced Swiss cheese; 1 unbaked 9-in (23-cm) shortcrust pie shell (see page 321); 3 eggs; 1½ cups (12 fl oz) cream; ¼ cup (2 fl oz) sherry; 1 teaspoon salt; ½ teaspoon nutmeg; pinch of paprika

Mix the crabmeat and cheese together and spread over the base of the pastry. Beat the remaining ingredients together, then pour over the crab and cheese mixture.

Bake in an oven preheated to 425°F (220°C) for 15 minutes, then reduce the temperature to 325°F (160°C) and cook for a further 20–30 minutes or until the filling is firm and golden.

Note: This recipe may be doubled and the pastry fitted into a jelly roll dish. Cut into finger-size pieces for appetizers.

Coulibiac

Crab Hotpot

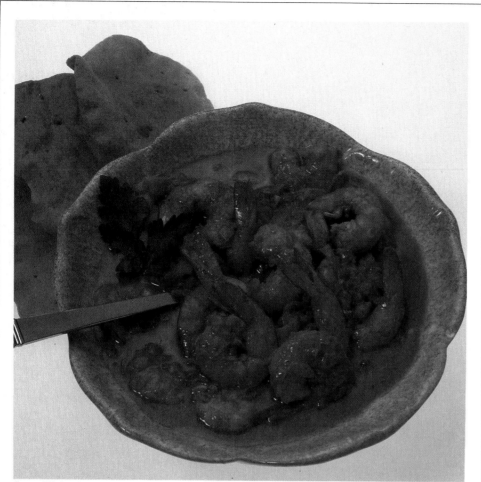
Creamed Shrimp Curry

Peel the shrimp, leaving the tail on. Cut down the back with a sharp knife, remove the intestinal tract and carefully press each shrimp open into a butterfly shape. Cut the fish fillet into 6 pieces. Prepare the vegetables. Cover and chill all prepared ingredients until just before frying.

Make the dipping sauce by combining the *dashi*, soy sauce and *mirin* in a pan. Bring to the boil, then allow to cool. Pour into individual sauce bowls. Put the grated *daikon* and ginger onto serving dishes to allow diners to add to the dipping sauce to suit individual taste.

Put the vegetable oil and sesame oil into a wok or deep skillet to heat. Make the batter, mixing all the ingredients quickly and lightly. Take care not to overmix — a few lumps are not a problem.

When the oil is very hot, dip a few items into the batter and fry 6–8 pieces of food at a time. Do not add more food or the temperature of the oil will be lowered. When the food is light brown and crisp, remove and drain, then serve immediately. Scoop out and discard any fragments of batter remaining in the oil before adding the next batch of ingredients.

It is essential that *tempura* be eaten while still hot and crisp; if you have a portable frying unit that can be brought to the table, this is ideal. Otherwise, as cook, you will need to make repeated trips between the kitchen and dining table to ensure the *tempura* is eaten immediately.

Creamed Shrimp Curry

Serves 4: 1¼ lb (625 g) raw shrimp, shelled; 1 small onion, grated; 1 garlic clove, crushed; 1 fresh red chili, seeded and chopped; ½-in (1-cm) piece fresh ginger, grated; 1-in (2.5-cm) piece lemon-grass, chopped; ½ teaspoon turmeric; 2 teaspoons curry powder; ½ teaspoon salt; ¼ teaspoon black pepper; 2 teaspoons sugar; 2 tablespoons vegetable oil; 1½–2 tablespoons fish sauce; 1 cup (8 fl oz) thick coconut milk; 3 tablespoons heavy cream

Wash the shrimp and devein if necessary. Dry on paper towels. Grind the onion, garlic, chili, ginger and lemongrass to a paste, then add the turmeric, curry powder, salt, pepper and sugar. Fry for 2 minutes.

Add the shrimp and cook until they change color, then stir in the fish sauce and stir briefly. Pour in the coconut milk mixed with the cream and simmer gently for 3–4 minutes. Serve with steamed rice.

D

Deep Fried Battered Seafood and Vegetables (Tempura)

Serves 6: 12 very large raw shrimp; 8 oz (250 g) white fish fillet; any of the following vegetables: 18 snow peas; 12 slices lotus root; 1 small eggplant, sliced ½-in (1-cm) thick; 6 fresh mushrooms (preferably shiitake*); 1 green bell pepper, cut into bite-size pieces; 1 large onion, cut in ½-in (1-cm) slices; 1 small bamboo shoot, cut in ½-in (1-cm) slices; edible chrysanthemum leaves or* shiso *leaves; oil for deep frying; ¼–½ cup (2–4 fl oz) sesame oil Tempura Batter: 4 oz (125 g) all purpose flour; 1 egg; 1 cup (8 fl oz) ice water; pinch of baking soda Dipping Sauce: ¾ cup (6 fl oz) light dashi; 3 tablespoons light soy sauce; 3 tablespoons sweet rice wine (mirin); 3 tablespoons finely grated giant white radish (daikon); 2 teaspoons finely grated fresh ginger*

Deep Fried Crab and Bean Curd Balls

Serves 4: 8 oz (250 g) fresh, frozen or canned crabmeat; 6½ oz (200 g) soft bean curd; 1 egg; ¼ teaspoon salt; 2 teaspoons light soy sauce; 1 scallion, very thinly sliced; 1½ teaspoons ginger juice (see page 209); oil for deep frying Dipping Sauce: 1 cup (8 fl oz) dashi; 2 tablespoons sweet rice wine (mirin); 2 tablespoons dark soy sauce; 4 oz (125 g) giant white radish (daikon), grated

Flake the crabmeat and put it into a bowl. Press the moisture from the bean curd by putting it into a colander with a lightly weighted plate on top for 30 minutes. Pat dry with paper towels, then push it through a sieve into the bowl with the crab. Beat the egg lightly, then mix well into the crab and bean curd. Add the salt, soy sauce, scallion and ginger juice and mix thoroughly.

Heat the oil in a deep skillet or wok. With wet hands, take a handful of crab mixture and squeeze out a ball through your thumb and clenched fingers. Scrape the ball off your hand with a spoon and drop into the very hot oil. Fry a few balls at a time for about 4–5 minutes, until golden brown, then drain on paper towels.

To make the sauce, combine the *dashi*, *mirin* and soy sauce in a pan and bring just to the boil. Put the *daikon* into individual dishes and prepare four sauce bowls for the hot sauce. When all the crab balls are cooked, divide between the serving bowls and serve with the hot sauce. Each diner adds a little *daikon* to the sauce, dipping the crab balls in just before eating.

F

Fillet of Turbot with Red Butter Sauce

Serves 4: 1 bottle of red Burgundy; 3 lb (1.5 kg) turbot fillets (or flounder); 8 tablespoons (4 oz) butter, chilled; ¼ cup (2 fl oz) heavy cream, whipped; salt and freshly ground black pepper; cayenne pepper

Boil the wine over high heat until reduced by one-quarter of the original volume.

Steam the fish fillets for about 10 min-utes, or until just cooked but still very firm. Remove and keep them warm.

Dice the hard butter and whisk it into the reduced wine over high heat. The butter should stay creamy. Just before the sauce reaches the boil, whisk in the whipped cream, then season with salt and freshly ground black pepper. Serve the fish fillets with the sauce poured over and sprinkled with a little cayenne pepper.

Fish and Fruit Salad Filipina

Serves 4-6: 1 lb (500 g) white fish fillets; ¼ cup (2 fl oz) lemon juice; 3 slices fresh pineapple, diced; 5-6 guavas, pitted and diced; 3 bananas, diced; 1 large firm ripe mango, peeled, pitted and diced; 1 Spanish onion, thinly sliced; 1-2 fresh red chilies, seeded and shredded; ¾ cup (6 fl oz) thick coconut milk; salt and black pepper

Cut the fish into narrow strips and mari-nate in the lemon juice for at least 6 hours. The citric acid in the fruit juice will ten-derize the fish, making cooking un-necessary. However, if preferred, the fish can be lightly steamed before marinating.

Arrange the drained fish and prepared fruit in a salad bowl. Garnish with the onion rings and shredded chili and pour the coconut milk over. Season with salt and pepper to taste. Chill before serving.

Fish Cutlets

Serves 4: 12 oz (375 g) steamed fresh fish, or canned fish; 1 tablespoon oil; 1 medium-size red or brown onion, finely chopped; ½ in (1 cm) fresh ginger, very finely chopped; 1-2 fresh green chilies, very finely chopped; 1 lb (500 g) baking potatoes, boiled and mashed; ½ teasoon turmeric; 1 teaspoon salt; ½ teaspoon white pepper; 2 eggs; 1 teaspoon lime or lemon juice; 1 tablespoon finely chopped fresh cilantro leaves; 1½ cups (6 oz) fine dried breadcrumbs; oil for shallow frying

Fillet the fish, flake fish and set aside. Heat the oil in a skillet and sauté the onion, gin-ger and chilies until soft. Combine the fish, fried ingredients, potatoes, turmeric, salt, pepper, 1 egg, lime juice and cilantro leaves, and mix well. Set aside until cold.

Shape the fish mixture into balls about 2 in (5 cm) in diameter, then flatten into rounds. Beat the remaining egg, then dip the cutlets into the egg and breadcrumbs to coat. If possible, chill for 30 minutes before frying in hot oil, a few moments on either side, until golden brown.

Fish in Coconut Sauce

Serves 4: 1¼ lb (625 g) thin fillets of white fish; 2 large onions; 2 green chilies; 1-in (2.5-cm) piece fresh ginger; 1½-in (4-cm) stalk lemongrass; 3 garlic cloves; 2 teaspoons dried shrimp, soaked; 1½ oz (45 g) shredded coconut; 1 cup (8 fl oz) thick coconut milk; 2 tablespoons coconut oil or vegetable oil; 2 heaped tablespoons finely chopped fresh cilantro leaves; 1 cup (8 fl oz) thin coconut milk; lemon juice or tamarind water; salt

Cut the fish fillets into 2-in (5-cm) squares and place in a dish. Thinly slice one onion and set aside. Mince the chilies, ginger, lemongrass, garlic, dried shrimp and coco-nut to a fairly smooth paste, then add the thick coconut milk. Pour over the fish and marinate for 1 hour.

Heat the oil and fry the remaining sliced onion until lightly colored. Add the fish pieces and cook briefly, then add the cilantro and pour over the thin coconut milk and marinade. Cover and simmer on low heat until the fish is cooked. Lift out the fish with a slotted spoon and place on a serving dish.

Continue to simmer the sauce until thick and creamy. Season to taste with the lemon juice or tamarind water and add salt. Pour over the fish and serve at once.

Fish and Fruit Salad Filipina

Fish in Taucheo Sauce

*Serves 4: 1 lb (500 g) white fish fillets or steaks;
½ cup (4 fl oz) oil; 2 slices fresh ginger; 1 garlic
clove; 1 fresh red chili, seeds removed; 1 medium-
size red or brown onion, sliced; 2 teaspoons salted
soybeans, lightly pounded; 1 teaspoon sugar;
1 teaspoon light soy sauce; ½ cup (4 fl oz) water;
¼ teaspoon salt*

Dry the fish thoroughly. Heat the oil in a
skillet until very hot and fry the fish, a few
pieces at a time, for just 1 minute on each
side. Remove and drain. Pour off all but 1
tablespoon of oil.

Pound the ginger, garlic and chili
together. Heat the oil and fry the sliced
onion for 2 minutes, then add the pounded
spices and stir-fry for 2–3 minutes, taking
care not to let it turn brown. Add the
soybeans and stir-fry for 1 minute, then
mix in the sugar, soy sauce, water and salt,
and simmer for 2 minutes. Add the fish and
simmer gently until cooked, turning from
time to time. The liquid should be reduced
to just a couple of tablespoons of thick
gravy.

Fish Soufflé

*Serves 6: 1⅓ lb (600 g) cooked fish fillets; 3 stale
rolls, soaked in water; 1 onion, finely chopped;
2 sprigs parsley, finely chopped; salt and freshly
ground black pepper; 1 cup (8 fl oz) sour cream;
4 eggs, separated; 3 anchovy fillets, cut into small
pieces; ½ cup (2 oz) grated Parmesan cheese*

Mince the fish, rolls (well squeezed out),
onion and parsley in a food processor. Add
the salt, pepper, sour cream and egg yolks.

Whip the egg whites until they are stiff
then fold them into the mixture. Mix in the
anchovies.

Pour the mixture into a buttered soufflé
dish and bake in an oven preheated to
400°F (200°C) for 30–40 minutes. Sprinkle
the top of the soufflé with the cheese 10
minutes before taking it out of the oven.
Serve immediately.

Fish with Cheese and Tomato Sauce

*Serves 4: 1½ lb (750 g) fresh fish fillets such as
snapper or bream; juice of 1 lemon; salt and freshly
ground black pepper; ¾ cup (3 oz) grated Cheddar
cheese; ¼ cup (2 fl oz) sour cream; ¼ cup (2 fl oz)
milk; 3 tablespoons chopped parsley; ¼ cup (2 fl oz)
tomato puree; 1½ tablespoons butter, cut into
pieces; 2½ tablespoons dry breadcrumbs;
1½ tablespoons grated Cheddar cheese for garnish*

Sprinkle the fish fillets with the lemon
juice, salt and pepper and allow them to
stand for 10 minutes.

Mix the grated cheese, sour cream, milk,
salt, pepper, parsley and tomato puree to a
smooth paste.

Arrange one layer of fish fillets in a buttered fireproof glass or earthenware dish.
Cover the fish with a layer of the cheese
mixture and continue with alternate layers,
finishing with a layer of the cheese mixture.

Cover the dish and bake in an oven
preheated to 400°F (200°C) for 10–15 minutes. Remove from the oven, sprinkle with
pieces of butter, breadcrumbs and cheese
and return the dish, uncovered, to the oven
for 15 minutes or until the top is brown.
This can also be done under the broiler.

Fish with Lime and Macadamia Nut Butter ⭐

*Serves 6: 6 pearl perch (sea bass, etc.) fillets each
weighing approx. 4 oz (125 g); seasoned flour;
8 tablespoons (4 oz) unsalted butter; 4 oz (125 g)
macadamia nuts, chopped; 3 tablespoons finely
chopped parsley; juice of 1 large lime; salt and
pepper*

Wipe the fish with paper towels, then coat
lightly in seasoned flour, shaking off the
excess.

Preheat a microwave browning/searing
skillet for 6 minutes. Add two-thirds of the
butter and quickly put in the fish. It is
important to put the butter in the pan just
before the fish is added, otherwise it will

Place the fillets on top of
the hot butter.

Spoon the butter over and
serve immediately.

burn. Microwave uncovered on HIGH
(100%) for 1 minute, then turn and microwave for a further 2 minutes on HIGH
(100%). Test the fish; it should flake easily
with a fork. Remove and keep warm.

Add the remaining butter and the
macadamia nuts. Microwave on HIGH
(100%) for 2–2½ minutes, stirring twice,
until golden. Spoon over the fish, leaving
the butter in the skillet. Add the parsley
and lime juice, salt and pepper and microwave on HIGH (100%) for 1 minute. Pour
over the fish and serve at once.

Fish with Tomatoes, Wine and Oregano

*Serves 6: 6 fish cutlets 1 in (2.5 cm) thick (use
halibut, snapper or any firm white-fleshed fish); salt
and freshly ground black pepper; juice of 1 lemon;
1 cup (250 g) canned peeled tomatoes, chopped;
3 tablespoons tomato puree; ½ cup (4 fl oz) dry
white wine; ½ cup (4 fl oz) olive oil; 1 garlic clove,
chopped; 2 teaspoons dried oregano; 3 fresh
tomatoes, peeled and sliced; 3 sprigs parsley,
chopped*

Arrange the fish cutlets in a baking dish
2 in (5 cm) deep. Sprinkle with salt, pepper
and lemon juice.

In a saucepan, combine the remaining
ingredients except the fresh tomato slices
and parsley. Simmer on low heat for 30
minutes. Pour the sauce over the fish,
arrange the fresh tomato slices on top and
sprinkle with parsley.

Bake the fish in an oven preheated to
400°F (200°C) for 30 minutes. Serve hot.

Fresh Fish Pie

*Serves 6–8: Court Bouillon: 1 cup (8 fl oz) white
wine; 3 cups (24 fl oz) water; 1 onion, sliced;
1 carrot, sliced; 1 teaspoon salt; 3 peppercorns
1½ lb (750 g) fish fillets (use firm, white-fleshed
fish); 4 tablespoons (2 oz) butter; 6 scallions,
chopped; 4 oz (125 g) mushrooms, sliced; 1 garlic
clove, chopped; 2 tablespoons all purpose flour;
½ cup (4 fl oz) cream; 14 oz (440 g) canned
condensed cream of oyster soup; ¼ teaspoon dried
tarragon; 3 tablespoons chopped parsley; 1 unbaked
9-in (23-cm) double shortcrust pie shell (see page
336)*

To make the court bouillon, place the
wine, water, onion, carrot, salt and peppercorns in a skillet and bring to the boil.

Reduce the heat and add the fish fillets.

Simmer for 20 minutes or until the fish flakes easily. Remove the fish from the stock and set aside. Strain the stock into a bowl and reserve ¾ cup (6 fl oz) for the sauce. The rest can be cooled, skimmed and frozen.

Meanwhile, to make the filling, heat the butter in a skillet, add the scallions, mushrooms and garlic, and sauté for a few minutes until the scallions are tender. Stir in the flour and cook 1 minute longer.

Remove from the heat and gradually add the reserved fish stock, stirring constantly. Add the cream, oyster soup and tarragon. Bring to the boil, stirring constantly until the sauce thickens. Flake the fish and add it to the sauce with the parsley. Cool.

Roll out the pastry and line a 9-in (23-cm) pie dish with half of it. Spoon the filling into the pastry shell and cover with the remaining pastry. Bake in an oven preheated to 375°F (190°C) for 20 minutes, reduce the oven temperature to 350°F (180°C) and bake for a further 20 minutes, or until the filling is firm and golden.

Fried Fish in Beer Batter

Serves 6: 6 large or 12 small fish fillets; juice of 1 lemon; salt and freshly ground black pepper; flour for dusting fish fillets; oil for frying; lemon wedges and parsley sprigs for garnish
Batter: 1¼ cups (5 oz) all purpose flour; 1 cup (8 fl oz) beer; 2 teaspoons olive oil; salt; 2 eggs, separated

Arrange the fish fillets in a glass dish and sprinkle them with lemon juice, salt and pepper. Leave to stand for 30 minutes.

Prepare the batter by whisking all the ingredients except the egg whites to a smooth liquid consistency. Beat the egg whites until they are stiff and fold them into the batter. Dust the fillets with the flour and dip them in the batter.

Heat the oil in a skillet and fry the fillets for 8-12 minutes until they flake easily and are golden brown. Drain them on paper towels and serve hot, garnished with lemon wedges and parsley.

Fried Squid Rings

Serves 4: 2 lb (1 kg) squid, cleaned and cut into rings ¼ in (5 mm) wide; 2 cups (16 fl oz) milk; 1½ cups (6 oz) all purpose flour; salt; 1½ cups (12 fl oz) water; oil for frying; freshly ground black pepper; 3 sprigs parsley, chopped; 1 lemon, cut into wedges for garnish

To tenderize the squid, soak it in the milk for 4-6 hours.

Dry the squid. Using ½ cup (2 oz) flour, dust the squid rings thoroughly. Make a batter by mixing the remaining flour, salt and enough water to make a liquid batter. Dip the squid into the batter and fry them until crisp and golden brown. Serve hot, sprinkled with salt, pepper and parsley, and garnished with lemon wedges.

Fried Trout with Almonds

Serves 4-6: 4-6 trout; salt and freshly ground black pepper; milk; all purpose flour; 8 tablespoons (4 oz) butter; 1 tablespoon oil; 4-6 tablespoons slivered almonds; juice of 1 lemon; 3 tablespoons finely chopped parsley

Season the cleaned trout with salt and a little pepper. Dip them in milk and then in flour. Melt half the butter with the oil and sauté the fish for 5 minutes each side or until golden brown and flakes easily. Remove the trout from the pan and keep warm.

Drain the fat from the pan and melt the remaining butter. Add the blanched, slivered almonds and cook, shaking the pan continuously until the almonds are golden brown. Add the lemon juice and parsley, and pour over the trout. Serve.

Fried Yellow Fish with Garlic Chives

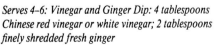

Serves 4-6: Vinegar and Ginger Dip: 4 tablespoons Chinese red vinegar or white vinegar; 2 tablespoons finely shredded fresh ginger
1½-lb (750-g) yellow fish (trout or grouper); 1 teaspoon salt; all purpose flour; 2 eggs, beaten; 8 cups (2 liters) oil for deep frying; 2-in (5-cm) piece fresh ginger, peeled; 10 garlic chives, shredded (or use 4-5 scallions); 1 tablespoon sesame oil; 1 teaspoon salt; 2 teaspoons rice wine or dry sherry

To make the dip, mix the vinegar and ginger at least 30 minutes before use. Reserve.

Clean the fish and score diagonally on both sides, cutting almost to the bones. Rub with the salt, then coat lightly with flour and brush with beaten egg. Coat with the flour again and set aside.

Heat a large wok and rub vigorously with the piece of ginger to prevent the fish from sticking. Heat the oil to smoking point. Carefully slide in the fish, holding it by its tail. Cook for 1 minute, then turn and cook the other side for 1 minute. Turn again and cook for 4 minutes on one side, then 4 minutes on the other side. Decrease the heat after the first side has cooked for about 2 minutes.

Lift out the fish on two spatulas and place it on a serving dish. Drain off the oil and wipe out the wok. Return about 3 tablespoons of the oil and fry the shredded garlic chives until softened. Add the sesame oil, salt and wine and stir in. Pour over the fish and serve at once with small dishes of vinegar and ginger dip.

H

Herb Marinated Shrimp

Serves 6: ½ cup (4 fl oz) olive oil; juice of 3 lemons; 1 tablespoon fresh oregano, chopped, or 1 teaspoon dried oregano; ½ teaspoon salt; freshly ground black pepper; 2 lb (1 kg) fresh jumbo shrimp, unshelled

To prepare the marinade, combine all ingredients except the shrimp in a screw-top jar and shake well. Place the shrimp in an enameled or glass dish and pour the marinade over. Refrigerate for 4 hours.

Preheat the broiler. Divide the shrimp into 6 portions and place them on six metal or bamboo skewers.

Broil for 2 minutes on each side, basting frequently with the marinade. When serving, pour the rest of the marinade over the shrimp and serve in their shells.

Hot and Spicy Squid

Serves 4: 1 lb (500 g) fresh small squid; beaten egg whites; all purpose flour; salt and cayenne pepper; olive oil for deep frying; lemon juice

Clean the squid under cold running water, removing the heads, stomachs, skin and fins. Rinse well and cut the tubular bodies into thin rings. Dip into the beaten egg whites. Heavily season approximately 1 cup of flour with salt and cayenne pepper. Pour into a paper or plastic bag and add the prepared squid. Shake vigorously.

Heat the olive oil in a wok or deep skillet to fairly hot and deep fry the squid rings until crisped on the surface and lightly colored. Drain well. Sprinkle with lemon juice before serving.

I

Italian Seafood Marinara

Serves 6: 2 lb (1 kg) cooked shellfish (oysters, scallops, shrimp, or rock lobster tails); ¼ cup (2 fl oz) olive oil; 2 garlic cloves, sliced; 1¾ lb (800 g) can tomatoes, sieved or pureed; 1½ teaspoons salt; 1 teaspoon oregano; 1 teaspoon chopped parsley; ¼ teaspoon pepper; ¼ cup (2 fl oz) red wine (optional); 1 lb (500 g) spaghetti or gemelle (spiral or corkscrew pasta)

Clean the shellfish, wash and drain, then sauté gently in medium hot oil for 5 minutes. Remove the shellfish from the skillet and keep warm. Add the garlic and sauté until golden. Stir in the tomatoes, salt, oregano, parsley, pepper and wine. Cook rapidly, uncovered, for 15 minutes or until thickened. Stir occasionally. If the sauce becomes too thick, add ¼–½ cup water. Add the shellfish and reheat gently. Meanwhile, cook the spaghetti and drain. Serve immediately with the sauce.

Hot and Spicy Squid

Mixed Seafood Hotpot

L

Lobster Thermidor

Serves 6: Buttered Breadcrumbs: 4 tablespoons (2 oz) butter; 1 cup (2 oz) fresh breadcrumbs 3 medium-size crayfish (rock lobster); 4 tablespoons (2 oz) butter; 1 small onion, finely chopped; 2 oz (60 g) mushrooms, chopped; 3 tablespoons all purpose flour; 2 cups (16 fl oz) milk; ¼ teaspoon dry mustard; ¼ teaspoon celery salt; 1 teaspoon salt; pinch of cayenne pepper; ⅔ cup (5 fl oz) cream; 2 egg yolks; 2 tablespoons dry sherry; 2 teaspoons lemon juice; 2–3 oz (60–90 g) grated cheese; lemon slices and parsley sprigs (garnish)

To make the buttered breadcrumbs, melt the butter in a saucepan, add the breadcrumbs and fry, stirring constantly, until golden brown.

Remove the crayfish claws and cut the crayfish in half lengthwise. Remove the meat, discard the coral (a long thread which is the digestive system) and cut the meat into 1-in (2.5-cm) cubes. Wash, dry and reserve the shells. Melt the butter in a saucepan and gently fry the onion and mushrooms for 2–3 minutes. Stir in the flour and cook over low heat for 1 minute. Add the milk and bring to the boil over medium heat, whisking continuously. Add the mustard, celery salt, salt and cayenne pepper, then stir in the cream, egg yolks, sherry, lemon juice and crayfish meat. Heat through and spoon the mixture into the crayfish shells. Sprinkle with grated cheese and buttered breadcrumbs.

Broil under a preheated broiler until golden brown. Garnish and serve hot.

M

Meeting Street Crab

Serves 6: 4 tablespoons (2 oz) butter; ¼ cup all purpose flour; 1 cup (8 fl oz) cream; ¼ cup (2 fl oz) sherry; 1 lb (500 g) crab, cooked and flaked; ¾ cup (3 oz) grated mature Cheddar cheese; salt and pepper; 1 baked 8-in (20-cm) shortcrust pie shell (see page 321)

Melt the butter in a pan, then stir in the flour until the mixture is bubbling. Remove from the heat and pour in the cream. Cook, whisking constantly, until the mixture has thickened. Gradually add the sherry and remaining filling ingredients.

Pour into the baked pie shell and bake in an oven preheated to 375°F (190°F) for 30–40 minutes or until golden.

Mixed Seafood Hotpot

Serves 4-6: 2 oz (60 g) dried rice vermicelli; 4-6 dried shiitake mushrooms; 1 lb (500 g) white fish fillets, with skin left on; 1 Japanese fish cake (kamaboko); 8–12 large raw shrimp; 1 medium-size carrot; 1 bunch (about 4 oz or/25 g) edible chrysanthemum leaves; 8 oz (250 g) white Chinese cabbage; 4 scallions; 4 cakes soft bean curd; 5 cups (1¼ liters) dashi or light chicken stock Dipping Sauce: ¼ cup (2 fl oz) light soy sauce; 2 tablespoons sake; ¼ cup (2 fl oz) lemon juice; 1 scallion; sprinkle of Japanese pepper (sansho)

Soak the transparent noodles in hot water for 1 minute, then drain and cut into 4-in (10-cm) lengths. Soak the dried mushrooms in hot water for 30 minutes, then squeeze dry, discard the stems and cut a cross in the center of each cap.

Cut the fish fillets into bite-sized pieces and carefully remove any bones. Cut the fish cake into ¼-in (5-mm) slices. Wipe the shrimp but do not peel.

Thinly slice the carrot and parboil in salted water. Rinse and dry the chrysanthemum leaves.

Shred the Chinese cabbage coarsely. Cut the scallions (including green tops) into 1½-in (4-cm) lengths. Wipe the bean curd, then cook under a hot broiler for 2–3 minutes on either side until lightly speckled. Cool, then cut into 1-in (2.5-cm) cubes.

Prepare the dipping sauce by putting the soy sauce and *sake* into a small pan and bringing just to the boil. Remove from the heat, cool, then add the lemon juice. Just before serving, slice the scallion (including the green top) very finely. Divide the dipping sauce equally into individual serving dishes; sprinkle with the scallion and a dash of Japanese pepper.

Just before the food is required, arrange all the prepared ingredients decoratively on one or two platters and bring to the table. Place a large pot over a burner in the center of the table and fill it with heated *dashi* or chicken stock. When it is simmering, add the sliced carrot and mushrooms and simmer for 1 minute. Add the fish fillets, fish cake and shrimp and simmer for 2 minutes. Add the chrysanthemum leaves, Chinese cabbage, scallions, bean curd and transparent noodles and cook for another 2 minutes. Diners can then help themselves to ingredients, dipping them into the sauce before eating.

Serve with rice in separate bowls and give each diner a soup bowl so that at the end of the meal the stock (which will have reduced and developed a rich flavor) can be enjoyed as a soup.

Mussels Marinière

Serves 1–2: 12 big mussels; 1 small onion, thinly sliced; ¾ cup (6 fl oz) dry white wine; 2 tablespoons (1 oz) butter; ½ teaspoon crushed garlic; pinch of white pepper; 2 tablespoons coarse breadcrumbs; 2 tablespoons chopped parsley

Place the well-scrubbed mussels into a saucepan with the onion, wine, butter, gar-

One Pot Salmon

lic and pepper. Cover and cook quickly over high heat until the mussels open (about 3 minutes). When they are all open, add the breadcrumbs and heat for 1 minute. Discard any shells that do not open. Garnish and serve hot in a soup plate.

Mussels Venetian Style

Serves 4: 1 cup finely chopped parsley; 3 garlic cloves, finely chopped; 1 cup (4 oz) fine dry breadcrumbs; salt and freshly ground black pepper; ¼ cup (2 fl oz) olive oil; 4 lb (2 kg) mussels, scrubbed

Combine the parsley, garlic, breadcrumbs, salt and pepper.

In a saucepan large enough to contain the mussels, heat most of the oil. Add the mussels, cover the pan and heat until all the shells have opened. Remove one half shell from each mussel and reserve the mussel liquid. Discard any unopened shells.

Spoon some of the breadcrumb mixture on top of each mussel, sprinkle with the remaining oil and place them under a preheated broiler to brown the breadcrumbs. Serve with some of the mussel liquid poured over.

O

One-Pot Salmon

Serves 4: 1½ lb (750 g) fresh or frozen salmon steaks; 8 dried shiitake mushrooms; 2 cakes soft bean curd; 4 oz (125 g) konnyaku; 4 oz (125 g) giant white radish (daikon); 4 oz (125 g) carrot; 8 oz (250 g) spinach; 8 oz (250 g) edible chrysanthemum leaves or watercress; 4 small leeks or 8 scallions; seven spice mixture (shichimi); Pon-Zu Sauce (see page 276)
Stock: 6 cups (48 fl oz) dashi; 3 tablespoons white miso; 2 tablespoons sweet rice wine (mirin); 1 tablespoon superfine sugar; salt to taste

Remove any scales from the fish but leave on the skin. Cut into bite-size pieces and remove any bones. Cover and set aside in the refrigerator.

Soak the mushrooms in hot water for 30 minutes, discard the stems and cut a cross in each cap. Broil the whole bean curd pieces for 2–3 minutes on either side under a hot broiler until lightly speckled, then cut into ¾-in (2-cm) cubes. Cut across the *konnyaku* cake to make slices about ¼ in (5 mm) thick and 1 in (2.5 cm) wide. Cook in boiling water for 3 minutes, then cool.

Cut a slit down the middle of each slice to within ½ in (1 cm) of each end and pull one end through the slit to give the appearance of a plait.

Cut the *daikon* in half lengthwise, then across into ¼-in (5-mm) thick slices. Simmer in water for 5 minutes, then drain, rinse and continue cooking in fresh water until just tender. Cut the carrot in a similar fashion and simmer in water until just tender.

Wash and dry the spinach and chrysanthemum leaves or watercress. Cut the small leeks or scallions diagonally into pieces about 1½ in (4 cm) long.

Arrange the salmon, mushrooms, bean curd and *konnyaku* on a platter and put the vegetables on another platter. Set a heating unit or fondue pot in the center of the table. Bring all stock ingredients almost to the boil in a heatproof casserole in the kitchen, then transfer to the table. Put in some of the fish, mushrooms, bean curd and *konnyaku* and simmer until the fish is half cooked. Add a selection of vegetables and continue simmering gently until cooked.

Each person helps himself to ingredients from the pot, sprinkling with a little seven spice mixture and dipping in Pon-Zu Sauce before eating. Add more items to the pot and continue cooking until they are finished. Serve the stock (which must never be allowed to boil as it will spoil the flavor) in soup bowls at the end of the meal and accompany with rice and pickles.

P

Poached Snapper Fillets with Herbed Butter

Poached Snapper Fillets with Herbed Butter

Serves 4: 10 oz (315 g) fresh snapper fillets; ½ cup (4 fl oz) dry white wine; 1 tablespoon butter; 1 bay leaf; pinch of freshly ground black pepper
Herbed Butter: 8 tablespoons (4 oz) butter; 1 tablespoon chopped parsley; 1 tablespoon chopped chives; 1 teaspoon chopped fresh basil; 1 teaspoon chopped fresh thyme; ½ teaspoon chopped fresh tarragon; ¼ teaspoon Dijon mustard

Place the fillets skin side down on a cutting board, hold firmly by the tail with the fingers of the left hand and use a narrow-bladed sharp knife to run between the fillet and skin, removing the skin completely. If necessary, rub your fingers with salt to pre-

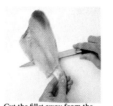

Cut the fillet away from the backbone.

Dot with butter.

vent them from slipping.

Place the fillets in a wide microwave-safe casserole and pour the wine over. Add the diced butter, the bay leaf and pepper. Cover and microwave on HIGH (100%) for 3 minutes. The fish should be almost cooked through. Rearrange in the casserole and set aside.

Place the butter in a small dish and soften on MEDIUM (50%) for 2 minutes. Add the herbs and mustard and whip until thoroughly mixed. Drain the liquid from the fish and discard the bay leaf. Cover thickly with the butter. Microwave on HIGH (100%) for 3 minutes, uncovered. Leave to stand, covered with aluminum foil, for 2 minutes, then serve. It is essential that the fish be completely covered with the butter to prevent dry patches.

Potage 'la Mer'

Serves 6: 8 oz (250 g) fresh, cleaned squid; 8 oz (250 g) white fish (flounder, bass, sea perch); 8 oz (250 g) shrimp; 8 oz (250 g) fresh scallops; 2 medium-size onions, very thinly sliced; 3 garlic cloves, crushed; ¼ cup (2 fl oz) olive oil; 13½-oz (425-g) can tomatoes, chopped; 4 cups (1 liter) water or well-flavored fish stock; 3 fish stock cubes, optional; 1 bay leaf; 8 spinach leaves, finely shredded; 2 scallions, finely shredded; 12-24 fresh oysters, removed from the shell

Clean and thoroughly rinse the squid. Cut into rings. Cube the fish. Peel and devein the shrimp and remove the black intestinal vein from the scallops.

Place the onions, garlic and olive oil in a very large microwave-safe casserole and cover. Microwave on HIGH (100%) for 3 minutes. Add the tomatoes, water or stock, stock cubes and bay leaf and microwave on HIGH (100%) for 10 minutes, covered. Give the dish a half turn, if necessary.

Add the cubed fish and microwave for 1 minute on HIGH (100%), then add the squid, shrimp, scallops, spinach and scallions and microwave, covered, on HIGH

(100%) for 3 minutes. The seafood should still be slightly opaque. Remove from the oven and add the oysters. Cover and leave to stand for 5–6 minutes. Serve with plenty of crusty French bread.

Add the cubed fish.

Place the seafood, spinach and scallions on top.

Potage 'la Mer'

Q

Quenelles of Pike

Serves 6: 2 lb (1 kg) fish fillets, chilled; 4 cups (1 liter) heavy cream; ½ teaspoon salt; cayenne pepper; ½ cup (4 oz) melted ghee or clarified butter; 3 eggs; 1½ cups (12 fl oz) Mornay Sauce (see page 109)

In a food processor, process the fish until very fine. Alternatively, rub the finely chopped flesh through a sieve. Place in a bowl set over ice and slowly incorporate the cream, beating with a wooden spoon. If an electric mixer is available, this can be done using a paddle attachment. The resulting mixture should have the consistency of a heavy mayonnaise.

Add the salt and pepper and slowly incorporate the butter and the eggs. Refrigerate the mixture for 24 hours.

Form the quenelles, one large or two smaller ones per person, using two spoons and rolling them into shape on a floured board. Gently poach them in simmering salted water for about 5 minutes. To serve, pour some mornay sauce over each quenelle and broil until the sauce browns a little.

R

Roasted Fish Parcels

Serves 4: 1 lb (500 g) white fish fillets; 1 tablespoon coriander seeds; 5 tablespoons grated or moistened shredded coconut; 4 shallots (or use Spanish onions), chopped; 4 scallions, chopped; 2 garlic cloves, chopped; 2-in (5-cm) piece lemongrass, chopped; 4 dried red chilies, soaked; ½-in (1-cm) piece fresh ginger, grated; 2 tablespoons chopped roasted peanuts; 2 tablespoons coconut or peanut oil; ½ teaspoon turmeric; 1 teaspoon salt; ½ teaspoon black pepper; ¾ cup (6 fl oz) thick coconut milk; banana leaf or aluminum foil; butter or oil

Cut the fish into thin slices approximately 2 in x ¾ in (5 cm x 2 cm). Roast the coriander seeds and the coconut in a dry pan over low heat or until lightly colored and fragrant, stirring continually to prevent burning. Grind to a coarse powder.

Grind the shallots, scallions, garlic, lemongrass, dried chilies, ginger and peanuts to a paste and fry for 1–2 minutes in the coconut or peanut oil. Add the turmeric, salt, pepper, ground coriander and coconut, and fry lightly, then pour in the coconut milk and mix well.

Cut the banana leaf or aluminum foil into 6-in (15-cm) squares. Hold the banana leaf pieces over a gas flame or other direct heat source for a few seconds to soften. Brush with butter or oil and place a spoonful of the coconut seasoning paste in the center. Press on a slice of fish and cover with more seasoning paste. Fold up and pin the ends with toothpicks or tie with cotton. Roast over a charcoal fire or under a moderately hot broiler until cooked through, approximately 10 minutes. Serve hot or cold.

S

Salmon Pie with Dill Sauce

Serves 6–8: 2 cups (4 oz) soft breadcrumbs; ½ cup (4 fl oz) milk; 1 egg, slightly beaten; 1 tablespoon chopped onion; 2 tablespoons finely chopped parsley; 1 tablespoon butter or margarine, melted; ¾ teaspoon salt; 16 oz (500 g) canned salmon, drained and flaked; 1 egg, well beaten; 4 medium-size potatoes, peeled, boiled and mashed
Dill Sauce: 1 tablespoon butter or margarine; 1 tablespoon all purpose flour; 1½ cups (10 fl oz) milk (or 1 cup milk with white wine added); 1 teaspoon sugar; ¾ teaspoon dried dill; ½ teaspoon salt; 1 tablespoon lemon juice; ½ cup (4 fl oz) sour cream

Combine the breadcrumbs, milk, egg, onion, parsley, butter and salt. Blend in the salmon and mix well. Spoon the mixture into an 8-in (20-cm) buttered pie dish. Beat the egg into the mashed potatoes and pipe or spoon the mixture around the edge of the pie. Bake in an oven preheated to 350°F (180°C) for 30–35 minutes.

Meanwhile, to make the sauce, melt the butter in a saucepan and stir in the flour. Add the milk, sugar, dill and salt. Cook until bubbling and thickened, stirring constantly. Combine the lemon juice and sour cream and gradually stir into the sauce.

Salmon Sautéed with Lemon

Serves 6: 1½ lb (750 g) salmon or salmon trout; 1 teaspoon salt; oil or butter; 2 lemons; 2 small cucumbers, about 5 in (13 cm) long

Cut the salmon into six steaks, across the body. Sprinkle with salt and let stand for several minutes. Rinse off and wipe dry. In a heavy-based pan, heat the oil or butter and sauté the fish gently for 4 minutes on each side. Sprinkle with the juice of 1 lemon during cooking.

When the fish is cooked, lift each slice onto a small plate, preferably rectangular, and decorate with cucumber fans and lemon butterflies prepared as follows.

Wash the cucumbers and cut each into 3 pieces. Slice each piece lengthwise into ¼-in (5-mm) slices, discarding the end pieces. To make cucumber fans, use a very sharp knife to cut each slice into strips, leaving the end ¼ in (5-mm) uncut. Gently press the "fan" ribs open.

Slice the remaining lemon into thin slices and make butterfly shapes by cutting away a small triangle from two opposite sides, leaving wing-like shapes.

Salmon Sautéed with Lemon

Sardines with Tomatoes

Serves 4: ⅓ cup (2 fl oz) olive oil; 8-12 fresh sardines (depending on size), cleaned; 3 tablespoons all purpose flour; salt; freshly ground black pepper; 2 garlic cloves, crushed; 2 lb (1 kg) tomatoes, peeled and chopped; 2 sprigs parsley, chopped

Heat the oil in a skillet, sprinkle the sardines with flour, season with salt and pepper, and fry briefly. Remove the sardines and set aside. In the same oil, sauté the garlic, add the tomatoes and simmer for 10 minutes. Add the sardines and simmer over low heat for 5 minutes. Season to taste and serve sprinkled with parsley.

Scallops Indienne

Serves 4: 1 lb (500 g) fresh scallops; 6 oz (185 g) fresh spinach or beet green, chopped; 2 tablespoons (1 oz) butter, cubed; 2 cups (16 fl oz) milk; 2½ tablespoons cornstarch; 2 teaspoons mild curry powder; 2 fish stock cubes (optional); pinch of ground ginger; salt and black pepper; pinch of nutmeg; lemon juice

Rinse the scallops and set aside in a microwave-safe dish. Place the spinach in a covered vegetable dish and add the butter. Microwave, covered, on HIGH (100%) for 3 minutes, then remove and leave to stand for 5-6 minutes.

In a 4-cup (1-liter) capacity jug mix the milk, cornstarch, curry powder, stock cubes, if used, and a large pinch each of ground ginger, salt and pepper. Microwave on HIGH (100%) for 3 minutes, then stir thoroughly. Microwave on HIGH (100%) a further 3 minutes, stirring once or twice. Set aside.

Cover the scallops with two sheets of very damp paper towel, tucking in the edges. Microwave on HIGH (100%) for 2 minutes, then rearrange the scallops. Microwave a further 2 minutes and rearrange again. Microwave a final 1-2 minutes on HIGH (100%).

Drain the spinach and, depending on your own taste, either leave it as it is or puree it in a food processor, adding salt, pepper and nutmeg to taste. Spread onto a serving dish. Use a slotted spoon to transfer the scallops to the spinach, spreading evenly. Pour the sauce over and add lemon juice to taste.

Place the diced butter on the spinach.

Microwave, then rearrange scallops.

Scallops Indienne

Scallops in Garlic Oyster Sauce

Scallops in Garlic Oyster Sauce 🇨🇳

Serves 4–6: 1½ lb (750 g) fresh scallops; 1 teaspoon crushed garlic; 1 tablespoon ginger wine or dry sherry; 5 oz (155 g) fresh beansprouts; 1 medium-size red bell pepper, or chili; 2 large scallions
Sauce: ⅔ (5 fl oz) chicken stock; 2 teaspoons dark soy sauce (mushroom soy); 2 teaspoons Chinese oyster sauce; 2 teaspoons cornstarch; ½ teaspoon sugar

Rinse the scallops and drain. Place in a dish and add half the garlic and the wine or sherry. Mix in lightly. Set the dish on a rack in a steamer. Cover and steam until the scallops are white.

In the meantime, rinse and drain the beansprouts. Shred the pepper or chili and the scallions and sauté together in about 1½ tablespoons of cooking oil with the remaining garlic until the beansprouts have softened.

Add the premixed sauce ingredients and bring quickly to the boil. Strain the scallops and add to the beansprouts. Heat through in the sauce, then serve.

Scallops with Shrimp and Mushrooms 🇨🇳

Serves 4: 12 large fresh scallops; 7 oz (220 g) raw shrimp, peeled; 2 teaspoons Chinese rice wine; 2 teaspoons light soy sauce; 6 dried Chinese mushrooms, soaked; 6 canned or fresh straw mushrooms; 1½ tablespoons oil; ½-in (1-cm) piece fresh ginger, shredded; 4 scallions, shredded; 1 teaspoon sugar; salt and white pepper; ⅔ cup (5 fl oz) light chicken or fish stock; 1 heaped teaspoon cornstarch; 2 egg whites

Wash the scallops in salted water and drain well. Cut the shrimp open down the backs and scrape out the dark veins. Wash well. Place the scallops and shrimp in a dish and pour over the wine and soy sauce. Marinate for 10 minutes.

Drain the mushrooms and remove the stems, then cut in half. Lightly boil the fresh straw mushrooms or drain the canned mushrooms and rinse in cold water. Cut in half.

Heat the oil and fry the ginger and scallions for 1 minute, then add the scallops and cook for 2 minutes. Mix in the mushrooms and season with sugar, salt and pepper. Add the shrimp and cook for another minute on moderate to low heat. Pour in the stock and bring to the boil. Thicken with cornstarch mixed with a little cold water. Stir in the lightly beaten egg whites, which will form white threads in the sauce. Do not stir again until the egg sets. Transfer to a serving dish at once.

Scallops with Shrimp and Mushrooms

Seafood Risotto 🇮🇹

Serves 4: 2 blue crabs or 1 small crayfish, cooked; 1 lb (500 g) shelled small shrimp, cooked; 2 carrots, chopped; 2 stalks celery, chopped; 1 onion, chopped; 2 tablespoons (1 oz) butter; 3 tablespoons olive oil; 3 tablespoons chopped parsley; 2 cups (12 oz) rice; salt and freshly ground black pepper; ½ cup (4 fl oz) dry white wine; approximately 2 cups (16 fl oz) fish stock

Chop the crab and shrimp. Sauté the carrots, celery and onion in the butter and oil, add the parsley and the rice, and season. Add sufficient wine and fish stock to cover the rice. Simmer until the rice is cooked and the liquid has been absorbed, adding more liquid as required. Stir in the seafood and cook for another 5 minutes. Season.

Seafood Tartlets 🇮🇹

Makes 48 tartlets: 1 quantity shortcrust pastry (see page 319); 1 tablespoon butter; 1 tablespoon all purpose flour; ½ cup (4 fl oz) fish stock or milk; ½ teaspoon pepper; pinch each of nutmeg and cayenne; ½ teaspoon salt; ⅓ cup (2½ fl oz) dry sherry or vermouth; ¾ cup finely chopped shrimp (or crab); ¾ cup finely chopped clams, drained; ¼ cup (½ oz) finely chopped parsley

Line the tartlet dishes with the pastry, prick well and bake in an oven preheated to 400°F (200°C) for 12–15 minutes or until golden brown.

Melt the butter in a heavy-based saucepan and stir in the flour. Cook for a few minutes without browning.

Whisk in the fish stock and cook, stirring until thickened and smooth. Add the seasonings and pour in the sherry. Stir in the seafood and simmer until hot, then finally add the parsley. Spoon the mixture into each tartlet. Serve hot.

Sea Trout Baked in Butter with Sorrel Sauce 🇬🇧

Serves 4–6: 1 tablespoon butter, melted; 1 large or 2 smaller trout; 1 large onion, chopped; 2 bay leaves, crumbled; salt and pepper; pinch of dried dill; sea salt; 1 cup (8 fl oz) dry white wine
Sorrel Sauce: 4 tablespoons (2 oz) butter; 3 scallions, finely chopped; 8 oz (250 g) fresh sorrel, chopped; ½ cup (2 oz) all purpose flour; 1¼ cups (10 fl oz) chicken stock; ½ teaspoon sugar; salt and pepper

Brush a large sheet of aluminum foil with melted butter and place the cleaned trout in the center. Stuff the cavity with the onion, bay leaves, salt and pepper and rub the skin with sea salt. Add the wine and loosely wrap the fish in the foil. Place in a baking dish and bake in an oven preheated to 375°F (190°C), allowing 10 minutes per lb (500 g).

When the trout is cooked, remove from the oven but leave it wrapped in foil for a further 20 minutes.

Meanwhile, make the sauce, melt the butter and gently sauté the scallions and sorrel for 10 minutes. Stir in the flour and add the stock, sugar and seasoning. Cook for a further 20 minutes, then blend the sauce until it is smooth and creamy. Return to the pan and reheat it gently.

When the fish is cooked, carefully remove the skin and the light-brown bits near the head. Serve the fish and the sauce separately.

Note: The fish may also be served cold. In this case, cool the sauce and mix it with 1 cup (8 fl oz) of mayonnaise.

Shrimp and Feta Cheese Casserole

Serves 4: 2 lb (1 kg) raw shrimp, in the shell; 8 scallions, finely chopped; 3 garlic cloves, crushed; 2 tablespoons olive oil; 1¼-lb (875-g) can tomatoes, chopped; ½ teaspoon dried oregano; salt and pepper; large pinch of sugar; ½ cup (1 oz) finely chopped parsley; 4 oz (125 g) feta cheese, finely diced

Peel the shrimp, leaving the tails and last section of the shell in place. Discard the heads and remove the intestinal veins. Rinse in cold water and drain well.

Place the scallions in a microwave-safe casserole of an 8-cup (2 liter) capacity with the garlic and olive oil. Cover with plastic wrap vented in one corner and microwave on HIGH (100%) for 3 minutes. Add the tomatoes, oregano, seasonings and half the parsley, and microwave on HIGH (100%) for 5 minutes. Add the shrimp and half the cheese, pushing them below the surface of the sauce. Scatter the remaining cheese on top. Cover and microwave on HIGH (100%) for 3 minutes, then stir and microwave a further 3–4 minutes. Stir again and microwave on HIGH (100%) for a further 3–4 minutes. The cheese on top will be stirred into the dish. Allow to stand for 4–5 minutes before serving. Garnish with the remaining parsley and serve hot with fresh bread, rice or pasta.

Remove and discard the intestinal vein.

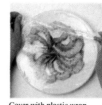
Cover with plastic wrap vented in one corner.

Shrimp and Feta Cheese Casserole

Shrimp Biriyani

Serves 4: 1½ lb (750 g) raw shrimp in shells; 4½ cups (1 liter) water; 1 large onion; 6 garlic cloves; 1-in (2.5-cm) piece fresh ginger; 4 dried chilies, soaked; 1 teaspoon cumin; 1 teaspoon black peppercorns; 2-in (5-cm) stick cinnamon; 6 cloves; 3 black cardamoms, crushed; ¼ teaspoon saffron powder; 1 tablespoon boiling water; 3 tablespoons ghee; 12 oz (375 g) long grain rice; 4 large tomatoes; salt; rose water (optional)

Remove the heads and shells from the shrimp, leaving the tails on. Place the shells and heads in a pot with water. Cover the pot, bring to the boil, then reduce the heat and simmer for 1 hour. Strain, reserving the liquid.

Pound the onion, garlic, ginger and chilies to a paste. Grind the cumin and black peppercorns coarsely. Mix in the broken cinnamon stick, cloves and cardamoms. Mix the saffron with the boiling water.

Melt the *ghee* in a large skillet and fry the rice until the grains are well coated, then add the onion paste and mix well. Fry for 3 minutes, stirring constantly, then add spice mixture and stir thoroughly.

Add the reserved stock, which should measure 3¼ cups. Bring to the boil and cook until the rice is almost tender and liquid has been absorbed. Add the shrimp, sliced tomato and salt to taste and continue to cook, tightly covered, until the rice is tender and the grains dry and well separated. The shrimp should be pink and cooked through. Splash rose water over and stir before serving.

Shrimp Curry

Serves 2: 12 oz (375 g) peeled raw shrimp; salt and pepper; 1 tablespoon coconut oil; ½-in (1-cm) piece fresh ginger, shredded; 2 teaspoons chili powder; 1 teaspoon grated fresh turmeric, or ⅓ teaspoon turmeric powder; 8 candlenuts, ground; 1-in (2.5-cm) piece lengkuas, sliced (optional); ½ teaspoon dried shrimp paste; ¾ cup (6 fl oz) fish stock; 1½ cups (12 fl oz) thin coconut milk; 1 stalk lemongrass; fresh cilantro, chopped, for garnish

Season the shrimp with salt and pepper and fry in coconut oil until pink. Remove and set aside.

Grind the ginger, chili powder, turmeric and candlenuts to a paste and fry in the oil for 3 minutes. Add the sliced *lengkuas* and shrimp paste, then pour over fish stock and bring to the boil. Reduce the heat and add the coconut milk and lemon grass, and boil briefly. Return the shrimp to the pan and cook for 3–4 minutes on moderate heat.

Season with salt and pepper to taste and garnish with chopped cilantro.

Shrimp in Black Bean Sauce

1 lb (500 g) medium-size raw shrimp; 1 tablespoon salted black beans; 1 tablespoon lard or oil; 1 tablespoon oyster sauce; 1 tablespoon Chinese rice wine or dry sherry; ½ teaspoon ginger juice (see page 209); 1 teaspoon sugar; 1 tablespoon water

Peel the shrimp, then rinse and dry. If using canned salted black beans, rinse under running water, then mash roughly with a fork. If using dried salted black beans, soak in water for 5 minutes and drain before mashing.

Heat the lard or oil until quite hot and stir-fry the shrimp for 1–2 minutes until they turn pink. Add the black beans, oyster sauce, wine, ginger juice and sugar, and simmer for a minute, stirring all the time. Add the water and cook for another 1–2 minutes or until the shrimp are done.

Shrimp Curry

Shrimp in Wine and Chili Sauce

Serves 2: 12 raw shrimp, peeled, approx. 8 oz (250 g); 5 garlic cloves, sliced; 3 slices fresh ginger, shredded; 1 large red chili, sliced; 2 scallions, sliced; 2 tablespoons oil; 2 egg whites; ½ cup (2 oz) cornstarch; oil for deep frying
Sauce: 2 teaspoons light soy sauce; 2 teaspoons sugar; ¼ cup (2 fl oz) dry sherry; ¼ cup (2 fl oz) chicken stock; small pinch of salt; 1 teaspoon cornstarch

Devein and wash the shrimp, then dry thoroughly and set aside. Mix the sauce ingredients.

Sauté the garlic, ginger, chili and scallions in the oil for 1 minute. Add the premixed sauce ingredients and bring to the boil. Stir on moderate heat for 2 minutes, then set aside.

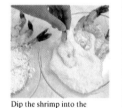

Add the premixed sauce ingredients.

Dip the shrimp into the batter.

Beat the egg whites to soft peaks, then fold in half the cornstarch. Dust the shrimp lightly with the remaining cornstarch, shaking off the excess.

Heat the oil for deep frying to hot. Dip the shrimp into the batter, then coat them lightly with remaining cornstarch. Deep fry, six at a time, until crisp. When all are done, reheat the oil and deep fry the shrimp again for about 30 seconds. Drain well.

Pour off the oil and reheat the pan. Add the sauce and bring to the boil, then pour over the shrimp and serve.

Shrimp Pie

Serves 4-6: 1 lb (500 g) raw shrimp, chopped; ½ cup chopped onion; 4 tablespoons (2 oz) butter; ¼ cup (1 oz) all purpose flour; 1½ cups fresh tomatoes, peeled, chopped and seeded; ½ cup sliced small mushrooms; 1 teaspoon seasoned salt; freshly ground pepper; 1 unbaked 8-in (20-cm) double shortcrust pie shell (see page 336); 2 hard-cooked eggs, coarsely chopped; 12 black olives, pitted and sliced

Sauté the shrimp and onion in the butter until shrimp lose their translucence and the onion is tender. Stir in the flour, then add the tomatoes, mushrooms, salt and pepper. Simmer, covered, for 15 minutes.

Roll out a little more than half the pastry and line a pie dish. Fill with the mixture and sprinkle the chopped eggs and olives over. Roll out the remaining pastry and cut into strips. Lay the strips across the pie, lattice style, and flute the edges. Brush with beaten egg, if desired.

Bake in an oven preheated to 450°F (230°C) for 20 minutes or until the crust is brown and the filling is bubbling.

Shrimp Satay

Serves 4: 1 lb (500 g) raw shrimp, shelled; ¼ teaspoon salt; ¾ teaspoon white vinegar; 1 small onion, grated; 1-2 garlic cloves, crushed; 1 fresh red chili, seeded and chopped; ½-in (1-cm) piece fresh ginger, grated; 1½ tablespoons vegetable oil; 2 bay leaves; 2 teaspoons ground almonds or cashew nuts; ½ teaspoon turmeric; ½ teaspoon sugar; ½ cup (4 fl oz) thick coconut milk; salt

Devein the shrimp and wash well. Pat dry with paper towels and season with the salt and vinegar. Grind the onion, garlic, chili and ginger to a paste and fry in the oil with the bay leaves until fragrant, approximately 2 minutes. Add the ground nuts, turmeric, sugar and coconut milk and season to taste with salt. Simmer, stirring, until the sauce thickens.

Divide the shrimp among six bamboo skewers. Do not use metal as this may affect the taste. Pour the sauce over and marinate for 2-3 minutes only. Grill over a charcoal fire or under the broiler until just cooked through. Serve with any remaining sauce.

Singapore Chili Crab

Serves 2-4: 2 medium-size raw crabs; 1 tablespoon tamarind; ¾ cup (6 fl oz) boiling water; 3 tablespoons oil; 2 medium-size onions, minced; 2-in (5-cm) piece fresh ginger, chopped; 4 fresh red chilies, finely chopped; 1-2 teaspoons chili powder; 2 teaspoons tomato paste; 1 tablespoon sugar, or to taste; 2 teaspoons cornstarch; fresh red and green chilies, sliced; scallions, chopped

Drop the crabs into boiling, slightly salted water and cook rapidly for 4 minutes. Remove, drain and leave to cool. Soak the tamarind in the boiling water. Chop the crabs into large pieces, if possible leaving

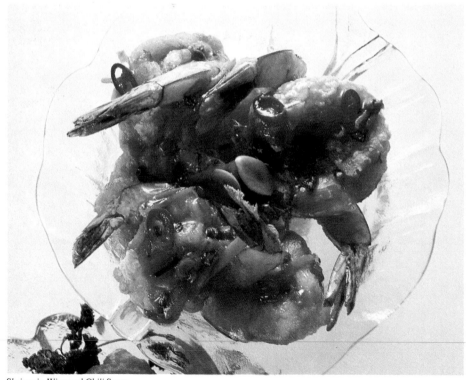

Shrimp in Wine and Chili Sauce

the legs attached to the body pieces. Remove the spongy gray portion and discard.

Heat the oil in a wok or large skillet and sauté the onions, ginger and chopped chilies for 2 minutes. Add the crab pieces and sprinkle the chili powder over, then pour in the strained tamarind water. Lower the heat and simmer for 4 minutes.

Remove the crab to a serving plate. Add the tomato paste and sugar to the sauce, thicken with cornstarch mixed with a little cold water and cook until the sauce thickens and clears slightly. Pour over the crab. Garnish with sliced chili and scallions.

Small Fried Fish with Sambal Stuffing

Serves 4: 6 small fish weighing about 4 oz (125 g) each (horse mackerel, mackerel or yellowtail); 4 shallots or ½ medium-size red or brown onion; 4 fresh red chilies; 1 slice lengkuas; *1 garlic clove; ¼ teaspoon dried shrimp paste; 4 candlenuts or macadamias; 1 stalk lemongrass; 1½ tablespoons oil; ½ teaspoon sugar; ½ teaspoon salt; extra oil for frying fish*

Wash, clean and dry the fish. Leave whole, but slit on either side of the backbone making a pocket on each side.

Grind the shallots, chilies, *lengkuas*, garlic, dried shrimp paste, candlenuts and lemongrass until fine. Heat 1½ tablespoons of oil and fry the ground ingredients for 2–3 minutes, then mix in the sugar and salt. Divide the fried mixture into six and stuff into the pockets along the backbone of each fish.

Heat the oil and fry the fish until cooked, turning to make sure each side is golden.

Sole Normande

Serves 6–8: 6–8 sole (or flounder), filleted; 1½ cups (12 fl oz) dry white wine; 2 tablespoons (1 oz) butter; ¼ cup (1 oz) all purpose flour; 1 cup (8 fl oz) fish stock; salt and pepper; 4 oz (125 g) button mushrooms, sliced; ½ cup (4 fl oz) cream; 12 oysters; 4 oz (125 g) peeled shrimp

Poach the sole fillets in the wine for 5 minutes or until just cooked. Drain the fillets well, reserving the liquid. Place in a covered dish and keep warm. Reduce the

Singapore Chili Crab

Sole Veronique

wine in which the fillets were cooked to approximately ½ cup.

In a clean saucepan, melt the butter and stir in the flour to make a roux. Add the fish stock, then the reduced wine, whisking well. Season to taste with salt and pepper and add the mushrooms. Simmer gently for 5 minutes. Add the cream, oysters and shrimp and cook for a few minutes longer, just until they are heated through. Pour the sauce over the sole fillets and serve immediately.

Sole Véronique

Serves 6: 1½ lb (750 g) fillets of sole or other small fish fillets; 1 cup (8 fl oz) water; ¾ cup (6 fl oz) dry white wine; 6 black peppercorns; 1 large scallion, trimmed; 5 oz (155 g) seedless green grapes; lemon juice
Sauce: 1 tablespoon butter; 2 tablespoons all purpose flour; ⅓ (2½ fl oz) cup milk; 2–3 tablespoons heavy cream; 2 egg yolks, beaten

Wash the fillets and dry on paper towels. Fold each piece in half and arrange in a well-buttered dish. Add the water, wine, peppercorns and scallion, and cover the dish with a piece of buttered paper. Place the dish in a large pan of boiling water or on a rack in a steamer and steam over moderately high heat for about 12 minutes.

When done, transfer the fish to a warmed serving plate. Cover with aluminum foil and keep it warm in a low oven with the door ajar while you make the sauce. Reserve 1¼ cups (10 fl oz) of the poaching liquid.

Peel the grapes and cut into halves. Sprinkle with a little lemon juice and set aside.

Melt the butter in a pan and add the flour. Cook briefly, then pour in the milk and the reserved stock. Stir until the sauce boils and thickens slightly, about 2 minutes, then remove from the heat. Mix the cream and egg yolks together and add to the sauce. Beat until smooth, then return to low to cook until the sauce is thick and creamy. Stir continually to prevent burning or curdling. Add the grapes, then pour the sauce over the fish.

Cover the dish with buttered paper.

Halve and pit the grapes.

Somerset Casserole

Serves 4: 1 lb (500 g) firm white fish, cut into small cubes; salt and freshly ground pepper; 3⅓ oz (100 g) button mushrooms, sliced; 2 tomatoes, peeled and sliced; ¾ cup (6 fl oz) cider; 2 scant tablespoons (1¾ oz) butter; ¼ cup (1 oz) all purpose flour; 8 oz (250 g) seasoned mashed potatoes; tomato slices and parsley sprigs for garnish; ½ cup (2 oz) grated cheese

Place the fish in a shallow buttered ovenproof dish and season with salt and pepper. Cover with mushrooms and tomatoes, add the cider and dot with half of the butter. Cover with aluminum foil and cook in an oven preheated to 375°F (190°C) for 20 minutes. Strain the cooking liquid and reserve.

Melt the remaining butter, add the flour and cook without coloring for 2–3 minutes, then add the cooking liquid. Cook for 2–3 minutes more. Pour the sauce over the fish and pipe a border of potatoes on top.

Increase the oven temperature to 450°F (230°C). Garnish the top with tomato slices, sprinkle it with cheese and bake until the top is brown. Serve garnished with parsley.

Sour Hot Fish Curry

Serves 4: 8–12 dried red chilies, soaked; 2 slices fresh ginger; 6–8 shallots or 1 medium-size red or brown onion; 3 garlic cloves; ½ teaspoon dried shrimp paste; 1 lb (500 g) fish cutlets about ¾ in (2 cm) thick (use Spanish mackerel or similar fish); ½ teaspoon salt; ½ teaspoon turmeric; ½ cup (4 fl oz) oil; 1 large red or brown onion, sliced; ¼ cup (2 fl oz) tamarind water (see page 392); ½ cup (4 fl oz) water; extra salt to taste; pinch of sugar

Grind the dried chilies, ginger, shallots, garlic and dried shrimp paste until fine, then set aside. Dry the fish cutlets and rub with salt and turmeric. Heat the oil in a skillet until quite hot and fry the fish for a couple of minutes on either side until golden. Drain and keep aside.

Pour out all but 1 tablespoon of the oil and gently fry the sliced onion until golden. Add the ground ingredients to the fried onion and cook gently, stirring frequently, for 2–3 minutes. Pour in the tamarind water and plain water and simmer for 1 minute. Add salt and sugar to taste, then put in the fried fish and continue cooking for another few minutes until the fish is cooked through.

Sour Hot Fish Stew

Serves 4: 1 lb (500 g) small pomfret or any white fish fillets or steaks; 2 stalks lemongrass; ½ in (1 cm) fresh turmeric or ½ teaspoon turmeric powder; 1 in (2.5 cm) lengkuas; 10–15 dried red chilies, soaked; 15–20 shallots or 2 medium-size red or brown onions; ½ teaspoon dried shrimp paste; 2 tablespoons oil; 1 tablespoon tamarind; 3 cups (24 fl oz) warm water; 2–3 teaspoons sugar; 1 teaspoon salt

Clean the fish and, if using pomfret, cut in half crosswise, keeping the heads on. Grind the lemongrass, turmeric, *lengkuas*, chilies, shallots and dried shrimp paste until fine. Heat the oil in a saucepan and fry the pounded ingredients gently for about 5 minutes.

Soak the tamarind in warm water for 10 minutes. Squeeze and strain, discarding the pulp and seeds, and add the liquid to the saucepan with the sugar and salt. Simmer uncovered for 5 minutes, then add the fish. Simmer for 5–10 minutes until the fish is tender.

Note: Fresh turmeric, lemongrass and *lengkuas* are necessary for the success of this recipe.

Southern Indian Fish Curry

Serves 4: Fish Curry Powder: 10 oz (300 g) coriander; 2½ oz (75 g) fennel; 2½ oz (75 g) dried red chilies; 1½ oz (45 g) cumin; 1 oz (30 g) fenugreek; 1 oz (30 g) black peppercorns; 1½ oz (45 g) turmeric powder
2 tablespoons oil; ½ teaspoon fenugreek seeds; 4 shallots or ½ medium-size red or brown onion, finely sliced; 2 slices fresh ginger, very finely chopped; 1–2 garlic cloves, very finely chopped; 1–2 small eggplants, quartered lengthwise, then cut in half crosswise; 3 heaped tablespoons fish curry powder; ½–1 teaspoon chili powder; 2 sprigs curry leaves; 1–2 tomatoes, quartered; 1 teaspoon salt; 4 small okra (ladies' fingers); ¾ cup (6 fl oz) water; ¼ cup (2 fl oz) tamarind water (see page 392); 1 cup (8 fl oz) coconut milk; 1 lb (500 g) fish fillets or cutlets

To make the fish curry powder, heat a pan and dry fry the spices one at a time until they turn light golden brown or give off a pleasant fragrance. Grind the whole spices, then mix in the ground spices, stirring to blend well. When cold store in an airtight container.

Heat the oil and gently fry the fenugreek seeds for 30 seconds. Add the shallots, ginger and garlic and fry, stirring frequently, for 2–3 minutes. Add the eggplants and fry for 2 minutes more.

Mix the fish curry powder to a stiff paste with a little cold water while the eggplant is frying. Add the spice paste and curry leaves to the pan and fry for a couple of minutes. Put in the tomatoes, salt, whole okra and water. Bring to the boil, add the tamarind water and simmer until the vegetables are half-cooked.

Add the coconut milk, stir and bring to the boil, then put in the fish and simmer gently until it is cooked and the gravy has thickened.

Spiced Fish Wrapped in Banana Leaves

Serves 4: 1 lb (500 g) white fish fillets; 4 candlenuts; 2 medium-size onions, chopped; 2 garlic cloves, chopped; ¼ teaspoon turmeric powder or 1 teaspoon grated fresh turmeric; 1-in (2.5-cm) piece fresh ginger, chopped; ½ teaspoon tamarind; 1 teaspoon salt; 1 tablespoon chili powder; 2 teaspoons coriander, ground; 2 teaspoons cumin, ground; ½ teaspoon daun kesom, chopped; banana leaves (or aluminum foil)

Cut the fish into thin slices about ½ in (1 cm) thick and 4 × 2 in (10 × 5 cm). Grind the candlenuts and mix to a paste with all the remaining ingredients, except the banana leaves. Hold the banana leaves over a flame to soften.

Coat each fish slice thickly with the ground ingredients and wrap in a small piece of well-greased banana leaf. Secure with toothpicks. Broil or toast over a charcoal fire for 8–10 minutes. Serve with the leaf partially torn away to display the fish.

Squid and Bamboo Shoot Salad

Serves 4: 6½ oz (200 g) squid; 8 oz (250 g) bamboo shoots; 1 cup (8 fl oz) dashi; 1½ tablespoons light soy sauce; 1 tablespoon sweet rice wine (mirin); 12 spinach leaves; 2 tablespoons white miso plus 1 tablespoon superfine sugar; 2 tablespoons dashi; ⅛ teaspoon Japanese pepper (sansho); 4 sprigs of watercress for garnish

Wash the squid and discard the head, tentacles and skin. Simmer whole in plenty of water for just 2 minutes. Cool, then cut into ½-in (1-cm) rings if using small squid. If large squid is used, cut into squares of about 1 in (2.5 cm). Set aside.

If possible, use canned winter bamboo shoots, which have a superior flavor. Rinse well under running water, then cut into slices. If the shoots are rather fat, it may be necessary to cut them lengthwise first to ensure you finish up with neat, bite-size slices. Combine the *dashi*, soy sauce and *mirin* in a pan and bring to the boil. Add the bamboo shoot slices and simmer, uncovered, for 10 minutes. Drain and cool.

Chop the spinach leaves finely and put into a blender with the *miso* and just 1 tablespoon of *dashi*. Blend, frequently scraping down the sides of the jar and gradually adding the rest of the *dashi* until you get a smooth sauce. Season with Japanese pepper.

Just before serving, combine the squid, bamboo shoots and dressing, mixing carefully. Put into individual bowls and garnish with a sprig of watercress.

Squid in Tamarind Sauce

Serves 4: 8 oz (250 g) small squid not more than 3 in (8 cm) long; 2 heaped tablespoons dried tamarind; ½ cup (4 fl oz) warm water; ¼ teaspoon salt; 2 tablespoons oil

Wash the squid and remove the reddish-brown skin but leave the heads intact.

Soak the tamarind in warm water for about 5 minutes, then squeeze with the fingers and strain through a sieve. Mix in the salt, then rub the squid with this liquid.

Just before cooking, pierce the black sacks just behind the eyes of the squid with a skewer. Heat a skillet without any oil and put in the squid. Cook over medium heat until all the liquid has come out of the squid and evaporated. Turn the squid over once or twice during this process. Add the oil and fry the squid for 1 minute, then serve.

Squid Stuffed with Nuts and Rice

Serves 6: 12 squid, each approximately 5 in (12 cm) long; ½ cup (4 fl oz) olive oil; 2 onions, finely chopped; 4 sprigs parsley, finely chopped; 1 cup (5 oz) cooked rice; 2 tablespoons pine nuts; 1 tablespoon tomato paste; ¼ cup (1½ oz) currants; salt and freshly ground black pepper; 1 cup (8 fl oz) dry white wine; ½ cup (4 fl oz) water

Under running water, clean the squid, making sure that the sack is not cut. Chop and retain the tentacles for the stuffing.

In half the oil, fry the onions until golden brown. Add the tentacles and cook for 5 minutes. Add the parsley, cooked rice, pine nuts, tomato paste, currants, salt and pepper and cook for a further 5 minutes. Cool.

The stuffing will swell during cooking, so stuff the squid lightly. Secure the openings with toothpicks. Pour the wine and water into a heavy-based oven dish and lay the squid side by side. Cover the dish with aluminum foil and bake in an oven preheated to 350°F (180°C) for 1 hour or until the squid are tender. Serve hot with the cooking juices poured over the squid.

Squid with Spicy Stuffing

Serves 4: 6–8 medium-size squid; 1 dried red chili, soaked; 2 shallots or ¼ medium-size red or brown onion; 1 tablespoon oil; 4 oz (125 g) peeled raw shrimp
Gravy: ½ teaspoon dried shrimp paste; 6 dried red chilies, soaked; 2 slices lengkuas; *6–8 shallots or 1 medium-size red or brown onion; 1 garlic clove; 2 tablespoons oil; ¼ cup (2 fl oz) tamarind water (see page 392); 1 stalk lemongrass, bruised; 1 cup (8 fl oz) thick coconut milk; ½ teaspoon salt*

Wash the squid and peel off the reddish-brown skin. Discard the transparent spine but keep the head. Grind the chili and shallots, then fry gently in oil for a couple of minutes. Add the shrimp and fry, stirring frequently, for 3–4 minutes.

Divide the fried mixture and stuff into each of the cleaned squid. Put the heads back on the top of each squid and fasten with a toothpick. You may need to make holes for the toothpick with a skewer or you will break a lot of toothpicks before getting them to penetrate the squid.

To make the gravy, grind the dried shrimp paste, soaked dried chilies, *lengkuas*, shallots and garlic, then fry gently in oil for 3–4 minutes. Add the tamarind water, lemongrass, coconut milk and salt and simmer, stirring constantly, until the gravy thickens. Put in the stuffed squid and simmer gently, with the pan uncovered, for about 5 minutes or until the squid are cooked.

Steamed Golden Carp

Serves 4–6: 1½-lb (750-g) golden carp or freshwater trout; 1 oz (30 g) Chinese or cured (Smithfield) ham; 4 dried black mushrooms, soaked for 25 minutes; 1 oz (30 g) canned bamboo shoots, drained; 1 scallion, trimmed and shredded; 3 slices fresh ginger, shredded; 3 oz (90 g) pork omentum, or use 3 slices streaky bacon; ¼ cup (2 fl oz) chicken stock; ¼ cup (2 fl oz) oil
Seasoning: 1¼ teaspoons salt; ½ teaspoon sugar; 2 teaspoons rice wine or dry sherry; 1 tablespoon softened lard

Clean the carp and score diagonally on one side at ¾-in (2-cm) intervals. Cut the ham into slices. Drain the mushrooms and remove the stems. Cut the caps in half. Thinly slice the bamboo shoots.

Place the fish on an oiled plate, score-side upwards. Insert the slices of ham, mushroom halves and bamboo shoot slices in alternate rows in the cuts. Arrange the scallion and ginger on top of the fish and sprinkle the seasonings evenly over it.

Place the pork omentum, if used, on top or arrange the streaky bacon so that it covers as much of the fish as possible. Pour the chicken stock over, then set the plate on a rack in a steamer and steam over high heat for about 20 minutes.

Test if the fish is done by pushing a fork into the thickest part. If the meat lifts cleanly from the bones it is ready. Lift out the plate. Remove the bacon or pork fat and discard.

Strain the liquid into a pan and bring to the boil. Adjust the seasoning to taste and thicken slightly, if preferred, with a thin solution of cornstarch and cold water. Pour over the fish.

Heat the oil to smoking point and pour it quickly over the fish. Serve at once.

Steamed Salmon with Roe

Steamed Salmon with Roe

Serves 4: 1 lb (500 g) fresh or frozen salmon steaks; salt; 1 tablespoon oil; 4 scant tablespoons salmon roe; 1 teaspoon sake; 4 oz (125 g) giant white radish (daikon), grated; ½ egg white, beaten; 4 lemon wedges
Sauce: 1 cup dashi; 2 tablespoons sweet rice wine (mirin); 1½ tablespoons light soy sauce; 1½ tablespoons rice vinegar; 2 teaspoons cornstarch; 2 teaspoons water; lemon wedges for garnish

Sprinkle the salmon steaks lightly with salt and set aside for 10 minutes. Before cooking, wipe the salmon with a paper towel to remove any moisture.

Heat the oil in a skillet and fry the salmon steaks over moderately high heat for 2–3 minutes each side. Remove from the heat and pat dry with a paper towel to remove all traces of oil. Cut the salmon into bite-size pieces, removing all bones but leaving on any skin. Divide the salmon pieces equally among four individual casseroles or one large casserole.

Mix the salmon roe carefully with the *sake*. Squeeze the *daikon* to expel all moisture, then carefully mix with the salmon roe, tossing gently with a fork. Add the egg white, mix well and spoon this mixture over each portion of salmon. Cover the casseroles tightly and steam over high heat for 5 minutes.

While the salmon is steaming, combine all sauce ingredients except the cornstarch and water in a pan and bring to the boil. Mix the cornstarch with the water and stir into the sauce. Lower the heat and cook gently, stirring, until the sauce clears and thickens slightly.

Remove the casseroles from the steamer, spoon over the sauce and garnish with a lemon wedge. Serve hot.

Steamed Whole Fish

Serves 4: 1 large or 2 small pomfret weighing total of 1 lb (500 g), or flounder, sole, John Dory or plaice; 1 teaspoon salt; ¼ teaspoon sugar; white pepper; 1½-in (4-cm) piece fresh ginger, finely shredded lengthwise; 2 scallions, finely chopped; 2 dried black mushrooms, soaked and shredded; 2 teaspoons melted lard, chicken fat or oil; 1 fresh red chili, shredded; fresh cilantro leaves
Gravy: about ½ cup (4 fl oz) stock or water; 2 teaspoons peanut oil; ¼ teaspoon sugar; ¼ teaspoon salt; ½ teaspoon sesame oil; 1 teaspoon oyster sauce

Clean the fish and make two diagonal cuts on both sides. Rub with salt, sugar and pepper. Leave to stand for 15 minutes.

Shred the ginger and scatter half of it on a deep plate. Put the seasoned fish on top. Cover with the remaining ginger, scallions, dried mushrooms and melted lard. Steam for 10–15 minutes. Test the fish with a skewer to make sure it is cooked.

To make the gravy, pour the liquid from the plate in which the fish was steamed and add sufficient stock or water to make ½ cup. Heat the peanut oil in a saucepan and add the stock and all other ingredients. Simmer for 1 minute.

Put the fish on a large serving platter and decorate with the chili and cilantro. Sprinkle liberally with pepper and pour the gravy over.

Stuffed Baby Squid in its Ink

Serves 4: 32 small squid; ½ cup (4 fl oz) olive oil; 2½ onions, finely chopped; 1 garlic clove, crushed; salt and freshly ground black pepper; 2 red or green bell peppers, seeded and chopped; 2 tomatoes, peeled, seeded and chopped; 1 garlic clove, whole, unpeeled; 1 slice white bread without crust; 2 cups (16 fl oz) fish stock; 12 triangular croutons

Clean the squid, reserve the ink and chop the tentacles finely. In a pan, heat half the oil and sauté two of the chopped onions, the garlic and the chopped tentacles until the onions are soft and transparent. Season

Steamed Whole Fish

to taste. Remove the ingredients but leave the oil in the pan for later use.

Mix the tentacles and onion well. With a teaspoon, spoon a little of the onion–tentacle mixture into each squid, making sure that it is not filled too firmly. Secure the opening with a toothpick.

To make the sauce, add the rest of the oil to the pan, heat it and sauté the chopped half onion, pepper, tomatoes, 1 whole unpeeled garlic clove and the bread. Add the fish stock mixed with the ink and cook over low heat for 2–3 minutes. Rub the sauce through a fine sieve or puree it in a processor, then rub through a sieve. Return the sauce to the pan, season and cook a few minutes. Gently add the squid and simmer until the squid is cooked and the sauce has thickened. Serve with small triangular croutons.

Stuffed Dried Mushrooms with Broccoli

Serves 4: 12 large dried black mushrooms; 2 cups (16 fl oz) warm water; 1 tablespoon oil; 2 garlic cloves, smashed and chopped ; ½ chicken stock cube; 2 teaspoons cornstarch; 1 tablespoon cold water; 8 oz (250 g) fresh or frozen broccoli
Filling: 8 oz (250 g) raw shrimp; 3½ oz (100 g) fresh or canned crabmeat; 3 water chestnuts; 1 tablespoon finely diced hard pork fat; ½ teaspoon salt; pinch of white pepper

Rinse the mushrooms in cold water, then leave to soak in 2 cups warm water for about 2 hours. Drain, reserving the soaking liquid. Discard the mushroom stems and squeeze the mushrooms dry. Heat the oil in a skillet and gently fry the garlic for about 15 seconds. Raise the heat and add the mushrooms. Stir-fry for 1 minute, then add the mushroom-soaking liquid and stock cube. Simmer very gently for about 1 hour or until the mushrooms are tender. Remove the mushrooms from the cooking liquid and drain. Thicken the cooking liquid with 1 teaspoon cornstarch mixed with cold water. Set this sauce aside.

While the mushrooms are simmering, prepare the filling. Peel the shrimp, flake the crabmeat and peel the water chestnuts. If you have a food processor, blend the water chestnuts and pork fat for about 30 seconds or until a rough paste results. Add the shrimp, crabmeat, salt and pepper and process for another few seconds. If you do not have a processor, chop all filling

Stuffed Dried Mushrooms with Broccoli

ingredients together with a cleaver to get a fine paste.

When the cooked, drained mushrooms have cooled sufficiently to handle, sprinkle the inside of each cap with a little cornstarch. Press on some of the filling, mounding it slightly. If desired, the mushrooms can now be stored in the refrigerator for several hours and the dish finalized just before the meal.

Put the stuffed mushrooms onto an enamel plate or low-sided bowl and steam for 20 minutes. Cook the broccoli until it is just tender. Arrange the mushrooms in the center of a serving platter. Pour any liquid that has accumulated in the steaming plate into the prepared sauce. Reheat and pour over the mushrooms. Arrange the broccoli around the edge of the serving platter, sprinkle the mushrooms with a little white pepper and serve immediately.

Stuffed Fillets of Sole

Serves 6: 4 tablespoons (2 oz) butter; 6 oz (185 g) peeled uncooked shrimp; 4 oz (125 g) cooked or canned crab or lobster meat; 2 tablespoons all

purpose flour; 1½ cups (12 fl oz) fish stock; ¼ cup (2 fl oz) cream; 2 tablespoons brandy; 3 oz (90 g) button mushrooms, cut in slivers; ½ cup (1 oz) fresh breadcrumbs; salt and freshly ground black pepper; 6 or 12 sole fillets, depending on size (John Dory may be used); 4 tablespoons (2 oz) melted butter

In a saucepan, melt the butter and lightly sauté the shrimp and the crab or lobster meat. Remove from the pan and set aside. Add the flour to the butter in the pan, stir and cook for 3 minutes. Slowly stir in the fish stock, then add the cream, brandy, mushrooms, breadcrumbs, crab, salt and pepper. Mix together well. Allow the mixture to cool so that the sauce thickens.

Place an equal part of the stuffing on each fillet, roll it up and secure it with a toothpick or some twine. Brush the bottom of a baking dish with some of the melted butter. Arrange the rolled fillets next to each other and brush them with the melted butter. Cover the dish with aluminum foil and bake in an oven preheated to 350°F (180°C) for 20–30 minutes. Serve hot.

Sugar Cane Sticks Coated with Shrimp

Serves 4–6: 6 pieces fresh sugar cane, peeled (each about 9 in or 23 cm long); 1½ lb (750 g) fresh raw shrimp, peeled and cleaned; ¼ teaspoon white pepper; 1 tablespoon fish sauce; 2 egg whites; 2 tablespoons oil; 8 scallions, finely chopped
Sauce: 1 tablespoon brown sugar; 1 tablespoon sugar cane juice (available canned), optional; 2 tablespoons fish sauce; 1 tablespoon roasted peanuts, crushed; 3 garlic cloves, chopped; 1 fresh red chili, chopped

Trim about 4 in (10 cm) of one end of each sugar cane stick to make that end slightly thinner than the rest of the stick. Wipe dry.

Chop the shrimp finely and season with white pepper and fish sauce. Bind with egg whites and knead to a smooth paste. Press a thin layer onto the trimmed end of each stick. Make the thickness of the shrimp about ½ in (1 cm), squeezing firmly onto the sticks. Brush with the oil and put under a preheated broiler or roast over a charcoal fire for about 6–7 minutes until lightly cooked. Brush with oil from time to time during cooking.

Remove from the fire and dip into the chopped scallions, coating lightly. Press the scallions onto the shrimp paste and return to the broiler or fire for another minute, turning frequently.

Mix the sugar with the sugar cane juice (if used) and fish sauce and stir until the sugar dissolves. Blend in the peanuts, garlic and chili and stir in a little water. Serve in small bowls with the sugar cane sticks.

Note: Bamboo or metal skewers can be used if sugar cane is not available, although the flavor of the dish will not be as good.

Sugar Cane Sticks Coated with Shrimp

Sweet and Sour Fish

Sweet and Sour Fish

Serves 4: 12 oz (375 g) white fish fillets (pearl perch or sea bass); 2 tablespoons (1 oz) butter; ½ medium-size green bell pepper; ½ medium-size red bell pepper; 2 scallions; 1 garlic clove; 1 slice canned pineapple, drained; ¼ cup (2 fl oz) white vinegar; ¼ cup (3 oz) light corn syrup; ¼ cup (2 fl oz) pineapple juice; 1 tablespoon dry sherry; 1 tablespoon cornstarch; salt and black pepper

Cut the fish into two or three pieces each and place in a wide microwave-safe casserole. Spread half the butter over the fish and sprinkle generously with pepper. Cover the dish and microwave on HIGH (100%) for 2 minutes, then rearrange the fish and set aside.

Trim the peppers and scallions and shred finely. Peel and thinly slice the garlic. Place in a microwave-safe vegetable dish with the remaining butter, cover and microwave on HIGH (100%) for 1½ minutes. Add the pineapple.

In a small jug, mix the vinegar, syrup and pineapple juice together, then add the sherry, cornstarch and seasoning. Pour over the peppers, re-cover and microwave on HIGH (100%) for 1 minute. Stir, microwave on HIGH (100%) a further minute, stir well, then microwave a final 1 minute on HIGH (100%) until the sauce is thick and clear. Pour over the fish and allow to stand for at least 5–6 minutes so the fish can absorb the flavors, then reheat on MEDIUM (50%) when ready to serve.

T

Tamarind Flavored Shrimp

Serves 4-6: 1¾ lb (875 g) raw shrimp, unshelled; oil for deep frying; 1 large onion, grated; 3-4 garlic cloves, crushed; 1-2 fresh red chilies, seeded and chopped; 1½ tablespoons tamarind pulp, mixed with ¼ cup (2 fl oz) boiling water; 1 tablespoon sugar, or to taste; salt and black pepper; pineapple chunks and cucumber slices for garnish

Deep fry the shrimp in their shells for 1 minute. Drain well. Pour off most of the oil and fry the onion and garlic until soft. Add the chopped chilies and stir on high heat for 30 seconds.

Remove the shells and legs from the shrimp leaving the heads and tails on. Return to the pan, strain over the tamarind water, then add the sugar and salt and pepper to taste. Bring to the boil and simmer for approximately 1½ minutes until the shrimp are cooked through and the liquid has been absorbed. Serve hot, garnished with the pineapple chunks and sliced cucumber.

Treasure Ship Fish

Serves 4-6: 1 whole fresh fish such as snapper or bream, weighing about 2-3 lb (1-1½ kg); salt; 2 teaspoons sweet rice wine (mirin); oil for deep frying; 2 tablespoons all purpose flour; daikon-chili garnish (see page 276)
Dipping Sauce: ¼ cup (2 fl oz) lemon or sour orange juice; ¼ cup (2 fl oz) Japanese light soy sauce; ¼ cup (2 fl oz) dashi

Clean the fish and make sure all the scales have been removed. Using a sharp pointed knife, cut along the backbone of the fish from just behind the head right down to the tail. Cut down to the bottom part of the fish and then along, so that you can remove the complete fillet. Turn the fish and repeat on the other side. Cut the fillets into pieces about ¾ in (2 cm) square, leaving on the skin. Set aside.

Rub the fish head, center bone and tail with a generous amount of salt. Using a piece of kitchen string, tie a knot around the tail of the fish, then bring the string up the body and around the head, tying firmly so that the tail of the fish is raised vertically.

Put the tied fish on a lightly greased rack over a baking dish and cook in an oven preheated to 450°F (230°C) for 10 minutes. Remove from the oven, brush the head, tail and skin with the *mirin* and return to the oven for another 5 minutes. Allow to cool to room temperature.

Put the Dipping Sauce ingredients into a saucepan, bring to the boil, then allow to cool. Serve in individual sauce dishes.

Just before serving time, heat a generous amount of oil in a wok or deep skillet. Put the flour into a plastic bag, add the fish pieces and shake gently. Remove the fish pieces from the bag and put into a sieve. Shake once more to remove excess flour, then deep fry the fish in very hot oil for about 4 minutes or until golden brown.

To serve, put the baked fish body (strings removed) onto a platter and carefully place the fried fish pieces on the center of the body. This fish is traditionally decorated with pieces of fresh pine. Place the prepared *daikon*-chili garnish on the platter.

Tuna and Chili Sambal

Serves 4: 8 oz (250 g) canned chunk tuna; 4-6 fresh red chilies; 6 shallots or 1 small red or brown onion; 2 stalks lemongrass; 4 candlenuts or macadamias; 2 tablespoons oil; 1 cup (8 fl oz) coconut milk;
3 fragrant lime leaves or young citrus leaves; 1-2 teaspoons lime or lemon juice; salt to taste

Drain the oil from the tuna and put into a bowl; set aside. Pound or grind the chilies, shallots, lemongrass and candlenuts together to a fine paste. Heat the oil in a skillet and gently fry the ground ingredients, stirring from time to time, for 5 minutes. Add the coconut milk and lime leaves. Bring to the boil, stirring constantly, then add the tuna. Simmer gently for about 3 minutes, then add the lime juice and salt. Serve with rice.

Tuna and Peppers in Soy Sauce

Serves 4: 1 lb (500 g) fresh tuna steaks; ⅓ cup (2½ fl oz) light soy sauce; 2 tablespoons sweet sherry or sweet rice wine (mirin); 1¼ tablespoons sugar; 1 large green bell pepper; oil

Cut the tuna into 18 pieces and place in a dish. Mix the soy sauce, sherry or *mirin* and sugar together until the sugar has dissolved. Pour over the fish and marinate for 10 minutes, turning occasionally.

Cut the pepper into squares, discarding the seed pod and cutting away the inner white ribs.

Heat 2 tablespoons of oil in a skillet.

Tuna and Peppers in Soy Sauce

Drain the tuna, reserving the marinade, and sauté with the peppers for about 2 minutes. Pour in the remaining marinade, cover the pan and simmer gently for a further 3 minutes. Serve hot with white rice.

Note: To serve as an appetizer or a snack, thread the tuna and peppers alternately on short bamboo skewers and cook in the same way.

Tuna Steak with Wine and Bacon

Serves 4: 1 tablespoon olive oil; 4 oz (125 g) bacon, coarsely chopped; 2 onions, sliced; 1½ lb (750 g) fresh tuna, cut into steaks 1¼ in (3 cm) thick; 1 cup (8 fl oz) dry white wine; salt and freshly ground black pepper

Heat the oil in a skillet and fry the bacon and onions until the onions are soft and the bacon starts to brown. Add the tuna and lightly fry on both sides. Pour in the wine and simmer over low heat for 10 minutes. Season and serve with the bacon, onions and cooking juice poured over the tuna.

W

Whiting Fillets Sandwiched with Scallop Mousseline

Serves 6: 12 whiting fillets (approximately 1 lb/ 500 g); 12 oz (375 g) scallops, with roe; 1 large egg; ¼ cup (2 fl oz) heavy cream; salt and white pepper; 4 tablespoons (2 oz) butter; dried or fresh dill

Wipe the fillets and place half, skin side downwards, in a buttered microwave-safe dish.

Drain the scallops and remove the black intestinal vein. Place them in a food processor and process until pureed. Add the egg, cream and a little salt and pepper. Process again. The texture should be quite thick. Transfer to the refrigerator for 20 minutes to firm up if it appears slightly creamy.

Spread the mixture thickly over the fillets and add a light sprinkling of dill. Cover with the remaining fillets. Dot with butter and sprinkle with more dill. Cover with

plastic wrap and vent. Microwave on MEDIUM-HIGH (70%) for 6½–7½ minutes. Non-carousel ovens: Give the dish a half-turn after 3–4 minutes. Sprinkle over a little extra salt to taste.

When done the filling should be firm and springy to the touch while the fish will be white and flake easily. Serve at once.

Whole Baked Fish Served on a Hot Plate

*Serves 4: 2-lb (1-kg) sea bass or snapper; 2 tablespoons oil; 2½ oz (75 g) pork belly (fresh bacon pancetta); 2-in (5-cm) piece fresh young leek, shredded; 1 fresh red chili pepper, shredded; 4 thick slices fresh ginger, shredded; 6 sprigs fresh cilantro
Seasoning A: ¾ teaspoon salt; 1 tablespoon rice wine; 2 teaspoons sesame oil; 1 tablespoon oil; 1¾ teaspoons five-spice powder
Seasoning B/Sauce: ¼ cup (2 fl oz) chicken stock; 1½ tablespoons rice wine or dry sherry; ¼ cup (2 fl oz) light soy sauce; 2 teaspoons dark soy sauce; 1 tablespoon sugar; ½ teaspoon salt; 2 tablespoons oil*

Cut the fish in half lengthwise, cutting right through the head, but do not sever along the top of the back, so the fish can be pressed out flat in one piece. Trim away the backbone. Leave the skin and scale intact. Place the fish in a large dish and cover with boiling water. Leave for 2 minutes, then drain well. Rub both sides with the seasoning A ingredients and leave for 25 minutes.

Heat a baking pan or large ovenproof dish and add the oil. Spread the fish, scales upwards, on the tray and arrange the ingredients on top. Bake in an oven preheated to 425°F (220°C) for about 30 minutes. Put a metal serving tray, preferably one with a sturdy wooden detachable base, in the oven while the fish is cooking so it heats through thoroughly.

Drain the pan juices in a wok and return the fish to the oven. Heat the wok and add the seasoning B/sauce ingredients. Bring to the boil and check the seasoning.

Remove the fish and the heated tray from the oven. Use two large spatulas to transfer the fish to the hot serving tray. Pour on the piping hot sauce and carry sizzling to the table.

Whole Baked Fish Served on a Hot Plate

192

POULTRY

A

Andalusian Duckling with Olives

Serves 4: 2 tablespoons olive oil; 3 tablespoons (1½ oz) butter; 3 onions, sliced; 2 carrots, sliced; 3-lb (1.5-kg) duckling; 1 tablespoon all purpose flour; 1 cup (8 fl oz) hot stock; salt and freshly ground black pepper; 1 cup (8 fl oz) Madeira or dry sherry; 3 tablespoons tomato paste; 2 sprigs parsley, finely chopped; 48 green olives, pitted

Use a large, heavy-based pan deep enough to accommodate the duckling. Heat the oil and butter in the pan, add the onions, carrots and duckling and fry over medium heat until the duckling is light golden brown. Remove the duckling and vegetables and keep them warm.

Stir the flour into the fat, cook for 2–3 minutes and, while whisking constantly, add the hot stock. Season. Add the wine, tomato paste and parsley, and cook for 5 minutes, stirring constantly. Put the duckling and vegetables back into the pan, cover and simmer over low heat for 1¼ hours or until the duckling is tender.

Put the duckling onto a serving plate. Remove all excess fat from the sauce, strain into a saucepan, add the olives and check the seasoning. Simmer just long enough to heat the olives. Pour the sauce over the duckling and serve.

Black Velvet Chicken

Austrian Roast Goose

Serves 6: 6–8-lb (3–4-kg) goose; 6 medium-size tart cooking apples, peeled and cored; 2 tablespoons finely chopped fresh marjoram; salt and freshly ground black pepper; 1 tablespoon drained and finely chopped capers; 1 tablespoon Hungarian paprika; ½ cup (4 fl oz) heavy sour cream; ½ cup (4 fl oz) water

Prick the skin of the goose all over with a skewer. Coat the apples with the marjoram, season with salt and black pepper and put inside the bird. Secure the cavity with toothpicks.

Season the skin with salt and black pepper and put the bird on a rack set over a roasting dish. Cook just below the center of an oven preheated to 400°F (200°C) for 2½–3 hours or until the bird is cooked. Baste the bird occasionally, removing and reserving the excess fat from the dish. Potatoes can be roasted in some of the goose fat for the last hour of cooking.

Transfer the goose to a heated carving dish, remove the toothpicks and keep hot. Drain the goose fat from the dish. Stir the capers and paprika into the pan juices on top of the stove. Add the sour cream and water, simmer gently and adjust the seasoning.

B

Black Velvet Chicken ★

Serves 8: 4 tablespoons (2 oz) butter; 2 large onions, halved and thinly sliced; 4–6 lb (2–3 kg) chicken thighs or other pieces; 1 teaspoon salt; 1 teaspoon freshly ground black pepper; ½ cup (2 oz) all purpose flour; 1 cup (8 fl oz) Guinness or dark ale; 1¾ cups (14 fl oz) champagne; ½ teaspoon nutmeg; 1 teaspoon dried thyme; 2 bay leaves; 8 oz (250 g) small button mushrooms, larger ones halved; 1¼ cups (10 fl oz) cream

Melt the butter in a large flameproof casserole and gently fry the onions until they are transparent. Add the chicken pieces and brown lightly on all sides. Season with the salt and black pepper. Put the uncovered casserole into an oven preheated to 425°F (220°C) and roast the chicken for 30 minutes.

Remove the casserole from the oven. Sprinkle the flour over the chicken, on top of the stove, and turn the pieces in the pan juices until the flour is the color of pale straw. Gradually add the Guinness or dark ale and champagne, stirring until the sauce simmers. Add the nutmeg, thyme and bay leaves. Cover and return to the oven for 30 minutes, or until the chicken is tender and the juices run clean when pierced with a skewer.

Shortly before the chicken is cooked, simmer the mushrooms in the cream for 3–4 minutes or until they are just tender. Strain the cream into the casserole. Arrange the chicken pieces on a heated serving dish and keep hot. On top of the stove, bring the sauce just to the boil, whisking constantly until slightly thickened. Adjust the seasoning and spoon the sauce over the chicken.

Broiled Chicken with Wine Sauce

Serves 4: 1 chicken; 4 oz (125 g) pale button mushrooms, sliced; 1 small onion, finely chopped; ½ teaspoon salt; freshly ground black pepper; 2 tablespoons vegetable oil or olive oil; 1 cup (8 fl oz) red wine; 2 parsley sprigs; 2 bay leaves; 2 sprigs of celery leaves or 1 celery stalk, quartered; vegetable oil; 1 teaspoon arrowroot; ½ cup (4 fl oz) chicken stock; watercress (optional)

Use kitchen scissors or poultry shears to halve the chicken. Cut first through the breastbone and then the spine. Trim away any small backbones and discard. Lay the bird in a shallow dish and set aside.

Mix the mushrooms in a small bowl with the onion, salt, black pepper, oil and wine. Pour over the chicken. Tie the parsley, bay leaves and celery leaves or celery stalk together and bury among the chicken halves. Cover and leave at room temperature for at least 2 hours, turning the chicken occasionally. The longer you leave them marinating the better — all day if you can, in which case marinate in the refrigerator.

When ready to cook, preheat the broiler to high. Lift the chicken halves from the marinade and pat dry with paper towels. Brush each side lightly with oil. Arrange the bird, skin side down, on a rack and broil for 4–5 minutes on each side, at the furthest point from the heat.

Slip the chicken from the rack into the broiler pan. Discard the herbs and pour the marinade over the bird. Lower the heat slightly and continue to cook, skin side up, for 10–12 minutes, basting frequently with the marinade. Arrange the cooked chicken on a heated serving dish and keep hot.

Pour the marinade into a saucepan. Mix the arrowroot with the chicken stock and stir into the pan. Cook, stirring constantly, until the sauce is clear and slightly thickened. Adjust the seasoning and spoon over the chicken. Garnish with the watercress and serve immediately.

Note: To marinate four halved chickens,

it is necessary to increase the marinade ingredients only by half.

Broiled Skewered Chicken (Yakitori)

Serves 4–6 (12 skewers): 2 lb (1 kg) chicken thighs and drumsticks; 6 scallions; seven spice mixture (shichimi) or assorted chili powder (togarashi) Sauce: ¾ cup (6 fl oz) dark soy sauce; ¼ cup (2 fl oz) sake; 2½ tablespoons sweet rice wine (mirin); 1½ tablespoons sugar

Bone the chicken and cut into 1-in (2.5-cm) squares, leaving on the skin. Trim the scallions, wash and cut the thick portion into 1-in (2.5-cm) lengths. Thread the chicken and scallions onto skewers, using 2–3 pieces of onion per skewer. The

Broiled Chicken with Wine Sauce

194

skewers can be covered with plastic wrap and refrigerated until needed.

Combine all sauce ingredients in a pan and bring just to the boil. Pour into a shallow dish long enough to hold a skewer and keep ready for dipping the skewers during cooking.

Cook the *yakitori* over charcoal or under a hot broiler for just 2 minutes on one side, then dip each skewer into the sauce and return to cook longer on the same side. After another couple of minutes, dip the skewers again and return to the heat, turning over so that the other side can brown. When the *yakitori* are cooked, dip one more time in the sauce, drain and serve on a large platter or individual platters, sprinkled with seven spice mixture or assorted chili powder.

C

Cantonese Fruit Chicken

Serves 4: ½ cup (4 fl oz) fresh orange juice; 8 fresh or canned lychees, stoned and quartered; 1 tablespoon tomato paste; 1 tablespoon light soy sauce; 3 tablespoons water; 2 tablespoons oil; 8 oz (250 g) boneless chicken, thinly sliced across the grain; 1 tablespoon cornstarch; 1 teaspoon salt

Mix the orange juice with the lychees, tomato paste, soy sauce and water and set aside. Heat the oil in a wok or skillet. Dust the chicken slices with the cornstarch seasoned with salt and stir fry for 2 minutes. Pour the fruit mixture over the chicken and stir gently until the sauce has thickened. Serve at once.

Cantonese Roast Duck

Serves 6: 3-lb (1½-kg) duck
Seasoning: 2 tablespoons soybean paste; 1 tablespoon rice wine or dry sherry; 1 teaspoon salt; 1 tablespoon sugar; ½ teaspoon powdered licorice root, or 1 small piece licorice root (optional), or use 1 star anise; 3 tablespoons finely chopped scallion; 1 tablespoon finely chopped fresh ginger; 1¼ teaspoons crushed garlic
Glaze: 2½ tablespoons malt sugar; ¼ cup (2 fl oz) white vinegar; 1½ tablespoons boiling water

Clean and dress the duck and blanch in boiling water for 2 minutes. Remove and

Cantonese Roast Duck

drain well. Tie a strong string around its neck, passing it beneath the wings to hold them away from the body. Hang in a well-ventilated place over a drip tray.

Mix the seasoning ingredients together and smear thickly over the inside of the duck. Secure the lower opening with poultry pins, or sew up.

Mix the glaze ingredients, stirring over a pan of boiling water if the malt sugar is slow to dissolve. Slowly pour over the duck's skin to coat evenly. Catch the drips and brush these onto the skin until thickly coated. Leave to dry for 1 hour.

Place the duck, breast side down, on a rack in a baking pan and bake in an oven preheated to 400°F (200°C) for 20 minutes, then reduce the heat to 325°F (170°C) and roast for a further 55 minutes, turning the duck once. If preferred, secure the duck on a rotisserie and cook on high heat for 25 minutes, then reduce to low for the remainder of the cooking.

Drain the pan juices into a pan and bring to the boil. Supplement with a little chicken stock or water if the amount is small. Check the seasonings and keep hot.

Cut the duck into serving portions or bite-size pieces as preferred and arrange on a serving plate. Pour the sauce over and serve at once.

Castilian Turkey

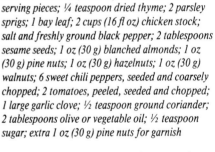

Serves 4-6: 4-5-lb (2-2.5-kg) turkey, cut into serving pieces; ¼ teaspoon dried thyme; 2 parsley sprigs; 1 bay leaf; 2 cups (16 fl oz) chicken stock; salt and freshly ground black pepper; 2 tablespoons sesame seeds; 1 oz (30 g) blanched almonds; 1 oz (30 g) pine nuts; 1 oz (30 g) hazelnuts; 1 oz (30 g) walnuts; 6 sweet chili peppers, seeded and coarsely chopped; 2 tomatoes, peeled, seeded and chopped; 1 large garlic clove; ½ teaspoon ground coriander; 2 tablespoons olive or vegetable oil; ½ teaspoon sugar; extra 1 oz (30 g) pine nuts for garnish

Put the turkey pieces into a heavy flameproof casserole with the thyme, parsley and bay leaf. Add the stock and bring to the boil over moderate heat. Reduce the temperature until the stock is simmering. Season with salt and black pepper to taste. Cover and simmer for 1-1¼ hours or until the turkey is almost tender. Remove the pan from the heat and let the turkey cool, uncovered, in the stock.

Mix the sesame seeds in a bowl with the nuts, chilies, tomatoes, garlic and coriander. Puree coarsely in a blender or food processor and set aside.

Using a slotted spoon, lift the turkey pieces from the stock and set aside. Strain the stock into a jug, discard the herbs and skim any excess fat from the top of the stock.

Heat the oil in a skillet and cook the nut puree for 5 minutes, stirring constantly. Stir enough of the reserved stock into the nut mixture to make a smooth sauce of coating consistency. Add the sugar, adjust the seasoning and simmer very gently for 2–3 minutes. Return the turkey to the casserole, pour the sauce over and cook over low heat for 20 minutes. Sprinkle with the extra pine nuts before serving.

Caucasian Fried Chickens ★

Serves 4–6: 2 small chickens, halved; 1 large garlic clove, halved; salt; ½ cup (4 fl oz) natural yogurt; 8 tablespoons (4 oz) butter; watercress for garnish

Flatten the birds and rub both sides with the garlic and salt. Lay cut side down on a baking sheet. Brush with the yogurt and roast in an oven preheated to 300°F (150°C) for 15 minutes.

Melt the butter in a large skillet over moderate heat. Place as many halves as the pan will hold, skin side down, in the hot butter. Press the chickens while they are frying. Cover with aluminum foil, put another pan on top and weight with anything heavy — cans of food or a heavy casserole. Reduce the heat until the chickens are gently sizzling. Fry for 8–10 minutes, turn the halves, replace the weight and cook for 10 minutes longer, until crisp and brown.

Keep the cooked halves hot at the bottom of the oven and finish cooking the rest in the same way. They will need a shorter frying time because of their longer precooking — 5–6 minutes on each side. Arrange the birds on a heated serving platter and garnish with watercress.

Charcoal-Roasted Duck Stuffed with Lotus Leaves

Serves 4–6: 5-lb (2½-kg) fairly fat duck; 1 teaspoon salt; 1 tablespoon rice wine or dry sherry; 6 dried or fresh lotus leaves; 12 large scallions, trimmed; 24 mandarin pancakes (see page 230); sweet bean paste or hoisin sauce; sugar; sesame oil (optional)

Caucasian Fried Chickens

Chicken Akbar

Glaze: 3 tablespoons malt sugar (or clear honey or light corn syrup); ½ cup (4 fl oz) boiling water

If possible, have the duck drawn through an incision beneath one wing. Rub the salt and wine inside the cavity and prop the body open with a short stick placed inside the breast cavity between the shoulders.

Soak the dried lotus leaves, if used, in boiling water until softened. If using fresh leaves, blanch in boiling water for 10 seconds. Drain and roll the leaves up together, then shred coarsely. Place the lotus leaves and two scallions into the cavity and tie a string around the neck, then under the wings. Hang in a well-ventilated area over a drip tray. Pour on several batches of boiling water to tighten the skin, then mix the malt sugar, or substitute, with the ½ cup boiling water and pour slowly and evenly over the duck. Leave for at least 6 hours until the skin is dry to the touch.

Charcoal-roast the duck on a rotisserie at 400°F (200°C), turning frequently until cooked through with a crisp and dark skin, about 1½ hours.

Using a sharp carving knife, pare off the crisp skin in pieces about 1⅔ in (4 cm) square and arrange on a plate. Cut the meat into bite-size pieces and serve on another plate. Save the carcass for soup or stock. Discard the lotus leaves.

Have the pancakes warm and ready. (They keep well if wrapped in aluminum foil.) Heat the sweet bean paste with sugar and sesame oil to taste, or use a prepared duck sauce (hoisin or plum). Cut the trimmed scallions into 2-in (5-cm) lengths and cut in half lengthwise.

To eat the duck, place a slice of scallion in the center of a pancake. Dip a piece of crisp skin into the sauce, followed by a piece of meat. Place on the pancake, add more scallion if desired and roll up, tucking in the end.

Chicken Akbar

Serves 4: 4 sheets filo pastry; 8 oz (250 g) boneless chicken breasts; 2 scallions, chopped; 1 small garlic clove, crushed; 1 tablespoon pine nuts; 1 tablespoon slivered almonds; 1½ tablespoons seedless raisins; 2 tablespoons (1 oz) butter; 1 teaspoon mild curry powder; 1 tablespoon all purpose flour; ¼ cup (2 fl oz) chicken stock; ¼ cup (2 fl oz) heavy cream; salt and black pepper

Cover the pastry with a damp paper towel until needed. Finely shred the chicken and mix with the scallions and garlic.

Sauté the nuts, raisins and chicken in the butter until the chicken is lightly colored. Sprinkle over the curry powder and cook briefly, then add the flour and cook for about 1 minute. Add the chicken stock and bring almost to the boil, stirring. Add the cream and seasoning, and simmer gently for about 2 minutes or until the sauce is thick. Remove from the heat and leave to cool slightly.

Fold each sheet of pastry in half to give rectangular shapes about 8 × 7 in (20 × 18 cm). Brush with melted butter. Place one-quarter of the filling on each piece of pastry, fold in the sides and then fold the pastry over the filling to completely enclose it. Press the edge to seal.

Heat about ½ in (1 cm) of mixed butter and oil and gently fry the pastries, two at a time, until golden. Drain and arrange on a serving plate. Serve hot.

Fold each sheet in half and brush with melted butter.

Fold the pastry over the filling to enclose it completely.

Chicken Amager

Serves 4: 2 tablespoons (1 oz) butter; 1 tablespoon vegetable oil; 3-4 lb (1.5-2 kg) chicken pieces; 1 large onion, chopped; 1 garlic clove, crushed; 1½ tablespoons all purpose flour; ¼ teaspoon cayenne or red pepper; ½ teaspoon Hungarian paprika; 1 teaspoon finely chopped fresh dill or ½ teaspoon dried dill; 2 cups (16 fl oz) chicken stock; salt and white pepper; 2 tablespoons Madeira; 1 large bay leaf; 8 oz (250 g) raw shrimp, peeled and deveined; 8 oz (250 g) fresh asparagus, blanched, or 11 oz (340 g) can asparagus spears, drained; ½ cup (4 fl oz) cream

Melt the butter with the oil in a skillet and brown the chicken pieces on all sides, without overcrowding the pan. Transfer to a casserole. Add the onion to the skillet and cook gently until transparent. Add the garlic and cook for 1 minute. Sprinkle the flour, cayenne or red pepper, paprika and dill over the onion mixture and stir for 1-2 minutes. Add the stock gradually, stirring constantly between additions until the sauce is smooth. Season with salt and pepper to taste. Stir the Madeira into the sauce and pour it over the chicken. Add the bay leaf to the casserole, cover and bake in an oven preheated to 375°F (190°C) for 40 minutes.

Add the shrimp and asparagus and cook, still covered, for 20 minutes, or until the chicken is tender. Stir the cream into the sauce, discard the bay leaf and adjust the seasoning before serving.

Chicken, Avocado and Orange Salad

Serves 4: 1 chicken; 1 bay leaf; 1 sprig each parsley and thyme; 2 garlic cloves, peeled; salt and black pepper; 2 tablespoons dry white wine; 1 ripe avocado; 2 oranges; ½ red bell pepper; 1 scallion Lime and Hazelnut Dressing: 3 oz (90 g) hazelnuts; 1 cup (8 fl oz) olive oil; ½ cup (4 fl oz) fresh lime juice or to taste; salt, pepper, cayenne; chopped parsley

Rinse and dry the chicken. Place the herbs and garlic in the cavity and season with salt and pepper. Rub the skin with more salt and pepper and place, breast side upwards, in an oven bag. Pour the wine into the bag. Secure the top with a strip of plastic cut from the top end of the oven bag. Pierce in several places.

Set the chicken in a microwave-safe dish and microwave on HIGH (100%) for 20 minutes. Test by inserting a meat thermometer into the thickest part of the thigh. It should register 190°F (88°C). Remove the chicken and leave to cool in the bag.

Place the hazelnuts on a plate and microwave on HIGH (100%) for 3 minutes. Transfer to a cloth and rub to remove the skins, then return to the oven and microwave on HIGH (100%) for a further 3-4 minutes until toasted. It will be necessary to stir and turn the nuts frequently for even coloring.

In a food processor, grind the nuts until still slightly coarse. Remove. Add the remaining sauce ingredients and process until well blended, then add the nuts and blend further. Pour into a jug.

Peel and slice the avocado. Peel the oranges, removing all pith, then cut into segments. Shred pepper and scallion.

When the chicken is cool, remove the skin and slice or pull the meat into shreds. Place in a salad bowl and lightly toss with the avocado, oranges, pepper and scallion. Stir the dressing before pouring over the salad.

Chicken, Avocado and Orange Salad

Chicken and Leek Pie

Chicken and Leek Pie

*Serves 4–6: 3 lb (1.5 kg) chicken thighs; 3 cups
(1½ pts) chicken stock or water; 1 quantity of
shortcrust pastry (see page 319); 3–4 leeks, split and
sliced; 1 hot red chili, seeded and thinly sliced;
2 tablespoons butter; 2 tablespoons all purpose
flour; ½ cup (4 fl oz) cream; salt and white pepper;
egg glaze*

Poach the chicken in the stock or water
until tender. Meanwhile, make the pastry,
then cover and chill before rolling. Lift the
cooked chicken from the stock and set
aside to cool, reserving the cooking liquid.

Blanch the leeks for 1 minute in some of
the boiling stock, strain and set aside.
Remove and discard the skin and chicken
bones, then cut the meat into chunky
pieces. Sprinkle with the sliced chili and set
aside.

Melt the butter, stir in the flour and cook
for 1–2 minutes without browning. Gradually add 1¼ cups of the reserved stock, stirring between each addition until the sauce
is smooth and thickened. Simmer for 2–3
minutes and remove from the heat. Add
the cream and season well with salt and
pepper.

Roll out half of the pastry to line a
9–10 in (23–25 cm) pie plate. Spread the
chicken and leeks over the pastry. Roll out
the remaining dough. Add some of the
sauce to the chicken and brush the pastry
edge lightly with water. Cover the pie,
trim, and seal the edges firmly. Cut a small
slit in the top of the pastry and decorate
with the trimmings if you wish. Brush
lightly with the egg glaze and bake in the
center of an oven preheated to 400°F
(200°C) for 30 minutes, or until the pastry
is crisp and golden.

Chicken and Orange Kebabs

*Serves 6: 3 oranges; 3–6 slices bacon; 1 lb (500 g)
cooked chicken; 24 small mushroom caps, sautéed
in butter; juice of 1 large orange; 4 tablespoons
(2 oz) butter*

Peel the oranges, remove the pith and cut
into segments. Remove the rind from the
bacon and fry gently, then dice. Remove
the skin and membrane from the chicken
and cut into 1-in (2.5-cm) cubes. Thread six
skewers alternately with the orange segments, chicken, cooked mushroom caps
and bacon. Brush with a mixture of orange
juice and melted butter and barbecue over
hot coals, turning once or twice, until
lightly browned on all sides. Serve
immediately.

Note: The kebabs may also be cooked
under a broiler.

Chicken and Seafood Fondue

*Serves 4: 2 whole chicken breasts, skinned, boned
and cut across the grain into 1-in (2.5-cm) strips;
12 raw shrimp, shelled and deveined; 24 fresh
oysters; 1 medium-size white radish, thinly sliced;
12 scallions, cut into 1-in (2.5-cm) lengths; 4 oz
(125 g) button mushrooms; 2 celery stalks, cut into
1-in (2.5-cm) lengths; 4 cups (1 liter) chicken stock;
4 oz (250 g) shirataki noodles, drained; 10 oz (315 g)
cooked long grain rice (optional); ⅓ cup (2½ fl oz)
light soy sauce; ¼ cup (2 fl oz) sake or dry sherry*

Arrange the prepared chicken, seafood and
vegetables attractively on a large platter
within easy reach of everybody. Bring the
chicken stock to the boil, add the shirataki
noodles and heat thoroughly. Strain the
stock into the fondue dish and serve the
noodles and rice on heated plates. Add half
of the soy sauce and the sake or sherry to
the chicken stock. Guests then poach their
own chicken, seafood and vegetables in the
simmering stock. Serve the remaining soy
sauce in a small dish for dipping.

Note: Shirataki noodles are available
from Asian food stores.

Chicken Balls Simmered with Daikon

Serves 4: 8 oz (250 g) boneless chicken, finely ground; 2 tablespoons dashi; 2 teaspoons light soy sauce; 2 teaspoons sweet rice wine (mirin); 2 teaspoons cornstarch; 1 lb (500 g) giant white radish (daikon); 4 cups (1 liter) water from washing rice; very finely shredded strips of lemon peel for garnish
Stock: 3 cups (24 fl oz) dashi; 1½ tablespoons light soy sauce; 1½ tablespoons sake; 1 tablespoon sugar

Mix the chicken thoroughly with the *dashi*, soy sauce, *mirin*, and cornstarch. Divide into eight portions. Use wet hands to shape the mixture into balls, then press flat into circles about ½ in (1 cm) thick. Bring the stock to simmering point and add the chicken balls. Simmer, uncovered, for 4 minutes. Remove and set aside, keeping the stock.

Peel the *daikon* and cut into ¾-in (2-cm) thick slices. Bevel the top and bottom slightly for a more attractive appearance. Put the water from washing the rice into a pan and boil the *daikon* slices for 5 minutes. Drain, rinse and put into the stock used for cooking the chicken balls. Simmer over low heat with a drop lid for about 30 minutes or until the *daikon* is tender. If you wish to prepare the dish in advance, take out the daikon and keep aside with the chicken balls.

When ready to serve, bring the stock almost to the boil, put back the chicken balls and *daikon* and simmer gently, uncovered, for 3 minutes. Taste the stock and adjust the flavor with a little more soy sauce or salt if preferred. Divide the *daikon* and chicken balls among four individual serving bowls. Moisten with 2-3 tablespoons of the cooking stock and garnish with shred of lemon peel.

Served with boiled rice.

Chicken Cooked with Soy Sauce and Lime Juice

Serves 4: 1 fresh chicken, weighing about 2½ lb (1.2 kg), or 2 lb (1 kg) chicken pieces; ¼ cup oil; 4 medium-size red or brown onions, sliced; 2-3 fresh red chilies, sliced; 2 tablespoons sugar; ¼ cup thick black soy sauce; ½ teaspoon salt; ¼ cup Chinese lime juice or lemon juice; 1 cup (8 fl oz) water

If using a whole chicken, cut it into small pieces. Heat the oil and gently fry the sliced onions and chili for 2 minutes, then add the chicken and fry a further 10 minutes, stirring from time to time. Sprinkle the sugar over the chicken and fry for 1 minute, then add the remaining ingredients and simmer gently, uncovered, until the chicken is tender and the sauce has thickened.

Chicken Divan

Serves 4: 1 lb (500 g) fresh broccoli, trimmed; ¾-1 lb (375-500 g) chopped cooked chicken; salt and pepper; 2 oz (60 g) toasted slivered almonds; 2 tablespoons grated Parmesan cheese
Sauce: 1½ cups (14 fl oz) milk; 1 small onion; 1 bay leaf; 4 tablespoons (2 oz) butter; 3 tablespoons all purpose flour; salt and white pepper; ½ cup (4 fl oz) cream; 1 tablespoon dry sherry

Cook the broccoli in lightly salted water until just tender. Drain and arrange in a shallow ovenproof dish with the flower ends against the rim of the dish.

To make the sauce, put the milk, onion and bay leaf in the top of a double boiler and cook over simmering water for 15 minutes. Strain the milk and discard the flavoring ingredients. Melt the butter in a saucepan, stir in the flour and cook gently for 2 minutes. Gradually add the strained milk, whisking constantly between additions until the sauce is thick and smooth. Season with salt and pepper to taste and simmer for 1 minute. Remove the pan from the heat and add the cream and sherry.

Fold the chicken into the sauce, adjust the seasoning and pour over the broccoli. Sprinkle with the almonds and cheese and bake in an oven preheated to 350°F (180°C) for 25-30 minutes. Serve immediately.

Chicken in Chilindrón Sauce

Serves 4-6: ½ cup (4 fl oz) olive oil; 1 garlic clove, chopped; 3-lb (1.5-kg) chicken, cut into pieces; salt and freshly ground black pepper; 1 onion, chopped; 2 red or green bell peppers, seeded and chopped; 1 tablespoon paprika; ¼ teaspoon saffron; 6½ oz (200 g) Spanish ham or prosciutto, cut into cubes; 8 oz (250 g) tomatoes, peeled and chopped; ½ small hot pepper, seeded and chopped

Chicken Divan

Heat the oil in a casserole and sauté the garlic until golden, then discard. Add the chicken pieces, season and brown on all sides. Remove the chicken and set aside. Sauté the onion and peppers until they are soft, then mix in the paprika, saffron, ham and tomatoes.

Mix the browned chicken pieces and the hot peppers into the sauce, cover and simmer over low heat for about 1 hour or until the chicken is tender. To serve, arrange the chicken pieces on a platter and cover with sauce.

Chicken in Cream Sauce

Serves 2: 1 small chicken; salt and ground pepper; 3 tablespoons (1½ oz) butter; 4 oz (100 g) bacon, diced; 8 button mushrooms; 4 pickling onions; 5 tablespoons cream; 5 tablespoons meat stock; 1½ teaspoons finely chopped rosemary

Split the chicken along the backbone and flatten out. Season lightly and sauté in the butter until almost cooked, then put into a casserole.

Sauté the bacon, mushrooms and onions in the remaining butter. Add the cream, meat stock and rosemary and bring it to the boil. Season to taste. Pour the sauce over the chicken, cover the casserole and cook in an oven preheated to 350°F (180°C) for about 25 minutes.

Chicken in Honey

Serves 4: 3-lb (1.5-kg) roasting chicken; chicken stock or water; 3 tablespoons honey; 3 tablespoons English mustard; 1 cup (4 oz) dry breadcrumbs; oil for deep frying

Poach the chicken in stock or water to cover for 45 minutes. When cool enough to handle, skin the bird and cut it into pieces.

Mix together the honey and mustard, and coat each piece of chicken. Roll the chicken pieces in breadcrumbs and refrigerate for 30 minutes. Heat the oil and deep fry the chicken pieces for 7–10 minutes or until golden brown. Serve with apple rings fried in butter.

Chicken in Rich Coconut Gravy

Chicken in Soy Sauce

Chicken in Rich Coconut Gravy

Serves 4: 1 whole chicken, weighing about 2½ lb (1.2 kg); ½ in (1 cm) fresh turmeric or ½ teaspoon turmeric powder; 2-in (5-cm) piece fresh ginger; 16 shallots or 2 medium red or brown onions; 2 garlic cloves; 3 stalks lemongrass; 6–8 fresh red chilies; 2 slices lengkuas; 3 tablespoons oil; 3 cups (24 fl oz) thick coconut milk; 1 pandan leaf; 1 teaspoon salt

Cut the chicken into about 14 pieces. Pound the fresh turmeric to obtain the juice, or mix the turmeric powder with a little water to make a paste. Rub the chicken with turmeric and set aside.

Grind the ginger, shallots, garlic, lemongrass, chilies and *lengkuas* to a fine paste. Heat the oil in a deep pan and gently fry the ground ingredients for about 5 minutes. Add the chicken pieces and fry for 5 minutes, stirring frequently so the chicken is thoroughly coated with the spices.

Add the coconut milk, *pandan* leaf and salt. Stir constantly until the coconut milk comes to the boil, then simmer, uncovered, until the chicken is tender and the gravy has thickened.

Chicken in Soy Sauce

Serves 4-6: 2½-lb (1.2-kg) roasting chicken; 5 scallions, trimmed; 5 thick slices fresh ginger; 1 teaspoon sesame oil (optional); 2 star anise Sauce: 2 cups (16 fl oz) chicken stock or water; 1 cup (8 fl oz) light soy sauce; ½ cup (4 fl oz) dark soy sauce; ½ cup (4 oz) sugar

Clean the chicken and wipe with paper towels. Put 2 scallions and 2 slices of ginger into the cavity. Rub the skin with the sesame oil, if used. Place the chicken in a wok or a deep pan on a small oiled rack to hold it just above the bottom of the pan. Place the star anise and remaining scallions and ginger in the pan on either side of the chicken.

Add the sauce ingredients and bring to a gentle boil. Cover the pan, reduce the heat and simmer slowly with the bubbles just occasionally breaking the surface, until the chicken is completely tender, about 50 minutes. Turn once to ensure even cooking.

Lift the chicken out of the stock with two slotted spoons and drain thoroughly. Cut into serving pieces and serve hot with a little of the poaching liquid as a sauce.

Note: A sliced fresh red chili and a piece of orange or tangerine peel can be added to the poaching liquid for flavor.

Chicken Kashmir

Serves 4–6: 3-lb (1.5-kg) chicken; 6 garlic cloves; 1-in (2.5-cm) piece fresh ginger; 1 green chili; 1 tablespoon lemon juice; 1 teaspoon garam masala; 1 teaspoon chili powder; ½ teaspoon salt; ¼ teaspoon turmeric; ½ cup (4 fl oz) plain yogurt; ½ teaspoon sugar; ¼ cup ghee; 1 tablespoon finely chopped fresh cilantro leaves
Curry paste: 1 large onion; 4 garlic cloves; 1-in (2.5-cm) piece fresh ginger; 6 cloves; 1 teaspoon black peppercorns; 1-in (2.5-cm) stick cinnamon; 1 heaped teaspoon fennel seeds; 2 tablespoons ground coriander; 6 black cardamoms; 1 teaspoon cumin; 1½ oz (45 g) ground almonds; 1 teaspoon salt; ¼ cup (2 fl oz) plain yogurt; ¼ teaspoon saffron powder; 2 tablespoons boiling water

Clean the chicken and wipe dry. Grind all ingredients except the yogurt and sugar to a paste, then stir in the yogurt and sugar. Rub over the chicken, inside and out. Leave for 2 hours to absorb the flavors. Roast in an oven preheated to 350°F (180°C) for 45 minutes or until almost cooked through, then remove from the oven and leave to cool completely.

To make curry paste, mince the onion with the garlic and ginger. Grind all spices to a fine powder and mix with the onion paste. Add the almonds, salt, yogurt and saffron steeped in boiling water. Rub this mixture over the cooked chicken.

Add the *ghee* to the pan and fry the chicken, basting frequently with *ghee* and the sauce, until done. Sprinkle with *garam masala* and chopped cilantro leaves before serving.

Chicken Kiev Macadamia

Serves 6: 6 large chicken breasts; salt and pepper; 12 tablespoons (6 oz) chilled butter; 3 garlic cloves, halved; 3 teaspoons chopped parsley; 1 cup (4 oz) all purpose flour; 2 eggs, beaten; ground macadamia nuts; oil for deep frying

Bone the chicken breasts and beat flat with a cleaver. Sprinkle on both sides with salt and pepper and lay them skin side down. In the center of each breast, put 2 tablespoons

(1 oz) chilled butter, ½ garlic clove, crushed, and ½ teaspoon chopped parsley. Fold the two shorter ends of each breast in towards the center, then overlap the two longer ends to make a tight package. Tie each breast securely with string.

Roll the breasts in flour seasoned with salt and pepper, dip in the beaten egg and finally roll in ground macadamia nuts. Press the nuts on firmly and chill for at least 30 minutes.

Fry the breasts in oil preheated to 375°F (190°C) for 5 minutes. Lift them out and gently remove the string. Return the breasts to the oil for 10–12 minutes or until cooked. Remove and drain on paper towels. Serve immediately.

Chicken Liver and Ham Gougère

Serves 4–6: Choux Pastry: 1 cup (8 fl oz) water; 8 tablespoons (4 oz) butter; 1 cup (4 oz) all purpose flour; pinch of salt; 4 jumbo eggs, lightly beaten
Filling: 4 tablespoons (2 oz) butter; 8 oz (250 g) chicken livers, skinned and trimmed; 1 large onion, halved and sliced; 2 oz (60 g) mushrooms, sliced; 1½ tablespoons all purpose flour; 1¼ cups (10 fl oz) chicken stock; 3 tablespoons dry red wine; 4 oz (125 g) coarsely chopped lean ham; 2 medium-size tomatoes, peeled, seeded, and cut into eighths; 8 green olives, pitted and quartered; salt and freshly ground black pepper
Topping: 1 tablespoon breadcrumbs, sautéed in 1 tablespoon butter; 1 tablespoon finely chopped parsley

To make the choux pastry, put the water and butter into a saucepan and bring just

Chicken Liver and Ham Gougère

to boiling point. Remove the pan from the heat, add all the flour and salt, and beat with a wooden spoon until the mixture is smooth and leaves the sides of the pan. Cool slightly. Gradually add the eggs, beating thoroughly until the mixture is shiny and smooth.

Spoon or pipe the choux pastry around the edge of a lightly oiled circular dish, leaving the center free. Bake in an oven preheated to 425°F (220°C) for 30–40 minutes, or until the pastry is crisp and golden.

Meanwhile, prepare the filling; melt half the butter in a skillet and quickly sauté the chicken livers on all sides until sealed. Remove from the pan. Reduce the heat, add the remaining butter and cook the onion until transparent. Add the mushrooms and turn in the pan juices until they are coated but still firm. Sprinkle with the flour, stir well and cook for 1 minute more. Gradually add the stock, stirring constantly until the sauce is smooth. Fold the reserved livers into the sauce with the wine, ham, tomatoes and olives. Simmer for 2–3 minutes and season with salt and black pepper to taste.

Spoon the liver mixture into the center of the pastry, sprinkle over the crumbs and parsley, and serve.

Chicken Marengo

Serves 4–6: 3–4 lb (1.5–2 kg) chicken pieces, skinned; salt and freshly ground black pepper; 2 tablespoons (1 oz) butter; 2 tablespoons olive oil; 2 medium-size onions, finely chopped; 2 garlic cloves, crushed; 1 tablespoon all-purpose flour; approx 1½ cups (12 fl oz) chicken stock; 3 tablespoons dry sherry or white wine; 3 tablespoons tomato paste; 4 parsley sprigs; 2 bay leaves; 2 sprigs celery leaves; 4 oz (125 g) button mushrooms, halved if large; 6–8 raw shrimp or crayfish, peeled, but with the heads left on; juice of ½ lemon; cayenne or red pepper; 4–6 eggs (optional)

Season the chicken pieces with salt and black pepper. Melt the butter with the oil in a large, heavy-based casserole. Quickly sauté the chicken pieces until golden on all sides. Lift the chicken from the pan and set aside.

Add the onions and garlic to the pan and cook over gentle heat until the onions are transparent. Sprinkle the flour into the pan, stir into the pan juices and cook for 1 minute without browning. Gradually add the stock, stirring between additions, until a smooth sauce forms. Stir in the sherry or wine and the tomato paste. Adjust the seasoning and simmer gently for 3–4 minutes. Tie the parsley, bay leaves and celery leaves together and add to the pan with the chicken, turning the pieces in the sauce until they are well coated. If the sauce is too thick, add a little more stock. Cover and simmer for 40 minutes.

Add the mushrooms to the casserole and simmer for 15 minutes. Lay the shrimp or crayfish on the chicken and cook for 10 minutes more. Lift the chicken, mushrooms and shrimp from the pan, arrange on a heated serving dish and keep hot. Bring the sauce to the boil and discard the herbs. Add the lemon juice and cayenne or red pepper to taste. Pour the sauce over the chicken and garnish, if you wish, with the eggs, which have been lightly fried or poached.

Chicken Mille-Feuille

Serves 4–6: 1 lb (500 g) package frozen puff pastry, thawed; 1½ tablespoons butter; 2 tablespoons all purpose flour; 1½ cups (12 fl oz) milk; ½ cup (4 fl oz) cream; salt and white pepper; 1 lb (500 g) chopped cooked chicken; 4 oz (125 g) lean ham, chopped; 4 scallions, finely chopped; 1 teaspoon green peppercorns, drained; Spanish paprika

Roll the pastry to approximately ¼-in (5-mm) thickness and cut into three rectangles, each about 10 × 4 in (25 × 10 cm). Sprinkle baking sheets lightly with water, arrange the pieces of pastry on them and chill for a few minutes. Bake in an oven preheated to 500°F (260°C) until well risen and golden. Leave to cool on wire racks before filling.

Melt the butter in a heavy-based sauce-

Chicken Mille-Feuille

pan, stir in the flour and cook gently for 1–2 minutes without browning. Add the milk gradually, whisking well between additions, until the sauce is thick and smooth. Simmer for 2–3 minutes. Remove from the heat and cover the surface closely with plastic wrap, to prevent a skin forming. Leave to cool before adding the cream. Season with salt and pepper to taste, remove 3 tablespoons of the cream sauce, and reserve.

Mix the chicken with the ham, scallions and green peppercorns and fold into the sauce. Spread half of the chicken mixture over one sheet of pastry. Put another pastry layer on top and spread with the remaining chicken mixture. Cover with the last sheet of pastry, drizzle the reserved sauce over and sprinkle with paprika.

Chicken Pie in Filo Pastry

Serves 8: 7 tablespoons (3½ oz) butter; 3 onions, chopped; 3 stalks celery, chopped; 1 garlic clove, crushed; 2 lb (1 kg) coarsely chopped raw chicken meat; ½ cup (2 oz) all purpose flour; 2 cups (16 fl oz) hot chicken stock; 6 eggs, whisked; 4 sprigs parsley, chopped; 4 sprigs dill, chopped; juice of 2 lemons; ⅛ teaspoon nutmeg; salt and freshly ground black pepper; ½ cup (4 fl oz) melted butter; 12 sheets filo pastry

Heat the butter in a large skillet and sauté the onions, celery and garlic for 5 minutes. Add the chicken meat and flour and fry for a further 5 minutes, stirring constantly. Reduce the heat and add the hot chicken

Chicken Marengo

stock, then simmer for 3 minutes. Take off the heat and while stirring constantly, add the whisked eggs. Stir in the parsley, dill, lemon juice, nutmeg, salt and pepper. With a little of the melted butter, grease a large baking dish.

On the bottom and up the sides of the dish, place 6 sheets of filo pastry, brushing each sheet generously with melted butter before the next is placed. Spoon the chicken mixture into this and fold the edges of the filo over the mixture. Cover the mixture with the remaining 6 sheets of filo pastry, brushing each sheet in turn with the melted butter. Brush the top with the remaining butter. Tuck the edges of the covering filo sheets around the inside edges of the baking dish. Bake in an oven preheated to 400°F (200°C) for 30 minutes or until golden. Serve hot.

Chicken Quiche

Serves 4–6: 8 oz (250 g) shortcrust pastry (see page 319); 1 tablespoon butter; 2 bacon slices, chopped, with rind removed; 6 scallions, chopped; 4 oz (125 g) button mushrooms, thinly sliced; 8 oz (250 g) chopped cooked chicken; 2 eggs; ¾ cup (6 fl oz) cream; salt and white pepper; 1 tablespoon finely snipped chives

Roll the pastry out thinly and use to line individual flan rings. Prick the bases lightly with a fork and line with aluminum foil. Bake blind in an oven preheated to 425°F (220°C) for 15 minutes, then reduce the temperature to 350°F (180°C).

Chicken Quiche

Chicken Rolls with Salad

Melt the butter and fry the bacon until the fat starts to run. Add the scallions and mushrooms, and cook until just softened. Cool slightly before mixing with the chicken. Beat the eggs with the cream and season with salt and pepper to taste. Divide the chicken mixture between the flan cases and pour some of the cream mixture over each. Bake for 15–20 minutes or until set and golden. Sprinkle with the chives and serve hot or chilled.

Chicken Rolls with Salad

Serves 4: Chicken Rolls: 1 oz (30 g) transparent vermicelli (optional); ½ lb (250 g) chicken meat; 4 scallions, chopped; 2 garlic cloves, crushed; ¾-in (2-cm) piece fresh ginger, grated; 4 dried black mushrooms, soaked in cold water for ½ hour; 2 egg whites; 2 teaspoons cornstarch; 2 teaspoons fish sauce; ¼ teaspoon white pepper; 24 sheets transparent rice paper or spring roll wrappers; oil for deep frying
Salad: 1 medium-size lettuce; 24 sheets transparent rice paper, dampened slightly (each about 8 in or 20 cm square), or use extra lettuce; 1 small cucumber; 1 small eggplant (optional); 3½ oz (100 g) beansprouts; 3½ oz (100 g) pickled vegetables (radish and carrot in vinegar and salt); small bunch mint leaves; small bunch sweet basil;
small bunch daun kesom; 3½ oz (100 g) rice vermicelli, cooked
Sauce: 2 scallions, finely chopped; 2 garlic cloves, crushed; 1 fresh red chili, minced; 1 tablespoon lemon or lime juice; ¼ cup fish sauce; sugar to taste; pinch of white pepper

Soak the vermicelli until soft, then drain. Boil the chicken meat until tender. Cool, then grind finely with the scallions, drained vermicelli, garlic, ginger and drained mushrooms. Knead to a smooth paste and bind with the egg white and cornstarch. Season with fish sauce and white pepper.

Divide the mixture between 24 rice sheets or spring roll wrappers and roll up tightly into small rolls, about 2 in (5 cm) long. Stick the ends down with a little water, or make a paste by mixing cornstarch with boiling water and use to glue the ends. Heat the oil and deep fry the chicken rolls until crisp and a golden brown. Lift out and drain.

To prepare the salad, wash the lettuce leaves and dry carefully; arrange on a plate with the rice paper sheets. Peel the cucumber and slice thinly. Wipe the eggplant and cut into very thin strips. Pour boiling water over the beansprouts to soften, splash with cold water and drain well. Shred the pickled vegetables. Wash the mint, sweet basil and *daun kesom*. Cut the rice vermicelli into 2-in (5-cm) pieces. Arrange all the vegetables, herbs and vermicelli on a serving plate.

Mix the sauce ingredients in a small saucepan, heat through, then allow to cool. Pour into a small bowl.

To prepare the salad rolls, line each sheet of rice paper with a lettuce leaf (or use two lettuce leaves instead of rice paper). Put a fried chicken roll on top and add a little of each of the vegetables, herbs, pickles and vermicelli. Roll up and dip into the sauce.

Chicken Russus

Serves 4: 3 large tomatoes, peeled, seeded and chopped; 3 tablespoons tomato paste; 2 bay leaves; 3 cloves; 1 small onion, halved; 1 cup (8 fl oz) water; salt and freshly ground black pepper; 2 slices of bread, with crusts removed; 1 lb (500 g) finely ground chicken; 1 large onion, finely minced or ground; ½ teaspoon turmeric; ½ teaspoon dried chervil or tarragon; 1 egg, lightly beaten

Put the tomatoes and paste into a small saucepan with the bay leaves, cloves and halved onion. Add the water and bring to the boil. Reduce the heat, season with salt and pepper to taste and simmer very gently, uncovered.

While the sauce is cooking, soak the bread in a little water. Mix the chicken with the onion, turmeric and chervil or tarra-gon. Season with about ½ teaspoon of salt and plenty of black pepper. Squeeze the water out of the bread. Mix the bread thoroughly with the chicken mixture, then add enough egg to bind the ingredients firmly together. Form the mixture into 1-in (2.5-cm) balls.

Discard the onion, bay leaves and cloves from the sauce and transfer it to a shallow pan, adding a little more water if the sauce is very thick — it should just coat the back of a spoon. Put the chicken balls into the sauce, cover and simmer for 20 minutes.

Chicken Sarma

Serves 4: 8 large cabbage leaves, or 16–20 grape leaves; 3 tablespoons (1½ oz) butter; 1 large onion, finely chopped; 1 garlic clove, crushed; 12 oz (375 g) raw chicken, ground; 1 cup rice; 3 oz (90 g) seedless raisins; salt and pepper; 2 tablespoons finely chopped parsley; 1 egg, lightly beaten; ¾ cup (6 oz) chicken stock; 1 tablespoon tomato paste; ½ teaspoon dried oregano; 2 tablespoons (1 oz) butter; 1 oz (30 g) fresh breadcrumbs

Use a sharp knife to pare down any thick stalk on the cabbage. Blanch the leaves in boiling salted water for 5 minutes. Drain, then spread cabbage leaves or grape leaves on a board.

Melt the 3 tablespoons (1½ oz) of butter and gently fry the onion until transparent. Add the garlic and chicken and cook until the chicken has browned lightly, stirring to break up any lumps. Mix in the rice and raisins, seasoning with salt and pepper to taste. Set aside to cool before adding the parsley and egg.

Divide the cooled filling between the leaves, folding and rolling each one into a parcel. Arrange the rolls in a flameproof serving dish or casserole. Mix the chicken stock with the tomato paste and oregano, bring quickly to the boil and season to taste. Pour over the rolls, cover and simmer for 15 minutes.

In the meantime, melt the butter, add the breadcrumbs and turn in the butter until they are crisp and golden. Sprinkle over the rolls and serve immediately.

Chicken Smothered with Oysters

Serves 4–6: 3–4 lb (1.5–2 kg) chicken pieces; salt and white pepper; 3–4 tablespoons vegetable oil; ¾ cup (6 fl oz) milk; 24 fresh or bottled (not canned) oysters, drained; ¾ cup (6 fl oz) cream

Season the chicken pieces with salt and pepper. Heat the oil in a skillet and quickly brown the chicken, transferring the pieces to a baking dish as they brown. Pour the milk over the chicken, cover and bake in an oven preheated to 400°F (200°C) for 40 minutes.

Mix the oysters with the cream and pour over the chicken. Cover and cook for 15–20 minutes longer, or until the chicken is tender. Transfer the chicken to a heated serving dish. Adjust the seasoning of the sauce and pour over the chicken. Serve immediately.

Chicken Stew with Peas, Mushrooms and Olives

Serves 4: 3-lb (1.5-kg) chicken, cut into pieces; salt and freshly ground black pepper; ½ cup (2 oz) all purpose flour; ¼ cup (2 fl oz) olive oil; 2 onions, chopped; 5 tomatoes, peeled and chopped; 1 teaspoon sugar (optional); 1 red or green bell pepper, seeded and chopped; water; 1 cup (6 oz) green peas; 4 oz (125 g) small button mushrooms; 1 cup chopped and pitted green or black olives; flour and water for thickening

Sprinkle the chicken with the salt, ground pepper and half the flour. Heat the oil in a casserole and brown the chicken pieces, then remove and set aside.

In the same oil, sauté the onions, add the tomatoes, sugar, salt and the chopped pepper, then simmer over low heat for 10 minutes. Add the chicken pieces and enough water to cover. Cover the casserole and simmer for 1 hour. Add the peas, mushrooms, olives and enough flour mixed with a little water to thicken the sauce. Simmer for 15 minutes, check the seasoning and serve hot.

Chicken Russus

Chicken Suprêmes Madeira

*Serves 4–8: 3 tablespoons (1½ oz) butter; 4–8
chicken fillets; salt and white pepper; ½ cup (4 fl oz)
strained orange juice; 3 tablespoons chicken stock;
3 tablespoons dry Madeira; finely grated peel of
2 oranges; 2 oz (60 g) pâté; extra Madeira;
½ teaspoon arrowroot; pimiento-stuffed olives,
sliced (optional)*

Melt the butter over low heat and fry the
chicken fillets for 3–4 minutes on each side.
They should be very lightly colored, not
brown. Season with salt and pepper to taste
and pour the orange juice, stock, Madeira
and half of the orange peel over. Cover and
simmer very gently for 20 minutes, or until
the fillets are tender. Turn the chicken once
during this time.

Beat the pâté until creamy, adding 1–2
teaspoons of Madeira if necessary to soften
it. Set aside. Transfer the cooked chicken
to a heated serving dish and top each fillet
with some of the creamed pâté. Sprinkle
lightly with the remaining orange peel and
keep hot.

Mix the arrowroot to a smooth paste
with 1 teaspoon of water and stir into the
pan juices. Simmer for 2 minutes, adjust
the seasoning and spoon a little over each
fillet, serving the rest separately. Garnish
the chicken with the sliced olives.

Chicken Vol-au-Vent

*Serves 6–8: 2 pieces frozen puff pastry, thawed;
1 egg; pinch of salt
Filling: 5 tablespoons (2½ oz) butter; 5 tablespoons
all purpose flour; ¼ cup (2 fl oz) dry white wine;
2½ cups (20 fl oz) chicken stock or water and
chicken bouillon cubes; salt and pepper; 2 drops
lemon juice; 1 lb (500 g) cooked chicken, diced; 4 oz
(125 g) button mushrooms; 1 egg yolk;
2 tablespoons cream; parsley sprigs for garnish*

Roll out the pastry to a 17 × 9-in (42.5 ×
23-cm) rectangle. Cut out an 8-in (20-cm)
circle of pastry and place on a greased baking sheet. Cut out a second 8-in (20-cm)
circle. Cut out a 5-in (12.5-cm) circle of
pastry from it and roll out and cut a 6-in
(15-cm) circle from it. Place on baking
sheet and mark in lattice fashion with a
knife.

Beat the egg and salt together. Brush a
thin layer of egg on the first circle of
pastry, taking care not to allow it to run

Chicken Suprêmes Madeira

down the edge of the pastry as this will
affect the rising. Take the second circle of
pastry with center removed and place carefully on top of the first. Brush egg over the
top of the double layer and the latticed
circle. Prick the center of the case with a
fork several times. Rest for 1 hour in a cool
place before baking.

Roll out the pastry scraps and cut out 18
leaves and 12 crescent shapes using a fluted
pastry cutter. Decorate the top edge of the
vol-au-vent with 12 leaves and the lattice-
marked pastry with 6 leaves. Brush with
egg. Place the crescent shapes on the baking sheet and brush with egg.

Bake in an oven preheated to 450°F
(230°C) for 10 minutes, remove the crescents quickly and continue the baking for
10 more minutes. Remove the lattice top.
Cover the vol-au-vent with waxed paper,
reduce the oven temperature to 350°F
(180°C) and bake for 5 minutes more.
Remove and place on a wire cooling rack.

To make the filling, melt the butter in a
small saucepan, add the flour and cook,
stirring, for 2–3 minutes. Add the white
wine and mix well, then add the hot
chicken stock a little at a time, stirring constantly to make a smooth sauce. Cook
gently for 10 minutes. Season with salt and
pepper. Stir in the lemon juice, chicken and
mushrooms. Reheat, then remove from
heat. Mix the egg yolk and cream together
and stir it into the sauce. Fill the hot vol-
au-vent case with the chicken mixture.
Arrange the crescents around the base.
Place the latticed top on the case and garnish with parsley.

Chicken with Crisp Hot Peppers and Orange Peel

*Serves 2: 12 oz (375 g) boneless chicken; 2 dried chili
peppers; 3 pieces dried orange peel; 3 cups (24 fl oz)
oil for deep frying; 1 slice fresh ginger; 2 scallions,
trimmed and sliced
Seasoning A: ¼ teaspoon salt; ½ teaspoon rice
wine or dry sherry; 2 teaspoons cornstarch
Seasoning B: ¼ teaspoon salt; 1½ teaspoons sugar;
1 tablespoon light soy sauce; ½ teaspoon white
vinegar; ½ teaspoon sesame oil; 1 tablespoon water;
½ teaspoon cornstarch*

Cut the chicken into small cubes and mix
with the seasoning A ingredients. Marinate
for 15 minutes. Cut the chilies into 3–4
pieces and the orange peel into 2–3 pieces.

Heat the oil to moderately hot and fry
the chilies and orange peel until both are
dark brown. Remove and set aside. Add
the chicken and fry until white and firm,
about 1½ minutes. Remove. Pour off all
but 2½ tablespoons of the oil and add the
ginger and scallions. Stir-fry briefly, then
return the chilies, orange peel and chicken,
and stir-fry together for 1 minute. Add the
premixed seasoning B ingredients and simmer until the chicken is well glazed with the
sauce, then serve.

Chicken with Egg-Lemon Sauce

*Serves 4: 8 chicken pieces; juice of 2 lemons;
1 teaspoon dried oregano; salt and freshly ground
black pepper; 4 tablespoons (2 oz) butter; 1 cup
(8 fl oz) dry white wine; 1 cup (8 fl oz) chicken stock;
3 eggs, separated; 1 tablespoon cornstarch
(optional, if thicker sauce is required); 2 sprigs dill,
chopped, for garnish*

Sprinkle the chicken pieces with the lemon
juice, oregano, salt and pepper and marinate for 2 hours.

In a casserole, heat the butter and fry the
chicken pieces until light brown but not
cooked. Add the wine and chicken stock.
Cover the pan, bring to the boil and braise
in an oven preheated to 350°F (180°C) for
1 hour.

Beat the egg whites with some salt until
stiff. Add the egg yolks and beat together.

Take the chicken pieces out of the casserole and arrange them on a serving platter.

Chicken with Tarragon

Take out 1 cup (8 fl oz) of the cooking juice and mix it with the cornstarch, if using. Pour it back into the casserole and heat, stirring, until it thickens. While whisking constantly, add a cup of the thickened cooking juice to the egg mixture. Then, while continuing to whisk vigorously, pour the egg mixture into the casserole. Heat until it thickens but do not boil. Taste and, if necessary, add more lemon juice, salt or pepper. To serve, pour the sauce over the chicken pieces and serve sprinkled with the dill. Serve with rice.

Chicken with Mushrooms and Cream

Serves 4: 8 tablespoons (4 oz) butter; 1 large chicken, disjointed; 12 small white onions, peeled; 8 oz (250 g) button mushrooms; 2 cups (16 fl oz) dry white wine; 1 cup (8 fl oz) chicken stock; 2 cups (16 fl oz) cream; salt and freshly ground black pepper; finely chopped parsley for garnish

Heat the butter in a heavy-based casserole and add the chicken pieces and the onions. Cook over medium heat for 5 minutes without letting the chicken pieces take on any color. Add the whole mushrooms, wine and stock, and simmer gently for 25 minutes or until the chicken is cooked. Transfer the chicken, onions and mushrooms to a serving dish and keep them warm. Pour the cream into the casserole dish and boil briskly for a few minutes. Adjust the seasoning and pour over the chicken. Serve garnished with a little chopped parsley.

Chicken with Peppers

Serves 4: 5 large green and red bell peppers; 1 large onion, sliced; 2 tablespoons (1 oz) butter; 3 tablespoons olive oil; 3-lb (1.5-kg) chicken, cut into pieces; salt and freshly ground black pepper; ½ cup (4 fl oz) dry white wine; 1½ lb (750 g) tomatoes, skinned and chopped; 1 cup (8 fl oz) chicken stock; 3 tablespoons chopped fresh basil

Blanch the peppers in boiling water for 1 minute. Drain, peel and seed, then cut into 1-in (2.5-cm) strips.

Sauté the onion in the butter and oil until light brown, add the chicken and brown it on all sides. Season with salt and pepper. Add the wine and cook until it has almost evaporated, then add the tomatoes and stock. Cover the pan and simmer over low heat, stirring occasionally, for 45 minutes or until the chicken is tender.

Transfer the chicken to a preheated serving plate, then reduce the pan juices by fast boiling. Pour them over the chicken and serve sprinkled with the basil.

Chicken with Tarragon

Serves 4: 8 tablespoons (4 oz) butter, softened; 1 teaspoon salt; freshly ground black pepper; 4 tablespoons chopped fresh tarragon or 1 tablespoon dried tarragon leaves; 3-4-lb (1.5-2-kg) chicken; tarragon sprigs for garnish

Cream the butter with the salt, grinds of black pepper and the tarragon. Carefully lift the skin of the chicken at the neck end and with your hand, loosen the skin over the breast. Spread half of the butter mixture over the breasts, under the skin. Put the remaining butter in the neck cavity, fold the skin over and secure with small poultry pins or coarse thread. Tie the legs loosely together and fold the wings under the body of the bird.

Put the chicken, breast side down, on a rack in a roasting dish and bake in an oven preheated to 400°F (200°C) for 30 minutes. Carefully turn the bird onto its back, using two spoons to avoid breaking the skin. Cook for 30–40 minutes longer, basting occasionally with the pan juices. Transfer the chicken to a heated serving dish, pour the pan juices over and garnish.

Crispy Home-Style Duck

Serves 6: 4-lb (2-kg) duck; 2 tablespoons Chinese brown peppercorns; 2 tablespoons salt; 2 tablespoons finely chopped scallion; 1 tablespoon finely chopped fresh ginger; 1 tablespoon rice wine or dry sherry; 1 tablespoon dark soy sauce; all purpose flour; 8 cups (2 liters) oil for deep frying; 12 mandarin pancakes (see page 230)

Clean and dress the duck. Fry the peppercorns in a dry wok for 2 minutes over moderate heat, then pour into a mortar and grind to a fine powder. Return the peppercorns to the wok and add the salt. Dry-fry together on moderate to low heat, stirring constantly to avoid burning, for 2 minutes.

Mix the spiced salt with the scallion, ginger and wine and rub over the duck thoroughly. Pour the remainder inside and leave for 2 hours.

Place the duck breast side up in a large dish and set on a rack in a steamer. Steam over high heat until the duck is completely tender, about 3 hours. Remove and leave to cool, then brush with the soy sauce and coat lightly with flour.

Heat the oil to smoking point, then reduce the heat slightly. Deep fry the duck, completely immersed in the oil if possible, for 3 minutes. Lift out and reheat the oil, then deep fry a further 3 minutes until the duck is very crisp and deeply colored on the surface.

Serve with the pancakes and with additional spiced salt.

Cumin Chicken

Serves 4-6: 3-4 lb (1.5-2 kg) chicken pieces; juice of 1 large lemon; ¼ cup (1 oz) all purpose flour; 1 teaspoon salt; 1 teaspoon cayenne or red pepper; ¼ cup (2 fl oz) ghee or butter; 1 large onion, finely chopped; 2 garlic cloves, crushed; 1-in (2.5-cm) piece of fresh ginger, peeled and finely grated; 2 teaspoons cumin seed; 1 cup (8 fl oz) cream; 1 cup (8 fl oz) natural yogurt; 2 strips of lemon peel, pared very finely

Brush the chicken pieces liberally with the lemon juice and set aside for 15 minutes. Mix the flour with the salt and cayenne or red pepper. Drain excess lemon juice from the chicken and dry with paper towels before lightly dusting with seasoned flour.

Melt the *ghee* or butter in a heavy-based skillet over moderate heat and lightly brown the chicken pieces on all sides. Remove them from the pan and set aside. Add the onion, garlic, ginger and cumin seed to the pan and cook fairly quickly until the onion is straw-colored but not browned. Add the cream, yogurt and lemon peel, stirring in well. Return the chicken to the pan, turning the pieces in the sauce until they are coated. Cover and simmer gently for 45–50 minutes, or until the chicken is tender and the juices run clear when pierced with a skewer.

Lift the chicken from the sauce, arrange on a heated serving platter with rice and keep hot. Increase the heat and reduce the sauce by boiling rapidly for a few minutes. Adjust the seasoning, discard the lemon peel and pour the sauce over the chicken.

Cumin Chicken (see page 207)

Deep Fried Marinated Chicken

D

Deep Fried Bean Curd, Shrimp and Chicken Fritters

Serves 4: 4 squares soft bean curd (or 16 pieces canned bean curd, drained); 2½ oz (75 g) shrimp meat, ground; 2 oz (60 g) boneless chicken, ground; 2 oz (60 g) pork fat, ground; 2 oz (60 g) pine nuts or toasted peanuts; cornstarch; 4 cups (1 liter) oil for deep frying
Seasoning: 2 egg whites, beaten; 1 teaspoon salt; 1 tablespoon minced onion and ginger; 1½ tablespoons cornstarch

Mash the bean curd with a fork and mix with the shrimp, chicken and pork fat. Add the seasoning ingredients and mix thoroughly. Blanch the pine nuts, if used, in boiling water for 1 minute. Drain, then dry and deep fry until golden. Drain and chop finely. Stir half into the bean curd mixture.

Press the mixture into an oiled square baking pan and decorate with the remaining chopped nuts, pressing on lightly. Set the pan on a rack in a steamer and steam over rapidly boiling water for 15–20 minutes or until firm.

Remove the pan from the steamer and invert onto a board. Cut the bean curd into pieces about 1½ × ¾ in (4 × 2 cm) and coat lightly with cornstarch.

Heat the oil to moderately hot and deep fry the fritters until golden brown. Drain and season generously with salt and pepper. Serve hot.

Deep Fried Chicken Livers with Spicy Dressing

Serves 2–4: 12 oz (375 g) fresh chicken livers; 6 cups (1½ liters) oil for deep frying; 1 tablespoon sesame oil; 3 tablespoons finely chopped scallion; 2 teaspoons finely chopped fresh ginger; 1½–2 teaspoons Chinese pepper-salt
Seasoning: 1½ teaspoons rice wine or dry sherry; ¼ teaspoon white pepper; 2 teaspoons sugar; 2 teaspoons grated fresh ginger
Batter: 2 eggs, well beaten; 3 tablespoons cornstarch; 3 tablespoons flour

Wash the livers and cut into bite-size

pieces. Mix with the seasoning ingredients and leave to marinate for 20 minutes. Make a thick batter with the eggs, cornstarch and flour, adding a little water. Beat well.

Heat the oil to smoking. Drain the chicken and dip into the batter, coating it thickly. Deep fry until well browned. Drain well.

Pour off the oil and wipe out the pan. Add the sesame oil and heat through, then return the chicken livers and add the scallion, ginger and pepper-salt. Stir on moderate heat until the chicken livers are cooked through, about 3 minutes. Serve.

Deep Fried Marinated Chicken

Serves 4: 1½ lb (750 g) fresh chicken pieces (thighs and breast); 3 tablespoons light soy sauce; 1½ tablespoons sweet rice wine (mirin); *1 teaspoon ginger juice (see Note); 6 tablespoons cornstarch; oil for deep frying; mustard*

Cut the chicken, leaving on the skin and bones, into bite-size chunks. Combine the soy sauce, *mirin* and ginger juice, and marinate the chicken for at least 30 minutes. Drain the chicken well, then pat dry with a paper towel or a kitchen cloth.

Put the cornstarch into a large plastic bag and add half the chicken pieces. Shake for a couple of moments, then remove the chicken pieces. Repeat with the remaining chicken, then shake the chicken pieces in a sieve to remove any excess cornstarch.

Heat plenty of oil in a deep pan until hot, then fry the chicken pieces, a few at a time, until crisp and golden brown. This should take 3–4 minutes. Remove from the oil, drain and serve on individual dishes with a little mustard.

Note: To make ginger juice, grate fresh ginger finely, then press through a garlic press.

Diced Chicken with Dried Chilies

Diced Chicken with Dried Chilies

Serves 4: 1 lb (500 g) raw chicken breast; 4 points star anise; 10 black peppercorns; 12 large dried red chilies; 1 teaspoon sugar; 1 teaspoon light soy sauce; ½ teaspoon white vinegar; ½ teaspoon Chinese rice wine or dry sherry; 2 teaspoons cornstarch; ¼ cup water; 6 tablespoons oil; 1 garlic clove, smashed; 1 slice fresh ginger, very finely chopped; 2 scallions, cut into 1-in (2.5-cm) lengths; few drops sesame oil

Cut the chicken into ½-in (1-cm) cubes. Pound or grind the star anise and pepper until fine. Remove stalks from the chilies, break into 1½-in (4-cm) lengths and shake to discard most of the seeds so that the chicken will not be too hot. Blend together the sugar, soy sauce, vinegar, wine, cornstarch and water. Set aside.

Heat the oil in a skillet until very hot, then fry the chicken for 2 minutes, stirring frequently. Remove the chicken from the pan and pour off half the oil. Fry the chilies over high heat, stirring constantly, until dark brown and crisp. Remove from the pan. Allow the oil to cool a little, then gently fry the ground spices, garlic and ginger for 1 minute. Add the blended mixture and scallions and cook for 30 seconds. Put the chicken and chilies back in the skillet and stir over medium heat for about 1 minute or until the chicken is thoroughly coated with sauce. Sprinkle with sesame oil and serve immediately.

Drunken Chicken

Serves 4: 1 small chicken, halved; 1 teaspoon salt; 2½ teaspoons sugar; 1¼ cups (10 fl oz) rice wine (see Note); 2 tablespoons oil; cilantro

Wash the chicken and place in a saucepan. Cover with boiling water and bring to the boil. Reduce the heat and simmer, tightly covered, for about 20 minutes.

Drain the chicken and place in a dish. Mix the remaining ingredients except the cilantro and pour over the chicken. Cover with plastic wrap and leave overnight to marinate. Garnish with fresh cilantro and serve cold.

Note: The yellow *Shao Hsing* wine is usually used. The dish has a strong flavor of wine and therefore a good quality wine should be used. Japanese *mirin*, not unlike a sweet sherry, is ideal. If using this, use less sugar.

Duck in Almond Sauce

Serves 4: 3 oz (90 g) lard; 1 duck liver or 2 chicken livers, chopped; 1 onion, sliced; 2 garlic cloves, crushed; 3-lb (1.5-kg) duck, cut into 8 pieces; ¼ cup (1 oz) all purpose flour; salt and freshly ground black pepper; 4 tomatoes, peeled and chopped; 20 blanched almonds, roasted; ½ cup (4 fl oz) dry sherry; 2 sprigs parsley, finely chopped

Heat the lard in a large skillet and lightly fry the liver. Remove and set aside. Sauté the onion and garlic. Remove and set aside with the liver. Remove most of the fat from the pan, sprinkle the duck pieces with flour, salt and pepper and fry them in the remaining fat until brown. Add the tomatoes, cover the pan and simmer over low heat.

In a food processor, blend the liver, onion and garlic with the almonds into a smooth paste. Mix in the sherry. Add the mixture to the duck, then add the parsley and adjust the seasoning. Cover and simmer over low heat for 1–1¼ hours or until the duck is tender. To serve, arrange the duck pieces on a platter and strain the sauce over.

Duck Melissa

Serves 4: 3–4-lb (1.5–2-kg) duck; 3 oz (90 g) coconut cream; 1 tablespoon water; 2 small garlic cloves, crushed; ½ teaspoon salt; ¼ teaspoon ground mace; ½ teaspoon cinnamon; 1 teaspoon turmeric; ¼ teaspoon ground cardamom; ¼ teaspoon ground cloves; 1¼ teaspoons ground fenugreek; 1½ teaspoons ground cumin; 1 tablespoon ground coriander; freshly ground black pepper; 1-in (2.5-cm) piece of fresh ginger, peeled and finely grated; 1 large onion, finely minced; juice of 1 lemon; 2 teaspoons mild chili sauce

Cut through the breastbone and open the duck. You will have to break the ribs here and there to press the duck flat. Thread a wooden skewer through the second wing joint on one side and out through the same joint on the other side. Push another skewer through the legs in the same way, to keep the bird flat. Prick the skin all over with a skewer.

Melt the coconut cream with the water in a small pan over low heat. Cool slightly and stir in the garlic, all the dry spices and then the ginger, onion, lemon juice, and chili sauce. Spread this paste over both sides of the duck and roast skin side down on a rack in a roasting dish. Cook in an oven preheated to 400°F (200°C) for 1¼–1½ hours, basting every 15 minutes or so with the pan juices. Turn the bird halfway through the cooking time.

When the duck is cooked, remove as many of the small bones as you can before transferring it to a hot serving dish. Skim as much fat from the surface of the sauce as possible. Either pour the sauce over the bird or serve it separately.

Note: This is a very good sauce for barbecued duck. Prepare the duck for roasting flat, mix the sauce ingredients, add ¾ cup (6 fl oz) of chicken stock and 3 tablespoons of redcurrant jelly and simmer for 2–3 minutes. Use to baste the bird frequently over the coals.

Duck Smoked with Camphor Wood and Tea Leaves

Serves 4: 3-lb (1.5-kg) duck; 2 tablespoons Chinese black tea leaves; 1 cup camphor wood chips (see Note); 2 cups (16 fl oz) water

Wash the duck and wipe dry. Line a wok with a double thickness of aluminum foil and put in the tea leaves, wood chips and the water. Bring to the boil.

Set a metal rack in the wok and place the duck on top. Cover and steam until the water has evaporated, then continue to cook for about 1¼ hours, turning the duck from time to time. After the water evaporates, the wood chips and tea leaves will dry out and begin to smoke, so the duck is cooked in a combination of steam and smoke — making it moist and aromatic and drawing out much of the excess fat.

Note: If unobtainable, hickory wood chips can be used.

Line a wok with foil; then add the wood chips, tea leaves and water.

Place a metal rack inside the wok and put the duck on top.

Duck with Honey

Serves 8: two 4-lb (2-kg) ducks, marinated in game marinade (see page 253) for 48 hrs; 2 teaspoons salt; 1 tablespoon chopped fresh basil or 1 teaspoon dried basil; freshly ground black pepper; 8 tablespoons (4 oz) butter; juice and finely grated peel of 1 large orange; juice of ½ lemon; 2 teaspoons Dijon mustard; ½ teaspoon salt; 1 lb 7 oz (720 g) honey; 2 large oranges, quartered; 2 teaspoons cornstarch; 2 tablespoons water; 4 tablespoons brandy (optional)

Remove the ducks from the marinade and pat dry with paper towels. Mix the salt with the basil and about ½ teaspoon of black pepper in a paper bag. Melt the butter and, off the heat, add the orange juice and peel, the lemon juice, mustard, salt and honey. Put 2 tablespoons of this honey mixture and a quartered orange into each duck cavity. Secure the opening with small poultry pins and lay the ducks side by side in a large roasting dish. Pour the remaining honey mixture over the birds and sprinkle with the herb mixture. Cover the dish completely with aluminum foil and roast the ducks in an oven preheated to 350°F (180°C) for 1¼–1½ hours. Remove the foil and roast the birds for 20–30 minutes longer, basting them frequently with the pan juices.

Transfer the cooked ducks to a heated serving dish and keep hot. Mix the cornstarch to a smooth paste with the water and stir into the pan juices. Bring to the boil on top of the stove and adjust the seasoning. Pour a little of the sauce around each bird and serve the rest separately. Warm the brandy, ignite and pour over the birds just before serving.

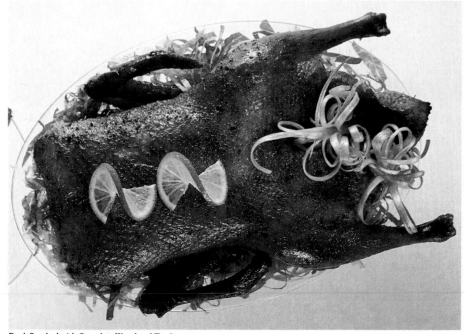

Duck Smoked with Camphor Wood and Tea Leaves

Duck Melissa

Duck with Sour Cherries ★

Serves 4–6: 6-lb (3-kg) duck; ½ teaspoon celery salt; salt and freshly ground pepper; ½ cup (4 fl oz) water; 8 tablespoons (4 oz) butter; 1½ cups (12 fl oz) chicken stock or water and chicken bouillon cube; ½ cup (4 fl oz) port; ½ cup (4 fl oz) cherry brandy; 2 tablespoons beurre manié; 1¾ lb (875 g) preserved sour cherries

Wipe the duck inside and out with a damp cloth. Sprinkle the cavity with celery salt, salt and freshly ground pepper to taste. Place the duck in a roasting pan breast side up and add the water to prevent scorching. Cover the breast and legs with a piece of cheesecloth rubbed with butter.

Roast the duck in an oven preheated to 400°–450°F (200°–230°C) for 30 minutes. Reduce the heat to 350°–375°F (180°–190°C) and continue cooking the duck until tender, about 1¼–1¾ hours. Transfer the duck to a heated platter.

Pour off all fat from the roasting pan, leaving only brown sediment, then deglaze the pan with chicken stock. Add the port and cherry brandy and blend in the beurre manié (see Note).

Put the roasting pan over a high heat and bring the sauce to the boil. Cook the sauce, stirring continuously, until it has slightly thickened. Drain the sour cherries, add to the sauce and heat through.

Carve the duck and pour half the sauce over it. Serve the remaining sauce separately in a sauceboat.

Note: To make the beurre manié beat together 2 tablespoons (1 oz) butter and 1 tablespoon of flour until smooth.

Duck with Wine and Anchovies 🇫🇷

Serves 4: duck giblets (not the liver); 2 cups (16 fl oz) water; 3 salt-packed anchovies, soaked in 2 tablespoons milk, or 6 canned anchovy fillets, drained; 1 tablespoon butter; 1 tablespoon olive oil or vegetable oil; 12 small pickling onions, peeled; 4-lb (2-kg) duck, quartered; 2 large garlic cloves, crushed; ½ teaspoon dried chervil; 1¼ cups (10 fl oz) dry white wine; 1 tablespoon tomato paste; freshly ground black pepper; juice of ½ lemon; 1 tablespoon butter; 1 tablespoon all purpose flour; 3 large tomatoes, peeled, seeded and coarsely chopped; 1 tablespoon finely chopped fresh cilantro or parsley

Duck with Honey (see page 210)

Bring the duck giblets to the boil in the water. Reduce the heat and simmer until the liquid has reduced to 1¼ cups (10 fl oz). Strain and reserve the stock.

If using salt-packed anchovies, soak them in milk for 10 minutes, rinse, remove the bones and chop finely. Melt the 1 tablespoon of butter with the oil in a heavy-based pan and quickly shake the whole onions in the hot fat until lightly browned on all sides. Remove and set aside. Add the duck quarters and sauté on all sides until brown. Drain all but 1 tablespoon of fat from the pan. Return the onions to the pan with the garlic, chopped anchovies, chervil,

reserved giblet stock, wine and tomato paste. Bring to the boil, season with black pepper to taste, more salt if necessary and the lemon juice. Reduce the heat, cover and simmer for 40–50 minutes, or until the duck is very tender.

Transfer the duck to a heated serving dish and keep hot. Mix the 1 tablespoon of butter with the flour and whisk small pieces into the sauce until it has thickened to your liking. Add the tomatoes and simmer for 5–6 minutes. Pour the sauce around the duck and serve sprinkled with the cilantro or parsley.

Duckling Stuffed with Apples and Raisins

Serves 4: ¾ cup (4 oz) seedless raisins; 1 cup (8 fl oz) white wine; 1 lb (500 g) apples, peeled, cored and chopped into small dice; 1 lb (500 g) white bread, cut into cubes; 1 cup (8 fl oz) brandy; pinch of cinnamon; salt and freshly ground black pepper; 3-lb (1.5-kg) duckling

Soak the raisins in the wine for 30 minutes, then combine with the apples in a saucepan, add the bread and soak for 10 minutes. Pour the brandy into the saucepan and flame. Add the cinnamon and season with pepper and salt. If the mixture is too liquid, cook until some of the liquid evaporates.

Spoon the stuffing into the duck cavity and secure the opening with skewers. Place in a baking dish and roast in an oven preheated to 350°F (180°C) for 1½ hours. Serve with the cooking juices poured over.

E

East Indies Barbecued Chicken

Serves 4-6: 2½-lb (1¼-kg) chicken; oil; salt
East Indies Sauce: 1 onion, finely chopped; 1 stalk celery, finely chopped; 2 tablespoons oil; 2 cups (16 fl oz) chicken stock or water and chicken bouillon cube; ½ cup stewed tomatoes; ¼ apple, peeled and finely chopped; 1½ tablespoons curry powder; salt and pepper

Sauté the onion and celery in oil until soft and golden. Add the chicken stock, stewed tomatoes, apple, curry powder and salt and pepper to taste. Simmer for 30 minutes.

Cut the chicken into eight pieces, brush each piece with oil and sprinkle with salt. Allow the chicken pieces to stand for 30 minutes. Barbecue the chicken over glowing coals, basting frequently with the sauce and turning the pieces from time to time until tender. Serve the barbecued chicken with the sauce and boiled rice. Accompany with chopped fresh pineapple, fruit chutney and chopped cashew nuts.

Note: The chicken may also be broiled.

Duck with Wine and Anchovies

Egyptian Omelet

Egyptian Omelet

Serves 4: 1 medium-size eggplant, quartered and thinly sliced; salt; 2 tablespoons (1 oz) butter; 1 tablespoon olive oil; 1 medium-size onion, coarsely chopped; 1 large garlic clove, crushed; ½ teaspoon dried mixed herbs; 4-8 oz (125-250 g) shredded cooked poultry or game; 2½-5 oz (75-155 g) cooked pasta (optional); freshly ground black pepper; 6-8 eggs, lightly beaten

Put the sliced eggplant into a strainer, sprinkle lightly with salt and leave for 20 minutes, until the juice starts to drain. Shake off any excess moisture and pat dry before using.

Melt the butter and oil in a 9-in (23-cm) omelet pan. Sauté the onion and garlic for 2 minutes. Reduce the heat, add the eggplant and cook until just softened. Sprinkle with the herbs and stir in the poultry or game, pasta or any other vegetables. Season to taste and pour the eggs over the mixture. Cook until almost set, then either brown the top under a very hot broiler or turn the omelet onto a plate and slide the unfinished side back into the pan to brown. Cut into wedges and serve immediately or leave until cooled before cutting.

Enchiladas

Serves 4: Filling: 1 tablespoon olive or vegetable oil; 1 large onion, chopped; 2 garlic cloves, crushed; 1 red bell pepper, seeded and chopped; two 15-oz (425-g) cans peeled tomatoes, crushed; 2 tablespoons tomato paste; 1 teaspoon powdered oregano; ½ teaspoon cayenne or red pepper; 1 teaspoon Mexican chili powder; ½-1 lb (250-500 g) chopped cooked poultry or game; salt Batter: 1 cup (8 fl oz) milk; 1 egg; 1½ teaspoons Hungarian paprika; 1 teaspoon chili powder; 8 tortillas; 4 oz (125 g) grated mozzarella cheese

To prepare the filling, heat the oil in a large skillet and brown the onion quickly. Reduce the heat and sauté the garlic and pepper gently until the pepper is just softened. Stir in the tomatoes, their liquid and the tomato paste. Sprinkle with the oregano, cayenne or red pepper and Mexican chili powder. Simmer for 5-6 minutes. Add the poultry or game, stir well and season with salt to taste. Simmer gently until the sauce has thickened. Reserve.

Beat the milk and egg with the paprika and chili powder in a shallow dish and leave to chill. Dip each tortilla in the egg mixture before refrying until browned on both sides.

Spoon the filling onto the tortillas and roll them up. Arrange in a lightly oiled baking dish. Pour any remaining sauce around the tortillas and sprinkle them with the grated cheese. Bake in an oven preheated to 350°F (180°C) for 15-20 minutes, or until the cheese has melted and is lightly browned.

F

Fried Chicken with Sweet Basil and Chili

Serves 2: 10 oz (315 g) chicken breast; 2 oz (60 g) chicken liver and giblets (optional); 2 tablespoons vegetable oil; ¼ cup very small green birds-eye chilies or 6 green chilies, sliced; 1 small bunch fresh basil leaves; 2 tablespoons parsley, finely chopped; 2 tablespoons fish sauce

Chop the chicken breast, liver and giblets into very small dice. Heat the oil and fry the chicken on moderate heat for 3 minutes, then add the chilies, half the basil and the chopped parsley. Cook, stirring frequently, for 5 minutes, then stir in the fish sauce.

Spoon the chicken and herbs onto a serving dish and surround with the remaining basil leaves.

Fried Diced Chicken with Sweet Bean Paste

Serves 4: 1 lb (500 g) chicken pieces; 2 eggs, well beaten; cornstarch; 5 cups (1¼ liters) oil for deep frying; 2 tablespoons sweet bean paste (see Note); 1 large scallion, trimmed and thinly sliced

Cut the chicken through the bones into bite-size pieces. Dip into the beaten egg, then coat thickly with cornstarch.

Heat the oil to smoking point and deep fry the chicken pieces for about 2 minutes. Lift out and drain well. Pour off all but 2 tablespoons of the oil. If the pan is floury, pour off all the oil, wipe out the wok and return 2 tablespoons of the oil.

Heat the oil and stir-fry the chicken briefly, then add the sweet bean paste and scallion and stir-fry together on moderate heat until the chicken is cooked through and well glazed with the sauce.

Note: Oyster sauce, hot bean paste, salted yellow beans or hot black bean sauce can be used in place of the sweet bean paste, adding a little sugar to taste. Add diced drained water chestnuts for variety.

G

Garlic Goose

Serves 6–8: 7–8-lb (3.5–4-kg) goose; 3 medium-size onions, halved; 2 stalks celery, quartered; 6 whole cloves; 6 black peppercorns; salt; ½ cup croutons Sauce: 1¾ cups (14 fl oz) milk; 4 garlic cloves, peeled; 3 egg yolks; ½ cup (4 fl oz) cream; salt and pepper

Put the goose into a large pan with the onions, celery, cloves and peppercorns. Add about 2 teaspoons of salt and enough cold water to cover the bird. Bring the water to simmering point, cover and simmer for 2 hours, or until the bird is tender. It must not be cooked until it is falling apart.

Meanwhile, make the sauce; put the milk and garlic in the top of a double boiler and simmer for 30 minutes, with the pan half-covered. Strain 1½ cups (12 fl oz) of the milk into a heavy-based saucepan and discard the garlic. Whisk the egg yolks into the milk and cook over very low heat, whisking all the time, until the milk begins to thicken. Add the cream and cook without boiling for 4–5 minutes. Season with salt and pepper to taste.

Carefully lift the cooked goose from the pan and cut into serving pieces. Arrange on a hot, deep serving dish and keep hot. Stir the croutons into the sauce and pour over the goose.

Gingered Chicken ★

Serves 4: 1 chicken, halved; 1 teaspoon salt; ½ teaspoon freshly ground black pepper; 1 teaspoon ground ginger; 6 tablespoons (3 oz) butter; 1-in (2.5-cm) piece of fresh ginger, peeled and finely grated; 1 small garlic clove, crushed; juice of 1 lemon

Season the chicken halves on each side with the salt, black pepper and ground ginger, rubbing the seasoning well into the skin. Melt the butter in a small pan, add the fresh ginger and garlic and sauté over very

Enchiladas (see page 213)

Garlic Goose

Remove any skin from the chicken pieces. Put the flour into a paper or plastic bag, add the chicken and shake until well coated.

Melt the butter in a large skillet and lightly cook the chicken pieces until they are the color of pale straw. Transfer from the pan to a casserole. Add the onions and celery to the pan and sauté for 3–4 minutes. Add the peppers and cook for 3 minutes. Stir in the mushrooms and sprinkle with the turmeric, stirring until the mushrooms are lightly coated with the pan juices. Add the wine and half the chicken stock and bring gently to the boil. Reduce the heat and season with salt and pepper to taste. Pour the mixture over the chicken, add the cream and cover.

Bake in an oven preheated to 350°F (180°C) for 45 minutes, or until the chicken is tender. Remove the casserole from the oven and strain off the cooking liquid. Keep the chicken and vegetables warm while finishing the sauce.

Melt the 1 tablespoon of butter in a small pan. Add the 1 tablespoon of flour and mash into the butter to form a smooth paste. Cook for 1 minute. Add a quarter of the reserved chicken liquid, whisking well. Repeat until all the liquid has been used and a smooth sauce forms. The sauce should just coat the back of the spoon. If it is too thick, thin with the remaining chicken stock. Adjust the seasoning and pour the sauce over the chicken and vegetables.

Goose Brûlée Attunga

Serves 4: ¾–1 lb (375–500 g) sliced cooked goose; 1 cup (8 fl oz) chicken stock; 3 tablespoons orange juice; finely grated peel of 1 orange; 2 tablespoons redcurrant jelly; salt and freshly ground black pepper; 1 orange, peeled and cut into segments; 3 oz (90 g) seedless raisins; 2 tablespoons brown sugar

Simmer the sliced goose in the chicken stock for 7–8 minutes. Mix the orange juice and peel with the redcurrant jelly.

Remove the goose from the stock and arrange in a shallow heatproof serving dish. Pour the orange juice mixture over the goose and season with salt and black pepper to taste. Pattern the orange segments and raisins over the top and sprinkle with the brown sugar. Broil until the sugar bubbles and glazes the surface. Serve immediately.

low heat for 3–4 minutes.

Put the chicken, skin side up, under a preheated broiler. Stir the lemon juice into the butter mixture and pour over the chicken. Broil for 10 minutes on high, reduce the heat to medium and cook for 10 minutes longer or until the juices run clear when pierced with a skewer. Turn the bird and baste with the sauce. Broil for 3–4 minutes more or until tender. Transfer to a heated serving dish, season the sauce if necessary and spoon over the chicken.

Golden Chicken Casserole

Serves 4–6: 3-lb (1.5-kg) chicken, cut into serving pieces; ¾ cup (3 oz) all purpose flour; 4 tablespoons (2 oz) butter; 4 medium-size onions, peeled and quartered; 2 stalks celery, cut into ¾-in (2-cm) pieces; 2 red bell peppers, seeded and coarsely chopped; 4 oz (125 g) button mushrooms, halved; ¼ teaspoon ground turmeric; ½ cup (4 fl oz) white wine; 1 cup (8 fl oz) chicken stock; salt and pepper; ½ cup (4 fl oz) cream; 1 tablespoon softened butter; 1 tablespoon all purpose flour

Goose Caprice

*Serves 4–6: Stuffing: 2 tablespoons (1 oz) butter;
2 tablespoons olive oil; goose liver or 2 chicken
livers, trimmed and chopped; 3 medium-size onions,
chopped; 6 oz (185 g) mushrooms, sliced; 2 large
green bell peppers, seeded and chopped; 2 stalks
celery, sliced; 6 oz (185 g) pimiento-stuffed olives,
sliced; salt and freshly ground black pepper; ½ cup
(4 fl oz) dry Marsala*
*7–8-lb (3.5–4-kg) goose; ¾ cup (6 fl oz) brandy;
½ cup (4 fl oz) chicken stock; salt and pepper*

To make the stuffing, melt the butter and
oil in a skillet and sauté the liver with the
vegetables and olives for 2–3 minutes.
Season lightly with salt and generously
with black pepper. Stir the Marsala into the
pan, cover and cook over low heat for 10
minutes. Remove the lid and stir the vegetable mixture until most of the liquid has
been absorbed. Remove from the heat and
leave to cool.

Spoon the cooled stuffing into the cavity
of the bird and close the opening with
coarse thread or poultry pins. Fold the
wings under the body and prick the goose
skin all over with a fine skewer. Put the
goose on a rack set over a roasting dish and
cook in an oven preheated to 500°F (260°C)
for 15 minutes. Reduce the temperature to
350°F (180°C) and roast for 3–3½ hours, or
until the bird is cooked. Cover the breast of
the goose loosely with aluminum foil if it
browns too quickly but remove the foil 1
hour before the end of cooking time.

Carefully transfer the goose to a heated
carving dish, discard the thread or pins and
leave to stand in a warm place before carving. Let the pan juices settle in the roasting
dish before skimming the fat from the surface. Bring the pan juices rapidly to the
boil and add the brandy and stock. Reduce
the heat and simmer for 2–3 minutes.
Adjust the seasoning and serve with the
goose.

Goose Cassoulet

*Serves 4–6: 5–6-lb (2.5–3-kg) goose, cut into serving
pieces; 4 oz (125 g) smoked pork loin, cut into small
dice; 1 medium-size onion, chopped; 2 large garlic
cloves, crushed; 2 slices bacon; 6 scallions, sliced;
2 cups (16 fl oz) goose stock or chicken stock;
1 teaspoon chili sauce; 15-oz (425-g) can chickpeas
(garbanzo beans), drained; 12 small pickling onions,
peeled; 1 garlic sausage, cut into ½-in (1-cm) slices;
cherry tomatoes, whole, or 3 medium-size tomatoes,
quartered*

Goose Brûlée Attunga (see page 215)

Goose Cassoulet

Preheat the broiler and brown the goose,
skin side up. When the fat starts to run,
turn the goose and broil for 3–4 minutes.
Set aside.

Lightly brown the pork loin in a large,
deep flameproof casserole. Add the onion,
garlic and bacon, and cook gently until the
onion is transparent. Put the goose into the
casserole with the scallions and distribute
the pork and vegetables around it. Add the
stock and chili sauce and bring to the boil
on top of the stove. Remove from the heat
and check the seasoning — there should be
enough from the smoked meats and chili
sauce, but adjust if necessary.

Cover and cook below the center of an
oven preheated to 325°F (160°C) for 2
hours, skimming excess fat from the surface of the pan from time to time. Add the
remaining ingredients. Re-cover the casserole and cook for 1 hour longer, until the
goose is tender. Skim fat from the surface
and adjust the seasoning before serving.

H

Herb-Roasted Turkey

*Serves 8–10: 10–12-lb (5–6-kg) turkey; stuffing
(optional); ½ cup (4 fl oz) melted butter; 2 garlic
cloves, crushed; 1 teaspoon dried basil; 1 teaspoon
salt; ½ teaspoon freshly ground black pepper;
½ teaspoon dried thyme; 1 teaspoon crushed
rosemary; ½ teaspoon dried marjoram; ½ teaspoon
Spanish paprika; rosemary sprigs for garnish*

If stuffing the bird, fill the cavities loosely
and close with poultry pins or coarse
thread. Fold the neck skin over the stuffing
and secure with pins. Tie the legs together
and tuck the wings under the body. Put the
bird on a rack in a roasting dish. Mix the
butter with the garlic, basil, salt, black pepper, thyme, crushed rosemary, marjoram
and paprika. Pour the herbed butter over
the turkey.

Roast in an oven preheated to 325°F
(160°C) for 15 minutes/lb (30 mins/kg),
remembering to include the stuffing weight
when calculating the cooking time. Cover
the breast and legs of the bird loosely with
aluminum foil for the first 2 hours of the
cooking time and baste with the pan juices
every 30 minutes.

When the turkey is cooked, transfer it to
a heated carving dish, cover and leave to
stand in a warm place for 10 minutes
before carving. Garnish the dish lavishly
with the rosemary sprigs and serve the
gravy separately.

Herb Roasted Turkey

Honey and Sesame Chicken Wings

Serves 6: 12 chicken wings (approx 2 lb/1 kg); ¼ cup (2 fl oz) light soy sauce; 1 tablespoon dry sherry; 2 teaspoons sesame oil; 2 tablespoons clear honey; 1 tablespoon white sesame seeds

Place the chicken wings in a wide microwave-safe dish and pour over the soy sauce, sherry and sesame oil. Soften the honey in the microwave, top removed, for 1 minute on MEDIUM (50%), then drizzle evenly over the wings. Cover with a lid or plastic wrap, vented in one corner, and microwave on HIGH (100%) for 5 minutes. Rearrange the chicken wings so that the parts towards the center of the dish are now at the outside, and microwave on HIGH (100%), covered, for a further 5 minutes. Rearrange the wings again, basting with the sauce, and microwave uncovered for a further 5 minutes. Remove and let stand for 5 minutes. Chicken wings should be cooked only to this point if being prepared in advance. Keep covered until ready to reheat.

Spread the sesame seeds on a plate and microwave on HIGH (100%) for 3 minutes. Set aside.

When ready to serve, remove the wings from the sauce, arrange the meaty parts outward on a roasting rack and brush with the sauce. Microwave, uncovered, on HIGH (100%) for 5–6 minutes until heated through and crisped on the surface. Sprinkle with the sesame seeds.

Hungarian Goose Loaf

Serves 4–6: 2 tablespoons (1 oz) goose fat or butter; 1 large onion, chopped; breasts from 1 goose, skinned and finely ground; 8 oz (250 g) goose or chicken livers, trimmed and finely chopped; 3 oz (90 g) sultana raisins; 3 slices of bread, with crusts removed, soaked in 3 tablespoons milk; salt and freshly ground black pepper; ½ teaspoon freshly grated nutmeg; 2 teaspoons Hungarian paprika; 1-2 teaspoons cracked black peppercorns

Heat the fat or butter in a skillet and quickly fry the onion until softened and lightly browned. Mix the onion and pan juices with the goose, livers and sultana raisins. Squeeze out the milk and mix the bread thoroughly with the goose mixture. Season with salt and black pepper to taste and add the nutmeg and the paprika.

Lightly oil a loaf pan and sprinkle the base with the cracked peppercorns. Spoon the goose mixture into the pan, pressing firmly into the corners. Level the top and cover loosely with aluminum foil. Bake in the center of an oven preheated to 350°F (180°C) for 50–60 minutes. Turn onto a heated serving dish and serve with the vegetables. To serve cold, cool the loaf in the pan before chilling.

J

Javanese Fried Chicken

Serves 4: 1 chicken, weighing about 2 lb (1 kg); 2 teaspoons coriander; 1 teaspoon turmeric; 1½ teaspoons salt; 8 shallots or 1 medium-size red or brown onion; 1 garlic clove; 1-2 fresh chilies; 2 slices lengkuas; 1 stalk lemongrass; 1½ cups (10 fl oz) coconut milk; 1 teaspoon palm sugar or brown sugar; oil for deep frying

Chili and Onion Sambal: 8–10 dried red chilies, soaked; 1 tablespoon dried shrimp, soaked and pounded; 4 shallots or ½ medium-size onion; pinch salt; 1–2 teaspoons lemon juice, or more to taste

Cut the chicken into serving pieces. Grind the coriander and mix with turmeric and salt. Rub this mixture into the chicken and set it aside.

Grind the shallots, garlic, chilies, *lengkuas* and lemongrass in a mortar and pestle, or put them in a blender with a little of the coconut milk finely and grind.

Put the ground mixture, coconut milk and sugar into a pan and bring to the boil, stirring constantly. Simmer for a couple of minutes, then add the chicken and cook, uncovered, for 20–30 minutes until the chicken is tender and the sauce almost completely evaporated. It will be necessary to turn the chicken pieces as they cook to ensure even cooking. The chicken can be left in the pan to soak in the remaining spicy liquid until just before it is required, or it can be kept in the refrigerator for a day.

To make the sambal, grind the chilies finely, then add the pounded dried shrimp. Pound until fine, then add the shallots and pound to make a paste. Add salt and lemon juice to taste.

To finish the chicken, heat plenty of oil in a deep pan and deep fry the pieces, a few at a time, for 2–3 minutes until golden brown. Serve with the Chili and Onion Sambal.

Korean Barbecue

K

Korean Barbecue

Serves 10–12: Beef Barbecue: 1 lb (500 g) lean beef (rump, sirloin, top round); 1½ tablespoons dark soy sauce; 1½ tablespoons light soy sauce; 1 scallion, chopped; 4 garlic cloves, chopped; 1-in (2.5-cm) piece fresh ginger, chopped; 2 tablespoons white sesame seeds, ground; pinch of white pepper; 3 tablespoons sesame oil
Chicken Barbecue: 1 lb (500 g) chicken breast meat; 2 tablespoons sugar; 1½ tablespoons light soy sauce; 6 scallions, chopped; ¾-in (2-cm) piece fresh ginger, chopped; 6 garlic cloves, chopped; 2 tablespoons white sesame seeds, ground; pinch of pepper; 2 tablespoons sesame oil
Pork Barbecue: 1 lb (500 g) pork shoulder, leg or tenderloin; 1½ teaspoons red pepper paste (kochujan); 2½ tablespoons sugar; 4½ tablespoons light soy sauce; 6 scallions, chopped; 1-in (2.5-cm) piece fresh ginger, chopped; 8 garlic cloves, chopped; 2 tablespoons white sesame seeds, ground; 1 tablespoon sesame oil

Cut the beef into ¼-in (5-mm) slices, then into small pieces. Sprinkle with soy sauce, then marinate in the remaining combined ingredients for 5 minutes.

Cut the chicken into small, thin slices, discarding the skin. Rub with sugar, then marinate in a mixture of the remaining ingredients, except the sesame oil, for 5 minutes. Sprinkle the sesame oil over and let stand for another minute.

Rub the pork with the red pepper paste, then sprinkle over the sugar. Mix all ingredients and marinate the meat in this sauce for at least 10 minutes.

Heat a griddle over a portable fire on the table. Cook the beef to preference, ideally rare, then serve the chicken and cook to taste, and lastly cook the pork. Serve with a selection of side dishes and dips of soy sauce and *kochujan* (see Note).

Shrimp may also be cooked on the barbecue. Marinate as in the preparation for chicken, omitting the sugar. Spareribs may be substituted for pork. Cut the meaty ribs into 2-in (5-cm) lengths and marinate in the same way. Cook until the meat is well done.

Note: To make *kochujan*, mix 2 tablespoons soybean paste, 2 tablespoons dark soy sauce and 1½–2 teaspoons chili powder. Let stand for 1 hour before using.

Kung Pao Chicken

Serves 4: 1 lb (500 g) boneless chicken breasts, or use slightly more chicken on the bone; 3 oz (90 g) raw peanuts; 5 fresh red chili peppers; ¾ cup (6 fl oz) oil; 3 scallions, trimmed and sliced; 5–6 garlic cloves, sliced; ¾ teaspoon Chinese brown vinegar
Seasoning A: 2 tablespoons light soy sauce; 2 tablespoons rice wine or dry sherry; 1 teaspoon sugar; 1½ teaspoons cornstarch; 1 tablespoon finely chopped scallion; 1½ teaspoons grated fresh ginger
Seasoning B/Sauce: ⅔ cup (5 fl oz) chicken stock; 2 tablespoons light soy sauce; 1 tablespoon rice wine or dry sherry; 1 teaspoon salt; 1½ teaspoons sugar; 1½ teaspoons cornstarch

Cut the chicken into bite-size pieces. Place in a dish with the seasoning A ingredients, mix well and leave for 20 minutes. Drop the peanuts into a pot of boiling water and leave for 2 minutes, then drain and remove the skins. Cut the chilies into quarters and discard the seeds for a milder taste.

Heat the oil and fry the chilies until they turn dark brown. Remove and set aside. Add the peanuts and fry until golden. Remove and drain well.

Pour off all but 2½ tablespoons of the oil and stir-fry the chicken for 2 minutes. Add the sliced scallions and garlic and stir-fry a further 30 seconds, then add the chili peppers and the premixed seasoning B/sauce ingredients. Cover and simmer until the chicken is tender, about 2 minutes. Cooking will take longer for chicken on the bone, so leave out the cornstarch until the chicken is done, then mix to a paste with cold water and use to thicken the sauce.

Stir in the vinegar and the peanuts and transfer to a serving plate. Serve at once.

L

Lemon Chicken

Serves 4–6: 3-lb (1½-kg) chicken; salt and white pepper; 1½ teaspoons sugar; 1½ teaspoons Chinese rice wine; 2 tablespoons instant custard powder; 2 egg yolks; oil for deep frying
Sauce: ¼ cup (2 fl oz) lemon juice; ¾ teaspoon white vinegar; ½ cup (4 fl oz) light chicken stock; ¼ cup (2 oz) sugar; 1 tablespoon cornstarch; 3–4 drops yellow food coloring; lemon slices

Prepare the chicken and pat dry. Mix the salt and pepper with the sugar and Chinese wine, and rub into the chicken inside and out. Let stand for 15 minutes. Place in a steamer and cook for 45 minutes. Leave to cool. Coat the bird with custard powder, then brush with beaten egg.

Heat the oil and carefully lower in the bird. Deep fry until the skin is golden brown and crisp. Lift out and drain well, then cut into serving pieces.

Put all sauce ingredients into a small saucepan and bring to the boil, stirring until it becomes clear. Check the taste and add more sugar or lemon as preferred. Pour over the chicken and garnish with lemon slices.

Lemon Chicken

M

Mango Chicken

Serves 4: 3½–4-lb (1¾–2-kg) chicken; 6 tablespoons (3 oz) butter; 2 large onions, thinly sliced; 6 slices fresh or canned mango; grated nutmeg; 3 strips of lemon peel; 1¼ cups (10 fl oz) chicken stock; salt and pepper; juice of 1 lemon; ½ cup (4 fl oz) cream; paprika

Disjoint the chicken and reserve the back and trimmings for stock.

Fry the chicken in half the butter until golden brown. Melt the remaining butter in a saucepan or flameproof casserole and sauté the onions until golden. Add the mango, increase the heat and cook for 3–5 minutes. Add the fried chicken, a little grated nutmeg, lemon peel, chicken stock and salt and pepper to taste.

Cover the pan and cook in an oven preheated to 350°F (180°C) for 1 hour or until the chicken is tender. Remove and keep warm. Discard the lemon peel, add the lemon juice and season to taste. Stir in the cream and bring to a gentle simmer. Pour the sauce over the chicken, sprinkle with paprika and serve with rice pilaf.

Note: 2–3 peeled, sliced peaches may be used instead of the mango.

N

Noodles with Chicken and Vegetables ⬤

Serves 6: 1½ lb (750 g) udon noodles, or spaghetti; 6 cups dashi or chicken stock; 6 dried Japanese black mushrooms, soaked in cold water for ½ hour; 12 scallions; 3 oz (90 g) chicken breast; ⅔ cup light soy sauce; ⅔ cup mirin or sake; 1½ teaspoons sugar; 2 oz (60 g) fish cake (kamaboko), sliced (optional); 6 eggs; sansho or chili powder

Soak the noodles for 20 minutes in cold water. Drain. Bring the stock to the boil, add the noddles and cook until tender. Remove the noodles from the stock, drain and spread on a tray to dry slightly.

Drain the mushrooms and remove stems. Clean the scallions and cut into 1-in (2.5-cm) pieces. Remove any skin and bones from the chicken and slice thinly. Return the stock to moderate heat, then add the chicken and mushrooms and cook until the chicken is tender. Remove the chicken and mushrooms from the soup with a slotted spoon and set aside. Season the soup with soy sauce, *mirin* and sugar. Add the scallions and fish cake, if used.

Return the noodles to the pan, reheat, then spoon into six large bowls. Add a mushroom and several pieces of chicken to each bowl. Break an egg on top of the noodles and add a sprinkling of *sansho* or chili powder. Cover the bowls and put in a hot oven or on a warming plate for 5 minutes before serving.

Noodles with Chicken and Vegetables

O

Orange Duck (Canard à l'Orange) 🇫🇷

Serves 4: 5–6-lb (2½–3-kg) duck; salt and pepper; dry white wine; 1½ teaspoons sugar; 1½ teaspoons vinegar; 1 cup (8 fl oz) chicken stock or water and chicken bouillon cube; juice of 4 oranges; juice of 1 small lemon; 2 tablespoons brandy; orange peel cut into julienne strips; orange segments and watercress for garnish

Wipe the duck with a damp cloth and truss. Rub all over with salt and pepper and roast in an oven preheated to 400°–450°F (200°–230°C) for 15 minutes, reduce the heat to 350°–375°F (180°–190°C) and continue to roast until cooked, about 1¼ hours. Baste every 20 minutes with the dry white wine.

In a small pan, melt the sugar and vinegar together until it caramelizes. Remove the duck from the oven and keep warm. Pour off excess fat from the roasting pan and add the chicken stock, scraping any sediment in well. Stir in the orange and lemon juice and brandy. Finally add the caramelized sugar and vinegar and cook the sauce slowly for 10 minutes.

Cut the duck into four portions and arrange on a large heated platter, pour the sauce over and sprinkle with julienne strips of orange peel. Garnish with orange segments and sprigs of watercress.

Peking Duck

Oyster Sauce Chicken in Parcels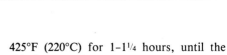

*Serves 2: 8 oz (250 g) boneless chicken breast;
several sheets of edible rice paper, cellophane or
waxed paper; sesame oil; 3 cups (24 fl oz) oil for
deep frying; small bunch of fresh cilantro, broken
into sprigs with stems removed
Seasoning: 1¼ teaspoons sugar; pinch of white
pepper; 1 tablespoon oyster sauce; 2 teaspoons
sesame oil; ¼ teaspoon grated fresh ginger;
1 tablespoon finely chopped scallion*

Skin the chicken breasts and cut across the grain into thin slices, about 2 × 1 in (5 × 2.5 cm). Mix with the seasoning ingredients and leave to marinate for 20 minutes.

Cut the paper into 5-in (12-cm) squares and brush one side with sesame oil. Place a slice of chicken on each paper, towards one corner. Add a sprig of cilantro and top with another chicken slice. Fold the closest corner over the chicken, then fold in the two sides and lastly the end flap, tucking it securely inside the other folds.

Heat the oil to moderate and fry the chicken parcels, turning once or twice, until they float to the surface, about 3 minutes.

Drain well, arrange on a serving plate and surround with fresh cilantro. Serve piping hot. If using cellophane or waxed paper, use scissors to cut an opening in the tops to facilitate removal of the chicken.

P

Peking Drumsticks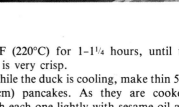

*Serves 4: 8 small drumsticks; 2–3 tablespoons
cornstarch; oil for deep frying
Marinade: 2 garlic cloves, crushed; 1-in (2.5-cm)
piece of green ginger, peeled and finely grated;
2 medium-size onions, chopped; 1 teaspoon salt;
¼ teaspoon five spice powder; 1 tablespoon brown
sugar; 3 tablespoons soy sauce; 2 tablespoons dry
sherry*

Arrange the drumsticks in a shallow dish. Mix all the ingredients for the marinade and pour over the chicken, turning, until well coated. Cover and leave at room temperature for 2–3 hours, turning the drumsticks occasionally.

Put the marinated chicken into a steamer and steam over rapidly boiling water for 20

Peking Drumsticks

minutes. Remove from the steamer and leave to cool.

Preheat the oil to 365°F (185°C). Dust the drumsticks lightly with the cornstarch and deep fry until crisp and golden.

Peking Duck

*Serves 4: 4-lb (2-kg) duck; 6 oz (185 g) sugar; 1 cup
(8 fl oz) water; salt; 1 quantity of pancakes (see page
230) with 1 teaspoon sesame oil; 1 tablespoon
sesame oil; 12 scallions, cut into 5-in (12-cm)
lengths; 1 cucumber, peeled and cut into strips;
Chinese plum sauce; hoisin sauce*

Put the duck in a bowl, pour boiling water over it and leave for a few seconds. Drain, dry the duck and tie the legs together. Hang the bird in a cool, airy place overnight.

The following day, put the sugar and water into a small pan and boil rapidly until syrupy but not caramelized. Brush the duck liberally with the syrup, sprinkle with salt and hang again until it is dry.

Put the duck on a rack set over a roasting dish and roast in an oven preheated to

425°F (220°C) for 1–1¼ hours, until the skin is very crisp.

While the duck is cooling, make thin 5-in (12-cm) pancakes. As they are cooked, brush each one lightly with sesame oil and stack them one on top of the other.

When ready to serve, peel the crisp skin from the duck, slice the meat thinly and arrange on a hot platter. Serve with the stack of pancakes and dishes of scallions, cucumber and sauces. Each pancake is then spread with sauce, crisp skin, duck and vegetables before being rolled.

Poached Chicken

*Serves 4: 3–4-lb (1.5–2-kg) chicken or fowl;
1 tablespoon bitters; stuffing (optional); chicken
stock or water; 4 medium-size onions, peeled;
4 small leeks, trimmed and split; 4 stalks celery, cut
into equal lengths; 4 medium-size carrots, trimmed;
1 bay leaf; a small parsley sprig; 2 cloves;
½ teaspoon dried thyme or sage; salt and freshly
ground black pepper*

Brush the chicken evenly with the bitters and put aside to dry. Brush again. If you

Pomeranian Roast Goose Stuffed with Prunes and Apples

1–1½ cups (2–3 oz) fresh coarse rye breadcrumbs; 2 tablespoons sugar; ⅔ cup (2½ oz) all purpose flour

Twenty-four hours before roasting, rub the goose with the salt and pepper and refrigerate.

Place the goose in a large saucepan with the onions and water, and simmer, covered, for 1 hour. Strain the stock, skim off the fat and reserve. Rub the goose again with salt and pepper.

Combine the prunes, apples, breadcrumbs, sugar, salt and pepper, and stuff the cavity of the bird. Use skewers to hold the opening together. Place the goose breast side down on a rack in a roasting pan and bake in an oven preheated to 425°F (220°C) for 45 minutes. Drain the fat from the roasting pan, reduce the temperature to 375°F (190°C) and roast the goose for a further 1–1¼ hours. Again, drain the fat from the pan. Turn the goose breast side up and increase the temperature to 475°F (240°C). Roast for 15 minutes or until the breast is golden brown. Remove the goose and keep warm.

Skim off the fat from the roasting pan, combine the flour with the reserved goose stock and add the mixture to the pan. Simmer slowly until the sauce thickens. Season and serve with the goose.

wish, stuff the bird, filling the cavity loosely. Sew the opening with coarse thread, tie the legs together and fold the wings neatly under the body, securing with poultry pins.

Choose a wide pan that is not too deep and which has a lid — the ideal vessel is a wok. Put the bird into the pan and add enough warm stock or water to reach just halfway up the sides of the chicken. Put the pan over a low to moderate heat and add the onions, leeks tied in a bundle, celery tied in a bundle and the carrots. Bring the stock or water almost to boiling point, remove any scum from the surface and immediately reduce the heat until the water is barely simmering. Add the bay leaf, parsley, cloves and herbs, seasoning with a little salt and pepper. Cover and simmer for 1½–2 hours, depending on the age of the bird. The legs should move very easily when the chicken is cooked.

Carefully lift the bird onto a heated serv-ing dish and remove the trussing string. Arrange the vegetables around the chicken before serving. Coat lightly with sauce or serve separately.

Note: If the chicken has been cooked in water, you will now have a well-flavored stock. Strain the liquid, freeze it and use to poach the next bird, and the next . . . The stock and the poached chickens will become better and better.

Pomeranian Roast Goose Stuffed with Prunes and Apples

Serves 6–8: 8–10-lb (4–5-kg) goose; salt and freshly ground black pepper; 2 onions, chopped; 3–4 cups (24 fl oz–1 liter) water; 2 cups (12 oz) pitted and chopped prunes; 4 apples, peeled, cored and diced;

Preserved Cucumber and Ginger Stewed Chicken with Beans

Serves 4–6: 1½ lb (750 g) chicken pieces; 4 oz (125 g) fresh or frozen lima beans (or fresh soybeans, shelled, if available); 1 oz (30 g) soy-preserved cucumber (see Note); 1 oz (30 g) soy-preserved ginger (see Note); ¼ cup (2 fl oz) softened lard or oil; 2 scallions, trimmed and diced; salt to taste; sesame oil (optional)
Seasoning A: ¼ teaspoon salt; ½ teaspoon sugar; 1 tablespoon light soy sauce; 1 tablespoon rice wine or dry sherry
Seasoning B/Sauce: ⅓ cup chicken stock or cold water; 1 tablespoon light soy sauce; ½ teaspoon rice wine or dry sherry; 2 teaspoons sugar

Wash the chicken and cut through the bones into bite-size pieces. Mix with the seasoning A ingredients and set aside for 20 minutes. Boil the lima or soybeans until just tender, then drain, refresh in cold water and drain again. Wash the cucumber

Poached Chicken

and ginger in warm water, drain well and cut into small shreds.

Heat the lard in a wok and stir-fry the chicken on moderate heat until almost cooked through, about 6 minutes. Add the cucumber, ginger and scallions, and stir-fry a further 1 minute. Stir in the premixed seasoning B/sauce ingredients and cover. Reduce the heat when boiling and simmer for 4 minutes. Add the beans and heat through. Adjust the seasoning with salt and stir in the sesame oil, if used. Transfer to a serving dish.

Note: Soy-preserved cucumber and ginger can be bought at Asian food stores, or can be made at home by infusing the cucumber or ginger in salted vinegar and soy sauce overnight.

Quick Chicken and Mango Curry

Q

Quick Chicken and Mango Curry ★

Serves 2: 8 oz (250 g) chicken breasts, skinned; 1 small onion, chopped; 2 slices fresh ginger, shredded; 2 tablespoons oil; 1½ teaspoons mild curry powder; 1 tablespoon all purpose flour; ½ teaspoon salt; ¾ cup (6 fl oz) water or chicken stock; 1 tablespoon compressed coconut cream (see Note); 4 slices fresh or canned mango; 1 tablespoon toasted slivered almonds

Cut the chicken breasts into cubes and sauté with the onion and the ginger in oil

until the chicken is well colored and the onion soft.

Sprinkle over the curry powder, flour and salt, mix well, then add the water and the finely chopped coconut cream. Bring almost to the boil, then reduce the heat and simmer gently, stirring, until the sauce thickens and the coconut has dissolved. Add the mango and nuts and serve on a bed of white rice.

Note: Or use ¾ cup (6 fl oz) of canned or fresh coconut milk.

R

Roast Duck with Horseradish 🏴󠁧󠁢󠁥󠁮󠁧󠁿

Serves 4: 4-lb (2-kg) duck; juice of 1 lemon; ½ teaspoon salt; freshly ground black pepper; 8 parsley sprigs; ½ cup (4 fl oz) dry red wine; 1 tablespoon all purpose flour; ¾–1 cup (6–8 fl oz) cream; 1 duck liver or 2 chicken livers, trimmed and finely chopped; 3 tablespoons prepared horseradish or 1½ tablespoons freshly grated horseradish; pinch of dried fennel; white pepper

Fold the wings under the body of the duck and place it on a rack set over a roasting dish. Pour some of the lemon juice into the cavity and the rest over the skin. Sprinkle the bird with salt and pepper and push the parsley into the cavity. Roast in an oven preheated to 400°F (200°C) for 20 minutes, until the fat starts to run, then reduce the heat to 350°F (180°C). Pour the wine over the duck and continue to cook, basting occasionally, for 1¼–1½ hours or until cooked.

Transfer the bird to a heated serving dish and keep hot while finishing the sauce. Skim 2 tablespoons of fat from the surface of the pan juices and mix to a smooth paste with the flour. Remove any remaining fat from the pan, pour the pan juices into a measuring cup, and add enough cream to make 1½ cups (12 fl oz). Stir the chopped liver into the roasting dish and cook for 1–2 minutes over gentle heat. Add the blended flour to the pan, stir in the liver and cook for 2 minutes. Gradually add the cream mixture, stirring constantly until the sauce is smooth. Stir in the horseradish and fennel, seasoning with pepper to taste and salt if necessary. Simmer for 2–3 minutes and serve with the duck.

Roast Goose Served with Braised Sauerkraut ▬

Serves 6–8: 1 goose, 8–10 lb (4.5 kg), ready for the oven; flour; 1 tablespoon diced butter
Stuffing: 8 oz (250 g) sausage meat; 2 tablespoons finely chopped parsley; 1 tablespoon chopped fresh thyme
Braised Sauerkraut: 1 onion, finely chopped; 8 oz (250 g) bacon and ham, chopped and mixed; 1½ lb (750 g) sauerkraut; salt and freshly ground black pepper; 1 lb (500 g) Knackwurst sausage (optional)

Mix the sausage meat with the parsley and thyme. Sprinkle the back of the goose with a little flour and the pieces of butter. Stuff the goose with the stuffing mixture.

Roast the goose in an oven preheated to 425°F (210°C) for 15 minutes, then reduce the oven temperature to 350°F (180°C) and continue roasting until the goose is tender, allowing about 25 minutes per lb (500 g). From time to time, drain off and reserve some of the fat.

Using 2 tablespoons of goose fat in a heavy-based pan, sauté the onion until it is soft and transparent. Add the bacon and ham and continue to cook gently. Drain the sauerkraut and rinse it well in fresh water. Drain it again. Place the washed sauerkraut on top of the onions, bacon and ham and mix all the ingredients together, seasoning well. Moisten with 1 cup of water, cover the pan and leave to cook very gently for 1 hour. 10 minutes before serving, add the sausages to the sauerkraut. Serve the goose on a bed of braised sauerkraut with the diluted pan juices poured over the top.

Roast Goose with 🏴󠁧󠁢󠁥󠁮󠁧󠁿 Apricot-Stuffed Apples

Serves 6: 8-lb (4-kg) goose; salt and pepper; 3 oz (90 g) dried apricots; ¾ cup (6 fl oz) water; 4 tart cooking apples, cored

Season the goose inside and out with salt and pepper. Truss and prick the skin all over to release the fat, then roast on a rack in an oven preheated to 425°F (210°C) for 15 minutes. Reduce the temperature to 350°F (180°C) and continue roasting, allowing 25 minutes per lb (500 g). Drain off excess fat during cooking.

Meanwhile, put the apricots into a small

saucepan with the water and bring to the boil. Cover and simmer until the apricots are tender. Remove the lid and cook until most of the liquid has evaporated. Puree the apricots in a blender or food processor or rub through a sieve.

Make sure that seeds and tough cores have been removed from the apples. Arrange them in a lightly oiled baking dish and fill the centers with the apricot puree. Bake in the oven, below the goose or duck, for 30–35 minutes. The apples should still be slightly firm when served.

Roast Goose with Baked Pears

Serves 6: Stuffing: 1 tablespoon vegetable oil; 2 slices bacon, chopped; 1 large onion, chopped; 1 goose liver, trimmed and chopped; 2 medium-size pears, peeled, cored and chopped; 2 oz (60 g) fresh breadcrumbs; 2 teaspoons dried chervil; salt and white pepper
6–8-lb (3–4-kg) goose; juice of 1 lemon; 1 teaspoon cracked black peppercorns; ½ teaspoon salt; 6 medium-size pears, peeled; 6 slices bacon

To make the stuffing, heat the oil in a small pan and quickly sauté the bacon until lightly browned. Reduce the heat, add the onion and cook until transparent. Add the liver and turn in the pan until sealed. Tip the contents of the pan into a bowl and mix with the pears, breadcrumbs, chervil and salt and white pepper to taste. The stuffing will be crumbly but will absorb some of the fat from the goose.

Spoon the stuffing loosely into the cavity of the bird and close the opening with toothpicks. Any extra stuffing can be used at the neck end or rolled into balls and roasted around the goose. Fold the wings under the body of the bird and loosely tie the legs together.

Prick the skin all over with a skewer and put the goose on a rack set over a roasting dish. Cook in an oven preheated to 350°F (180°C) for 20 minutes. Mix the lemon juice with the cracked peppercorns and salt and pour over the hot bird. Roast for 2–2½ hours longer, basting occasionally with the pan juices and removing and reserving excess fat from the roasting dish when you do so.

About 50 minutes before the goose is ready, roll the pears in the fat in the baking pan and bake under the goose until tender. While the pears are cooking, roll the bacon

Roast Goose with Baked Pears

Roast Goose with Apricot-Stuffed Apples

slices and secure with cocktail picks. Broil for 5–6 minutes when needed.

Remove the toothpicks and serve the cooked bird on a heated carving dish with the baked pears and the bacon rolls.

Roast Turkey with Cherry Stuffing

Serves 8-10: 10–12-lb (5–6-kg) turkey, with giblets; salt; 2½ cups (20 fl oz) water; freshly ground black pepper; 4 tablespoons (2 oz) butter; 1½ tablespoons all purpose flour
Stuffing: 15-oz (425-g) can pitted black cherries; 1 egg; ⅓ cup (3 fl oz) kirsch; 6 oz (185 g) soft breadcrumbs; 2 teaspoons dried mixed herbs; 4 tablespoons (2 oz) butter; 1 large onion, finely chopped; turkey liver, trimmed and chopped; 2 slices bacon, chopped; 1 lb (500 g) finely ground lean veal; 1 lb (500 g) pork sausage meat; salt and pepper

Put the turkey giblets (not the liver) into a saucepan with 1 teaspoon of salt and the water. Bring to the boil, reduce heat and simmer very gently for 30 minutes. Strain and reserve the stock. Season the turkey inside and out with salt and black pepper and set aside while you make the stuffing.

To make the stuffing, drain the juice from the cherries into a mixing bowl and reserve the fruit. Add the egg and kirsch to the juice and mix together. Stir in the breadcrumbs and herbs, and set aside. Melt the butter in a large skillet, and sauté the onion over low heat until softened. Stir in the liver and bacon and cook for 2 minutes. Crumble the veal into the pan and mix with the onion, using a fork to break up any lumps. Combine the onion mixture with the soaked crumbs and the sausage meat, mixing thoroughly and seasoning well with salt and pepper.

Spoon the stuffing and the reserved cherries loosely into the cavity of the bird. Fold the neck skin over the stuffing and secure with coarse thread, then close the vent with toothpicks. Fold the wings under the body, fasten with poultry pins and tie the legs together. Put the bird on a rack in a roasting dish. Melt the butter and pour over the turkey. Cover the breast loosely with a piece of aluminum foil and roast just below the center of an oven preheated to 325°F (160°C) for 3½ hours, basting occasionally.

Increase the temperature to 500°F (260°C), remove the foil and roast for 30–40 minutes longer, until the bird is

cooked and golden. Remove the thread and pins and transfer the bird to a heated carving dish. Leave to stand in a warm place for 10 minutes before carving.

Skim excess fat from the roasting dish, stir the flour into the pan, and cook over moderate heat until lightly browned. Gradually add the giblet stock, stirring between additions, until the gravy reaches the consistency you prefer. Season to taste and simmer for 2–3 minutes. Serve separately.

S

Sake-Steamed Chicken

Serves 4: 12 oz (375 g) boneless chicken breasts, without the skin; ¼ cup sake; ¼ teaspoon salt; 1 teaspoon horseradish powder (wasabi); 2 teaspoons finely grated fresh ginger; 2 teaspoons light soy sauce

Slice the chicken breasts into ½-in (1-cm) strips. Sprinkle with *sake* and salt and leave to marinate for 10 minutes. Put into a shallow bowl in a steamer. Do not cover the bowl. If using a metal rather than bamboo steamer, put a small towel under the lid to absorb any moisture. Steam the chicken over high heat for 15–20 minutes or until cooked.

While the chicken is steaming, mix the horseradish powder with cold water to make a paste. Put a dab of *wasabi* and ½ teaspoon of ginger on individual serving dishes.

When the chicken is cooked, divide among the serving dishes. Add soy sauce to the steaming liquid and spoon a little of this over each portion. Serve immediately.

Salt-Baked Chicken

Serves 4: 1 fresh chicken, weighing about 2½ lb (1.2 kg); 2 teaspoons ginger juice (see page 209); 2 teaspoons Chinese rice wine or dry sherry; 2 teaspoons peanut oil; 3 scallions, including green tops, chopped; 4 large sheets parchment paper; 6 lb (3 kg) coarse salt
Peanut Oil Sauce: 1-in (2.5-cm) piece fresh ginger; 1 scallion, very finely chopped; 3 tablespoons peanut oil; ¼ teaspoon sesame oil; 1 tablespoon oyster sauce

Rub inside of the chicken with ginger juice and rice wine, then rub the skin with oil. Stuff the scallions inside the chicken and wrap it with two layers of parchment paper (make sure you use parchment paper, not waxed paper).

Heat salt in a deep casserole for about 10 minutes or until very hot. Remove half the salt. Bury the chicken breast side down in the remaining salt, then completely cover

Sake-Steamed Chicken

with the salt just removed. Cover the pan and cook in an oven preheated to 350°F (180°C) for 1 hour.

Meanwhile, make the peanut sauce. Chop the ginger as finely as possible, then mix with remaining ingredients.

Remove the chicken from the salt, discard the wrapping paper and cut the chicken into serving pieces. Serve with the peanut oil sauce.

Sambal Chicken

Serves 4–6: 1¼ lb (625 g) boneless chicken; 1 teaspoon salt; ¼ teaspoon black pepper; 3 tablespoons vegetable oil; pineapple and cucumber chunks
Marinade: 1 large onion, grated; 3–4 garlic cloves, crushed; 1-in (2.5-cm) piece fresh ginger, grated; 2-3 dried red chilies, soaked; 1 teaspoon toasted shrimp paste; 3 tablespoons lemon juice; 3 tablespoons water; 2-3 teaspoons sugar

Skin the chicken and cut into bite-size pieces. Thread onto twelve bamboo skewers and rub with the salt, pepper and a little of the oil.

To make the marinade, grind the onion, garlic, ginger, drained chilies and shrimp paste together and add the lemon juice, water and sugar. Pour over the chicken, rub in and leave for 2 hours.

Brush the chicken with oil and cook on a charcoal barbecue or under the broiler until cooked through. Brush occasionally with any remaining marinade and more oil and turn frequently while cooking. Serve hot with the pineapple and cucumber chunks.

Skewered Chicken and Pork Adobo

Serves 4: 12 oz (375 g) pork fillet; 8 oz (250 g) boneless chicken; ½ teaspoon salt; 1 teaspoon black pepper; 1 bay leaf; 1 whole head garlic, crushed; ½ cup (4 fl oz) white vinegar; ¼ cup (2 fl oz) thick coconut milk; 2 teaspoons sugar; vegetable oil; black pepper

Cut the pork and chicken into bite-size cubes and thread onto thin metal or bamboo skewers. Season with the salt and pepper. Arrange the skewers in a wide saucepan and add the bay leaf and crushed garlic. Pour the vinegar and leave to marinate for 30 minutes, then add the

Salt-Baked Chicken

Skewered Chicken and Pork Adobo

coconut milk and sugar with enough water to just cover the skewers. Bring to the boil, then reduce the heat and simmer until the liquid has been completely absorbed.

Heat shallow oil in a large skillet and fry the skewered meats on high heat or cook under the broiler until crisped on the surface. Brush with a little oil first. Season with freshly milled black pepper and serve hot.

Skewered Chicken Meatballs with Radishes

Serves 4: 1 lb (500 g) boneless chicken, minced; 1 egg; 2 tablespoons vegetable oil; 1 teaspoon salt; 1 teaspoon sugar; ½ teaspoon grated lemon peel (optional); 2 tablespoons thin soy sauce; ¼ cup dashi; 1 tablespoon sweet sherry; 1 tablespoon sugar; oil for deep frying; ¾ teaspoon cornstarch; 12 small red radishes, trimmed

Mix the chicken with the egg, vegetable oil, salt, sugar and lemon peel if used and squeeze through the fingers until sticky. Form into walnut-size balls using wet hands.

Bring the soy sauce, dashi, sherry and sugar to the boil and keep warm. Heat the oil to fairly hot and fry the chicken balls until golden. Drain and transfer to the sauce. Add the cornstarch, mixed with a little cold water, and simmer until the sauce has reduced to a sticky glaze on the meatballs.

Shake the pan to turn the balls as they may break up if a spoon is used. Blanch the radishes, if preferred, in boiling water and thread one onto each of twelve thin metal or bamboo skewers. Add several chicken balls to each and serve at once.

Skewered Chicken Meatballs with Radishes

Sliced Roast Duck with Broccoli

Serves 4: ½ cold roast duck; 1 lb (500 g) fresh broccoli, broken into florets; 2 scallions, trimmed and sliced; ⅓ cup (2½ fl oz) oil or softened lard; 2 slices fresh ginger, shredded; ½ teaspoon sesame oil (optional); ½ teaspoon white vinegar (optional) Seasoning: ½ teaspoon salt; ¾ teaspoon sugar; 1 teaspoon light soy sauce; 2 teaspoons rice wine or dry sherry; ⅓ cup (2½ fl oz) chicken stock; ¾ teaspoon cornstarch

Bone the duck and cut into bite-size pieces, then fry in a wok with the oil or lard until lightly browned. Add the broccoli and scallions, and fry a further 3 minutes, stirring constantly.

Add the ginger and seasoning ingredients and bring to the boil. Stir until thickened. Add the sesame oil and vinegar, if used, and transfer to a serving plate.

Spicy Barbecued Chicken ★

Serves 4: 1 whole fresh chicken, weighing about 3 lb (1.5 kg); 8–10 shallots or 1 medium-size red or brown onion; ½-in (1-cm) piece fresh ginger; 10 fresh red chilies; 1 tablespoon coriander, freshly ground; 1 teaspoon cumin, freshly ground; 1½ cups (12 fl oz) thick coconut milk; 1 stalk lemongrass, bruised; 1 teaspoon salt; 1 fragrant lime leaf or young citrus leaf (optional); 1 lime or lemon, quartered

Wash the chicken, dry and cut in half lengthwise. Grind together the shallot, ginger and chilies, then mix in the freshly ground spices. Rub this mixture into the chicken and let it stand while preparing the gravy.

Put the coconut milk, lemongrass, salt and lime leaf into a pan and bring to the boil, stirring constantly. Simmer for 2 minutes, then put in the chicken halves and simmer uncovered, turning several times, until the chicken is tender. The cooked chicken can be stored in a refrigerator for up to 24 hours before barbecuing.

Heat a barbecue or broiler, and oil the metal grid. Barbecue or broil the chicken halves for about 5 minutes on either side until golden brown. Squeeze over the lime or lemon juice when serving. Cut into smaller pieces before serving if desired.

Steamboat

Steamboat

Serves 6: 10 cups (2½ liters) chicken stock; 2 tablespoons vegetable oil; 1-in (2.5-cm) piece fresh ginger, sliced; 1 fresh red or green chili, sliced; 8 scallions, chopped; 12 medium-size raw shrimp; 4 oz (125 g) pork leg or shoulder; 4 oz (125 g) rump, sirloin or fillet steak; 4 oz (125 g) chicken breast; 8 oz (250 g) fish fillets (bream, perch, whiting); 4 oz (125 g) cuttlefish (optional); large bunch fresh spinach, lettuce or Chinese cabbage leaves; chili sauce; 3 tablespoons light soy sauce; 3 garlic cloves; 1-in (2.5-cm) piece fresh ginger, shredded; 2 teaspoons sugar; 6 eggs (optional)

Bring the stock to a rapid boil and add the vegetable oil, sliced ginger, sliced chili and scallions. Reduce the heat and simmer for 10 minutes, then pour into the steamboat or other suitable pot which can be heated at the table.

Peel and devein shrimp, leaving the tails on. Slice the pork, beef and chicken thinly. Cut the fish fillets into thin strips. Clean and slice the cuttlefish. Wash the vegetables and shake out excess water. Separate the leaves. Arrange the meat, shrimp and fish attractively on a plate with the vegetables. Keep the eggs aside.

Mix the soy sauce, crushed garlic, shredded ginger and sugar, stirring until the sugar has dissolved. Pour into several small dishes. Spoon the chili sauce into several small dishes.

The ingredients are cooked individually at the table by each diner, using wooden chopsticks or small wire baskets. Fondue forks could also be used. When the stock begins to bubble, cook the ingredients and dip into either of the sauces.

When all ingredients have been consumed, carefully break the eggs into the stock and poach lightly. These are eaten with the remaining highly enriched soup.

Stir-Fried Beansprouts with Chicken

Serves 4: 9 oz (280 g) fresh beansprouts; 6 oz (185 g) boneless chicken; 2 tablespoons oil
Seasoning A: 1 egg white, beaten; ½ teaspoon salt; 1 teaspoon rice wine or dry sherry; 2 teaspoons cornstarch
Seasoning B: ½ teaspoon salt; ½ teaspoon sugar; ¼ teaspoon ground black pepper; ½ teaspoon rice wine or dry sherry; ½ teaspoon sesame oil; 1 tablespoon cold water; ½ teaspoon cornstarch

Remove the roots and pods from the sprouts and wash well. Dry thoroughly on a kitchen towel.

Thinly slice the chicken, then cut into fine shreds. Place in a dish with the seasoning A ingredients, mix well and leave for 15 minutes.

Heat the oil in a wok and stir-fry the beansprouts for 1 minute. Push to one side of the pan and add the chicken shreds. Stir-fry until white, about 1½ minutes, then mix in the bean sprouts and add the premixed seasoning B ingredients.

Stir on high heat until thoroughly mixed, then serve.

Stuffed Roast Turkey

Stuffed Goose with Applesauce

Serves 8: Stuffing: 1½ lb (750 g) cooked, diced potatoes; 2 onions, chopped; 3 slices bacon, chopped; salt and freshly ground pepper; liver of the goose, chopped; 2 tablespoons parsley, chopped; 1 tablespoon fresh sage or 2 teaspoons dried
6–8-lb (3–4-kg) goose; 1 cup (8 fl oz) chicken stock in which the goose giblets have been cooked
Applesauce: 8 oz (250 g) peeled, cored apples, cut into pieces; ½ cup (4 fl oz) chicken stock; 2 tablespoons (1 oz) butter; 1 tablespoon sugar; pinch of nutmeg; salt

Mix all the stuffing ingredients together and spoon them into the cavity of the bird. Secure the opening with a skewer.

Place the bird, breast side down, on a rack in a roasting pan and roast in an oven preheated to 400°F (200°C) for 45 minutes. Reduce the oven temperature to 325°F (160°C) and continue roasting for 1 hour. Pour off any excess oil in the pan.

At the end of the hour, turn the bird breast side up and roast at the same tem-perature for 30–45 minutes, until the breast is golden brown. During this time, baste with the cooking juices and the stock. If necessary, add a further cup of stock.

Meanwhile, prepare the applesauce: cook the apples in the stock until they are tender, then purée in a blender or food processor. Add the butter, sugar and pinch of nutmeg and serve hot with the goose.

The goose should be carved and arranged on a serving platter with the stuffing surrounding the pieces of meat.

Stuffed Roast Turkey

Serves 8–10: 1 turkey, 8–10 lb (4–5 kg), prebasted; juice of 2 lemons; 1 teaspoon grated lemon peel; salt and freshly ground black pepper
Stuffing: 2 onions, finely chopped; 3 stalks celery, finely chopped; 2 tablespoons oil; 12 oz (375 g) ground veal-pork mixture; turkey liver, chopped; 2 cups (12 oz) cooked rice; 1 cup (8 fl oz) red wine; ½ cup (2 oz) pine nuts or chopped almonds; ½ cup (2½ oz) currants; ½ teaspoon nutmeg; 1 teaspoon dried oregano; 4 sprigs parsley, finely chopped; ½ teaspoon cinnamon; 4 oz (125 g) feta cheese, crumbled

Rub the cavity of the turkey with half of a mixture of lemon juice, lemon peel, salt and pepper. Let it stand while preparing the stuffing.

To make the stuffing, sauté the onions and celery in the oil. Add the ground meat and liver, and fry for 5-8 minutes. Add the rice and wine and cook for 10 minutes. Mix in the rest of the ingredients, combine well together and if necessary adjust the seasoning. Stuff the mixture into the turkey cavity and secure the openings with skewers. Rub the skin with the rest of the seasoned lemon juice, then cover with aluminum foil.

Roast the turkey in an oven preheated to 350°F (180°C) for 2½ hours with the foil. Remove the foil and continue cooking for 1 more hour or until cooked and golden brown. When cooked, let it stand for 10-15 minutes before carving.

Arrange the carved pieces in the middle of a serving platter and place the stuffing around it. Do not worry if some parts of the turkey are undercooked. After carving, and while preparing a gravy from the cooking juices, put the platter in the turned-off oven to keep warm. The underdone parts will set during that time. An overcooked turkey would be dry and tasteless.

T

Tandoori Chicken

Serves 4: 1 fresh chicken, weighing about 2 lb (1 kg); 1 tablespoon melted ghee *or butter*
Marinade 1: 1 teaspoon salt; ½ teaspoon turmeric; ½ teaspoon chili powder; ¼ teaspoon white pepper powder; pinch of ground cloves; 1 teaspoon crushed garlic; 1½ tablespoons lemon juice
Marinade 2: ¼ cup plain yogurt; 1 heaped tablespoon fresh cilantro leaves, pounded; 1 heaped tablespoon mint leaves, pounded; 1 tablespoon cumin, finely ground; ½ teaspoon salt; 1 teaspoon crushed fresh ginger; 1 teaspoon white vinegar; ¼ teaspoon cinnamon; ⅓ teaspoon cardamom; few drops orange food coloring (optional)

Remove the feet, head and skin from the chicken and make deep cuts in the thighs and breast. Combine all ingredients for Marinade 1 and rub well into the chicken. Leave in the refrigerator for about 3 hours.

Combine the ingredients for Marinade 2 and rub evenly all over the chicken, making sure some of the marinade penetrates the

slits. Refrigerate for at least 6 hours.

Brush the barbecue grill with *ghee* or butter and cook the chicken over hot coals, brushing from time to time. Cook until the chicken is done and has turned a rich reddish-gold. If cooking the chicken in a rotisserie or oven, roast for about 45 minutes at 400°F (200°C).

Serve the chicken with tomato and cucumber salad, wedges of fresh lime or lemon and mint chutney.

Thai Peppered Chicken

Serves 4: 6 chicken thighs; 2 garlic cloves, crushed; 1-in (2.5-cm) piece fresh ginger, grated; 2 teaspoons black peppercorns; 2 tablespoons chopped fresh cilantro, including the root and stems; 2 tablespoons thick soy sauce; 2 tablespoons vegetable oil; 1½ teaspoons sugar

Prick the chicken all over. Grind the garlic, ginger, peppercorns and cilantro to a paste and rub into the chicken. Wrap in plastic wrap and leave for at least 2 hours.

Mix the soy sauce, vegetable oil and sugar. Brush over the chicken. Broil or cook on a charcoal barbecue until crisped on the surface and cooked through. Brush occasionally with the sauce during cooking. Serve hot.

Thai Peppered Chicken

Threaded Chicken with Peppers

Serves 4: 3 tablespoons cornstarch; 1 teaspoon salt; 6 oz (185 g) boneless chicken, cut into matchstick strips; 2 tablespoons vegetable oil; 1-in (2.5-cm) piece fresh ginger, peeled and halved; 1 tablespoon butter; 1 dried red chili, seeded and finely chopped; 1 red bell pepper, seeded and cut into matchstick strips; 1 green bell pepper, seeded and cut into matchstick strips; 1 teaspoon sugar; 2 teaspoons vinegar; 2 teaspoons light soy sauce; 2 tablespoons chicken stock; 1 tablespoon dry sherry

Put the cornstarch and salt into a bag, add the chicken strips and shake until they are lightly coated. Heat the oil in a wok or skillet, add the ginger and cook for 1 minute to flavor the oil. Discard the ginger and add the chicken strips to the hot oil. Stir-fry for 1 minute, then remove the chicken and set aside.

Add the butter to the oil with the chili and toss for 1 minute. Add the strips of red and green bell pepper and stir-fry for 1 minute. Sprinkle with the sugar, stir in the vinegar, soy sauce and stock, and cook for 1 minute. Return the chicken to the pan, add the sherry and stir the mixture for a minute or so until the chicken is very hot.

Three Courses of Peking Duck

Serves 4-6: Dish 1: 1 Peking duck, freshly roasted (see page 221); 12 mandarin pancakes; 1 young leek or 6 scallions, trimmed and sliced; ½ cup (4 fl oz) duck sauce
Dish 2: 2 tablespoons softened lard or frying oil; 1-2 teaspoons fresh red chili peppers, shredded; 4 oz (125 g) fresh beansprouts; 1 scallion, trimmed and shredded; ¼ teaspoon grated fresh ginger; ½ teaspoon finely chopped garlic; 1 tablespoon rice wine or dry sherry; ½ teaspoon salt
Dish 3: 6 cups (1½ liters) chicken stock; 2 tablespoons evaporated milk; 1 scallion, trimmed and sliced; 1 slice fresh ginger; 5 oz (155 g) young Chinese green vegetables, trimmed; 1¼ teaspoons salt; 2-3 teaspoons rice wine or dry sherry
Mandarin Pancakes: 1½ cups (6 oz) flour; ½ cup (4 fl oz) boiling water; sesame oil
Duck Sauce: 2 tablespoons sesame oil; ½ cup sweet bean paste; ½ cup (2 oz) sugar; ½ cup (4 fl oz) water

To make the pancakes, sift the flour into a mixing bowl and pour in the water. Work

Tandoori Chicken

Tikka Chicken

Serves 4–6: 1½ lb (750 g) chicken breasts;
1 medium-size onion; 3 garlic cloves; 1-in (2.5-cm)
piece fresh ginger; ¼ cup (2 fl oz) plain yogurt;
2 teaspoons white vinegar; 2 teaspoons chili powder;
2 teaspoons ground coriander; 1 teaspoon ground
cumin; ½ teaspoon turmeric; salt; lemon juice;
garam masala; lettuce leaves; onion rings; lemon
wedges

Cut the chicken into 2-in (5-cm) squares
and press flat.

Grind the onion, garlic and ginger to a
paste and mix with the yogurt. Add the vinegar and spices, and rub into the chicken
well. Leave for 3 hours to marinate.

Sprinkle the chicken with salt and thread
onto skewers. Place under a hot broiler or
over a charcoal barbecue and cook until
tender and crisp.

Sprinkle the chicken with lemon juice
and *garam masala* and serve on a bed of
lettuce leaves surrounded with onion rings
and lemon wedges.

Turkey Cobbler

Serves 4: Cobbler Dough: 2 cups (8 oz) self-rising
flour; ½ teaspoon salt; 8 tablespoons (4 oz) butter;
milk
2 tablespoons (1 oz) butter; 2 tablespoons vegetable
oil; 2 medium-size carrots, thinly sliced; 1 large
onion, chopped; 2–3 sweet chilies, seeded and
sliced; 4 oz (125 g) button mushrooms, halved or
sliced; salt and white pepper; 1 tablespoon all
purpose flour; 1 cup (8 fl oz) turkey stock or chicken
stock; ½ cup (4 fl oz) cream; 1 lb (500 g) cubed
cooked turkey; milk

To make the dough, sift the flour and salt
into a hot mixing bowl. Rub the butter into
the flour until it resembles fine
breadcrumbs. Add enough milk to make a
soft but not sticky dough. Knead lightly
and turn onto a lightly floured board.

Melt the butter with the oil in a
flameproof baking dish. When the fat is
sizzling, add the carrots and onion, and
brown lightly. Reduce the heat, then add
the chilies and mushrooms, and stir with
the other vegetables. Season lightly with
salt and pepper, sprinkle with the flour and
mix thoroughly. Cook for 1–2 minutes
before gradually adding the stock. Stir
until thickened and smooth. Remove the
dish from the heat.

Stir the cream into the vegetable mixture
with the turkey. Adjust the seasoning and

with the handle of a wooden spoon until
the dough is well combined. When cool
enough to handle, knead briskly for 10
minutes. Cover with a damp cloth and
leave in a warm place for 15 minutes.

Roll the dough into a long sausage shape
and divide into 18 pieces. Cover the roll
with a damp cloth while working each
piece. Press two pieces into small round
cakes and brush one side of each with
sesame oil. Press the two oiled surfaces
together, then roll out together until paper-
thin.

When all are rolled out, heat a heavy-
based skillet and rub with an oiled cloth.
Cook the pancakes on moderate heat until
brown flecks appear on the underside.
Turn and cook the other side, then peel
apart and fold the two pancakes into triangular shapes. Wrap in a cloth until ready
to serve.

The pancakes can be stored in plastic
bags in the refrigerator or freezer until
needed. To reheat spread on a plate and set

on a rack in a steamer. Steam for 6–8 minutes. Serve at once.

For the sauce, heat the sesame oil in a
wok and add the remaining ingredients,
mixing thoroughly. Simmer, stirring, until
the sauce thickens, about 2 minutes. Store
in an airtight jar. Keeps for several weeks.

Slice the crisp skin of the roasted duck
into bite-size pieces and serve with the pancakes, sauce and sliced leek or scallion.

Slice off the meat and place the carcass in
a soup pot with the dish 3 ingredients. Simmer for 15 minutes.

In the meantime, stir-fry the chili, beansprouts, scallion, ginger and garlic in the
lard or oil for 1½–2 minutes. Add the sliced
meat and stir-fry a further 1½ minutes,
then sizzle the wine onto the sides of the
pan and add salt to taste. Serve with
steamed white rice.

Check the seasoning of the soup, lift out
the carcass and scrape the meat into the
soup. Pour into a tureen and serve as the
last course.

bake in an oven preheated to 350°F (180°C) for 20–25 minutes. Roll the cobbler dough to a thickness of ½ in (1 cm) and cut into 2-in (5-cm) circles. Arrange on a baking sheet, brush lightly with milk and bake on a shelf above the turkey for 12–15 minutes, until golden. (They can be cooked directly on top of the turkey mixture for 20–25 minutes but are more crisp when cooked separately.) Arrange the cooked cobbler over the turkey and serve hot.

Turkey Paprikash

Turkey Cobbler

Turkey Fillets in Sour Cream

Serves 8: fillets from a 12-lb (6-kg) turkey; seasoned fine breadcrumbs; 2 eggs; 2 tablespoons water; pinch of salt; butter for frying; 1 tablespoon finely chopped onion; 1 tablespoon finely chopped parsley; ¼ cup (2 fl oz) water; 1¼ cups (10 fl oz) sour cream; 1 tablespoon all purpose flour

Remove the breast meat from the turkey and cut each fillet into uniform pieces. Dip the pieces in the breadcrumbs, then in the eggs beaten with 2 tablespoons of water and salt, and finally dip again in the crumbs.

Brown the fillets on both sides in hot butter and transfer them to a baking dish. Sprinkle the turkey with the onion and parsley and add ¼ cup water. Pour the sour cream over the fillets, cover the dish and

bake in an oven preheated to 375°F (190°C) for 15 minutes. Reduce the heat to 250°F (120°C) and bake the fillets for 45 minutes or until they are tender. Remove, cover and increase the heat for the last few minutes of cooking to crisp the top. Transfer the turkey to a heated platter. Stir the flour into the sauce in the dish and cook for a few minutes. Strain over the turkey and serve hot.

Turkey Paprikash

Serves 4–6: 1 tablespoon vegetable oil; 8 oz (250 g) smoked bacon cut into ½-in (1-cm) slices; 1 large onion, coarsely chopped; 4–5-lb (2–2.5-kg) turkey, cut into serving pieces; 1–2 tablespoons Hungarian paprika; 3 tablespoons water; 1½ cups (12 fl oz) light sour cream; salt and freshly ground black pepper

Heat the oil in a heavy-based flameproof casserole until moderately hot. Add the bacon and cook on both sides until lightly browned, then mix in the onion and cook for a few minutes until golden. Remove the bacon and onion from the pan and set aside. Brown the turkey pieces in the

flavored oil, adding a little more if necessary. Sprinkle with the paprika, return the bacon and onion to the pan, add the water and cover very tightly. Simmer very gently for 1–1½ hours or until the turkey is tender. Add a little more water if necessary.

When the turkey is cooked, arrange it with the bacon in a heated serving dish. Skin any excess fat from the pan juices and stir in the sour cream. Simmer gently for 1–2 minutes, season to taste and strain into a serving jug.

Turkey Provençale

Serves 6: 4–5-lb (2–2.5-kg) turkey, skinned and disjointed; ⅓ cup (2½ fl oz) olive oil; salt and freshly ground black pepper; 4 large onions, halved and thickly sliced; 3 garlic cloves, crushed; 6 medium-size tomatoes, peeled and sliced; 2 large red bell peppers, skinned, seeded and thickly sliced; 1 small can anchovies, drained and chopped; 1 teaspoon dried basil; 1 cup (8 fl oz) dry white wine

Brush the turkey with some oil and season with salt and black pepper. Toss the onions, garlic, tomatoes and peppers with the anchovies and basil. Spread a thick layer of the mixture over the base of a heavy-based flameproof casserole. Season and arrange the turkey in the pan. Pack the remaining vegetable mixture over the turkey, season again and pour the remaining oil into the casserole with the wine.

Put the pan over a moderate heat and bring the liquid to a very slow simmer. Cover tightly, using aluminum foil or paper to ensure a close seal. Reduce the heat even more and simmer for 2–2½ hours. The turkey should be very tender.

Lift the turkey pieces from the pan, discarding the bones. Arrange on a heated serving dish and keep hot. Stir the soft vegetables together and beat lightly with a wooden spoon. Adjust the seasoning, reheat until the mixture bubbles and spoon over the turkey.

Turkey with Ham and Olives ★

Serves 6–8: 8-lb (4-kg) turkey; salt and pepper; 8 oz (250 g) raw ham, chopped; 24 olives; 3 garlic cloves, sliced; 6 peppercorns, crushed; 1 tablespoon ground walnuts; ½ teaspoon ground cloves; ½ teaspoon cinnamon; 2 onions, quartered; 2 oranges, sliced; 3 parsley sprigs; 1 bay leaf; ¾ cup (6 fl oz) dry sherry

Wash and dry the turkey and rub the body cavity with salt and pepper. Combine the ham with the olives, garlic and peppercorns, and place inside the bird. Skewer and truss the bird and rub the skin with a mixture of the ground walnuts, cloves and cinnamon.

Enclose the turkey in a cheesecloth bag and tie or wrap securely in greased aluminum foil. Cook the turkey in simmering water to cover for approximately 1½ hours, depending on the age of the bird, or until it is almost tender.

Remove the bag and place the turkey in a baking dish. Add the onions, oranges, parsley sprigs, bay leaf and dry sherry. Cover the dish and cook the bird in an oven preheated to 300°–325°F (150°–160°C) until it is tender, about 1½ hours. Remove the turkey and cut into serving pieces. Arrange on a heated serving platter. Strain the sauce in the baking dish and pour it over the bird before serving.

V

Viennese Fried Chicken

Serves 4–6: 1 tablespoon Hungarian paprika; 4 tablespoons (2 oz) butter; 1 small can anchovy fillets, drained; 6 chicken thighs, skinned and boned; salt; ¼ cup (1 oz) all purpose flour; 2 eggs; 1 tablespoon vegetable oil; 1 cup (4 oz) dry breadcrumbs; oil

Combine the paprika with the butter and anchovy fillets in a blender or food processor and mix until smooth. Shape the flavored butter into a roll or rectangle and wrap in aluminum foil. Chill thoroughly in the refrigerator.

Cut through the center of each piece of chicken to form two thin slices. Season lightly with salt and dust with the flour. Beat the eggs with the oil. Dip the chicken slices into the egg mixture and coat with the crumbs. Put aside to allow the coating to set.

Heat the oil to a depth of ½ in (1 cm) in a shallow pan and fry the chicken over moderately high heat until crisp and golden, turning once. Transfer the chicken to a heated serving dish. Slice the anchovy butter into pats and serve on top of the chicken.

W

Wild Duck with Mashed Taro Stuffing and Oyster Sauce

Serves 4–6: ½ 4-lb (2-kg) wild duck (or use domestic duck); 2 tablespoons dark soy sauce; 8 cups (2 liters) oil for deep frying; 2 scallions, trimmed and shredded; 4 slices fresh ginger, shredded; 1½ star anise, broken; 1½ teaspoons Chinese brown peppercorns; cornstarch
Stuffing: 1 lb (500 g) taro, sweet potato or potato, peeled; ¾ cup (3 oz) taro flour, potato flour or cornstarch; ½ cup (4 fl oz) boiling water; ¼ cup (2 fl oz) softened lard or pastry shortening; 1½ teaspoons salt; ½ teaspoon ground black pepper; 2 dried black mushrooms, soaked and finely diced; 2 tablespoons cooked ham, finely diced
Sauce: 1½ tablespoons oyster sauce; 1½ tablespoons light soy sauce; ½ cup (4 fl oz)

chicken stock; 1 teaspoon sugar; pinch of salt; pinch of ground black pepper; 2 teaspoons cornstarch; 2 tablespoons finely chopped scallion*

Wash the duck and blanch in boiling water. Drain well. Rub with the soy sauce and leave for 15 minutes, then deep fry in smoking hot oil until well colored, about 3 minutes. Remove and drain well.

Place the duck on a plate, cut side upward, and sprinkle over the shredded scallion, ginger, star anise and the peppercorns. Set the plate on a rack in a steamer and steam over rapidly boiling water for 1¾ hours.

Boil the taro or potato until soft enough to mash smoothly. Mix the taro flour with the boiling water and add to the mashed taro. Work in the lard, salt, pepper and the diced ingredients, and knead into a smooth paste.

Remove the duck and wipe dry, then carefully bone it, keeping its original shape. Discard the spices, onion and ginger, and sprinkle with cornstarch. Spread the stuffing over the inside of the duck in a thick layer, smoothing the top and edges. Coat lightly with cornstarch.

Reheat the oil and slice the stuffed duck carefully into the oil. Deep fry until golden brown and the stuffing is crisp. Carefully lift onto a cutting board and cut into bite-size pieces. Arrange on a plate of shredded lettuce.

Bring the sauce ingredients, except the scallions, to the boil and simmer until thickened, then add the scallions. Pour over the duck or serve as a dip.

Wine and Chicken Casserole (Coq au Vin)

Serves 4: 3-lb (1.5-kg) chicken and giblets; 2 tablespoons (1 oz) butter; ½ cup (4 fl oz) Marc de Bourgogne or brandy; ½ cup (2 oz) all purpose flour; salt and freshly ground black pepper
Marinade: 2 onions, roughly chopped; 2 carrots, sliced; 2 stalks celery, cut in ½-in (1-cm) lengths; 2 scallions, roughly chopped; 1 garlic clove, chopped; 2 sprigs thyme, chopped; 2 bay leaves; 4 sprigs parsley, chopped; 2 cloves; 3 cups (24 fl oz) dry red Burgundy; ½ cup (4 fl oz) wine vinegar; ¼ cup (2 fl oz) olive oil

Cut the chicken into pieces, place them into a large container and add all the marinade ingredients. Marinate overnight.

Take out the chicken pieces and brown

them lightly in the butter. Add the Marc or brandy and flame. Transfer the chicken pieces, the marinade, including all its ingredients, and the giblets to a flameproof casserole dish. Cover and simmer for approximately 1½ hours, checking the chicken to see if it is tender.

Strain the cooking liquid into a saucepan and add the chicken pieces. Mix the flour with some water and pour it into the cooking liquid. Slowly boil the liquid, stirring constantly until it thickens. Season and serve with sautéed button mushrooms and small onions.

Y
Yogurt Chicken

Serves 6: 3-lb (1.5-kg) chicken; 1 teaspoon turmeric; 1 tablespoon ground coriander; 1 teaspoon cumin; 1½ teaspoons chili powder; ½ teaspoon fenugreek seeds, ground; 1 large onion, chopped; 2 garlic cloves, crushed; 1-in (2.5-cm) piece fresh ginger, minced; 1½ cups (12 fl oz) plain yogurt; ¼ cup ghee; 1 large onion; 3 garlic cloves; 3 black cardamoms, peeled; 3 cloves; 1-in (2.5-cm) stick cinnamon; salt and black pepper; lemon juice; fresh cilantro leaves or mint, chopped

Wipe the chicken and cut into large pieces. Place in a bowl and rub with turmeric. Make a paste with the spices, onion, garlic and ginger. Mix with the yogurt, pour over the chicken and leave to marinate for 2 hours. Turn several times.

Heat the *ghee* and fry the sliced onion and garlic until soft. Add the cardamoms, cloves and cinnamon stick, then add the marinated chicken and cook until well colored. Add any remaining marinade and enough water to just cover the chicken. Cover and simmer until tender. Season to taste with salt, pepper and lemon juice. Garnish with fresh cilantro or mint.

Wine and Chicken Casserole (Coq au Vin)

GAME

A

Australian Venison Roast

Serves 6–8: 3 oz (90 g) ham fat, chilled and cut into ¼-in (5-mm) strips; 4 lb (2 kg) venison cut from the rump or fillet, trimmed of fat; 1 large onion, halved and sliced; 12 juniper berries, bruised; ¼ teaspoon white pepper; 1½ teaspoons salt; 3 tablespoons gin; 3 tablespoons olive oil; 1½ cups (14 fl oz) passionfruit juice, sieved of seeds (about 12 passionfruit); 1 tablespoon butter; 1 tablespoon all purpose flour

Using a larding needle, "sew" the ham strips all over the surface of the venison. Put the venison into a plastic bag or large lidded bowl with the onion, juniper berries, pepper and salt. Shake the gin in a screwtop jar with the oil and passionfruit juice and pour into the bag or bowl. Seal and marinate for two days, turning the container occasionally.

Lift the venison from the marinade and put it into a roasting dish. Pour the marinade over and roast in an oven preheated to 500°F (260°C) for 20 minutes. Reduce the temperature to 325°F (160°C) and cook for 2 hours, basting the meat frequently with the pan juices.

Transfer the venison to a heated dish, cover and leave to stand in a warm place for 10 minutes before carving. Strain the pan juices into a saucepan. Work the butter and flour together and add, in small pieces, to the sauce. Whisk each addition until the sauce is thickened and smooth. Adjust the seasoning and simmer for 2–3 minutes. Carve the venison thinly and serve the sauce separately.

Note: Larding needles are readily available at kitchenware shops. Their barbed hinge allows a lardon to be easily pulled through the surface of the meat. Chilling the larding fat before slicing makes the job easier.

B

Basque Pheasant

Serves 4–6: 2 pheasants; salt and freshly ground black pepper; 3 tablespoons goose fat or olive oil; 1 large onion, finely chopped; 2–3 small carrots, coarsely chopped; 3–4 cups (24 fl oz–1 liter) chicken stock; 2 sprigs parsley; 2 bay leaves; 1 sprig thyme or celery leaves; 1 large garlic clove, peeled; 4 chorizo sausages; 8 slices bacon, rind removed; 13 oz (410 g) long-grain rice
Tomato Sauce: 2 tablespoons goose fat or olive oil; 1 lb (500 g) tomatoes, peeled, seeded and coarsely chopped; 3 red bell peppers, seeded and cut into ½-in (1-cm) strips; 2 teaspoons Spanish paprika; salt and pepper

Season the pheasants inside and out with salt and pepper and tie the legs together. Heat the goose fat or oil in a large heavy-based pan and brown the onion and carrots lightly over moderate heat. Add the pheasants and brown on all sides, turning them frequently. Arrange the pheasants side by side in the pan and add just enough stock to cover them. Tie the herbs together to make a bouquet garni and add to the stock with the whole clove of garlic. Cover and simmer gently for 15–20 minutes, depending on the size of the birds. Add the sausages and bacon. Cover and simmer for 20 minutes more, or until the birds are tender.

While the birds are cooking, bring a large pan of water to the boil, add 2 teaspoons of salt and stir in the rice. Cook the rice for 10 minutes, strain and add a little more salt if necessary. Spread in the top of a steamer set over 2 cups (10 fl oz) of simmering water. Lay a folded cloth on top of the rice, cover and steam for 15 minutes. If you do not have a steamer, leave the rice in the colander and steam over a saucepan in the same way.

To make the tomato sauce, heat the goose fat or oil in a small pan. Add the tomatoes and peppers, and cook over fairly high heat, stirring constantly until the sauce is thick. Season with paprika, salt and pepper. Reduce the heat to very low and keep the sauce hot.

Spread the rice over a heated serving dish. Lift the pheasants from the casserole and cut into serving pieces, discarding as many small bones as you can. Arrange the pheasants on the rice and keep hot. Cut the sausages and bacon into bite-size pieces, arrange on the serving dish and surround the pheasants with the tomato sauce. Serve.

Braised Pheasant with Mushrooms

Serves 2: 1 pheasant, dressed; juice of 1 lemon; salt and freshly ground black pepper; 3 tablespoons (1½ oz) butter; 4 thin slices bacon; 1 small onion, finely chopped; ½ cup (4 fl oz) Madeira or sweet sherry; 1 cup (8 fl oz) beef stock; 8 oz (250 g) button mushrooms, thinly sliced; ¼ cup (2 fl oz) cream; 1 teaspoon all purpose flour

Paint the pheasant with half the lemon juice and sprinkle with salt and pepper. Melt the butter in a heavy-based casserole and brown the pheasant. Wrap the bird in the bacon and secure the bacon with string. Sprinkle the outside with the rest of the lemon juice and brown the bacon on all sides. Add the onion, half the Madeira or sherry and the stock. Cover and braise over low heat. Gradually add the rest of the Madeira. Total braising time, depending upon the age of the bird, is between 45 and 90 minutes. Twenty minutes before the bird is ready, add the mushrooms.

Mix the cream with the flour and add it to the cooking juices. Cook gently for another 5 minutes and season. Remove the bacon, carve the bird and return the pieces to the casserole with the sauce and mushrooms.

Braised Stuffed Partridge with Port Alcantara

Serves 2: 1 cup (2 oz) soft breadcrumbs; 2 tablespoons oil; 1¾ oz (50 g) liver pâté; 2 tablespoons finely chopped sweet pickled cucumbers; salt and freshly ground black pepper; 1 partridge; ½ cup (4 fl oz) port; ½ cup (4 fl oz) dry white wine

Soak the breadcrumbs in the oil for 10 minutes. In a bowl, combine the breadcrumbs, pâté, pickles, salt and pepper. Mix well and spoon the stuffing into the bird. Sew up the opening or secure it with skewers.

Place the bird in a bowl with the wines and season with salt and pepper. Cover and refrigerate for 24 hours, turning the bird occasionally.

Place the bird and the wine marinade in a heavy-lidded casserole, cover, bring to the boil and simmer over low heat for 1½ hours. Remove the bird and boil the sauce rapidly until reduced by half.

To serve, cut the bird lengthwise into

two, making sure that the stuffing stays in the cavities. Arrange on a decorative platter, skin side up, and serve masked with the sauce.

Broiled Quails

Serves 4: 8 quails; juice of 1 lime or 1 small lemon; 4 tablespoons (2 oz) butter, melted; salt and freshly ground black pepper; lime twists or lemon twists for garnish

Split each quail through the backbone and trim the spinal bones away. Carefully open the birds, lay them cut side down on a board and press along the breastbone with the heel of your hand. Fold the legs and secure in place with a small skewer.

Mix the lime or lemon juice with the butter and brush liberally over each side of the quails. Preheat the broiler and cook the birds at medium to high heat for 12–15 minutes, basting once during this time with the lemon butter. Season before serving and garnish with a citrus twist.

Broiled Snipe with Juniper Butter

Serves 4: 8 snipe, trussed; 10 juniper berries; 8 tablespoons (4 oz) unsalted butter; salt and freshly ground black pepper; 8 round croutons

Preheat the broiler to low and arrange the snipe on their sides, well spaced, in the pan.

Put the juniper berries into a small pan with the butter and stab them a few times with a fork. Melt the butter over low heat and simmer for 3–4 minutes, until the butter is imbued with the flavor of the berries. Pour the butter over the snipe, season with salt and black pepper and set the pan at the lowest point from the heat. Broil for 3–7 minutes on each side, basting frequently. Serve the snipe very hot on the croutons and glazed with the juices from the pan.

Alternatively, the snipe can be cooked, barbecue fashion, over glowing coals and basted with the juniper butter.

C

Casserole of Rabbit with Lentils

Serves 4: 3 tablespoons olive oil; 7 oz (220 g) lentils, soaked; 1 small onion, sliced; 2 tablespoons goose fat or butter; 3 slices bacon, with rind removed; 1 rabbit, cut into serving pieces; freshly ground black pepper; 1 sprig thyme; 1 sprig celery leaves; 1 bay leaf; ¾ cup (6 fl oz) cider; 1 teaspoon dried mint; 1 garlic clove, unpeeled; salt

Heat the olive oil in a heavy-based pan, add the lentils and onion and simmer over gentle heat until most of the oil has been absorbed. In another pan, melt the goose fat or butter and sauté the bacon until lightly browned. Add the rabbit and brown lightly. Season with black pepper and add the herbs tied together to form a bouquet garni. Pour the cider over, cover and simmer for 40–50 minutes, until tender.

In the meantime, add the mint, garlic, salt and black pepper to the lentils with enough water to cover. When the water is simmering, cover and cook until the lentils are tender. Strain and add to the rabbit. Adjust the seasoning before serving.

Creole Rabbit

Serves 4: 2 tablespoons (1 oz) butter; 2 tablespoons olive oil; 1 rabbit, cut into serving pieces; 2 medium-size onions, chopped; 3 tablespoons chopped parsley; 2 garlic cloves, crushed; 3 large tomatoes, peeled and chopped; 1 cup (8 fl oz) beef bouillon; ½ cup (4 fl oz) dry sherry; 2 tablespoons rum; 1 teaspoon ground hot red chili; salt and freshly ground black pepper; 1 tablespoon lemon juice; 3 oz (90 g) ground hazelnuts

Melt the butter and oil in a heavy-based, flameproof casserole and brown the rabbit pieces on all sides. Lift the browned rabbit from the pan and set aside. Add the onions, parsley and garlic to the casserole and sauté over low heat until the onions are transparent. Stir in the tomatoes, stock, sherry and rum. Bring to the boil, then reduce the heat and simmer gently for 3–4 minutes.

Sprinkle the chili, salt and black pepper over the rabbit and return it to the casserole. Spoon the sauce over the rabbit, cover and simmer over low heat for 2 hours, or until tender.

Stir the lemon juice into the sauce with the hazelnuts. Simmer uncovered for 4–5 minutes, adjust the seasoning and serve from the casserole.

F

Farmer's Rabbit Pie

Serves 4: 1 large rabbit; 2½ cups (20 fl oz) dry red wine; 4 bay leaves; 6 oz (185 g) onions, chopped; salt and freshly ground pepper; seasoned all purpose flour; 4 tablespoons (2 oz) butter; 2½ cups (20 fl oz) brown sauce; 8 oz (250 g) mushrooms, sliced; 6½ oz (200 g) ground mixed pork and veal; 2 tablespoons brandy; ground mace; 12 oz (375 g) puff pastry; egg wash (1 egg yolk mixed with a little cold water)

Cut the rabbit into eight pieces and marinate for 48 hours in a mixture of wine, bay leaves, onions, salt and pepper.

Dry the meat, dust it with seasoned flour and fry in the butter until brown. Cook the marinade until reduced by half and add it to the meat. Add the brown sauce and mushrooms, cover and cook for 1½ hours. Cool the mixture and take the meat off the bones.

Combine the ground pork and veal, brandy, mace, salt and pepper and roll into twelve balls. Arrange the rabbit meat, sauce and meatballs in a pie dish, cover with the rolled-out pastry and brush it with the egg wash. Bake in an oven preheated to 375°F (190°C) for 30–45 minutes or until the pastry is golden brown.

G

Grouse Casserole with Dumplings

Serves 6: 2 mature grouse; 1¼ cups (10 fl oz) chicken stock; 12 oz (375 g) lean chuck steak or round steak; 2 tablespoons vegetable oil; 1 large onion, thinly sliced; salt and freshly ground black pepper; 3 sprigs parsley; 1 bay leaf; 1 sprig thyme; ½ cup (4 fl oz) port or red wine; freshly grated nutmeg
Liver Dumplings: 3 tablespoons grouse or goose fat or melted butter; 3 eggs, lightly beaten; ½ cup (4½ oz) fine matzo meal; reserved grouse liver, finely chopped; salt to taste; 1 teaspoon snipped chives

Broiled Quails

Guinea Fowl en Papillote

Quarter the grouse, trim away the wing tips and backbones and reserve the livers. Simmer the bones in the chicken stock for 30 minutes.

Cut the steak across the grain into ½-in (1-cm) slices. Heat the oil and brown the steak quickly. Remove the steak from the pan, add the grouse and lightly brown the meaty side of the quarters. Add the onion and turn until lightly coated with the pan juices.

Layer the grouse, steak and onion in a casserole, seasoning each layer lightly with salt and black pepper. Tie the herbs together to form a bouquet garni and bury it in the casserole. Strain the stock, season to taste and pour a scant cup over the grouse. Add the port or wine and a light sprinkling of nutmeg. Cover tightly and bake in an oven preheated to 300°F (150°C) for 1 hour.

To make the dumplings, mix the cooled melted fat with the eggs. Put the matzo meal into a bowl with the salt. Make a well in the center, then pour in the egg, liver and chive mixture and mix until well blended. Chill for 30 minutes, then form into balls.

Arrange the dumplings on top of the meat, replace the lid, and cook for another hour. Remove the lid for the last 10 minutes to allow the top to brown. Discard the bouquet garni before serving.

Grouse Pie

Serves 4-6: Swag Pastry: 2 cups (250 g) all purpose flour; ¼ teaspoon salt; ¼ teaspoon cayenne pepper; 10 tablespoons (5 oz) butter; 1½ teaspoons lemon juice; 1½ tablespoons ice water
1 mature grouse; 8 oz (250 g) stewing steak, cut into ¾-in (2-cm) cubes; 2 tablespoons all purpose flour; salt and freshly ground black pepper; 2 slices bacon, with rind removed, cut into strips; 2-3 hard-cooked eggs, quartered; 1 medium-size onion, chopped; 4 oz (125 g) mushrooms, sliced; ½ cup (4 fl oz) beef stock; 2 teaspoons tomato paste

To prepare the pastry, sift the flour, salt and cayenne into a mixing bowl. Cut the butter into small pieces and rub into the flour. Mix to a firm dough with the lemon juice and water. Chill for 30 minutes.

Cut the grouse into eight pieces, trimming away the backbones and wing tips and removing as many small bones as possible. Dust the grouse and steak with the flour, season generously with salt and black pepper and arrange in a deep pie dish with the bacon, eggs, onion and mushrooms.

Mix the stock with the tomato paste and pour into the dish.

Roll out the pastry to cover a pie dish and trim the edges. Cut a vent in the top of the pie and decorate with pastry leaves. Bake in an oven preheated to 500°F (260°C) for 20 minutes. Reduce the oven temperature to 400°F (200°C), cover the pastry with aluminum foil or waxed paper and bake for 1¼ hours longer.

Guinea Fowl en Papillote

Serves 4: 2 guinea fowl, halved and trimmed; salt and freshly ground black pepper; 1 egg white, lightly beaten; 2 tablespoons finely chopped parsley
Sauce: 4 medium-size carrots, thinly sliced; 1 cup (8 fl oz) veal stock or chicken stock; 8 scallions, chopped; 4 oz (125 g) button mushrooms, halved; 1 cup (8 fl oz) champagne or dry white wine; 1 tablespoon butter; 1 tablespoon all purpose flour; ½ cup (4 fl oz) cream; white pepper

Season the guinea fowl with salt and pepper and steam over simmering water for 20 minutes, until just tender.

Meanwhile, to prepare the sauce, poach the carrots in the stock for 4-5 minutes, until they begin to soften. Add the scallions and mushrooms and simmer for 1 minute. Strain the vegetables and reserve.

Add the champagne to the stock and bring rapidly to the boil. Reduce the heat. Work the butter into the flour and whisk small pieces into the stock until it has a light coating consistency. Simmer for 2-3 minutes and remove from the heat. Add the cream, adjust the seasoning and reserve.

Cut four oval-shaped pieces of paper large enough to contain the birds and allow for securing the edges. Make a fold across the center.

Remove the skin and bones from the guinea fowl. Brush the paper with oil and spread out on baking trays. Place one portion of guinea fowl on one half of each piece of paper and divide the reserved vegetables from the sauce between the parcels. Brush the edges of the paper with egg white, spoon the sauce over the birds and sprinkle with a little parsley. Fold the top half of the paper over the bird, matching the paper edges together. Prepare the parcels one by one or the egg white will dry. Roll to seal, crimping or pleating where necessary. Bake for 10-15 minutes in an

oven preheated to 400°F (200°C) until the paper is puffed and crisp. Serve the parcels individually on hot plates.

Note: When sealing the parcels, any particularly stubborn spots can be "fixed" with a paper clip, peg or pin. Remove the hardware before serving!

Guinea Fowl Royale

Serves 4: 3 tablespoons butter; 2 tablespoons vegetable oil; 2 medium-size onions, halved and sliced; 1 medium-size green bell pepper, seeded and sliced; 1 medium-size red bell pepper, seeded and sliced; 2 medium-size carrots, thinly sliced; 2 stalks celery, sliced; 2 guinea fowl, quartered; salt and freshly ground black pepper; juice and finely grated peel of 1 lemon; ½ cup (4 fl oz) dry white wine; ½ cup (4 fl oz) port

Heat the butter and oil in a flameproof casserole. Mix the vegetables together and fry very gently in the fat until they begin to soften but are not brown. Lift the vegetables from the pan with a slotted spoon and set aside. Add the guinea fowl to the casserole and turn in the pan juices, adding a little more butter if necessary. Cook gently until they begin to color slightly. Season with salt and black pepper. Add the lemon juice and peel with the wine and port. Cover and simmer very gently for 35-40 minutes, until the birds are tender. Lift them from the casserole, arrange on a heated serving dish and keep hot.

Sprinkle the reserved vegetables lightly with salt and pepper, return them to the casserole and simmer for a few minutes until they are heated through but still crisp. Adjust the seasoning and spread the vegetables around the guinea fowl before spooning the sauce over the birds.

H

Hare Stew

Serves 4-6: 2 lb (1 kg) hare or rabbit meat cut into cubes; 4 tablespoons (2 oz) butter; 1 large onion, chopped; 2 cups (16 fl oz) beef stock; 2 tablespoons tomato puree; 2 bay leaves; 8 juniper berries, crushed; ½ teaspoon crushed caraway seeds; ½ teaspoon dried thyme; 2 tablespoons paprika; salt and freshly ground black pepper; 1 cup (8 fl oz) sour cream

Guinea Fowl Royale (see page 239)

In a heavy-lidded casserole, lightly sauté the meat in the butter. Add the onion and fry until it is soft and transparent, then mix in the stock, tomato puree, bay leaves, juniper berries, caraway seeds, thyme, paprika, salt and pepper. Cover and simmer over low heat for 50 minutes. Add the cream, mix well and simmer gently for a further 5 minutes. If necessary, adjust seasoning. This is traditionally served with potato dumplings, lettuce salad, apple and cranberry compote.

Hare with Prune Sauce

Serves 4–6: 1 hare, disjointed; 4 tablespoons (2 oz) butter, melted; 2 oz (60 g) fresh breadcrumbs; salt and freshly ground black pepper
Sauce: 8 oz (250 g) prunes, pitted; 2 oz (60 g) ground almonds; 1½ cups (12 fl oz) dry red wine; ½ cup (4 fl oz) beef stock; 2 tablespoons wine vinegar; ¼ teaspoon cinnamon; 1 teaspoon sugar; salt and pepper

Brush the pieces of hare liberally with the butter and roll in the breadcrumbs. Season with salt and black pepper and place in a casserole. Cook, uncovered, in an oven preheated to 350°F (180°C) for 20 minutes while you prepare the sauce.

Puree the prunes in a blender or food processor. Add the ground almonds and 1 cup of the wine, blend thoroughly and pour into a saucepan. Simmer over gentle heat, gradually adding the remaining ingredients. Season with salt and pepper to taste.

Pour the sauce over the hare. Cover and simmer for 1–1¼ hours, or until the hare is tender. Serve from the casserole or transfer to a heated serving dish.

Hare with Sour Cream Sauce

Serves 6: 1 saddle of hare, larded with strips of pork fat; 1 teaspoon salt; 1 teaspoon paprika; all purpose flour; 8 tablespoons (4 oz) butter; 2 cups (16 fl oz) sour cream; ½ cup (4 fl oz) beef stock; ¼ cup (2 fl oz) vinegar; 1 bay leaf; ½ teaspoon dried thyme; juice of ½ lemon; 1 tablespoon capers; 1 tablespoon beurre manié (see page 387)

Rub the larded saddle of hare with salt and paprika and sprinkle it generously with

Hare with Prune Sauce

flour. Brown on all sides in the heated butter in a roasting pan. Pour over the hot sour cream, beef stock and vinegar. Add the bay leaf and thyme.

Roast in an oven preheated to 375°F (190°C) for approximately 1 hour, or until tender, depending on the age of the hare. Baste every 15 minutes. Remove the hare and keep warm. Strain the pan juices and add the lemon juice and capers. Stir in the beurre manié. Bring the mixture to a boil and serve separately with the roast hare.

Honeyed Rabbit ⭐

Serves 4: 1 rabbit, cut into serving pieces; juice of 2 lemons; 3 tablespoons honey; 6 tablespoons all purpose flour; ½ teaspoon white pepper; 1 teaspoon salt; 1½ tablespoons sesame seeds; 1 teaspoon dried tarragon; 3 tablespoons butter; 3 tablespoons olive oil; watercress or scallion curls

Put the rabbit into a shallow dish. Mix the lemon juice and honey together in a small pan, heating gently until the honey has dissolved. Pour the mixture over the rabbit, turning each piece until well coated. Marinate for 1-2 hours, turning the rabbit occasionally.

Mix the flour with the pepper, salt, sesame seeds and tarragon. Spread over a sheet of paper. Lift each rabbit piece from the marinade, draining off any excess liquid. Coat with the seasoned flour.

Melt the butter with the oil in a heavy-based, flameproof casserole. Fry the rabbit, turning each piece until evenly browned. Drizzle the remaining marinade over the rabbit, cover and bake in an oven preheated to 350°F (180°C) for 30 minutes. Remove the lid and cook for 30 minutes longer or until tender, basting occasionally with the pan juices. Transfer to a heated dish and garnish before serving.

Hunter's Hare

Serves 4-6: 1½ lb (750 g) hare; 6 juniper berries; 4 cloves; 1 small garlic clove, unpeeled; salt and freshly ground black pepper; 1 cup (8 fl oz) red wine; 6 oz (185 g) bacon; 1 tablespoon oil; 2 large onions, coarsely chopped; 1 tablespoon Hungarian paprika; 1½ teaspoons dried mixed herbs; 12 small white onions; sour cream (optional)

Put the hare into a saucepan with the juniper berries, cloves, garlic and ½ teaspoon

each of salt and black pepper. Add the wine and just enough cold water to cover the meat. Simmer the hare gently for 30-40 minutes, then remove from the heat and cool slightly in the cooking liquid. Remove the hare from the pan and reserve the stock. Cut the meat into cubes and set aside.

Fry the bacon in a pan over moderate heat until the fat starts to run, adding a little oil if there is insufficient fat. Fry the chopped onions until golden. Reduce the heat a little and add the hare. Sprinkle with the paprika and herbs and transfer to a casserole. Set aside.

Bring the reserved liquid to the boil, adjust the seasoning and strain into the casserole. Cover and bake in an oven preheated to 350°F (180°C) for 30 minutes. Add the white onions and cook for 30-40 minutes longer, or until the hare is tender. Adjust the seasoning and serve very hot. Offer the sour cream separately.

J

Jugged Hare

Serves 4-6: 1 hare; 2 tablespoons Cognac; 2 tablespoons olive oil; salt and pepper; 1 onion, thinly sliced; dry red wine; 8 oz (250 g) bacon, diced; 2 tablespoons (1 oz) butter; 20 small white onions; 2 tablespoons all purpose flour; bouquet garni; 20 cooked mushrooms; croutons

If possible, obtain a fresh hare and save the blood and the liver. Cut the hare into serving pieces and place in a bowl with the Cognac, oil, a little salt and pepper and the onion. Cover with dry red wine. Allow to stand in a cool place for several hours, preferably overnight.

Cook the bacon in butter in a large heavy-based saucepan. Drain the bacon as soon as it browns and put to one side. Sauté the onions in the butter-bacon fat mixture. Drain the hare, add to the butter and brown well.

Sprinkle over the flour and cook until lightly browned. Add sufficient wine marinade to cover. Add the bouquet garni, cover the pan and simmer gently for 40-45 minutes. Add the mushrooms and simmer a further 5 minutes. Transfer the hare to a warm serving dish. Spoon the mushrooms, reserved bacon and onions around the hare. Stir the reserved blood and liver into

the sauce and cook for 2-3 minutes. Strain the sauce over the hare and vegetables. Serve garnished with croutons.

M

Mango Quails

Serves 8: 16 quails; salt and freshly ground black pepper; 2 tablespoons (1 oz) butter; 2 tablespoons vegetable oil; 1 small garlic clove, peeled; 1 medium-size onion, finely chopped; 1 large or 2 small fresh mangoes, pitted and sliced, or 15-oz (425-g) can sliced mangoes; 1½ teaspoons very finely grated lemon peel; 2 whole cloves; ¼ teaspoon cinnamon; ¼ teaspoon ground coriander; 1½ teaspoons all purpose flour; ¾ cup (6 fl oz) chicken stock; 2-3 tablespoons lemon juice; ¾ cup (6 fl oz) cream; hard-cooked quail eggs or thin lemon slices for garnish

Season the quails inside and out with salt and black pepper, then secure the wings to the body with cocktail picks.

Heat the butter and oil in a skillet and sauté the garlic clove without browning for 2 minutes, to flavor the fat. Discard the garlic and lightly brown the quails on all sides, cooking only a few at a time. Transfer to a casserole large enough to hold them upright without crowding.

Add the onion to the skillet and sauté over low heat until transparent. Add the mangoes and fry with the onion for 2 minutes, turning once or twice. Using a slotted spoon, transfer the mangoes and onion to the casserole, spreading the mixture over and between the quails.

Add the lemon peel and cloves to the skillet and sprinkle with the cinnamon, coriander and flour. Stir until blended into the pan juices, then cook for 1 minute. Gradually add the chicken stock and 2 tablespoons of the lemon juice, stirring constantly until the sauce is smooth. Simmer for 1 minute, adjust the seasoning and, if desired, add a little more lemon juice. Pour the sauce over the birds, cover and simmer for 30-35 minutes, until the quails are tender.

Carefully lift the birds from the casserole, arrange on a heated serving dish and keep hot. Bring the sauce quickly to the boil, reduce the heat, stir in the cream and simmer for 1-2 minutes. Adjust the seasoning before pouring the sauce over the quails. Garnish with quail eggs or lemon slices.

Mango Quails (see page 241)

Paprika Hare

Marinated Roast Quails

Serves 4: half quantity game marinade (see page 253); 8 quails; 8 oz (250 g) pâté; 4 tablespoons (2 oz) butter; 8 small slices of ham fat; 1¼ cups (10 fl oz) dry white wine; 2 tablespoons lemon juice; 3 tablespoons redcurrant jelly; salt and white pepper; lightly fried quail eggs or watercress for garnish

Put the quails into a dish, pour the marinade over and let stand for 24 hours. Lift the quails from the marinade, drain and pat dry thoroughly.

Stuff the birds with the pâté, about 2 tablespoons to each bird, and secure the openings with cocktail picks. Melt the butter in a deep, heavy-based roasting dish until foaming. Add the quails, turning in the butter until they are browned on all sides. Arrange the quails, breast side up, compactly in the dish and cover each breast with a piece of ham fat. Add ¾ cup (6 fl oz) of the wine and the lemon juice to the pan.

Roast the birds in an oven preheated to 400°F (200°C) for 15–20 minutes, or until tender. Baste the quails frequently with the pan juices and discard the ham fat 5 minutes or so before the end of the roasting time. Remove the birds from the pan, discard the picks and keep hot on a heated serving dish.

Skim any fat from the surface of the pan juices. Add the remaining wine with the redcurrant jelly and bring to the boil. Gently boil until the sauce has reduced and thickened slightly. Adjust the seasoning and spoon a little of the sauce over each bird. Garnish with quail eggs or watercress.

Note: The game marinade can be kept in the refrigerator for future use.

P

Paprika Hare

Serves 4: 1½ teaspoons salt; 3-4 teaspoons Hungarian paprika; meat of 1 hare, sliced; 2 tablespoons goose fat or butter; 2 large onions, coarsely chopped; 1-1½ cups (8-12 fl oz) water; 1 lb (500 g) noodles; 1 tablespoon vegetable oil; 1 tablespoon butter or olive oil; 1 cup (8 fl oz) sour cream

Mix the salt with the paprika in a large paper bag. Shake the slices of hare in the bag until coated on all sides.

Melt the fat or butter in a heavy-based pan and quickly sauté the onions until golden. Reduce the heat a little and brown the hare slices on all sides. Add 1 cup of the water, shake the pan and cover tightly. Simmer gently for 40–50 minutes, adding a little more water from time to time if the hare looks dry. Towards the end of cooking time, boil the noodles in boiling salted water with the oil added until tender. Strain and toss with the butter or oil. Keep hot while you finish the sauce.

When the hare is cooked, pour the sour cream into the pan. Stir the ingredients together and adjust the seasoning. Serve very hot on the bed of noodles.

Partridge Pie

Serves 6: Cream Cheese Pastry: 2 cups (8 oz) all purpose flour; ½ teaspoon salt; 4 tablespoons (2 oz) butter; 2 oz (60 g) cream cheese; 3–4 tablespoons ice water; lightly beaten egg
3 roasted partridges; 1½ tablespoons butter; 1½ tablespoons vegetable oil; 1 lb (500 g) lean stewing veal, cut into small dice; salt and freshly ground black pepper; 4 oz (125 g) lean ham, cut into chunky pieces; 4 oz (125 g) trimmed and sliced button mushrooms; 2 tablespoons finely snipped chives; 1½ tablespoons finely chopped parsley; 2 teaspoons dry mustard; ½ cup (4 fl oz) chicken stock; ½ cup (4 fl oz) medium dry sherry; 1 small egg, lightly beaten

Marinated Roast Quails

Sift the flour and salt into a mixing bowl. Cut the butter and cheese into small pieces and rub into the flour until the mixture resembles fine breadcrumbs. Add 3 tablespoons of water and mix quickly with one hand to form a dough. Use more water if the dough is dry and crumbling. Knead lightly, shape into a ball, wrap in plastic wrap and chill until required.

Slice the meat from the partridges and cut into bite-size pieces. Put the meat in a mixing bowl and set aside.

Melt the butter and oil in a skillet and when the fat is sizzling, add the veal and fry, turning occasionally, for 5 minutes, or until the meat is lightly browned. Season the veal, then add the ham and mushrooms, and cook for 1 minute.

Mix the veal mixture and the herbs with the partridge meat. Blend the mustard smoothly with the stock and sherry, then pour it over the partridge and mix well. Spoon the filling into a deep, medium-size pie dish and put to one side.

Roll the pastry to a circle about ¾ in (2 cm) larger than the top of the pie dish. Cut a ½-in (1-cm) strip around the dough and press the strip onto the rim of the dish. Moisten the pastry strip with cold water, cover the dish with the pastry and press firmly to form a good seal. Trim and crimp the edges. Decorate the top of the pie with leaves made from the pastry trimmings, make a small slit in the top with a sharp knife and brush all the pastry with the beaten egg. Bake the pie in an oven preheated to 350°F (180°C) for 50 minutes or until the pastry is crisp and golden.

Partridges with Chestnuts and Red Cabbage

Serves 4: 8 oz (250 g) chestnuts; salt; 2 tablespoons (1 oz) butter; 2 tablespoons vegetable oil; 4 oz (125 g) bacon, cut into small dice; 4 partridges; freshly ground black pepper; approximately 1½ lb (750 g) shredded red cabbage; 1 small onion, finely chopped; 1½ tablespoons drained capers; 1¾ cups (14 fl oz) dry white wine

Carefully make small slits in the shells of the chestnuts, drop them into a pan of boiling salted water and boil for 15 minutes. Drain the chestnuts and remove their shells and inner skins while they are still hot.

Melt the butter and oil in a large skillet and lightly brown the diced bacon. Remove from the pan and reserve. Add the par-

tridges to the pan and brown lightly on all sides. Remove from the pan and season with salt and black pepper.

Mix the cabbage with the onion and capers, add to the skillet and turn until lightly coated with the pan juices. Season lightly and pack half the mixture over the base of a casserole large enough to hold the partridges in one layer. Arrange the partridges, breast sides up, on the cabbage. Add the chestnuts and bacon and cover with the remaining cabbage mixture. Pour the wine over, cover the casserole with a sheet of aluminum foil and the lid and simmer for 1½–2 hours, or until the birds are tender when pierced with a fork.

Pheasant Ballottine

Serves 6–8: 2 young pheasants; freshly ground black pepper; ¼ teaspoon ground allspice; 3 tablespoons (1½ oz) butter; ¾ cup (6 fl oz) sherry; 15-oz (425-g) can peeled tomatoes; 10 slices prosciutto
Stuffing: 2 tablespoons (1 oz) butter; 1 large onion, finely chopped; 8 oz (250 g) ground lean veal; 1 oz (30 g) coarsely chopped pistachios; 1½ cups (4 oz) soft fresh breadcrumbs; ½ teaspoon dried marjoram; 6 oz (185 g) chicken livers, skinned and coarsely chopped; salt and pepper

Cut through the backbone of the pheasants. Pry the cut open and trim the backbone away. Flatten the birds and with a very sharp knife, remove the ribs and breastbone, saving the trimmings for stock. Place the birds on a board, cut side down, and flatten by pressing along the breast with the heel of your hand. Turn them and sprinkle with the black pepper and allspice. Set aside and make the stuffing.

To make the stuffing, melt the butter in a heavy-based pan and quickly sauté the onion until softened but not brown. Tip the contents of the pan into a mixing bowl. Add the veal, pistachios, breadcrumbs, marjoram and chicken livers. Mix thoroughly, seasoning with salt and pepper to taste.

Divide the stuffing between the birds. Sew the sides together with a poultry needle and coarse thread, pressing the pheasants back into shape by molding them around the stuffing. Tie the legs together and pin the wings into position, using heavy cocktail picks or poultry pins.

Melt the butter in a flameproof casserole large enough to hold both birds and brown them, one at a time. Start with the breasts and turn until they are evenly browned on all sides. Put the birds side by side in the casserole over low heat. Warm the sherry and pour over the pheasants. Simmer the sherry for 2–3 minutes until it begins to glaze in the pan. Crush the tomatoes and pour with the liquid from the can around the birds. Cover and bake in the center of an oven preheated to 350°F (180°C) for 45–60 minutes, depending on the size of the birds.

Carefully lift the pheasants from the casserole. Remove the thread and pins, and cover the breast of each bird with a slice of prosciutto. Arrange on a heated serving dish and keep hot. Strain the juices from the casserole into a small pan. Bring to the boil, adding a little more sherry if the sauce is too thick. Adjust the seasoning and pour over the pheasants.

Note: As only wing and leg bones are left in the pheasants they can very easily be carved at the table. Alternatively, the birds can be sliced before coating with the sauce. If you use a very sharp knife, you can carve the birds on the serving dish without disturbing their shape, then coat with the sauce.

Pheasant in a Pot

Serves 3–4: 2 tablespoons (1 oz) butter; 1 or 2 pheasants, loosely trussed; 4 slices fatty bacon; 2 medium-size onions, halved and sliced; 2 large carrots, sliced; 2 leeks, split and sliced; 4 stalks celery, sliced; 4 sprigs parsley; salt and freshly ground black pepper; ½ cup (4 fl oz) chicken stock; 3 tablespoons dry sherry

Melt the butter in a flameproof casserole. Add the pheasants, covering the breasts with the bacon. Pack the vegetables and parsley around the sides and season lightly with salt and black pepper. Cover and cook over medium heat for a few minutes or until the vegetables start to sweat. Reduce the heat and simmer gently for 40–50 minutes or until the pheasants are tender.

Remove and discard the bacon, arrange the pheasants on a heated serving dish and keep hot. Pour the stock over the vegetables, bring to the boil and stir in the sherry. Adjust the seasoning and serve the vegetables in a separate dish.

Pheasant in Cider

Serves 4: 4 tablespoons (2 oz) butter; 2 small pheasants; juice of 1 lemon; 2 sprigs rosemary, finely chopped; 2 sprigs thyme, finely chopped; salt and freshly ground pepper; 3 cooking apples, peeled, cored and sliced; ½ teaspoon cinnamon; 1 cup (8 fl oz) cider; ¼ cup (2 fl oz) cream; finely chopped parsley for garnish

In a casserole, melt half of the butter and brown the pheasants. Remove the pheasants from the casserole and sprinkle the insides with lemon juice, rosemary, thyme, salt and pepper.

Melt the rest of the butter and lightly sauté the apples. Return the pheasants to the casserole and pour over a mixture of cinnamon, cider and cream. Cover the casserole and put it in an oven preheated to 350°F (180°C) for 50–60 minutes or until the pheasants are tender. Season to taste, split the pheasants into two lengthwise and place them on a heated serving platter. Arrange the apples around, pour the sauce over the birds and serve sprinkled with parsley.

Pheasant with Bacon and Sour Cream

Serves 4: 2 pheasants; 2 thick slices fatty bacon, halved, with rind removed; 2 tablespoons (1 oz) melted butter; 1 cup (8 fl oz) sour cream; salt and freshly ground pepper; ½ cup (4 fl oz) cream

Carefully loosen the skin over the breasts of the pheasants. Insert a piece of bacon under the skin over each breast. Pull the skin back into position and brush the birds liberally with the melted butter. Fold the wings under the body of the birds, tie the legs together and put them into a casserole.

Roast, uncovered, in an oven preheated to 350°F (180°C) for 15 minutes, or until the birds begin to brown. Pour the sour cream over the pheasants and season lightly with salt and black pepper. Cover and cook for 40–55 minutes longer.

Transfer the birds to a heated serving dish and keep hot. Stir the cream into the pan juices. Simmer gently until the sauce has thickened, adjust the seasoning and serve with the pheasants.

Pheasant with Bacon and Sour Cream

Pheasant with Peaches

Serves 4: 2 pheasants; salt and freshly ground black pepper; 2 tablespoons (1 oz) butter; 2 tablespoons oil; 4 slices bacon, halved, with rind removed; 4 large fresh peaches, poached (see Note) or two 15-oz (425-g) cans peach halves, with juice reserved; 2 tablespoons dry sherry or brandy; finely grated peel of 1 orange; juice of 1 lemon; 1 bay leaf; 1½ teaspoons cornstarch

Lightly season the pheasants inside and out with salt and black pepper. Tuck the wings under the body, secure with toothpicks and tie the legs together.

Heat the butter and oil in a heavy, flameproof roasting dish. Brown one bird at a time, turning frequently until golden on all sides. Remove the pan from the heat, set the pheasants side by side and lay the bacon over the breasts. Mix 1½ cups (12 fl oz) of the reserved peach juice with the sherry or brandy, orange peel and lemon juice. Push the bay leaf between the birds and pour the juices over.

Roast the birds in an oven preheated to 350°F (180°C) for 45–60 minutes or until the juices run clear from a thigh pierced with a fine skewer. Take the pheasants from the dish and quarter them, removing and discarding the spine bones. Kitchen scissors or shears make this an easy job. Arrange the pheasants on a heated serving dish and keep hot.

Add the prepared peach halves to the pan, and mix them into the pan juices for a few minutes until they are very hot. Lift them carefully with a slotted spoon and arrange with the pheasants. Mix the cornstarch to a smooth paste with 2 tablespoons of water. Add to the pan juices, stirring constantly until the sauce has thickened and cleared. Adjust the seasoning, discard the bay leaf and spoon the sauce over the pheasants.

Note: To poach fresh peaches, halve the peaches and discard the stones. Lay them in a shallow pan with 1¼ cups (10 fl oz) of water. Simmer for 2 minutes, turn the fruit and simmer for another 2 minutes. Remove the pan from the heat, skin the peaches and set them aside until ready to use.

Pigeon Pie

Serves 4–6: ½ cup (4 fl oz) chicken stock; 3 tablespoons dry sherry; 1 tablespoon brandy; salt and pepper; 1 quantity of Cream Cheese Pastry (see page 243); egg glaze (see Note)
Pigeon Filling: 4 tablespoons (2 oz) butter; 1 lb (500 g) lean stewing veal, cut into bite-size cubes; 4 oz (125 g) mushrooms, sliced; 4 oz (125 g) lean ham pieces, chopped; meat of 3 cooked pigeons, skinned and chopped; 2 tablespoons finely chopped parsley; 2 tablespoons Dijon mustard; salt and freshly ground black pepper

To make the filling, melt the butter in a large skillet and lightly brown the veal on all sides. Reduce the heat a little, add the mushrooms and ham, and stir the ingredients together, cooking for 2–3 minutes or until the juices start to run from the mushrooms. Remove the skillet from the heat and tip the contents into a bowl. Add the pigeon meat, parsley, mustard and seasonings, mixing together thoroughly.

Spoon the filling into a medium-size pie dish. Pour the stock, sherry and brandy into the dish and adjust the seasoning.

Set aside while you roll out the pastry to the shape of the pie dish, about 1 in (2.5 cm) larger than the overall size. Trim a ½-in (1-cm) strip from the sides of the rolled pastry. Moisten the rim of the pie dish with water and press the ribbon of dough onto the rim.

Brush the pastry-covered rim lightly with water and lift the rolled pastry onto the pie. Trim the edges with a sharp knife and crimp or pinch to seal. Use the pastry trimmings to decorate the pie. Cut a slit in the center and brush with the egg glaze. Bake the pie in an oven preheated to 350°F (180°C) for 50–55 minutes, until the pastry is golden. Serve immediately.

Note: To make the egg glaze, whisk 1 egg with a little salt.

Pigeons with Cherries ★

Serves 4: 5 tablespoons (2½ oz) butter; 4 pigeons; 1 medium-size onion, finely chopped; 2 oz (60 g) pine nuts; 1 tablespoon all purpose flour; 2 cups (16 fl oz) chicken stock; 1 bay leaf; 2 sprigs celery leaves; 1 small celery stalk, quartered; 3 sprigs parsley; salt and white pepper; 1 lb (500 g) cherries, stoned; ⅓ cup (2½ fl oz) cream; 4 round croutons for garnish

Melt 3 tablespoons of the butter in a large pan, add the pigeons and turn them in the butter until lightly browned. Remove and set aside. Add the onion to the pan and fry

Pigeons with Cherries

Quails Poached in Port

Quails with Cherry Stuffing

gently until transparent. Stir in the pine nuts and fry for 2–3 minutes until they are lightly colored. Sprinkle the flour into the pan, stir and cook for 2 minutes until straw-colored. Gradually add the stock, stirring constantly to form a smooth sauce. Simmer gently for 2–3 minutes.

Tie the bay leaf, celery leaves or celery and parsley together to make a bouquet garni and push deeply into the sauce. Season very lightly with salt and pepper and return the birds to the pan, spooning some sauce over each one. Cover and simmer for 35–40 minutes, until the pigeons are tender.

When the birds are cooked, lift them carefully from the sauce, arrange on a heated serving dish and keep hot. Discard the bouquet garni and raise the heat to bring the sauce nearly to boiling point. Allow the sauce to bubble and reduce by a quarter.

In the meantime, melt the remaining butter in a skillet and fry the cherries for 3–4 minutes until they are very hot. Add the cherries with their pan juices and the cream to the sauce. Bring back almost to boiling point and adjust the seasoning before pouring over the pigeons. Serve garnished with the croutons.

Q

Quails Poached in Port

Serves 6: 12 quails; 1 cup (8 fl oz) ruby port; 1 cup (8 fl oz) strongly flavored veal or game stock (see Note)

Place the cleaned quails in a casserole just large enough for them to fit closely together. Add the port and stock. Cover and poach on HIGH (100%) for 3 minutes, then turn and rearrange. Microwave on MEDIUM (50%) for 8–10 minutes until the quails are tender. (Non-carousel ovens: Give the dish a quarter-turn every 3 minutes.) The poaching liquid can be transferred to a saucepan and rapidly boiled until reduced to about one-third of its original volume, or use only 1 cup (8 fl oz) of the liquid and thicken it with 1 tablespoon cornstarch. Boil on HIGH (100%), stirring several times, for 3–4 minutes.

Note: Well-reduced stock is needed to give the strong, rich taste required.

Quails with Cherry Stuffing

Serves 4: Cherry Jelly: 15-oz (425-g) can black cherries; juice of 1 lemon; 1½ teaspoons unflavored gelatin
8 quails; 1½ teaspoons salt; freshly ground black pepper; 4 tablespoons (2 oz) butter, melted
Stuffing: 6 tablespoons (1 oz) fresh breadcrumbs; ⅛ teaspoon dried marjoram; 1 pork sausage, skinned; 1 truffle, finely chopped (optional); 1 egg, lightly beaten; salt and pepper

To make the cherry jelly, drain the syrup from the cherries into a measuring cup. Reserve twenty cherries for the stuffing. Add enough lemon juice to the cherry syrup to make 1 cup of liquid. Pour 2 tablespoons of the cherry juice into a small bowl and sprinkle the gelatin over the surface. Let stand for 2–3 minutes. Stand the bowl in a saucepan containing a little hot water and heat gently until the gelatin has melted. Strain into the remaining cherry liquid, pour into a shallow dish and cover. Refrigerate until set.

To prepare the stuffing, mix the breadcrumbs with the marjoram and sausage until crumbly and well blended. Chop the twenty cherries reserved from the jelly and add with the truffle, mixing lightly together. Add only enough egg to bind the ingredients. The mixture should not be too wet.

Season the quails inside and out with the salt and black pepper. Divide the stuffing between the quails and very loosely secure each cavity with toothpicks. Pin the wings to the sides of the bird and loosely tie the legs together. Arrange the birds, breast side up, in a roasting dish and pour the melted butter over them. Roast just above the center of an oven preheated to 475°F (240°C) for 15–20 minutes, or until the birds are tender.

To serve, remove the pins and trussing strings, arrange the quails on a hot serving platter and surround with the vegetables. Serve the jelly separately, chopping it lightly before putting it in a serving bowl.

Note: To make Duck with Cherry Stuffing: double the stuffing ingredients, making the cherry jelly in the same way. Preheat the oven to 350°F (180°C). Spoon the cherry stuffing into a 4-lb (2-kg) duck. Prick the skin and close the cavity. Cook on a rack in a roasting dish for 1½–2 hours, until tender.

Quails with Herb Sauce

Serves 4: 2–3 tablespoons goose fat or butter; 8 quails; salt and white pepper; 1 sprig thyme; 1 sprig marjoram; 1 sprig rosemary; 1 bay leaf; ¾ cup (6 fl oz) dry white wine; ½ cup (4 fl oz) chicken stock or veal stock; 1 tablespoon very finely chopped parsley; 1 tablespoon butter; 1 tablespoon all purpose flour

Heat the fat or butter in a flameproof casserole and quickly brown the quails on all sides. Season lightly with salt and pepper. Tie the thyme, marjoram, rosemary and bay leaf together to form a bouquet garni. Add the herbs to the pan with the wine and stock. Bring to the boil. Cover tightly, using aluminum foil or paper to make a good seal. Cook in an oven preheated to 350°F (180°C) for 35–45 minutes.

Carefully transfer the quails to a heated serving dish and keep hot. Discard the bouquet garni and stir the parsley into the liquid. Work the butter and flour together and add in small pieces to the pan, whisking between each addition, until the sauce has a light coating consistency. Adjust the seasoning and spoon over the birds.

R

Rabbit with Maple Sauce

Serves 4: 2 tablespoons butter or goose fat; 1 tablespoon vegetable oil; 6 scallions, sliced; 4 slices bacon, with rind removed; 1 rabbit, cut into serving pieces; 1 tablespoon all purpose flour; salt and freshly ground black pepper; 1 teaspoon cayenne pepper; 1 garlic clove, crushed; 2 tablespoons lemon juice; 3 tablespoons water; 3 tablespoons maple syrup; 3 tablespoons cream

Heat the butter or goose fat and oil in a flameproof casserole. Toss the scallions with the bacon in the hot fat until lightly browned. Push the mixture to one side of the pan and lightly brown the rabbit pieces on all sides. Distribute the scallions and bacon evenly between the rabbit pieces and sprinkle with the flour. Turn the rabbit in the pan juices until the flour has been absorbed. Season with the salt, black pepper and cayenne pepper. Add the garlic, lemon juice and water. Stir together and trickle the maple syrup over the rabbit. Cover and simmer over low heat for 1–1¼

Roast Saddle of Hare (see page 250)

hours, or until the rabbit is tender.

Transfer the rabbit to a heated serving dish and keep hot. Stir the cream into the pan and heat through without boiling. Adjust the seasoning and spoon the sauce over the rabbit.

Rabbit with Prunes in Cider Sauce

Serves 6: 6 oz (185 g) prunes, pitted; 3 cups (24 fl oz) dry cider; 6 rabbit joints (hindquarters and saddle pieces); 4 tablespoons (2 oz) butter; 1 lb (500 g) scallions, finely chopped; fresh thyme; salt and freshly ground black pepper; 6 tablespoons Calvados, warmed

Marinate the prunes in the cider for several hours. Drain.

Wipe the rabbit joints. Melt half the butter in a flameproof casserole dish and fry the rabbit pieces until evenly browned on all sides. Add the scallions and the thyme and cook gently until the scallions are soft, but not brown. Season with salt and freshly ground black pepper. Pour in the warmed Calvados and ignite. When the flames have died down, pour in the cider and simmer very gently, uncovered, until the rabbit is very tender, about 45 minutes.

While the rabbit is cooking, sauté the prunes gently in the rest of the butter, taking care to keep turning them so that they do not burn. When the rabbit is cooked, transfer the pieces to a serving dish with the prunes and keep warm. Increase the heat under the casserole dish and reduce the liquid in which the rabbit has been cooking until it is a rich consistency. Correct the seasoning. Pour over the rabbit pieces and the prunes and serve.

Roast Grouse

Serves 4: 4 young grouse, each weighing about 12 oz (375 g); salt and freshly ground black pepper; 4 tablespoons (2 oz) butter; 4 slices fatty bacon; 2 teaspoons all purpose flour; 1 cup (8 fl oz) rich game stock or beef stock; 1 tablespoon brandy; watercress for garnish

Reserve the livers and dry the grouse thoroughly with paper towels. Season inside and out with salt and black pepper and place a tablespoon of butter inside each bird. Fasten a bacon slice securely over each grouse, fold the wings close to the body and tie the legs loosely together.

Place the birds on a rack set over a roasting dish and cook in an oven preheated to 425°F (220°C) for 25-30 minutes, a little longer if the birds are large. Baste frequently. Drop the livers into the roasting dish 10 minutes before the end of the cooking time and discard the bacon.

Arrange the grouse on a heated serving dish, removing the trussing string, and keep them hot. Mash the livers into the pan juices in the roasting dish. Stir in the flour and cook over low heat for 1 minute. Gradually add the stock and stir constantly until the gravy is lightly thickened. Add the brandy, adjust the seasoning and simmer for 2-3 minutes. Garnish the grouse with watercress and strain the gravy into a sauceboat.

Roast Guinea Fowl Jerez

Serves 4: 2 oz (60 g) chicken livers, trimmed; salt; 2 guinea fowl; 6 tablespoons (3 oz) butter; 4 slices ham; 4 oz (125 g) mushrooms, sliced; 1 tablespoon all purpose flour; ½ cup (4 fl oz) chicken stock; ½ cup (4 fl oz) dry sherry; freshly ground black pepper

Season the chicken livers lightly with salt and divide between the cavities of the birds. Fold the wings under the body and tie the legs loosely together. Put the birds on a rack set over a roasting dish. Melt 4 tablespoons (2 oz) of the butter and pour over the birds. Roast in an oven preheated to 500°F (260°C) for 25-30 minutes, or until cooked.

Spread the slices of ham over the base of a broiler pan, cover with the sliced mushrooms and dot with the remaining butter, cut into tiny pieces. Shortly before the fowl are cooked, preheat the broiler and cook the ham and mushrooms for 5-6 minutes. Transfer the ham to a heated serving dish, arrange the guinea fowl on top and surround with the mushrooms. Keep warm while you finish the sauce.

Stir the flour into the pan juices in the roasting dish and cook on top of the stove until lightly browned. Gradually add the stock and sherry, stirring constantly until the sauce has thickened. Simmer for 2 minutes, adjust the seasoning and spoon over the guinea fowl.

Roast Guinea Fowl with Brie

Serves 4: 2 guinea fowl; freshly ground black pepper; 2 tablespoons (1 oz) butter; 4 oz (125 g) Brie; juice of 1 lemon; 1 teaspoon finely chopped fresh marjoram or ¼ teaspoon dried marjoram; ½ cup (4 fl oz) port; 3 tablespoons cream; salt

Season the guinea fowl inside and out with pepper. Melt the butter until sizzling, then lightly brown the birds on all sides. Remove from the pan and set aside.

Mash the Brie with a fork and mix with the lemon juice and marjoram. Put half of the cheese mixture into the cavity of each bird. Fasten the wings to the body with poultry pins but do not close the cavity. Put the birds in a roasting dish, pour over the port and cover loosely with aluminum foil. Roast in an oven preheated to 400°F (200°C) for 45-50 minutes.

Remove the dish from the oven and halve the guinea fowl, discarding the spinal bones. Transfer to a heated serving dish. Stir the port into the pan juices, on top of the stove, and simmer for 2-3 minutes. Add the cream and, stirring constantly, reheat without boiling until the sauce is smooth and well blended. Adjust the seasoning, adding salt if necessary. Spoon the sauce over the birds and serve immediately.

Note: Pheasant can be prepared in the same way. Roast for 45-50 minutes in a hot oven.

Roast Partridge

Serves 4: 4 young partridges, trussed; salt and freshly ground black pepper; 8 fatty bacon slices, with rind removed; 4 tablespoons (2 oz) butter, melted; 2 tablespoons redcurrant jelly; ½ cup (4 fl oz) port; parsley for garnish

Season the partridges with salt and black pepper and secure two bacon slices over each bird. Arrange the birds breast side up in a roasting dish and pour the butter over. Roast in an oven preheated to 400°F (200°C) for 25-30 minutes, basting the partridges two or three times. Discard the bacon for the last 5 minutes of the cooking time.

Transfer the birds to a serving platter and keep warm. Skim excess fat from the juices in the roasting dish. Stir in the redcurrant jelly and the port, and boil rap-

Roast Partridge

idly for 2–3 minutes. Season to taste. Garnish the partridges lavishly with parsley and glaze with the sauce before serving.

Roast Pheasant

Serves 4: 2 pheasants; salt and freshly ground black pepper; 1 teaspoon Spanish paprika; 4 slices of fat ham, pork, or bacon; 2 tablespoons melted goose fat or butter; 3 tablespoons dry red wine; redcurrant jelly

Season the pheasants inside and out with salt and black pepper and sprinkle the paprika over the skin. Cover the breasts with the fat ham. Fold the wings under the body and tie the legs together.

Put the birds into a roasting dish, pour the melted fat over and roast in an oven preheated to 350°F (180°C) for 45–60 minutes, basting every 15 minutes with the pan juices. Remove the fat covering the breasts 10 minutes before the end of the cooking time. The birds are cooked when the juices run clear from a thigh pierced with a fine skewer.

Transfer the pheasants to a heated serving dish, halve or carve as for chicken and leave to stand in a warm place. Remove any excess fat from the roasting dish, add the wine and boil for 1–2 minutes. Adjust the seasoning and serve with the pheasants. Serve the redcurrant jelly separately.

Roast Pheasants with Wild Rice Stuffing

Serves 4: Wild Rice Stuffing: 2 oz (60 g) wild rice; ¼ teaspoon salt; 1½ tablespoons butter; 1 tablespoon finely snipped chives; 1 oz (30 g) finely chopped prosciutto; white pepper
2 pheasants; 4 tablespoons (2 oz) butter; 1 teaspoon Spanish paprika; salt and freshly ground black pepper; 2 fatty bacon slices; ⅓ cup (2½ fl oz) dry red wine; redcurrant jelly (optional)

Rinse the rice thoroughly under cold water, then put into a pan with water to cover. Simmer for 2 minutes, strain and repeat the process twice more.

Cover the rice with boiling water again, add the salt and simmer for 5 minutes. Strain and add the butter, chives and prosciutto. Season to taste, then cool.

Stuff the birds loosely and close the cavity with toothpicks. Truss the pheasants and rub the skin liberally with the butter. Sprinkle with the paprika, salt and black pepper.

Put the birds side by side in a roasting dish. Cover the breasts with the bacon and roast in an oven preheated to 400°F (200°C) for 45–60 minutes, or until the juices run clear from a thigh pierced with a fine skewer.

Transfer the birds to a heated serving dish and leave to stand for a few minutes before carving. Remove excess fat from the roasting dish, add the wine and boil rapidly for 2 minutes. Season to taste and serve with the pheasants. Accompany with redcurrant jelly if desired.

Roast Pheasant

Roast Pigeons Wonga with Banana Stuffing

Serves 4: Banana Stuffing: 2 bananas, coarsely chopped; ¾ cup (2 oz) fresh breadcrumbs; 1 oz (30 g) finely grated beef suet; 1 oz (30 g) coarsely chopped walnuts; 1 teaspoon dried mixed herbs; 1 tablespoon finely chopped parsley; 1 egg, lightly beaten; salt and pepper
4 pigeons; 1 tablespoon all purpose flour; salt and pepper; juice of 1 lemon; 2 tablespoons (1 oz) butter; ½ cup (4 fl oz) chicken stock or white wine; 1 banana, sliced and brushed with lemon juice for garnish; 12–14 walnut halves for garnish

To make the banana stuffing, mix the bananas in a bowl with the breadcrumbs, suet, walnuts, dried herbs and parsley. Add only enough of the egg to bind the ingredients together — the mixture should be fairly dry but not too crumbly. Season with salt and pepper to taste.

Lightly fill the pigeons with the stuffing, remembering that it will expand when cooked. Secure the opening with thread or poultry pins. Dredge the pigeons lightly with the flour seasoned with salt and pepper. Arrange the birds in a roasting dish with the lemon juice and butter. Cover the breasts with buttered paper and roast in an oven preheated to 400°F (200°C) for 15 minutes. Remove the paper and cook for 15–20 minutes longer, or until the birds are tender, basting them occasionally with the pan juices.

To serve, spread the accompanying vegetable on a heated serving dish and arrange the pigeons on top. Keep hot in a warm oven while you finish the sauce. Mix the stock or wine into the pan juices, stirring any sediment into the sauce. Adjust the seasoning, spoon a little sauce over each bird and serve the rest separately. Garnish the dish with the sliced banana and the walnut halves.

Roast Quails and Juniper Berry Sauce

Serves 4: 24 juniper berries, bruised; 8 quails; 8 fatty bacon slices, with rind removed; 3 tablespoons melted goose fat or butter; freshly ground black pepper; 2 teaspoons all purpose flour; 3 tablespoons beef bouillon; 3 tablespoons port; salt

Put three juniper berries into the cavity of each bird. Fasten the wings to the body and wrap each bird with bacon. Put the quails compactly in a roasting dish, pour the melted fat over and season with black pepper. Roast in an oven preheated to 400°F (200°C) for 15–20 minutes.

Transfer the quails to a heated serving dish and leave to stand in a warm place. Pour off all but 1 tablespoon of the fat from the roasting dish. Stir the flour into the pan juices and cook for 1 minute before adding the stock, port and remaining berries. Stir constantly until the gravy is smooth. Adjust the seasoning and serve with the quail.

Variation: The quails can be flavored in a variety of ways, rather than with the juniper berries. Roast them with a hot chili in the cavity, a small bunch of fresh herbs, or a piece of peeled fresh ginger.

Roast Quails with Rice

Serves 4: 8 quails; salt and freshly ground pepper; 8 bacon slices; 1½ cups (12 fl oz) meat stock; 1 onion, finely chopped; butter; ¾ cup (5 oz) rice; 1 sprig each of thyme, oregano and rosemary, finely chopped; 1 chicken liver, finely chopped; finely chopped parsley

Season the birds inside and out, cover with the bacon and roast in an oven preheated to 350°F (180°C) for 30 minutes or until cooked. Occasionally baste with stock.

In a saucepan sauté the onion in a little butter. Pour the cooking juices from the quails and the rest of the stock into the saucepan with the onion, then add the rice and herbs. Bring to the boil, then reduce the heat, cover and simmer until the rice is cooked. Season and stir in the chicken liver. Heat to cook the liver.

Spoon the rice onto a preheated serving platter, arrange the quails on top and sprinkle with parsley.

Roast Saddle of Hare

Serves 4–6: saddle and hind legs of hare; salt and freshly ground black pepper; 4 thin slices of pork or ham fat; 2 tablespoons melted goose fat or vegetable oil; ½ cup (4 fl oz) game stock or beef stock; ½ cup (4 fl oz) port; watercress for garnish
Cumberland Sauce: 1 medium-size orange; ½ cup (4 fl oz) boiling water; ½ cup (4 fl oz) redcurrant jelly; juice of ½ lemon; 1 teaspoon Dijon mustard; ⅓ cup (2½ fl oz) port

Using a sharp knife, carefully remove any shiny membrane from the hare. Position the legs close to the body and season lightly with salt and black pepper. Put the hare into a roasting dish, cover with the pork fat and pour the melted fat or oil over. Roast in an oven preheated to 400°F (200°C) for 30 minutes.

Meanwhile, prepare the sauce; remove the orange peel with a vegetable peeler and cut into a fine julienne. Blanch in boiling water until soft. Drain and refresh in cold water.

Put 3 tablespoons of orange juice into a pan with the redcurrant jelly, mustard and port. Bring rapidly to the boil, reduce the heat and simmer for 5 minutes. Cool, then add the peel. Reserve.

Mix the stock with the port and bring to the boil in a small pan. Remove the fat from the hare and discard. Pour the port mixture over and cook for 15 minutes longer.

Transfer the hare to a heated serving dish and keep hot. Reduce the pan juices rapidly until syrupy. Glaze the hare with the sauce and garnish with watercress before serving with the Cumberland sauce.

Roast Venison

Serves 4–6: 3–4 lb (1.5–2 kg) venison fillet; 1 quantity of game marinade (see page 253); 3–4 tablespoons melted goose fat or butter; 1½ tablespoons all purpose flour; ½ cup (4 fl oz) water; 3 tablespoons port; salt and white pepper

Put the venison into a bowl, pour the marinade in and refrigerate for five or six days, turning occasionally.

Remove the venison from the marinade and dry thoroughly. Strain the marinade and reserve ½ cup for the gravy, discarding the flavoring ingredients.

Stand the venison on a rack set over a roasting dish, pour the melted fat or butter over and roast in an oven preheated to 350°F (180°C) for 25 minutes/lb (50 minutes/kg). Cover the meat loosely with aluminum foil after the first 30 minutes of the cooking time. Baste the meat occasionally with the pan juices.

Transfer the cooked venison to a heated serving dish and leave to stand in a warm place while you prepare the gravy. Pour off all but 3 tablespoons of the pan juices.

Whisk the flour into the dish until well incorporated with the juices and sediment. Gradually add equal quantities of the reserved marinade and water to the pan, whisking constantly until the gravy is smooth. Add the port and season with salt and pepper to taste. Simmer for 3–4 minutes, adding more marinade and water if the gravy is too thick. Strain, spoon a little over the venison and serve the rest separately.

Roast Woodcocks with Orange Sauce

Serves 4: 4 tablespoons (2 oz) butter, softened; 4 woodcocks, trussed; salt and freshly ground black pepper; ham fat or fat bacon; juice and finely grated peel of 1 large orange; 4 slices of bread, with crusts removed, crisply fried in butter; ½ cup (4 fl oz) dry white wine; ½ cup (4 fl oz) rich game stock or chicken stock; 2 extra teaspoons butter; 1 large orange, peeled and thinly sliced for garnish

Spread the butter liberally over the woodcocks and season with salt and black pepper. Tie a piece of ham fat or bacon over each bird and place on a rack set over a roasting dish. Roast in an oven preheated to 475°F (240°C) for 12–15 minutes, basting frequently.

While the birds are cooking, blanch the orange peel for a few minutes in a little boiling water. Prepare the fried bread and arrange over the base of an ovenproof serving dish. Remove the birds from the oven and reduce the temperature to 350°F (180°C). Discard the fat or bacon, arrange the birds on the prepared bread and return them to the oven.

Add the wine and stock to the drippings in the roasting dish. Bring to the boil, then simmer for 2–3 minutes. Add the strained orange juice and season to taste. Stir the extra butter in and spoon the sauce over the birds. Garnish with the orange slices.

S

Salmis of Grouse

Serves 4: 6 tablespoons (3 oz) butter; two 1-lb (500-g) grouse; salt and freshly ground black pepper; 2 slices ham fat or fatty bacon; 1 medium-size onion, finely chopped; 1 garlic clove, finely chopped; 3 small carrots, finely chopped; 4 tablespoons all purpose flour; 1 cup (8 fl oz) chicken stock; 1 cup (8 fl oz) red wine; 2 parsley sprigs; 1 bay leaf; 1 sprig thyme; 6 oz (185 g) mushrooms, thinly sliced; 3 tablespoons port; triangular fried croutons

Place 1 tablespoon of the butter inside each bird and season inside and out with salt and black pepper. Fold the wings close to the breast and tie the legs together. Drape the ham fat or bacon over the birds and place them on a rack set over a roasting dish. Roast the birds in an oven preheated to 500°F (260°C) for 15 minutes, basting frequently and using a little extra butter if necessary.

While the birds are roasting, melt the remaining butter in a saucepan and fry the onion, garlic and carrots until just softened. Sprinkle the flour over the vegetables and cook over low heat for a minute or so, stirring occasionally. Add the stock and wine, whisking constantly to form a smooth sauce. Bring almost to the boil, then simmer for 3–4 minutes. Tie the herbs together to form a bouquet garni, add to the sauce and season lightly. Simmer for a few minutes more.

Remove the grouse from the oven and discard the fat or bacon and the trussing string. Quarter the birds, trim away the backbone and wing tips and remove the skin. Many of the small bones can also be discarded at this point. Arrange the grouse in a heatproof dish and scatter the mushrooms over.

Add the port to the simmering sauce, discard the bouquet garni and adjust the seasoning. Strain the sauce over the grouse and simmer over low heat for 10 minutes, or until the birds are just cooked through. Arrange the croutons around the salmis.

Salmis of Grouse

Salt-Baked Guinea Fowl

Serves 4: 2 guinea fowl; 6–7 lb (3–4 kg) rock salt

Tie the legs of each bird loosely together and tuck the wings under the body. Spread about 1 in (2.5 cm) of salt over the base of a flameproof casserole and heat on top of the stove for 4–5 minutes. Arrange the birds on the salt and firmly pack enough salt over and around them to bury them completely. Cover and bake in an oven preheated to 400°F (200°C) for 50 minutes. Remove the guinea fowl from the casserole, scrape off any salt which clings to them and halve or carve them before serving.

Sliced Pheasant Sautéed with Bamboo Shoots and Mustard Greens

Serves 4: 8 oz (250 g) boneless breast of pheasant (or use wild duck, domestic duck or pigeon); 3 oz (90 g) canned winter bamboo shoots, drained; 1½ oz (45 g) salted mustard root, soaked for 20 minutes; ¼ cup (2 fl oz) oil or softened lard; 2 scallions, trimmed and diced; 2 slices fresh ginger, shredded; ½ teaspoon white vinegar (optional); 1 teaspoon sesame oil (optional)
Seasoning A: 1 egg white, beaten; ¼ teaspoon salt; 1½ teaspoons sesame oil (optional); ½ teaspoon cornstarch
Seasoning B/Sauce: ½ cup (4 fl oz) chicken stock; 1 tablespoon light soy sauce; ½ teaspoon rice wine or dry sherry; ¼ teaspoon salt; pinch of white pepper; ¼ teaspoon sugar; ½ teaspoon cornstarch

Blanch the pheasant breasts in boiling water for 1 minute, drain and slice thinly, then cut into narrow shreds. Mix the meat with the seasoning A ingredients and leave to marinate for 20 minutes. Shred the bamboo shoots and the drained mustard root.

Heat the oil or lard in a wok until smoking and sauté the pheasant on high heat for 1½ minutes. Remove and sauté the bamboo shoots for 1 minute, then add the scallions and ginger and sauté briefly before returning the meat.

Add the shredded mustard root and fry for a few seconds, then pour in the premixed seasoning B/sauce ingredients and cook, stirring, until the sauce thickens.

Season with vinegar and sesame oil, if used, and transfer to a warmed serving plate.

T

Tamarillo Rabbit

Serves 4: 1 rabbit, cut into serving pieces; 2 tablespoons all purpose flour; ½ teaspoon salt; ½ teaspoon white pepper; 2–3 tablespoons butter; 1 tablespoon olive oil or vegetable oil; 1 large onion, chopped; 2 medium-size carrots, thinly sliced; 4 tamarillos, quartered; 1 cup (8 fl oz) chicken stock; 1 tablespoon honey; 1 tablespoon finely snipped chives

Dust the rabbit pieces with the flour seasoned with salt and pepper. Melt the butter in a shallow pan and lightly brown the rabbit on all sides. Transfer the pieces to a flameproof casserole. Add the oil to the butter and sauté the onion and carrots until golden. Reduce the heat and add the tamarillos, chicken stock and honey. Simmer gently for 2–3 minutes. Adjust the seasoning and pour the mixture over the rabbit. Cover and simmer for 1 hour, or until the rabbit is tender. Remove and discard the tamarillo skins as they loosen. Serve from the casserole or transfer to a heated serving dish. Sprinkle with the chives.

Tangy Braised Game Birds

Serves 4: 1 wild duck or pheasant; 1 slice bacon, finely chopped; 1 onion, finely chopped; 2 tablespoons (1 oz) butter; 2 tablespoons all purpose flour; 2 cups (16 fl oz) chicken stock; 2 tablespoons white wine; salt and pepper; ¼ cup (2 fl oz) orange juice (for duck) or redcurrant jelly (for pheasant); 10 soaked dried apricots (for duck) or 10 button mushrooms (for pheasant); triangles of toast

Place the dressed bird in a roasting pan and roast in an oven preheated to 350°F (180°C) for 20 minutes. Cut the bird into small serving pieces, then fry the bacon and onion in hot butter in a large heavy-based skillet. Stir in the flour, then add the stock and wine gradually, stirring until the sauce boils. Season with salt and pepper and add the orange juice or the redcurrant jelly.

Place the pieces of bird in the sauce and simmer gently until tender, about 45 minutes. Add the apricots or the mushrooms 10 minutes before serving and cook gently. Arrange the braised bird with the apricots

Salt-Baked Guinea Fowl

or mushrooms on a hot plate and boil the sauce rapidly until reduced by half. Pour over the braised bird and serve with small toast triangles.

Thirlmere Forest Casserole of Venison

Serves 4–6: Marinade: 1 onion, chopped; 1 carrot, chopped; ½ stalk celery, chopped; 6 peppercorns; 4 juniper berries, crushed; 2 tablespoons olive oil; red wine
2½ lb (1.25 kg) venison; 1 tablespoon olive oil; 5 oz (155 g) fatty bacon, cut into strips; 8 oz (250 g) onions, chopped; 8 oz (250 g) carrots, chopped; 8 oz (250 g) celery, chopped; 1 cup (4 oz) all purpose flour; salt; 1–2 tablespoons redcurrant jelly

Place all the marinade ingredients except the wine into a large bowl, put the venison on top and pour over enough red wine to cover the meat. Leave to marinate for 24 hours, turning occasionally.

Remove the venison from the marinade, dry it well with paper towels and cut it into 1-in (2.5-cm) cubes. Heat the oil in a skillet and add the bacon and venison. Fry on all sides to seal the meat. Add the vegetables, then the flour and stir well. Add sufficient strained marinade to almost cover the meat and vegetables, then simmer the liquid, stirring constantly, until it has thickened.

Cover the pan and cook very slowly for 2–4 hours depending upon the age of the meat. Test after 2 hours — the meat should not be chewy but it must not fall apart either. Add the redcurrant jelly to taste. Traditionally this is served with potatoes in their jackets and red cabbage.

V

Venison Braise

Serves 4–6: Game Marinade: 2 large carrots, sliced; 3 medium-size onions, sliced; 6 black peppercorns, crushed; 3 whole cloves; 3 juniper berries; 2 bay leaves, crumbled; 2 garlic cloves, quartered; 4 parsley sprigs; 4 cups (1 liter) red wine; 1½ cups (12 fl oz) olive oil; 1½ cups (12 fl oz) wine vinegar
3–4 lb (1.5–2 kg) venison haunch; 2 stalks celery; 1 sprig thyme; 2 sprigs parsley; 1 bay leaf; 3 tablespoons goose fat or vegetable oil; 2 medium-size carrots, sliced; 2 medium-size onions, sliced;

¾ cup (6 fl oz) beef stock; salt and freshly ground black pepper; 1 tablespoon tomato paste; redcurrant jelly or Cumberland sauce (see page 250); 1 tablespoon butter; 1 tablespoon all purpose flour

Trim all fat from the venison and put it into a large, shallow bowl. Combine all ingredients for the marinade. Pour over the venison and marinate for three days.

Remove the meat and dry thoroughly. Strain and reserve the marinade. Cut the leaves from the celery and tie with the thyme, parsley and bay leaf into a bouquet garni.

Heat the fat or oil in a deep flameproof casserole and brown the venison on all sides. Remove and add the sliced carrots, onions and celery. Reduce the heat, cover and cook gently until the vegetables begin to sweat.

Put the venison on top of the vegetables with the bouquet garni. Pour ½ cup of the reserved marinade and the stock over. Season to taste and bring the liquid to the boil. Cover with aluminum foil and the lid. Braise just below the center of an oven preheated to 375°F (190°C) for 2½–3 hours, or until the meat is very tender.

Transfer the venison from the pan to a heated carving dish and keep hot. Strain the cooking liquid into a saucepan and leave to stand for 1–2 minutes until the fat rises. Skim the surface or blot with paper towels. Add the tomato paste and 1 tablespoon of redcurrant jelly and simmer the gravy for 2–3 minutes. Work the butter and flour together and add to the sauce in small pieces, whisking thoroughly between each addition. Adjust the seasoning and simmer for 2 minutes. Carve the venison and arrange on a heated serving dish. Spoon a little of the gravy over the meat and serve the rest separately.

Note: The marinade can be stored in the refrigerator for later use.

Venison Pepper Stew

Serves 4–6: 2 lb (1 kg) venison (neck, shoulder or breast meat), cut into cubes; 2 cups (16 fl oz) dry red wine; 3 bay leaves; 8 juniper berries, crushed; ½ teaspoon dried thyme; 1 onion, studded with 6 cloves; 6 peppercorns; 2 slivers of lemon peel; 4 oz (125 g) bacon, diced; salt and freshly ground black pepper; 2 cups (16 fl oz) beef stock; ½ cup (4 fl oz) sour cream; 3 tablespoons redcurrant jelly, heated to liquefy; white pepper; ½ teaspoon grated lemon peel

Place the meat in a marinade of wine, bay leaves, juniper berries, thyme, onion and cloves, peppercorns and lemon peel. Refrigerate for 24 hours. Drain the meat and reserve the marinade.

Lightly sauté the bacon to render the fat. Add the venison to the pan and fry until brown. Season and add 1 cup of the stock. Cover and simmer over low heat for 50 minutes or until the meat is tender. During that time, gradually add the rest of the stock and all the strained marinade. Add the sour cream, redcurrant jelly, sufficient white pepper to make the stew quite peppery and the lemon peel. Continue cooking gently for a further 5 minutes. Season to taste. Serve with Spätzle (see page 130), stewed apples and cranberries.

Venison Rolls

Serves 6: 6 thin slices venison steak; 3 slices fatty bacon; 4 oz (125 g) venison scraps or ground beef; 1 small onion, finely chopped; 1 tablespoon oil; 4 oz (125 g) mushrooms, finely chopped; 2 tablespoons fine breadcrumbs; salt and pepper; 1 tablespoon all purpose flour; ½ cup (4 fl oz) red wine; 1 cup (8 fl oz) beef stock; 1 tablespoon tart jelly

Beat the venison steak with a cleaver until ¼ in (5 mm) thick. Remove the rind from the bacon and cut each slice in half.

Prepare the filling by grinding the scraps of venison or, if not available, use ground beef. Fry the onion in heated oil until soft and golden. Add the mushrooms and cook for 1 minute, then add to the meat and stir in the breadcrumbs. Season lightly.

Spread a little stuffing on each piece of venison and roll up. Wrap in the bacon strips and secure with either cocktail picks or string. Place the rolls side by side in a heavy-based casserole and sauté over heat until brown on all sides. Sprinkle the flour over the meat, then add to the wine, stock, salt and pepper. Bring to the boil, then lower the heat and cover. Simmer for 1 hour or until the meat is tender. Lift out the rolls and remove the cocktail picks or string. Keep the rolls hot. Stir in the jelly and pour over the rolls. Serve hot with rice.

Wrapped Quails with Grapes

Venison Sautéed with Leeks

*Serves 2: 10 oz (315 g) fresh venison fillet or rump;
2 fresh young leeks; ¼ cup (2 fl oz) oil; 1 teaspoon
sesame oil; ½ teaspoon white vinegar
Seasoning A: ¼ teaspoon salt; 1 teaspoon sugar;
2 tablespoons light soy sauce; 1 tablespoon rice wine
or dry sherry; 2 teaspoons sesame oil; 1 tablespoon
finely chopped scallion; 1½ teaspoons grated fresh
ginger; 1½ teaspoons cornstarch; 1 tablespoon oil
Seasoning B: ½ teaspoon salt; ¾ teaspoon sugar;
2 tablespoons light soy sauce; 1 tablespoon rice wine
or dry sherry*

Cut the meat across the grain into thin
slices, then into shreds, and place in a dish
with the seasoning A ingredients. Mix well
and leave for 1 hour.

Thoroughly wash the leeks and cut into
2-in (5-cm) pieces, then shred finely lengthwise. Heat the oil in a wok or skillet and
fry the leeks until softened. Push to one
side of the pan and add the meat. Sauté
until it changes color, then cook for a further minute. Stir in the sesame oil and add
the seasoning B ingredients, sizzling the soy
and wine separately onto the sides.

Mix in the leeks and cook, stirring, until
the meat is just done. Transfer to a warmed
serving plate. Sprinkle over the vinegar and
stir in lightly.

Venison Stew

*Serves 4: 1 lb (500 g) venison; 2 onions, sliced;
3 tablespoons olive oil; 1 slice fatty bacon, chopped;
1 bay leaf; 6 peppercorns; 2 teaspoons tomato
paste; 2 cups (16 fl oz) water; small sprig of
rosemary; 1 garlic clove, crushed; ½ cup (4 fl oz)
dry red wine; salt and pepper*

Cut the venison into 1-in (2.5-cm) cubes.
Fry the onions in hot oil in a large saucepan, add the bacon and fry. Stir in the
meat, bay leaf and peppercorns, and cook
for 2-3 minutes until the meat is lightly
browned. Add the tomato paste, water,
rosemary, garlic and wine. Season to taste
with salt and pepper. Bring to the boil,
reduce the heat and simmer covered for 2
hours, stirring occasionally and adding
more water if necessary. Test the tenderness of the meat by piercing with a fork.
Adjust the seasoning and serve.

W
Wild Duck Casserole

*Serves 4: 4 wild ducks; bouquet garni (see page 387);
dry red wine; oil; salt and pepper; 16 small white
onions; 6 tablespoons (3 oz) butter; ½ cup (4 fl oz)
dry white wine; 8 oz (250 g) mushrooms, sliced*

The wild ducks should be well cleaned and
the end feathers singed over a flame. Place
in an earthenware or stainless steel bowl
and add a bouquet garni. Cover with dry
red wine and leave in a cool place for at
least 1 day, preferably 2-3 days.

When ready to cook, drain the ducks
well. Sauté in hot oil in a large flameproof
casserole, turning until seared all over.
Pour over the strained marinade and allow
to come gently to the boil. Season to taste.
Lower the heat, cover and simmer gently
until the ducks are cooked, about 1-1½
hours depending on age and size.

Prepare the small white onions and sauté
in butter, turning to soften all over. Do not
allow to color. Pour over the dry white
wine and gently poach until tender. Do not
overcook. Sauté the mushrooms in butter
for 5 minutes. Add the onions and mushrooms to the ducks just before serving. If
necessary, thicken the sauce with a little
arrowroot blended with cold water. Serve
with small boiled potatoes tossed in butter.

Woodcock Casserole

*Serves 4: 4 woodcocks; 4 tablespoons (2 oz) butter;
2 medium-size onions, sliced; 1 large red bell
pepper, seeded and sliced; 1 large garlic clove, finely
chopped; salt and freshly ground black pepper;
1½ tablespoons all purpose flour; ½ cup (4 fl oz)
dry white wine; cooked rice*

Halve the woodcocks through the backbone and breast. Trim the backbone away
and cut the wings to the first joint. Place
the trimmings in a pan with 1¼ cups of
cold water. Bring to the boil, then simmer
for 15 minutes. Strain and set aside.

Melt 2 tablespoons of the butter in a
large, shallow pan. Add the onions, red
pepper and garlic, and stir until lightly
coated with the butter. Cover and cook the
vegetables over low heat for 10 minutes.
Season lightly with salt and black pepper
and spread over the base of a casserole.

Add about ½ teaspoon of salt and pepper to the flour and dust over the wood-

cocks. Melt the remaining butter in the pan
in which the vegetables were cooked and
briskly fry the bird until browned.
Arrange, skin side up, on the vegetables.
Add 1 cup of the strained stock to the pan
drippings with the wine. Bring to the boil
and season to taste before pouring over the
woodcocks. Cover the casserole tightly and
cook for 35-45 minutes, depending on the
size of the birds.

Arrange the woodcocks on a serving dish
with a border of rice and keep hot. Stir the
liquid and vegetables remaining in the casserole until smooth. Adjust the seasoning
and reheat, if necessary, before spooning
over the birds.

Wrapped Quails with Grapes

*Serves 4: 8 quails; salt and freshly ground black
pepper; 8 oz (250 g) seedless grapes; 3 tablespoons
(1½ oz) butter; 8 slices of prosciutto; 1 small can
vine leaves; 1 cup (8 fl oz) veal or chicken stock;
½ cup (4 fl oz) dry white wine; 2-3 tablespoons
coffee liqueur; 1 tablespoon cream*

Season the quails inside and out with salt
and black pepper. Put 5-6 grapes in the
cavity of each bird and tie the legs together.
Melt the butter over moderate heat in a
heavy-based, flameproof casserole. Brown
the birds on all sides. As soon as they are
browned, lift them carefully from the pan
and leave until cool enough to handle.

Lay a slice of prosciutto over the breast
of each bird and completely overwrap with
vine leaves. Secure the leaves in position
with a length of coarse thread, criss-
crossing once over the breast before tying.
Arrange the birds in the casserole and pour
the stock and white wine over them. Cover
and bake in an oven preheated to 425°F
(220°C) for 15 minutes. Remove the lid and
cook for 5-10 minutes longer, until the
birds are tender. Remove the casserole
from the oven and reduce the temperature
to 200°F (100°C). Arrange the quails on a
heated serving platter and keep them hot.

Boil the pan juices rapidly until reduced
by half. Lower the heat and add the
remaining grapes to the pan with the coffee
liqueur. Simmer gently for 2 minutes. Lift
the grapes from the sauce with a slotted
spoon and arrange over and around the
quails. Stir the cream into the sauce and
heat through briefly without boiling.
Adjust seasoning and pour sauce over.

MEAT

A

Apples with Fried Calf's Liver, Berlin Style

Serves 4: 8 tablespoons (4 oz) butter; 2 onions, cut into thin slices and pushed into rings; 1½ lb (750 g) cooking apples, peeled, cored and sliced; salt and freshly ground black pepper; 1 lb (500 g) calf's liver, cut into ¼-in (5-mm) slices; flour

Melt half the butter in a skillet. Fry the onion rings and apple slices until they are light brown. Season with salt and pepper. Set aside and keep hot. Dust the liver slices with flour. Fry them in the remaining butter, allowing approximately 2 minutes each side. Do not overcook. Serve the liver slices garnished with the apples and onions.

Assorted Livers in Coconut Chili Sauce

Serves 4: 1 lb (500 g) liver (chicken, lamb or calf); 2 tablespoons oil; 1½ cups (12 fl oz) coconut milk; ¼ cup (2 fl oz) tamarind water; 1 teaspoon salt; 1 teaspoon sugar; 1 stalk lemongrass, bruised
Spice Paste: 3 candlenuts or macadamias; 6–8 shallots or 1 medium-size red or brown onion; 2 garlic cloves; 8–10 dried red chilies, soaked; 1 thick slice lengkuas; 1 teaspoon dried shrimp paste

Wash and slice the liver. If using chicken livers, leave whole. Grind the spice paste ingredients together until fine. Heat the oil and fry the spice paste gently for 3–4 minutes, then add the liver and continue cooking for another 2 minutes. Add the coconut milk, tamarind water, salt, sugar and lemongrass and simmer, uncovered, until the liver is cooked and the gravy has thickened.

Note: To make the tamarind water, soak 1 heaped tablespoon of pulp in ¼ cup warm water for 5 minutes. Squeeze to extract all juice from the fibrous matter. Strain before using.

B

Baby Lamb Stew

Serves 6–8: 4 lb (2 kg) baby lamb, cut into pieces; salt; 1 tablespoon paprika; 3 bay leaves; 8 oz (250 g) lamb's liver; 2 cups (16 fl oz) dry white wine; 2 garlic cloves, crushed; 3 slices bread, fried in oil, cut into pieces

In a bowl, combine the meat, salt, paprika, bay leaves, liver and wine. Refrigerate for 12 hours.

Transfer the meat to a casserole, bring to the boil, then cover and simmer over low heat for 1½ hours. Take out the liver, cut it into small pieces and put it into a food processor. Add the garlic and bread, then blend to a paste. Add the paste to the lamb, season and cook over low heat for 10 minutes. Serve hot.

Insert the garlic and herbs into the lamb.　　Put dish into the steamer.

Baby Lamb with Herbs and Garlic

Serves 4–6: 2½-lb (1¼-kg) leg of young lamb; 6–8 sprigs fresh rosemary; 6–8 sprigs fresh thyme; 6–8 sprigs fresh sage or oregano; 6 garlic cloves; 1¼ teaspoons salt; ½ teaspoon ground black pepper

Trim the lamb and puncture at regular intervals with the point of a sharp knife. Insert the sprigs of herbs and the peeled whole cloves of garlic into the holes. Rub the lamb with the salt and pepper.

Place in a dish and set in a steamer. Add water, cover and steam over gently boiling water for about 1¾ hours, or until tender.

Drain well. Carve at the table or slice the meat and arrange overlapped on a serving plate. Pour the liquid from the dish into a small jug to serve as the gravy.

Baked Country Ham with Cumberland Sauce

Serves 8: country ham weighing 5 lb (2.5 kg), soaked overnight in cold water; cloves; 1¼ cups (10 fl oz) cider
Glaze: ¼ cup dark brown sugar; 1 teaspoon dry mustard; pinch of mace; grated peel and juice of 1 orange
Cumberland Sauce: juice and peel of 2 oranges or 1 orange and 1 lemon; 4 tablespoons redcurrant jelly; 1 teaspoon dry mustard; ½ cup (4 fl oz) port or red wine; salt and black pepper; pinch of ground ginger

Drain the ham and put it into a large pan. Cover with fresh cold water, bring to the boil and simmer for 1 hour. Wipe the meat dry, wrap it loosely in aluminum foil and bake in an oven preheated to 350°F (180°C) for 45 minutes.

Remove the ham from the oven and carefully lift off the skin. To do this, lift the corner of the skin with a knife and pull the skin back with your fingers. If it is cooked, it should come away easily. Score the fat in a diamond pattern with a sharp knife.

Mix together all the glaze ingredients, then spread it over the fat. Stud the fat with cloves, pour the cider around the meat and bake for a further 20 minutes, basting occasionally with the cider, until the glaze is crisp and golden.

Meanwhile, to make the Cumberland Sauce, cut the fruit peel into fine matchsticks. Blanch for 5 minutes in boiling water, then drain. Heat the jelly and mustard together over low heat, stirring until smooth. Add the fruit juice, wine, pepper, salt and ginger. Stir in the peel and simmer for about 5 minutes, then pour into a sauce boat or glass bowl and serve cold.

Baked Stuffed Leg of Lamb, Kashmiri Style

Serves 6: 3-lb (1½-kg) leg of lamb; 3 oz (90 g) dried apricots; 2 medium-size onions; 4 garlic cloves; 1½ oz (45 g) seedless raisins; 1½ oz (45 g) blanched almonds; 2-3 thin slices fresh ginger; 2 tablespoons (1 oz) butter; 2 teaspoons dried mint; 1 tablespoon garam masala or mild-flavored curry powder; 3 whole cloves; ½ teaspoon cinnamon; ¼ cup (1 oz) dry breadcrumbs; salt and pepper; extra garam masala or curry powder

Using a thin-bladed sharp knife, work around the lamb bone until it can be removed, leaving a good-size cavity. Extend the cavity by cutting into the meatiest part of the leg without cutting through the skin. Set aside.

Soak the dried apricots in warm water to cover. Very finely chop the onions and garlic. Chop the raisins. Toast the almonds in a microwave on HIGH (100%) for 1¾ minutes, then set aside.

Finely chop the ginger. Place in a microwave-safe covered dish with the onions and garlic, and add the butter. Microwave on HIGH (100%) for 4 minutes. Drain the apricots and squeeze out all excess water, then chop finely. Mix into the onions, adding the raisins, nuts, mint, spices, breadcrumbs and a large pinch each of salt and pepper. Mix well.

Place the lamb in a microwave-safe dish, stuff the prepared filling into the cavity and stand the lamb shank upwards to cover the filling. Prick all over with a sharp knife or skewer and rub on a generous amount of *garam masala* or curry powder.

Roast in an oven preheated to 250°F/120°C for about 1 hour, until the lamb shows no pink liquid when pricked in the thickest part. A temperature probe may not register accurately in the meat prepared in this way and is best avoided. Slice to serve and accompany by plain boiled rice and a salad.

Bavarian-Style Sauerbraten

Serves 8-10: 4 lb (2 kg) boned shoulder of beef; 3 tablespoons all purpose flour; 4 tablespoons (2 oz) butter; 1 lemon, thinly sliced; sugar to taste; salt; ½ cup (4 fl oz) sour cream
Marinade: 4 cups (1 liter) beer; 2 cups (16 fl oz) water; 1 lemon, quartered; 2 bay leaves; 1 onion, sliced; 2 cloves; 1 tomato, peeled and chopped; 6 peppercorns

Put the meat into a shallow dish. Combine all the ingredients for the marinade and pour it over. Refrigerate for 2-3 days, turning the meat several times. Remove the meat and strain the marinade.

Wipe the meat dry, dust it with flour and brown it in hot butter on all sides. Add 1 cup of strained marinade, the lemon slices, sugar and salt. Simmer the meat in a covered saucepan for 2½-3 hours or until tender. Remove the meat. Puree and strain the cooking juice. Add the sour cream and reheat the sauce but do not boil. Serve the sauce poured over the sliced meat. Traditionally this dish is accompanied by potato dumplings and red cabbage.

Beef and Vegetable Hotpot

Serves 4-6: 1½ lb (750 g) well-marbled beef steak such as rump; 12 fresh or dried shiitake mushrooms; 2 cakes soft bean curd; 8 oz (250 g) white Chinese cabbage; 5 oz (155 g) edible chrysanthemum leaves (optional); 8 oz (250 g) bamboo shoots; 4-6 scallions; 8 cups (2 liters) dashi; salt; soy sauce
Garnishes: 2 scallions, very finely sliced; daikon-chili garnish (see page 276); pon-zu sauce (see page 276)
Sesame Sauce: 2 oz (60 g) white sesame seeds; ½ cup (4 fl oz) dashi; 2 tablespoons light soy sauce; 1 tablespoon sweet rice wine (mirin); 1 tablespoon sake; 2 teaspoons superfine sugar

Make the sauces first. Prepare the pon-zu sauce as directed. To make the sesame sauce, toast the seeds in a dry pan over low to moderate heat until golden brown, stirring constantly. While still warm, pound to a paste with a mortar and pestle or grind in a blender. Add the *dashi* gradually, blending well after each addition, then combine with the rest of the ingredients. Both sauces can be made well in advance, although the sesame sauce is best eaten within a couple of hours of serving.

Prepare all the ingredients, arranging on one or two large platters for serving. If possible, have the butcher cut the meat into paper-thin slices; otherwise, chill it in the freezer until firm enough to cut very thinly across the grain.

If using dried mushrooms, soak in warm water until softened, then discard the stems. Cut the caps of dried or fresh mushrooms with a cross. Cut the bean curd into 1-in (2.5-cm) cubes. Separate the leaves of

Baby Lamb with Herbs and Garlic

Chinese cabbage, then cut across in 2-in (5-cm) lengths. Wash the chrysanthemum leaves and drain well. Wash the bamboo shoots thoroughly, slice and boil in water for 2–3 minutes. Rinse and drain. Cut the scallions into 2-in (5-cm) lengths.

Prepare the garnishes before cooking time; arrange the scallions and *daikon*-chili garnish on small plates and put a little of both sauces into individual sauce bowls.

Put the steam boat or fondue on the table and fill about two-thirds full with *dashi*. Add sufficient salt and light soy sauce to give flavor but do not over-season as the stock will reduce during cooking and the flavor will intensify.

Each diner adds his or her own food to the simmering pot; the beef needs only a few seconds' cooking so it is held in a pair of chopsticks and swished around in the stock before being dipped in either of the sauces and eaten. Scallion and *daikon*-chili garnish can be added to the pon-zu sauce according to taste. Serve with rice and a dish of pickles.

When all the food is finished and the stock has reduced, ladle it into soup bowls, sprinkle with a little scallion and serve.

Note: A heatproof casserole set over a burner can also be used for cooking.

Beef in Coconut Sauce with Cabbage

Beef in Coconut Sauce with Cabbage

Serves 2: 12 oz (375 g) lean beef (sirloin, round, top round); ½ teaspoon salt; 2 teaspoons dark soy sauce; 2 cups (16 fl oz) thin coconut milk; 4 dried chilies, crumbled; 1-in (2.5-cm) piece fresh ginger, shredded; 3 garlic cloves, crushed; 8 shallots or 2 small red onions, sliced; 1 heaped tablespoon roasted peanuts, crushed; 1 tablespoon brown sugar; 1½ teaspoons cornstarch; 1 lb (500 g) Chinese cabbage or white cabbage; 2 medium-size carrots; 2 fresh red chilies, sliced

Cut the beef into thin strips. Season with salt and soy sauce and let stand for 10–15 minutes.

Pour 1¼ cups coconut milk into a saucepan and add the crumbled chilies, ginger, garlic and sliced shallots. Bring almost to the boil, then add the marinated meat. Turn the heat down, cover and simmer until the meat is tender. Stir in the roasted peanuts and brown sugar, and add salt to taste. Thicken the sauce with cornstarch mixed with a little cold water. Remove from the heat and set aside, keeping warm.

Wash the cabbage and cut into 3-in (8-cm) pieces. Scrape or peel the carrots and slice very thinly. Cook in slightly salted boiling water for 2–3 minutes, then drain. Put the cabbage into a pan with a little salt and remaining coconut milk. Simmer on low heat until the cabbage is cooked but still slightly crisp.

Arrange the cabbage in a serving dish; top with the carrots and the cooked beef. Pour over the sauce and garnish with sliced red chilies.

Beef in Spicy Coconut Gravy

Serves 4: 1 lb (500 g) top round; 6–8 shallots or 1 medium-size red or brown onion; 3 slices lengkuas; 1-in (2.5-cm) piece fresh ginger; 5–10 dried red chilies, soaked; 2 stalks lemongrass; 1 garlic clove; 6 tablespoons freshly grated coconut or ¼ cup packaged coconut; 2½ tablespoons oil; 2½ cups (20 fl oz) coconut milk; 1 leaf fresh turmeric, very finely shredded (optional); 1 teaspoon salt; 1 teaspoon sugar

Cut the beef into 2-in (5-cm) dice. Grind the shallots, *lengkuas*, ginger, chilies, lemongrass and garlic together until fine. Gently fry the grated coconut in a dry pan, stirring constantly until golden brown.

Allow to cool slightly, then pound to a paste.

Heat the oil in a skillet and gently fry the ground shallot mixture for 4–5 minutes. Add the pounded coconut and fry for another minute, then put in the beef and stir-fry until it changes color. Add all other ingredients and stir, lifting the coconut milk and pouring it back into the skillet until it comes to the boil. Reduce the heat and simmer, uncovered, until the meat is tender. If the sauce threatens to dry out before the meat is cooked, add a little hot water.

Reduce the sauce until all that remains is a very thick coating on the meat. The oil will come out of the coconut milk and the meat will start to fry in it.

Beef Olives

Serves 4: 4 oz (125 g) veal, ground; 2 oz (60 g) ham, finely chopped; ½ cup (1 oz) fresh breadcrumbs; 2 sprigs parsley, chopped; salt and freshly ground pepper; 1 egg, lightly beaten; 1 lb (500 g) rump steak, cut into 4 thin slices and lightly beaten; 2 tablespoons (1 oz) butter; 2 onions, sliced; 1¾ cups (14 fl oz) beef stock; ½ cup (4 fl oz) dry red wine; 1 tablespoon tomato puree

To make the stuffing, mix together the veal, ham, breadcrumbs, parsley, salt, pepper and egg. Divide it into quarters and spread it on the steak slices. Roll them up and tie with thread or string.

In a casserole, melt the butter and sauté the onions. Add the rolled beef olives and lightly brown. Add the stock, wine, tomato puree and season to taste. Cover the casserole and simmer over very low heat for 1½ hours. To serve, arrange the olives on a heated platter. The sauce may be thickened with flour and strained over the meat.

Beef Samosas

Makes 36: 1 package large spring roll wrappers Filling: 6 oz (185 g) lean beef or lamb, finely ground; 1 medium-size cooked potato, diced; ¼ cup cooked green peas; 1 medium-size onion, grated; 1 garlic clove, crushed; ½-in (1-cm) piece fresh ginger, grated; 2 teaspoons garam masala; ½ teaspoon chili powder; ¼ teaspoon turmeric; 1 teaspoon salt; ¼ teaspoon black pepper; 2 tablespoons ghee or butter; 1 tablespoon lemon juice; 1 tablespoon chopped fresh cilantro or mint; oil for deep frying

Cover the spring roll wrappers with a damp cloth until needed.

Mix all the filling ingredients except the *ghee*, lemon juice and chopped herbs and fry in the *ghee* or butter until just cooked through. Sprinkle over approximately 2 tablespoons of water and increase the heat until the liquid has evaporated. Remove from the heat and add the lemon juice and herbs. Stir well and leave to cool.

Cut the spring roll wrappers into 1¾-in (4-cm) strips, then cut each piece in half, turn one end over to make a triangular shaped pocket, then turn again in the opposite direction. Fill the cavity with a spoonful of the cooled filling and continue folding until the whole strip has been used and a triangular shaped pastry results. Seal the end with water or a paste made from flour and water.

Heat the oil to fairly hot and deep fry the samosas, several at a time, until golden and crisp. Serve hot with a fresh mint chutney.

Beef Steak and Kidney Pie

Serves 4-6: Suet Pastry: 4 cups (1 lb) all purpose flour; pinch of salt; 8 tablespoons (4 oz) margarine; 4 oz (125 g) suet or lard; cold water; egg wash (1 egg yolk mixed with a little cold water)
1 lb (500 g) stewing steak; 4 oz (125 g) kidneys; 2 onions, chopped; beef stock; salt and pepper; 2 tablespoons cream

To make the pastry, sift the flour and salt together into a bowl. Cut the margarine and suet or lard into small pieces and rub it in with your fingertips. Add enough cold water to make a firm dough. Wrap in plastic wrap and refrigerate until ready to use.

Cut the steak and kidney into small cubes, discarding all fat. Put the meat, onion, salt and pepper into a pan and cover it with beef stock. Bring to the boil, then simmer for about 2 hours or until the meat is tender.

Roll out the pastry into two rounds and line an 8-in (20-cm) pie dish with one of them. Spoon the steak and kidney into it and cover with the remaining pastry, pressing the edges down well. Cut a hole in the center of the top crust. Paint the pie with egg wash and bake in an oven preheated to 350°F (180°C) for 1 hour or until the pastry is golden brown. Just before serving, pour the cream through the hole in the crust.

Note: It's a good idea when preheating the oven to heat up a baking sheet at the same time. The bottom crust of the pie, cooked on the hot sheet, will bake quickly and is less likely to become soggy.

Beef Vindaloo

Serves 4-6: 2 lb (1 kg) beef steak (chuck, round or knuckle) or 3 lb (1½ kg) oxtail; 3 tablespoons coriander; 1 tablespoon cumin; 6 cloves; 2-in (5-cm) stick cinnamon; 1½ teaspoons black peppercorns; 2 teaspoons fenugreek seeds; 1 teaspoon fennel seeds; 6 dried chilies, soaked; 8 garlic cloves; 1 large onion; 1-in (2.5-cm) piece fresh ginger; ¼ cup (2 fl oz) white vinegar; 3 tablespoons ghee; 2 bay leaves; 2 cups (16 fl oz) beef stock; salt to taste

Trim the meat and cut it into 2-in (5-cm) cubes. Set aside. Grind the spices from coriander to fennel to a fine powder. Grind the chilies with the garlic, onion and ginger. Mix the spice powder with the vinegar and rub it into the meat well. Pour over the onion paste and leave the meat to marinate for 2 hours.

Heat the *ghee* in a large casserole and fry the meat until very deeply colored. Add the bay leaves and stock, bring to the boil, then simmer until the meat is very tender, about 1 hour. Season to taste with salt and refrigerate overnight if time permits. Reheat before using.

Note: If using oxtail, cut into sections and prepare in the same way, cooking until the meat falls from the bones.

Beef with Celery and Button Mushrooms

Serves 2: 8 oz (250 g) rump steak, very finely sliced; 1½ cups (12 fl oz) oil; 1 slice fresh ginger, very finely chopped; 2 garlic cloves, smashed and chopped; 4-5 large stalks celery, cut diagonally in ½-in (1-cm) slices; 1 cup canned button mushrooms, halved if large; 2 teaspoons oyster sauce; 1 fresh red chili, cut in very fine lengthwise strips
Marinade: 1 tablespoon cornstarch; 1 teaspoon baking soda; 2 tablespoons water; 1 tablespoon peanut oil; 1 teaspoon thick black soy sauce; 1 teaspoon light soy sauce; 1 teaspoon sesame oil; 1 teaspoon salt; ½ teaspoon sugar; ¼ teaspoon white pepper

Combine all marinade ingredients in a bowl. Add the beef, stir well, then leave to marinate for about 30 minutes.

Heat the oil in a skillet until very hot.

Beef Steak and Kidney Pie

Drain the beef thoroughly, then deep fry for just 30 seconds. Remove and drain on a paper towel.

Pour out all but 2 tablespoons of oil, then fry the ginger and garlic gently for 30 seconds. Raise the heat and add the celery. Stir-fry for 2 minutes, then put in the button mushrooms and stir-fry for 1 minute. Lower the heat slightly, cover the skillet and cook until the celery is just cooked but still crisp. Remove lid, add the beef and oyster sauce, and stir-fry over high heat for 30 seconds. Put into a serving bowl or on a platter. Decorate with the chili and serve immediately.

Braised and Stuffed Green Cabbage

Serves 6–8: 2 tablespoons (1 oz) butter; 1 large onion, finely chopped; 1 cup (2 oz) fresh white breadcrumbs; 1 cup (8 fl oz) beef stock; 1 lb (500 g) fresh ground pork; 1 garlic clove, crushed; rosemary; thyme; ¼ cup finely chopped parsley; salt and pepper; 1 egg; 1 head cabbage; 4 strips streaky bacon

Melt the butter, add the onion and sauté slowly until tender but not brown. Soak the breadcrumbs in ½ cup of beef stock for 5 minutes. Drain through a sieve, pressing out as much liquid as possible. Put the onions and the breadcrumbs into a mixing bowl. Add the minced pork, garlic, rosemary, thyme, parsley, salt, pepper and egg, and beat vigorously together.

Blanch the whole cabbage in boiling salted water for several minutes, then rinse under cold running water, drain well and remove the core. Spread out the cabbage, starting with the outer leaves. Remove the inner heart, chop it finely and add to the forcemeat stuffing. Stuff the heart first with a ball of the forcemeat stuffing. Close the leaves around this. Fill the next layer of leaves and close them, and so on, reforming the shape of the cabbage. Wrap the cabbage in thin strips of bacon and tie it with string to keep its shape. Carefully transfer the stuffed cabbage to a heavy braising pan. Pour the remaining ½ cup of stock over it, cover the pan and braise gently in an oven preheated to 325°F (160°C) for 45 minutes. Drain the cabbage, carefully transfer it to a round serving dish and untie the string. Reduce the cooking liquid over a high heat and pour a little over the cabbage. Serve the rest separately.

Braised Beef and Eggplant

Serves 4–6: 2 lb (1 kg) eggplant cut into 2-in (5-cm) cubes; salt; ¾ cup (6 fl oz) olive oil; 2 lb (1 kg) shin beef, cut into 2-in (5-cm) cubes; freshly ground black pepper; 3 onions, chopped; 1 garlic clove, crushed; 5 tomatoes, peeled and chopped; 2 tablespoons tomato puree; 1–2 cups (8–16 fl oz) dry red wine or water; ½ cup (2 oz) all purpose flour

Sprinkle the eggplant cubes with salt and place them in a colander. Cover them with a weighted plate for 30 minutes.

Heat 2 tablespoons of the oil in a saucepan or casserole and brown the meat on all sides. Season. In a skillet, heat 2 tablespoons of oil and sauté the onions and garlic until the onions are golden brown. Add the sautéed onions and garlic, the tomatoes, tomato puree and wine or water to the meat, cover the casserole and simmer over low heat for 1 hour.

Remove the eggplant from the colander, dry with paper towels, dust with flour and fry in the remaining oil until light brown. Add them to the meat and simmer for a further 30 minutes. Serve hot.

Braised Lamb with Fruit and Nuts

Serves 4–6: 1½ lb (750 g) boned young lamb, leg or shoulder; 3 cups (24 fl oz) water; 1 tablespoon lemon juice; 2 bay leaves; 2-in (5-cm) stick cinnamon; 4 tablespoons ghee; 2-in (5-cm) piece fresh ginger, shredded; 6 garlic cloves, crushed; 2 large onions, chopped; 6 green cardamoms, crushed; 2 tablespoons ground coriander; 3 cloves; 1 tablespoon white poppyseeds; 1½ oz (45 g) ground almonds; 1 teaspoon black pepper; 2 tablespoons finely chopped fresh mint; ¾ cup (6 fl oz) plain yogurt; 2 teaspoons garam masala; 1 teaspoon chili powder; salt; 1½ oz (45 g) raisins, soaked; 1 oz (30 g) golden raisins, soaked; 1½ oz (45 g) blanched, slivered almonds; ¼ teaspoon saffron; 1 tablespoon boiling water; 1½ teaspoons rose water (optional)

Place the trimmed lamb in a pan and add the water, lemon juice, bay leaves and cinnamon. Cover and bring to the boil, then reduce the heat and simmer for about 1 hour or until very tender. Skim several times during cooking. Remove the meat and reduce the liquid to about ¾ cup.

Heat 3 tablespoons of *ghee* and fry the

ginger, garlic and onions until soft. Grind the cardamoms, coriander, cloves, poppyseeds, almonds and black pepper to a powder and add to the pan. Fry for 3 minutes, stirring frequently. Add the mint and yogurt and simmer until the sauce is thick and creamy.

Add the meat and spoon the sauce over it. Braise until heated through and well seasoned. Add the reserved stock and simmer uncovered, until the liquid has been completely absorbed or evaporated. Sprinkle the *garam masala*, chili powder and salt over.

Melt the remaining *ghee* and fry the drained fruit and nuts gently for 5 minutes. Add to the pan. Mix the saffron with the boiling water and rose water and add to the pan. Pour over the meat and heat through.

Braised Pork and Leek Rolls (Teriyaki)

Serves 4–6: 6 leeks or 12 Japanese leeks; 6 very thin slices pork shoulder or leg; ⅓ cup (2½ fl oz) light soy sauce; ⅓ cup (2½ fl oz) sake or mirin; 2 tablespoons sugar; vegetable oil; 2 small cucumbers; 2 tablespoons white vinegar; 2 teaspoons salt; 1 tablespoon sugar

Wash the leeks, remove the roots and green tops, and cut into pieces the same length as the width of each slice of pork. Wrap the pork securely around one piece of leek or two pieces of Japanese leek and secure with toothpicks.

Mix the soy sauce, *sake* or *mirin* and sugar, stirring until the sugar dissolves. Heat 1 in (2.5 cm) oil in a skillet and cook the rolls on moderate heat, turning to brown evenly.

Wash and dry the cucumbers and cut into wedges about 1 in (2.5 cm) long, then sprinkle with a mixture of vinegar, salt and sugar. Set aside to marinate.

Drain the oil from the pan when the pork is partially cooked and pour in the prepared sauce. Simmer on low heat for 6–7 minutes, turning the pork frequently. Remove the rolls from the pan and cut each piece into two or three pieces. Stand these upright on small, flat plates and garnish each with several pieces of drained cucumber.

Bring the remaining sauce to the boil and cook until reduced to a thick glaze. Spoon a little over each portion of meat before serving.

Braised Pork and Leek Rolls (Teriyaki)

Braised Pork Ribs

Serves 4: 1 lb (500 g) meaty pork ribs; oil for deep frying; 1 medium-size red or brown onion, finely chopped; 2 garlic cloves, smashed and chopped; 2 slices fresh ginger, very finely chopped; ½ fresh red chili, sliced (optional); 2 scallions, cut in 1-in (2.5-cm) lengths; 1 or 2 dried black mushrooms, soaked and shredded; 1 tablespoon salted soybeans, mashed lightly; 1 teaspoon Chinese rice wine or dry sherry
Marinade: ½ teaspoon salt; ½ teaspoon sugar; 1 teaspoon light soy sauce; 1 teaspoon thick black soy sauce; ½ teaspoon sesame oil; pinch of white pepper; 2 teaspoons cornstarch
Gravy: ½ cup (4 fl oz) water; 1 teaspoon sugar; ½ teaspoon light soy sauce; ½ teaspoon thick black soy sauce; few drops sesame oil; white pepper

Cut the ribs into 1½-in (4-cm) pieces. Combine the marinade ingredients and rub into the pork ribs. Let stand for 30 minutes. Drain the ribs and deep fry in hot oil for just 1 minute. Remove and drain.

Pour out all but 1½ tablespoons of oil and gently fry the onion, garlic, ginger and chili for 3–4 minutes, then add the ribs and all other ingredients, except the wine. Stir-fry for 1 minute, then add the wine and cook for another minute.

Combine all gravy ingredients and add to the ribs. Cover the pan and simmer until the ribs are cooked. Remove the lid, stir, and continue cooking until the sauce is almost completely dried up. Serve with white rice.

Burgundy Beef (Boeuf Bourguignonne)

Serves 6: 3 lb (1.5 kg) top round; flour; ¼ cup oil; 7 tablespoons (3½ oz) butter; 4 oz (125 g) salt pork, diced; salt and freshly ground black pepper; ¼ cup brandy, warmed; 2 carrots, chopped; 1 leek, chopped; 4 scallions, chopped; 1 large onion, chopped; 1 garlic clove, crushed; 1 calf's foot (optional); bouquet garni (see page 387); ½ bottle red Burgundy; beef stock, to cover; 1 tablespoon all purpose flour; 18 pickling onions; 18 button mushrooms; sugar; lemon juice; chopped parsley

Cut the beef into cubes and roll them in flour. Heat 2 tablespoons of oil with 2 tablespoons of butter in a large heavy-based skillet and sauté the salt pork until crisp and brown. Transfer the pork to a large earthenware casserole. Brown the beef well on all sides in the fat remaining in the pan and season with salt and freshly ground pepper. Pour the warmed brandy over the meat and ignite. Let the flame burn away and add the meat to the casserole. Cook the carrots, leek, scallions, onion and garlic in the remaining fat in the skillet, stirring until they are browned. Transfer the vegetables to the casserole dish with the meat. Add the calf's foot and the bouquet garni to the casserole. Pour over all but ¼ cup of the wine and just enough beef stock to cover the contents of the casserole. Cover and put into an oven preheated to 300°F (150°C). Reduce the heat to 250°F (120°C) and cook for 2 hours. The secret of a good burgundy beef is very slow, gentle cooking.

Skim off all fat from the sauce. On a saucer, work together 1 tablespoon of flour with 1 tablespoon of soft butter to make a beurre manié. Stir this mixture into the casserole. Cover and cook very gently for a further 2 hours.

Brown the small onions in 1 tablespoon butter with a pinch of sugar. Add the remaining ¼ cup of red wine, cover and cook very gently until the onions are almost tender. Keep warm. Sauté the mushrooms in the remaining oil and butter and a little lemon juice. Keep warm. When the meat is tender, remove the calf's foot and bouquet garni. Correct the seasoning and add the onions and mushrooms. Sprinkle with chopped parsley and serve.

C

Cabbage Rolls

Makes 12: 3-lb (1.5-kg) cabbage; 12 oz (375 g) coarsely ground pork; 1 large onion, chopped; 1 large tomato, chopped; 2 tablespoons (1 oz) butter; 1½ tablespoons all purpose flour; 1½ teaspoons sweet paprika; salt and black pepper; 2 teaspoons chopped parsley; ¼ teaspoon dried oregano; 1 egg, beaten
Tomato Sauce: 1 medium-size onion, finely chopped; 1 large tomato, chopped; 1 garlic clove, crushed; 1 tablespoon butter; ½ teaspoon sugar; salt and black pepper; ½ cup (4 fl oz) heavy cream

Separate the cabbage leaves and select 12 large ones for the rolls. Trim away the central stems. Place the leaves and about 4 oz (125 g) of the remaining cabbage in a pan. Cover with boiling water and simmer gently for about 5 minutes until the leaves have softened. Drain well.

Fry the pork, onion and tomato in the hot butter for about 5 minutes, stirring frequently. Add the flour and paprika, salt and pepper to taste and the herbs. Cover and simmer gently for 5–6 minutes. Remove from the heat and leave to cool for about 10 minutes.

Stir the egg into the pork mixture. Chop the blanched excess cabbage finely, squeeze to remove as much water as possible and mix into the pork mixture.

Divide the filling among the 12 prepared leaves and roll up each to enclose the filling. Place in a dish, seam side downwards, and place in a steamer or rack set in a pan. Steam, tightly covered, for about 45 minutes, adding more water as needed.

In a separate saucepan, prepare the sauce. Sauté the onion, tomato and garlic in the hot butter until soft. Add the sugar, salt and pepper to taste and simmer gently until thick. Stir in the cream just before using.

To serve the cabbage rolls, drain and arrange on a plate, then pour the sauce over.

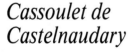

Cover the cabbage with boiling water and simmer.

Fold the cabbage over the filling and roll up tightly.

Cassoulet de Castelnaudary

Serves 8–10: 4 cups (1 liter) water; 1 lb (500 g) lean salt pork, in one piece; 8 oz (250 g) fresh pork rind (optional); 1 lb (500 g) garlic pork sausage, fresh or smoked; 16 cups (4 liters) chicken stock; 2 lb (1 kg) dry white beans, soaked overnight; 3 whole peeled onions; 3 garlic cloves, finely chopped; 1 teaspoon dried thyme; bouquet garni (see page 387); salt and freshly ground black pepper
Pork and Lamb: 8 oz (250 g) pork fat, diced; 1 lb (500 g) pork neck, cut in 2-in (5-cm) chunks; 1 lb (500 g) boned lamb shoulder, cut in 2-in (5-cm) chunks; 2 onions, finely chopped; 2 stalks celery,
finely chopped; 1 garlic clove, finely chopped; 1 cup (8 fl oz) dry white wine; 1 1/2 lb (750 g) firm ripe tomatoes, peeled, seeded and chopped (or substitute 2 cups drained canned tomatoes); 1 bay leaf; salt and freshly ground black pepper
Topping: 1 1/2 cups (6 oz) fine dry breadcrumbs; 1/2 cup (3/4 oz) finely chopped fresh parsley

Put the water, salt pork and pork rind (if using) into a pan and bring to the boil. Simmer for 15 minutes, then drain the meat and reserve. Using a sharp knife, pierce a few holes in the sausage.

Pour the stock into a large, heavy-based pan and add the beans, sausage, salt pork and pork rind. Bring to the boil, skimming off all scum that rises to the surface. When the stock looks clean, add the whole onions, garlic, thyme, bouquet garni, salt and pepper. Reduce the heat and simmer, uncovered, for 45 minutes, adding more stock if necessary. Remove the sausage and reserve.

Simmer the beans for another 30–40 minutes or until tender. Using a slotted spoon, transfer the salt pork and rind to a plate and discard the onions and bouquet garni. Strain the stock, skim off any fat and reserve all ingredients.

In a heavy-based skillet, sauté the diced pork fat until crisp and brown. Remove and reserve. Pour off all but 2–3 tablespoons of rendered fat into a bowl.

Heat the remaining fat and sauté the pork neck and lamb in batches until golden brown, adding more fat if necessary. Transfer the meat to a large ovenproof casserole.

Drain off the excess fat, then fry the onions for 5 minutes. Mix in the celery and garlic and sauté for 2 minutes more, scraping the pan well. Pour in the wine, bring it to the boil and cook over high heat until reduced by half. Scrape the contents of the pan into the casserole. Gently stir in the tomatoes and bay leaf and season.

Bring to the boil, then transfer the casserole to an oven preheated to 325°F (160°C) and bake for 1 hour, adding stock if necessary. Transfer the meat to a bowl. Skim off all fat from the juices in the casserole, then strain these juices into the bean stock, discarding the vegetables.

To assemble the cassoulet; peel the sausage and cut it into 1/4-in (5-mm) slices and dice the salt pork and rind. In a large, heavy-based casserole, spread a thick layer of beans and arrange the sausage, pork, pork rind, pork fat, braised pork and lamb on top. Cover with another layer of beans and meat, then top with beans and sliced sausage. Pour in the bean stock until it almost covers the beans, then spread the breadcrumbs over. Spread 3–4 tablespoons of reserved pork fat over the breadcrumbs.

Bring the casserole to the boil on top of the stove, then bake uncovered in an oven preheated to 350°F (180°C) for 1 1/4 hours or until the crust is firm and golden. Sprinkle with parsley and serve.

Chili Pork Spareribs

Serves 4–6: 1 1/2 lb (750 g) meaty pork spareribs or "five flowered" pork; 6 cups (1 1/2 liters) oil for deep frying; 3 scallions, trimmed and sliced; 3 thick slices fresh ginger, chopped; 1 fresh red chili pepper, shredded (optional); 1 teaspoon finely chopped garlic (optional)
Seasoning A: 1 egg white, beaten; 1 tablespoon finely chopped scallion; 2 teaspoons finely chopped fresh ginger; 1 teaspoon salt; 1/4 teaspoon white pepper; 1 tablespoon rice wine or dry sherry; 1 tablespoon oil; 2 tablespoons cornstarch
Seasoning B/Sauce: 2 tablespoons hot bean paste; 3 1/2 cups (28 fl oz) chicken stock; 2 tablespoons light soy sauce; 1 tablespoon rice wine or dry sherry; 1/2 teaspoon salt; 1 tablespoon sugar

Cut the ribs or pork into bite-size chunks and place in a dish with the seasoning A ingredients. Mix well and leave for 30 minutes.

Heat the oil to fairly hot and deep fry the pork until golden, cooking in several lots to keep the oil hot. Drain and transfer to a casserole. Pour off all but 2 tablespoons of the oil and add the scallions, ginger, chili and garlic, if used. Stir-fry briefly, then add the hot bean paste and stir-fry for several seconds. Add the chicken stock and remaining seasoning B/sauce ingredients and bring to the boil.

Pour over the pork and cover. Simmer until the pork is completely tender, about 1 1/4 hours. Transfer the pork to a serving plate with a slotted spoon and thicken the sauce, if necessary, with a thin solution of cornstarch and cold water. Check the seasonings and pour over the pork.

Note: For a more substantial dish, surround the pork with braised fresh green vegetables and serve with boiled thick egg noodles.

Chinese Beef Steak

Serves 4: 1 lb (500 g) round steak, cut ½ in (1 cm) thick; 2 tablespoons oil; 1 garlic clove, finely chopped
Marinade: 1 tablespoon light soy sauce; 1 tablespoon barbecue sauce; 2 tablespoons peanut oil; 1 teaspoon Chinese rice wine or dry sherry; ½ teaspoon sesame oil; 1 teaspoon baking soda; 1 tablespoon cornstarch; 1 egg, beaten
Gravy: ¾ cup (6 fl oz) water; 1 tablespoon Worcestershire sauce; 1 tablespoon tomato sauce; 1 teaspoon oyster sauce; 1 teaspoon sugar; ½ teaspoon salt

Cut the meat into 1½-in (4-cm) squares. Combine all the marinade ingredients and marinate the meat for 8 hours in the refrigerator, stirring occasionally.

Remove the meat from the marinade and drain. Heat the oil in a large skillet and cook the garlic until it turns golden. Discard the garlic, raise the heat and quickly fry the meat for 2 minutes on each side.

Heat the gravy ingredients and pour over the browned meat. Cover the pan and simmer gently until the meat is tender and the gravy has reduced.

Chinese Cabbage Rolls

Serves 4–8: ½ medium-size cabbage or 1 Chinese cabbage; 8 slices fresh ginger, shredded; 1 cup (8 fl oz) beef stock; 1 tablespoon dry sherry; 1 tablespoon light soy sauce
Stuffing: 1 lb (500 g) ground lean pork; 4 dried Chinese mushrooms; 2 oz (60 g) canned bamboo shoots, drained and finely chopped; 2 scallions, finely chopped; 1 teaspoon grated ginger; 2 teaspoons dark soy sauce; 2 teaspoons dry sherry; 1 teaspoon sugar; salt and black pepper

To prepare the stuffing, place the pork in a dish and squeeze through the fingers until smooth and pastelike. Place the mushrooms in a small bowl with 1 cup (8 fl oz) water and cover with plastic wrap vented in one corner. Microwave on MEDIUM-HIGH (70%) for 4 minutes, or until the mushrooms have softened. Drain, reserving the liquid, and chop finely. Mix the mushrooms and remaining stuffing ingredients with the pork.

Remove eight large pieces or whole leaves from the cabbage and cut away the central white ribs. Place the leaves in a plastic bag and microwave on HIGH (100%) for 2 minutes until softened.

Chinese Beef Steak

Divide the stuffing among the cabbage leaves and wrap each into a compact parcel. Shred the remaining cabbage and place in the bottom of a casserole with the shredded ginger. Arrange the cabbage rolls on top. Add ½ cup (4 fl oz) of the mushroom liquid, the beef stock, sherry and soy sauce. Cover with plastic wrap vented in one corner. Microwave on HIGH (100%) for 10 minutes. (Non-carousel ovens: Give the dish a half turn after 5 minutes.) Stand for 5 minutes, then serve with the cabbage and white rice. The sauce can be thickened with cornstarch.

Coconut Beef

Serves 4: 1 lb (500 g) round or sirloin steak; 1 tablespoon ground coriander; ½ teaspoon powdered sweet basil, or 2 teaspoons chopped fresh basil; 1 tablespoon brown sugar; 2 teaspoons tamarind; 3 garlic cloves, crushed; 3 medium-size onions, grated; 2 tablespoons oil; salt and pepper; 2 daun salam or bay leaves; 5 oz (155 g) freshly grated coconut, or 3½ oz (100 g) moistened shredded coconut

Slice the beef thinly. Grind the coriander, basil, brown sugar and tamarind to a paste and mix with the garlic and onions.

Heat the oil in a skillet and fry the seasoning paste for 5 minutes, stirring occasionally. Season the beef with salt and pepper and add to the pan. Cook over high heat until very well browned. Remove and keep warm.

In a dry pan, stir together the coconut and the *daun salam* or bay leaves. Turn the heat down low and stir the coconut as it cooks. It burns very quickly, so do not stop stirring at any time. When the coconut is lightly browned, add the meat and cook until warmed through.

Corned Beef

*Serves 6–8: 3 lb (1½ kg) corned beef brisket, trimmed; ⅓ cup (2½ fl oz) white wine vinegar; ⅓ cup (3 oz) sugar; 1½ cups (12 fl oz) water; 6 black peppercorns; 3 whole cloves; 2 bay leaves; 1 medium-size onion, sliced
Vegetables: 6 medium-size potatoes, peeled and halved; 1 large wedge cabbage, quartered; 6 small onions, peeled and an X cut in the bases; 6 medium-size carrots, peeled*

If the meat is very salty, soak it in cold water for 3–4 hours, changing the water twice.

Put the vinegar, sugar and water into a casserole or oven bag and stir or shake until the sugar has dissolved. Add the remaining ingredients and the meat. Cover the casserole with plastic wrap vented at one edge or tie the top of the bag with plastic or string and pierce in several places near the closure.

Place the meat in its bag in a dish deep enough to hold the cooking liquids should the bag split. Microwave on HIGH (100%) for 10 minutes, then continue on MEDIUM (50%) for 1¼–1½ hours until the meat is very tender. Turn several times during cooking.

Add the vegetables halfway through the cooking. Add an extra 8–10 minutes' cooking time. If using a temperature probe, set for 155°F (70°C).

Coconut Beef

Crown Roast of Lamb

Serves 6: 1 crown roast of lamb with 12 ribs; 1 cup (4 oz) all purpose flour; ¼ cup (2 oz) tomato puree; 1 cup (8 fl oz) port; 2½ cups (20 fl oz) chicken stock; salt and pepper

Trim the lamb and cover the bones with aluminum foil. Roast in an oven preheated to 350°F (180°C) for 45 minutes, then keep it warm while you make the gravy.

Skim the fat from the pan juices and stir in the flour. Put the roasting pan over high heat and stir well until the flour has browned. Add the tomato puree, port, stock, salt and pepper. Bring to the boil,

stirring constantly, and simmer for 3–4 minutes or until the gravy is smooth. Place paper frills on the lamb bones and serve with vegetables, redcurrant jelly and the gravy.

Crumbed Pork Slices

Crumbed Pork Slices

*Serves 4: 8 oz (250 g) pork loin cut in ½-in (1-cm) slices; 3 tablespoons light soy sauce; 3 tablespoons sweet rice wine (mirin)); ½ teaspoon ginger juice (see page 209); 1 egg, lightly beaten; 1 cup (8 oz) soft, white homemade breadcrumbs, or dried if preferred; oil for shallow frying; 4 oz (125 g) cabbage, finely shredded; 4 lemon wedges (garnish)
Tonkatsu Sauce: ¼ teaspoon English mustard powder; 3 tablespoons dark soy sauce; 1 tablespoon sake; 1 tablespoon tomato sauce; 1½ teaspoons Worcestershire sauce*

Put the pork into a shallow dish. Combine the soy sauce, *mirin* and ginger juice and leave the pork to marinate for 20 minutes. Drain the pork well, then dip each slice into the beaten egg, then into the breadcrumbs, pressing firmly to coat well on both sides. Put the crumbed slices on a plate, cover with plastic wrap and refrigerate for at least 1 hour. The pork can be left much longer if desired.

Combine all the sauce ingredients, stirring to mix well, then pour into individual sauce bowls.

Heat about ¼ in (5 mm) of oil in a skillet and cook the crumbed pork for about 3 minutes on either side until golden brown. Drain and cut each slice across into bite-sized portions. Divide among 4 serving plates. Arrange the shredded cabbage next to the pork and garnish with a lemon wedge. Serve hot.

Chinese Cabbage Rolls (see page 263)

Crown Roast of Lamb (see page 264)

D

Danish Meatballs

Makes 36: 8 oz (250 g) lean veal; 8 oz (250 g) lean pork; 4 oz (125 g) beef steak; 4 oz (125 g) cooked ham; 1 medium-size onion; 1 teaspoon salt; ½ teaspoon black pepper; 1 large egg; 1 teaspoon baking soda; ¼ cup (1 oz) dry breadcrumbs; ⅓ cup (2½ fl oz) cream; oil
Dill Mayonnaise: 2 tablespoons mayonnaise; 1½ tablespoons heavy cream; ¾ teaspoons dried dill; ½ teaspoon caraway seeds

Finely grind the meats, ham and onion, then add the remaining ingredients, mixing thoroughly. Chill for 1 hour, then make 36 meatballs and flatten each slightly.

Heat about 1 in (2.5 cm) oil to moderate and fry the meatballs, about eight at a time, until golden brown, about 5 minutes. Drain well. Serve warm or cold with Dill Mayonnaise.

To make the Dill Mayonnaise, mix the ingredients together about 2 hours before use.

Flatten the meatballs slightly.

Fry until golden brown.

Danish Meatballs

Deep Fried Meatballs (Kofta)

Serves 4: 1 lb (500 g) very finely ground lamb or beef; 1 medium-size red or brown onion; 1 garlic clove; 1 slice fresh ginger; 1 fresh green chili; 1 heaped tablespoon finely chopped fresh cilantro or mint leaves; 2 teaspoons garam masala; 2 heaped tablespoons plain yogurt; 1 teaspoon salt; oil for deep frying

Put the meat into a deep bowl. Chop the onion, garlic, ginger and chili together until very fine, then mix with the meat. Add the cilantro or mint leaves, *garam masala*, yogurt and salt, and mix well. Leave to stand for at least 30 minutes to allow the yogurt to tenderize the meat.

Put plenty of oil into a deep frying pan and heat. Shape the meat into balls about 1 in (2.5 cm) and deep fry until golden brown. Do not overcook. Drain and serve with rice and chutney.

E

Emmentaler Schnitzel

Serves 4: 4 veal schnitzels; seasoned flour; 1 egg, lightly beaten with 2 tablespoons water; ½ cup (2 oz) fine dry breadcrumbs; 3 tablespoons grated Emmentaler cheese; oil; 4 slices Emmentaler cheese

Dust the schnitzels in the seasoned flour, dip them in the egg wash and coat with a mixture of breadcrumbs and cheese.

Fry the schnitzels in oil until light brown and cooked through, then put into a heatproof serving dish. Put a slice of cheese on each piece of meat and broil under a preheated broiler until the cheese melts.

English Oxtail with Dumplings

Serves 8: 4 oxtails, cut into pieces; seasoned flour; 1 oz (30 g) dry English mustard; 4 oz (125 g) onions, chopped; 4 oz (125 g) mushrooms, chopped; 2 bay leaves; 4 oz (125 g) carrots; salt and freshly ground black pepper; 1¼ cups (10 fl oz) dry red wine
Brown Sauce: 4 onions, chopped; 6 tablespoons (3 oz) dripping; 5 tablespoons all purpose flour; 5 cups (1¼ liters) beef stock or water; 3 tablespoons Worcestershire sauce; 3 tablespoons vinegar
Dumplings: 4 oz (125 g) suet; 4 cups (1 lb) all purpose flour; 1 tablespoon baking soda; salt and pepper; water; chopped parsley for garnish

Soak the oxtail in cold water for 24 hours.

To make the Brown Sauce, sauté the onions in the dripping until they are browned. Drain off the fat. Add the flour and cook until it browns, then pour in the stock or water and stir until it boils. Add the Worcestershire sauce and vinegar, and simmer for 10 minutes. Strain and reserve.

Dry the oxtail and roll in a mixture of seasoned flour and mustard. Place in a dry skillet or casserole and fry. The oxtail will render its own fat. Add the onions, mushrooms, bay leaves, carrots, salt and pepper, and sauté lightly. Add the wine and the reserved brown sauce. Cover the pan and simmer the oxtail for 2½ hours or until the meat is tender and falls off the bone.

Meanwhile, to make the dumplings, mix together the suet, flour, baking soda, salt and pepper, then add enough water to make a firm soft dough. Roll into 16 small balls and simmer in a pan of salted water for about 30 minutes.

To serve, garnish with parsley and serve with dumplings, broad beans and boiled new potatoes.

Fillet of Beef in Filo Pastry , Stuffed with Pecans and Mushrooms

Fricassée of Veal with Mushrooms

Serves 4: 1½ lb (750 g) veal shoulder or breast, boned; 3 tablespoons (1½ oz) butter; 2 tablespoons all purpose flour; 2½ cups (20 fl oz) veal or chicken stock or water and chicken bouillon cube; salt and pepper; 8 small white onions; 8 button mushrooms; 1 egg yolk; 2 tablespoons cream; few drops of lemon juice; chopped parsley for garnish

Cut the veal into 1-in (2.5-cm) cubes and fry slowly in the butter without coloring. Stir in the flour and cook over a low heat for 5 minutes. Add the stock slowly, stirring continuously, and bring to the boil. Season lightly, cover and simmer gently for 30 minutes. Remove the veal with a slotted spoon.

Adjust the consistency and seasoning if necessary and strain into a clean saucepan. Add the veal and onions and simmer for 15 minutes, then add the mushrooms and cook a further 15 minutes or until the vegetables are tender.

Mix the egg yolk with the cream and stir into the fricassée over a low heat or preferably shake the pan gently until thoroughly mixed. Do not boil. Stir in the lemon juice and serve sprinkled with chopped parsley.

F

Fillet of Beef in Filo Pastry, Stuffed with Pecans and Mushrooms

Serves 6: 2 lb (1 kg) rib fillet; 4 tablespoons (2 oz) butter; 5 sheets filo pastry; salt and black pepper Stuffing: ½ medium-size onion, finely chopped; 2 tablespoons (1 oz) butter; ½ cup (2 oz) pecans, chopped; 2½ oz (75 g) fresh mushrooms, chopped; 1 tablespoon chopped parsley; 1 teaspoon grated lemon peel; 1 egg yolk; salt and pepper

Trim the fillet, removing the skin and fat, and slit down one side so that it can be opened flat.

To make the stuffing, place the onion and butter in a small covered dish and microwave on HIGH (100%) for 2 minutes. Add the remaining stuffing ingredients, seasoning generously. Rub the meat with black pepper and place on a micro-wave roasting rack. Cover with a piece of waxed paper and microwave on MEDIUM-HIGH (70%) for 5 minutes. Turn and microwave a further 5 minutes on MEDIUM-HIGH (70%) after draining off the pan juices. Remove from the oven and let stand uncovered to cool.

Soften the butter in a small jug or dish on MEDIUM-HIGH (70%) for 1 minute. Brush each sheet of filo pastry lightly with the butter and stack together. Wrap the meat in the pastry and place, folded edges downwards, on an oven tray. Brush the top of the pastry with the remaining butter. Bake in an oven preheated to 425°F (230°C) for about 18 minutes until the pastry is well colored.

Check the internal temperature with a meat thermometer; rare meat should be 140°F (60°C), medium 145–155°F (65–70°C) and well done 165°F (75°C). Allow to stand for at least 5 minutes before carving. Slice across the fillet so that each serving has a wrapping of pastry and a layer of the stuffing in the center.

G

Goulash

Serves 4: 1¼ lb (625 g) veal steak; 2 tablespoons olive oil or cooking oil; 1 medium-size onion, finely chopped; ¾ teaspoon sweet paprika; salt; ½ cup (4 fl oz) water; ½ cup (4 fl oz) sour cream

Cut the veal into small cubes and sauté in two or three batches in the oil until evenly colored. Remove and keep warm.

Add the onion and fry until lightly colored and softened. Return the meat and add the paprika and salt. Pour in about ½ cup of water, cover the pan and braise gently for about 1½ hours or until the meat is completely tender.

Add a splash of hot water from time to time during cooking to prevent the dish drying up and sticking to the pan. Just before serving stir in the sour cream and heat through.

Greek Meatballs

Makes 48 egg-size meatballs: 1 onion, finely chopped; 1 tablespoon olive oil; 2 lb (1 kg) finely ground lamb, beef or veal; 4¼ cups (8 oz) soft breadcrumbs; 2 teaspoons finely chopped mint; 3 sprigs parsley, finely chopped; 2 teaspoons salt; freshly ground black pepper; juice of 1 lemon; 2-3 tablespoons Ouzo, or ½ cup (4 fl oz) dry red wine; 2 eggs, lightly beaten; ½ cup (2 oz) all purpose flour; ⅔ cup (5 fl oz) olive oil

Lightly fry the onion in 1 tablespoon of oil until golden. Combine all ingredients except the flour and the oil for frying. Knead well until the mixture is blended and smooth. Shape it into egg-size balls and roll in the flour. Fry the balls in hot oil, rolling them until they are brown on all sides.

H

Ham Curry ★

Serves 4: 1 lb (500 g) country ham; 1 tablespoon cumin seeds; 10 dried red chilies, soaked; 3 tablespoons olive oil; ¾ cup (6 fl oz) red wine vinegar; ¼ teaspoon fenugreek seeds; ½ teaspoon brown mustard seed; 1 sprig curry leaves; ½ cup prunes; 8 green olives; sugar to taste (optional)

Cut the ham into 1-in (2.5-cm) cubes, leaving on any skin. Taste a small piece of ham and if it is very salty, soak in cold water for about 15 minutes.

Ham Curry

Toast the cumin seeds in a dry saucepan, then grind to a powder. Pound or grind the soaked chilies and mix with the cumin. Heat 1 tablespoon of olive oil and gently fry the chili–cumin mixture for 3-4 minutes. Mix the fried spices with the vinegar and put into a glass or china bowl. Add the meat, stir well and leave to marinate for 2 hours.

Heat the remaining 2 tablespoons olive oil (in an earthenware casserole if possible) and gently fry the fenugreek, mustard seed and curry leaves for about 1 minute, taking care the fenugreek seeds do not turn brown. Add the drained meat (keeping the marinade aside) and fry gently, stirring frequently, until the meat changes color and the juices have dried up. Add the marinade and sufficient cold water to just cover the meat. Cover the casserole and simmer gently until the meat is tender. Add the prunes and olives and cook a further 10 minutes. Taste and add sugar if desired. Serve with white rice.

Hawaiian Pork Chops

Serves 2: two 7-oz (210-g) pork loin or butterfly pork chops; ¼ cup (2 fl oz) pineapple juice; 2 teaspoons sweet chili sauce, or chili and garlic sauce; 2-3 teaspoons light soy sauce; ¼ teaspoon freshly ground black pepper; ½ teaspoon grated fresh ginger; 2 tablespoons (1 oz) unsalted butter; 2 slices pineapple

Trim the excess fat from the chops. Mix the remaining ingredients, except the butter and pineapple, in a dish and add the chops. Baste with the marinade, then leave for at least 1 hour, turning once or twice. Drain thoroughly, reserving the marinade. Pat the chops dry with paper towels.

Preheat a browning dish for 5 minutes. Spread the softened butter over the chops and drop into the dish when ready. Microwave on HIGH (100%) for 1 minute, then turn and microwave on HIGH (100%) for 1 minute more. Turn to the first side, add the marinade and microwave on MEDIUM (50%) for 2 minutes. Turn again, place a slice of pineapple on the top of each chop and cover. Microwave on MEDIUM (50%) for 6-8 minutes until the chops are tender when pierced with a fork. Season lightly with salt. Serve with rice.

Honey Baked Ham

Honey Baked Ham

Serves 4-6: 1½ lb (750 g) middle section of uncooked ham; 3 tablespoons honey; 3 tablespoons sugar; 3 tablespoons oil; 1 large sheet cellophane paper; 2 lotus leaves (optional)

Steam the ham for 30 minutes, then remove the skin, fat and bone, and cut into thin slices. Mix the honey, sugar and oil. Arrange the ham slices on the cellophane paper in a block and pour the honey mixture over. Wrap the cellophane around the ham, then wrap in lotus leaves or aluminum foil.

Place the ham on a baking sheet and bake in an oven preheated to 350°F (180°C) for 2 hours. Leave to cool for 15 minutes before removing the wrappers.

Hot Bean Curd with Pork

Serves 4: 3-4 large squares soft bean curd, weighing a total of about 1½ lb (750 g); 1½ tablespoons oil; 4 garlic cloves, smashed and chopped; 3 dried black mushrooms, soaked and shredded; 8 oz (250 g) ground lean pork; 1½-2 tablespoons hot bean paste; ½ cup (4 fl oz) beef stock; 1 tablespoon dark soy sauce; 1 tablespoon light soy sauce; 2 teaspoons cornstarch; 2 tablespoons water; 1 teaspoon sesame oil; 1-2 scallions, finely chopped

Cut the bean curd into ¾-in (2-cm) cubes and put in a colander to drain. Heat the oil and gently fry the garlic for 15 seconds, then add the mushrooms and stir-fry for another 15 seconds. Put in the pork, raise the heat a little and stir-fry for 3 minutes. Add the bean paste and stir-fry for 30 seconds, then pour in the stock and both lots of soy sauce. Cook for 2 minutes, then add the cornstarch combined with water. Stir and add the bean curd pieces. Cook, stirring gently, for 1 minute, then serve immediately sprinkled with sesame oil and scallions.

Hungarian Cabbage Rolls

Serves 6: 12 large cabbage leaves; 1 oz (30 g) bacon, finely chopped; 3 onions, finely chopped; 1 garlic clove, crushed; 1 lb (500 g) ground pork-veal mixture; 1 cup cooked rice; 2 eggs, lightly beaten; 2 tablespoons paprika; 1 sprig marjoram, finely chopped; salt and freshly ground black pepper; 2 lb (1 kg) sauerkraut, rinsed in cold water and drained; 1 cup (8 fl oz) water; 1 cup (8 fl oz) tomato puree; 3 tablespoons (1½ oz) butter; 2 tablespoons all purpose flour; 1 cup (8 fl oz) sour cream

Blanch the cabbage leaves in a large saucepan of boiling salted water. Drain and leave to cool.

In a skillet, fry the bacon, add the onions and garlic, and sauté until the onions are transparent. Place the onions in a mixing bowl, add the ground meat, rice, eggs, paprika and marjoram, and season with salt and pepper. Mix together well.

Put approximately 2 tablespoons of the mixture in the center of each cabbage leaf. Roll up the leaf, starting at the thick end. Fold the sides over and roll the cabbage leaf tightly.

In a large, heavy-based casserole, spread out the sauerkraut and arrange the cabbage rolls on top. Mix the water and the tomato puree and pour it over the rolls. Cover the casserole and simmer for approximately 1 hour. Transfer the cabbage rolls to a dish and keep warm.

In a small skillet, melt the butter and stir in the flour until the roux browns slightly, add the cream and continue cooking until the sauce thickens. Mix the sauce into the sauerkraut and simmer for 10 minutes; taste and, if necessary, adjust the seasoning. To serve, arrange the sauerkraut on a serving dish and place the cabbage rolls on top of it with the sauce poured over.

Irish Beef Stew

Kebabs of Ground Lamb (Sheek Kebab)

I
Irish Beef Stew

Serves 4-6: 1½ oz (45 g) dripping or lard; 1 lb (500 g) shin beef cut into 1-in (2.5-cm) cubes; 3 carrots, sliced; 2 onions, sliced; 3 stalks celery, chopped; ¼ cup (1 oz) all purpose flour; 2 cups (16 fl oz) beef stock; 1 tablespoon tomato paste; salt and freshly ground pepper; 8-12 small potatoes; 4-6 slices of bacon, cut into large pieces

Melt the fat in a heavy-based pan or casserole and brown the meat to seal. Take out the meat and in the remaining fat, fry the vegetables until slightly browned. Mix in the flour, gradually pour in the stock, add the tomato paste and season to taste.

Return the meat to the pan, cover and cook in an oven preheated to 325°F (160°C) for 45 minutes. Place the potatoes on top, cover again and continue cooking for a further 45 minutes or until the potatoes and meat are done. Broil the bacon and serve the stew garnished with the bacon.

K
Kebabs of Ground Lamb (Sheek Kebab)

Serves 4-6: 1½ lb (750 g) boneless lamb, finely ground; ¼ teaspoon saffron; 2 tablespoons water; 2 teaspoons cumin, ground; 1 large onion, chopped; 3 garlic cloves, crushed; 2½ tablespoons finely chopped fresh cilantro; 1½ teaspoons salt; 3 tablespoons ghee; dried green mango powder (amchur); lime wedges, onion rings and lettuce leaves for garnish

Mix all ingredients except 1 tablespoon of *ghee* and the dried green mango powder together and knead until smooth. Divide the mixture into 2-in (5-cm) balls and flatten each into a sausage shape. Insert a flat metal skewer along each kebab, press firmly onto the skewer and roll across the bottom of a plate to give an even shape.

Melt the remaining *ghee* and brush each kebab lightly. Cook under a hot broiler or on a charcoal barbecue until well browned on the surface and cooked through. Brush with more *ghee* during cooking to keep moist. Remove from the heat and sprinkle with the mango powder. Serve with lime wedges, onion rings and lettuce leaves.

Konigsberg Meatballs

*Serves 6: 1 cup (2 oz) fresh breadcrumbs;
1 lb (500 g) lean beaf, ground; 8 oz (250 g) pork,
ground; 2 scallions, chopped; ½ teaspoon grated
lemon peel; juice of ½ lemon; 1 tablespoon juice
from jar of capers; 2 anchovy fillets, chopped;
1 teaspoon salt; freshly ground black pepper;
2 eggs, beaten; 1 egg white, beaten; 3-4 cups
(24 fl oz-1 liter) beef stock
Caper Sauce: 2 tablespoons (1 oz) butter; 1 scallion,
chopped; 2 tablespoons all purpose flour; ½ cup
(4 fl oz) white wine; 1 egg yolk; 1 tablespoon capers;
juice of ½ lemon; salt and freshly ground pepper*

Soak the breadcrumbs in water, then squeeze out and add to the ground beef and pork. Mix together well. Add the scallions, lemon peel, lemon and caper juice, anchovies, salt and pepper. Combine all ingredients, then add the beaten eggs and egg white. When the mixture is smooth, form it into 2-in (5-cm) meatballs.

Bring the stock to the boil and while it is boiling rapidly, add the meatballs, making sure not to add too many at one time. Poach them for approximately 15 minutes or until they rise to the surface. Remove the meatballs with a slotted spoon and keep them warm. Strain the cooking juice and set it aside.

Meanwhile, make the caper sauce. Melt the butter in a saucepan. Add the scallion and cook until it is soft. Stir in the flour and cook for a few minutes. Add 2½-3 cups of the strained cooking juice. Pour in the wine and simmer for a few minutes until the mixture is smooth and thick. Reduce the heat, then mix in the egg yolk. Make sure that the sauce does not boil as it will curdle. Add the capers and lemon juice, and season to taste. If the sauce is too thick, add more stock. To serve, add the meatballs to the sauce and gently reheat. Traditionally, they are served with potatoes and a green bean salad.

Korean Hotpot

*Serves 4: 6 oz (185 g) liver; salt and pepper; sesame
oil; 3 oz (90 g) tripe; 3½ oz (100 g) ground beef;
1 egg; ½ medium-size carrot; 6 dried mushrooms,
soaked in cold water for 30 minutes; 1 green bell
pepper; 1 fresh red chili; 3½ oz (100 g) canned
bamboo shoots, drained; 3½ oz (100 g) beef steak;
12 gingko nuts; 4 walnuts; 4½ cups (1⅛ liters) beef
stock; 1 tablespoon light soy sauce
Vinegar Soy Sauce Dip: ¾ cup (6 fl oz) light soy
sauce; 3 tablespoons white wine vinegar;
3 tablespoons ground sesame seeds; 2 teaspoons
finely chopped scallions*

Slice the liver thinly, then rub with salt and pepper and fry for 2 minutes on each side in a little sesame oil. Slice the tripe and boil for 5 minutes in slightly salted water. Drain. Mix the ground beef with the egg and a little salt and pepper, and roll into small balls. Fry in sesame oil until lightly browned.

Scrape the carrot and cut into long thin strips. Drain the mushrooms, remove the stems and cut into quarters. Remove the seeds and stem from the peppers and slice thinly. Remove the seeds from the chili and slice. Slice the bamboo shoots.

Put the beef into the freezer until firm, then cut into wafer-thin slices, season with salt and pepper and fry for 2 minutes in a little sesame oil. Arrange the liver, tripe and beef in a charcoal hotpot or metal fondue pot (or use an electric frying pan on lowest heat setting). Add the vegetables, then the meatballs, gingko nuts and walnuts. Pour the stock over and add 1 teaspoon salt and soy sauce. If the stock is made from a stock cube, do not add extra salt. Bring to the boil and simmer for 12-15 minutes.

Serve straight from the pan using wooden chopsticks. Small bowls of soy sauce and the combined ingredients of Vinegar Soy Sauce Dip should be placed on the table. When all meat and vegetables have been eaten, serve the soup in small bowls.

L
Lamb and Potato Curry

*Serves 4-6: 1 lb (500 g) lean lamb, shoulder or leg;
8 oz (250 g) peeled potatoes; oil for deep frying;
2 black cardamoms; ¼ teaspoon fennel seeds;
1 tablespoon ground coriander; ¾ teaspoon
turmeric; 1-in (2.5-cm) piece fresh ginger; 4 garlic
cloves; 2 green chilies; ½ cup plain yogurt;
3 tablespoons ghee; 2 large onions; 1½ teaspoons
black mustard seeds; ½ teaspoon chili powder; salt
and pepper; garam masala; fresh cilantro leaves,
finely chopped*

Trim the lamb and cut into 1½-in (4-cm) cubes. Cut the potatoes into ¾-in (2-cm) dice. Heat the oil and fry the potatoes until well colored. Remove and drain well.

Grind the seasonings from cardamoms to chilies to a fairly smooth paste and rub into the meat cubes. Place in a dish and pour the yogurt over. Leave for 2 hours to marinate.

Heat the *ghee* and fry the lamb until well colored. Add any remaining marinade, the sliced onions and cover with water. Bring to the boil, cover and simmer until the meat is very tender. Add the fried potatoes and mustard seeds and season with chili powder, salt, pepper and *garam masala* to taste. Heat through, transfer to a serving dish and garnish with chopped cilantro.

Lamb Biryani

*Serves 8: Garnish: 8 shallots or 1 medium-size red or
brown onion, finely sliced; 3 tablespoons ghee or
butter; ½ cup raw cashew nuts, split in half; ½ cup
seedless raisins; fresh cilantro leaves
Curry: 1 medium-size red or brown onion, chopped;
1-in (2.5-cm) piece fresh ginger, finely chopped;
4 garlic cloves, finely chopped; 1½-in (4-cm) stick
cinnamon; 6 cloves; 6 cardamom pods, slit and
bruised; ½ teaspoon freshly ground black pepper;
½ teaspoon black cumin seeds (optional);
3 tablespoons meat curry powder (see page 274);
1½ lb (750 g) boneless leg lamb, cut in 1-in (2.5-cm)
cubes; 3-4 tomatoes, coarsely chopped; ½ cup
(4 fl oz) plain yogurt; ½ cup (4 fl oz) water;
1 teaspoon salt; 2 tablespoons chopped mint
Rice: 4 cups Basmati rice; 1 tablespoon salt
Additional items: 2 tablespoons ghee or butter;
½ cup (4 fl oz) evaporated milk; yellow food
coloring (optional); few drops rosewater*

Prepare the garnish first. Pat the sliced shallots dry. Heat the *ghee* and fry the shallots gently until golden brown. Drain and set aside. Fry the cashews very gently in the same *ghee*, stirring constantly, until golden brown. Drain and set aside. Fry the raisins in *ghee* for just 1 minute, drain and set aside, leaving *ghee* in the pan. When the fried garnishes are cold, store in an airtight container.

To prepare the curry, gently fry the onion, ginger and garlic in the leftover *ghee* for 2 minutes. Add the cinnamon, cloves, cardamom, pepper and black cumin, and continue frying for another 2 minutes. Combine the curry powder with enough cold water to form a stiff paste. Add the paste to the pan and fry for 2 minutes, then put in the lamb and fry until it changes color. Add the tomatoes and cook until they begin to soften, then put in the yogurt and stir for a moment or two before adding the water, salt and mint. Cover the pan and cook meat gently until it is soft and the gravy has almost dried up. If there is more than about ¼ cup of gravy left, cook with the lid off the pan to reduce.

While the curry is cooking, prepare the rice. Wash thoroughly in several changes of water, then drain in a sieve or colander for at least 15 minutes. Heat a large saucepan of water with 1 tablespoon salt added, and when it is boiling vigorously, pour in the rice in a thin stream, stirring all the time. Stir until the water comes back to the boil, then continue boiling with the lid off the pan for 5 minutes. Drain the rice thoroughly.

To assemble the *biryani*, melt 1 tablespoon of *ghee* in a very large casserole. Swirl around so that the sides of the casserole are greased. Mix half the reserved garnish ingredients with the rice and spread half the rice on the bottom of the casserole. Arrange the meat over this, then top with the remaining rice. The *biryani* can be left aside for several hours at this stage.

Roughly 30 minutes before the *biryani* is required, melt 1 tablespoon *ghee* and combine with the evaporated milk, yellow food coloring and rosewater. Spoon this mixture over the top of the assembled casserole, cover tightly and put in an oven preheated to 300°F (150°C) for 30 minutes. Serve piled onto a large platter with the remaining garnish ingredients and fresh cilantro leaves scattered on top. *Biryani* goes well with onion *sambal* (see page 279) and cucumber mixed with yogurt.

Lamb in Spinach Puree

Serves 4–6: 1½ lb (750 g) leg or shoulder of lamb; 3 tablespoons ghee; 3 garlic cloves, crushed; 1-in (2.5-cm) piece fresh ginger, grated; 4 black cardamoms, crushed; 1 tablespoon ground coriander; ½ green chili, finely chopped; 2 teaspoons black mustard seeds, ground; 1 teaspoon turmeric; 1½ cups (12 fl oz) water; 2 teaspoons salt; 1½ lb (750 g) fresh or frozen leaf spinach; pinch of freshly grated nutmeg; 1½ teaspoons sugar; 1 tablespoon white poppy seeds, ground; ¼ cup (2 fl oz) plain yogurt; salt; ½ cup (4 fl oz) heavy cream

Trim the meat and cut into 1½-in (4-cm) cubes. Heat the *ghee* in a casserole or heavy-based saucepan and fry the garlic for 2 minutes. Add the ginger, crushed cardamoms, coriander, chili and mustard seeds, and fry on moderate heat for 2 minutes. Add the meat and sprinkle the turmeric

over. Stir to coat the meat thoroughly with the spices and cook for 5 minutes.

Pour over ½ cup water, cover the pan and cook for 20 minutes. Add the remaining water and salt, and cook, covered, until the lamb is tender and most of the liquid has been absorbed.

Drain the frozen spinach, or wash and drain the fresh spinach, discarding stems. Chop finely and put into a saucepan with the nutmeg, sugar, poppy seeds and yogurt. Cover and cook until tender. Add salt to taste and blend to a puree. Mix the spinach into the meat and heat through, stirring to mix the two sauces well. Add cream and reheat. Check the seasoning and serve hot.

Lamb on Skewers (Souvlákia)

Serves 6: 1 cup (8 fl oz) olive oil; juice of 2 lemons; ½ cup (4 fl oz) dry red wine; 1 garlic clove, crushed; 2 bay leaves; ½ teaspoon salt; freshly ground black pepper; 1½ tablespoons dried oregano; 3 lb (1.5 kg) lamb from a leg, cut into 1½-in (4-cm) cubes; 3 green bell peppers; 2 onions, each cut into 6 wedges; 12–18 small button mushrooms; 3–4 tomatoes, cut into quarters

In a large bowl, combine the oil, lemon juice, wine, garlic, bay leaves, salt and pepper and oregano. Mix well and add the meat.

Lamb on Skewers (Souvlákia)

Halve the green peppers, remove and discard the seeds, cut the peppers into 1-in (2.5-cm) squares. Blanch the peppers and onions for 5 minutes, then rinse in cold water and add them to the marinade. Marinate for 24 hours. Two hours before broiling the skewers, add the mushrooms and the tomatoes to the marinade.

Allow 1 skewer per person. Divide all the ingredients equally among the six skewers; thread a piece of lamb, pepper, onion, mushroom and tomato, and then repeat. Leave room at the end of each skewer for easy holding and turning. Broil either over an open charcoal fire or under a broiler for 15 minutes or until cooked to taste. While broiling, baste frequently with the marinade.

Lamb with Olives

Serves 4: 6 tablespoons olive oil; 4 lamb leg steaks, about ½ in (1 cm) thick; salt and freshly ground black pepper; 1 cup (5 oz) black olives, pitted and chopped; ½ teaspoon dried oregano; 3 tablespoons chopped green bell pepper; juice of ½ lemon

In a skillet, heat the oil and brown the steaks on both sides. Drain off some of the fat and season. Add the olives, sprinkle with the oregano, add the green bell pepper and lemon juice, and simmer for 4–5 minutes or until cooked to taste. Serve.

Lancashire Steak Pie

Serves 4: 1 tablespoon vegetable oil; 1 large onion, finely chopped; 1 small stalk celery, finely chopped; 8 oz (250 g) ground beef; salt and pepper; 1 tablespoon Worcestershire sauce; 1 quantity shortcrust pastry (see page 319); 6 slices blood sausage

Heat the oil in a pan and sauté the onion and celery for about 5 minutes or until the onion is transparent. Add the ground beef, salt, pepper and Worcestershire sauce, and cook until the meat is well browned.

Roll out the pastry and, using two-thirds of it, line a shallow round pie dish. Spoon in the meat mixture and arrange the blood sausage slices on top. Roll out the remaining pastry and cover the pie with it, crimping the edges together. Bake in an oven preheated to 350°F (180°C) for 30–35 minutes or until the pastry is golden.

Leg of Lamb Marinated in Wine with Juniper Berries

Leg of Lamb Marinated in Wine with Juniper Berries

Serves 4: 1½ lb (750 g) leg of lamb; 20 juniper berries, lightly crushed; 4–5 garlic cloves, peeled and slivered; 10 small sprigs fresh rosemary; freshly ground black pepper; 3 cups (24 fl oz) dry white wine; 2 large onions, thinly sliced; 4 slices fat bacon

Although this must be prepared in advance, it is worth the effort and planning for its superb game-like taste. It should prove a particular favorite for those who are not fond of the natural smell of lamb.

Trim excess fat from the lamb and use a sharp knife to pierce the meat all over. Insert the juniper berries, garlic and rosemary into the incisions. Rub the meat with the pepper and place in a deep glass or china dish. Pour the wine over and arrange the sliced onions on top. Cover the dish tightly with plastic wrap and place in the refrigerator for up to 48 hours. Turn the lamb from time to time.

When ready to cook, drain thoroughly and wipe with paper towels. Dust generously with salt to flavor and crisp the surface. Place on a microwave roasting rack. Snip the bacon rind to prevent it curling and place over the lamb. Cover with a piece of waxed paper and microwave on MEDIUM-HIGH (70%) for 16–19 minutes for medium-rare and 22–25 minutes for

273

well done. Turn the roast so that it cooks evenly and drain the juices into the marinade. Half way through cooking, add ½ cup (4 fl oz) of the marinade to the dish. When done, remove from the oven, wrap in aluminum foil or cover with a dome lid and allow to stand for 10 minutes.

Serve the bacon and the marinated onion, separated into rings, with the lamb. Return the drained pan juices to the dish and heat on HIGH (100%) for 1–2 minutes until boiling. If desired, thicken with cornstarch and add salt and pepper to taste.

Note: This lamb can be cooked on combination (mix) setting, allowing an approximate cooking time of 15–20 minutes per 1 lb (500 g) for medium and 17–24 minutes per 1 lb (500 g) for well done. If using a temperature probe, set for an internal temperature of 145°F (65°C) for medium or 165–175°F (75–80°C) for well done.

Lentils with Bacon

Serves 6: 12 oz (375 g) green lentils, soaked overnight; 5 cups (1¼ liters) beef stock; 2 potatoes, diced; 3 tablespoons vinegar; 3 tablespoons sugar; salt and freshly ground black pepper; 8 oz (250 g) bacon, chopped; 2 onions, finely chopped; 3 tablespoons finely chopped parsley

In a heavy-based saucepan, simmer the lentils in the beef stock for 45 minutes or until soft. Add the potatoes and cook for a further 15 minutes, then mix in the vinegar, sugar, salt and pepper. In a skillet, brown the bacon, add the onions and fry lightly. Add the bacon, onions and parsley to the lentils and mix well. Serve hot.

M

Malay Beef Stew

Serves 4: 1 lb (500 g) beef top round; 8–10 shallots or 1½ medium-size red or brown onions, finely sliced; 1 thick slice fresh ginger, very finely chopped; 1–2 garlic cloves, smashed and chopped; 3 tablespoons oil; 3 tablespoons meat curry powder (see below); 1 tablespoon water; ¼ cup (2 fl oz) tamarind water (see page 392); 1 stalk lemongrass, bruised; ¼ whole nutmeg, grated; 1 teaspoon fenugreek seeds; 4 medium-size potatoes, peeled and quartered
Meat Curry Powder: 10 oz (300 g) coriander seeds;

2½ oz (75 g) cumin seeds; 2½ oz (75 g) fennel seeds; 2½ oz (75 g) dried red chilies; 1½ oz (45 g) black peppercorns; 1½ oz (45 g) cinnamon sticks; 10 whole cardamom pods; 10 whole cloves; 1½ oz (45 g) turmeric

Cut the beef into slices ½ in (1 cm) thick and about 1½ in (4 cm) square. Fry the shallots, ginger and garlic gently in hot oil in a skillet until golden. Mix the curry powder with water to form a paste, then add to the skillet and fry, stirring constantly, for 2 minutes. Add the beef and continue frying until it changes color and is well coated with spices.

Put in just enough water to cover the meat and add the tamarind water, lemongrass, nutmeg and fenugreek seeds. Cover and simmer until the meat is just tender, then add the potatoes and continue simmering until the potatoes are soft and the gravy has thickened.

To prepare the curry powder, dry fry each spice except the turmeric separately until heated and giving off a pleasant fragrance. Cool slightly, then grind a little at a time to a fine powder. Add the turmeric, mix well, then store in an airtight container when cold.

Note: The curry powder will keep for several months and can be used as a base for all meat curries and combined with other spices for different flavors.

Ma Po Bean Curd

Serves 4: ½ cup (4 fl oz) oil; 6 squares soft bean curd; 3 oz (90 g) ground beef; 3 oz (90 g) ground pork; 8 garlic cloves, finely chopped; 4 scallions, finely chopped; 1½ tablespoons hot bean paste; ¼ teaspoon white pepper, or 1½ teaspoons chili oil; 3 tablespoons dark soy sauce; ½ cup (4 fl oz) beef stock; 2 teaspoons cornstarch; 1½ teaspoons sesame oil

Heat the oil in a skillet. Drain the bean curd and carefully cut into cubes, then fry without stirring, to avoid breaking the cubes. Cook to a light golden brown, then lift out and set aside.

Add the ground beef and pork to the pan and fry until light brown, then add the garlic, scallions, bean paste, pepper or chili oil and soy sauce. Cook for 3 minutes, then add the beef stock mixed with cornstarch.

Bring the liquid to the boil, reduce the heat and simmer until the sauce has thickened and the meat is well seasoned.

Return the bean curd and cook for 2 minutes. Transfer to a serving dish and splash with the sesame oil.

Marinated Roast Pork Fillet ★

Serves 2: 2 pork fillets (approx. 1 lb/500 g)
Marinade: 1 tablespoon oil; 1 tablespoon light soy sauce; 2 tablespoons liquid from preserved ginger or 2 teaspoons grated fresh ginger; 1 tablespoon sugar; 2 teaspoons dry sherry; 1 teaspoon five spice powder; red food coloring

Trim the fillets, removing all fat and skin. Mix the marinade ingredients together, stirring until the sugar has dissolved. Put the fillets into a glass or china dish and pour the marinade over. Cover with plastic wrap and leave for 2–4 hours, turning from time to time. Drain well, then place on a metal rack over a dish to catch the drips. Cook in an oven preheated to 350°F (180°C) for 12–13 minutes, turning once. Serve cold, thinly sliced, with soy sauce and mustard.

Marinated Roast Veal

Serves 6: 2 cups (16 fl oz) dry white wine; 2 garlic cloves, crushed; 1 tablespoon paprika; ¼ cup (2 fl oz) olive oil; salt and freshly ground pepper; 3 lb (1.5 kg) rolled veal shoulder; 1½ cups (12 fl oz) water; 2 tablespoons vinegar; 3 tablespoons finely chopped mixed pickles

Combine the wine, garlic, paprika, oil, salt and pepper, and marinate the veal for two days, turning occasionally.

Place the meat on a rack set in a roasting pan and roast in an oven preheated to 350°F (180°C) for 1½–2 hours. Occasionally baste with the marinade. When cooked, keep the meat warm.

Pour the remaining marinade and cooking juices into a saucepan, add the water, vinegar and pickles, and boil rapidly until reduced to 2 cups (16 fl oz). Season to taste. Serve the meat cut into slices with a little of the sauce poured over it. Serve the rest of the sauce separately.

Note: Traditionally the veal is served with baked potatoes and a vegetable, especially spinach puree, cooked with garlic and oil.

Ma Po Bean Curd

Meat Pie — Stage Coach Inn

Serves 6–8: 3 lb (1.5 kg) beef (chuck or round); or pork tenderloin, cut into cubes; ½ cup (2 oz) all purpose flour; salt and pepper; ¼ cup (2 fl oz) oil; 4 tablespoons (2 oz) butter; 1½ cups sliced onion; 1 garlic clove, minced; two 14 oz (440-g) cans condensed beef consommé; 1 bay leaf, crushed; 1 teaspoon dry mustard; 2 teaspoons soy sauce; 2 teaspoons Worcestershire sauce; 1 cup shelled peas; ½ cup finely diced carrot; 1 quantity shortcrust pastry (see page 319)

Toss the meat cubes in flour mixed with salt and pepper. Brown the meat quickly, a few cubes at a time, in hot oil and butter, removing them as they brown. Add the onion and garlic and fry until tender.

Return the meat to the pan, then add the consommé, 1 can of water and the remaining seasonings. Bring to the boil, reduce the heat, cover and simmer for 1½ hours or until tender. Add the vegetables.

Place the mixture into a casserole or individual casserole dishes. Top with the pastry, rolled to ⅛ in (3 mm) thick. Bake in an oven preheated to 450°F (230°C) for 30–35 minutes or until the crust is brown.

Mixed Grill (Teppanyaki)

Serves 6: Pon-zu Sauce: ½ cup (4 fl oz) light soy sauce; ½ cup (4 fl oz) lemon juice; 2 tablespoons sweet rice wine (mirin); 2 tablespoons dried bonito flakes (hana-katsuo)
Seafood Sauce: ½ cup (4 fl oz) mayonnaise; 1 tablespoon tomato sauce; few drops of freshly squeezed garlic juice
Daikon-Chili Garnish: 3-in (8-cm) piece giant white radish (daikon); 1 fresh red chili
Additional Garnishes: 1 lemon; 2 scallions
1½ lb (750 g) piece of sirloin or fillet (tenderloin) beef, cut ¾ in (2 cm) thick; 6–12 large raw shrimp; 1 lb (500 g) boneless chicken; 1 medium-size eggplant; 6 large fresh shiitake or button mushrooms; 8 oz (250 g) beansprouts; 2 medium-size onions; 2 green bell peppers; optional extras: 6 oysters in the shell, 1–2 fresh squid, 1 sweet potato

Prepare the sauces and garnishes first. To make pon-zu sauce, combine the soy sauce, lemon juice and *mirin* in a small pan and bring just to the boil. Remove from the heat, add the dried bonito flakes, leave to stand for 1 minute, then strain and set the sauce aside.

To make the seafood sauce, combine all ingredients and mix well.

Poke three holes into the *daikon* with a chopstick. Cut the chili lengthwise into three strips and push each into a hole in the *daikon*. Grate it finely, then squeeze the grated mixture to expel the liquid. Cover and keep cool.

Cut the lemon into eight wedges. Slice the scallions, including green tops, very finely. Cover and keep cool.

Arrange the beef on a large platter. Wash and dry the shrimp, but do not peel or discard the head and tails. Trim the whiskers if they are long.

Cut the chicken into six pieces, pricking the skin with a fork. Cut the eggplant across in ½-in (1-cm) slices, leaving the skin on. Remove the stems from the mushrooms. Wash the beansprouts thoroughly, removing any tails and black skins. Cut the onions in slices ½ in (1 cm) thick. Cut each green pepper into six pieces. If using oysters, rinse and drain, but leave in the shell. If using squid, discard the head and tentacles and peel off the skin. If using sweet potato, peel and cut in ½-in (1-cm) slices. Arrange all these ingredients attractively on one or two platters and bring to the table.

If you have a sauce dish with several compartments, put a little pon-zu, seafood sauce, *daikon*-chili garnish and sliced scallion into each, arranging the lemon wedge on one corner of the scallion. Otherwise, serve in several small serving dishes.

Heat a large electric skillet and place it in the middle of the table. Add just enough oil to grease the bottom and start cooking the food, a few pieces at a time. Normally, the delicately flavored seafood such as shrimp, squid and oysters are cooked first, followed by the chicken, then the beef and vegetables, with the beansprouts being left until last. Cut the beef, chicken and squid into bite-size pieces when serving.

Each batch of food is eaten as soon as it is cooked, with each diner mixing garnishes into the pon-zu sauce to taste and dipping the food into one of the sauces before eating. Normally the seafood is eaten with a squeeze of lemon or the seafood sauce, the other foods with pon-zu.

As each round of food is being enjoyed, the next batch is sizzling away in the pan. Most items take only a few minutes to cook, although the sweet potato should be put in the pan well in advance of when it is required.

A bowl of rice with pickles is usually served at the end of a teppanyaki dinner.

Mongolian Lamb

Serves 2: 9 oz (280 g) lean lamb; ¼ cup (2 fl oz) oil; 1 small leek, shredded; 1 small carrot, parboiled and thinly sliced; 2 teaspoons toasted white sesame seeds
Seasoning A: 2 teaspoons sugar; 1 teaspoon crushed garlic; 2 tablespoons dark soy sauce; 2 tablespoons rice wine or dry sherry; 1 tablespoon sesame oil; 2 teaspoons cornstarch
Seasoning B/Sauce: ¼ cup (2 fl oz) cold water; 1 tablespoon light soy sauce; 1 tablespoon rice wine or dry sherry; 1 tablespoon sesame oil; ¼ teaspoon salt; 1 teaspoon sugar; 1¼ teaspoons cornstarch

Partially freeze the meat, cut into wafer-thin slices across the grain, then into pieces about 2 in (5 cm) square. Mix with the seasoning A ingredients and leave for about 45 minutes.

Heat the oil in a wok and stir-fry the shredded leek until lightly colored. Push to one side of the pan and add the sliced carrot. Stir-fry briefly, then push aside. Heat the pan to very high and stir-fry the lamb until lightly colored.

Place the skillet or steak pan on another heat source to thoroughly heat through. Pour the premixed seasoning B/sauce ingredients onto the meat and stir in the vegetables. Heat to boiling point, then pour into the prepared hot pan and garnish with the sesame seeds. Carry sizzling to the table.

Note: Fillet (tenderloin) of beef can also be used.

Moussaka

Serves 4: 2 egg yolks, beaten; 1 cup (8 fl oz) milk; salt and freshly ground pepper; 1 small onion, sliced; ½ cup (4 fl oz) olive oil; 4 eggplants, sliced; 1 lb (500 g) cooked lamb from the leg, ground; ½ cup (4 fl oz) beef stock; ½ cup (4 fl oz) fresh tomato sauce (see page 138)

Combine the egg yolks, milk, salt and pepper, and cook over low heat, stirring constantly until it is like a thick custard. Set aside to cool.

Sauté the onion in 1 tablespoon of the oil until golden brown. Lightly fry the eggplant slices in the remaining oil. Oil the bottom and sides of a casserole 6½ in (16 cm) in diameter and 2 in (5 cm) deep. Cover the bottom with a layer of eggplant and place some of the ground meat and fried onions on top. Repeat the layers until the ingredients are all used. Pour the beef stock and tomato sauce on top and cover with the custard. Bake the dish in an oven preheated to 350°F (180°C) for at least 1 hour or until the top has formed a golden brown crust. Serve hot or cold.

Mutton and Eggplant Curry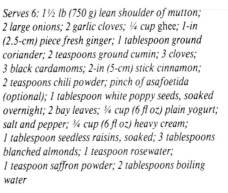

Serves 4–6: 1 lb (500 g) lean mutton or lamb, shoulder or leg; 3 medium-size eggplants; salt; 1½ tablespoons white poppy seeds; 1 teaspoon fennel seeds, crushed; 1 tablespoon ground coriander; 1¼ teaspoons ground cumin; 1½ teaspoons black peppercorns, crushed; ¾ teaspoon powdered turmeric or 1½ teaspoons grated fresh turmeric; 1-in (2.5-cm) piece fresh ginger; 8 shallots or 3 small red onions; 3 garlic cloves; 4 tablespoons ghee or oil; 3 curry leaves, or 1 bay leaf; 3 cloves; ¾-in (2-cm) stick cinnamon; 2 cups (16 fl oz) thin coconut milk; ½ cup (4 fl oz) thick coconut milk; lime juice or wedges of fresh lime

Cut the meat into ¾-in (2-cm) cubes. Cut the eggplant in half lengthwise, then into 2-in (5-cm) pieces. Sprinkle with salt, cover and allow to stand for 10 minutes to draw out the bitter juices.

Grind the poppy seeds, fennel, coriander, cumin and peppercorns together and mix with the turmeric. Peel the ginger and shred finely. Mince the shallots and garlic.

Heat the *ghee* or oil in a large skillet and fry the onions and garlic with the ginger for 3 minutes. Add the ground seasonings and fry for 5 minutes, stirring frequently. Put in the cubed meat, curry or bay leaves, cloves and cinnamon stick. Cook on moderate heat for 10 minutes, stirring to coat the meat well.

Rinse the eggplant, wipe and add to the pan, cooking for another 5 minutes. Pour the thin coconut milk over and bring almost to the boil. Lower the heat and cook for about 25 minutes or until the meat and eggplant are tender. Stir in the thick coconut milk and cook until the sauce thickens slightly.

Season to taste with salt and lime juice. Spoon into a serving dish. If serving with lime wedges, arrange around the edge of the dish.

Note: If using mutton, do not add the eggplant when frying the meat. Simmer the meat in thin coconut milk until almost tender, then add the eggplant and cook for another 20–25 minutes before adding the thick coconut milk.

Mutton and Eggplant Curry

Mutton Korma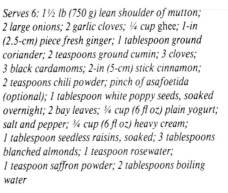

Serves 6: 1½ lb (750 g) lean shoulder of mutton; 2 large onions; 2 garlic cloves; ¼ cup ghee; 1-in (2.5-cm) piece fresh ginger; 1 tablespoon ground coriander; 2 teaspoons ground cumin; 3 cloves; 3 black cardamoms; 2-in (5-cm) stick cinnamon; 2 teaspoons chili powder; pinch of asafoetida (optional); 1 tablespoon white poppy seeds, soaked overnight; 2 bay leaves; ¾ cup (6 fl oz) plain yogurt; salt and pepper; ¾ cup (6 fl oz) heavy cream; 1 tablespoon seedless raisins, soaked; 3 tablespoons blanched almonds; 1 teaspoon rosewater; 1 teaspoon saffron powder; 2 tablespoons boiling water

Trim the mutton and cut into 2-in (5-cm) cubes. Slice the onions thinly and crush the garlic, then fry in 3 tablespoons of hot *ghee* until soft. Shred the ginger and add to the pan with the mutton cubes. Fry until well colored, turning frequently. Add the coriander and all spices to the bay leaves and stir on moderate heat for 3 minutes.

Pour in the yogurt and stir to coat the meat thoroughly and mix with the spices. Cover and simmer until the meat is tender and the liquid has been completely absorbed. Splash in a little water and add salt and pepper to taste.

Add the cream and raisins, and cover

Mutton Korma

4 tablespoons (2 oz) ghee or butter; 2 medium-size red or brown onions, grated; ½ cup (6 fl oz) plain yogurt; 2 medium-size tomatoes, skinned and chopped; 1 lb (500 g) leg lamb, cut into cubes; 1 teaspoon salt; ½ cup (4 fl oz) water

Prepare the spice paste first. Fry the coriander, poppy seeds, cumin, cardamom, peppercorns and nutmeg in a dry pan over low heat until they smell fragrant. Set aside. Cook the coconut in the same manner, stirring frequently, until it turns golden. Grind the cooked spices and coconut together finely. Grind the almonds, ginger and garlic together, then mix with the ground spice and coconut mixture, adding the chili and turmeric powder.

Heat the *ghee* in a deep skillet and gently fry the grated onion for 2–3 minutes. Add the spice paste and continue frying gently for another 3–5 minutes. Slowly add the yogurt, stirring constantly, then add the tomatoes and cook for 5 minutes. Put in the lamb and salt, and continue cooking until the meat changes color. Add the water, cover the pan and cook over low heat, stirring occasionally, until the meat is tender and the liquid has reduced to a thick sauce.

O

Osso Bucco

Serves 4: 4 veal shanks; 1 onion, chopped; 2 stalks celery, chopped; 2 oz (60 g) bacon, diced; 2 tablespoons (1 oz) butter; ⅔ cup (5 fl oz) dry white wine; pinch of thyme; 1 bay leaf; 2 garlic cloves, crushed; 1 lb (500 g) ripe tomatoes, skinned, seeded and chopped; ¼ cup (2 oz) all purpose flour; salt and pepper; 1 tablespoon oil; grated peel of ½ lemon; chopped parsley for garnish

Ask the butcher to cut the veal shanks into 2-in (5-cm) pieces across the leg bone. Sauté the onion, celery and bacon in butter. Add the wine, thyme and bay leaf, and simmer slowly for 20 minutes. Add the garlic and tomatoes and cook for a further 5 minutes.

Roll the veal in seasoned flour and fry in hot oil until light brown. Place the fried veal in an ovenproof casserole with the vegetables and tomato sauce. Cook in an oven preheated to 325–350°F (160–180°C) for 1½ hours. Just before serving, add the lemon peel. Sprinkle with chopped parsley and serve with a rice pilaf.

---

again. Continue to simmer until the meat is very tender and the sauce thick. Add a little more water if needed.

Fry the almonds in 1 tablespoon of *ghee* until golden and stir into the sauce. Add the rosewater and saffron mixed with the boiling water. Heat through for 10 minutes on low heat.

Mutton Mysore

Serves 4: 1 lb (500 g) lean mutton or lamb; 2 garlic cloves; 1 heaped teaspoon finely chopped mint; 1 teaspoon salt; 1–2 teaspoons chili powder; ½ teaspoon ground cumin; ½ teaspoon turmeric; 1 teaspoon vinegar; 1 teaspoon sugar; 1 teaspoon light soy sauce; 2 tablespoons ghee or butter

Cut the meat into pieces about ½ in (1 cm) thick.

Pound the garlic with the chopped mint and salt, then combine the pounded mixture with the spices, vinegar, sugar and soy sauce. Rub well into the meat and leave to

stand for 30 minutes.

Heat the *ghee* or butter gently in a heavy-based pan and add the meat. Do not add any water. Cover the pan and cook over very low heat, stirring from time to time, until the meat is tender. Remove the lid to allow any moisture to evaporate, and continue cooking until the meat fries to a rich brown color.

N

North Indian Lamb Curry

Serves 4: Spice Paste: 1 tablespoon ground coriander; 1 teaspoon white poppy seeds (optional); 1 teaspoon cumin seeds; 4 cardamom pods; 12 black peppercorns; small chunk nutmeg (about ⅛ of a nut); 2 heaped tablespoons shredded coconut; 10 almonds (15 if not using poppy seeds); 1-in (2.5-cm) piece fresh ginger; 6 garlic cloves; 1–2 teaspoons chili powder; ½ teaspoon turmeric

P

Pan-Fried Pork in Sweet Ginger Sauce ⬤

Serves 4: 10 oz (315 g) pork loin slices cut ¼ in (5 mm) thick; 2 tablespoons light soy sauce; 1 tablespoon ginger juice (see page 209); 1 tablespoon sake; 12 snow peas or 8 green beans; 4 oz (125 g) giant white radish (daikon), grated; 1 tablespoon rice vinegar; 4 teaspoons sugar; ¼ teaspoon salt; 1 tablespoon oil

Put the pork into a shallow bowl. Combine the soy sauce, ginger juice and *sake* and pour over the pork. Leave to marinate for about 20 minutes.

Boil the snow peas or beans in lightly salted water until just cooked but still firm. Drain and cool under running water so they retain their bright green color. If using beans, cut into 1½-in (4-cm) lengths. Keep peas or beans aside.

Squeeze out the moisture from the *daikon*, then combine with the vinegar, 1 teaspoon sugar and salt. Mix well, cover and set aside.

Remove the pork slices from the marinade, drain and pat dry. Heat the oil in a skillet and cook the pork over a moderately high heat for 2 minutes on each side. Add the marinade and remaining 3 teaspoons of sugar. Lower the heat slightly and continue cooking for 1–2 minutes, turning the pork over once so that it becomes well coated with the sauce. Remove the pork and cut into bite-size portions. Arrange on individual serving plates, then pour over the sauce (there should be about 2 tablespoons left). Garnish each serving with vinegared *daikon* and the snow peas or beans. Serve hot.

Parsi Meat, Lentil and Vegetable Stew (Dhansak) with Brown Rice

Serves 6–8: 12 oz (375 g) mixed lentils (black, yellow, red, etc.), and chickpeas; 1½ lb (750 g) lamb shoulder or leg; 3 oz (90 g) pumpkin; 4 oz (125 g) spinach; 1 large onion; 3 tablespoons chopped fresh cilantro; 2 teaspoons turmeric; 2 teaspoons salt; 4 dried chilies, soaked; 3 tablespoons boiling water; 1-in (2.5-cm) piece fresh ginger; 6 garlic cloves; 2 green chilies; 2 teaspoons tamarind; 3 cloves; 2-in (5-cm) stick cinnamon; 3 green cardamoms; 1 teaspoon black mustard seeds; 1 tablespoon ground coriander; 2 teaspoons ground cumin; 3 tablespoons ghee; 3 tablespoons chopped fresh cilantro; salt and pepper; 1 large onion, finely chopped

Brown Rice: 10 oz (315 g) long grain rice; 2 large onions, finely chopped; 2 tablespoons ghee; 4 cloves; 2 black cardamoms; 2-in (5-cm) stick cinnamon; salt and pepper; sugar

If using hard lentils like black or green lentils or chickpeas, soak overnight, then boil in unsalted water for 3 hours to soften. Place all lentils, well washed, into a saucepan and add the meat cut into ½-in (1-cm) dice. Cover with water to 3 in (8 cm) above the level of the ingredients and bring to the boil. Simmer for at least 1 hour.

Peel and slice the pumpkin, chop the spinach and slice the onion. Add the pumpkin, spinach, cilantro, onion, turmeric and salt to the pan and cook until the meat and lentils are tender, adding more water if necessary. Transfer the meat to another pan. Mash the lentils with the vegetables or put into a blender to puree.

Grind the seasonings (from dried chilies to green chilies) to a paste. Soak the tamarind in water and add to the paste together with the cloves, cinnamon, cardamom and mustard seeds. Add the ground coriander and cumin.

Heat the *ghee* and fry the seasonings for 4 minutes, then add the cilantro, salt, pepper and finely chopped onion. Cook for a further 3 minutes, then put in the lamb and cook until well colored. Add the lentil puree and adjust the seasoning to taste. Keep warm.

Wash the rice and drain well. Fry the onions in *ghee* until very well colored. They should be very dark brown, almost black. Add the spices and rice, and cover with water to 1¼ in (3 cm) above the rice. Cover and bring to the boil. Simmer until cooked through. Season to taste with salt, pepper and sugar. Serve with the dhansak.

Peppered Fillet Steaks (see page 280)

Parslied Leg of Lamb

Serves 6: 1 leg of lamb, about 5 lb (2.5 kg); 1 garlic clove, slivered; sprigs of thyme; 2 tablespoons finely chopped parsley; 3 tablespoons fresh breadcrumbs

Trim off any excess fat from the lamb. Insert slivers of garlic and small sprigs of thyme into slits cut in the lamb. Roast in an oven preheated to 400°F (200°C) for about 1 hour with a little water in the pan to prevent it from sticking.

Mix the parsley with the breadcrumbs in a bowl. About 10–15 minutes before the leg is cooked, coat it with the breadcrumb and parsley mixture, taking care to press the mixture well into the fatty surface so that it adheres. Return the meat to the oven and roast until the surface turns golden. Arrange on a serving dish, garnished with watercress.

Pepper Steak with Artichoke Hearts

Serves 4: 2 lb (1 kg) fillet steak; oil; 1 tablespoon cracked black peppercorns; coarse salt; 8 tablespoons (4 oz) butter or margarine; 1 tablespoon lemon juice; 1 teaspoon Dijon mustard; 1 teaspoon chopped fresh tarragon; salt; 7 oz (220 g) canned artichoke hearts, halved

Trim the steak and cut it into serving portions. Brush with the oil and press cracked peppercorns into each side, then sprinkle with coarse salt, freshly ground, if possible.

Broil the steaks, place in a warm serving dish and keep warm. Melt the butter and add the lemon juice, mustard, tarragon, salt to taste and the artichoke hearts. Allow the artichokes to heat through then pour over the steak. Serve hot.

Note: If you cannot buy pepper already cracked, place whole peppercorns between folded paper towels and pound with the blunt side of a steak mallet, or a rolling pin, until pepper resembles coarse breadcrumbs.

Peppered Fillet Steaks

Serves 2: 3 tablespoons (1½ oz) unsalted butter; 2 tablespoons lightly cracked black peppercorns; 2 garlic cloves, crushed (optional); two 6-oz (185-g)

eye fillet (tenderloin) steaks; 2 tablespoons brandy or Cognac; ½ cup (4 fl oz) heavy cream*

Preheat the browning dish for 5–6 minutes. Mix the butter, peppercorns and garlic, and spread over both sides of the steaks. Drop the steaks onto the dish and microwave on HIGH (100%) for 1 minute, then turn and microwave a further 1–1½ minutes or until done to taste. Remove to a warmed plate. Add the brandy to the dish and microwave on HIGH (100%) for 30 seconds, then add the cream. Stir well and microwave for 1½ minutes. Pour over the steaks.

Pickled Pork with Sauerkraut

Serves 4: 2 tablespoons (1 oz) lard; 2 onions, chopped; 1½ lb (750 g) sauerkraut; 2 cooking apples, peeled, cored and roughly chopped; 6 juniper berries, crushed; freshly ground black pepper; 2 cloves; 1 garlic clove, crushed; 2 cups (16 fl oz) beef stock or water; 2 knuckles of pickled pork

In a large lidded saucepan, melt the lard and lightly fry the onions. Add the sauerkraut, apples, juniper berries, pepper, cloves, garlic and stock, and cook for 10 minutes. Make a well in the sauerkraut, add the meat and cover with sauerkraut. Cover the saucepan and simmer over very low heat for 2 hours. Remove the pork from the pan, take the meat off the bones and cut it into serving pieces. If necessary, season the sauerkraut, place it on a serving platter and arrange the meat on top of it. Serve with boiled potatoes or dumplings.

Pork and Veal English Pie

Serves 6–8: Hot-water Pastry: 2½ cups (10 oz) all purpose flour; 1 egg yolk; ⅔ cup (5 fl oz) water; 6 tablespoons (3 oz) lard; ½ teaspoon salt 2 egg yolks; 1 lb (500 g) shoulder of veal, ground; 8 oz (250 g) fatty bacon, ground; 2 eggs, well beaten; ½ teaspoon salt; 1 tablespoon grated lemon peel; pinch of cayenne pepper; pinch each of ground mace and nutmeg; 1 tablespoon chopped parsley; ¼ teaspoon dried basil or thyme; 8 oz (250 g) lean veal, diced; ground nutmeg and allspice; salt and pepper; 8 oz (250 g) pork, diced; 1 egg white; 1–1½ cups (8–12 fl oz) strong gravy or stock

To make the pastry, sift the flour into a warmed bowl. Make a well in the center, add the egg yolk and cover it with a little flour. Heat the water, lard and salt in a saucepan until just boiling. Pour immediately into the flour and mix with a wooden spoon until the dough is cool enough to handle. Knead until smooth, then roll into a ball, cover and allow to rest for 10 minutes, keeping it warm.

Roll out the pastry and cut out 2 rounds for the top and bottom crusts and a long piece to fit the sides of the mold.

Fit the pastry base into a greased cake pan or springform pan. Join the pastry sides to the base with egg yolks.

Combine the ground veal, bacon and beaten eggs together. Blend in the salt, lemon peel, cayenne, mace, nutmeg, parsley and basil. Thinly line the pastry with the meat mixture. Cover with a layer of diced veal, and season with nutmeg, allspice, salt and pepper. Cover with a layer of pork, then a layer of ground meat mixture and a layer of diced veal, seasoning well. Repeat until the meat is about 1 in (2.5 cm) above the rim of the mold, finishing with a layer of the meat mixture.

Brush the edges of the top pastry with egg yolks. Carefully place it on top of the pie and pinch the edges firmly together. Cut a hole in the middle of the top crust. Decorate with pastry leaves, if desired, sticking them on with egg white. Brush the top with egg yolk.

Bake in an oven preheated to 450°F (230°C) until the pastry begins to brown. Cover the pie with aluminum foil and reduce the oven temperature to 350°F (180°C). Bake for a further 1½ hours or until the meat feels tender when forked through the hole.

Remove the pie from the oven and place a funnel in the hole in the crust. Carefully pour the boiling gravy or stock into the pie through the funnel. Seal the hole with an extra baked circle of pastry. The pie should be served cold.

Pork and Vegetable Casserole

Serves 4: 1 lb (500 g) pork loin (with a little fat); 2 teaspoons oil; 8 slices giant white radish (daikon), cut into ¼-in (5-mm) slices; 2 small carrots, diced; 4 medium-size or 8 small potatoes, diced; 2 cups (16 fl oz) water; 3 slices fresh ginger; 2 tablespoons sweet rice wine (mirin); ½ cup (4 fl oz) sake; 2 tablespoons sugar; 4 tablespoons dark soy sauce; 4 oz (125 g) snow peas or green beans, cut into 2-in (5-cm) lengths

Cut the pork into pieces about 1 in (2.5 cm) square and ½ in (1 cm) thick. Heat the oil in a heavy-based pan and brown the pork over high heat, stirring frequently for 10 minutes. Add the *daikon*, carrots and potatoes and continue cooking, stirring all the time, for another 2–3 minutes. Add enough water to just cover the contents of the pan, then add the ginger, *mirin*, *sake*, sugar and soy sauce. Cover with a drop lid and simmer gently until the pork and vegetables are tender.

String the snow peas or beans and cook in boiling, lightly salted water until just done but still bright green. Drain and put under cold running water for a few seconds.

Divide the pork, vegetables and snow peas or beans among 4 serving bowls and spoon over some of the cooking liquid. Serve with white rice.

Pork Casserole with Herb Scone Top

Serves 4: 1¾ lb (875 g) lean shoulder of pork; 2 tablespoons fine whole-wheat flour; salt and pepper; 1 onion, chopped; 2 garlic cloves, chopped; 2 oz (60 g) preserved ginger; 6 prunes, pitted; 1 bouquet garni (a bay leaf and a sprig each of marjoram, parsley and thyme tied together) or 2 teaspoons dried bouquet garni; 1¼ cups (10 fl oz) red wine
Herb Scone Top: 6 tablespoons (3 oz) butter; 1½ cups (6 oz) self-rising flour; pinch of salt; 2 tablespoons chopped parsley; cold water to mix

To prepare the filling, dice the pork and roll it in flour, salt and pepper. Place in a casserole with the other ingredients, adding the wine last. Cook, covered, on the middle shelf of an oven preheated to 325°F (160°C) for 2 hours.

Meanwhile, make the herb scone top.

Rub the butter into the flour and salt, add the parsley, then stir in enough cold water to make a stiff dough. Roll out lightly on a floured surface. Remove the lid, take out the bouquet garni if using fresh herbs and place the herb scone dough on top, marking it into squares with a knife.

Turn heat up to 450°F (230°C) and bake a further 10–15 minutes. Serve hot.

Pork Chops in Fruit Sauce

Serves 6: 6 pork chops, approx. 2 lb (1 kg); salt and black pepper; 1 egg white, beaten; 1 cup (4 oz) dry breadcrumbs; 8 tablespoons (4 oz) butter
Fruit Sauce: 1 cup (6 oz) canned black cherries or plums; 2 cloves; ½ teaspoon cinnamon; grated peel of ¼ lemon; ¼ cup (2 fl oz) Madeira or Port

Season the chops with salt and pepper. Brush with the egg white and coat with the crumbs, shaking off any excess. Chill for 1 hour to set the crumbs.

Melt the butter and fry the chops, two or three at a time, until cooked through and golden brown, about 7 minutes. Lift out and keep warm while the remaining chops are cooked.

Blend half the fruit with the juice to a smooth puree, then heat in a small saucepan with the spices, lemon peel and wine. Simmer for 2–3 minutes.

When all the chops are cooked, return them to the pan, pour the sauce and remaining fruit over and simmer gently for 4–5 minutes before serving. Alternatively, the sauce may be served separately.

Pork Chops in Fruit Sauce

Pork in Soy Sauce

Serves 4: 1 lb (500 g) pork (belly, shoulder or loin); 2 teaspoons oil; 4 garlic cloves, smashed and chopped; 1 tablespoon sugar; ¼ cup thick black soy sauce; 1 cup (8 fl oz) water; ½-in (1-cm) stick cinnamon; ¼ teaspoon five spice powder; 2-3 hard-cooked eggs, shelled (optional)

Cut the pork into cubes about 1½ in (4 cm) square. Heat the oil and fry garlic gently for 15 seconds. Raise the heat and add the pork. Fry, stirring constantly, to seal the meat, then lower the heat slightly and sprinkle in the sugar. Cook for 1 minute, then add all other ingredients (except eggs) and simmer until the pork is tender. If using eggs, add during the last 5 minutes of cooking.

Pork Pies

Makes 4: Filling: 1 lb (500 g) lean pork; 3¾ cups (30 fl oz) water; salt and pepper; 1 small carrot; 1 stalk celery; 1 small onion; pinch of thyme; 1 apple, peeled and thickly sliced
1 quantity Hot Water Pastry (see page 280); egg for glazing
Jelly: 1¼ cups (10 fl oz) pork stock; 2 teaspoons gelatin

To prepare the filling, place the pork in a saucepan with water to cover. Add the seasoning, chopped vegetables and thyme. Bring to the boil and simmer for 15 minutes. Remove the pork and cut into ½-in (1-cm) cubes. Strain the remaining liquid.

Divide the prepared pastry into eight pieces, four being a little larger. Roll out the larger pieces one at a time and line four 3-in (8-cm) deep foil pie dishes, molding up to the top with the fingers. Fill each pastry case with the diced pork and lay apple slices on top. Roll out the remaining pieces of pastry for the pie tops.

Brush the beaten egg around the edge of the pie, lay the tops on and seal the edges together with the fingers. Trim with scissors, then press the fingers around the edge to form a fancy edge. Cut two slits in the top of the pies and fold back the pastry. Brush with egg.

Make four decorative leaves and a bud for each pie from leftover pastry. Arrange the leaves on the top around the hole. Place the bud in the center of the leaves. Brush all over with egg glaze.

Bake the pies in an oven preheated to 400–450°F (200–230°C) for 30 minutes or until golden brown, lower the oven temperature to 350–375°F (180–190°C) and bake for a further 15 minutes, covering the pies with waxed paper if becoming too brown. Remove from the oven and cool.

To make the jelly, put the stock and gelatin into a saucepan. Stir until the gelatin has dissolved and season to taste. The jelly should be cooled slightly before using. Remove the bud from the pie with a sharp pointed knife. Pour the jellied stock into each pie with a funnel, then replace the bud. Allow to set before serving.

Pork Satay

Serves 4: 25-30 bamboo satay skewers; 1 lb (500 g) boneless pork loin; 1 stalk lemongrass; 8 shallots or 1 medium-size red or brown onion; 2 teaspoons coriander seeds; ½ teaspoon turmeric; 1 teaspoon salt; 2 teaspoons brown sugar; ¼ cup oil; ¾ cup canned crushed pineapple
Satay Sauce: 8 dried chilies, soaked; 8 shallots; 1 garlic clove; 4 candlenuts or macadamias; 1 stalk lemongrass; ½ cup raw peanuts or ½ cup crunchy peanut butter; 2 tablespoons oil; 1 cup (8 fl oz) coconut milk; 2 teaspoons tamarind soaked in ¼ cup water; 1 teaspoon brown sugar; salt

Soak the bamboo *satay* skewers in cold water for an hour or so to make them less likely to burn during broiling. Cut the pork into pieces ¾ in (2 cm) square and ½ in (1 cm) thick.

Slice the lemongrass finely, then grind or pound together with the shallots to make a paste. Toast the coriander, then grind to a powder and mix with the shallot paste, turmeric, salt, sugar and 1 tablespoon of oil. Put in the pork pieces and stir to coat with the mixture. Leave for at least 2 hours.

To make the satay sauce, pound the chilies, shallots, garlic, candlenuts and lemongrass until fine. Lightly roast the peanuts and pound coarsely.

Heat the oil in a saucepan and gently fry the ground items (except peanuts) for 5 minutes, stirring from time to time. Add the coconut milk and bring slowly to the boil, stirring continuously. Add the tamarind water, brown sugar, peanuts or peanut butter and salt. Simmer gently for a couple of minutes. Thin the sauce with a little boiled water if desired. Finely chop the crushed pineapple and mix into the sauce. Serve at room temperature.

Thread 4-5 pieces of pork onto each skewer. Brush with oil and cook over charcoal or under a broiler until cooked. Serve with sauce, pieces of raw onion and cucumber chunks.

Pork Vindaloo

Serves 4-6: 2½ lb (1¼ kg) lean leg pork, cubed; 4 medium-size onions, thinly sliced; 4-6 garlic cloves, chopped; 1½ teaspoons grated fresh ginger; ¼ cup (2 oz) ghee or cooking oil; 2-3 tablespoons prepared curry paste; 2 tablespoons distilled white vinegar; 1 cinnamon stick; ½ teaspoon turmeric; 1 cup (8 fl oz) water

Prepare the pork and set aside. Place the onions, garlic, ginger and *ghee* or oil in a microwave-safe casserole and cover. Microwave on HIGH (100%) for 6 minutes. Add the pork and mix into the onions well. Cover and microwave on HIGH (100%) for 3 minutes, then rearrange the pork, bringing the outside pieces into the center. Microwave on HIGH (100%) a further 3 minutes. Add the curry paste, vinegar, cinnamon stick, turmeric and water. Cover again and microwave on HIGH (100%) for 5 minutes, then on MEDIUM-LOW/SIMMER (30%) for 30 minutes. Stir and rotate dish and microwave on LOW (20%) for a further 30 minutes. Stir in salt to taste.

The very slow cooking allows the meat to tenderize while absorbing the full flavor of the spices. Leave to stand for 10 minutes.

While the curry is simmering, prepare the accompaniments of sliced ripe banana tossed in shredded coconut, chopped tomato, onion and apple dressed with vinegar, sugar, salt and pepper.

Pot Roast Stuffed Steak

Serves 6-8: 3-4 lb (1½-2 kg) corner cut of top round; 3 tablespoons dripping or oil; 1 cup (8 fl oz) water
Stuffing: 1 small onion, chopped; 2 tablespoons (1 oz) butter; 1 cup (2 oz) soft breadcrumbs; ½ teaspoon mixed herbs; ½ teaspoon salt; pinch of pepper

Cut a pocket in the meat. Sauté the onion in hot butter in a saucepan until tender and lightly browned. Add the breadcrumbs, herbs and seasonings and mix together. Lightly press the stuffing into the pocket. Close the opening with meat skewers or by sewing it with a large needle and cotton.

Pork Vindaloo

Heat the dripping in a large heavy-based saucepan and brown the meat on all sides. Pour off the fat. Add the water, cover and cook gently for 2½–3 hours, until the meat is tender. Add a little more water if necessary during cooking. Serve hot with gravy in the saucepan.

R

Red Barbecued Pork

Serves 4: 1 lb (500 g) pork fillet or boneless loin, in one piece; 2 garlic cloves, crushed; 1 tablespoon honey; 1 tablespoon light soy sauce; 2 teaspoons Chinese rice wine or dry sherry; 1 teaspoon tomato sauce; ½ teaspoon five spice powder; pinch of powdered ginger; red food coloring (optional)

Cut the pork lengthwise into strips about 1½ in (4 cm) thick. Combine all other ingredients. Marinate the pork in this for at least 2 hours, turning from time to time.

Put the pork strips on a greased rack set over a pan of water and roast in an oven preheated to 450°F (230°C) for 45 minutes, basting with the marinade every 15 minutes. Allow to cool. Cut into thin slices when serving.

Roast Beef and Yorkshire Pudding

Serves 6–8: Yorkshire Pudding: 2 cups (8 oz) all purpose flour; pinch of salt and pepper; 2 eggs; 1¼ cups (10 fl oz) milk; ¾ cup (5 fl oz) water; dripping 7½ lb (3.5 kg) rib roast at room temperature

Mix the flour, salt and pepper together. Make a well in the center, add the eggs and gradually pour in the milk and water to make a batter. Allow the batter to stand for an hour before use.

Place the roast on top of a rack, fat side up, and roast for 30 minutes in an oven preheated to 475°F (240°C). Reduce the heat to 350°F (180°C) and roast the meat for 2 hours or until cooked to taste. Forty-five minutes before the end of cooking, heat the dripping in a mold and pour in the Yorkshire Pudding batter. Bake until brown and risen. Remove the roast from the oven and let it stand for 15 minutes before carving. Serve with its cooking

Roast Beef & Yorkshire Pudding

Roast Pickled Pork

juices, Yorkshire Pudding and horseradish.

Note: Use a meat thermometer: 140°F (60°C) for rare, 149-150°F (60-70°C) for medium and 167°F (75°C) for well done.

Roast of Lamb ⭐

Serves 4: 1 crown roast of lamb (approx. 12 cutlets); 1 stalk celery, including leaves, finely chopped; 2 garlic cloves, crushed; 1 medium-size onion, finely chopped; 3 tablespoons (1½ oz) butter; 3 oz (90 g) fresh mushrooms, finely chopped; 1 cup (5 oz) cooked rice; 2 tablespoons pine nuts; 2 tablespoons seedless raisins; 1 tablespoon grated lemon peel; pinch each of thyme, rosemary and sage; 1 tablespoon chopped parsley; salt and black pepper; 1 egg

Prepare the crown roast and place on a microwave-safe roasting dish.

In a vegetable dish, place the celery, garlic, onion and butter. Cover and microwave on HIGH (100%) for 4 minutes, then add the mushrooms and microwave a further 1½ minutes on HIGH (100%), covered. Mix in the remaining ingredients, then pile into the center of the roast. If the cavity is too small to contain all the stuffing, the remainder can be placed in an oven (cooking) bag and cooked alongside the roast. Bake in an oven preheated to 300°F (150°C) for 18-22 minutes per 1 lb (500 g) (include weight of stuffing when calculating cooking time). Let stand for 5 minutes before carving.

Roast Pickled Pork ▬

Serves 6-8: 6½ lb (3 kg) boned rolled loin of pickled pork (boned leg may also be used); rock or sea salt; 1 tablespoon caraway seeds; 2-3 cups (16-24 fl oz) beef stock for basting

Put the meat into a baking dish and sprinkle the top with rock or sea salt and caraway seeds. Place the meat in an oven preheated to 350°F (175°C) and roast for 2-2½ hours, basting occasionally with the beef stock.

When the meat is cooked, keep it in a warm place for approximately 20 minutes before carving to allow the juices to settle. Drain the fat from the cooking juices, add more beef stock and cook until it has reduced to a thicker consistency. Serve this gravy with the meat. Carve the meat into thin slices and serve.

Roast Pork with Crackling and Applesauce

Serves 6: 3 lb (1½ kg) pork leg roast; 2 tablespoons oil; 1 teaspoon salt or seasoning/coloring salt Applesauce: 3 tart green apples; 2 tablespoons water

Score the rind thoroughly. Brush with the oil and rub with the salt. Place on a rack in a dish or in a roasting pan with the rind upwards. Add ½ cup (4 fl oz) water. Cover with a piece of waxed paper to prevent splatters. Microwave on MEDIUM (50%) for 17 minutes, then drain off the pan liquids and turn so that the rind is downwards. Microwave a further 17 minutes on MEDIUM (50%) and return, rind side upwards. Microwave a final 10-20 minutes on MEDIUM (50%). Remove from the oven and insert a meat thermometer. Temperature should be 165°F (75°C). Cut off the rind, then wrap the roast in aluminum foil and leave to stand for 10-15 minutes.

Place the rind between two pieces of paper towel and cook on HIGH (100%) for 3-5 minutes until well crisped. The uncooked rind should be rubbed with oil and salt and microwaved on HIGH (100%) between two double thicknesses of paper towel for 8-10 minutes. Remove top paper for last 2 minutes of cooking. Use the pan drippings for gravy.

To make the applesauce, peel, core and thinly slice the apples and place in a microwave-safe dish with a vacuum-sealed lid. Add the water and cover. Microwave on HIGH (100%) for 6 minutes. Mash or puree in a food processor. Serve warm with roast pork, or as a dessert, adding sweetener to taste.

Roast Spare Ribs 🇺🇸

Serves 4: 1½ lb (750 g) pork spare ribs; 4 garlic cloves, crushed; ½ cup (4 fl oz) thick soy sauce; ½ cup (4 fl oz) dry sherry; ½ cup (4 oz) sugar; ¼ cup (2 fl oz) vegetable oil; 2 teaspoons sesame oil; ½ cup (4 fl oz) water

Divide the ribs and cut into 2-in (5-cm) pieces. Trim off any excess fat. Mix the remaining ingredients together, stirring to dissolve the sugar. Arrange the pork in a baking pan and pour on the prepared sauce. Cover with aluminum foil and marinate for at least 5 hours.

Place the pan in an oven preheated to 375°F (190°C) and roast for 25 minutes, then remove the foil and conpanue cooking until the sauce has reduced to a sticky glaze on the ribs. Drain off the excess fat. Serve hot.

Roast Stuffed Loin of 🇬🇧 Lamb with Marmalade Sauce

Serves 4: 1½ lb (750 g) loin of lamb; seasoning salt flavored with rosemary Stuffing: ¾ cup (1½ oz) fresh soft breadcrumbs; 1 small egg, beaten; 1 small onion, chopped; 2 garlic cloves, crushed; ½ cup (1 oz) finely chopped parsley; ½ teaspoon dried mixed herbs and/or rosemary; 1½ teaspoons mixed grated lemon and orange peel; ½ teaspoon salt; black pepper Sauce: 2 tablespoons orange or lemon marmalade; 1 tablespoon orange liqueur or dry sherry; ⅔ cup (5 fl oz) veal or beef stock (or pan drippings); ½ teaspoon light soy sauce; 1 tablespoon cornstarch

Have your butcher bone the loin and trim off excess fat.

Mix the stuffing ingredients together and spread evenly across the meaty part of the loin. Roll up so that the thin, flap end is on the outside. Tie at intervals with twine.

Prick the surface to release the fat. Season generously with salt and place on a roasting rack in a dish or in a microwave roasting dish. Cover with a piece of waxed paper and microwave on MEDIUM (50%) for 15 minutes. Remove the gravy from the dish and turn the roast. Season and roast a further 15 minutes on MEDIUM (50%). Turn again, remove the gravy and continue roasting on MEDIUM (50%) until done. Remove from the oven and insert a thermometer. Wrap in aluminum foil and leave to stand for 10 minutes. The internal temperature should rise from about 155°F (70°C) to 165-175°F (75-80°C) on standing.

Mix the sauce ingredients together in a jug, adding the meat drippings, but not the fat, from the roasting dish. Microwave on HIGH (100%) for 3 minutes, stirring occasionally, until thickened. Remove string from the lamb and cut into four portions. Coat with sauce.

Roast Stuffed Loin of Lamb with Marmalade Sauce (see page 285)

Roast Suckling Lamb

*Serves 6: ½ side of baby lamb, cut into 6 portions;
salt and freshly ground black pepper; 1½ cups
(12 fl oz) water; 1½ cups (12 fl oz) dry white wine;
2 garlic cloves, crushed; 2 sprigs thyme, chopped*

Place the lamb pieces in a baking dish,
sprinkle with salt and pepper, and add the
water. Bake in an oven preheated to 400°F
(200°C) for 30 minutes. Add the wine, garlic and thyme, turn the meat and return it
to the oven for 45 minutes more. Baste
occasionally. Serve hot with the cooking
liquid, fried potatoes and lettuce salad.

Rosemary-Smoked Steaks

*Serves 4: 4 sirloin (striploin/porterhouse) steaks,
each approx. 7 oz (220 g); 2 tablespoons beef
dripping (fat) or cooking oil and butter mixed;
2-3 large sprigs fresh rosemary*

Trim the steaks if necessary. Heat the fat in
a wok and quickly brown the steaks on
both sides to seal and color. Remove, then
drain the wok and rinse.

Place the rosemary in the wok and set a
rack over it. Arrange the steaks on the
rack. Cover the wok and smoke for 12-15
minutes until the steaks are cooked to individual taste. Serve at once, garnished with
rosemary.

Note: The wok can also be used in conjunction with a barbecue fire to make
delectable broiled steaks with a smoky
flavor. Prepare a charcoal or wood-chip
fire and allow it to burn down to glowing
coals. Set a rack over the fire and place the
steaks on top to sear quickly on both sides.
Dampen branches of fresh rosemary (or
use handfuls of well-soaked hickory chips)
and place on the fire. Cover with an
upturned wok and allow the steaks to
smoke until cooked to taste.

Place the rosemary into a
foil-lined wok.

Arrange the steaks on a
rack.

Rosemary-Smoked Steaks

Sesame Beefballs

S

Sesame Beefballs

*Serves 2: 12 oz (375 g) lean steak; 1½ oz (45 g) fat
pork; 3 dried black mushrooms, soaked; 1½ oz
(45 g) canned bamboo shoots; ¾ cup chopped
vegetables (celery, cabbage, onion, carrot);
2 scallions, chopped; 2 teaspoons thin soy sauce;
2 teaspoons dry sherry; ½ teaspoon salt;*

*¼ teaspoon white pepper; 1 tablespoon cornstarch;
oil for deep frying; beaten egg; 2 tablespoons hoisin
sauce; 1 tablespoon thin soy sauce; 2 teaspoons
sugar; 1 tablespoon white sesame seeds*

Finely grind the steak with the fat pork,
mushrooms (stems removed) and bamboo
shoots. Add the chopped vegetables and
scallions and season with the soy sauce,
sherry, salt and pepper. Squeeze through
the fingers until sticky and bind with the
cornstarch. Form into walnut-size balls.

Heat the oil to fairly hot. Dip the balls
into the beaten egg and deep fry until well
colored. Remove and drain. Pour off all
but about 2 tablespoons of the oil and add
the remaining ingredients. Bring to the
boil, then return the meatballs and shake in
the pan until coated with the sauce and
deeply colored. Serve with rice or noodles.

Shish Kebabs

*Serves 4: 1 lb (500 g) leg of lamb cut into 1½-in
(4-cm) cubes; salt and pepper; 4 green and red bell
peppers, seeded and cut into large pieces;
4 tomatoes, cut into quarters; 12-16 small pickling-
type onions, blanched; 4-5 potatoes, peeled, partly
cooked and cut into thick slices; oil for frying*

Season the meat with salt and pepper, then
arrange the ingredients on skewers, alternating the meat and vegetables but starting
and finishing with meat.

Heat the oil in a large skillet and fry the
kebabs until the meat and vegetables are
cooked. Towards the end of the cooking
add a little water. Season and serve hot on
a bed of cooked rice.

Sichuan Beef Stew

*Serves 4-6: 2 lb (1 kg) stewing/braising beef;
4 scallions, trimmed and halved; 1-in (2.5-cm) piece
fresh ginger, sliced and bruised; 3 star anise;
3 pieces dried orange peel; ¼ cup (2 fl oz) softened
lard or oil to taste; cornstarch
Seasoning: 2 teaspoons finely chopped garlic;
1 tablespoon Chinese brown peppercorns; ½ cup
(4 fl oz) light soy sauce; 2 tablespoons dark soy
sauce; ⅓ cup rice wine or dry sherry; 2 tablespoons
sweet bean paste; 1 tablespoon hot bean paste;
2 teaspoons sugar*

Cut the meat into 2-in (5-cm) cubes and
place in a deep pan with the scallions, ginger, star anise and orange peel. Cover with

water and bring to the boil, skim, then simmer for 2 hours, tightly covered over low heat.

Heat the lard or oil in a skillet and fry the seasoning ingredients for 1 minute, then pour into the pan and re-cover. Simmer a further 1 hour or until the meat is very tender. Transfer the meat to a serving dish and thicken the sauce to taste with a paste of cornstarch and cold water. Pour over the meat after discarding the onion, ginger, star anise and orange peel.

Spicy Ground Meat

Serves 4: 1 lb (500 g) ground lean lamb or beef; 2 tablespoons ghee or butter; 1 large onion, chopped; 2 slices fresh ginger, very finely chopped; 1 garlic clove, smashed and chopped; 1½-in (4-cm) stick cinnamon; 6 cloves; 4 cardamom pods, slit and bruised; ½ teaspoon turmeric; ½ teaspoon chili powder; 1 large tomato, chopped; 3 tablespoons plain yogurt; 1 teaspoon salt; 2 teaspoons garam masala; 1 cup frozen green peas (optional)

Break the meat up with a fork. Heat the *ghee* and gently fry the onion, ginger, garlic and whole spices for 3–4 minutes. Add the turmeric and chili powder, fry for a few seconds, then put in the meat and stir-fry until it changes color. Cover the pan and cook for 10 minutes, then add the tomato, yogurt, salt and *garam masala*, and cook for another 5 minutes. If using frozen peas, add now and continue cooking until both the meat and peas are tender.

Steamboat

Serves 8: 6–8 cups light stock, made with chicken and beef bouillon cubes; 2 teaspoons Chinese rice wine or dry sherry; 2 teaspoons sesame oil; sprinkle of white pepper; fried onion flakes (see page 151); 16 hard-cooked quails' eggs (optional); 8 oz (250 g) Chinese rice vermicelli; 8 eggs
Meat and Fish: 8 oz (250 g) lean pork, finely sliced; 8 oz (250 g) round steak, finely sliced; 8 oz (250 g) raw shrimp, peeled; 1–2 white fish steaks or fillets, cubed; 6½ oz (200 g) fish balls; 1 chicken breast, sliced; 2 chicken livers, sliced
Vegetables: leafy green vegetables such as lettuce, Chinese celery cabbage, chrysanthemum leaves, watercress, beet greens; bunch of scallions, cleaned and cut in 6-in (15-cm) lengths; fresh red or green chilies, stuffed with fish ball mixture; slices of bitter gourd, stuffed with fish ball mixture; 8 dried black

Steamboat

mushrooms, soaked; 2–3 cakes hard bean curd, cubed
Sauces: soy sauce with sesame seeds; soy sauce with ginger; bottled chili sauce; bottled plum sauce; hot mustard

Prepare the stock by boiling together the stock, rice wine, sesame oil and pepper for 3 minutes. Put into a steamboat or other utensil and sprinkle with the onion flakes.

Arrange the meat, fish and vegetables attractively on large platters and place on the table. If preparing in advance, don't tear or cut the vegetables and keep the ingredients tightly covered in the refrigerator.

Soak the Chinese rice vermicelli in hot water for 5 minutes, then divide among eight soup bowls and place on the table. Put the eggs in a bowl and set on the table.

Place the prepared sauces in individual sauce bowls and put beside each diner.

To cook the food, each person lowers a few morsels into the boiling stock and leaves them for a minute or two, then removes them with a small wire mesh ladle or pair of chopsticks. When all the meat, fish, quails' eggs and vegetables have been finished, and the stock has reduced and enriched, pour it over the noodles in the soup bowls and break in a whole egg, stirring to cook it. This rich soup brings the meal to an end.

Note: A fondue or deep saucepan placed over a burner can be used instead of a steamboat.

Steamed Meat and Cabbage Loaf

Serves 4-6: 8 oz (250 g) lean beef, finely ground; 8 oz (250 g) lean pork, finely ground; 3 eggs; 1½ tablespoons all purpose flour; 1 teaspoon salt; 1 lb (500 g) white Chinese cabbage; ½ cup (4 fl oz) dashi; 1 teaspoon light soy sauce

Combine the ground beef and pork with 1 beaten egg, the flour and salt, mixing well. Set aside. Separate the cabbage leaves and boil in plenty of salted water until tender but not falling apart. Drain well and press out any moisture. This is important as cabbage tends to give off a lot of liquid and may make the loaf watery.

Select a 6-in (15-cm) square dish at least 1½ in (4 cm) deep. Carefully line the bottom with half the cabbage leaves, spreading the leaves open to overlap each other. Beat 1 egg and smear it over the cabbage. Put in the meat, pressing down well with the back of a spoon, to cover the cabbage evenly. Beat the remaining egg and distribute it over the top of the meat. Cover with the remaining cabbage leaves and press down gently. Cover the dish with aluminum foil.

Set the dish in a steamer and cook over fast boiling water for 45 minutes. Remove from the steamer and allow to cool slightly, or if preferred, leave until it reaches room temperature. To serve, cut the loaf into rectangles and put in individual dishes. Pour off the liquid that remains in the cooking dish and combine with the *dashi* and soy sauce. Pour a little of this over each serving.

Steamed Pork and Yam Slices

Serves 4: 1 lb (500 g) belly pork, in one piece; 2 teaspoons thick black soy sauce; 1 cup (8 fl oz) oil; 2 garlic cloves, smashed and chopped; 8 oz (250 g) yam, peeled; 8–10 lettuce leaves
Gravy: 6 tablespoons pork stock; 1 tablespoon light soy sauce; 1 teaspoon thick black soy sauce; 1 teaspoon cornstarch; 1 teaspoon sugar; 1 teaspoon sesame oil; 2 teaspoons salted soy beans, mashed; ¼ teaspoon white pepper

Simmer the pork in water to cover for 20 minutes. Reserve the stock. Rub the meat with 2 teaspoons black soy sauce and set aside. Heat the oil and fry the garlic until golden. Discard the garlic. Fry the pork in the garlic-flavored oil, skin side up, for 3 minutes. Turn and fry the other side for 2 minutes. Drain and allow to cool, then cut into slices about ½ in (1 cm) thick. Cut the yam into slices ¼ in (5 mm) thick and fry in hot oil for 2–3 minutes. Drain.

Combine all gravy ingredients, put into a pan and simmer for 5 minutes. Rub into the pork and yam slices, then put in a bowl, alternating the pork and yam. Cover the bowl and put in a steamer. Cook for 1¾–2 hours or until the pork and yam are tender.

Plunge the lettuce leaves in boiling water with a dash of oil added. Drain and arrange on a large serving platter. Put alternate slices of pork and yam on top of the lettuce and serve.

Stir-Fried Beef with Vegetables

Serves 4: 6 oz (185 g) fillet (tenderloin) steak; 1 tablespoon light soy sauce; 2 teaspoons dry sherry; 1 teaspoon cornstarch; ½ teaspoon sugar; 1 small green bell pepper; 1 small red bell pepper; 1 fresh red chili; 1 stalk celery; 1 small carrot; 2 oz (60 g) canned sliced bamboo shoots, drained; 2 slices fresh ginger, shredded; cooking oil

Stir-Fried Beef with Vegetables

289

Sauce: ¼ *cup (2 fl oz) chicken stock; 2–3 teaspoons* hoisin *sauce; 1 teaspoon dry sherry; ¾ teaspoon cornstarch*

Very thinly slice the beef, cutting across the grain, then cut into narrow strips. This is much more easily achieved if the meat is partially frozen. Place in a dish and add the soy sauce, sherry, cornstarch and sugar. Mix well and leave at room temperature for 20 minutes.

Trim away the inner ribs and seed pods from the peppers and chili, and cut into narrow strips. Cut the celery, carrot and bamboo shoots into julienne (matchstick) strips. Mix the sauce ingredients together in a small jug and set aside. (Make a paste of the cornstarch and some of the liquid before adding to the sauce.)

Heat the wok and add about 2 tablespoons of cooking oil. Stir-fry the beef on high heat until evenly and lightly colored. Remove and keep warm.

Add the vegetables and ginger and stir-fry until beginning to soften, about 2 minutes, then pour in the sauce and boil rapidly for 30 seconds. Return the beef and continue to cook on high heat until the sauce has thickened. Serve at once.

Stuffed Shoulder or Breast of Veal

Serves 6–8: 3–4 lb (1.5–2 kg) shoulder or breast of veal, boned; 2 tablespoons (1 oz) butter; ¼ cup (2 fl oz) olive oil; 1 garlic clove, crushed; 8 oz (250 g) veal, finely ground; 5 oz (155 g) calf's or lamb's brains, chopped; 5 oz (155 g) calf's or lamb's sweetbreads, chopped; salt and freshly ground black pepper; 2 tablespoons fresh marjoram, chopped; ½ cup (2 oz) fresh peas; 2 oz (60 g) artichoke hearts, chopped (optional); ¼ cup (1 oz) grated Parmesan cheese; 2 oz (60 g) shelled pistachio nuts; 3 eggs, hard-cooked; 8–12 cups (2–3 liters) veal stock; (if not available, use water and add the following: 1 large onion, chopped; 2 carrots, chopped; 1 stalk celery, chopped; 2 bay leaves; 12 peppercorns; 1 teaspoon salt)

Ask the butcher to bone the shoulder or breast, making sure that it forms the largest possible flat piece.

Heat the butter and the oil, add the garlic and sauté the minced veal, brains and sweetbreads. Season and add the marjoram. Cook until lightly browned. In a food processor or grinder, process the meat mixture to a fine texture. In a bowl, mix the

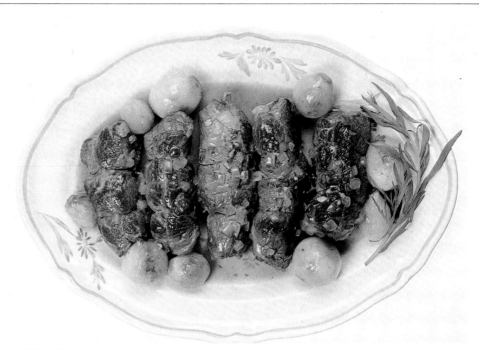

Stuffed Veal Olives

meat, peas, artichoke hearts, cheese and pistachio nuts. Taste and, if necessary, adjust the seasoning.

Spread the stuffing on the shoulder or breast, place the hard-cooked eggs in a row and roll the meat around the stuffing. Using twine, bind the roll and wrap it in cheesecloth. Place the roll in a saucepan and cover it with veal stock. Bring it to the boil, reduce the heat and simmer for 2–2½ hours. Cool the roll in the stock, remove it from the cooking liquid and refrigerate. Carve the roll into slices to serve. It can also be eaten hot.

Stuffed Veal Olives

Serves 6: 1½ lb (750 g) veal, cut into thin steaks Stuffing: 3 oz (100 g) veal, ground; 3 oz (100 g) pork, ground; 2 egg yolks; 1 slice bacon, chopped; 2 slices white bread, crumbed; 2 sprigs parsley, chopped; ½ garlic clove, crushed; 1 sprig thyme, chopped; ½ onion, chopped and lightly fried; salt and pepper; 2–4 tablespoons (1–2 oz) lard; 2 cups (16 fl oz) veal or beef stock; ½ cup (4 fl oz) cream

Cut the veal into 5 × 4-in (12 × 10-cm) pieces and lightly beat them with a meat mallet.

In a mixing bowl, combine the ground veal, pork, egg yolks, bacon, crumbs, parsley, garlic, thyme and onion. Season to taste and mix together well.

Spread out the veal pieces and distribute the stuffing equally among them. Roll up with the stuffing inside and secure the rolls with toothpicks or tie them with fine thread. Melt the lard in a skillet and lightly fry the veal olives.

Pour the stock into an ovenproof dish large enough to snugly hold the veal olives. Cover the dish with aluminum foil and put it into an oven preheated to 350°F (175°C). Cook for approximately 30 minutes.

Remove the veal olives and keep them hot. Transfer the cooking juices to a saucepan and reduce by one-quarter. Add the cream, pepper and salt to taste. Serve the veal olives arranged on a serving platter, masked with the sauce.

Sukiyaki

Serves 4: 1½ lb (750 g) sirloin (striploin/porterhouse, loin) steak in one piece; 4 squares soft bean curd (see Note); 2 medium-size onions; 8 scallions; 2 bunches watercress or spinach; 8 dried Japanese black mushrooms, soaked; 6 oz (185 g) shiitaki *noodles or Chinese "glass" noodles, or mung bean vermicelli; 2–3 pieces fresh beef suet; 4 eggs Sauce: 1 cup (8 fl oz) light soy sauce; 1¼ cups (10 fl oz) Japanese dashi (see Note); ½ cup (4 fl oz) sake (rice wine) or mirin (sweet rice wine); 2½ tablespoons sugar*

Dice the bean curd.

Cut a cross in the top of each mushroom.

Drain the noodles well.

Fry the meat quickly, adding the other ingredients.

Sukiyaki

Trim the steak and cut into very thin slices. This can be done more easily if the meat has been partially frozen beforehand to make it firm. Arrange the meat on one or two platters.

Cut the bean curd into small cubes and place with the meat. Peel and slice the onions. Trim the scallions and leave whole. Rinse the vegetables and shake off excess water, then remove the stems. Drain the mushrooms when softened and remove the stems. Cut a cross in the top of each to decorate and to allow it to cook quicker. Drop the noodles into boiling water to soften, then drain well. Mix the sauce ingredients together in a jug.

When ready to cook, set up an electric or portable wok in the center of the table. Heat the wok and rub the suet over the bottom until well greased.

Hand each diner a fresh egg, to be beaten in his or her own bowl. This will be used as a dip, in conjunction with some of the prepared sauce.

Bring the meat platter and the other ingredients to the table, placing them within easy reach of the diners. Hand each person a pair of wooden chopsticks.

Fry the meat quickly, then splash on a little of the sauce to flavor. Cook portions of the remaining ingredients separately in the center, until done to taste, adding plenty of the sauce. The diners help themselves to meat, vegetables and noodles, dipping them into the egg and sauce before eating.

Note: If bean curd is not available, peel and slice a sweet potato and cut a bell pepper into squares to substitute.

If *dashi* is unobtainable, use chicken stock powder mixed with water and add ½ cup of orange juice.

Swedish Meatballs with Dill Sauce

Serves 4: 1 lb (500 g) lean ground veal; 1 medium-size onion, very finely chopped; 1 large potato, boiled, peeled and mashed; ⅓ cup (1½ oz) dry breadcrumbs; 1 large egg, beaten; ⅓ cup (2½ fl oz) sour cream; ¼ teaspoon freshly ground black pepper; ¼ teaspoon freshly grated nutmeg; 2 tablespoons chopped parsley
Dill Sauce: 2 tablespoons (1 oz) butter; 1½ tablespoons all purpose flour; ½ cup (4 fl oz) cream; ¼ cup (2 fl oz) sour cream; ¼ cup (2 fl oz) veal stock; salt and black pepper; 1 tablespoon dried dill, or ½ cup (1 oz) chopped fresh dill

Mix the meatball ingredients together, beating briskly with a wooden spoon until the mixture is smooth and light. With wet hands, form the mixture into 24 balls. Arrange in two circles around the edge of a microwave-safe pie plate and cover with a piece of waxed paper. Microwave on HIGH (100%) for 8 minutes, then turn and rearrange the meatballs, moving the inside row to the outside and vice versa. Re-cover and microwave on MEDIUM-HIGH (70%) a further 10–12 minutes until no pink shows on the inside. (Non-carousel ovens: Give dish a half-turn after 5 minutes.) Transfer to a warmed serving dish.

To prepare the Dill Sauce, add the butter to the dish and microwave on MEDIUM (50%) for 45 seconds, then sprinkle over the flour and stir in well, incorporating the pan drippings. Add the creams and stock and season to taste with salt and pepper. Stir in the dried dill. Microwave on HIGH (100%) for 3–3½ minutes, stirring twice, until the sauce is thick and creamy. Add fresh dill at this stage if used. Pour over the meatballs and serve.

Swedish Meatballs with Dill Sauce (see page 291)

Sweet Beef Satay

Serves 4: 1 lb (500 g) fillet or sirloin steak;
1 medium-size onion, grated; 2–3 garlic cloves,
crushed; 1-in (2.5-cm) piece fresh ginger, grated;
2 tablespoons peanut oil; 1 tablespoon ground
coriander; 1 teaspoon ground cumin; 2 tablespoons
thick soy sauce; 3 tablespoons brown sugar;
1 teaspoon lemon juice; 2 tablespoons thick coconut
milk; ½ teaspoon turmeric; salt

Cut the beef into thin slices, then into strips
about 1 in (2.5 cm) wide. Fry the onion,
garlic and ginger in the oil until fragrant
and add the coriander, cumin, soy sauce
and brown sugar. Mix well and stir in the
lemon juice, coconut milk, turmeric and
add salt to taste. Rub into the meat and
thread onto bamboo skewers, passing the
skewers through the meat from one side to
the other, pleating the meat along the
skewers. Pour over any remaining marinade and leave for 2 hours.

Broil, brushing with the marinade until
crisped on the surface and just cooked
through. Sweet beef satay can be served
with peanut sauce (see page 117) or with
bite-size cubes of cucumber or pineapple.

Székely Goulash

Serves 4–6: 2 lb (1 kg) shoulder of pork, cut into
large cubes; 12 oz (375 g) onions, chopped; 6
tablespoons (3 oz) lard; ½ teaspoon caraway seeds,
crushed; 1 garlic clove, crushed; 2 sprigs dill,
chopped; 1–2 cups (8–16 fl oz) beef stock; 2 lb (1 kg)
sauerkraut, rinsed in cold water and drained;
1 teaspoon paprika; 1 cup (8 fl oz) sour cream; salt

In a large saucepan, lightly sauté the meat
and the onions in the hot lard. Add the
caraway seeds, garlic, dill and the stock.
Simmer for 45 minutes. Stir in the
sauerkraut and the paprika, and simmer
for a further 30 minutes. Before serving,
add the sour cream, heat gently and if
necessary, season.

Sweet and Sour Pork Vietnam Style

Serves 4: 1¼ lb (625 g) meaty pork spare ribs; 1 egg;
1 heaped tablespoon all purpose flour; 1 heaped
tablespoon cornstarch; 2 teaspoons sugar;
1½ teaspoons salt; ½ teaspoon pepper; vegetable
oil; 3 garlic cloves, crushed; 2 tablespoons fish
sauce; 12 lettuce leaves; small bunch mint;
1 tablespoon finely chopped parsley or fresh cilantro
leaves; 1 medium-size tomato, sliced; 1 medium-size
cucumber, sliced
Sauce: ½ cup (4 fl oz) white vinegar; 6 tablespoons
sugar; ½ cup (4 fl oz) light beef or chicken stock;
2 fresh red or green chilies, finely chopped;
1 teaspoon black peppercorns, crushed; 1 teaspoon
cornstarch; red food coloring (optional)

Divide the ribs and chop each into 2-in
(5-cm) pieces. Wash and dry thoroughly.
Beat the egg and mix with the flour, cornstarch, sugar, salt and pepper, and enough
water to make a smooth, not too thick batter. Coat the ribs.

Pour 2 in (5 cm) oil into a wide pan and
heat to smoking point. Fry the ribs on high
heat until well crisped and deep golden
brown. Remove from the pan and drain off
most of the oil. Add the garlic and fry for
1 minute, then return the ribs and season
with the fish sauce. Cook, stirring
frequently, for 3 minutes, then turn the
heat off and let stand while the sauce is prepared.

Mix the vinegar, sugar and stock in a
small saucepan and bring to the boil. Add
the chilies and peppercorns and thicken
with cornstarch mixed with a little cold
water. Add red food coloring, if desired,
and cook until the sauce thickens and
clears. Pour over the ribs and simmer for
a further 2 minutes.

Wash the lettuce leaves and wipe dry.
Line a serving plate with the leaves and
arrange the pork ribs on top. Sprinkle with
finely chopped parsley or cilantro leaves.
Garnish with sprigs of mint and surround
with tomato and cucumber slices.

Sweet and Sour Pork Vietnamese-Style

T

Tamale Pie

Serves 10–12: 1½ cups (8 oz) yellow cornmeal (polenta); 1½ teaspoons salt; 6 cups (1½ liters) boiling water; 8 oz (250 g) pure pork sausage meat, ground; 1 garlic clove, crushed; 2 large onions, chopped; 1 small green bell pepper, chopped; 1 stalk celery, chopped; 1½ lb (750 g) beef, finely ground; 2 teaspoons salt; 1 tablespoon chili powder; pinch of cayenne; 1-lb 9-oz (780-g) can tomatoes; 2½ cups whole kernel corn; 1 cup pitted black olives; 1½ cups (6 oz) grated Cheddar cheese

Stir the cornmeal and salt into boiling water in the top of a double boiler over direct heat. Cook, stirring well, until smooth and thickened, then place the pan in the bottom section of the double boiler half filled with hot water. Cover and cook for 1 hour.

In a large skillet, fry the sausage meat for 10 minutes, then drain off the excess fat. Add the garlic, onions, green pepper and celery, and cook for about 5 minutes. Add the beef, stirring until it is lightly browned, adding salt, chili powder and cayenne while cooking. Add the tomatoes and corn, and simmer for 15 minutes.

Grease a large shallow baking dish 10 × 14 in (25 × 30 cm) and line the bottom and sides with the hot cornmeal. Add the meat mixture. Press the olives here and there, then spoon the remaining cornmeal over the meat. Sprinkle with cheese. Bake in an oven preheated to 350°F (180°C) for about 1 hour.

Teriyaki Steaks

Serves 2: two 5-oz (155-g) fillet (tenderloin) steaks; 4 tablespoons (2 oz) unsalted butter; 5 scallions, trimmed and shredded; 2 thin slices fresh ginger, shredded; ¼ cup (2 fl oz) teriyaki sauce

Preheat the browning dish for 5–6 minutes. Spread half the butter over the steaks. Drop onto the dish when ready and microwave on HIGH (100%) for 30 seconds, then turn and microwave on the other side for 30 seconds on HIGH (100%). Remove from the dish and keep warm.

Add the remaining butter and microwave on HIGH (100%) for 30 seconds, then add the scallions and ginger. Microwave on HIGH (100%) for 2 minutes, then add the sauce and microwave on HIGH (100%) for

30 seconds. Return the steaks, baste with the sauce and microwave on MEDIUM (50%) for 3–4 minutes until done to taste, turning several times.

V

Veal Escalopes with Chicken Liver Croutons

Serves 4: 1 lb (500 g) thin slices of veal, cut either from the fillet or the inside of the leg; ½ cup (2 oz) all purpose flour; salt and freshly ground black pepper; juice of 1 lemon; 4 tablespoons (2 oz) butter; 8 slices fresh French bread; ½ cup (4 oz) ghee; 2 slices ham, finely chopped; 4 oz (125 g) chicken livers, finely chopped

Cut the veal into 2-in (5-cm) square slices, each weighing approximately 1 oz (30 g). Allow 3–4 slices per person. Beat them flat, dust with flour, season and sprinkle with half the lemon juice.

Fry the veal in half the butter, set aside and keep hot. To prepare the chicken liver croutons, fry the slices of bread in the clarified butter. Remove and drain. Brown the ham lightly in the remaining butter, then add the livers and the rest of the lemon juice. Season, cover the pan and cook gently for 8–10 minutes. Spread the liver on the fried bread. Arrange the croutons around the sides of a preheated serving dish and place the escalopes in the center.

Veal Pizzaiola

Serves 4: 2 lb (1 kg) veal steak; 2 tablespoons oil; 1½ lb (750 g) tomatoes, skinned and chopped; 2-3 garlic cloves, chopped; 1 tablespoon chopped oregano; salt and pepper

Cut the veal into serving portions. Heat the oil in a large skillet, add the veal and fry on both sides to seal. Add the tomatoes, garlic, oregano, salt and pepper, and simmer over medium heat. When the meat is cooked, take out and keep hot. Simmer tomato mixture a little longer. Return the veal to the pan to heat through. Serve with the rich sauce poured over the veal steaks.

Vegetable Salad Rolls

Serves 4-6: Wrappers: 2½ cups (10 oz) all purpose flour; 1¼ cups (5 oz) rice flour; 1 tablespoon salt; 1 tablespoon oil; 3 cups (24 fl oz) water; 2 eggs; 24 lettuce leaves
Filling: 1 tablespoon oil; 1 small onion, chopped; 4 garlic cloves, crushed; 4 oz (125 g) green beans, sliced; 2 small carrots, grated; 5 oz (155 g) cabbage, shredded finely; 1 small sweet potato, peeled and grated, or 3 oz (90 g) thinly sliced palm hearts; 3½ oz (100 g) pork, finely diced; ¼ cup (2 fl oz) water; 3 oz (90 g) raw shrimp, peeled and finely diced; light soy sauce; salt and pepper
Sauce: ¼ cup brown sugar; 1½ tablespoons cornstarch; 1½ tablespoons dark soy sauce; 1 teaspoon salt; 2 cups (16 fl oz) beef stock; 4 garlic cloves, crushed

To prepare the wrappers, sift the flour, rice flour and salt into a bowl. Beat in the oil, water and eggs, and beat for 2 minutes. Leave to stand for 1 hour.

To prepare the filling, heat the oil and fry the onion and garlic until soft. Add all vegetables and sauté for 2 minutes, then add the pork and stir on moderate heat for 6 minutes. Pour in the water, cover and cook for 3 minutes.

Remove the lid, add the shrimp and season with soy sauce, salt and pepper to taste. Simmer, stirring, until the liquid has evaporated and the ingredients are cooked through. Allow to cool before using.

To prepare the sauce, mix the sugar, cornstarch, soy sauce and salt in a small saucepan. Pour in the stock and bring to a rapid boil. Cook over high heat, stirring frequently, until the sauce thickens.

Add the garlic to the sauce. Stir in and simmer for a further 2 minutes. Pour into one or two small sauce dishes.

To cook the wrappers, heat a well-oiled omelet pan and rub the base with a paper towel. Pour in just enough prepared batter to thinly coat the pan, swirling so it spreads as evenly as possible. Cook the pancake on moderate heat until it can be easily lifted. Lift and turn. Cook the other side to a light golden color. Cook all batter and stack the prepared pancakes between pieces of waxed paper.

Wash the lettuce leaves and dry thoroughly. Line each pancake with a lettuce leaf. Spoon on a generous amount of the filling and roll up. Serve with the sauce.

Teriyaki Steaks

Vegetable Salad Rolls (see page 294)

Venetian Risotto with Lamb

*Serves 4: 1 onion, chopped; 2 tablespoons (1 oz)
butter; 2 tablespoons oil; 8 oz (250 g) lean lamb (or
mutton), diced; 3 tomatoes, skinned and chopped;
1 cup (8 fl oz) dry white wine; salt and freshly
ground black pepper; beef stock; 2 cups (12 oz) rice;
¼ cup (1 oz) grated Parmesan cheese*

Sauté the onion in the heated butter and
oil, then add the meat and brown it. Add
the tomatoes, wine and salt and pepper.
Pour in ½ cup of stock. Cover the saucepan
and simmer until the meat is cooked,
approximately 20 minutes.

Stir in the rice. Let the rice absorb the
cooking liquid, then add more stock. Continue cooking in this way until the rice is
cooked, about 12–15 minutes. Make sure
that the end result is not too wet. Add the
cheese just before serving.

Vindaloo

*Serves 4: 1 lb (500 g) pork; 1 heaped tablespoon
cumin seeds; 1 tablespoon brown mustard seed;
1 teaspoon black peppercorns; 2 cardamom pods;
4 cloves; ½-in (1-cm) stick cinnamon; 4–6 garlic
cloves; 1½-in (4-cm) piece fresh ginger; 16 dried red
chilies, soaked; ½ teaspoon turmeric; 1 teaspoon
salt; 1 teaspoon sugar; ½ cup (4 fl oz) white vinegar;
½ cup (4 fl oz) oil*

Cut the meat into pieces 2 in (5 cm) square
and ¾ in (2 cm) thick. Grind the cumin,
mustard seed, peppercorns, cardamom,
cloves and cinnamon, and set aside. Grind
the garlic, ginger and chilies. Combine all
ingredients except the oil and leave to stand
in a glass or porcelain bowl for at least 4
hours.

Heat the oil in a pan (do not use aluminum) until moderately hot. Drain the meat,
keeping the marinade aside, then fry until
it changes color. Add the marinade, cover
the pan and cook over very low heat, stirring occasionally, until the meat is tender.

Wiener Schnitzel

W

Wiener Schnitzel

*Serves 6: 6 veal steaks, approx. 1¼ lb (625 g ;
ground black pepper; 1½ tablespoons lemon juice;
½ cup (2 oz) seasoned flour; 2 large eggs, beaten;
2 cups (8 oz) dry breadcrumbs; 6 tablespoons (3 oz)
butter; ⅓ cup (2½ fl oz) olive or cooking oil
Lemon and Mustard Sauce: 3 egg yolks; salt and
pepper; 1½ tablespoons lemon juice;
1¾ tablespoons Dijon mustard; 8 tablespoons
(4 oz) butter*

Pound the steaks out very thinly, using a
meat mallet or rolling pin, taking care not
to break through at any point. Grind a
little black pepper over one side of each
steak and sprinkle over the lemon juice.
Leave for about 15 minutes.

Coat the steaks lightly with the seasoned
flour, shaking off the excess. Dip into the
beaten egg, then coat with the crumbs.
Arrange side by side on a tray and chill for
1 hour to set the crumbs.

Heat the butter and the oil. Fry the
schnitzels three at a time, for about 3 minutes on each side. Drain thoroughly and
keep warm while the remaining steaks are
cooked.

To make the lemon and mustard sauce,
beat the egg yolks lightly with a pinch of
salt and pepper. Add the lemon juice and
the Dijon mustard, and mix well. Place the
bowl over a pan of almost boiling water.

Cut the butter into small cubes and
slowly whisk it into the sauce, whisking
between additions. When all the butter has
been added, continue to whisk gently until
the sauce is thick and creamy. Do not allow
the water to boil, or the sauce will curdle.
Serve at once.

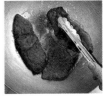

Fry the schnitzels and drain
well.

Slowly whisk in the butter.

VEGETARIAN

A

Asparagus in Butter

Serves 6: 1½ lb (750 g) asparagus; 1 teaspoon salt;
6 tablespoons (3 oz) butter, melted

Trim the asparagus, removing the hard end portion if necessary. Scrape any hard skin from the stalk and wash and tie in three bundles. Place the bundles, with tips uppermost, in a saucepan containing 1 in (2.5 cm) of boiling salted water. If this is not possible, place bundles on their sides in the saucepan. Simmer, covered, for 20–30 minutes, then lift out and drain. Serve with melted butter.

B

Baked Stuffed Potatoes

Serves 6: 6 large, even-size potatoes; salt;
4 tablespoons (2 oz) butter; ½ cup (4 fl oz) hot milk;
1 egg (optional); 1 tablespoon chopped chives or scallions; 1 oz (30 g) Parmesan cheese

Scrub the potatoes and roll in salt. Bake in an oven preheated to 400°F (200°C) for 1–1½ hours or until tender. Cut the top off each potato and scoop out the pulp; beat with the butter, hot milk and egg until light and fluffy. Season and flavor with the chopped chives. Pile the mixture back into the potato skins, sprinkle with cheese and reheat before serving.

Broiled Bean Curd with Miso Topping

Bean Curd Skin "Noodles" with Young Soybeans

Bean Curd Skin "Noodles" with Young Soybeans

Serves 2–4: 2 sheets dried bean curd skin, about 12 in (30 cm) square; 8 oz (250 g) fresh or frozen young soy or lima beans; ⅓ cup (2½ fl oz) oil or softened lard
Seasoning: ¾ teaspoon salt; ½ teaspoon sugar;
1 tablespoon light soy sauce; 1 teaspoon rice wine or dry sherry

Cover the bean curd skins with a wet cloth until softened, then cut into noodle-like shreds. Boil the soy or lima beans in lightly salted water until beginning to soften, about 5 minutes. Drain. Rub off the outer skin of lima beans, if used.

Heat the oil in a wok and stir-fry the beans for 2½ minutes on moderate heat. Add the noodles and stir-fry for 1½ minutes, then add the seasoning ingredients, sizzling the soy sauce and wine separately on to the sides of the pan. Stir in and transfer to a warmed serving plate.

Broiled Bean Curd with Miso Topping

Serves 4: 4 cakes soft bean curd; 8 sprigs watercress for garnish
White Miso Dressing: 6½ oz (200 g) white miso;
1½ tablespoons sake; 1½ tablespoons sweet rice wine (mirin); 1½ tablespoons superfine sugar;
5 tablespoons dashi; 2 egg yolks
Red Miso Dressing: 5 oz (155 g) red miso;
2 tablespoons white miso; 1½ tablespoons sake;
1½ tablespoons sweet rice wine (mirin);
1½ tablespoons superfine sugar; 5 tablespoons dashi;
2 egg yolks

Drain the bean curd, wrap each piece in a towel and put into a colander. Place a lightly weighted plate on top. Leave for 30 minutes to remove excess moisture.

Combine all ingredients for the white miso dressing and mix with a wooden spoon until smooth. Put in the top of a double boiler (or in a small pan set in a larger pan of boiling water) and stir over moderate heat until the dressing thickens. This will take about 10 minutes. Allow the white miso dressing to cool. Repeat the procedure for red miso dressing.

Ideally, this dish should be cooked over a charcoal fire; alternatively it can be cooked under a very hot broiler. Cut each cake of bean curd in half and skewer with two thin bamboo skewers pushed fairly close together into each piece of bean curd. Broil for about 3 minutes on each side until the surface of the bean curd is lightly browned, then spread white miso dressing on 4 pieces of bean curd to a thickness of about ¼ in (5 mm). Spread the red miso dressing on the remaining pieces of bean curd. Put back over the charcoal or under the broiler and cook the miso-covered side for 1 minute. Remove from the heat, place a sprig of watercress on the top of each piece of bean curd and serve hot.

Note: The *miso* dressing can be kept for at least 6 months in the refrigerator. It can also be mixed with a variety of seafood and vegetables to make a salad.

Broiled Leeks with Miso Dressing ▪

Serves 4: 4 Japanese leeks; 2 teaspoons peanut or soya oil
Miso Dressing: 2 tablespoons red miso;
1 tablespoon powdered sugar; 1 tablespoon sweet rice wine (mirin); 1 tablespoon dashi

Cut off the bottoms of the leeks and trim off the green, top portion. Cut leeks into 1½ in (4 cm) lengths and thread onto bamboo skewers. Brush both sides of the leeks with oil and cook under a hot broiler, turning once, until tender.

Combine all ingredients for the *miso* dressing, stirring to mix well. When the leeks are tender, reduce the heat of the broiler to very low. Spread the *miso* dressing carefully on one side of the skewered leeks, and put back under low heat to dry out the dressing. This should take about 2 minutes; take care the dressing does not burn. Serve hot.

Note: Japanese leeks or 'long onions', as they are called, are thinner than their Western counterpart, with a diameter of about ¾–1 in (2–2.5 cm) and a white stem of about 14–16 in (35–40 cm) in length. Their flavor is milder than that of Western leeks, although the latter can be used as a substitute. The *miso* topping can also be used on eggplant.

C

Cannelloni with Spinach and Ricotta Stuffing ▮▮

Serves 4: 1 lb (500 g) spinach; 8 oz (250 g) ricotta or cottage cheese; 7 oz (220 g) Parmesan cheese, freshly grated; 2 egg yolks; salt and freshly ground black pepper; generous pinch of nutmeg; 12 oz (350 g) cannelloni
Béchamel Sauce: 4 tablespoons (2 oz) butter; 2 oz (60 g) all purpose flour; 2 cups (16 fl oz) milk, warmed

Cannelloni with Spinach and Ricotta Stuffing

Remove the stems and stalks from the spinach, wash well and cook for 2–3 minutes, tightly covered, in the absolute minimum of water. Chop finely. Squeeze out any excess water.

In a bowl, combine the spinach, ricotta cheese and 3 oz (90 g) of the grated Parmesan. Beat the egg yolks lightly and add them to the bowl. Season with a pinch of salt, plenty of black pepper and the nutmeg.

Boil the cannelloni in boiling salted water until al dente. Drain. Using a teaspoon, fill the cannelloni with the spinach–cheese mixture.

Prepare the béchamel by melting the butter in a heavy-based pan and stirring in the flour to make a roux. After 3 minutes, pour in the warmed milk all at once and whisk until smooth. Cook slowly, barely bubbling, over a low heat for 20 minutes, stirring now and then, until the béchamel has the consistency and texture of thick cream.

Spread a shallow layer of the béchamel in the bottom of a buttered ovenproof dish, arrange the cannelloni rolls in a single layer on top, dust with the remainder of the Parmesan cheese and pour the balance of the sauce evenly over all. Bake in an oven preheated to 350°F (180°C) until the sauce is bubbling and slightly browned. Serve at once with the lightest possible dusting of grated nutmeg.

Cheese Fondue

on the stove and add the cheese a little at a time, stirring constantly so that it gradually melts. When all the cheese has melted, add the kirsch. Transfer the pan to a chafing dish and place it in the middle of the table. Each guest has a fondue fork and a pile of bread cubes or parboiled vegetables, ready to dip into the gently bubbling cheese.

Note: If kirsch is unavailable, brandy may be substituted.

Rub the pan with garlic.   Add the cheese, a little at a time.

Cheese Fondue Pie

Serves 4: 2 cups (16 fl oz) cream; 3 eggs, beaten; 8 oz (250 g) Swiss cheese, finely diced; salt and pepper; pinch of nutmeg; 1 unbaked 9-in (23-cm) shortcrust pie shell (see page 321)

Mix all the filling ingredients together and pour into the unbaked pastry shell. Bake in an oven preheated to 325°F (160°C) for 30–45 minutes or until firm. Cool. Cut into small pieces and serve.

Cheese Soufflé

Serves 4: butter for greasing; ¼ oz (7 g) fresh white breadcrumbs; 2¼ oz (65 g) grated Parmesan cheese; 3 tablespoons (1½ oz) butter; 3 tablespoons all purpose flour; 1¼ cups (9 fl oz) milk; 4 egg yolks; 5 egg whites; ¾ teaspoon salt; ¼ teaspoon freshly ground black pepper; pinch of cayenne pepper; ¼ teaspoon paprika; 1 oz (30 g) grated Gruyère cheese

Grease the inside of a 6-in (15-cm) soufflé dish with butter, then sprinkle with breadcrumbs and ¼ oz (7 g) Parmesan cheese. Cut a band of waxed paper about 7 in (17 cm) wide and long enough to go around the outside of the dish with a 2-in (5-cm) overlap. Fold in half lengthwise, butter the top half of one side of the paper and tie around the soufflé dish with string.

Melt the butter in a saucepan, stir in the flour and cook over gentle heat for about

Cheese and Tomato Flan

Serves 6: 1 unbaked 9-in (23-cm) shortcrust pie shell (see page 321); 1 cup (5 oz) grated aged cheese; 1 white onion, finely chopped; 2 teaspoons chopped fresh oregano or ½ teaspoon dried oregano; 5 oz (155 g) canned tomato paste; 3 tablespoons water; ½ teaspoon salt; freshly ground pepper; 1 egg; stuffed olives

To make the filling, sprinkle half the cheese into the prepared pie shell and sprinkle with onion and oregano. Mix the tomato paste, water, salt and pepper, and spoon over evenly. Beat the egg, spoon over all, then sprinkle with the remaining cheese. Decorate with the sliced olives.

Place the flan in an oven preheated to 450°F (230°C), reduce the heat to 400°F (200°C) immediately and bake until set, about 25–30 minutes. Leave for a few minutes before removing the flan ring. Slide the flan on to a flat serving dish.

Cheese Fondue

Serves 4-6: 1 garlic clove; 1 cup (8 fl oz) dry white wine; salt and white pepper; 1½ lb (750 g) Gruyère cheese, sliced; 1 tablespoon kirsch; cubes of French bread, slightly stale

Rub a heavy-based pan or fondue dish with the garlic. Pour the white wine into the pan with the salt and pepper. Simmer the wine

1 minute. Add the milk and whisk continuously over medium heat until the mixture thickens and boils. Simmer for 5 seconds. Remove from the heat and add the egg yolks one at a time, beating well. Stir in the seasonings, then the grated cheese in two additions.

Whisk the egg whites until stiff peaks form. Stir a heaped tablespoon of whisked egg whites into the sauce to lighten it; then with a spatula, lightly fold in the remaining egg whites. Gently pour the soufflé mixture into the prepared soufflé dish and bake in an oven preheated to 400°F (200°C), for 35–40 minutes or until browned and well risen. Serve immediately.

Grease the inside of a soufflé dish.

Add the egg yolks one at a time.

Fold in the beaten egg whites.

Chinese Mixed Vegetables

Serves 4: 1 medium-size carrot; 1 stalk celery; 1 small onion; 2 oz (60 g) canned bamboo shoots, drained; 3 oz (90 g) canned young corn cobs, drained; 6 dried Chinese mushrooms, soaked; 12 canned button mushrooms, drained; 6 canned water chestnuts, drained; 1 bunch Chinese greens; 2 slices fresh ginger, shredded; 2½ tablespoons vegetable oil
Sauce: 2 tablespoons water; 2 teaspoons Chinese oyster sauce; 1 teaspoon dry sherry; 1 teaspoon sugar; 1 teaspoon cornstarch; ¼ teaspoon salt

Peel and thinly slice the carrot, cutting diagonally. String the celery if necessary and slice similarly. Peel the onion and cut into wedges from top to root. Thinly slice the bamboo shoots and cut the corn into halves. Drain the soaked mushrooms and remove the stems. Halve the button mush-

Cheese Soufflé

Chinese Mixed Vegetables

rooms and water chestnuts. Thoroughly wash the greens and chop diagonally.

Heat the oil in a wok or skillet and stir-fry the raw vegetables for about 2 minutes, then add the canned vegetables and ginger and stir-fry until just tender.

Add the premixed sauce ingredients and bring to the boil. Simmer briefly and serve hot.

Diagonally slice the carrot.

Cut the onion in wedges.

Diagonally slice the Chinese greens.

Chinese Mixed Vegetables

Chinese Vegetable Omelet

Serves 2: 4 eggs; 2 oz (60 g) canned bamboo shoots; 3 dried Chinese mushrooms, soaked; 1 small carrot; ½-in (1-cm) piece fresh ginger; 8 chives; 1 scallion; pinch of salt; white pepper; 1 teaspoon sesame oil; 1 teaspoon cornstarch; 2 tablespoons water; 3 tablespoons oil; fresh cilantro leaves or fresh red chili

Beat the eggs lightly and set aside. Cut the bamboo shoots into thin shreds, drain the mushrooms and cut into thin shreds. Scrape the carrot and cut into matchstick pieces. Shred the ginger and chives and cut the scallion into 1-in (2.5 cm) lengths.

Season the eggs with salt and pepper, then add the sesame oil and cornstarch mixed with water and set aside. Heat the oil and fry the vegetables until slightly softened. Pour in the egg and stir the vegetables evenly through the egg. Cook on low heat until the egg is set underneath. Cut into half and turn. Cook the other side, then slide onto a serving plate. Garnish with sprigs of cilantro or shreds of red chili.

Cold Lentil Cakes in Yogurt Sauce

Serves 2: 8 oz (250 g) yellow lentils, soaked overnight; 1 medium-size onion; 2 teaspoons salt; 2 teaspoons garam masala; ½ teaspoon chili powder; 2 teaspoons baking soda; pinch of asafoetida (optional); ghee or oil for deep frying; 2½ cups (20 fl oz) plain yogurt; 1 tablespoon heavy cream (optional); salt and pepper; sugar; 2 teaspoons finely chopped mint for garnish

Rinse the lentils and drain well. Put into a heavy duty grinder and grind to a smooth paste. It may be necessary to add a little water to prevent the machine clogging. Mince the onion and add to the lentil paste with the salt, *garam masala*, chili powder, baking soda and asafoetida (if used). Mix thoroughly, then form the paste into walnut-size balls using wet or greased hands. If needed, add a little all purpose flour to bind.

Heat the oil and drop in several balls at a time. Deep fry to a light golden brown. Lift out and drain thoroughly. Fry a second time for about 2 minutes on moderate heat and drain well.

Whip the yogurt and cream (if used) and season with salt, pepper and sugar to taste. Place the lentil cakes in a serving dish and pour the yogurt sauce over. Garnish with chopped mint. Chill slightly, leaving for at least 1 hour before serving to allow lentil cakes to soften.

Cream Curry of Mushrooms, Peas and Tomato

Serves 2: 6 oz (185 g) canned button mushrooms; 6 oz (185 g) frozen green peas; 4 medium-size tomatoes; 3 tablespoons ghee; 1½ teaspoons garam masala; ¼ teaspoon fennel; pinch of salt and pepper; ⅓ teaspoon turmeric; ¾ cup (6 fl oz) heavy cream; 1 tablespoon finely chopped cilantro leaves; ½ teaspoon chili powder (optional)

Drain the mushrooms and thaw the peas. Drop the tomatoes into boiling water, count to seven and lift out. Peel and cut into wedges, discarding the seeds if preferred.

Heat the *ghee* and fry the *garam masala* and fennel for 1 minute. Add the tomato and fry until slightly softened, then add the

mushrooms and peas, and cook briefly. Season to taste with salt and pepper. Add the turmeric and cream, and simmer until heated through. Stir in the chopped cilantro leaves and garnish with a sprinkling of chili powder.

Crustless Vegetable Pie

Serves 6–8: ¼ cup (2 fl oz) olive oil; 1 lb (500 g) eggplant, cut into ½-in (1-cm) cubes; 1 onion, chopped; 2 garlic cloves, chopped; 1 green bell pepper, chopped; 4 medium-size mushrooms, sliced; 1 small zucchini, sliced; ½ teaspoon each dried basil, oregano and tarragon; ½ teaspoon salt; pepper to taste; 2 tomatoes, peeled and chopped; 4 eggs, lightly beaten; ½ cup (2 oz) grated Parmesan cheese; 8 oz (250 g) mozzarella or Swiss cheese, grated; paprika

Heat the oil in a skillet and fry the eggplant, onion, garlic and bell pepper, stirring often, until the vegetables are tender. Add the mushrooms, zucchini, herbs, salt, pepper and tomatoes. Cook, stirring, until all the liquid has evaporated and allow to cool.

Beat the eggs with half the Parmesan cheese, then blend into the vegetable mixture. Pour half of the mixture into a well-greased 10-in (25-cm) pie dish or 9-in (23-cm) square baking dish. Sprinkle with half of the mozzarella. Top with the remaining vegetable mixture, then with the remaining cheeses. Sprinkle with paprika.

Bake in an oven preheated to 400°F (200°C) for 25–30 minutes or until golden brown. This dish may be served hot or cold.

D

Deep Fried Bean Curd with Sauce

Serves 4: 8 oz (250 g) soft bean curd; all purpose flour; oil for deep frying; 1 oz (30 g) grated giant white radish (daikon), with the moisture squeezed out; 1 scallion, very finely chopped
Sauce: 1 cup (8 fl oz) dashi; 2 tablespoons light soy sauce; 1 tablespoon sweet rice wine (mirin)

Wrap the bean curd in several layers of paper towel and place in a colander. Rest

Stuffed Ladies' Fingers (see page 315) and Cream Curry of Mushrooms, Peas and Tomato

a lightly weighted plate on top and stand for 30 minutes to expel any moisture. Cut bean curd into 1-in (2.5-cm) squares, then roll in flour, shake in a sieve or colander to remove any excess and deep fry in plenty of hot oil until golden brown. Drain and put on paper-lined bamboo serving plates.

Combine the *dashi*, soy sauce and *mirin* in a pan and bring almost to the boil. Divide between individual sauce bowls and add a little grated *daikon* and scallion to each. Serve immediately.

Deep Fried Bean Curd with Sauce

Dhal Curry with Coconut

Serves 2: 7 oz (220 g) red lentils; 1¾ cups (14 fl oz) thin coconut milk; ½ teaspoon saffron powder; 1 green chili, thinly sliced; 1-in (2.5-cm) stalk lemongrass, finely chopped; 1 cup (8 fl oz) thick coconut milk; salt and black pepper; 2 curry leaves; 1 tablespoon ghee; 3 scallions, sliced; chili powder

Wash the lentils well and soak in cold water to cover for 2 hours. Drain well and put into a saucepan with the thin coconut milk, saffron, chili and lemongrass. Bring to the boil, then cover and leave to simmer until the lentils are almost tender. Add the thick coconut milk, salt and pepper, and continue to cook until the lentils are mushy.

Crumble the curry leaves and fry in *ghee* with the sliced scallions for 2 minutes. Stir into the dhal and add chili powder to taste. Heat through briefly.

E
Eggplant Curry

Serves 4: 4 small or 2 medium-size eggplants, total weight about 12 oz (375 g); 1 teaspoon salt; ¼ teaspoon turmeric; ½ cup (4 fl oz) oil; 1 teaspoon ground coriander; ½ teaspoon cumin; ¼ teaspoon fennel; ¼ teaspoon brown mustard seed; pinch of fenugreek; ½ teaspoon chili powder; 1 medium-size onion, sliced; 1 garlic clove, finely chopped; 1 cup (8 fl oz) coconut milk; ½ teaspoon salt; 2 teaspoons vinegar

Cut the eggplant across in slices. Sprinkle with salt and turmeric and fry in hot oil for 2 minutes on either side. Roast the coriander, cumin, fennel, mustard seed and fenugreek in a dry pan until dark brown, then grind finely. Add the chili powder and enough cold water to make a stiff paste.

Heat 2 tablespoons of oil and fry the onion and garlic until soft. Add the spice paste and fry 2–3 minutes more, adding a little more oil if the mixture sticks to the pan. Pour in the coconut milk and bring to the boil, stirring constantly. Simmer for a few minutes until the coconut milk thickens. Put in the fried eggplant and salt, and simmer for 3–5 minutes. Add the vinegar, cook a moment longer, then serve.

Eggplant Sichuan Style

Serves 2–4: 12 oz (375 g) eggplant; ¼ cup (2 fl oz) oil; 2 tablespoons sesame oil; 6 scallions; 8 garlic cloves; ½-in (1-cm) piece fresh ginger; 2 tablespoons hoisin sauce; 1½ teaspoons sugar; 2 tablespoons dark soy sauce; 1½ teaspoons Chinese brown vinegar; ⅓ cup (2½ fl oz) water; 2 teaspoons cornstarch; 2 teaspoons sesame oil

Wipe the eggplants and remove the stalks but do not peel. Cut into 1-in (2.5-cm) thick slices. Heat the oil, add the sesame oil and fry both sides of the eggplant for 1 minute. Turn the heat down and cook until soft, then remove from the pan and drain on paper towels.

Chop the scallions, garlic and ginger finely. Add to the pan with a little more oil if needed and fry for 1 minute. Add the remaining ingredients except the cornstarch and sesame oil and bring to the boil. Simmer for 3 minutes, then return the eggplant and cook for 10 minutes on moderate to

low heat. Thicken the sauce with cornstarch mixed with a little cold water and cook until clear. Sprinkle the sesame oil over.

Note: Thinly sliced red chili can be added at the same time as the scallions to make this dish more piquant.

F
Fettuccine and Three Cheese Pie

Serves 4–6: 12 oz (375 g) fettuccine; 8 tablespoons (4 oz) butter; 2 oz (60 g) pecorino cheese, freshly grated (or substitute Parmesan cheese); 4 oz (125 g) mozzarella cheese, diced; 4 oz (125 g) Gruyère cheese, diced; 1 teaspoon dry mustard; ½ teaspoon salt; freshly ground black pepper; dry breadcrumbs; 1 egg; fresh basil, oregano or parsley, and tomato or mozzarella for garnish

Cook the fettuccine in boiling salted water until al dente. Drain well and transfer to a large mixing bowl. While still hot, add the butter, then the grated pecorino and the two other cheeses. Mix gently, then add the mustard, salt and plenty of black pepper.

Thickly butter a 10-in (25-cm) round, ovenproof dish with sloping sides. Sprinkle a layer of breadcrumbs over the butter, beat the egg until frothy and pour into the dish. Roll the dish to distribute the egg evenly over the crumbs, then sprinkle on another layer of crumbs. Shake the dish upside down to get rid of any excess, then spoon the filling into the baking dish.

Bake in an oven preheated to 400°F (200°C) for 15–20 minutes. The breadcrumbs should be nicely browned. After removing from the oven, allow to stand for a few minutes in a warm place, then invert the pie onto a plate. Garnish with the herbs, tomato slices and mozzarella.

Fusilli with Cauliflower and Tomato Sauce

Serves 4: 1 small cauliflower; 12 oz (375 g) fusilli; 1½ teaspoons oil; 1 small onion, minced; 2 garlic cloves, minced; 1-lb (500-g) can peeled tomatoes; 4 chopped basil leaves (or ¼ teaspoon dried basil); 1 sprig oregano (or ¼ teaspoon dried oregano); 2 tablespoons chopped parsley; salt and freshly ground black pepper; 1 oz (30 g) pine nuts; 2 oz (60 g) Parmesan cheese, freshly grated; 2 small ripe tomatoes for garnish

Remove the stalks and leaves from the cauliflower and break into florets. Bring the minimum of salted water to the boil, and simmer the florets until just tender. Drain and keep just warm in a colander over hot water. Reserve the cooking water.

Cook the pasta in ample boiling, salted water for 10–15 minutes or until al dente.

Heat the oil in a heavy-based skillet and gently sauté the onion and the garlic. Do not allow the garlic to brown. Pour in the tomatoes, basil and oregano, 1 tablespoon of parsley and salt and pepper to taste.

Simmer for 6–7 minutes, stirring often, then blend in a food processor or blender, together with the pine nuts, until the sauce is smooth. Add the reserved cauliflower liquid if the sauce is too thick. Place about two-thirds of the cauliflower in a large pot and pour the sauce over. Cook and stir gently, so as not to break up the florets, until the sauce covers the cauliflower pieces.

Drain the pasta thoroughly and place in a warmed serving bowl. Toss carefully with the sauce; sprinkle with the remaining parsley and the Parmesan cheese. Garnish with small cauliflower pieces arranged in the center and a ring of thin tomato slices around the edge.

Fusilli with Cauliflower and Tomato Sauce

Hotpot of Vegetables and Bean Curd

Serves 2–4: 8 squares soft bean curd; 1 medium-size carrot; 12 dried Chinese mushrooms, soaked; 4 scallions; 2 oz (60 g) canned bamboo shoots; 1 oz (30 g) cloud ear fungus, soaked; 8 cups (2 liters) water; soy sauce to taste; Chinese brown vinegar to taste

Slice or dice the bean curd and set aside. Scrape the carrot and slice thinly. Drain the mushrooms and cut each in half. Chop the scallions. Thinly slice the bamboo shoots and drain the cloud ear fungus.

Bring the water to the boil in a flameproof casserole and drop in the carrot, mushrooms, scallions, bamboo shoots and fungus. Boil for 10 minutes, then add the bean curd. Simmer gently for a further 10 minutes. Season to taste with soy sauce and/or Chinese brown vinegar.

Hotpot of Vegetables and Bean Curd

L

Lentil and Vegetable Curry

Serves 4: 1¼ cups (7½ oz) yellow or red lentils; 2 slices fresh ginger; 3–4 garlic cloves, halved lengthwise; 2 shallots or ¼ medium-size red or brown onion; 1 fresh green chili, quartered, ½ teaspoon salt; 1 teaspoon oil or butter; ½ teaspoon turmeric
Vegetables: 2 small potatoes, quartered; 1 carrot, thickly sliced; 4 small okra (ladies' fingers); 1 small eggplant, quartered lengthwise; 4 green beans, cut into 1½-in (4-cm) lengths; 2 tomatoes, quartered
Additional items: ¼ cup tamarind water (see page 392); 1 tablespoon oil; ½ teaspoon brown mustard seed; 2 dried red chilies, broken into 1-in (2.5-cm) lengths; 1 sprig curry leaves; 3–4 shallots or ½ medium-size red or brown onion, very thinly sliced; ¼ cup thick coconut milk (optional)

Rinse the lentils and soak for 15 minutes. Put into a saucepan with the ginger, garlic, shallots, chili, salt, oil and turmeric with enough water to cover by ½ in (1 cm). Simmer gently until the lentils are soft. Add the vegetables and cook until soft, adding a little more water if necessary.

Add the tamarind water to the saucepan. Heat the oil and gently fry the mustard seed, chilies, curry leaves and shallots for 2–3 minutes, then add to the lentils and vegetables. Stir in the coconut milk and cook a further minute. Serve hot.

Lentil Fritters with Yogurt ★

Serves 2: 1 cup (6 oz) yellow lentils; 2 tablespoons all purpose flour; 2 scallions, finely chopped; 1 fresh red chili, seeded and chopped; 2 teaspoons garam masala; 1 teaspoon ground cumin; 1 teaspoon chili powder; 1 teaspoon salt; oil for deep frying; 2 cups (16 fl oz) plain yogurt; ground cumin for garnish; chopped fresh cilantro or mint for garnish

Soak the lentils for at least 3 hours, then drain and grind to a smooth paste. If using the blender it will be necessary to add a little water. Drain this off, then squeeze out as much excess liquid as possible. Make into a stiff paste with the flour, scallions, fresh chili, spices and salt, and roll into walnut-size balls. Flatten each slightly.

Heat the oil to moderately hot and deep fry the fritters, several at a time, until cooked through and golden, approximately 5 minutes. Drain well.

Whip the yogurt, adding salt to taste, and pour into a bowl. Add the fritters and garnish with the ground cumin and chopped herbs. Chill for at least one hour before serving.

M

Macaroni and Cheese

Serves 4: 8 tablespoons (4 oz) butter; ¾ cup (3 oz) all purpose flour; 3 cups (24 fl oz) milk, warmed; ½ teaspoon salt; ⅛ teaspoon cayenne pepper; pinch of white pepper; 1 teaspoon dry mustard; 3 oz (90 g) Gruyère cheese, grated; 3 oz (90 g) Cheddar cheese, grated; 2 oz (60 g) dry breadcrumbs; 12 oz (375 g) elbow macaroni; 1½ oz (45 g) Parmesan cheese, freshly grated; parsley for garnish; 1 large ripe tomato for garnish

In a heavy-based pan, melt 6 tablespoons (3 oz) of the butter and blend in the flour to make a roux. Cook 4–5 minutes over low heat. Pour in the warm milk all at once and whisk until smooth. Season to taste. Sprinkle in the dry mustard and whisk again. Cook a further 2–3 minutes.

Slowly add the Gruyère and the Cheddar, stirring gently to allow the cheeses to melt into the sauce. Continue cooking over a very low heat until the sauce has the consistency of cream. If it seems too thick, dilute with a little extra milk. Set aside.

Melt the remaining butter in a small saucepan, add the breadcrumbs and cook gently over a medium heat for 1–2 minutes.

Cook the macaroni in boiling salted water until al dente, drain and transfer to

Malay Vegetable Salad

a well-buttered casserole dish. Pour over the cheese sauce and mix well. Spoon the butter and breadcrumb mixture over the top, then sprinkle the Parmesan cheese evenly over all.

Bake in an oven preheated to 350°F (180°C) for 15–20 minutes or until the crust is golden. Garnish with a sprig of parsley and a thin tomato slice for each serving.

Malay Vegetable Salad

Serves 2–4: Sauce: 2 heaped tablespoons roasted peanuts; 4 dried chilies, soaked; 1 tablespoon sugar; pinch salt; 1 tablespoon tamarind; ½ cup (4 fl oz) boiling water
5 oz (155 g) beansprouts; ½ small cucumber; 1–2 hard-cooked eggs; 2 tomatoes; 1 tablespoon peanut oil; 1 cake hard bean curd; 4 shallots or 1 medium-size red onion; 12 lettuce leaves; 4 oz (125 g) noodles, cooked; 1 fresh red chili, to garnish

Prepare the sauce first. Grind the peanuts coarsely. Pound the chilies and add to the peanuts together with the sugar and salt. Soak the tamarind in the boiling water, then strain. Pour all sauce ingredients except the tamarind water into a small saucepan and bring slowly to the boil. Stir in the tamarind water and beat until the sauce is smooth and rather thick.

To prepare the salad, clean the beansprouts and scald with boiling water. Drain and allow to cool. Wipe the cucumber and slice finely. Cut the cooked eggs and tomatoes into wedges.

Heat the oil in a small skillet and fry the bean curd until golden. Cool and shred. Peel the shallots or onion and slice thinly. Fry in a very little oil until slightly crisp. Remove and set aside.

Arrange the lettuce in a bed on a flat platter and top with the beansprouts, shredded bean curd and noodles. Decorate with egg, tomato and the cucumber. Pour the peanut sauce over, garnish with the sliced chili and serve chilled. Accompany with shrimp crackers.

Mushrooms with Breadcrumbs and Scallions

Serves 6: 1 lb (500 g) button mushrooms; 6 tablespoons (3 oz) butter; juice of ½ lemon; 2 tablespoons oil; 1 tablespoon chopped scallions; 2 heaped tablespoons fresh breadcrumbs; 1 garlic clove, finely chopped; 1 tablespoon finely chopped parsley

Trim and wash the mushroom caps, reserving the stalks. Melt the butter with the lemon juice in a heavy-based pan and simmer the mushroom caps for a few minutes, then drain.

Heat the oil in a clean pan and sauté the mushrooms until they brown slightly. Chop the mushroom stalks and combine with the scallions, breadcrumbs, garlic and parsley. Add this combination to the mushrooms and cook for five minutes, stirring regularly. Arrange the mushrooms on a dish, sprinkle with a little lemon juice and chopped parsley and serve.

N

Neapolitan Pizza

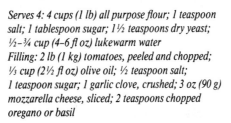

Serves 4: 4 cups (1 lb) all purpose flour; 1 teaspoon salt; 1 tablespoon sugar; 1½ teaspoons dry yeast; ½–¾ cup (4–6 fl oz) lukewarm water
Filling: 2 lb (1 kg) tomatoes, peeled and chopped; ⅓ cup (2½ fl oz) olive oil; ½ teaspoon salt; 1 teaspoon sugar; 1 garlic clove, crushed; 3 oz (90 g) mozzarella cheese, sliced; 2 teaspoons chopped oregano or basil

Place the flour on a board, make a well in the center and add the salt and sugar. Dissolve the yeast in a little of the water and leave in a warm place until it is frothy and bubbling. Stir it into the flour, adding enough water to make a soft dough. Beat and pummel the dough until it becomes smooth, then hit the ball of dough against the board until it is smooth and elastic. Divide into four parts, form into balls and leave in a warm place for 2–2½ hours or until well risen.

To make the filling, sauté the tomatoes in half the hot olive oil with the salt, sugar and garlic for 30 minutes. Roll out the balls of dough into rounds about ¼ in (5 mm) thick and place them on a greased baking

sheet. Spread the cooked tomatoes over the rounds and place the slices of cheese on top. Sprinkle with the oregano or basil and pour over the remaining olive oil. Place the baking sheet in an oven preheated to 400°F (200°C) and bake for about 30 minutes. Serve hot.

P

Pilau

Serves 4: 1 heaped tablespoon slivered almonds; 3 tablespoons ghee or butter; 8 shallots or 1 medium-size brown or red onion, finely sliced; 2 slices fresh ginger, finely chopped; 1 clove garlic, finely chopped; 3 cardamom pods, slit and bruised; 4 whole cloves; 1½-in (4-cm) stick cinnamon; 2 cups (8 oz) Basmati rice, washed and drained; 1 heaped tablespoon seedless dark or golden raisins; 2½ cups (18 fl oz) water; 1 teaspoon salt; fried onion flakes; fresh cilantro leaves

Fry the almonds gently in hot *ghee* until golden. Drain and set aside.

In the same *ghee*, gently fry the shallots, ginger, garlic and spices until golden. Add the rice and raisins and cook for 3 minutes, stirring constantly, to coat the rice with *ghee*. Add the water and salt, and bring quickly to the boil. Partly cover the pan and boil until every drop of water has evaporated and holes appear in the surface of the rice. Turn the heat as low as possible, cover tightly and leave the rice to dry out for 20 minutes. Fluff up with a fork and let the pan stand over very low heat for another 10 minutes.

Serve garnished with fried almond slivers, fried onion flakes and cilantro leaves.

Piperade

Serves 4–6: 1 tablespoon (½ oz) butter; 1 tablespoon (2 fl oz) oil; 12 oz (375 g) onions, thinly sliced; 1 lb (500 g) green bell peppers, cored, seeded and coarsely chopped; 2 lb (1 kg) tomatoes, peeled, seeded and chopped; 3 garlic cloves, crushed; bouquet garni; salt and freshly ground black pepper; 8–10 eggs, separated; chopped parsley for garnish

Heat the butter and oil in a large skillet, then sauté the onions until they begin to soften. Add the peppers and cook for 2–3 minutes. Stir in the tomatoes, garlic, bouquet garni, salt and pepper. Simmer gently for 30 minutes.

Remove the vegetables from the heat and discard the bouquet garni. Beat the egg whites until stiff. Mix with the egg yolks and add to the cooked vegetable mixture. Stir quickly with a wooden spoon over moderate heat until the mixture thickens and is blended, with a light and foamy mousse-like consistency. Garnish with parsley and serve immediately.

Potato Gnocchi with Tomato Sauce

Serves 6: 12 oz (750 g) baking potatoes; 1½ cups (6 oz) all purpose flour; pinch of salt; pinch of nutmeg; 1 egg, lightly beaten; 2 cups (16 fl oz) fresh tomato sauce (see page 135); Parmesan cheese, freshly grated; freshly ground black pepper

Choose medium to large potatoes and, if possible, have them of even size, with unbroken skins. Boil in plenty of salted water until the insides are soft.

Using an oven glove, peel the potatoes while they are still hot, discard the skins, put the centers into a bowl and mash until smooth.

Sift in the flour and mix the potatoes well. Add the salt, nutmeg and egg. Mix until well blended, then turn the dough onto a floured board and knead until smooth. If the dough is still a little sticky, use extra flour to correct the consistency and continue kneading until the dough is very smooth and elastic.

Divide the dough into four parts. Set one part aside to work with and cover the others with plastic wrap or place in a covered bowl. Using your hands, roll out the dough into a long rope, about the thickness of your forefinger. Cut this rope into ¾-in (2-cm) lengths, then push each portion against the concave side of the

tines of a floured fork. Your finger will make an indentation on one side and the tines will form ridges on the other. This thins down the center of the gnocchi and gives them some ridges which the sauce can adhere to.

As you make the individual gnocchi, space them out on a sheet of lightly floured paper towel. Repeat the process with the other portions of dough. Cook 30–40 at a time in plenty of boiling salted water until the gnocchi rise to the surface. Remove from the water with a slotted spoon, cover with plenty of hot tomato sauce and sprinkle with Parmesan cheese and black pepper.

Pumpkin Gnocchi

Serves 4: 1 lb (500 g) pumpkin; salt; pinch of nutmeg (optional); 1½ cups (6 oz) all purpose flour; 5 tablespoons (2½ oz) butter, melted; 2 oz (60 g) Parmesan cheese, freshly grated

Choose a pumpkin of good color, carefully peel off all the green skin, remove the seeds and chop into 10–12 pieces. Gently boil the pumpkin in the minimum of lightly salted water for 15–20 minutes, stirring occasionally, until it is quite tender. Drain well and pass through a sieve or food mill.

Transfer the pumpkin to a bowl, add a pinch of salt and, if desired, a pinch of nutmeg. Add the flour a little at a time. The quantity suggested may be too much or too little, depending on how starchy the pumpkin is. Keep adding and stirring until you have reached the stage where the dough is pliable but not tacky.

Turn the dough onto a floured board and knead well to distribute the pumpkin and flour evenly. Roll tennis ball-size pieces into a rope about ½ in (1 cm) in diameter. Cut off ¾-in (2-cm) lengths, form into balls and then flatten one side with a fork.

Cook the gnocchi in a large pot of boiling salted water, a few at a time. They are cooked when they rise to the top. Transfer with a slotted spoon to a heated serving bowl, add the melted butter and the Parmesan, mix thoroughly and serve.

Piperade

Potato Gnocchi with Tomato Sauce

Pumpkin Gnocchi (see page 308)

R

Rice and Cheese Balls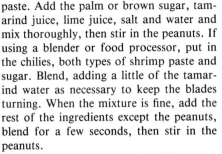

Serves 4: 2 eggs; 2 cups cooked risotto (use leftovers if available); 4 oz (125 g) mozzarella or Bel Paese cheese, cut into ½-in (1-cm) cubes; ¾ cup (3 oz) dried breadcrumbs; olive or vegetable oil for frying

Lightly whisk the eggs and gently add them to the risotto. Take 1 tablespoon of risotto and put it on the palm of your hand. Place a cube of cheese on top of the rice and place another tablespoon of rice on top of the cheese. Form into a ball.

Roll each ball carefully in the breadcrumbs. Fry them in hot oil and drain well.

Ricotta-Stuffed Cannelloni with Tomato Sauce

Serves 4–6: 12 cannelloni; 3 cups (15 oz) ricotta or cream cheese; 2 eggs; ¾ cup (4 oz) Parmesan cheese, freshly grated; salt and pepper; pinch of nutmeg; 4–6 large ripe tomatoes, skinned and chopped; 1 cup (8 fl oz) olive oil; 4 tablespoons (2 oz) butter

Cook the cannelloni in boiling salted water until al dente, then add 1–2 cups cold water and set aside until ready to fill.

Mix the ricotta cheese, eggs and one-third of the Parmesan cheese thoroughly. Season to taste with salt, pepper and nutmeg.

Place the prepared tomatoes in a saucepan and cook uncovered to a thick pulp, stirring occasionally. Remove from the heat and stir in the oil gradually.

Drain the cannelloni and fill with the ricotta cheese mixture. Place side by side in a single layer in a buttered shallow baking dish. Pour the tomato sauce around the cannelloni, sprinkle with the remaining Parmesan cheese and dot with the butter. Bake in an oven preheated to 350°F (180°C) for 20 minutes or until cooked and bubbling. Serve at once.

S

Salad with Spicy Gravy

Serves 4: Sauce: ½ cup raw peanuts; 3–4 fresh red chilies; 1 teaspoon dried shrimp paste, well toasted; 1 tablespoon thick shrimp paste; 1 tablespoon palm sugar or brown sugar; ¼ cup (2 fl oz) tamarind water (see page 392); 1 tablespoon Chinese lime juice or lemon juice; ½ teaspoon salt; 1 tablespoon water
Salad: 4 oz (125 g) beansprouts; ½ yam bean or 1 cup sliced water chestnuts or hard green pear; large handful spinach leaves; 2–3 squares hard bean curd; oil for frying; 1 small cucumber; salt; 1–2 pieces long fried Chinese doughnut (optional); 1 pink ginger bud (optional); 2–3 lengthwise slices of slightly underripe pineapple

Prepare the sauce first. Gently fry the peanuts in a dry pan, stirring frequently, until light brown and cooked. Allow to cool slightly, then rub with the hands to loosen the skins. Shake and blow to discard the skins. Grind the peanuts coarsely, using a mortar and pestle or electric blender.

Pound the chilies and dried shrimp paste together, then blend in the thick shrimp paste. Add the palm or brown sugar, tamarind juice, lime juice, salt and water and mix thoroughly, then stir in the peanuts. If using a blender or food processor, put in the chilies, both types of shrimp paste and sugar. Blend, adding a little of the tamarind water as necessary to keep the blades turning. When the mixture is fine, add the rest of the ingredients except the peanuts, blend for a few seconds, then stir in the peanuts.

Blanch the beansprouts in boiling water for just 30 seconds, then rinse under running water to refresh. Peel the yam bean and cut into coarse slices. Steam the vegetable leaves until just cooked, then chop coarsely and set aside. Deep fry the bean curd in hot oil for about 4–5 minutes, turning until golden brown on both sides. Drain and cut into thick slices. Scrape the skin of the cucumber with a fork, rub salt into the skin, then rinse and slice the cucumber.

Cut the Chinese doughnut, if using, into 1½-in (4-cm) lengths. Slice the pink ginger bud very finely and cut the pineapple into chunks. Arrange all vegetables and other items except the pink ginger bud attractively in piles on a large platter. Sprinkle with pink ginger bud, pour over the sauce and serve immediately.

Salad with Spicy Gravy

Sicilian Stuffed Tomatoes

Serves 6: 12 small to medium-size tomatoes (about 1¼ lb (625 g); 1 medium-size onion; 1 tablespoon butter; ¼ cup (2 fl oz) olive oil; 3 oz (90 g) mushrooms; 3 oz (90 g) Cheddar cheese, grated; 1 teaspoon dried oregano; ½ teaspoon salt; freshly ground black pepper; 1 cup (4 oz) dry breadcrumbs

Cut the tops from the tomatoes and set aside. Scoop out the seeds and soft flesh inside and reserve for another use. Set the tomatoes upside down in a dish to drain.

Very finely chop the onion and place in a microwave-safe vegetable dish with the butter and 1 tablespoon of the olive oil. Cover and microwave on HIGH (100%) for 3 minutes.

Finely chop the mushrooms and add to the onions. Microwave on HIGH (100%) for 2 minutes, then add the grated cheese, herbs, seasonings and crumbs, and mix together well. Spoon into the tomato cases and return to the dish. Pour a little of the remaining olive oil into each tomato and cover with the caps. Sprinkle the remaining crumb mixture over the tomatoes and sprinkle on any remaining olive oil, or dot with butter.

Bake in an oven preheated to 360°F (180°C) for about 45 minutes or until the tomatoes are tender. Serve hot or cold.

Smoked Vegetarian "Duck"

Serves 4: 10 sheets dried bean curd skin; 1 medium-size carrot; 4 dried black mushrooms, soaked for 25 minutes; ¼ cup (2 fl oz) oil; 1 cup (8 oz) sugar Seasoning: 1 cup (8 fl oz) light soy sauce; 1 tablespoon dark soy sauce; 1 tablespoon sesame oil; 1½ tablespoons sugar; ¼ teaspoon salt

Wipe the bean curd skins with a damp cloth to clean and soften. Set two aside and roll the others up. Shred coarsely. Peel and dice the carrot and parboil. Drain well. Squeeze the water from the mushrooms, remove the stems and dice the caps.

Heat the oil and stir-fry the carrot and mushrooms for 1 minute. Add the shredded bean curd skins and stir-fry for 2 minutes on moderate heat. Add half the premixed seasoning ingredients and cook a further 1 minute.

Place the two remaining sheets of bean

Spaghetti alla Pizzaiola

curd skin on a board and brush with some of the remaining seasoning ingredients. Divide the stir-fried vegetables and bean curd skin between the two sheets, arranging in a 2-in (5-cm) strip across the center of each piece. Pour on some of the remaining sauce, then fold in the sides and then the two larger flaps to produce two long flat sausage shapes. Press in the sides to form into a square-sided, rectangular shape. Place the two rolls in a dish and pour the remaining sauce over.

Leave for 1 hour to absorb the sauce, then set the dish on a rack in a steamer and steam for 10 minutes. Drain any water or sauce from the dish and discard. Wipe out the pan and add the sugar. Heat until the sugar begins to smoke, then place the dish on a rack over the sugar, cover the pan tightly and smoke for 5 minutes. Remove and cut diagonally into thick slices. Serve hot or cold.

Spaghetti alla Pizzaiola

Serves 4–6: 3 tablespoons olive or vegetable oil; 1 lb (500 g) onions, finely chopped; 1 tablespoon finely chopped garlic; 3 lb (1.5 kg) tomatoes, blanched, peeled and coarsely chopped; 8 oz (250 g) tomato paste; 1 tablespoon finely chopped fresh basil, or 1 heaped teaspoon dried basil; 1 tablespoon dried oregano; 1 teaspoon salt; 1 bay leaf; freshly ground black pepper; sugar; 1 lb (500 g) spaghetti; Parmesan cheese, freshly grated (optional)

Heat the oil in a large saucepan and sauté the onions until they are translucent, then add the garlic and cook a few minutes longer, stirring all the time. Add the tomatoes, tomato paste and all the seasonings, stir well, then bring to the boil and reduce the heat to low. Simmer very gently for at least 1 hour, adding water if the sauce becomes too thick. Take out the bay leaf and check for taste, adding salt, pepper or a little sugar as desired.

Cook the spaghetti in a large pan of boiling salted water until al dente, drain and arrange on a preheated serving plate. Pour over enough sauce to flavor the pasta and serve with freshly grated Parmesan cheese in a side dish.

Spaghetti and Cabbage

Serves 4-5: 1 onion, chopped; 2 tablespoons olive oil; 2 tablespoons (1 oz) butter; 1 cabbage, 1½-2 lb (750 g-1 kg); pinch of nutmeg; salt and freshly ground black pepper; 12 oz (375 g) spaghetti; 2 oz (60 g) Parmesan cheese, freshly grated

Sauté the onion in the hot oil and butter until turning golden. Do not let it become too soft.

Discard the hard core from the cabbage, wash, and cut into thick slices. Add the cabbage to the saucepan, season with the nutmeg, salt and pepper and mix together gently. Cook, covered, in the water clinging to the cabbage leaves for 25–30 minutes. Check now and then, stir, and add 1–2 tablespoons of water if necessary.

While the cabbage is cooking, boil the spaghetti in boiling salted water until al dente. Drain very briefly — it should not be too dry. Mix with the cabbage and onion in the saucepan and transfer to a heated serving dish. Sprinkle with Parmesan cheese.

Spaghetti and Spinach Frittata

Serves 4: 2 tablespoons oil; 2 medium-size onions, very thinly sliced; 2 large garlic cloves, finely chopped; 8 oz (250 g) spinach; 4 oz (125 g) spaghetti; salt and freshly ground black pepper; pinch of nutmeg; 6 eggs, lightly beaten; 4 oz (125 g) Cheddar cheese, grated; parsley; 1 or 2 ripe tomatoes for garnish; Parmesan cheese, freshly grated (optional)

Heat the oil in a heavy-based skillet and cook the onions and garlic until soft and golden. Remove from the heat and set aside.

Cook the spinach in the minimum of water, squeeze dry, chop finely, and place

Spaghetti and Spinach Frittata

in a large bowl. Break the spaghetti into short lengths and boil in salted water until al dente. Melt a little butter through the drained pasta to keep the pieces separate.

Season the spaghetti to taste with the salt, pepper and nutmeg, then fold in the eggs and the cheese. Return the skillet to the heat, add the egg mixture to the onions and garlic, and cook over a moderate heat until it has just set — it should not be too stiff, but the bottom of the mixture should have browned slightly.

Take the pan off the heat and place under a broiler. Cook the top surface of the frittata until it turns light brown. Invert onto a serving plate and decorate with a little chopped parsley or a few parsley

sprigs and wedges of tomato. Cut the frittata as you would a cake, and sprinkle with Parmesan cheese.

Spinach Pie (Spanakopita)

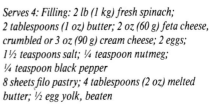

Serves 4: Filling: 2 lb (1 kg) fresh spinach; 2 tablespoons (1 oz) butter; 2 oz (60 g) feta cheese, crumbled or 3 oz (90 g) cream cheese; 2 eggs; 1½ teaspoons salt; ¼ teaspoon nutmeg; ¼ teaspoon black pepper 8 sheets filo pastry; 4 tablespoons (2 oz) melted butter; ½ egg yolk, beaten

Thoroughly wash the spinach using three or four changes of cold water. Drain well and pick off the leaves. Squeeze out the excess water and chop finely. Sauté in the butter, in a tightly covered pan, until tender. Shake the pan occasionally to turn the spinach, but do not lift the lid for at least the first 7 minutes. Remove from the heat and add the cheese, eggs and seasonings. Mix well.

Brush a pie dish with melted butter, then arrange a layer of filo pastry on top. Brush generously with melted butter and cover with a second piece. Continue until half the filo has been used, then pour the spinach filling over. Top with the remaining pastry, brushing each sheet generously with melted butter, and brush the top surface with the beaten egg yolk. Bake in an oven preheated to 350°F (180°C) for 45 minutes or until golden.

Note: Keep the filo pastry covered with a damp tea towel while using, otherwise it will dry out and crack.

Stuffed Eggplant

Serves 6: 3 medium-size eggplants; 1 large onion; 5 garlic cloves; 2 fresh red chilies; 1-in (2.5-cm) piece fresh ginger; 4-in (10-cm) stalk lemongrass; 1 teaspoon turmeric; 3 large tomatoes; 2 teaspoons salt; 2 teaspoons oil

Put the eggplants into a saucepan and cover with water. Bring to the boil and simmer for about 10 minutes until softened. Drain and cool.

Mince the onion, garlic, chilies, ginger and lemongrass and mix with turmeric and salt. Peel, seed and chop the tomatoes and add to the onion and spices. Cut the eggplants in half lengthwise and scoop out the pulp, taking care not to break through the skin. Chop the eggplant pulp and mix with all other ingredients.

Put the oil into a small skillet and sauté all ingredients on moderate to low heat for 5 minutes, stirring constantly. Fill the shells with the mixture, rounding the tops neatly. Bake in an oven preheated to 400°F (200°C) for about 6 minutes.

Spinach Pie (Spanakopita)

Stuffed Eggplant

Trenette with Pesto Sauce

Stuffed Ladies' Fingers

*Serves 4: 12 oz (375 g) large okra (ladies' fingers);
2 medium-size tomatoes; 1 tablespoon brown sugar;
2 tablespoons lemon juice; 2 teaspoons fennel seeds,
coarsely ground; ¾ teaspoon turmeric;
1 tablespoon ground coriander; 1 tablespoon ghee;
salt; chili powder; 2 tablespoons vegetable stock*

Wash the okra, trim the tops and cut a slit along each piece. Peel and finely chop the tomatoes and mix with the brown sugar, lemon juice and spices. Stuff the mixture into the okra and place in a flameproof dish.

Melt the *ghee* and add to the dish. Sprinkle with the salt and chili powder and add the vegetable stock. Cover and cook in an oven preheated to 350°F (180°C) until the okra are tender, then remove the lid and continue cooking until the pan juices have been absorbed.

T
Trenette with Pesto Sauce

*Serves 4: 1 tightly packed cup basil leaves;
2 tablespoons pine nuts; 2 garlic cloves; coarse or
rock salt; ½ cup (4 fl oz) olive oil (no substitutions);
2 tablespoons Parmesan cheese, freshly grated;
2 tablespoons pecorino cheese, freshly grated (or
substitute Romano, or double the quantity of
Parmesan); 12 oz (350 g) trenette (fettuccine)*

Put the basil, nuts, garlic and salt into a blender and blend, scraping down the sides now and then. Slowly add the oil and continue blending until the mixture is smooth. Next add the cheeses and give the blender one more short run. If the paste is too thick, thin it down with 1–2 teaspoons olive oil.

Cook the trenette in plenty of boiling salted water until al dente. Drain very briefly so that some of the cooking water still adheres to the pasta.

Transfer most of the pesto to a preheated serving dish. Add the trenette and toss well. Spoon a little pesto sauce on top of each serving.

V

Vegetable Caraway Pie

Serves 6: 1 cauliflower; 1 green or red bell pepper; 4 eggs, hard-cooked; 2 carrots; 2 oz (60 g) shelled almonds; 4 tablespoons (2 oz) butter or margarine; 12 scallions; 1 tablespoon chopped parsley
Topping: 4 tablespoons (2 oz) butter; 4 tablespoons all purpose flour; 1 ¼ cups (10 fl oz) milk; ½ teaspoon caraway seeds; salt and pepper; 1 cup (4 oz) dry breadcrumbs; ½ cup (2½ oz) grated cheese; 2 teaspoons paprika

Wash the cauliflower and break it into florets. Boil in salted water for 5 minutes and drain. Cut the pepper into strips, discarding the seeds. Shell and quarter the eggs. Wash the carrots and grate coarsely. Brown the almonds in butter. Wash the scallions and chop finely. Mix all ingredients together, including the parsley, in a greased ovenproof dish.

To make the topping, melt the butter in a saucepan, stir in the flour, then add milk, stirring until thickened. Add the caraway seeds, salt and pepper. Pour over the vegetables, then top with breadcrumbs, cheese and paprika. Bake in an oven preheated to 375°F (190°C) for 20–30 minutes until heated through and the cheese has melted.

Vegetable Cutlets in Curry Sauce

Serves 4: 1 lb (500 g) baking potatoes; ½ teaspoon chili powder; 2 teaspoons salt; ½ teaspoon pepper; 2 teaspoons garam masala; 3 tablespoons finely chopped cilantro leaves; 2 eggs; gram flour (besan); oil or ghee
Curry Sauce: 1 large onion; 1-in (2.5-cm) piece fresh ginger; 4 garlic cloves; 2 teaspoons garam masala; ½ teaspoon fennel seeds; 3 tablespoons ghee; 3 tomatoes; ¾ cup (6 fl oz) cream; ½ teaspoon turmeric; chili powder

Peel the potatoes and boil until soft. Drain and mash. Add the chili powder, salt, pepper, *garam masala* and cilantro, and bind the mixture with the eggs and gram flour. Shape into cutlets.

Heat about 1 in (2.5 cm) oil or *ghee* in a pan and fry the cutlets until golden brown. Turn to color evenly. Lift out and drain well.

Vegetables in Coconut Milk

To prepare the curry sauce, mince the onion with the ginger and garlic. Add the *garam masala* and fennel, and fry in *ghee* for 4 minutes, stirring frequently. Peel the tomatoes, chop finely and add to the pan. Fry for 4 minutes. Add about ¼ cup water and bring to the boil, then reduce the heat and stir in the cream. Season to taste with salt and pepper and add the turmeric. Stir well. Place the vegetable cutlets in the sauce and heat through. Transfer to a serving dish and garnish with chili powder.

Vegetables in Coconut Milk

Serves 4: 6 oz (185 g) green beans; 8 oz (250 g) Chinese cabbage or white cabbage; 1½ large onions; 2 medium-size tomatoes; 2 fresh chilies; 2 tablespoons vegetable oil; 2 garlic cloves, crushed; ⅓ teaspoon turmeric; ½ teaspoon chili powder (optional); salt; 1¼ cups (10 fl oz) thin coconut milk; 1 tablespoon tamarind water, made with 1½ teaspoons tamarind (see page 392)

Cut the beans into 2-in (5-cm) lengths. Chop the Chinese cabbage and wash, shaking out excess water. Chop the onions

coarsely, peel and chop the tomatoes and slice the chilies.

Heat the oil in a skillet and fry the garlic and onion for 2 minutes, then put in the beans, turmeric, chili powder (if used), sliced chilies and salt. Pour in ½ cup coconut milk and stir well. Cook on moderate heat for 5 minutes, then add the cabbage and cook for a further 4 minutes.

Pour over the remaining coconut milk, bring almost to the boil then turn the heat down low. Add the tomato and tamarind water and simmer for 1–2 minutes. Stir continually to prevent the coconut sauce curdling. Add salt to taste.

Vegetable Kugel ★

Serves 6–8: 4 medium-size potatoes; 3 medium-size carrots; 1 large zucchini; 1 large onion; 2 garlic cloves, crushed; 2 eggs, beaten; ¼ cup (½ oz) chopped parsley; ¾ cup (1½ oz) fresh whole-wheat breadcrumbs; ¼ cup (1 oz) milk powder; 1 teaspoon salt; black pepper; ¾ cup (6 fl oz) heavy cream; 1 cup (4 oz) grated cheese

Grate the potatoes, carrots, zucchini and onion, and mix with the remaining ingredients, except the cheese. Transfer to a greased baking dish about 9 in (23 cm) in diameter. Smooth the top. Bake in an oven preheated to 350°F (180°C) for 30 minutes. Cover with the cheese and bake for a further 10–15 minutes, or until the sides come away from the dish and the kugel feels firm on top.

Vegetable Lasagne

Serves 4: 1 medium-size onion, finely chopped; 6 tablespoons (3 oz) butter; 2 large artichokes; 10 oz (315 g) green peas, fresh or frozen; 1 bunch spinach, or 8 oz (250 g) frozen, chopped spinach; freshly ground black pepper; salt; ½ cup (2 oz) all purpose flour; 2 cups (16 fl oz) milk; 12 oz (350 g) lasagne; 3 oz (90 g) Parmesan cheese, freshly grated; 4 oz (125 g) Gruyère cheese, grated (or substitute Emmenthal); nutmeg; dried breadcrumbs

Using a large, heavy-based pan, lightly fry the onion in 2 tablespoons (1 oz) hot butter until golden.

Cut off the leaves of the artichokes and remove the choke. Cut hearts into quarters lengthwise and cook in a minimum of lightly salted boiling water. Separately, cook the peas and the spinach. Squeeze the spinach to remove as much water as possible and chop it roughly. Put the well-cooked and drained artichokes through a food mill. Now combine all the cooked vegetables in the pan with the onion, a grind of black pepper and a good pinch of salt. Set aside.

To make the béchamel sauce, melt the remaining butter and stir in the flour to make a roux. Cook gently, then whisk in the warmed milk, bring to the boil and cook, whisking, until thickened and creamy.

Cook the lasagne in boiling salted water until almost al dente, then plunge into cold water and dry on clean tea towels.

Butter an ovenproof dish and line it with the lasagne. Spread a layer of the vegetable mixture over, then a thin layer of the béchamel and a good sprinkle of the mixed cheeses. Repeat with pasta, vegetables, béchamel and cheeses until the dish is full, finishing with a layer of béchamel. Grate a little nutmeg over the top, then sprinkle the breadcrumbs evenly over all. Dot with small knobs of butter and a further sprinkle of the two cheeses.

Bake in an oven preheated to 375°F (190°C) until the crust is nicely browned.

Vegetable Samosas

Serves 4–6: 2 cups (8 oz) all purpose flour; ¾ teaspoon salt; 1 large egg; 1 egg yolk; 2 tablespoons ghee or margarine; 2–4 tablespoons water; oil for deep frying
Filling: 1 large cooked potato, diced; ¼ cup (1 oz) finely chopped cabbage or cauliflower; ¼ cup (1 oz) cooked green peas; 1 medium-size onion, grated; 1 garlic clove, crushed; ½-in (1-cm) piece fresh ginger, grated; 1 green chili, seeded and finely chopped; 2 teaspoons finely chopped fresh cilantro or mint; 1 teaspoon ground coriander; 1 teaspoon salt; 2–3 tablespoons butter or ghee; 1 tablespoon lemon juice

Sift the flour and salt into a bowl and make a well in the center. Add the egg and egg yolk and the softened *ghee* or margarine. Work into the flour, then add enough water to make a firm dough. Knead lightly, then wrap in plastic until needed.

Mix the filling ingredients, except the butter or *ghee* and lemon juice, and sauté in the hot butter for 2–3 minutes, stirring continually. Remove from the heat and add the lemon juice. Stir well, then leave to cool.

Roll the pastry out very thinly on a floured surface and cut out rounds with a fluted 2½-in (6.5-cm) pastry cutter. Place a spoonful of the cooled filling in the center of each, run a wet finger around the edges and fold each in half. Pinch the edges together to seal.

Heat the oil to fairly hot and deep fry the samosas, several at a time, to a deep golden brown. Lift out and drain well. Serve with a sweet chili sauce or chopped mint and cucumber mixed with yogurt.

Vermicelli with Green Sauce

Serves 6–8: 4 tablespoons (2 oz) soft butter; 2 tablespoons chopped fresh basil; 2 tablespoons chopped parsley; 8 oz (250 g) softened cream cheese; ⅓ cup (2 oz) Parmesan cheese, freshly grated; ¼ cup (2 fl oz) olive oil; 1 garlic clove, crushed; ¾ teaspoon freshly ground pepper; ⅔ cup (5 fl oz) boiling water; 10 oz (315 g) vermicelli or thin spaghetti; Parmesan cheese for serving

In a bowl, cream together the butter, basil, parsley, cream cheese, Parmesan cheese, oil, garlic and pepper. Stir in the boiling water until smoothly combined.

Cook the vermicelli in plenty of boiling

salted water until al dente. Drain well, then arrange on a warm platter, pour the sauce over and sprinkle with Parmesan cheese.

W

Waldorf Salad

Serves 4–6: 1 green apple; 1 red apple; juice of ½ lemon; 1 cup finely chopped celery; ½ cup walnuts, broken; ¼ cup (2 fl oz) mayonnaise; crisp lettuce cups; 1 red apple, thinly sliced, brushed with lemon juice to prevent discoloration

Chill the apples, core and dice, then pour the lemon juice over the apples. Combine the apples with the celery, walnuts and mayonnaise. Serve piled into lettuce cups and garnished with slices of red-skinned apple.

Z

Zucchini Pie

Serves 8: 1 unbaked 10-in (25-cm) shortcrust pie shell (see page 336); 1 lb (500 g) zucchini, thinly sliced; ¼ teaspoon salt; 8 oz (250 g) Swiss cheese, cut into very small cubes; 3 eggs; 1 cup (8 fl oz) cream, heated; ¼ teaspoon basil; pinch of cayenne pepper

Roll out the pastry on a lightly floured board to ⅛ in (3 mm) thick. Line a pie dish, trim and flute the edge, then refrigerate.

Place the zucchini in a bowl, add the salt, cover with boiling water and allow to stand for 3 minutes, then drain. Sprinkle the pastry with cheese, then top with zucchini.

In a bowl, beat together the eggs, hot cream and seasonings until just blended. Pour over the pie. Bake in an oven preheated to 375°F (190°C) for 30–35 minutes, or until the pastry is golden and the custard puffy. Serve warm.

DESSERTS

A

Almond Fingers ★

Makes 36: 1 cup (4 oz) all purpose flour;
¼ teaspoon salt; 1 cup (8 fl oz) water; 2 tablespoons
(1 oz) butter; 2 large eggs; 2 tablespoons ground
almonds; 1¼ cups (10 fl oz) water; 1½ cups (12 oz)
sugar; 1½ teaspoons orange or rose flower water;
oil for deep frying

Sift the flour and salt onto a piece of waxed
paper. Bring 1 cup of water to the boil with
the butter, then quickly pour in all the flour
and beat with a wooden spoon until the
mixture leaves the sides of the pan and
becomes shiny and smooth. Cook gently
for about 5 minutes, stirring from time to
time, then remove from the heat and transfer to a mixing bowl. Leave to partially
cool, then gradually beat in the eggs and
the almonds. Set aside for 10 minutes.

In a saucepan, boil the 1¼ cups of water
with the sugar, stirring just until the sugar
dissolves. Simmer for about 10 minutes or
until the syrup begins to look sticky but has
not taken on any color. Remove from the
heat and add the flower water. Set aside to
cool.

Heat the deep frying oil to moderate.
Roll the dough into small finger shapes,
using wet hands to prevent sticking. Slide,
several at a time, into the oil and fry for
8-10 minutes until golden and puffed out.
It is essential that the oil is not too hot or
the pastries will cook too quickly on the
outside and remain soft and sticky inside.

Remove with a slotted spoon and transfer to the cool syrup. As each batch is
cooked, remove the previous batch from
the syrup and place on a rack to drain.

Pour into the boiling water.

Mix until shiny and smooth.

Apple and Ginger Crisp

When done, the pastries can be garnished with finely chopped walnuts, toasted
almonds or pistachio nuts. Or they can be
sprinkled with a mixture of cinnamon and
sugar just before serving.

Angel Kiwi Tarts

Serves 6-8: 4 egg yolks; ½ cup (4 oz) sugar;
⅛ teaspoon salt; ⅓ cup (2½ fl oz) lime juice;
1 teaspoon gelatin, softened in a little cold water;
1 teaspoon grated lime peel; 1 cup (8 fl oz) cream;
3 kiwi fruit, peeled and chopped (or mashed);
6 meringue shells; 2 kiwi fruit, peeled and sliced, for
garnish

In the top of a double boiler, with the
beater on low, stir together the egg yolks,
sugar, salt, lime juice and gelatin. Cook
over hot water, just under boiling, stirring
constantly until it thickens. Stir in the peel.
Remove from the heat, cover with plastic
wrap and chill.

Beat the cream until it is thick. Then
with the same beaters, beat the chilled egg
yolk mixture. Fold in the cream and
chopped kiwi fruit. Spoon into the
meringue shells. Refrigerate for 1-2 hours.
Garnish with slices of kiwi fruit.

Note: For Angel Strawberry-Kiwi Tarts,
add ½ cup sliced strawberries and 2 kiwi
fruit, peeled and chopped.

Apple and Ginger Crisp

Serves 6: 6 firm cooking apples; 2 tablespoons
chopped preserved ginger; ½ cup (3 oz) soft brown
sugar; ½ cup (1½ oz) rolled oats; ½ cup (2 oz) self-
rising flour; ½ cup (3 oz) dried, mixed fruits;
1 teaspoon ground ginger; 6 tablespoons (3 oz)
butter

Peel, core and thinly slice the apples and
arrange in a microwave-safe pie dish. Scatter the preserved ginger evenly over the
apple and stir in lightly.

Mix the sugar, oats, flour, fruit and
ground ginger together in a bowl. Soften
the butter on MEDIUM (50%) for 2 minutes and stir evenly into the oat mixture.
Spread over the apples. Microwave on
HIGH (100%) for 5 minutes, then rotate
the dish and microwave on HIGH (100%)
for a further 4-5 minutes.

The top can be lightly browned and
crisped by placing under a preheated
browning element or a broiler for a few
minutes. Serve hot or cold with custard.

Apple and Honey Pancake Gâteau

*Serves 4: Filling: 1½ lb (750 g) cooking apples;
½ lemon; cinnamon; powdered sugar; honey
1¼ cups (10 fl oz) crêpe batter (see page 339).*

To make the filling, peel the apples, core and cut into thick slices. Grate the lemon peel and add to the apples with the lemon juice. Set on a low heat in a heavy-based saucepan and allow to soften. Stir occasionally to prevent sticking. When soft, beat with a wooden spoon, add a pinch of cinnamon and, if too tart, sweeten with powdered sugar.

Cook the crêpes (see page 339) and leave unfolded. Spread one crêpe with honey and then the apple mixture. Transfer this to a round ovenproof dish and continue in layers, ending with an uncovered crêpe. Sprinkle a little extra cinnamon mixed with powdered sugar over the finished dish and serve with a bowl of whipped cream.

Apple Dumplings

*Serves 6: Shortcrust Pastry: 2 cups (8 oz) all purpose flour; 1 teaspoon salt; 6 oz (185 g) shortening;
5-6 tablespoons water
1 cup (8 oz) sugar; 2 cups (16 fl oz) water;
1 teaspoon lemon juice; 3 tablespoons (1½ oz) butter; ½ teaspoon cinnamon; 6 apples, peeled and cored; ½ cup (3 oz) brown sugar; 1 tablespoon cinnamon; ¼ cup (1 oz) chopped walnuts (optional); ¼ cup (2 oz) seedless raisins (optional); butter*

To make the pastry, sift the flour and salt into a bowl. Add half the shortening and cut in with a knife until the mixture resembles fine breadcrumbs. Cut in the remaining shortening until the mixture forms pieces the size of peas. Sprinkle over 1 tablespoon of water at a time, mixing lightly until the dough can be gathered into a ball. Mix until smooth and elastic, then roll into a ball, wrap in plastic wrap and allow to rest for 20 minutes or until required.

Roll out the pastry to a thickness of ⅛ in (3 mm). Cut into 7-8-in (18-20-cm) squares, depending upon the size of the apple. Heat the sugar, water, lemon juice, butter and ½ teaspoon of cinnamon in a saucepan. When the sugar has melted, boil for 3 minutes.

Place a cored apple on each pastry

Apple Pie

square. Mix the brown sugar and remaining cinnamon together and fill the apple cavity with it (plus walnuts and/or raisins if desired). Dot each apple with a knob of butter and cover with pastry. Overlap the edges, moisten with water and seal. With a wide spatula, lift the apples to a shallow baking dish. Pour the hot syrup around the apples.

Bake in an oven preheated to 425°F (220°C) for 40-45 minutes. Serve with cream, plain or whipped, or ice cream.

Apple Fritters

*Serves 6: 1½ cups (6 oz) all purpose flour; salt;
3 eggs; 1 cup (8 fl oz) beer; 3-4 apples, peeled, cored and cut into slices ½ in (1 cm) thick; oil for deep frying; ½ cup (4 fl oz) sugar mixed with cinnamon*

Place the flour and the salt in a mixing bowl, add the eggs and slowly stir in the beer to make a thick batter.

Heat the oil in a large pan. Dip the apple slices in the batter and deep fry until they are golden brown. Serve them warm, sprinkled with the cinnamon sugar.

Apple Pie

Serves 6-8: 1 unbaked 9-in (23-cm) double shortcrust pie shell (see page 336); ½-¾ cup (4-6 oz) sugar; pinch of salt; ¾ teaspoon cinnamon; 4-5 cups sliced apples (approx. 1½ medium-size apples per cup); 1 tablespoon butter

Line a pie dish with pastry. Mix together the sugar, salt and cinnamon. Toss the sliced apples through the mixture. Place this mixture into the pastry-lined pan and dot with butter. Cover with the top crust and cut slits in the top.

Bake in an oven preheated to 425°F (220°C) on the lowest shelf of the oven for about 1 hour or until the crust is nicely browned and the apples are transparent. Serve with cream, whipped cream, ice cream, cheese or any favorite sauce.

Note: Prepare the pastry and line the dish before preparing the apple filling. Once the top crust has been added to the pie, immediately freeze or bake.

Apple Snow

*Serves 4: 5–6 medium-size apples; 2 egg whites;
2 tablespoons brandy or rum; ⅓–½ cup (3–4 oz)
vanilla-flavored sugar; juice of 1 lemon or orange*

Core the apples and place them in a baking
dish. Bake in an oven preheated to 375°F
(190°C) for 30–40 minutes or until they are
soft. Let the apples cool, then peel. In a
food processor or blender, puree the apples
and chill.

Meanwhile, whisk the egg whites with
the brandy or rum and the sugar (the quantity of sugar used depends on the acidity of
the apples). Add the lemon or orange juice.
While vigorously whisking the mixture,
add the apple puree. The final results
should be firm but frothy. Serve very cold
in glass dessert dishes.

Apple Soufflé

*Serves 4–6: 4 tablespoons (2 oz) butter; ½ cup (2 oz)
all purpose flour; 1¼ cups (10 fl oz) hot milk; pinch
of salt; 5 egg yolks; ½ cup (4 oz) sugar; ½ teaspoon
vanilla; 3 tablespoons Calvados; ½ large apple,
peeled, chopped into small pieces and cooked in
water until tender; 6 macaroons; 6 egg whites*

Melt the butter in the top of a double
saucepan. Add the flour and cook, stirring,
until well blended. Add the hot milk and
salt. Cook the sauce, stirring constantly,
until smooth and thick, then cool slightly.

Beat the egg yolks with the sugar and the
vanilla and mix well with the cooled sauce.
Stir in 2 tablespoons of Calvados and the
cooked apple pieces. Line a buttered soufflé
dish with the macaroons and sprinkle them
with the remaining tablespoon of
Calvados.

Beat the egg whites until stiff, but not
dry, then fold into the cooled sauce mixture. Pour into the prepared soufflé dish.
Bake in the center of an oven preheated to
350°F (180°C) for 35 minutes or until the
soufflé is puffed and golden. Serve immediately.

Apple Strudel

*Makes one large strudel: Strudel Pastry: 1½ cups
(6 oz) all purpose flour; 1 egg yolk; salt;
¼ tablespoon oil; ¼ cup (2 fl oz) lukewarm water;
juice of ½ lemon; 16 tablespoons (8 fl oz) melted*

*butter; 1 tablespoon sugar
4 oz (125 g) roasted almonds, finely chopped; 3 lb
(1½ kg) apples, peeled and sliced; 5 oz (155 g)
seedless raisins; ⅓ cup (3 oz) sugar*

To make the pastry, mound the flour on a
pastry board. Make a well in the center and
add the egg yolk, salt, oil, water and lemon
juice. Mix the ingredients, using a knife.

Knead the dough with your hands until
it becomes elastic and leaves the board
freely. Place the dough into a preheated
stainless steel bowl, cover and keep warm
for 30 minutes.

Spread a tablecloth on a table and
sprinkle the cloth with flour. Place the
dough in the center of the cloth and
sprinkle it with flour. Flatten it slightly
with a rolling pin. Brush the dough with
approximately ¼ cup of the melted butter.

Place your hands, palms upward, under
the dough and while lifting it, pull and
stretch it in all directions until it becomes
thin and transparent. If there are any thick
edges left, cut them off with a knife. The
sheet of thin dough should be approximately rectangular in shape.

Spoon the chopped almonds on about
two-thirds of the dough. Mix together the
rest of the filling ingredients and arrange
them over the almonds. Sprinkle with ¼
cup of the melted butter.

To roll the strudel, lift the end of the
cloth nearest to you and, starting from the
end with the filling, continue lifting the
cloth, which will cause the strudel to roll
over and over. Lift the strudel with the
cloth and finally, roll it from the cloth into
a greased baking dish. With a pastry brush,
brush the remaining butter onto the surface
of the strudel.

Bake in an oven preheated to 450°F
(230°C) for 10 minutes, then reduce the
heat to 400°F (200°C) and bake for 20 minutes more or until the strudel is crisp and
brown. Before serving sprinkle with sugar.

Apple Tart
from Alsace

*Serves 6: 4 large cooking apples, peeled, cored and
thinly sliced; 1 unbaked 9-in (23-cm) shortcrust pie
shell (see page 321); 4 tablespoons sugar; 2 eggs;
1 tablespoon all purpose flour; ½ cup (4 fl oz) milk
or cream; kirsch or brandy*

Arrange the slices of apple on the pastry
base in circles, then sprinkle with 1 tablespoon of the sugar.

Bake in an oven preheated to 425°F
(210°C) for 10 minutes.

In a mixing bowl, whisk the eggs, mix in
the flour and add the milk or cream, whisking all the time. Add the remaining sugar.
Sprinkle a little kirsch or brandy into this
mixture. Pour onto the hot partly cooked
tart. Bake the tart for a further 20 minutes,
until the top is cooked and the pastry
golden brown.

Note: This tart can also be made with
stoned plums or cherries.

Apricot and
Almond Tart

*Serves 6–8: ¾ quantity (6 oz) Pâte Sucrée (see page
338); ¼ cup (1 oz) ground almonds
Filling: 1¼ cups (10 fl oz) heavy cream; 1¾ lb
(875 g) canned apricot halves; 6 tablespoons (3 oz)
apricot jelly; 2 teaspoons arrowroot, or cornstarch;
blanched toasted almonds, for decoration*

Make the pastry according to the recipe,
adding the ground almonds with the sugar.
Chill well.

Roll the pastry out thinly and line an 8-in
(20-cm) deep-sided flan tin or a 9-in
(23-cm) shallow-sided flan tin. Bake blind
in the top of an oven preheated to 425°F
(220°C) for 10–15 minutes or until the
pastry is set in shape. Remove the blind
filling, reduce the oven temperature to
375°F (190°C), and bake for a further
10–15 minutes or until the pastry is cooked.
Cool on a wire rack; after a few minutes
remove the pastry from the flan tin, then
leave until cold.

To make the filling, whip the cream until
thick. Drain the canned apricots well and
reserve ½ cup (4 fl oz) of juice. Place the
apricot juice and the jelly in a saucepan
and dissolve the jelly over a medium heat.
Strain the juice and jelly mixture and
return to the saucepan. Blend the arrowroot smoothly with a little extra apricot
juice, add it to the saucepan and bring to
the boil, stirring continuously until the
glaze clears and thickens. Cool but do not
allow to set.

To finish the tart, spread whipped cream
over the bottom of the pastry shell, then
top it neatly with apricot halves. Decorate
with toasted almonds placed between the
apricot halves. Brush the glaze over the
fruit and allow it to set before serving.

Note: Canned peaches may be used
instead of apricots.

Apricot Cheese Tart

Serves 6–8: 2 cups (8 oz) canned apricot halves; 1 tablespoon apricot liqueur or brandy; 8 oz (250 g) cream cheese, softened; 1 tablespoon powdered sugar; 1 teaspoon grated lemon peel; ½ cup (2 oz) pistachio nuts, chopped; 1 baked 8-in (20-cm) shortcrust pie shell (see page 321); ⅓ cup redcurrant jelly

Drain the apricots and reserve ¼ cup of the juice. Pour the liqueur over the apricots. Cream the cheese until soft and blend with the apricot juice, sugar, lemon peel and nuts. Spread evenly over the baked shell.

Arrange the apricots, rounded side up, over the cream cheese filling. Sprinkle over any remaining liqueur. Beat the jelly until it is smooth and syrupy. Spoon and brush over the apricots. Chill for 3–4 hours.

Apricot Cheesecake

Serves 6: Biscuit Base: 8 oz (250 g) plain sweet cookies; 8 tablespoons (4 oz) butter; pinch of nutmeg or cinnamon
1 lb (500 g) cream cheese; 8 oz (250 g) cottage cheese; 1 teaspoon vanilla; 4 eggs; 1 cup (8 oz) sugar; 1¾ lb (875 g) canned apricots; 1 tablespoon sugar; 1 teaspoon lemon juice; 1 tablespoon cornstarch

To make the biscuit base, crush the cookies finely. Melt the butter and add to the crushed cookies with the nutmeg or cinnamon. Mix well. Spread over the base and sides of an 8-in (20-cm) springform pan and press firmly. Refrigerate for 1 hour.

Meanwhile, make the filling; press the cheeses through a fine sieve, blend with the vanilla and beat until creamy. Beat the eggs until frothy, then beat in the sugar gradually until the mixture is thick and foamy. Continue beating while adding the cheese in small portions, mixing each time until smooth. Chop or mash 5–6 of the drained apricots and stir into the mixture. Spoon into the biscuit base and press down smoothly. Bake in an oven preheated to 325°F (160°C) for 35–40 minutes. Allow to cool in the oven with the door ajar.

Chop or mash the remaining apricots, adding 1 tablespoon sugar and lemon juice. Blend the cornstarch with ½ cup apricot syrup and add to the fruit. Bring to the boil, stirring constantly, then simmer for a few minutes. Cool and spread over the top of the cheesecake. Refrigerate overnight and remove from the pan before serving.

Apricot Nut Cream Pie

Serves 8: 1½ cups (7 oz) dried apricots; 2 teaspoons lemon juice; ⅓ cup (2½ fl oz) brandy; 1 cup (8 fl oz) cream; 2 egg yolks; 1 cup (5 oz) powdered sugar; ¾ teaspoon vanilla; ¼ teaspoon salt; ¾ cup (3 oz) toasted pecans or hazelnuts, finely chopped; 1 baked 9-in (23-cm) shortcrust pie shell (see page 321)

Place the apricots in a saucepan and cover with water. Bring to the boil and simmer until tender. Drain. Beat or blend to make a lumpy puree. Chill. Stir in the lemon juice and brandy.

In a large bowl, beat the cream until thick. In another bowl, beat the egg yolks with the sugar, vanilla and salt until smooth and creamy. Fold into the whipped cream, then fold the apricot puree into this mixture. Blend in the nuts, leaving a few out for a garnish.

Spoon the apricot mixture into the baked pie shell. Cover. Chill for 3–4 hours, or overnight. Garnish with nuts.

Apricot Pie

Serves 6: Basic Shortcrust Pastry: 1 cup (4 oz) all purpose flour; ½ teaspoon salt; 6 tablespoons (3 oz) butter; 3-4 tablespoons water
¾ cup cooked, lightly sweetened, dried apricot puree; ½ teaspoon grated lemon peel; 1 tablespoon lemon juice; 1 tablespoon brandy or Marsala; 3 egg whites; ⅛ teaspoon salt; ⅛ teaspoon vanilla; ½ cup (4 oz) sugar; 1 cup (8 fl oz) cream, whipped

Sift the flour and salt into a mixing bowl and cut in half the butter until it resembles fine breadcrumbs. Cut in the remaining butter and mix until it resembles pieces the size of peas. Gradually sprinkle over the water, mixing and gathering the dough into a ball. Wrap in plastic wrap and chill for 20 minutes.

Roll the pastry out on a floured board to ⅛ in (3 mm) thick and slightly larger than an 8-9-in (20-23-cm) pie shell. Fit the pastry into the dish and trim edges. Bake in an oven preheated to 350°F (180°C) for 20-25 minutes or cooked and firm.

Apricot and Almond Tart

In a small bowl, blend the apricot puree with the peel, lemon juice and brandy. Whisk the egg whites with the salt and vanilla until soft peaks form. Gradually beat in the sugar. Beat until the mixture is stiff and glossy, then fold it into the fruit puree.

Fill the pie shell with the mixture and bake in an oven preheated to 325°F (160°C) for 20 minutes. Serve warm with whipped cream.

B

Baked Devonshire Apple Dumplings

Serves 4: 8 oz (250 g) shortcrust pastry (see page 319) (see Note); 4 apples, each weighing about 4 oz (125 g); ¼ cup (2 oz) sugar; 4 cloves; 1 egg yolk, mixed with a little cold water

Roll out the pastry fairly thinly and cut it into 4 squares big enough to completely enclose an apple. Peel and core the apples, fill the centers with sugar and pierce each one with a clove. Place an apple on each pastry square, brush the edges of the pastry with water and fold it over to completely seal the apple. Decorate the tops with scraps of pastry cut into shapes. Brush the pastry with the egg yolk and water mixture. Place the apples on a lightly greased baking sheet and bake in an oven preheated to 350°F (180°C) for 30–45 minutes or until the pastry is golden brown and the apples are cooked. Serve with whipped cream.

Note: For a sweet shortcrust pastry, add 6 tablespoons (3½ oz) sugar to the basic recipe.

Bakewell Pudding

Serves 8: 8 oz (250 g) sweet shortcrust pastry (see page 319) (see Note); 2 tablespoons (1 oz) raspberry jelly; 4 eggs; ½ cup (4 oz) sugar; 8 tablespoons (4 oz) butter, melted; 1¼ cups (4 oz) ground almonds

This dish is usually made in a traditional oval Bakewell pudding tin with sloping sides; however, an 8-in (20-cm) flan mold may be used instead. Line the greased dish or flan mold with the pastry. Cover the pastry with the jelly.

Beat the eggs and sugar until the mixture is pale and creamy. While stirring constantly, pour in the butter. Mix in the almonds and pour it over the jelly. Bake in an oven preheated to 400°F (200°C) for 30–35 minutes or until the filling has set.

Note: Add 6 tablespoons (3½ oz) sugar to the basic recipe.

Banana Cakes

Makes 24: 5 large bananas; 1 cup (3½ oz) colored green pea flour or substitute arrowroot and green food coloring; ¼ cup (2½ oz) sugar, or to taste; pinch of salt; 2½ cups (20 fl oz) thin coconut milk; 1½ cups (12 fl oz) water

Steam the bananas in their skins for about 10 minutes or until soft. Set aside to cool, then slice.

Put the flour, sugar and salt into a saucepan and add the coconut milk and water. Bring to the boil, stirring continually, and simmer until the paste turns thick and begins to clear.

Cut a banana leaf or aluminum foil into 6-in (15-cm) squares and place a spoonful of the mixture on each. Add a slice of banana and top with a little more batter. Fold the leaf or foil around the mixture to make a square shape. Tie with thread or secure with toothpicks. Set aside to cool, then place in the refrigerator until set completely. Serve wrapped or with the wrapper torn away at the top.

Banana Cream Pie

Serves 6–8: ½ cup (4 oz) sugar; 2 tablespoons cornstarch; ¼ teaspoon salt; 2 teaspoons gelatin; 2 cups (16 fl oz) milk; 3 egg yolks; 1½ tablespoons butter or margarine; 2 teaspoons vanilla; ¾ cup (6 fl oz) cream; 3 medium-size bananas; 1 baked 9-in (23-cm) shortcrust pie shell (see page 321); juice of ½ lemon; ⅓ cup redcurrant jelly

In a saucepan, combine the sugar, cornstarch, salt and gelatin. Beat in the milk and the egg yolks. Cook over a low heat, stirring constantly, until the mixture is smooth and thickened, about 15 minutes. Stir in the butter and vanilla. Cover the surface with plastic wrap and chill.

Whip the cream. Slice 2 of the bananas, fold into the cream, then into the custard mixture. Spoon into the baked pie shell, chill until set. Slice the remaining banana

and sprinkle with the lemon juice. Heat the jelly in a small saucepan, until just melted. Drain the banana slices and pat dry. Arrange the slices over the custard and brush over with redcurrant jelly.

Banana Fritters

Serves 4: 1 cup (4 oz) all purpose flour; 1 egg, lightly beaten; 1 tablespoon melted butter; ½ cup (4 fl oz) milk; 1 egg white, stiffly beaten; 3 tablespoons sugar; 3 tablespoons brandy; 6 bananas, thickly sliced; all purpose flour; oil for deep frying; powdered sugar

Mix half the flour with the egg, butter and milk to make a smooth batter. Fold in the stiffly beaten egg white. Refrigerate for 1 hour.

In the meantime, mix the sugar and brandy until the sugar dissolves. Pour it over the bananas in a bowl and set aside for 30 minutes. Turn occasionally to make sure that all slices are well marinated. Remove the bananas from the marinade, then drain, dust in flour and dip them in the batter. Deep fry in hot oil until golden brown on both sides. Let the oil drain off and serve them warm, sprinkled with powdered sugar.

Basic Custard Pie

Serves 6: 4 eggs; ½–⅔ cup (4–5 oz) sugar; ½ teaspoon salt; ⅓ teaspoon nutmeg; 2½ cups (20 fl oz) hot milk; 1 teaspoon vanilla; 1 unbaked 9-in (23-cm) shortcrust pie shell (see page 321)

Place the eggs in a bowl and beat slightly. Beat in the sugar, salt, nutmeg, milk and vanilla. Pour into the pastry-lined dish.

Bake in an oven preheated to 450°F (230°C) for 15 minutes. Reduce the temperature to 350°F (180°C) and bake for a further 25–30 minutes. Sprinkle with extra grated nutmeg.

Note: Custard and cream pies must be refrigerated and must not be kept for more than 2–3 days.

Bavarian Strawberry Pie

Serves 10–12: ¼ cup (2 oz) sugar; ¼ teaspoon salt; 1 tablespoon gelatin; 1 cup (8 fl oz) milk; 2 egg yolks, lightly beaten; 2 teaspoons vanilla; 2 egg whites; ¼ cup (2 oz) sugar; 1 cup (8 fl oz) heavy cream, whipped; 1 baked 10-in (25-cm) shortcrust pie shell (see page 348); 2 cups strawberries, hulled, for garnish; powdered sugar

In the top of a double boiler, mix the sugar, salt and gelatin together. Add the milk and egg yolks and blend in. Place the mixture over hot (but not boiling) water, stirring constantly until slightly thickened, then remove from the heat. Stir in the vanilla. Cover with plastic wrap and cool — this will prevent the mixture from forming a skin.

Beat the egg whites until foamy. Gradually add the sugar and beat until stiff. Fold the whipped cream into the gelatin mixture, then add the egg whites. Chill until slightly thickened. Spoon into the baked cold pie shell. Chill until firm. Top with strawberries and sprinkle with powdered sugar.

Black-bottom Pie

Black-Bottom Pie

Serves 8: ¾ quantity (6 oz) Pâte Sucrée (see page 338)
Filling: 2 oz (60 g) unsweetened chocolate; 1¾ cups (14 fl oz) milk; 3 large eggs, separated; ½ cup (4 oz) sugar; 1 tablespoon cornstarch; 1 tablespoon gelatin; ¼ cup (4 fl oz) cold water; 1 tablespoon rum; pinch of cream of tartar; ¼ cup (2 oz) powdered sugar; grated chocolate for decoration

Roll the pastry out thinly and line a 10-in (25-cm) pie pan.

Bake blind in an oven preheated to 425°F (220°C) near the top rack for 10 minutes. Remove the blind filling and bake for another 10 minutes or until cooked. Allow to cool on a wire rack.

To make the filling, melt the chocolate over gently simmering water in the top of a double boiler. Scald the milk. Mix the egg yolks with ½ cup sugar and the cornstarch. Stir in the hot milk, then transfer to a saucepan and bring to a boil, stirring continuously. Remove from the heat. Measure out 1 cup of this custard and stir into the melted chocolate.

Soak the gelatin in ¼ cup cold water, then add this to the remaining custard to dissolve. Add the rum and allow to cool.

Whisk the egg whites with cream of tartar until soft peaks form and add the powdered sugar gradually, whisking continuously. Fold the egg whites into the remaining custard.

Pour the chocolate custard into the pie crust and chill until set. When firm, swirl the rum-flavored custard mixture on top, then chill again until firm. Serve decorated with grated chocolate sprinkled on top.

Black Forest Chiffon Pie

Serves 12: Filling: 13½ oz (425 g) canned pitted dark sweet cherries, well drained; 3 tablespoons kirsch (or cherry brandy); 2 eggs, separated (at room temperature); 1 cup (8 fl oz) milk; ½ teaspoon vanilla; 7 tablespoons (3½ oz) sugar; 2½ oz (75 g) unsweetened chocolate, coarsely grated; 1 tablespoon gelatin; ¼ teaspoon salt; 1 cup (8 fl oz) heavy cream
1 baked 10-in (25-cm) shortcrust pie shell made with 2 cups (8 oz) all purpose flour and ¾ cup (6 oz) shortening (see page 336)

Reserve six cherries, if desired, for garnishing. Chop the remaining cherries in half and marinate in kirsch.

In a saucepan, whisk the egg yolks, milk, vanilla and ¼ cup (2 oz) sugar until well blended. Sprinkle the chocolate and gelatin evenly over the mixture. Cook, stirring constantly, over a low heat until the chocolate and gelatin have completely dissolved, about 15 minutes. Stir in 1 tablespooon of kirsch. Cover and refrigerate until the mixture is slightly set, about 1 hour.

In a small bowl, whisk the egg whites and salt on a high speed until stiff peaks form. Gradually whisk in the remaining sugar until the mixture is stiff and glossy. Beat the cream until thick. With a spatula, fold the cherry mixture into the chocolate mixture. Then fold in the cream and egg whites. Turn into the baked pastry shell. Chill for 4 hours or overnight.

Buco Pie

*Serves 6–8: 1 unbaked 8-in (20-cm) double
shortcrust pie shell (see page 336); 2 cups young
coconut, finely slivered; ¾ cup (6 oz) sugar; ½ cup
(4 fl oz) coconut milk; ½ cup (4 fl oz) evaporated
milk; 2 tablespoons cornstarch; 2 eggs, well beaten;
½ teaspoon salt*

Line an 8-in (20-cm) pie dish with half the
pastry. Blend the remaining ingredients
together in a saucepan. Cook, stirring constantly, until the mixture has thickened.
Pour it into the pie dish and top with the
remaining pastry.

Bake in a preheated oven to 400°F
(200°C) 30–40 minutes or until the top has
browned. Serve cold.

Buttermilk Lemon Pie

*Serves 6–8: 2 egg yolks, lightly beaten; ⅓ cup (3 oz)
sugar; 1 tablespoon all purpose flour; ½ teaspoon
salt; 2 tablespoons (1 oz) butter, melted; 1 cup
(8 fl oz) buttermilk; 2 tablespoons lemon juice;
½ teaspoon grated lemon peel; 2 egg whites;
2 tablespoons sugar; ¼ teaspoon vanilla; 1 unbaked
9-in (23-cm) shortcrust pie shell (see page 321)*

Blend the eggs into a mixture of sugar,
flour and salt. Stir in the cooled melted butter, buttermilk, lemon juice and lemon
peel. Beat the egg whites until frothy.
Gradually add 2 tablespoons sugar. Beat
until soft peaks form. Beat in the vanilla.
Fold the meringue into the buttermilk mixture. Spoon into the pastry shell.

Bake in an oven preheated to 450°F
(230°C) for 10 minutes. Reduce the oven
temperature to 350°F (180°C) for 20–25
minutes longer. Cool until the filling sets.
Serve warm or cold.

C

Caramel Custard

*Serves 6: ½ cup (4 oz) sugar; 2½ cups (20 fl oz)
milk; 3 eggs; 1 teaspoon vanilla; pinch of salt*

Heat the sugar in a small saucepan over
medium heat until it caramelizes. Watch

Caramel Custard

Cheesecake Pie

continuously and move the saucepan around so the caramel colors evenly. Remove from the heat.

Carefully pour half the milk down the side of the saucepan (it foams up quickly). Put back over low heat until all the caramel dissolves in the milk; remove. Beat the eggs, stir in the remaining milk, vanilla and salt, add the caramel mixture, and mix together.

Grease six custard cups and pour in sufficient custard to come within about ½ in (1 cm) of the top. Place in a baking pan with about ¾-in (2-cm) depth of water and bake in an oven preheated to 350°F (180°C) until set, about 20–30 minutes. Leave standing for about 5 minutes, then turn out and serve hot. If preferred cold, leave in the molds, refrigerate and turn out when required.

Caramel Sponge Dessert

Serves 6: 6 tablespoons sugar; ¼ cup (2 fl oz) water; 2½ cups (20 fl oz) milk; 3 eggs; extra ¼ cup (2 fl oz) sugar; 1 cup (2 oz) soft cake crumbs; vanilla; ½ cup (2 oz) sugar for meringue

Caramelize the sugar and half the water in a saucepan. Carefully add the remainder of the water and boil over medium heat until the sugar has dissolved. Add the milk and heat.

Separate the eggs and beat the yolks with the extra sugar. Add the hot (not boiling) milk and pour it onto the cake crumbs. Flavor with vanilla. Pour the mixture into a buttered pie dish. Whisk the egg whites until foamy, then gradually add the sugar, whisking until stiff peaks form. Spoon the meringue over the custard mixture. Bake in an oven preheated to 325°F (160°C) for 40–45 minutes and serve hot.

Caramelized Apple Tart

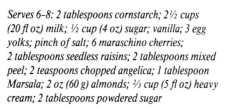

Serves 4: 2 tablespoons (1 oz) butter; ⅓ cup (3 oz) sugar; 5 apples, peeled, cored and sliced in rounds Pastry: 10 tablespoons (5 oz) butter; 2 cups (8 oz) all purpose flour; pinch of salt; 1 egg

Butter the bottom of a Teflon-coated pie dish. Sprinkle with the sugar. Arrange the apples on the sugar, overlapping them slightly.

Prepare the pastry by rubbing the butter into the flour and salt. Bind with the egg and a little cold water if necessary. Knead until the dough is smooth and elastic, then form into a ball, wrap in plastic wrap and leave in the refrigerator for 20 minutes. Roll the pastry out thinly and cut a round to cover the pie dish.

Bake the pie in an oven preheated to 350°F (180°C) for approximately 25 minutes. When the tart is cooked, place the pie on a hot plate and caramelize the apples until golden. Cool, then turn out onto a serving dish. Serve with whipped cream.

Caramelized Oranges

Serves 6: 6 seedless oranges; 1 cup (8 oz) sugar; 1¼ cups (10 fl oz) water; 1 tablespoon orange liqueur

With a very sharp knife, peel off the orange zest only and cut it into very fine strips. Place the strips in a saucepan and add just enough water to cover. Simmer them for 5–6 minutes. Peel the oranges carefully, removing all traces of white pith.

In a large saucepan combine the sugar and water and simmer, stirring constantly, until the sugar has dissolved. Boil the syrup for approximately 5 minutes, add the oranges and simmer for 2–3 minutes. Remove the oranges and arrange them on a serving platter.

Put the strips of orange peel into the syrup and boil gently until the syrup reaches the soft ball stage (see Note). Cool the syrup slightly, then add the orange liqueur. Cool the syrup and pour it, together with the strips of peel, over the oranges. Serve chilled.

Note: Soft ball stage has been reached when the sugar forms a soft ball when a little is dropped into a saucer of cold water. Alternatively, the sugar will reach 239°F (115°C) on a candy thermometer.

Cassata

Serves 6–8: 2 tablespoons cornstarch; 2½ cups (20 fl oz) milk; ½ cup (4 oz) sugar; vanilla; 3 egg yolks; pinch of salt; 6 maraschino cherries; 2 tablespoons seedless raisins; 2 tablespoons mixed peel; 2 teaspoons chopped angelica; 1 tablespoon Marsala; 2 oz (60 g) almonds; ⅔ cup (5 fl oz) heavy cream; 2 tablespoons powdered sugar

Blend the cornstarch to a smooth paste with a little of the milk. Add the sugar to the rest of the milk and heat gently. When nearly boiling, add the blended cornstarch, stir until boiling, then simmer for a further 2–3 minutes. Remove from the heat, stir in the vanilla to taste and cool slightly. Beat the egg yolks and gradually stir into the cooled milk. Return to the pan, lower the heat and stir for 1–2 minutes. Put aside until nearly cold, then pour into refrigerator trays and freeze until firm.

Chop the cherries and raisins, put into a bowl with the chopped peel and angelica, then stir in the Marsala and leave for 30 minutes.

Toast the almonds in the oven and chop. Whip the cream until thickening, then gradually beat in the remaining sugar. When thick, mix in the fruit and almonds. Chill well. Allow the frozen custard to soften slightly, spread a layer over the base and sides of a mold and quickly return to the freezer. When firm, spoon the fruit mixture into the center and cover with the remaining custard. Cover with aluminum foil and freeze until firm.

Cheesecake Pie

Serves 6–8: 8 oz (250 g) cream cheese, softened; ½ cup (4 oz) sugar; ½ teaspoon vanilla; ¼ teaspoon salt; 2 tablespoons lemon juice; 2 eggs; 1 unbaked 8-in (20-cm) biscuit crumb crust (see page 321); 1 cup (8 fl oz) sour cream; 2 tablespoons brown sugar; ½ teaspoon vanilla; fresh strawberries for garnish

Beat the cream cheese until fluffy then gradually beat in the sugar, vanilla, salt and lemon juice. Add the eggs, one at a time, beating thoroughly after each addition. Pour the mixture into the crumb crust. Bake in an oven preheated to 325°F (160°C) for 25–30 minutes.

Combine the sour cream, brown sugar and vanilla and spoon over the top of the pie. Bake for a further 10 minutes. Cool, then chill for 4–6 hours. Garnish with strawberries or other fresh fruit.

Cheese-Crusted Apple Pudding ★

Serves 6: 6 tart apples, peeled and sliced; 1 tablespoon lemon juice; ¾ cup (6 oz) sugar; ¾ teaspoon cinnamon; ½ teaspoon nutmeg; 1 unbaked 9-in (23-cm) cream cheese pastry shell for a one-crust pie (see page 332)

Select a baking dish into which apples fit snugly. Sprinkle them with lemon juice and toss with the sugar, cinnamon and nutmeg. Place them in the buttered baking dish. Arrange the pastry over the top. Turn under and flute the edges and cut a vent in the center. Bake in an oven preheated to 400°F (220°C) for 35-40 minutes. Serve warm.

Cherry Clafoutis

Serves 6: 1½ lb (750 g) black cherries, pitted; 4 eggs; pinch of salt; ½ cup (4 oz) sugar; ½ cup (2 oz) all purpose flour; 4 tablespoons (2 oz) butter; 1 cup (8 fl oz) milk; powdered sugar for sprinkling

Butter a wide shallow ovenproof dish generously. Put the pitted cherries into the dish. Beat the eggs lightly in a bowl, then whisk in the salt and the sugar. Blend in the flour. Melt half of the butter and beat into the batter. Pour in the milk, beating well. Pour this batter over the cherries and dot with the remaining butter. Bake in an oven preheated to 400°F (200°C) for 35-40 minutes or until the batter has set. Sprinkle with sugar and serve either hot or cold, accompanied by whipped cream.

Chess Pie — Southern Style

Serves 8-12: 8 tablespoons (4 oz) butter, softened; ⅛ teaspoon salt; 2 teaspoons vanilla; 1⅓ cups (11 oz) sugar; 4 egg yolks, well beaten; 1 unbaked 8-in (20-cm) shortcrust pie shell (see page 321)

Cream the butter, salt and vanilla together. Gradually add the sugar, beating until fluffy. Add the egg yolks. Beat the mixture until it is soft and fluffy. Spoon the filling into the pie shell and bake in an oven preheated to 425°F (220°C) for 10 minutes.

Reduce the oven temperature to 325°F (160°C). Bake for 40-50 minutes longer, or

Chilled Raspberry Whip

until a knife inserted halfway between the edge and the center of the pie comes out clean. Serve warm or cool.

Chilled Raspberry Whip

Serves 4: 1 lb (500 g) raspberries; 1¼ cups (10 fl oz) heavy cream, whipped; ½ cup (4 oz) powdered sugar

Set a few raspberries aside for decoration and crush the rest. Add the whipped cream and the sugar, and mix together. Take a soufflé dish and make a collar with waxed paper. Pour in the mixture and place in the coldest part of the refrigerator. When ready to serve, remove from the refrigerator and remove the paper collar. Decorate the top with the remaining raspberries and a little icing sugar and serve.

Chocolate-Coated Pears with Loganberry Sauce

Serves 6: 6 firm but ripe pears; 4-5 slices fresh ginger; 1 cinnamon stick; ¾ cup (6 oz) powdered sugar; 2 cups (16 fl oz) dry white wine; 13½-oz (425-g) can loganberries or raspberries; 5 oz (156 g) semisweet chocolate; 2 tablespoons vegetable shortening

Peel the pears, leaving on the stems. Place the ginger, cinnamon stick, sugar and wine in a microwave-safe deep dish and stir until the sugar has dissolved. Put in the pears and cover. Microwave on HIGH (100%) for 5 minutes, then on MEDIUM (50%) for 20-30 minutes. The time will depend on the ripeness of the pears — when ready they should be tender but still holding their shape. Turn the pears and rotate the dish several times during cooking so they are done evenly. Allow to stand for 3-4 minutes, then transfer to a rack to drain and cool.

Puree the berries in a blender or food processor and strain through a fine sieve to remove the seeds. Chill. (If using fresh raspberries or other berries that don't need to be cooked, puree them with a little powdered sugar.)

Break the chocolate into squares and place in a jug with the shortening. Cover with plastic wrap and microwave on MEDIUM (50%) for 4 minutes. Remove from the oven and stir until smooth and shiny. Dip the pears into the chocolate, coating evenly. Return to the rack to firm. Coat a second and even a third time until the chocolate is used up. Chill thoroughly.

To serve, pour some of the berry puree onto each plate and stand a pear in the center. Garnish if liked with blanched strips of orange peel.

Plain poached pears can be served to those who prefer less rich desserts. Thicken some of the poaching liquid with cornstarch or arrowroot and pour over the pears. Serve with lightly whipped cream.

Place pears in a deep dish and cover.

Break the chocolate into pieces with vegetable shortening.

Chocolate-Coated Pears with Loganberry Sauce

Chocolate Ice Cream Roll

Serves 6–8: 4 large eggs, separated; scant ⅔ cup (4 oz) powdered sugar; pinch of salt; 3 tablespoons cornstarch; 3 tablespoons dark cocoa; 1½ tablespoons rum or Marsala; 1 liter vanilla or coffee ice cream; 3 oz (90 g) swemisweet chocolate; ⅔ cup (5 fl oz) heavy cream; ½ teaspoon vanilla; chopped walnuts; extra chocolate

Grease and line a jelly roll pan, 10 × 14 in (25 × 35 cm), with greased, waxed paper or aluminum foil.

Beat the egg yolks and half the sugar together. Add the salt to the egg whites and whisk until stiff, then add the remaining sugar and beat until dissolved. Fold the meringue into the egg yolk mixture. Sift the cornstarch and cocoa together and sift gently on top. Pour the rum or Marsala around the edge and fold lightly. Spread the mixture evenly in the pan.

Bake in an oven preheated to 375°F (190°C) until springy, about 15–20 minutes. Turn onto a clean, damp tea towel and roll up. Unroll, then reroll without the tea towel. Let cool completely.

Have the ice cream slightly soft and spread it quickly on the unrolled cake. Roll up and wrap in clear plastic wrap or aluminum foil. Freeze overnight or until the ice cream sets.

Put chocolate into a bowl and stand in hot (not boiling) water over heat until melted, then add the cream and stir. Cool, then add the vanilla. Stand in a bowl of ice. Beat until thick, then quickly spread the chocolate mixture over the roll, roughing it with a fork. Sprinkle with chopped walnuts and grate a little extra chocolate over. Wrap and freeze until serving time.

Chocolate Mousse

Serves 6: 1⅓ cups semisweet chocolate chips; ⅓ cup (2½ fl oz) black coffee or water; 1 tablespoon butter; 2 tablespoons brandy or rum (optional); 4 eggs; 1¼ cups (10 fl oz) whipping cream

Melt the chocolate with the coffee in the top of a double boiler or in a heatproof bowl over gently boiling water. Remove from the heat and stir in the butter and brandy or rum, if desired. Separate the eggs and add the yolks one at a time to the warm chocolate mixture, stirring continu-ously. Whip the whites until stiff and stir into the chocolate mixture.

Pour the mousse into small mousse pots or small individual glass dessert dishes and chill until set. Serve with a little cream poured over the surface, or whip the cream and pipe a large rosette onto each mousse.

Chocolate Pie

Serves 8–12: 1 unbaked 10-in (25-cm) shortcrust pie shell (see page 348); 4 oz (125 g) semisweet chocolate; 4 tablespoons (2 oz) butter; 1 can evaporated milk; 3 tablespoons cornstarch; 1 tablespoon sugar; ¼ teaspoon salt; 3 eggs; 1 teaspoon vanilla; 1⅓ cups (4 oz) shredded coconut; ½ cup (2 oz) chopped cashews or hazelnuts

Chill the pastry shell. Melt the chocolate with the butter over low heat. Stir until blended. Remove from the heat and gradu-ally blend in the milk. Mix the cornstarch, sugar and salt together. Beat this mixture into the eggs and vanilla, then gradually blend in the chocolate mixture. Pour the filling into the pie shell and sprinkle the coconut and nuts over the top.

Bake in an oven preheated to 375°F (190°C) for 45 minutes or until the top is puffed. The filling will be soft, but will set as it cools. Cool for at least 4 hours before serving.

Coconut Cream Pie

Serves 4–6: 1 unbaked 7-in (18-cm) shortcrust pie shell (see page 321)
Filling: ½ cup (4 oz) powdered sugar; 1 tablespoon arrowroot; pinch of salt; ¾ cup (6 fl oz) water; drops of almond extract; drops of vanilla; 2 egg whites; ¾ cup (6 fl oz) heavy cream; ¾ cup (2 oz) shredded coconut

Chill the pastry shell.

Bake the pie crust blind in an oven preheated to 375°F (190°C) for 7 minutes. Remove the blind filling and paper, and bake for 15 minutes more or until the pastry is evenly golden and crisp. Allow to cool on a wire rack.

To make the filling, put 5 tablespoons of the powdered sugar, the arrowroot, salt and water into a small saucepan. Cook over low heat until smooth and clear. Add 1 drop of almond extract and 2 drops of vanilla to flavor. Allow to cool.

Beat the egg whites until stiff peaks form, then stir into the sugar mixture. Pour into the cooled pie shell.

Whip the cream and sweeten it with the remaining 1¼ tablespoons of powdered sugar, adding a drop each of almond extract and vanilla. Fold in half the coco-nut and spread it over the pie. Sprinkle the top with the remaining coconut.

Set in the freezer for 30 minutes, then remove to the refrigerator. Serve chilled.

Coconut Fruit Pie

Serves 4–6: 2–3 tablespoons raspberry, strawberry or apricot jam; 1 unbaked 9-in (23-cm) shortcrust pie shell (see page 321); 2–3 oz (60–90 g) seedless raisins or currants; 8 tablespoons (4 oz) butter; 1 cup (8 oz) sugar; 2 eggs; 2 cups (6 oz) shredded coconut; ¼ teaspoon vanilla or almond extract; cream for serving

Spread the jam evenly over the pastry shell. Sprinkle the fruit over the jam.

Soften the butter in a mixing bowl, then add the sugar and eggs and beat for 30 seconds. Add the seedless raisins, coconut and vanilla. Mix well and pour over the fruit, spreading the mixture as evenly as possible.

Bake in an oven preheated to 400–450°F (200–230°C) for 10 minutes, then reduce the temperature to 350–375°F (180–190°C) and bake for a further 15–25 minutes until the coconut topping is evenly browned and the center feels firm. Do not overcook. Serve warm with cream.

Note: Leftover pie can be cut into small pieces when cold and kept for 2–3 days.

Coconut Pancakes

Serves 4–6: 2½ cups (20 fl oz) thin coconut milk; 3½ oz (100 g) rice flour; 3 eggs; ½ cup (4 oz) sugar; 3 oz (90 g) shredded coconut; green and pink food coloring; pinch of salt; oil; ¼ cup shredded or grated coconut

Make a thin batter by mixing the coconut milk, rice flour, eggs and sugar together. Whisk for 5 minutes, then fold in the shredded coconut. Divide the batter into three portions. Color one pink, one bright green and leave one plain. Add a little salt to each and beat well. Leave for at least 20 minutes.

Cherry Pie (see page 330)

Wipe a 6-in (15-cm) omelet pan with an oiled cloth and heat through. When ready, pour in a thin layer of batter and swirl the pan to thinly cover the bottom. Cook the pancake on moderate heat until flecked with brown underneath. Flip over and cook the other side. Roll up in the pan and slide onto a plate. Cook all pancakes and stack the different colors in groups on a serving plate. Garnish with coconut.

Coffee Mousse in Meringue Shell

Serves 8–12: 4 egg whites; pinch of salt; ½ teaspoon lemon juice; ¾ cup (6 oz) sugar
Filling: 2 tablespoons instant coffee; 1 tablespoon gelatin; ⅓ cup (2½ fl oz) boiling water; 3 egg yolks; ⅛ teaspoon salt; ½ cup (3 oz) powdered sugar; 3 egg whites; 2 cups (16 fl oz) heavy cream; ½ teaspoon vanilla; ½ cup (2 oz) coarsely chopped nuts for garnish; curled chocolate for garnish

To make the meringue, beat the egg whites with salt until they hold a soft shape. Add the lemon juice, then gradually add the sugar. Beat until stiff peaks form. Spread half of the mixture in a lightly oiled 10-in (25-cm) pie dish. With a teaspoon, arrange mounds of meringue around the rim. Bake in an oven preheated to 300°F (150°C) for 50–55 minutes, until crisp but still white. Cool away from drafts.

For the filling, dissolve the coffee and gelatin in boiling water and stir until dissolved. In a bowl, beat the egg yolks, salt and powdered sugar until the mixture is light and fluffy. Stir in the gelatin mixture and chill until it has thickened slightly.

Beat the egg whites with a pinch of salt until stiff. Beat the cream and vanilla until thick. Fold the cream into the custard, then lastly fold in the egg whites. Spoon the mixture into the shell and garnish with nuts and/or grated or curled chocolate. Chill.

Cherry Pie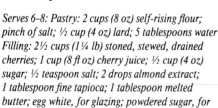

Serves 6–8: Pastry: 2 cups (8 oz) self-rising flour; pinch of salt; ½ cup (4 oz) lard; 5 tablespoons water
Filling: 2½ cups (1¼ lb) stoned, stewed, drained cherries; 1 cup (8 fl oz) cherry juice; ½ cup (4 oz) sugar; ½ teaspoon salt; 2 drops almond extract; 1 tablespoon fine tapioca; 1 tablespoon melted butter; egg white, for glazing; powdered sugar, for glazing

To make the pastry, sift the flour and salt into a bowl and cut in the lard, rubbing it in until the mixture resembles fine breadcrumbs. Add the water and mix in with a knife until a rough dough forms. Refrigerate the dough for 30 minutes.

Combine all the ingredients for the filling and allow to stand for 15 minutes.

Line a deep 8-in (20-cm) pie dish with two-thirds of the pastry. Fill with the cherry mixture. Roll out the remaining pastry and use to cover the pie. Pinch the edges and make four slits on the top of the pastry. Glaze the pastry with egg white and sprinkle powdered sugar over the top. Bake in an oven preheated to 375°F (190°C) for 35 minutes.

Country Rhubarb Tart

Serves 6–8: 1 unbaked 9-in (23-cm) shortcrust pie shell (see page 321); 3 cups rhubarb, cut into ½-in (1-cm) slices; ½–¾ cup (4–6 oz) sugar; 2 eggs; 1 teaspoon vanilla; 2 tablespoons all purpose flour; pinch of salt; pinch of ground cloves (optional); 1 cup (8 fl oz) light cream or half and half

Chill the pie shell until ready to fill.

In a bowl, toss the rhubarb with 3 tablespoons of the sugar and spread evenly over the pastry. In the same bowl, lightly beat the eggs. Stir in the vanilla, flour, salt, cloves, remaining sugar and cream. Pour over the rhubarb.

Bake on the lowest shelf of an oven preheated to 350°F (180°C) for 40 minutes, or until the filling is set. Cool. Refrigerate, if not served within 3 hours.

Cream Cheese Pancakes

Serves 4: 4 tablespoons (2 oz) butter; 3 tablespoons (1½ oz) sugar; 2 egg yolks; 8 oz (250 g) cottage or cream cheese; 3–6 tablespoons sour cream (use only if the cheese is too dry); 4 egg whites, stiffly beaten; 2 tablespoons seedless raisins; 8 pancakes (see page 339); powdered sugar

Cream the butter with the sugar and egg yolks. Add the cheese and, if necessary, the sour cream. Fold in the egg whites and raisins.

Divide the filling into eight parts and spread it over the pancakes. Roll the pancakes and serve dusted with a little powdered sugar.

Cream Party Pie with Macaroon Crust

Serves 12–15: 2 cups (7 oz) fine macaroon crumbs (about 30 macaroons); ¼ cup (2 oz) powdered sugar; 8 tablespoons (4 oz) melted butter
Filling: ¼ cup (2 oz) sugar; 1 tablespoon gelatin; ¼ cup (1 oz) all purpose flour; pinch of salt; 2 egg yolks; 1 cup (8 fl oz) milk; ¼ cup (2 fl oz) sherry; 1 cup (3 oz) coarse almond macaroon crumbs (about 12 macaroons); 2 tablespoons sherry or Marsala; 1 cup (8 fl oz) heavy cream, whipped; 4 egg whites, stiffly beaten

Mix the macaroon crumbs, sugar and melted butter together. Press into the sides and bottom of a 10-in (25-cm) pie plate. Chill.

To make the filling, in a saucepan, mix the sugar, gelatin, flour and salt. In a small bowl, beat the egg yolks, milk and sherry until blended, then stir it into the gelatin mixture. Cook over a low heat, whisking constantly until the mixture comes to the boil. Set the mixture in a pan of iced water for about 15 minutes or until cool, stirring occasionally.

Sprinkle the macaroon crumbs with the sherry. Mix well, then stir into the cooled gelatin mixture. Fold this mixture into the cream and then into the stiffly beaten egg whites. Turn the mixture into the crust, mounding it high in the center. Chill for at least 4 hours or overnight. Garnish with slightly sweetened cream and toasted almonds.

Crumbed Cherry Pie

Serves 6: 2 × 16-oz (500-g) cans dark sweet cherries, pitted and well drained; 1 baked 9-in (23-cm) shortcrust pie shell (see page 321); 1 teaspoon grated orange peel; ¾ cup (3 oz) cake or cookie crumbs; ⅓ cup (3 oz) sugar; 8 tablespoons (4 oz) soft butter; 2 tablespoons sugar; 1 teaspoon cinnamon

Place the cherries in the baked pie shell and sprinkle with the orange peel. In a bowl, blend the crumbs, sugar and butter together. Spread over the cherries. Sprinkle with the sugar mixed with the cinnamon.

Bake in an oven preheated to 375°F (190°C) for 10 minutes. Serve with softened ice cream, whipped cream or sour cream.

Note: For a variation, soak the cherries in port or kirsch for 1 hour, then boil the marinade with 1 tablespoon of sugar until reduced to a glaze, whip with cream, and spoon over the pie.

Crusted Pineapple Slices

Serves 6: 1 large pineapple; ½ cup (3 oz) seedless raisins, chopped; ¼ cup (1 oz) walnuts, chopped; 2 egg whites; 2 teaspoons lemon juice; 1 scant cup (6 oz) powdered sugar; ½ teaspoon grated lemon peel; flaked or shredded coconut

Remove the skin from the pineapple, cut into slices and remove the core. Fill the cavity of each slice with a mixture of raisins and walnuts.

Combine the lightly beaten egg whites, lemon juice, sugar and lemon peel in a heatproof bowl. Beat briskly over boiling water for 5 minutes, then remove from the heat and fold in the coconut. Cool slightly and pile onto each pineapple slice. Brown the tops lightly under a medium-hot broiler and serve at once.

Crustless Blueberry Pie

Serves 6-8: 4 cups blueberries; ½ cup (2 oz) all purpose flour; ¼ cup (2 oz) sugar; ⅛ teaspoon salt; ½ teaspoon cinnamon; ⅛ teaspoon mace; 3 tablespoons (1½ oz) butter or margarine Lemon Sauce: 1 cup (8 fl oz) nonfat yogurt; 3 tablespoons lemon juice; 1 teaspoon grated lemon peel; ¼ teaspoon vanilla

Spread the blueberries in an 8-in (20-cm) round or square baking dish. Into a small bowl, sift the flour, sugar and spices. Rub in the butter with the fingertips until the mixture is the consistency of pea-size crumbs. Sprinkle over the berries.

Bake in an oven preheated to 375°F (190°C) for 35-45 minutes, or until the berries bubble and the crust browns.

Meanwhile, prepare the Lemon Sauce. Mix the yogurt with the lemon juice, grated lemon peel and vanilla. Serve with the warm pie.

D

Devonshire Junket

Serves 6-8: 4 cups (1 liter) milk; ¾ cup (5 fl oz) brandy; ¼ cup (2 oz) sugar; 2 tablespoons rennet; 1 cup (8 fl oz) Devonshire clotted cream or heavy cream; ¾ teaspoon cinnamon; 2 tablespoons sugar

Warm the milk and brandy to blood temperature. Stir in the sugar and rennet and leave to set. Just before serving, garnish with the clotted cream and sprinkle with cinnamon and sugar. The junket may also be decorated with apricot or strawberry jam.

E

English Treacle Tart

Serves 6-8: 1 unbaked 9-in (23-cm) double shortcrust pie shell (see page 336); 1 apple, peeled and grated; 1 cup (4 oz) fresh breadcrumbs; juice and peel of 1 lemon; ½ teaspoon salt; ¼ teaspoon ginger; 1½ tablespoons sugar; 1½ tablespoons

milk; 2 tablespoons warmed treacle or golden syrup; extra milk; powdered sugar

Line a pie dish with half the pastry. Mix all the ingredients together except the extra milk and sugar. Spread over the pastry. Make a lattice top with the remaining pastry, brush lightly with the milk and sprinkle with sugar.

Bake in an oven preheated to 375°F (190°C) for 40 minutes or until the filling has set.

F

Floating Islands in Blackberry Sauce

Serves 4: 14-oz (450-g) can blackberries; ½ teaspoon salt; 2 egg whites; 1 tablespoon powdered sugar

Pour the blackberries and their liquid into a blender and puree, then pass through a fine sieve to remove the seeds. Heat gently and set aside.

Floating Islands in Blackberry Sauce

Bring about 5 cups of water to a gentle boil and add the salt.

Whisk the egg whites until firm, then add the sugar and continue whisking until it forms stiff peaks and is very shiny. Drop tablespoons of the mixture into the water. Poach about six at a time for 4–5 minutes on one side, then flip over and cook on the other side for the same time. Remove the meringues with a slotted spoon.

Reheat the berry puree gently, then pour into a wide shallow serving dish. Float the meringues on top. Serve as soon as the last batch is cooked.

Note: Lightly sweetened cream can accompany this light and tangy dessert.

Whisk the egg whites until stiff peaks form.

Poach spoonfuls of the mixture in simmering water.

Fluffy Rhubarb Pie

Serves 6: 3 egg yolks; 1 cup (8 oz) sugar; 2 tablespoons all purpose flour; ¼ teaspoon salt; 2 tablespoons frozen orange juice concentrate; 1 tablespoon soft butter; 2½ cups rhubarb, cut into ½-in (1-cm) pieces; 3 egg whites; ½ teaspoon vanilla; 1 unbaked 8-in (20-cm) shortcrust pie shell (see page 321); ½ cup (2 oz) chopped macadamias or walnuts

Beat the egg yolks; add two-thirds of the sugar mixed with the flour, salt, orange juice and butter. Beat until smooth. Stir in the rhubarb.

Beat the egg whites until soft peaks form, then gradually add the remaining sugar, beating until stiff. Add the vanilla, then gently fold the meringue into the rhubarb mixture. Pour into the pastry shell and sprinkle with nuts.

Bake in an oven preheated to 325°F (160°C) for 50–55 minutes. Serve slightly warm with cream, whipped cream (sweet or sour), or softened ice cream.

French Fruit Tart with Cream Cheese Crust

Serves 12–16: Cream Cheese Pastry: 2 cups (8 oz) all purpose flour; ½ teaspoon salt; 16 tablespoons (8 oz) butter or margarine, cut into small pieces; 8 oz (250 g) cream cheese, softened; egg wash (1 egg yolk, beaten with ½ teaspoon water)
Filling: 1 package vanilla-flavored instant pudding and pie filling; 1¼ cups (10 fl oz) milk; ¼ teaspoon vanilla; ¼ teaspoon almond extract; ½ cup (4 fl oz) cream; 1 can pineapple slices, drained (reserve juice); 1 can peach slices, drained (reserve juice); 1 cup kiwi fruit, sliced; 3 bananas, sliced; 2 cups strawberries (or raspberries), hulled; ¼ cup (2 oz) sugar; 2 teaspoons lemon juice

To make the pastry, in a bowl, sift the flour and salt. Cut or rub in the butter until the mixture resembles coarse crumbs. Mix in the cheese lightly until the pastry holds together, then form the pastry into a ball and wrap in plastic. Chill 3–4 hours.

On a lightly floured baking sheet, with a floured rolling pin, roll two-thirds of the pastry into a rectangle about 15 × 13 in (38 × 33 cm). Refrigerate the remaining third.

With a pastry brush, paint the four edges with the egg wash. Roll the remaining third of pastry and cut into 1-in (2.5 cm) strips and place along the sides. Decorate the corners with fancy pastry shapes, if desired. With a fork, prick the bottom of the pastry well.

Bake on the bottom shelf of an oven preheated to 425°F (220°C) for 12–15 minutes.

To make the filling, prepare the pudding mix according to directions, but use 1¼ cups (10 fl oz) of milk and the vanilla and almond extracts. In a small bowl, beat the cream until it is thick, then gently fold into the pudding mix. Spread the mix over the bottom of the baked pie shell.

Cut the pineapple slices in half. Attractively arrange the fruits (strawberries may be sliced or left whole) over the pie base. Combine the sugar, lemon juice and ½ cup (4 fl oz) fruit juices in a small saucepan. Bring to the boil, stirring until the sugar has dissolved. Simmer for 10 minutes or until the juice is syrupy. Lightly brush or spoon the syrup over the fruit.

Fresh Peach Pie

Serves 6–8: 4–6 ripe peaches (mangoes may be used as an alternative); ¼–⅓ cup (2–3 oz) sugar; juice of 1 lemon; 5 teaspoons cornstarch; ⅓ cup (3 oz) sugar; 2 drops almond extract; ¼ teaspoon vanilla; 1 tablespoon butter; 1 baked 9-in (23-cm) shortcrust pie shell (see page 321)

Peel and slice the peaches and place them in a medium-size bowl. Sprinkle with the sugar and lemon juice and refrigerate for 1 hour. Pour off the remaining juice into a cup. If it doesn't measure 1 cup, pour some water over the peaches and drain until it measures 1 cup. Brandy or peach liqueur may also be added to make up the difference.

Mix the cornstarch with ⅓ cup sugar in a small saucepan. Add the juice and cook, stirring constantly, until the mixture is thick and clear. Add the almond and vanilla extracts, the butter and a pinch of salt.

Place the peaches in the baked pie shell, then spoon over the thickened sauce. Refrigerate until set. Serve with whipped cream.

Fried Fruit Pies

Makes approximately 18 pies: Pastry: 2 cups (8 oz) all purpose flour; 1 teaspoon salt; ½ teaspoon nutmeg; ½ teaspoon baking soda; 8 tablespoons (4 oz) butter; 1 tablespoon vinegar; 3–4 tablespoons cold water; oil for deep frying
1¾ cups thick stewed applesauce (or apricots, peaches or berries); ½ teaspoon nutmeg; ½ teaspoon cinnamon; pinch of ground cloves (optional); 1½ tablespoons lemon juice

Sift the flour, salt, nutmeg and soda together into a bowl. Cut or rub in the butter until a fine even texture is achieved. Add the vinegar and enough water to hold the pastry together so that it is not sticky. Make it into a ball, then wrap in plastic or waxed paper and chill for at least 1 hour.

Roll the pastry out to ⅛-in (3-mm) thickness and cut into 2–3-in (5–7.5-cm) squares.

Mix all the filling ingredients together. Place a spoonful of fruit filling on the center of each square. Fold in half to form a triangle and press the edges firmly together. Chill, then deep fry in hot oil for about 3 minutes or until golden. Serve hot with whipped cottage or cream cheese, yogurt, sour cream or ice cream.

Fried Ricotta

Serves 4: 2 eggs; 1 lb (500 g) ricotta, in one piece; 2 tablespoons all purpose flour; oil for frying; 7 tablespoons (3½ oz) sugar

Whip the eggs in a bowl. Carefully, so as not to break it up, cut the ricotta into slices ½ in (1 cm) thick. Dust the pieces with flour, dip them in the eggs and fry in the oil until golden brown. Serve hot, sprinkled with sugar.

Frosted Sesame Melon

Serves 4–6: 1 honeydew melon; 1 cup cottage cheese; 1 tablespoon honey; 1 teaspoon lemon juice; ¼ cup sesame seeds; 1 egg white; ⅔–¾ cup shredded coconut; scented geranium leaves (if available) or lettuce leaves

Peel the melon, slice off the top and scoop out the seeds. In a mixing bowl, blend together the cottage cheese, honey and lemon juice until creamy. Toast the sesame seeds in a dry skillet over gentle heat, tossing until golden brown. Stir into the cheese mixture, then press into the melon cavity and secure the top with wooden toothpicks.

With a pastry brush, coat the melon all over with lightly beaten egg white, then carefully roll in the coconut until the melon is frosted all over. Chill in the refrigerator. To serve, cut the melon into rings and place each one on a large scented geranium leaf or a lettuce leaf.

Frosty Lemon Pie with ★ Berry Sauce

Serves 6–8: 2 egg whites; pinch of salt; ⅔ cup (5 oz) sugar; 2 teaspoons grated lemon peel; ⅓ cup (2½ fl oz) lemon juice; few drops yellow food coloring (optional); 1 cup (8 fl oz) heavy cream; 1 baked 8-in (20-cm) shortcrust pie shell (see page 321); ½ cup cookie crumbs
Berry Sauce: 1 cup berries (blackberries, raspberries, strawberries), crushed; 1 teaspoon lemon juice; 3 tablespoons sugar; 1 tablespoon brandy; pinch each of nutmeg and cinnamon

Whisk the egg whites with the salt until soft peaks form, then gradually whisk in the sugar, peel, juice and food coloring. Fold in the whipped cream. Turn into the pie shell and top with the cookie crumbs. Chill or freeze.

To make the berry sauce, mix all the ingredients together and chill. Serve with the pie.

Frozen Banana Pie

Serves 8–10: ½ cup (1½ oz) shredded coconut; 2 cups (7 oz) cracker crumbs; 4 tablespoons (2 oz) soft butter or margarine; ¼ cup (1½ oz) brown sugar; 2 oz (60 g) unsweetened chocolate, finely grated; ⅛ teaspoon cinnamon; ⅛ teaspoon allspice; 1 cup (8 fl oz) heavy cream; 1 cup (8 oz) light corn syrup; 1 teaspoon vanilla; ⅛ teaspoon salt; 4–5 bananas, mashed

In a 9-in (23-cm) pie dish, mix the coconut, crumbs, butter, brown sugar, chocolate and spices together. Press firmly around the bottom and sides of the dish. Bake in an oven preheated to 375°F (190°C) for 5–8 minutes. Cool.

In a small bowl, beat the cream until thick. In a large bowl, beat the syrup, vanilla, salt and bananas until smooth. Fold in the whipped cream. Spoon the mixture into the crust.

Freeze for at least 4 hours or until firm. For easier serving, allow the pie to stand at room temperature for 10–15 minutes before you are ready to serve it. Garnish with slices of banana.

Frozen Chocolate Velvet Pie

Serves 10–12: Meringue Nut Crust: 2 egg whites; ⅛ teaspoon salt; ¼ cup (2 oz) sugar; 2 cups (8 oz) walnuts or hazelnuts, finely chopped
¼ cup (2 fl oz) water; 3 tablespoons light corn syrup; 2 teaspoons vanilla; 1 cup chocolate chips; ⅔ cup (5 fl oz) sweetened condensed milk, chilled; 1½ cups (12 fl oz) heavy cream

To make the crust, whisk the egg whites with the salt until soft peaks form. Gradually add the sugar and whisk until stiff and glossy. Fold in the nuts. Spread over the bottom and sides of an 8-in (20-cm) pie dish. Bake in an oven preheated to 400°F (200°C) for 12 minutes. Cool.

To make the filling, in a small saucepan, bring the water and corn syrup to the boil.

Stir. Remove from the heat. Add the vanilla and chocolate bits, stirring until the chocolate has melted. Cool. Pour all but 2 tablespoons of the chocolate mixture into the condensed milk and cream. Using an electric mixer, blend at a low speed until mixed, then on a high speed until soft peaks form. Pour into the cooled crust. Freeze.

Decorate with the remaining chocolate mixture. Wrap and keep frozen until about 25 minutes before serving. For easier slicing, dip the knife in warm water before and during cutting.

Fruit Basket

Serves 4: 1 large papaya; 2 bananas; 1 wedge of watermelon; 1 mango; 1 salak, hard green pear or apple; 4 thin slices pineapple; lemon or lime juice; 1 tablespoon brown sugar

Remove two sections from the top half of the papaya to form a basket with a handle along the center. Scoop out the seeds, then carefully scoop out the papaya flesh with a melon baller.

Slice the other fruit or cut into cubes and arrange the fruit and papaya balls attractively in the basket. Sprinkle with lemon or lime juice and brown sugar and chill before serving.

Serve with cream or thick sweetened coconut milk. For extra flavor add a splash of white rum.

Fruit Turnovers

Makes 9–12 turnovers: Flaky Pastry: 1 quantity basic shortcrust pastry (see page 319); 5 tablespoons (2½ oz) butter 2½ cups cooked, sliced fruit, drained; 2 tablespoons each of sugar and cinnamon, mixed together; juice of ½ lemon; 1 tablespoon butter

To make the pastry, roll out the short pastry to ⅛-in (3-mm) thickness on a lightly floured board. Dot the butter pieces evenly over the surface. Roll up the pastry like a jelly roll, then roll out again into a rectangle. Fold into thirds, then in half and seal the edges. Wrap the dough in plastic and chill for 20 minutes.

Roll the pastry out to a thickness of ⅛ in (3 mm) and cut into 5-in (13-cm) squares. Place the fruit on the squares and sprinkle with the sugar–cinnamon mixture and lemon juice. Dot with butter. Moisten the edges with water, fold into triangles and seal. Flute the edges or use a fork and gently press. Cut slits on the top, and brush with milk and sprinkle with sugar, if desired.

Bake in an oven preheated to 475°F (240°C) for 15-20 minutes until lightly browned.

G

German Apple Pancake

Serves 4-6: 2 large green (cooking) apples; ¼ cup (1½ oz) seedless raisins; 1 tablespoon powdered sugar; 1 teaspoon cinnamon; 6 tablespoons (3 oz) butter; 1 tablespoon brandy (optional); 3 eggs; ¼ cup (1 oz) all purpose flour; ⅓ cup (2½ fl oz) milk; 1 tablespoon sugar; pinch of salt; 2 teaspoons brown sugar (optional)

Peel, core and slice the apples and place in a pan with the raisins, sugar, cinnamon and half the butter. Cover and cook very gently for about 7 minutes or until the apples are tender. Increase the heat, splash in the brandy if used and cook for a further minute.

Cook the apples over low heat until tender.

Spoon the apples onto the half-cooked pancake.

Beat the eggs with the flour and milk for 2 minutes, then add the sugar and salt, and beat again until dissolved. Melt the remaining butter in a pan and pour in the batter. Cover and cook very gently for 10 minutes.

Spread the apples over the top of the pancake, re-cover the pan and cook for a further 12-15 minutes until the pancake is firm and slightly puffed. Do not allow it to cook too quickly. Slide the pancake onto a plate and sprinkle on the brown sugar, if used. Serve at once. If desired, decorate with whipped cream and cinnamon.

German Chocolate Tarts

Makes 18-24 tarts: Pastry: 2 oz (60 g) unsweetened chocolate, grated; 1 cup (4 oz) all purpose flour; ¼ cup (1½ oz) brown sugar; ½ teaspoon salt; 6 tablespoons (3 oz) butter or margarine; 1 tablespoon water; 1 teaspoon vanilla

Filling: 2 oz (60 g) unsweetened chocolate; 5 tablespoons (2½ oz) butter or margarine; 1⅔ cups (13 fl oz) evaporated milk; 3 eggs, beaten; 1 teaspoon vanilla; ¼ teaspoon salt; ⅔ cup (5 oz) sugar
Topping: ⅔ cup (2 oz) shredded coconut, toasted; ½ cup (2 oz) walnuts, chopped

To make the pastry, stir the chocolate, flour, brown sugar and salt together in a bowl. Cut or rub in the butter until the mixture resembles coarse crumbs. Combine the water and vanilla. Stir into the flour mixture, then quickly knead the dough until it is smooth and elastic. Form into a ball and allow to rest for 20 minutes. Divide the pastry into 18-24 portions and press into muffin pans. Bake in an oven preheated to 375°F (190°C) for 10-12 minutes, then cool.

Meanwhile, to make the filling, melt the chocolate and butter over a low heat, stirring constantly. Remove from the heat. Blend in the evaporated milk and stir into the eggs. Add the vanilla, salt and sugar and mix well. Spoon into the chocolate shells and bake at 375°F (190°C) for 7-8 minutes.

Sprinkle the coconut and nuts over the top. Return to the oven and bake for a further 6-8 minutes or until the top is set. Cool in the pans. Loosen the shells gently and remove.

German Apple Pancake

Gingered Figs in Brandy

Serves 4–6: 8 oz (250 g) dried figs; 3 oz (90 g) crystallized ginger, diced; 3 oz (90 g) seedless raisins; ¾ cup (6 fl oz) brandy; ¼ cup (2 oz) sugar; ¾ cup (6 fl oz) water

Place all the ingredients into a covered dish or deep jug. Stir until the sugar has almost dissolved. Microwave on HIGH (100%) for 4 minutes, then on MEDIUM-LOW (40%) for 20 minutes, covered. Remove from the oven and leave for several hours before serving with lightly whipped cream or ice cream.

For a touch of luxury, drizzle melted dark chocolate over the figs before serving.

Golden Pear Pie

Serves 6–8: 3 cups pears, peeled and sliced; juice and grated peel of 1 lemon or orange; ½ cup (4 oz) sugar; 2 tablespoons all purpose flour; ¼ teaspoon nutmeg; ⅓ teaspoon cinnamon; 1 unbaked 9-in (23-cm) double shortcrust pie shell (see page 336); 1 tablespoon butter; ½ cup (2 oz) Cheddar cheese, grated

Gently mix the pears with the lemon juice and peel. Stir in the sugar, flour, nutmeg and cinnamon. Spoon into the pastry-lined pie dish. Dot with butter and sprinkle with cheese.

Top the pie with a crust or a lattice-type crust. Bake in an oven preheated to 425°F (220°C) for 15 minutes. Reduce the heat to 350°F (180°C) and bake a further 20–25 minutes. Serve warm or cold.

Golden Pumpkin Pie

Serves 6: scant 2½ cups (12 oz) mixed dried fruits; 1 tablespoon brown sugar; 1 teaspoon grated lemon peel; 1 green apple, grated; 1–2 tablespoons brandy or sweet sherry; 1 unbaked 9-in (23-cm) shortcrust pie shell (see page 321); 2 eggs; ½ cup (3 oz) brown sugar; ¼ teaspoon salt; 1 cup (8 fl oz) evaporated milk; ¾ cup cooked mashed pumpkin; whipped cream and walnuts for decoration

Combine the first four ingredients with the brandy or sweet sherry and spoon into the uncooked pastry shell. Beat the eggs with the remaining brown sugar and salt, mix in the evaporated milk and pumpkin, then stir

over a low heat until warmed but not boiling.

Carefully pour the fruit mixture into the pie, then bake in an oven preheated to 450°F (230°C) for 10 minutes. Reduce the heat to 375°F (190°C) and bake a further 30–40 minutes, or until the custard has set. Let stand for 5 minutes, then prick the surface of the custard with a fork or skewer. Sprinkle a little extra brandy or sherry over and, when cool, decorate with whipped cream and walnut pieces.

Green Tea Ice Cream

Serves 4–6: 4 cups (1 liter) milk; ⅔ cup (5 oz) sugar; 6 egg yolks, lightly beaten; 1 tablespoon (½ oz) powdered green tea; ⅓ cup (2½ fl oz) boiling water; or 4 oz (125 g) sweet green tea mix

Combine the milk, sugar and egg yolks in the top half of a double boiler, or in a saucepan that will fit into another saucepan full of almost boiling water. Cook over moderate heat, stirring constantly, until the mixture thickens into a custard. Remove from the heat.

Whisk the powdered green tea with the boiling water and stir into the custard. If using sweet green tea mix, make the custard with just the milk and egg yolks, then sprinkle over the sweet green tea mix, stirring to dissolve.

Pour the tea-flavored custard into a wide, shallow dish and let cool. Put in the freezing compartment of the refrigerator and leave until the mixture becomes icy around the edges. Remove, put into a bowl or food processor and blend vigorously to break up the ice. Return to the freezer, allow to set until almost solid, then repeat the blending once more. Freeze until serving time. Alternatively, put the mixture into an electric ice cream maker and churn until thick.

Green Tea Ice Cream

Green Tomato Pie

Serves 8-10: Shortcrust Pastry: 1 cup (8 oz) all purpose flour; 1 teaspoon salt; ¾ cup (6 oz) shortening; 5-6 tablespoons water
9 green tomatoes, finely chopped; 1 cup (5 oz) seedless raisins; 1 cup (5 oz) brown sugar, firmly packed; 4 tablespoons (2 oz) butter; 2 tablespoons cider vinegar; 2 tablespoons white wine; 2 tablespoons brandy; ¾ teaspoon cinnamon; ½ teaspoon allspice; ½ cup (2 oz) chopped walnuts (optional)

To make the pastry, sift the flour and salt into a bowl. Cut in the shortening until the mixture resembles fine breadcrumbs. Cut in the remaining shortening until the mixture resembles coarse crumbs. Add the water gradually, gathering the mix into a ball. Knead the dough lightly just until it is smooth and elastic. Wrap in plastic and allow to rest in the refrigerator for 20 minutes.

Roll the dough out to ⅛-in (3-mm) thickness and use to line a 10-in (25-cm) pie dish.

Place the tomatoes, raisins, sugar, butter, vinegar and wine in a heavy-based saucepan. Bring to the boil, then simmer for 45 minutes or until very thick, stirring occasionally. Remove from the heat.

Stir in the brandy, spices and nuts. Cool. Spoon in the filling, then top with a lattice pastry, or if desired, a top crust. Bake in an oven preheated to 325°F (160°C) for 25-35 minutes or until the crust is golden. Serve warm or cool with sour cream sauce, brandy sauce, softened ice cream or orange sauce.

H

Hawaiian Macadamia Nut Pie

Serves 8-12: 1 cup (4 oz) unsalted macadamia nuts, chopped; ⅓ cup (3 oz) sugar; 1½ tablespoons cornstarch; 1 tablespoon gelatin; ½ teaspoon salt; 4 oz (125 g) cream cheese, softened; ⅓ cup (2½ fl oz) sour cream; 1 teaspoon grated lemon peel; 1⅓ cups (11 fl oz) milk; 2 eggs, separated; 3-4 tablespoons rum; 3 tablespoons sugar; 1 cup (8 fl oz) cream; 1 baked 10-in (25-cm) shortcrust pie shell (see page 348)

Place the nuts on a baking sheet and bake in an oven preheated to 350°F (180°C) for 5-8 minutes until golden brown. Keep an eye on them and stir once, as they can turn brown quickly. Cool.

Blend the sugar, cornstarch, gelatin and salt together. Add the cream cheese and beat until fluffy. Gradually add the sour cream and lemon peel. Slowly add the milk, blending until smooth. This may all be done in a blender or food processor.

Spoon the mixture into the top of a double boiler and cook over hot, not boiling, water until thick and smooth, stirring constantly. Beat a little of the mixture into the egg yolks, then pour the eggs back into the remaining mixture, beating constantly for 3-4 minutes. Remove from the heat and allow to cool slightly. Stir in the rum.

Beat the egg whites until they form soft peaks. Gradually add 3 tablespoons sugar and beat until stiff. Fold 1-2 tablespoons of egg white mixture into the egg yolk mixture, then fold the two together. Cool.

Whip the cream and fold into the filling with about half of the chopped nuts. Pour into the pie. Chill for at least 3 hours or overnight, covered. Sprinkle with the remaining nuts.

High Hat Berry Cream Pie

Serves 6-8: 1 unbaked 9-in (23-cm) shortcrust pie shell (see page 321); 3 cups berries (strawberries, blackberries, raspberries, etc), halved; 1 cup (8 fl oz) sour cream; ½ teaspoon vanilla; 1¼ cups (10 oz) sugar; ¾ cup (3 oz) all purpose flour; ½ teaspoon salt; 2 tablespoons fine dry breadcrumbs; 2 tablespoons brown sugar; 1 tablespoon melted butter

Prepare the pastry and line the pie dish.

Wash, sort and hull the berries and dry with paper towels. Turn the berries into the pastry shell. Place the sour cream in a bowl. Blend in the vanilla, sugar, flour and salt. Pour over the berries. Sprinkle the top with breadcrumbs, sugar and butter blended together.

Bake in an oven preheated to 450°F (230°C) for 10 minutes. Reduce the heat to 350°F (180°C) and bake for 30 minutes or until the topping is lightly browned. Cool.

Honey Ice Cream with a Coulis of Blackcurrants

Serves 4: 2 cups (16 fl oz) milk; ½ vanilla bean or ½ teaspoon vanilla; 4 egg yolks; ½ cup (4 oz) sugar; ½ teaspoon grated orange or lemon peel; 2 tablespoons cream; 3 tablespoons honey; ½ cup blackcurrants (raspberries or strawberries may be used); 1 tablespoon sugar dissolved in ¼ cup (2 fl oz) boiling water; 4 mint leaves

Boil the milk with the vanilla bean and let it stand for 10 minutes. Whisk the egg yolks and sugar together until pale and frothy. Remove the bean from the milk and, while whisking the egg yolks, pour the hot milk into them. Return the milk–egg mixture to the saucepan and cook over low heat, stirring constantly, until the mixture is thick enough to coat the back of a spoon. Add the orange or lemon peel and the cream and honey. Cool the mixture, then refrigerate until chilled.

Partially freeze the mixture, then return it to the mixer or blender, whip it again and return it to the freezer.

To make the coulis, rub the berries through a sieve and add the sugar syrup. Refrigerate. To serve, spoon the coulis on the bottom of the plate and put a scoop of ice cream on top. Garnish with the mint leaves.

Honey Nut Pastries

Makes 18: 6 sheets filo pastry; 5 tablespoons (2½ oz) butter; ¼ cup (2 oz) sugar; ⅓ cup (2½ fl oz) water; 2 teaspoons honey; 1½ teaspoons lemon juice; 1 small strip lemon peel; ghee or oil for frying
Filling: 4 oz (125 g) coarsely ground almonds; 1 egg yolk; 3 tablespoons powdered sugar; ¾ teaspoon cinnamon; ¼ teaspoon nutmeg

Thaw the pastry if frozen and keep wrapped in a damp kitchen towel until needed. Melt the butter and set aside.

Cut the pastry lengthwise into strips, then brush with butter.

Roll the filling up in the pastry tightly.

Boil the sugar, water, honey and lemon juice together for 2 minutes. Add the lemon peel and continue to boil until syrupy, a further 5-6 minutes, then set aside to cool.

Mix the filling ingredients together. Cut the pastry sheets lengthwise into three even-sized strips. Brush lightly with the melted butter and fold each in half to give pieces about 8 × 4 in (20 × 10 cm). Brush one side with more butter and place a spoonful of the filling towards one end. Fold the two sides in about ¾ in (2 cm) and fold the bottom over the filling. Roll up tightly, brushing a little more butter on the end flap before pressing into place.

When all the pastries are rolled, heat about 1 in (2.5 cm) of *ghee* to moderate. Fry the pastries, about six at a time, until golden. Place in the pan with the end flaps downwards at first to prevent them unrolling during cooking. Turn carefully using two large spoons.

When golden on both sides, drain well on paper towels and arrange on a plate. Pour on the syrup and leave to cool before serving.

Honey Nut Pastries

Hot Fruit Salad Flambé ★

Serves 6: 2 oranges; 2 ripe pears; 1 apple; 1 banana; 1 pint strawberries; 1-2 kiwi fruit; 6 passionfruit or 4-oz (125-g) can passionfruit in syrup (optional); ½ cup (4 oz) sugar; ¼ cup (2 fl oz) water; ½ cup (4 fl oz) apricot nectar; ¼ cup (2 fl oz) Cognac, brandy or orange liqueur

Peel the oranges, removing all pith. Then cut each segment from its skin. Peel, core and slice the pears and apple. Peel and diagonally slice the banana. Hull the strawberries and cut the larger ones in half. Peel and thinly slice the kiwi fruit.

Place the sugar and water in a microwave-safe dish, preferably not plastic as the heat of the sugar may melt or buckle it. Microwave on HIGH (100%) for about 7 minutes or until the syrup has turned a pale golden color. Add the apricot nectar and stir. Add the passionfruit (if used) and the fruit and cover. Microwave on HIGH (100%) for 1-2 minutes until the fruit is just tender. In a small jug, microwave the liqueur on HIGH (100%) for 30 seconds, then flame. Pour over the fruit and serve at once with lightly whipped cream or ice cream.

Hot Fruit Salad Flambé

Hungarian Love Letters

Makes 30: Pastry: 2 cups (8 oz) all purpose flour; 2 tablespoons sugar; ½ teaspoon salt; 10 tablespoons (5 oz) butter, chilled and cut into small bits; 4 egg yolks, slightly beaten ½ cup (2 oz) walnuts, coarsely chopped; 1 teaspoon grated lemon peel; 2 egg whites; ½ teaspoon salt; ¼ cup (2 oz) sugar; ½ teaspoon cinnamon; egg wash (1 egg yolk, beaten with 1 teaspoon water); 2 tablespoons powdered sugar; ½ teaspoon cinnamon

To make the pastry, sift the dry ingredients into a large bowl. Cut or rub in the butter until the mixture resembles coarse breadcrumbs. Gradually add the egg yolks. Gather the dough into a ball. It will be crumbly. With the fingers and hands, squeeze and work the dough until it is well blended and smooth. Shape into a ball and flatten, then divide in half. Wrap and place in the refrigerator for 1 hour. While the pastry is chilling, make the filling.

Mix together the walnuts and lemon peel and set aside. Beat the egg whites and salt until foamy. Gradually beat in the sugar mixed with cinnamon until peaks form. Fold in the nut mixture.

Roll out half the dough on a lightly floured board into a rectangle ⅛ in (3 mm) thick. Work quickly as the dough can become sticky. Don't allow it to stick to the board and dust with flour when necessary. Trim off the uneven edges.

Cut the pastry into 3-in (7.5-cm) squares. Place 1–2 teaspoons of the filling in the center of each square. Bring the opposite corners together, overlapping in the center to make an envelope shape. Place on a baking sheet and brush with egg wash.

Bake in an oven preheated to 350°F (180°C) for 20–30 minutes or until lightly browned. Remove the turnovers with a spatula to wire racks. Cool slightly. Sift powdered sugar and cinnamon over the top. Repeat with the remaining pastry.

K

Kentucky Tarts

Serves 6–8: 2 eggs; ⅔ cup (5 oz) sugar; 4 tablespoons (2 oz) butter or margarine, melted; 2 tablespoons bourbon; ½ teaspoon vanilla; ½ cup (2 oz) all purpose flour; ½ cup (2 oz) chopped pecans; ½ cup chocolate chips, chopped (or grated semisweet chocolate); 1 quantity shortcrust pastry (see page 319); whipped cream and pecan halves for garnish

Place the eggs in a bowl and beat lightly. Gradually add the sugar and beat well. Add the butter, bourbon and vanilla. Gradually add the flour, mixing well after each addition. Stir in the nuts and chocolate. Roll the pastry out to ⅛-in (3-mm) thickness and use to line 6–8 tartlet tins.

Bake in an oven preheated to 400°F (200°C) for 20–30 minutes. Cool. Top with whipped cream and pecan halves.

Kiwi Pie

Serves 12: Pâte Sucrée: 2 cups (8 oz) all purpose flour; ½ teaspoon salt; ½ cup (4 oz) powdered sugar; 8 tablespoons (4 oz) unsalted butter; 2 egg yolks or 1 egg; 1 teaspoon iced water, if necessary 10 large kiwi fruit; 1 cup (8 fl oz) heavy cream; 1 cup (8 oz) powdered sugar, sifted; 2 large eggs; ¼ cup (2 fl oz) brandy or Cointreau; additional ¼ cup (2 oz) powdered sugar, for dusting

To make the pastry, sift the flour and salt onto a board. Make a well in the center and add the sugar, butter and egg yolks. Combine the butter and egg yolks, then quickly mix in the flour and sugar until the mixture resembles coarse breadcrumbs. Add enough water to form the dough into a ball, then knead until smooth and elastic. Wrap in plastic and allow to rest for 20 minutes or until required.

Roll the pastry out to ⅛-in (3-mm) thickness and use to line a 12-in (30-cm) pie pan. Bake blind in an oven preheated to 425°F (220°C) on the top rack for 10 minutes or until the pastry is set in shape. Remove the blind filling, reduce the oven temperature to 375°F (190°C) and bake for another 10–15 minutes or until the pastry is golden. Stand the pan on a wire rack to cool.

To make the filling, peel the kiwi fruit and cut into ¼-in (5-mm) slices. In a bowl, combine the cream, sugar, eggs and brandy, and beat until well mixed.

Arrange the slices of kiwi fruit in overlapping circles on the pie crust. Pour the egg mixture over, then brush over all the fruit. Bake at 375°F (190°C) for 40 minutes.

Preheat the broiler. Cover the pastry edge with aluminum foil, sieve extra powdered sugar over and place under the broiler for 3–5 minutes or until the top is lightly caramelized. Remove the pie from the pan. Serve hot or at room temperature with whipped cream.

L

Latticed Chocolate Rum Pie ★

Serves 6: 14-oz (396-g) can evaporated milk; 2 envelopes gelatin; ¾ cup (6 fl oz) milk; 1 cup (8 oz) sugar; pinch of salt; 2 eggs, separated; 4 oz (125 g) semisweet chocolate; ¼ cup (2 fl oz) rum; 1 teaspoon vanilla; 1 baked 9-in (23-cm) shortcrust pie shell (see page 321); 1¼ cups (10 fl oz) heavy cream

Pour the evaporated milk into an ice cube tray and freeze until mushy around the edges. Soften the gelatin in ¼ cup of the milk. Combine three-quarters of the sugar with the salt, egg yolks and softened gelatin in the top of a double boiler and mix well. Cook over boiling water until the mixture thickens slightly, then remove from the heat.

Melt half the chocolate, add and beat until smooth. Chill until slightly thickened. Whip the chilled evaporated milk until thick. Fold the whipped milk, rum and vanilla into the chocolate mixture and pour into the baked pie shell. Chill thoroughly.

To serve, whip the cream. Beat the egg whites until frothy, then add the remaining sugar gradually and continue to beat until soft peaks form. Fold into the whipped cream and spread over the pie. Shave the remaining chocolate into curls and sprinkle over the top of the whipped cream mixture in a lattice pattern.

Layered Pancakes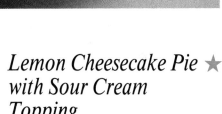

Serves 4–6: Pancake Batter: 1¼ cups (5 oz) all purpose flour; 2 eggs, lightly beaten; 1 egg yolk; 1 cup (8 fl oz) milk; 1 teaspoon sugar; pinch of salt; butter for frying
5 oz (150 g) walnuts, ground; 4 oz (½ cup) powdered sugar; 7 oz (220 g) cream cheese; 3 egg yolks, lightly beaten; 1 oz (30 g) seedless raisins; ¼ cup (2 oz) cocoa; 6 oz (185 g) apricot jam; 5 egg whites, stiffly beaten with some sugar and a few drops of vanilla; 1 tablespoon vanilla sugar

To make the pancake batter, whisk the flour, eggs, egg yolk, milk, sugar and a pinch of salt. Leave to stand for 20 minutes. Lightly grease a heavy-based skillet, then pour in enough batter to lightly coat the base, rotating the pan to spread the mixture evenly. When brown underneath, turn and cook the other side. Stack on a plate and keep warm while cooking the remaining pancakes.

The filling ingredients will make four different types of filling. *Filling No. 1:* combine the walnuts with one-third of the sugar; set aside. *Filling No. 2:* cream the cheese with a further one-third of the sugar, the egg yolks and raisins; set aside. *Filling No. 3:* combine the cocoa with the rest of the sugar; set aside. *Filling No. 4:* plain apricot jam.

Butter a soufflé dish, preferably the same diameter as the pancakes. Place a pancake on the bottom of the dish and on top of that place one-third of the walnut–sugar mixture. Place another pancake on top and spread it with one-third of the cream cheese mixture. Put another pancake on top and sprinkle it with the cocoa and sugar mixture, then add another pancake and spread it with one-third of the apricot jam. Repeat the layers, finishing with a layer of apricot jam.

Put the dish into an oven preheated to 350°F (175°C) and bake for 30 minutes. Turn down the heat and spread the top layer of jam with the beaten egg whites. Return the dish to the oven and leave it long enough for the meringue to set and brown slightly on top. Serve hot, sprinkled with the vanilla sugar.

Lemon Cheesecake

Lemon Cheesecake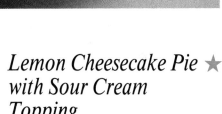

Serves 6: 6 tablespoons (3 oz) butter; 6½ oz (200 g) shortbread cookies
Filling: 1 lb (500 g) cream cheese; ¾ cup (6 oz) sugar; 2 tablespoons lemon juice; peel of 1 lemon, grated; 3 eggs; 1¼ cups (10 fl oz) heavy cream; nutmeg

Soften the butter in a microwave for 1½ minutes on MEDIUM (50%). Place the cookies in a plastic bag and crush with a rolling pin into fine crumbs. Mix with the butter and press into a 9-in (23-cm) microwave-safe round dish.

Beat the cream cheese until smooth and softened. Add the sugar, lemon juice and peel, then add the eggs one at a time, beating well between additions. Stir in the cream and mix thoroughly. Pour into the prepared crumb crust and bake in an oven preheated to 300°F (150°C) for 40–45 minutes until the center feels just firm and the sides have come away from the dish. Remove from the oven, sprinkle with nutmeg and allow to cool completely.

Lemon Cheesecake Pie ★ with Sour Cream Topping

Serves 6–10: Cookie Crumb Crust: 1¼–1½ cups (10 oz) cookie crumbs (plain, chocolate, etc.); 1–2 tablespoons sugar (optional); 4 tablespoons (2 fl oz) melted butter; ⅛ teaspoon salt
Filling: 8 oz (250 g) cream cheese, softened; 2 tablespoons (1 oz) butter; ½ cup (4 oz) sugar; 2 tablespoons all purpose flour; 1 egg; ⅔ cup (5½ oz) milk; ¼–½ cup (2–4 fl oz) lemon juice; 1 tablespoon grated lemon peel
Sour Cream Topping:1 cup (8 fl oz) sour cream; ½ teaspoon vanilla; 1–2 tablespoons brown sugar

Combine all ingredients for the crust, leaving a portion of crumbs for the top. Press into an 8–9-in (20–23-cm) pie dish.

Cream the cheese and butter together. Gradually add the sugar mixed with the flour, then blend in the egg and milk. Stir in the lemon juice and peel. Pour onto the unbaked crust and sprinkle with crumbs.

Bake in an oven preheated to 350°F (180°C) for 35–40 minutes. Cool and chill.

The sour cream topping, which is optional, is made simply by beating the ingredients together and pouring over the chilled cheesecake.

Lemon Egg Custard

Serves 6: 6 whole eggs; 3 egg whites; 1½ cups (12 fl oz) milk; 1½ tablespoons clear honey; 2 teaspoons cornstarch; ¾ teaspoon grated lemon peel
Topping: 1 lemon; 2 tablespoons sugar; ½ cup (4 fl oz) water

Beat the eggs and egg whites together. Add the milk, honey and cornstarch and beat until smooth. Stir in the lemon peel.

Pour the mixture into six oiled heatproof dishes. Cover with aluminum foil and set on a rack in a steamer. Add water to just below the rack, cover and steam over gently boiling water for about 15 minutes until the custard is set.

In the meantime, peel the lemon and very finely shred the peel after scraping away the pith. Place in a saucepan with the sugar and water, and bring to a slow boil. Stir until the sugar has dissolved, then simmer gently until the syrup turns a light golden color and is slightly sticky. Add about 1 tablespoon of lemon juice and stir on moderate heat until any toffee lumps that form have dissolved. Pour a little over each custard and serve hot.

If preferred, omit the lemon juice from the toffee. Chill the custards, top with the toffee and chill again until hard. Serve cold with whipped cream.

Pour the custard into six oiled heatproof dishes.

Cut all pith off the lemon peel, then shred finely.

Boil the peel in the sugar syrup until the syrup is golden.

Lemon Meringue Pie

Serves 4–6: 1 unbaked 8-in (20-cm) shortcrust pie shell (see page 321); 1 egg white
Filling: ¼ cup (2 oz) cornstarch; ¾ cup (6 oz) sugar; 1½ cups (12 fl oz) water; ¼ cup (2 fl oz) lemon juice; grated peel and juice of 1 lemon; 2 eggs, separated; 4 tablespoons (2 oz) butter; ¼ cup (2 oz) powdered sugar, for meringue

Roll out the pastry thinly and use to line an 8-in (20-cm) pie plate. Crimp the edges well, bringing the pastry up quite high on the rim. Prick the base of the pastry with a fork and brush with beaten egg white. Bake in an oven preheated to 375°F (190°C) for 20 minutes.

To make the filling, place the cornstarch, sugar and water into a saucepan. Blend well and bring to a boil, stirring until the mixture thickens. Lower the heat and cook for a few minutes longer. Stir in the lemon juice, lemon peel, egg yolks and butter. Beat well until smooth and shiny, then pour immediately into the prepared pie shell.

Whisk the egg whites with a pinch of salt until stiff. Add the sugar gradually, whisking to a stiff meringue. Spread the meringue over the lemon filling to the edges of the pastry and swirling the meringue into peaks.

Bake for 15 minutes. Allow to cool before cutting.

Lemon Soufflé Pie

Serves 6–8: 2 eggs, separated; ½ cup (4 oz) sugar; ¼ cup (2 fl oz) lemon juice; 1 tablespoon grated lemon peel; 1 tablespoon gelatin; ¼ cup (2 fl oz) cold water; ½ cup (4 fl oz) heavy cream, whipped; whipped cream and chopped nuts for garnish; 1 baked 9-in (23-cm) shortcrust pie shell (see page 321)

In the top of a double boiler, combine the egg yolks, sugar, lemon juice and peel over hot water. Cook, stirring constantly, until the sugar dissolves and the mixture thickens. Remove from the hot water and beat until cool.

Lemon Egg Custard

Sprinkle the gelatin over the cold water and allow to soften for 1 minute. Stir over a low heat until the gelatin has completely dissolved, then stir into the lemon mixture and fold into the whipped cream. Stand this mixture in a bowl of iced water. Occasionally stir lightly until the mixture starts to thicken.

Meanwhile, whisk the egg whites until stiff and fold into the lemon mixture. Pour into the baked pie shell. Refrigerate until set, at least 3 hours or overnight. Garnish with whipped cream and nuts.

Light Banana Soufflé

Serves 4: 6 bananas, thinly sliced; 5 tablespoons sugar; juice of ½ lemon; ½ cup (4 fl oz) port; 6 egg whites; ½ teaspoon vanilla

Butter a soufflé mold and sprinkle it with a little sugar. Mix the bananas with 2 table-spoons sugar, lemon juice and port. Pour the mixture into the mold.

Whisk the egg whites with the remaining 3 tablespoons of sugar and the vanilla to a glossy stiff meringue. Spoon it on top of the bananas and bake in an oven preheated to 350°F (180°C) for 20–30 minutes or until golden and well risen. Serve immediately.

Linzertorte

Serves 6-8: 1 cup (4 oz) all purpose flour; 2 tablespoons (1 oz) powdered sugar; 1½ teaspoons cocoa; ½ teaspoon cinnamon; ½ teaspoon baking powder; pinch of ground cloves (optional); pinch of salt; 4 oz (125 g) ground almonds; 8 tablespoons (4 oz) butter; milk or kirsch; 1½ cups (1 lb) raspberry, currant or strawberry jam; egg for glazing; whipped cream

Sift all dry ingredients except the almonds into a mixing bowl, then add the almonds. Rub in the butter, add the milk or kirsch if required and mix to a dry dough. Knead only until the ingredients are combined, then rest in refrigerator for 30 minutes.

Roll out two-thirds of the mixture and press onto the base of an 8-in (20-cm) greased springform pan. Spread the jam on top. Roll out the remaining pastry, cut into ½-in (1-cm) strips and arrange crosswise on top, using the last one as an edging around the side of the tart. Press down lightly. Chill again.

Brush with beaten egg and bake in an

Linzertorte

oven preheated to 400°F (200°C) for 35–40 minutes. Cool in the pan, then serve with whipped cream.

Note: The Linzertorte can also be decorated with raspberries and served with a bowl of fresh raspberries.

Little Ginger Puddings

Little Ginger Puddings

Serves 6: 1½ cups (6 oz) self-rising flour; 6 tablespoons (3 oz) butter; ⅓ cup (3 oz) powdered sugar; ¼ cup (1½ oz) chopped ginger preserved in syrup; 2 eggs, beaten; ¼ cup (2 fl oz) lukewarm milk; ¼ cup (2 fl oz) syrup from preserved ginger

Sift the flour onto a piece of paper. Cream the butter and sugar together, then add the ginger and beat well. Add the eggs, mixing thoroughly, then the sifted flour. Lastly stir in just enough of the milk to make a mix-ture of soft dropping consistency.

Pour a little of the ginger syrup into the bottom of six buttered single-serving dishes. Divide the batter among the dishes and cover each with a piece of buttered aluminum foil.

Place the dishes into a baking dish so they fit snugly and pour in enough water to come halfway up the sides of the dish. Bake in an oven preheated to 350°F

(180°C) for about 1 hour or until the puddings feel firm and springy to the touch and have loosened from the sides of the dishes. Turn out onto dessert plates and serve hot with whipped cream or custard.

Note: Drained canned mandarin segments, heated in additional ginger syrup with a touch of slivered ginger, transform this simple pudding into a memorable dessert.

Loganberry Soufflé

Serves 6: 3 eggs, separated; 3 generous tablespoons (3 oz) powdered sugar; 1 cup (8 fl oz) loganberry juice; 1 tablespoon gelatin; 1¼ cups (10 fl oz) heavy cream; ½ cup loganberries; whipped cream and extra loganberries for decoration

Tie a band of double waxed paper, or single waxed paper with a layer of aluminum foil, around the outside of a china soufflé dish, to stand 2–3 in (5–7.5 cm) above the dish.

Whisk the egg yolks, sugar and ⅔ cup loganberry juice in a heatproof bowl over boiling water until thick and light. Dissolve the gelatin in the remaining ⅓ cup loganberry juice and stir quickly into the whisked mixture. Both mixtures should be at body temperature to combine smoothly and to prevent the soufflé separating.

Whip 1¼ cups cream and fold into the mixture with the loganberries. Whisk the egg whites until stiff, then gently fold into the mixture, using a tablespoon or a plastic spatula. Pour into the prepared soufflé dish and place in the refrigerator to set.

When set, remove the paper carefully, unrolling from the soufflé and easing it off with a clean knife dipped in cold water. Decorate the top of the soufflé with swirls of whipped cream and extra loganberries.

Note: The loganberries may be soaked in maraschino or kirsch liqueur before adding to the soufflé mixture. Canned loganberries or stewed fresh loganberries may be used.

M

Macaroon Raspberry Torte ★

Serves 6: 4 egg whites; ¾ cup (6 oz) sugar; ½ cup (2 oz) finely chopped walnuts; 2 tablespoons (1 oz) melted butter; ¼ cup (1 oz) all purpose flour; cornstarch; 1 cup (8 fl oz) heavy cream; 2 tablespoons powdered sugar; rum or brandy; 3 cups fresh or frozen raspberries; whipped cream for decoration

Whisk the egg whites until stiff, then gradually whisk in the sugar, beating well after each addition. Fold in the chopped nuts, cooled melted butter and flour, and mix gently.

Grease three baking sheets and dust lightly with cornstarch. Mark a circle in the middle of each, about 10 in (25 cm) across, using a saucepan lid as a guide. Divide the mixture equally among the sheets. Spread out and smooth carefully to fill the circles.

Bake in an oven preheated to 350°F (180°C) for 15–20 minutes, until golden brown. Remove, loosen at once with a spatula and lift off the baking sheets. Cool on wire cooling racks.

Beat the cream in a bowl placed over a bowl of ice cubes until slightly thickened, then add the powdered sugar, flavor with a little rum or brandy and continue beating until stiff. Carefully fold in two-thirds of the raspberries. Sandwich the rounds of meringue together with the cream filling. Decorate with the remaining raspberries and extra cream.

Madeira Pudding

Serves 4: 2 tablespoons sugar dissolved in 2 tablespoons (1 fl oz) water; 1 cup (8 oz) sugar; 1 tablespoon vinegar; 2 eggs; 6 egg yolks; 1¾ cups (14 fl oz) hot milk; ¼ cup (2 fl oz) Madeira or port

Dissolve the sugar–water mixture over low heat and cook over moderate heat until the mixture turns a light amber color. Pour this caramel into a pudding mold, turning to coat the bottom and sides.

In a bowl, combine the sugar, vinegar, eggs and egg yolks and whisk until the sugar dissolves and the mixture is pale yellow. Slowly add the hot milk and the Madeira or port. Pour the mixture into the caramel-lined mold and place in a pan with

enough water to come halfway up the sides of the mold. Cover and bake in an oven preheated to 325°F (160°C) for 45–60 minutes or until it sets.

Allow it to cool, then refrigerate. To serve, unmold onto a decorative plate.

Melon in Port

Serves 6: 1 large or 2 small cantaloupes; ¼ cup (2 oz) sugar; 1½ cups (12 fl oz) port

Cut the melon in half and remove the seeds. Scoop out the flesh with a melon baller and place in individual serving dishes. Sprinkle with sugar and pour over the port. Allow to stand for at least 30 minutes and chill before serving.

Mince Pie Alaska

Serves 6–8: 1 baked 8-in (20-cm) shortcrust pie shell, chilled (see page 321); 2 cups (16 fl oz) vanilla ice cream; ¼ cup (2 oz) glacé cherries (or cherries and pineapple), chopped; 1 tablespoon brandy or rum; 1 cup fruit mincemeat; 3 egg whites; pinch of salt; 6–8 tablespoons sugar

Into the baked pastry shell, spread the slightly softened ice cream mixed with cherries and brandy. Spread the mincemeat over the top.

Whisk the egg whites with salt until soft peaks form. Gradually add the sugar, whisking until stiff and glossy. Pile the meringue on top of the pie, covering the edges of the pastry so that air can't penetrate and cause shrinkage. Bake in an oven preheated to 450°F (230°C) for 5–8 minutes. Serve immediately.

Note: The pie can be frozen after adding the mincemeat. Wrapped in plastic, it will keep for 2 months.

Loganberry Soufflé

Papaya Agar Agar

N

Neapolitan Strawberry Ice Cream

Serves 6: 1½ cups (12 fl oz) heavy cream; ½ cup (4 oz) powdered sugar; 1½ cups (12 fl oz) thick strawberry puree

Turn the freezer control to the coldest setting at least 1 hour in advance. Whip the cream with the sugar until thick, then gently fold in the pureed strawberries. Transfer the mixture to empty ice cube trays and freeze for 1–2 hours. Tip the frozen mixture into a bowl and break it up with a hand beater. Return the mixture to the trays and freeze for a further 1–2 hours. Repeat the beating process, then finally refreeze for 2–3 hours before serving.

Nut Fudge Pie

Serves 10–12: 1 cup (8 oz) chocolate bits; 4 eggs; 1 teaspoon vanilla; 1 cup (8 fl oz) light corn syrup or maple syrup; ½ teaspoon salt; 1½ tablespoons butter or margarine, melted; 1½ cups (6 oz) cashews, macadamias or pecans, coarsely chopped; 1 unbaked 10-in (25-cm) shortcrust pie shell (see page 348)

Melt the chocolate pieces in a small bowl over hot water. In a medium-size bowl beat the eggs, vanilla, syrup, salt and butter, and stir in the melted chocolate. Spread the nuts over the bottom of the pastry. Pour over the egg mixture. Bake in an oven preheated to 350°F (180°C) for 50–60 minutes. Cool.

Nutmeg Banana Custard

Serves 4: 2-in (5-cm) vanilla bean or 1 teaspoon vanilla; 2 cups (15 fl oz) milk; 2 egg yolks; 1 egg; 1 tablespoon (1 oz) sugar; 2 tablespoons (1 oz) butter, cut into pieces; 3 ripe bananas, sliced; ½ teaspoon nutmeg; cream for serving

Split the vanilla bean and place in a saucepan with the milk. Heat together slowly, then stand on one side just before the milk boils. Remove the vanilla bean. (Alter-

natively add vanilla to the milk and heat in the same way.)

Beat the egg yolks and egg with the sugar, pour a little of the milk onto them and return to the saucepan. Add the butter. Beat over a low flame with a rotary beater until thick. Remove the saucepan from the heat and beat a little longer. Pour into a jug and allow to cool. When cold, pour into a serving dish over the bananas. Chill. Sprinkle with the nutmeg and serve with cream.

Note: Peeled and segmented oranges may be used instead of bananas.

O

Old-Fashioned Butterscotch Pie

Serves 6–8: 4 tablespoons (2 oz) butter; ¾ cup (4 oz) brown sugar; ¾ cup (6 fl oz) boiling water; 2 tablespoons cornstarch; 1 tablespoon all purpose flour; ½ teaspoon salt; 1 cup (8 fl oz) milk; 2 large egg yolks, slightly beaten; 1 teaspoon vanilla; 1 baked 8-in (20-cm) shortcrust pie shell (see page 321)

Melt the butter in a heavy-based pan and add the sugar. Cook until foaming, about 2 minutes, stirring constantly. Pour in the boiling water and remove from the heat.

In a saucepan, mix together the cornstarch, flour and salt. Gradually add the milk and stir until smooth. Pour in the brown sugar mixture. Cook over low heat until it comes to a boil, stirring constantly. Boil for 1 minute, then remove from the heat.

Stir a little of the mixture into the egg yolks, then blend it all together in the saucepan. Boil for 1 minute, then remove from the heat and stir in the vanilla. Set it aside to cool, stirring occasionally.

Pour the mixture into the baked pie shell, chill and serve with whipped cream or top with meringue. Garnish with toasted nuts if desired.

Orange Custard

Serves 4: ¾ cup (6 fl oz) freshly squeezed orange juice, strained; ¾ cup (6½ oz) sugar; ⅓ cup (2½ fl oz) water; 8 egg yolks; 1 whole egg

Stir the juice, sugar and water until the sugar dissolves. Bring it to the boil and simmer for 10 minutes. Cool.

Lightly beat the egg yolks and egg together. Mix the syrup and beaten eggs and pour into a mold. Place the mold in a dish filled with hot water, cover with aluminum foil and bake in an oven preheated to 350°F (180°C) for 30 minutes or until the custard sets. Cool and chill if desired. Serve turned out onto a platter.

P

Papaya Agar Agar

4 cups (1 liter) water; 3½ teaspoons agar agar powder; ¼ cup (2 oz) sugar, or more to taste; 1 medium-size ripe papaya (pawpaw); 1½ tablespoons lime juice or lemon juice; mint leaves for garnish

Put the water into a saucepan and sprinkle the agar agar powder on top. Bring to the boil, stirring constantly, then simmer for 5 minutes to completely dissolve the powder. Add the sugar, stir to dissolve, then leave to cool.

Peel the papaya and discard the seeds. Chop the flesh into large chunks and pulverize in a blender or food processor to get a fine pulp. If you do not have a blender, press through a sieve or a food mill. When the agar agar liquid is cool but not yet starting to set, stir in the papaya pulp and lime juice, mixing well. Taste and adjust the sugar to suit your taste. Pour into a large decorative mold and refrigerate until serving time. Unmold onto a large glass plate, garnish with mint leaves, if desired, and serve.

Paradise Chiffon Pie

Serves 6: 2 envelopes (14 g) unflavored gelatin; 2 tablespoons cold water; 3 bananas; 2 passionfruit; 2 tablespoons lemon juice; 1 teaspoon grated lemon peel; 3 eggs; 1 scant cup (6 oz) powdered sugar; ⅔ cup (5 fl oz) heavy cream; 1 baked 9-in (23-cm) shortcrust pie shell (see page 321); toasted almond halves

Soften the gelatin in the cold water and dissolve over boiling water. Mash the bananas and stir in the passionfruit pulp, lemon juice and peel, egg yolks and half the sugar. Cook in the top of a double boiler over boiling water, stirring frequently, until the mixture thickens.

Remove from the heat, add the dissolved gelatin and cool. Chill until partially set. Whisk the egg whites until stiff and frothy, add the remaining sugar and beat until thick. Fold into the partially set banana mixture with the whipped cream. Spoon into the cooked pastry shell and chill well. Decorate with almond halves.

Passionfruit Flummery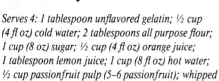

Serves 4: 1 tablespoon unflavored gelatin; ½ cup (4 fl oz) cold water; 2 tablespoons all purpose flour; 1 cup (8 oz) sugar; ½ cup (4 fl oz) orange juice; 1 tablespoon lemon juice; 1 cup (8 fl oz) hot water; ½ cup passionfruit pulp (5–6 passionfruit); whipped cream or ice cream for serving

Soak the gelatin in cold water. Mix the flour and sugar in a saucepan, then add sufficient orange juice to blend to a smooth paste. Add the remaining orange juice, lemon juice and hot water. Stir over heat until it boils and thickens. Add the soaked gelatin and stir until dissolved.

Cool, then empty into a mixing bowl and chill until it starts to thicken. Beat well until very thick and at least doubled in volume. Add the passionfruit and beat well again. Spoon into a serving bowl and chill until set. Serve with whipped cream or ice cream topped with a little more passionfruit.

Passionfruit Pavlova

Serves 8–10: 6 egg whites, at room temperature; ⅛ teaspoon cream of tartar; 1 cup (8 oz) sugar; 1 tablespoon cornstarch; 2 teaspoons white vinegar; cornstarch for dusting
Topping: 1¼ cups (10 fl oz) heavy cream, chilled; 1 teaspoon vanilla; 2 teaspoons powdered sugar; pulp of 4 large passionfruit (or ½–¾ cup canned passionfruit pulp)

Whisk the egg whites (preferably in a large glass bowl) until stiff and glossy. Combine the cream of tartar, sugar and cornstarch, and gradually add to the egg whites, beating well after each addition. Sprinkle the

vinegar over the surface and fold in lightly — do not overmix.

Grease the base and sides of an 8-in (20-cm) springform pan and dust with cornstarch, shaking off any excess. Pile the meringue into the pan, spreading to form a slight depression in the center.

Place into an oven preheated to 400°F (200°C), close the door, and immediately reduce the temperature to 250°F (120°C). Bake for 1¼–1½ hours.

Open the oven door and leave the meringue standing in the oven for 15 minutes before removing to a draft-free area. Carefully loosen the springform pan rim and allow to cool. The meringue may sink slightly in the center. Carefully lift the meringue onto a flat platter, removing the pan base.

To make the topping, whip the cream, vanilla and powdered sugar until thickened and firm. Spoon onto the meringue and lightly spread it. Spoon the passionfruit pulp over the cream and chill until ready to serve.

Notes: For ease of slicing, use a large knife dipped repeatedly into hot water.

Where passionfruit is unavailable, substitute sliced kiwi fruit.

Peaches in Wine

Serves 4: 2 cups (16 fl oz) dry red wine; ¼ cup (2 oz) sugar; 1 stick cinnamon, 2 in (5 cm) long; ½ cup (4 fl oz) brandy; 4–8 freestone peaches, peeled and halved

Mix the wine, sugar, cinnamon and brandy until the sugar has dissolved. Place the peaches in a bowl, pour the mixture over the peaches, cover the bowl with plastic wrap and refrigerate for 4 days. Serve cold in individual dessert bowls.

Pear and Apple Pie ★

Serves 8–10: 3½ cups canned pear halves, drained and sliced; 2 cups tart apples, peeled and sliced; ⅓ cup (3 oz) sugar; 2 tablespoons all purpose flour; ¼ teaspoon salt; ½ teaspoon cinnamon; ¼ teaspoon nutmeg (or mace); ½ cup (3 oz) seedless raisins; 1 teaspoon grated lemon peel; 1 tablespoon lemon juice; 1 unbaked 10-in (25-cm) shortcrust pie shell (see page 348)
Crumb Topping: 2½ cups (10 oz) all purpose flour; ½ cup (3 oz) brown sugar; ½ teaspoon salt;

Passionfruit Pavlova

6 tablespoons (3 oz) butter; ½ cup (2 oz) chopped walnuts

In a large bowl, gently combine the pears and apples. Mix together the sugar, flour, salt, cinnamon and nutmeg and add to the pear mixture with the raisins, peel and lemon juice. Blend gently. Turn into the unbaked pastry shell. Top with the crumb topping.

To make the topping, mix together the flour, brown sugar and salt, and cut or rub in the butter. Stir in the chopped walnuts. Bake in an oven preheated to 400°F (200°C) for 15 minutes. Cover with aluminum foil and bake 20–30 minutes more or until the apples are tender.

Pear Pie ★

Serves 10-12: 1½ cups (12 fl oz) pineapple juice; ¾ cup (6 oz) sugar; 6 pears, peeled, cored and cut into halves or quarters; 3 tablespoons cornstarch; 1 tablespoon butter; ½ teaspoon vanilla; ¼ teaspoon salt; 1 baked 10-in (25-cm) orange pastry shell (see page 348 and Note); toasted almonds or macadamias

In a skillet, bring 1 cup of pineapple juice and the sugar to the boil. Add the pears and simmer until they are tender, basting the pears as they poach. Lift out and drain.

Combine the remaining pineapple juice with the cornstarch and pour it into the syrup in the skillet. Cook, stirring constantly, until bubbling and thickened. Cook for a further minute, then remove from the heat. Stir in the butter, vanilla and salt. Cool, without stirring, about 5–8 minutes.

Pour half of the sauce into the baked pastry shell. Arrange the pears on top. Spoon over the remaining sauce. Chill. Garnish with whipped cream and sprinkle with toasted almonds or macadamias.

Note: Add the grated peel of ½ orange to the basic recipe.

Pears in Red Wine

Serves 6: 6 ripe but firm pears; ½ cup (4 oz) sugar; 1½ cups (12 fl oz) red wine; 1½ cups (12 fl oz) water; 1 tablespoon vanilla sugar (see Note); 1 tablespoon cornstarch

Peel the pears and set aside. Mix the sugar, wine and water together and bring to the

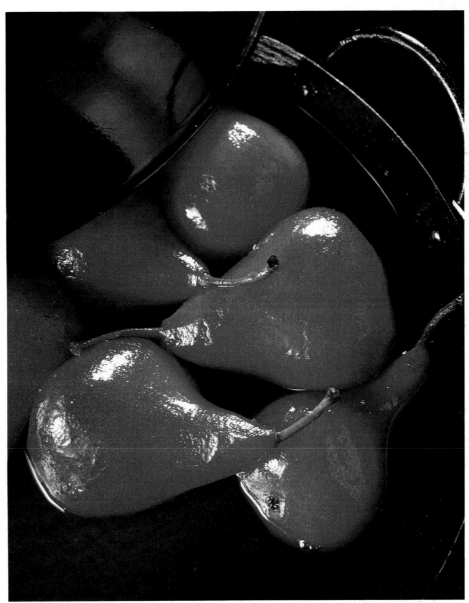

Pears in Red wine

boil, stirring until the sugar has dissolved.

Add the pears and vanilla sugar and reduce the heat. Partially cover the pan and gently poach the pears for about 1¼ hours until they are very tender but still holding their shape. The syrup should be reduced to about 1¼ cups.

Use a slotted spoon to lift the pears from the pan and transfer to glass dessert dishes.

Mix the cornstarch with an equal amount of cold water and slowly stir into the syrup. Stir on moderate heat until the sauce is thick and transparent. Spoon over the pears. Serve hot with whipped cream.

Note: Finely ground sugar infused with the flavor of vanilla — by storing a vanilla bean in a jar of powdered sugar. If unobtainable, substitute 1 teaspoon of vanilla extract.

Add the pears to the sugar-wine syrup and poach gently.

Transfer the cooked pears to glass dessert dishes.

Pear Tart ★

Makes one 10-in (25-cm) tart: 2 cups (8 oz) all purpose flour; ¼ cup (2 oz) sugar; 8 tablespoons (4 oz) butter, cut into cubes; water; 3 apples, peeled and cored; 8 pears, peeled and cored; 6 tablespoons (3 oz) sugar; 1¼ cups (10 fl oz) dry red wine; juice of ½ lemon; pinch of cinnamon; pinch of ground cloves; 2 tablespoons redcurrant jelly; whipped cream

To make the pastry, combine the flour and sugar, add the butter and rub it with your fingertips until it is the consistency of firm breadcrumbs. Pour in enough water to make a firm pastry dough and knead quickly until smooth and elastic. Do not overwork the dough. Wrap in plastic and chill for 2 hours.

Cut the apples and two of the pears into small slices and cook them with the sugar, wine, lemon juice, cinnamon and cloves until soft. Drain in a strainer and reserve the juice.

Halve the remaining pears and cook them in the juice until tender but still firm. Set aside.

Roll out the dough to approximately ⅛ in (3 mm) thick and 2 in (5 cm) larger than the pan. Line the pan with pastry, making the sides double thickness. Prick with a fork.

Combine the juice with the cooked apple and pear slices and rub them through a sieve to make a puree. Return to the saucepan and cook until reduced to a thick puree. Set aside to cool.

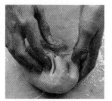
Quickly knead the dough until it is smooth and elastic. Do not overwork.

Roll the dough out to an even ⅛ in (3 mm) thickness.

Lift the dough onto the rolling pin and fit the pastry into the tart case.

Roll the rolling pin over the tart to trim the edges.

Spread the puree over the pastry and bake in an oven preheated to 425°F (220°C) for 30 minutes. Arrange the pear halves in concentric circles on top and bake 10 more minutes. When the tart has cooled slightly but the pears are still lukewarm, spread them with the redcurrant jelly. Chill until the jelly sets. Cut the tart into slices and serve with whipped cream.

Pecan Pie 🇺🇸

Serves 6-8: 1¼ cups (10 oz) cooked mashed pumpkin; ¼ teaspoon salt; 1¼ cups (10 fl oz) milk; 2 large eggs; ¼ cup (2 oz) sugar; ⅓ cup (2 oz) brown sugar; 1 teaspoon cinnamon; ⅓ teaspoon each ginger and nutmeg; ¼ teaspoon ground cloves; 1 unbaked 9-in (23-cm) shortcrust pie shell (see page 321); pecans and whipped cream for garnish

Beat all the ingredients together except the pie shell, pecans and cream. Pour the mixture into the unbaked pie shell and bake in an oven preheated to 400°F (200°C) for 45-55 minutes. The center may still look soft but will set later. Serve with nuts and cream when slightly warm but set.

Peil Wyke Raspberry Syllabub 🇬🇧

Serves 6-8: 2½ cups (20 fl oz) heavy cream; ½ cup (4 oz) powdered sugar; 10 oz (315 g) fresh raspberries; 1 tablespoon water; 4 egg whites; 5 fl oz (150 ml) dry white wine

Whip the cream until thick, then fold in the powdered sugar. Put the raspberries and water in a pan and stew over gentle heat for a few minutes. Leave to cool.

Whisk the egg whites until they form stiff peaks, then fold them into the cream mixture. Gently fold in the raspberries and wine, then spoon into champagne glasses. Serve decorated with a raspberry and a raspberry leaf.

Peil Wyke Raspberry Syllabub

Persimmon Crunch Pie ★

Serves 6–8: ⅓–½ cup (3–4 oz) sugar; 2 tablespoons quick tapioca; ½ teaspoon each grated orange and lemon peel; ¼ teaspoon each cinnamon and nutmeg; 2 tablespoons lemon juice; 4 cups firm persimmons, peeled and sliced; 1 unbaked 9-in (23-cm) shortcrust pie shell (see page 321)
Crunchy Topping: 8 tablespoons (4 oz) butter or margarine; ¾ cup (4 oz) brown sugar; ¾ cup (3 oz) all purpose flour; ¼ teaspoon salt; ¼ cup (1 oz) finely chopped nuts (optional)

Mix the sugar and tapioca together. Stir in the grated peel, spices, lemon juice and persimmons, mixing gently until blended. Allow this mixture to stand while making the pastry and topping. Taste, to make sure it is as sweet or tart as you would like it.

To make the topping, cream the butter and brown sugar together, then blend in the flour and salt. Add the nuts if desired. Pour the fruit filling into the pie shell and sprinkle with the crunchy topping.

Bake on the lowest rack of an oven preheated to 375°F (190°C) for 50–55 minutes or until the filling is bubbling hot and the pastry browned. Cool until the pie is just warm. Serve with custard topping, lemon gelato or softened vanilla ice cream.

Pineapple Custard

Serves 4–6: 3 tablespoons cornstarch; 2¾ cups (22 fl oz) milk; 6 egg yolks, well beaten; 13 oz (400 g) canned pineapple with juice; sugar (optional); heavy cream

Mix the cornstarch and milk. While stirring, boil it until the mixture thickens. Add the beaten egg yolks, stirring over low heat. Do not boil.

Add the finely chopped pineapple and 2–3 tablespoons of the pineapple juice. Taste and, if necessary, add some sugar, stirring until the sugar has dissolved. Pour the mixture into a serving dish and refrigerate. Serve with sweetened plain or whipped cream.

Pineapple Sherbet

Serves 6: 15 oz (470 g) canned crushed pineapple; 2 teaspoons unflavored gelatin; 1 tablespoon water; 2 tablespoons lemon juice; ½ cup (4 fl oz) cold milk; 2 egg whites; 2 scant tablespoons powdered sugar; crème de menthe or sugared mint sprigs for serving

Drain the pineapple and reserve ½ cup fruit pulp. Soften the gelatin in water, then dissolve over low heat. Put the remaining pineapple pulp, pineapple juice and lemon juice in an electric blender and mix to a puree. Add the dissolved gelatin and milk, and mix until blended.

Pour into a refrigerator tray and freeze until set. Whisk the egg whites until stiff peaks form, then add the sugar gradually and beat until dissolved. Place the frozen mixture into a mixing bowl, beat well, then fold in the whisked egg whites. Empty into a refrigerator tray and freeze until set. Serve topped with the reserved pineapple pulp and a drizzle of crème de menthe or a sugared mint sprig.

Plum Pie

Serves 6–8: 2 lb (1 kg) fresh tart red plums, pitted and quartered; ¼ cup (2 fl oz) water; 1 cup (8 oz) sugar; ¼ cup (1 oz) cornstarch; ¼ teaspoon salt; 2 tablespoons brandy; 1 unbaked 9-in (23-cm) shortcrust pastry shell (see page 321)
Crumble Topping: ⅓ cup (1½ oz) all purpose flour; ⅓ cup (3 oz) sugar; ½ teaspoon cinnamon; ¼ teaspoon nutmeg; pinch of ground cloves; 4 tablespoons (2 oz) butter

Place the plums and water in a saucepan, cover and cook over medium heat for 3–4 minutes. Stir together the sugar, cornstarch, salt and brandy, and stir into the plums. Cook over low heat, stirring constantly, for 5 minutes or until thick and clear. Remove from the heat and cool.

Meanwhile, make the crumble topping. Mix together the flour, sugar, cinnamon, nutmeg and cloves. Cut in the butter and mix until it resembles coarse breadcrumbs.

Spoon filling into the pie shell. Sprinkle with the crumble topping and bake in an oven preheated to 400°F (200°C) for 30–35 minutes.

Prune Parfait Pie ★

Serves 8–10: 1 package lemon gelatin; 1 cup (8 fl oz) boiling water; 2 cups vanilla ice cream; 1 cup prunes, stewed and pureed; 1 baked 9-in (23-cm) shortcrust pie shell (see page 321); whipped cream and nuts for topping

In a large bowl, dissolve the gelatin in boiling water. Stir until dissolved. Add the ice cream, chopped into pieces, to the hot liquid. Stir until dissolved and blended. Chill until thickened, for about 10–20 minutes, then beat until fluffy. Fold in the prunes and spoon the mixture into the baked pie shell.

Chill until set for about 1 hour or overnight. Top with whipped cream and nuts.

Pumpkin Ice Cream Pie

Serves 6–8: 1 prepared 9-in (23-cm) crumb crust (see page 321); 2 cups vanilla ice cream; 1 cup mashed pumpkin; ¾ cup (4 oz) brown sugar; ½ teaspoon cinnamon; ¼ teaspoon ginger; ¼ teaspoon ground cloves; ¼ teaspoon salt; ¼ cup (2 oz) mixed candied peel; ¼ cup (2 fl oz) orange juice (or orange liqueur); 1 cup (8 fl oz) cream; toasted macadamias, chopped, for garnish

Put the pie shell into the freezer. Remove the ice cream, allowing it to soften just enough to spread evenly over the bottom of the crumb crust. Place in the freezer.

In a saucepan, combine the pumpkin, sugar, spices and salt. Heat just until the sugar has melted. Blend in the peel and orange juice. Chill.

Whip the cream and fold into the pumpkin mixture. Spoon over the ice cream. Freeze. Garnish with macadamia nuts.

Q

Quick Cherry Strudel

Serves 6: 15 oz (470 g) canned cherries; ¾ cup (3 oz) very finely chopped walnuts; ¼ cup (2 oz) sugar; 2 teaspoons grated lemon peel; 1 teaspoon cinnamon; 4 tablespoons (2 oz) butter; ¾ cup (1½ oz) soft white breadcrumbs; 8 oz (250 g) commercial puff pastry; extra melted butter; powdered sugar

Stone and halve the cherries, put into a sieve and drain thoroughly. Mix together the walnuts, sugar, lemon peel and cinnamon. Pour the melted butter over the crumbs and stir to combine.

Roll the pastry out on a well floured clean tea towel to a thin oblong about 14 × 20 in (35 × 50 cm), with the longer side of pastry nearest to you. Brush with the extra melted butter and spread the crumbs over, leaving a 2-in (5-cm) margin of pastry all round.

Arrange the cherries parallel with the longer edge of the pastry and near the center. Fold in the sides of the pastry and brush the folds with melted butter. Roll up and put on a greased large baking sheet. Brush all over with melted butter.

Bake in an oven preheated to 475°F (240°C) for 10 minutes, reduce to 400°F (200°C) and bake another 25–30 minutes, or until golden brown, brushing with melted butter every 10 minutes. Dust with sifted powdered sugar and serve warm.

R

Raisin Prune Pie

Serves 6–8: 1½ cups (8 oz) seedless raisins, chopped; 1½ cups (9 oz) pitted prunes, finely chopped; 1 cup (8 fl oz) water; ⅓ cup (3 oz) sugar; 1 teaspoon lemon juice; ½ teaspoon each vanilla and cinnamon; ⅛ teaspoon ground cloves; ½ cup (2 oz) walnuts, finely chopped; 1 unbaked 9-in (23-cm) double shortcrust pie shell (see page 336); 1 tablespoon butter

Place the raisins, prunes and water in a saucepan, cover and bring to the boil. Reduce the heat and simmer for 20 minutes. Cool slightly, then lightly drain. Stir in the sugar, lemon juice, vanilla, cloves and nuts.

Spoon the filling into the prepared pie shell, then dot with the butter. Cover with pastry and trim. Crimp the edges and cut slits for the steam to escape. Bake on the bottom rack of an oven preheated to 375°F (190°C) for 35–45 minutes. Serve warm.

Raspberry Fool

Serves 12: 3 lb (1½ kg) raspberries; 1¼ cups (10 oz) water; 1 cup (8 oz) sugar; 1¼ cups (10 oz) heavy cream; ⅔ cup (5 oz) whipped cream for decoration
Vanilla Custard: 1¼ cups (10 oz) milk; ½ teaspoon vanilla; 3 tablespoons sugar; 3 egg yolks

Clean the raspberries and place in a large saucepan with the water and sugar. Stew the raspberries until soft, then cool and rub through a sieve to remove seeds.

To make the custard, gently heat the milk to body temperature, then add the vanilla. Whisk the sugar and egg yolks until smooth. Add a little warmed milk, stirring constantly, then add the remaining

Raspberry Fool

milk. Return to the heat and cook, stirring constantly, until the custard thickens to the consistency of cream. Do not boil.

Whip the cream and mix with the custard and raspberry puree. Serve in a glass bowl or in individual glasses. Decorate with whipped cream.

Note: Frozen raspberries or fresh boysenberries may be used instead of fresh raspberries.

Red Fruit Dessert

Serves 4-6: 6 cups (1½ liters) redcurrant juice; 4-6 tablespoons honey (depending on the acidity of the fruit juice); 1 cup (8 oz) dry red wine; ⅔ cup (3 oz) cornstarch; fruit for garnish

Bring the fruit juice to the boil, then add the honey and wine. Mix the cornstarch with a little water. Reduce the heat and add the cornstarch to the juice, stirring vigorously. Continue stirring and boil slowly for 1–2 minutes. To serve, pour the mixture into dessert glasses and refrigerate. Garnish with the same type of fruit which has been used for the juice.

Note: If redcurrant juice is unavailable, use the juice or puree of strawberries, raspberries, plums or cherries.

Refrigerator Cheesecake

Serves 10–12: 8 oz (250 g) plain sweet cookies; 8 tablespoons (4 oz) butter; 2 teaspoons cinnamon Filling: 1 tablespoon unflavored gelatin; ¼ cup (2 fl oz) lemon juice; 12 oz (375 g) cream cheese; finely grated peel of 2 lemons; 3 eggs, separated; ½ cup (3½ oz) powdered sugar; 1¼ cups (10 fl oz) heavy cream or sour cream; pinch of salt; whipped cream and strawberries, pineapple or passionfruit for decoration

To make the crust, crush the cookies finely. Melt the butter, add the crumbs and cinnamon and mix well. Grease the base and sides of an 8-in (20-cm) springform pan.

Press and mold the crumb mixture over the base and sides of the pan to make a firm crust. Bake in an oven preheated to 375°F (190°C) for 8 minutes, then cool and chill.

To make the filling, add the gelatin to the lemon juice, stand in hot water and heat until dissolved. Cool a little. Beat the

Refrigerator Cheesecake

cream cheese with the lemon peel; add the egg yolks, half the sugar and the dissolved gelatin. Beat well until the mixture is smooth. Beat the cream until thick. Whisk the egg whites and salt until stiff, then beat in the remaining sugar gradually until stiff peaks form. Fold the cream cheese mixture, cream and meringue lightly but thoroughly together.

Carefully spoon into the prepared cookie crust. Chill until set. Serve topped with whipped cream. If desired, decorate with strawberries, pineapple or passionfruit.

S

Sachertorte

Serves 6: 16 tablespoons (8 oz) butter, softened; ¾ cup (5½ oz) powdered sugar; 10 egg yolks; 8 oz (250 g) semisweet chocolate, melted and cooled; 12 egg whites, stiffly beaten; 1⅔ cups (6½ oz) all purpose flour; whipped cream for serving Apricot Glaze: ¼ cup (3 oz) apricot jam; hot water; 1-2 tablespoons apricot brandy (optional) Chocolate Fondant Icing: 1¾ cups (14 oz) sugar; ¼ teaspoon cream of tartar; 1 cup (8 fl oz) boiling water; ½ cup melted semisweet chocolate

Cream the butter and sugar, then beat in the egg yolks two at a time, making sure that they are well incorporated before adding the next two. Add the chocolate and mix well. Gently fold in the beaten egg whites, at the same time gradually adding the sifted flour. Fold in carefully.

Butter and flour a springform pan and pour in the batter. Bake the cake in an oven preheated to 350°F (175°C) until it is puffy and dry. Test by inserting a thin skewer in the center — it should come out clean and dry.

Remove the ring of the springform and rest the cake for one or two days.

To make the apricot glaze, heat the apricot jam in a double boiler, thinning it down with a little hot water. Add the apricot brandy if desired.

To make the chocolate fondant icing, combine the sugar and cream of tartar in a heavy-based saucepan. Add the boiling water and stir until the sugar has dissolved. Cook the syrup, without stirring, until it reaches the thread stage or 240°F (115°C) on a sugar thermometer. Remove the fondant from the heat and pour it onto a metal surface. With a spatula, work it until it cools, then knead it into a smooth mass. This should be done as quickly as possible. Place the fondant in an airtight container and store it in the refrigerator.

Heat the fondant in the top of a double boiler over simmering water and add the melted chocolate. Thin the fondant to a spreadable consistency with boiling water.

Spread the top and sides of the cake with a thin layer of apricot glaze. Pour the fondant icing onto the cake and quickly tilt it in all directions to spread the icing. If the fondant gets too stiff, it can be reheated to the required consistency. Serve with whipped cream.

Shoo-Fly Pie

Serves 8–10: 1½ cups (6 oz) all purpose flour; 1 cup (5 oz) brown sugar; ½ teaspoon cinnamon; ⅛ teaspoon ground cloves; ¼ teaspoon ginger; ½ teaspoon nutmeg; ½ teaspoon salt; 1 teaspoon baking soda; 8 tablespoons (4 oz) butter or margarine; 1 cup (8 oz) treacle or light corn syrup; 1 cup (8 fl oz) boiling water; 2 eggs, well beaten; 1 unbaked 9-in (23-cm) shortcrust pastry shell (see page 321)

In a bowl, combine the flour, sugar, spices, salt and half the soda. Cut or rub in the butter until the mixture resembles coarse crumbs.

In a medium-size bowl, mix together the treacle, boiling water, remaining soda and the eggs. Add 1 cup of the flour–butter mixture and stir until it is well blended. Pour into the unbaked pastry shell and sprinkle the remaining flour mixture evenly over the top.

Bake on the lowest rack of an oven preheated to 375°F (190°C) for 50 minutes, or until the filling is just set in the center. Cool completely.

Note: Half a cup of finely chopped nuts may be stirred into the treacle mixture.

Sour Cream Raisin Pie

Serves 6–8: 1 unbaked 9-in (23-cm) shortcrust pastry shell (see page 321); ½ cup (4 oz) sugar; 2 tablespoons all purpose flour; ½ teaspoon cinnamon; ¼ teaspoon nutmeg; ¼ teaspoon salt; 1 egg, beaten; 1½ cups (12 fl oz) sour cream; 1½ cups (8 oz) seedless raisins

Mix the sugar, flour, spices and salt together. Blend into the egg mixed with the sour cream. Mix in the raisins. Pour into the prepared pie shell. Bake in an oven preheated to 450°F (230°C) for 40 minutes, then reduce the oven temperature to 350°F (180°C) and bake for 20–25 minutes longer. Cool slightly. Serve warm with cream or ice cream, if desired.

Southern Brown Sugar Pie

Serves 6–8: 1 unbaked 9-in (23-cm) shortcrust pie shell (see page 321); 4 tablespoons (2 oz) soft butter or margarine; 2 cups (10 oz) light brown sugar; 4 eggs, well beaten; 2 tablespoons cream; 1 tablespoon all purpose flour; 1 tablespoon vanilla; ¼ teaspoon salt; ¼ teaspoon nutmeg (optional)

Chill the pie shell for 1 hour. In a bowl, cream together the butter and brown sugar until the mixture is light and fluffy. Add the eggs, the cream and flour blended together, then the vanilla, salt and nutmeg. Mix well. Pour into the chilled pie shell.

Bake on the bottom rack of an oven preheated to 450°F (230°C) for 12 minutes. Reduce the temperature to 350°F (180°C) and bake for 20–30 minutes more or until the center is just set. Serve warm with vanilla or coffee ice cream.

Spicy Coconut Pudding

Serves 4: 2 large eggs; 2 cups (16 fl oz) milk; 3 tablespoons whole milk powder; ½ cup (4 fl oz) thick coconut milk; 3 green cardamoms, crushed; ½ teaspoon grated fresh nutmeg; ½ teaspoon cinnamon; ½ cup (4 oz) dark molasses; 2 tablespoons brown sugar

Beat the eggs lightly. Mix the milk with the milk powder and coconut milk and heat until just beginning to boil. Add the spices and stir in the molasses. Mix thoroughly. Pour the mixture into the beaten eggs and pour into an ovenproof bowl. Set in a larger bowl of water and bake in an oven preheated to 350°F (180°C) for about 1 hour or until the pudding is set. Sprinkle the brown sugar over and raise the heat to crisp the top. Serve warm or cold.

Steam-Baked Carrot Ring

Serves 6–8: 4 tablespoons (2 oz) butter or margarine, softened; ½ cup (4 oz) sugar; 2 eggs; 1 teaspoon pumpkin pie spice; ¼ teaspoon salt; ¾ cup (2 oz) soft white breadcrumbs; ⅓ cup (1½ oz) seedless raisins; ½ cup (2 oz) chopped walnuts; 1 cup cooked, mashed carrots, cooled; 2 tablespoons sweet sherry; 2 tablespoons evaporated milk

Cream the butter and sugar. Add the eggs one at a time and beat well before adding the spices, salt and breadcrumbs. Mix in the raisins, walnuts, mashed carrots, sherry and evaporated milk.

Turn the mixture into a well-greased and crumb-coated fluted ring mold and cover securely with greased aluminum foil. Stand in a baking pan containing 1–1½ in (2.5–4 cm) boiling water and bake in an oven preheated to 350°F (180°C) for 55–60 minutes. Serve hot with custard sauce, cream or ice cream.

Steam-Baked Carrot Ring

of the way up the side of the mold. Bring the water to a boil and simmer over low heat for 1 hour, then turn the pudding out onto a serving dish. Whip the cream with the 3 tablespoons powdered sugar and vanilla until stiff peaks form. Serve the pudding hot with the whipped cream presented separately in a bowl.

Strawberries à La Romanoff

Serves 6: 1 cup (8 fl oz) heavy cream; 2½ cups (20 fl oz) vanilla ice cream; 2 lb (1 kg) strawberries; sugar; 1 liqueur glass Cointreau

Whip the cream until stiff. Soften the ice cream slightly and fold in the cream. Put into freezer trays and freeze until firm.

Wash and hull the strawberries and add sugar to taste, reserving a few strawberries for decoration. Chill. Before serving add the Cointreau to the strawberries. Soften the ice cream and fold in the strawberries. Decorate with a few reserved strawberries and serve at once.

Strawberries and Oranges with Port

Serves 4: 8 oz (250 g) strawberries, hulled; ½ cup (4 fl oz) port; 2 oranges, peeled and thinly sliced; 2 tablespoons sugar; ½ cup (4 fl oz) heavy cream, whipped with 1 teaspoon sugar and ½ teaspoon vanilla

Marinate the strawberries in the port for 30 minutes. Add the orange slices and sugar and refrigerate for 1 hour. Serve with the whipped cream.

Strawberries à la Romanoff

Steamed Chocolate Pudding

Serves 6-8: 1½ cups (12 oz) powdered sugar; 8 oz (250 g) semisweet chocolate, cut into chunks; 1 teaspoon instant coffee; 16 tablespoons (8 oz) softened unsalted butter; 10 egg yolks; 10 oz (300 g) blanched almonds, coarsely chopped and roasted; 10 egg whites, stiffly beaten; 2 cups (16 fl oz) cream; additional 3 tablespoons powdered sugar; ⅛ teaspoon vanilla

Sprinkle 2-3 tablespoons of the sugar into a greased 8-cup (2-liter) pudding mold to

coat the bottom and sides. Melt the chocolate in a double boiler and mix in the coffee.

In a large mixing bowl, cream the butter and the remaining sugar. Add the egg yolks one at a time, beating constantly, then add the chocolate. Beat until the mixture is smooth. Add the almonds. Fold one quarter of the egg whites into the egg–chocolate mixture, then gradually mix it into the rest of the egg whites. Pour the mixture into the pudding mold, smooth the top and cover the mold.

Place the mold in a large saucepan and pour in enough water to come two-thirds

Strawberry and Lime Tart ★

Serves 6-8: ½ cup (4 oz) sugar; ⅓ cup (2½ fl oz) lime juice; 3 egg yolks; 3 tablespoons grated lime peel; 2 tablespoons (1 oz) soft butter; 1 unbaked 9-in (23-cm) shortcrust pie shell (see page 321); 1 cup sliced strawberries (garnish); sweetened whipped cream

In a bowl, beat the sugar, lime juice, egg yolks, lime peel and butter until fluffy.

Spread the mixture over the unbaked pie shell and cover loosely with aluminum foil.

Bake on the lowest rack of an oven preheated to 400°F (200°C) for 30–35 minutes, until the filling is set. Allow to cool. Top with strawberries and serve with sweetened whipped cream or softened ice cream.

Strawberry Crêpes Royale

Serves 5–6: Crêpe Batter: 1¼ cups (5 oz) all purpose flour; ¼ teaspoon salt; ½ teaspoon baking powder; 2 teaspoons sugar; 2 eggs; 1 teaspoon vanilla, rum or brandy extract; 2 tablespoons light vegetable oil; 2 cups (16 fl oz) milk; water as required; butter or oil for frying
2 tablespoons sweet sherry; 8 oz (225 g) cream cheese, softened; 2 tablespoons powdered sugar; 1½ teaspoons grated orange peel; ¼ cup (2 fl oz) orange juice; 20–24 strawberries, hulled and sliced; ¾ cup (6 fl oz) apricot preserves; additional 2 tablespoons sweet sherry; 2 tablespoons (1 oz) butter or margarine, melted; ½ cup (2 oz) flaked almonds; sour cream for serving

To make the crêpes, sift the flour, salt, baking powder and sugar into a bowl and make a well in the center.

Beat the eggs with the extract, oil and milk. Pour into the flour mixture gradually, whisking until the mixture is a smooth, creamy consistency. Set aside for at least 30 minutes, then whisk in sufficient water to produce a thin cream consistency.

Heat a shallow crêpe or omelet pan and grease lightly with the butter or oil. Pour in 2–3 tablespoons of the batter and tilt the pan to coat the base, pouring off any excess batter.

Cook over medium-high heat until the underside is lightly browned. Carefully flip or turn over and cook another minute. Make the remaining crêpes in a similar way, placing a strip of waxed paper between each while stacking to complete the required number.

To prepare the filling, lightly brush one side of each crêpe with the sweet sherry. Combine the cream cheese, powdered sugar, orange peel and juice, and spoon about 2 tablespoons across each crêpe. Roll up loosely and arrange in a single layer in a well-greased shallow casserole.

Spoon the sliced strawberries over the crêpes. Combine the apricot preserves, remaining sweet sherry and melted butter,

Strawberry Crêpes Royale

and spoon this over the top. Scatter with almonds and loosely cover with aluminum foil.

Bake in an oven preheated to 350°F (180°C) for 15–20 minutes. Serve at once, with a spoonful of sour cream on top.

Note: To flambé the crêpes, carefully pour a little flaming brandy over the crêpes just before serving.

Strawberry Pastries

Serves 10–12: 10–12 unbaked shortcrust patty shells (see page 319); 1 lb (500 g) strawberries (frozen or fresh); 8 oz (250 g) cream cheese, softened; 2 tablespoons sour cream; 2 tablespoons Cointreau or orange liqueur; ¼ cup (2 oz) sugar; grated peel of 1 orange

Prick the base of the patty shells with a fork and bake in an oven preheated to

400°F (200°C) for 8-12 minutes or until lightly browned. Allow the pastry shells to cool before removing them.

Slightly thaw the strawberries if frozen. Whip the cream cheese until it is soft, then beat in the sour cream, Cointreau, sugar and orange peel until fluffy. Spread the shells with this mixture and top with strawberries.

Stuffed Figs

Serves 4: 12 ripe fresh figs; ¼ cup (1 oz) chopped mixed nuts; 1 tablespoon sweetened cocoa; 1 tablespoon mixed candied fruit, chopped; 1 tablespoon honey; 2 tablespoons powdered sugar

Cut the figs in half vertically and from each piece, scoop out one teaspoon of flesh. In a bowl, mix the flesh with the rest of the ingredients, except the powdered sugar. Spoon this mixture back into the figs. Put the two halves together and serve them dusted with the powdered sugar.

Summer Berry Pudding

Serves 6: 1½ lb (750 g) soft berries (raspberries, strawberries, redcurrants, mulberries or blackberries); ½ cup (4 fl oz) water; ¾-1 cup (6-8 oz) sugar, depending on fruit; 6-8 thin slices bread, crusts removed and cut into strips; brandy or kirsch; extra fruit for decorating; whipped cream for serving

Hull and clean the fruit and stew slowly with the water and sugar in a covered saucepan until the fruit has slightly softened.

Line a greased pudding mold with the strips of bread. Half fill the center with the drained fruit and sprinkle with a little brandy or kirsch. Cover with strips of bread. Add the remaining fruit and ¼ cup of the juice, mixed with a little more brandy or kirsch. Cover with a "lid" of bread strips, then a sheet of aluminum foil and a plate. Put a heavy weight on top of the plate and leave in the refrigerator overnight. To serve, loosen around the edge with a knife, turn out onto a flat plate. Decorate with reserved fruit and serve with whipped cream.

Note: Spongecake fingers may be used in place of the strips of bread.

T
Tart of St. James

Serves 6-8: 8 eggs; 2 cups (1 lb) sugar; 2⅓ cups (9½ oz) all purpose flour; 16 tablespoons (8 oz) butter, softened; 1 cup (8 fl oz) water; 4½ cups (1 lb) ground almonds; 1 teaspoon grated lemon peel; powdered sugar

Cream the eggs with the sugar until pale yellow, light and fluffy. Add the flour, butter and water. Beat in an electric beater for 15 minutes, then add the almonds and lemon peel.

Pour the mixture into a greased round baking pan and bake in an oven preheated to 350°F (180°C) for 30-40 minutes or until the custard has set. Serve sprinkled with powdered sugar and cut into wedges.

Toffeed Apple

Serves 6: 2 large cooking apples; 1½ tablespoons white sesame seeds; oil for deep frying
Batter: 1 cup (4 oz) all purpose flour; 2 tablespoons cornstarch; 1 egg, beaten; 1 cup (8 fl oz) water
Toffee: 1 tablespoon sesame oil; 2 cups (1 lb) sugar

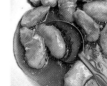

Dip the apple slices into the batter.   Turn until the apples are coated.

Peel, core and slice the apples and set aside. Mix the batter ingredients together, beating until smooth.

Heat the oil to hot. Dip the apple pieces one by one into the batter, then deep fry until crisp. Drain. When all the apple pieces have been done once, reheat the oil and fry again for 1½ minutes to crisp the batter. Drain well and place on a plate near the cooking area.

Heat the ingredients for the toffee, stirring occasionally, until the sugar has melted and turned to a light toffee color. Add the sesame seeds and the apple pieces and turn quickly but carefully in the toffee until evenly coated. Remove to the plate, which should be lightly oiled to prevent sticking.

Serve at once with a dish of iced water.

To eat, each piece of apple should be separated from the others and dipped into the water, where the toffee will solidify.

Tropical Fruit Flambé

Serves 4: 4 slices canned pineapple; 1 ripe but firm banana; 1 passionfruit; 2 tablespoons (1 oz) butter; 2½ tablespoons soft brown sugar; ¼ cup (2 fl oz) lime juice; ¼ cup (2 fl oz) pineapple juice; 1¼ tablespoons brandy; 2 teaspoons dark rum; whipped cream

Drain the pineapple. Peel the banana and cut in half lengthwise, then in half again to give four pieces. Open the passionfruit and set aside.

Melt the butter, add the pineapple and banana, and sauté gently until the banana is beginning to soften. Sprinkle the brown sugar over, then add the juices. Heat the brandy and rum together in a metal ladle and flame. Pour into the pan and boil briefly. Transfer the fruit to dessert dishes and top with whipped cream. Decorate with the passionfruit juice and seeds, and serve.

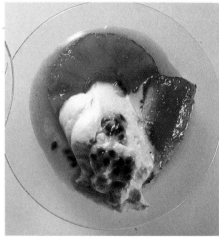

Tropical Fruit Flambé

Tropical Fruit Tart

Serves 8-12: Cream Cheese Pastry: 4 oz (125 g) cream cheese, softened; 8 tablespoons (4 oz) soft butter; 1 cup (4 oz) all purpose flour; ½ teaspoon salt
Orange Glaze: ⅔ cup (5½ fl oz) orange juice (or part brandy); 2 tablespoons sugar; 1 teaspoon

Toffeed Apple

Upside-Down Pudding

lemon juice; 2 teaspoons cornstarch
1 cup (8 fl oz) vanilla-flavored yogurt; ½ papaya,
peeled, seeded and cut into strips; ½ fresh
pineapple, peeled, cored and cut into slices;
1 orange, peeled, sliced and cut into half slices;
½ cup kiwi fruit, peeled and sliced; 8–12
strawberries, sliced

To make the pastry, beat together the cream cheese and butter until light and fluffy. Stir in the flour and salt until well blended. Chill for 4 hours, then roll out to fit a 9-in (23-cm) pie dish. Bake in an oven preheated to 375°F (200°C) for 15 minutes or until cooked and firm. Cool.

To make the glaze, mix all the ingredients together in a saucepan. Bring to the boil, then reduce the heat and simmer until thickened. Cool.

Over the prepared crust, spread the yogurt evenly. Attractively arrange the fruit in sections and spoon over the glaze. Chill 1–2 hours before serving.

U

Upside-Down Pudding

Serves 6: 4 tablespoons (2 oz) butter or margarine;
½ cup (3 oz) brown sugar; a selection of dried
apricots, prunes, pineapple, cherries, chopped
walnuts or almonds
Cake Mixture: 4 tablespoons (2 oz) butter or
margarine; ½ cup (3½ oz) powdered sugar or
brown sugar; 1 large egg; 1 teaspoon vanilla;
1¼ cups (5 oz) self-rising flour; pinch of salt;
3 tablespoons milk; cream or ice cream for serving
(optional)

Beat the butter and brown sugar until well mixed and spread on the bottom and a little way up sides of a well-greased deep 8-in (20-cm) cake pan, bottom-lined with greased waxed paper. Arrange the prepared selected fruit and nuts in a pattern on top of butter and sugar.

To make the cake mixture, cream the butter and sugar, add the egg and vanilla and beat well together. Sift the flour and salt, and stir half into the creamed mixture. Add the milk, then the remaining flour, mixing until smooth. Carefully spread in the prepared pan.

Bake in an oven preheated to 375°F (190°C) for about 30 minutes or until cooked. Let stand for a few minutes, then

White Radish with Sweet Miso Filling

turn out onto a serving dish and remove the paper. Serve either warm or cold with cream or ice cream if desired.

V

Vanilla Creamed Rice Pudding

Serves 4: 1 tablespoon short-grain rice; 2½ cups
(20 fl oz) milk; 1 tablespoon sugar; 1 teaspoon
butter; 2-in (5-cm) vanilla bean; 1 teaspoon nutmeg

Stir the rice, milk and sugar together in a buttered ovenproof dish. Add the vanilla pod and sprinkle the top with nutmeg. Bake in an oven preheated to 325°F (160°C) for 2–2½ hours. Stir the pudding gently once or twice during cooking, slipping a spoon under the skin to do so.

Serve hot or cold. When serving cold, remove the skin and sprinkle top with sugar and more nutmeg. When convenient, take out the vanilla bean, wash and dry and keep in a jar of sugar until used again.

W

White Radish with Sweet Miso Filling

Serves 4: 5 white radishes, about 7 oz (220 g) each;
3½ oz (100 g) white miso; 3 tablespoons mirin;
2 tablespoons sugar, or to taste; ⅓–½ cup water

Choose round, squat radishes or cut top sections from giant white radish. Put the radishes in a large saucepan and boil for 10 minutes. Remove and drain. Allow to cool, then with a very sharp vegetable knife, remove the skin and slice off the top, leaving the stem attached. Cut a hollow in the center of each radish for the filling. Remove the center, taking care not to damage the sides of the radishes. Carve the top to fit as a lid, leaving the stem attached as the handle.

Mix the *miso, mirin* and sugar in a small saucepan, adding enough water to make a paste of medium consistency. Bring to the boil, turn heat down and simmer for 2–3 minutes, stirring continually. Remove the sauce from the heat and cool slightly, then

Zabaione

pour into the radish cups. Set the lids in position and carefully place the filled radishes in a steamer or on a dish over a saucepan of boiling water. Steam for 10 minutes over high heat. Serve in small flat bowls, decorated with small blossoms or leaf sprigs.

The flavor of the sweet *miso* should permeate the radish, giving this usually sharply flavored vegetable a delicate, slightly sweet taste.

Note: If radishes are unavailable substitute turnips or small squash.

Z

Zabaglione Pie

Serves 6–8: ¼ cup (2 oz) sugar; 2 teaspoons unflavored gelatin; ½ cup (4 fl oz) Marsala or sherry; 6 egg yolks; 1 tablespoon brandy; 1 teaspoon vanilla; 1 cup (8 fl oz) cream, whipped; 3 egg whites; ⅛ teaspoon cream of tartar; ¼ teaspoon salt; 2 tablespoons powdered sugar; 1 baked 9-in (23-cm) shortcrust pie shell (see page 00); chocolate curls for garnish

In the top of a double boiler, mix together the sugar and gelatin. Stir in the wine, then the beaten egg yolks. Cook over hot water, stirring constantly, until thickened. Remove from the heat. Stir in the brandy and vanilla, then cool. Fold in the whipped cream.

Beat the egg whites until foamy and then add the cream of tartar and salt. Beat until stiff, gradually adding the powdered sugar. Fold this mixture into the cream and custard mixture. Spoon into the baked pie shell and garnish with chocolate curls if desired. Chill.

Zabaione

Serves 4: 6 egg yolks; 2 whole eggs; ½ cup (4 oz) powdered sugar; 1 cup (8 fl oz) Marsala

In a bowl, beat the yolks and the whole eggs together with the sugar until they are white and frothy. Stir in the Marsala and pour the mixture into a double boiler. While the water is boiling, whisk the mixture with a hand beater, making sure that it does not get too hot and curdle. As soon as it thickens, pour the zabaione into glass dishes and serve immediately.

Cakes, Cookies & Tea Breads

A

Alsatian Yeast Cake (Kugelhupf)

Serves 8-10: ½ cup (3 oz) seedless raisins; 3 tablespoons kirsch (optional); 1 oz (30 g) fresh yeast; 1 cup (8 fl oz) milk, warmed; ⅓ cup (3 oz) sugar; 1 lb (500 g) all purpose flour; ½ teaspoon salt; 2 eggs, beaten; 14 tablespoons (7 oz) butter, softened; 2 oz (60 g) almonds, chopped; powdered sugar for dusting

Soak the raisins in the kirsch, if using. If not, cover the raisins with tepid water and leave for 20 minutes. Drain.

Blend the yeast with half the warm milk, 1 teaspoon sugar and just enough of the flour to give the consistency of thin cream. Leave in a warm place for 20 minutes until frothy.

Sift the remaining flour into a bowl. Add the salt. Stir in the remaining sugar. Beat in the eggs and the rest of the milk. Knead in the softened butter and work the dough until it comes cleanly away from the sides of the bowl. Add the yeast mixture and beat for a few minutes. Cover with a damp cloth and leave in a warm place for 1 hour until well risen and doubled in size. Knead the dough on a lightly floured board and incorporate the raisins.

Butter a kugelhupf mold or 12-in (30-cm) ring mold. Scatter the almonds in the mold. Press the dough into the mold; it should only half fill it. Cover with a damp cloth again and leave in a warm place for 2 hours or until the dough has risen almost to the top of the pan.

Bake in an oven preheated to 325°F (160°C) for 45 minutes. If the top appears to be browning too quickly, cover it with aluminum foil. Leave the kugelhupf in the mold for at least 30 minutes before turning out. Dust liberally with sifted powdered sugar when cool. Serve within a day or two of baking. Kugelhupf is at its best when eaten fresh.

Apple Amber

Anzac Cookies

Makes 48: 8 tablespoons (4 oz) butter; 1 tablespoon light corn syrup; 1 teaspoon baking soda; 2 tablespoons boiling water; 1 cup (3 oz) rolled oats; 1 cup (3 oz) shredded coconut; 1 cup (4 oz) all purpose flour; 1 cup (8 oz) sugar

Melt the butter and syrup in a large saucepan over a low heat. Add the baking soda mixed with the boiling water.

Combine the dry ingredients in a mixing bowl and pour the melted mixture into the center. Mix to a moist but firm consistency, then drop teaspoons of the mixture onto cold greased baking sheets. Bake in an oven preheated to 300–325°F (150–160°C) for 20 minutes or until golden brown. Cool before removing to a wire rack.

Apple Amber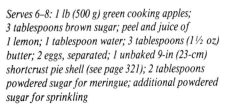

Serves 6–8: 1 lb (500 g) green cooking apples; 3 tablespoons brown sugar; peel and juice of 1 lemon; 1 tablespoon water; 3 tablespoons (1½ oz) butter; 2 eggs, separated; 1 unbaked 9-in (23-cm) shortcrust pie shell (see page 321); 2 tablespoons powdered sugar for meringue; additional powdered sugar for sprinkling

Peel, core and slice the apples. Put the apples, brown sugar, strips of lemon peel and water into a saucepan. Cover and cook gently until the apple is very soft. Remove the lemon peel and puree the apple in a food processor. Cut the butter into small pieces and add with the egg yolks and lemon juice to the hot puree. Blend well.

Roll out the pastry and use to line a deep 9-in (23-cm) pie dish. Crimp the edges or, using the cut-off scraps of pastry, decorate the edges with small circles of pastry placed overlapping all around the rim of the pie. Brush the pastry shell with a little lightly beaten egg white. Pour in the apple mixture.

Bake in an oven preheated to 350°F (180°C) for 30 minutes or until the pastry is crisp and golden.

Prepare the meringue topping in the meantime. Whisk the egg whites until stiff, then fold in the powdered sugar gently, using a large metal spoon. When the pastry is cooked and golden, remove the pie from the oven and increase the oven temperature to 375°F (190°C). Pile the meringue on top of the apple, taking the meringue to the edges of the pastry. Sprinkle with a little extra powdered sugar.

Bake for 15 minutes or until the meringue is golden. Serve warm or cold.

Apricot Crunchies

Makes 20–24: ½ cup lightly crushed cornflakes; 2 cups (8 oz) self-rising flour; ½ teaspoon salt; 3 tablespoons sugar; 2 tablespoons (1 oz) butter or margarine, melted; 1 egg, beaten; ½ cup (4 fl oz) milk ; ½ cup (2 oz) chopped dried apricots; additional 4 tablespoons (2 oz) butter or margarine, melted; 3 tablespoons brown sugar; ½ cup (2 oz) chopped nuts

Grease small muffin tins and lightly coat the insides with the cornflakes.

Sift the flour, salt and sugar into a bowl. Combine the melted butter, egg, milk and apricots and add to the flour mixture. Mix into a soft dough, then turn onto a lightly floured board, pat out to 1 in (2.5 cm) thick and cut into 20–24 pieces. Dip each piece in the extra melted butter, then toss in a mixture of the combined brown sugar and nuts. Place one piece into each muffin cup.

Bake in an oven preheated to 400°F (200°C) for 17–20 minutes. Turn out to cool on cake racks and eat while very fresh.

Apricot Nut Loaf ⭐

Makes one 8 × 4-in (20 × 10-cm) loaf cake: ½ cup (2 oz) chopped dried apricots; sweet sherry; 1 egg; 1 cup (8 oz) sugar; 6 tablespoons (3 oz) butter or margarine, melted; 2 cups (8 oz) all purpose flour; 1 tablespoon baking powder; ½ teaspoon baking soda; ¼ teaspoon salt; ½ cup (4 fl oz) orange juice; 1 cup (4 oz) chopped walnuts

Soak the dried apricots in sufficient sweet sherry to cover for 1 hour. Drain the apricots well and reserve ¼ cup of the liquid.

Beat the egg until frothy. Gradually add the sugar, beating until well mixed. Stir in the cooled butter. Sift the flour, baking powder, baking soda and salt over the egg–sugar mixture and fold through in alternate batches with the orange juice and reserved apricot liquid. Add the walnuts and fold in lightly. Turn into an 8 × 4-in (20 × 10-cm) loaf pan lined with greased waxed paper.

Bake in an oven preheated to 325°F (160°C) for 75–80 minutes. Remove from the oven and allow to stand for 5–6 minutes before turning out onto a cake rack to cool. Store in an airtight container for 1–2 days before cutting into slices.

Austrian Almond Torte

Makes one 8½ × 4½-in (21.5 × 11.5-cm) torte: 4 oz (125 g) unsweetened chocolate; 4 eggs, separated; scant ⅔ cup (4 oz) powdered sugar; 4 oz (125 g) ground almonds
Decoration: 2 oz (60 g) unsweetened chocolate; ⅔ cup (5 fl oz) cream; 2 teaspoons powdered sugar; vanilla; coarsely chopped toasted almonds

To make the cake, melt the chocolate over hot water, stirring occasionally, then cool. Beat the egg yolks with the powdered sugar until thick and creamy, then slowly beat in the chocolate.

Whisk the egg whites until stiff, then fold into the chocolate mixture. Sprinkle the ground almonds over the surface, a little at a time, folding in gently after each addition.

Pour into a loaf pan approximately 8½ × 4½ × 2¾ in (21.5 × 11.5 × 7 cm), lined with greased waxed paper. Bake in an oven preheated to 350–375°F (180–190°C) for about 45 minutes. Leave in the pan for a few minutes before turning the cake out. Cool on a wire rack.

To decorate the cake, melt the remaining chocolate over hot water; cool. Whip the cream until thickening, add the sugar and beat until thick. Stir in the vanilla to taste. Slowly and carefully stir in the chocolate (cream must be at room temperature before the chocolate is added). Chill well, and spread all over the cake. Top with the almonds.

Note: Bake the cake the day before it is to be cut.

B

Baklava

Makes 30 pieces: 16 tablespoons (8 oz) melted unsalted butter; 1 lb (500 g) walnuts, finely chopped; 8 oz (250 g) almonds, blanched and finely chopped; ¼ cup (2 oz) sugar; 2 teaspoons cinnamon; ¼ teaspoon ground cloves; 1 lb (500 g) filo pastry
Syrup: 1 scant cup (7 oz) sugar; 1 cup (12 oz) honey; 2 cups (16 fl oz) water; juice of 1 lemon; 2 whole cloves; 1 sliver of lemon peel

With a little of the melted butter, brush the inside of a 13 × 9 × 2-in (33 x 23 x 5-cm)

baking pan. In a bowl, mix together the nuts, sugar, cinnamon and cloves. Over the bottom of the pan, place 10 sheets of filo pastry, each sheet generously brushed with butter before the next is placed. Sprinkle the top sheet with some of the nut–sugar mixture. Place 2 buttered sheets of filo pastry on top and sprinkle with the nut mixture. Repeat this process until all the nut mixture is used up. There should be 15–20 layers. Trim along the edges and brush the top with the remaining butter. Score the top layer diagonally with parallel lines.

Bake in an oven preheated to 325°F (160°C) for 30 minutes. Move up to the top of the oven and bake for a further 30 minutes. If the top browns too quickly, cover with aluminum foil.

While the baklava is baking, prepare the syrup. Combine all ingredients, heat and stir to dissolve the sugar. Bring to the boil and boil briskly for 10 minutes. Strain, cool and pour half the syrup over the hot baklava. Let it stand for 30 minutes, then pour over the remainder of the syrup. Leave overnight before cutting.

Banana Cake

Makes one 8-in (20-cm) cake: 8 tablespoons (4 oz) butter; scant ¾ cup (5 oz) powdered sugar; 2 eggs; ¾ cup mashed banana (about 2 large bananas); ¼ cup (2 fl oz) milk, warmed; 1 teaspoon baking soda; 2 cups (8 oz) all purpose flour; 1 teaspoon baking powder; ⅛ teaspoon salt
Vienna Icing: 1¼ cups (8 oz) powdered sugar; 8 tablespoons (4 oz) butter; 1 tablespoon sugar; ½ tablespoon sherry; 4–5 drops vanilla

Cream the butter and sugar until light, white and fluffy, then add the beaten eggs gradually, beating well after each addition. Beat in the mashed banana. Combine the warm milk and baking soda and mix into the banana mixture. Sift the flour, baking powder and salt and stir into the banana mixture. Spread the mixture into a deep 8-in (20-cm) cake pan lined with greased waxed paper. Bake in an oven preheated to 350–375°F (180–190°C) for 40–45 minutes.

To make the icing, sift the powdered sugar, then cream the butter and half the sugar gradually, beating until creamy. Beat in the sherry alternately with the remaining sugar. Stir in the vanilla. When the cake is cool, coat the top and sides with the icing.

Clockwise from top: Date and Peanut Ragamuffins (see page 371), Apricot Crunchies, Spice and Sugar Swirls (see page 383), Nut Pumpkin Gems (see page 380)

Bavarian Apple Strudel

Makes 2–3 strudels: 2 cups (8 oz) all purpose flour; pinch of salt; 1–2 tablespoons oil or 1 tablespoon melted butter; 1 egg; approximately ½ cup (4 fl oz) lukewarm water; melted butter or oil for brushing the pastry; powdered sugar
Apple Filling: 1 cup (8 fl oz) sour cream; 3–4 lb (1.5–2 kg) apples; ¼–½ cup (2–4 oz) sugar, depending on the sweetness desired; ⅓ cup (2 oz) seedless raisins; ½ cup (2 oz) finely chopped hazelnuts or almonds; 3–4 tablespoons toasted breadcrumbs (optional)

Place the flour and salt into a mixing bowl and make a well in the center. Add the oil or butter, egg and water. Stir until the dough is soft and comes away from the sides of the bowl. Transfer the dough to a floured board and knead for approximately 15 minutes or until it is soft and pliable. Depending on the number of strudels to be made, divide the dough into 2–3 portions. With a pastry brush, lightly paint the pieces with oil so that they do not dry out. Cover the dough with the heated mixing bowl and allow it to stand for 30 minutes.

Place a large cloth on the pastry board and on top of this roll out one of the pieces of dough with a warm rolling pin, ensuring that the dough does not stick. Brush it frequently with some oil or melted butter. Using your hand, spread out the sheet of dough as thinly as possible. Try to shape the piece into a rectangular form so that it will be easier to roll into the strudel.

Spread the sour cream over the rolled-out dough leaving a 1-in (2.5-cm) margin of dough on each side. Peel and core the apples, cut them into slivers and arrange them on top of the sour cream. Sprinkle with the sugar, raisins and the hazelnuts or almonds. If the mixture is too liquid, the breadcrumbs may be used.

Roll the strudel into shape with the aid of the cloth, brushing the pastry with warm oil or melted butter. Place on a buttered baking dish, brush it with more oil or melted butter and bake in an oven preheated to 450°F (230°C) for 30–45 minutes. When the strudel is crisp and golden, let it stand for a few minutes. Sprinkle it with powdered sugar and serve it cut into 2-in (5-cm) slices.

Berlin Doughnuts

Makes 12–14: 1 oz (30 g) fresh yeast; 1 cup (8 fl oz) lukewarm milk; pinch of salt; 1 lb (500 g) all purpose flour; ⅓ cup (3 oz) sugar; 3 egg yolks; 6 tablespoons (3 oz) butter, melted; grated lemon peel; 2 tablespoons rum or kirsch; apricot or rosehip jelly for filling; egg-milk mix for sealing; oil for deep frying; powdered sugar mixed with cinnamon for dusting

In a large bowl, break up the yeast and gradually add the milk, dissolving the yeast. Add the salt and enough flour to work into a soft dough. Cover with a tea towel and let stand in a warm place for about 1 hour.

Add the sugar, egg yolks, butter, lemon peel, rum or kirsch and the remaining flour to the dough. Beat vigorously and then let the dough rise for a further 30 minutes. Beat the dough down, then roll it out on a floured board to a thickness of 1 in (2.5 cm).

Cut the dough into rounds with a 3-in (7.5-cm) cookie cutter. Place a teaspoon of jelly on one round, brush the edges with an egg-milk wash and place a second round on top. Press to seal. Pierce a small hole over the jam. Place the doughnuts on a floured board, cover them with a slightly heated tea towel and let them stand until they increase in size by half.

Preheat 2 in (5 cm) oil to 375°F (190°C). With a large spoon, carefully place some of the doughnuts (top down) into the oil. Cover and cook for 2–4 minutes, then remove the lid. Check that the underside is nice and brown, then turn the doughnuts. Deep-frying time should be 6–8 minutes. Carefully remove the doughnuts with a slotted spoon and place them next to each other on paper towels. Repeat this procedure until all the doughnuts are cooked. When they have cooled, sprinkle them with cinnamon sugar and serve.

Black Forest Cherry Cake

Black Forest Cherry Cake

Makes one 9–10-in (23–25-cm) cake: 8 tablespoons (4 oz) butter; ½ cup (4 oz) sugar; 6 egg yolks; few drops vanilla; 4 oz (125 g) unsweetened chocolate, grated; 1¼ cups (4 oz) ground almonds; 1 cup (4 oz) self-rising flour; 6 egg whites, beaten stiffly; ¼ cup (2 fl oz) kirsch; ¼ cup (2 fl oz) cherry syrup from preserved cherries
Filling and Topping: 3 cups (24 fl oz) heavy cream; ¼–⅓ cup (2–3 oz) powdered sugar; 3 tablespoons kirsch; 1½ lb (750 g) pitted preserved sour cherries, chopped; 8 oz (250 g) unsweetened chocolate curls; fresh cherries with stems, drained and rinsed

Cream the butter and gradually add the sugar (reserve 1–2 tablespoons for the egg whites) and egg yolks. The mixture should be light and frothy. Gradually mix in the vanilla, chocolate, almonds and flour. Finally, fold in the egg whites, beaten with the reserved sugar. Pour the mixture into a buttered and floured springform pan and bake in an oven preheated to 350°F (180°C) for 45–60 minutes. Cool for a few minutes, then remove the cake from the pan.

When cold, cut the cake horizontally in three slices. Mix the kirsch and cherry syrup and sprinkle the slices with the mixture.

For the filling and topping, whip the cream with the sugar and kirsch. Fold in the cherries. Spread each layer with the whipped cream mixture and put them together. Spread the top and sides with the remaining cream. Sprinkle the side with the chocolate curls and decorate the top with the cherries.

Blue Ribbon Sponge Sandwich

Makes two 7-in (18-cm) sponges: 3 eggs; ½ cup (4 oz) powdered sugar; 1 cup (4 oz) all purpose flour; 1 tablespoon cornstarch; 2 teaspoons baking powder; ¼ teaspoon salt; 2 teaspoons butter or margarine; ¼ cup (2 fl oz) very hot water; ½ teaspoon vanilla

Separate the eggs and place the whites in a clean, dry glass bowl. Beat with an electric beater, hand beater or whisk to stiff white foam. Add the powdered sugar 1 tablespoon at a time and beat well after each addition — the sugar must be completely dissolved. Fold in the egg yolks lightly and gently.

Sift the flour with the cornstarch, baking powder and salt twice, then sift this again over the egg mixture. Don't mix it in yet.

Melt the butter in the hot water, add the vanilla extract and carefully pour down the side of the bowl into the egg mixture. Now, using a rubber spatula and with a gentle folding motion, mix the dry ingredients and the liquid through the eggs and sugar. Pour the mixture gently into two greased and floured deep 7-in (18-cm) layer cake pans. Be careful to avoid knocking or banging either the bowl or the pans. Spread lightly to even the surface.

Bake in an oven preheated to 350°F (180°C) for 22–25 minutes, preferably both pans on the same oven shelf so that both sponges will be evenly cooked and browned. Remove from the oven and allow to stand for 1 minute away from drafts, then turn carefully onto a fine mesh cake rack or a tea towel over a cake rack to cool.

Topping and Filling Variations:
Plain Sponge: Fill with raspberry jam and dust the top with sifted powdered sugar.
Cream Sponge: Fill with fresh whipped cream and dust the top with powdered sugar.
Strawberry Sponge: Fill and top with fresh whipped cream and decorate the top with whole or sliced strawberries.

Blue Ribbon Sponge Sandwich

Brazil Nut Stars ★

Makes 40 cookies: 2 large eggs, well beaten; 2 cups (10 oz) brown sugar, firmly packed; 1½ teaspoons vanilla; 1¾ cups (7 oz) all purpose flour; ½ teaspoon baking powder; 1 lb (500 g) Brazil nuts, finely chopped; powdered sugar for dusting

To the well-beaten eggs, add the sugar and vanilla and whisk until light and foamy.

In a separate bowl, sift the flour and baking powder together, then mix in the nuts. Combine the two mixtures, mixing well to form a dough. Cover the bowl and refrigerate for several hours.

Roll out the dough between two sheets of waxed paper. Remove the paper and cut out fancy shapes such as stars. Arrange on greased baking sheets.

Bake in an oven preheated to 350°F (180°C) for 12–15 minutes or until they are lightly browned. Turn onto wire racks to cool, then dust with powdered sugar.

Brownies

Makes 16 brownies: 2 oz (60 g) unsweetened chocolate; 8 tablespoons (4 oz) butter; 1 cup (8 oz) sugar; 2 eggs, well beaten; 1 cup all purpose flour, sifted; 2 teaspoons vanilla; 1 cup (4 oz) finely chopped pecans

In a double boiler, melt the chocolate and butter with the sugar. Pour this gradually onto the well-beaten eggs, beating after each addition. Add the flour and vanilla, mixing well. Spread into a greased and floured, square cake pan and sprinkle the top with the nuts.

Bake in an oven preheated to 350°F (180°C) for 20–25 minutes. Cut into squares and allow to cool on wire racks.

C

California Orange Cake

Makes one 9-in (23-cm) cake: 8 tablespoons (4 oz) butter or margarine, softened; 1 cup (8 oz) sugar; 1 egg, beaten; ½ teaspoon vanilla; 2 cups all purpose flour; 1 teaspoon baking powder; 1 teaspoon baking soda; ¼ teaspoon salt; 1 teaspoon cinnamon; 1 cup (8 fl oz) sour milk; 1 large orange; 1 cup (4 oz)

Brazil Nut Stars and Cinnamon Shapes (see page 370)

chopped walnuts or pecans; 1 cup seedless raisins; ½–¾ cup (1½–2 oz) shredded coconut for topping

Cream the butter and sugar. Add the egg and vanilla and beat well.

Sift the dry ingredients together, then sift again over the creamed mixture and fold in alternately with the sour milk.

Peel the orange, removing as much of the white membrane as possible. Chop very finely and mix in a bowl with the chopped nuts and raisins. With a slotted spoon, spoon out one-quarter to one-third of this mixture and lightly fold it into the cake mixture. To the remaining orange–nuts–raisins mixture, add the coconut and set aside until after baking.

Spoon the cake mixture into a well-greased 9-in (23-cm) square cake pan and bake in an oven preheated to 350°F (180°C) for 40–45 minutes. Remove from the oven and allow to stand for 5 minutes.

Preheat the broiler. Carefully spread the reserved orange–nuts–raisins mixture over the top of the cake and toast lightly under the broiler. Remove from the heat and allow to stand for another 5 minutes, then carefully turn out on to a cake rack that has been covered with waxed paper. Invert the cake to top side and allow to cool.

Caramel Layer Cake ★

Makes two 8-in (20-cm) layers: 1½ cups (12 oz) powdered sugar; ½ cup (4 fl oz) hot black coffee — plus water, as required; 2 cups (8 oz) all purpose flour; 1 tablespoon baking powder; ½ teaspoon salt; 8 tablespoons (4 oz) butter or margarine, softened; 2 eggs, beaten
Caramel Frosting: 2 tablespoons sugar; 6 tablespoons (3 oz) butter or margarine; 6 tablespoons (3 oz) evaporated or rich milk; 1 teaspoon vanilla; 3 cups (15 oz) powdered sugar, sifted
Mock Cream Filling (see page 369)

Spoon ¼ cup of the sugar into a small heavy-based saucepan and dissolve over low heat without stirring. Allow to boil to a rich brown caramel (smoke will appear). Remove from the heat and slowly but very carefully add the hot coffee, stirring until all lumps dissolve. Return to low heat if the mixture cools before the lumps dissolve. Let the liquid cool, then pour into a measuring cup and add enough water to make 14 tablespoons (7 fl oz).

Sift the flour, baking powder and salt together twice and set aside.

Beat the butter with the remaining 1¼ cups powdered sugar until creamy. Add the beaten eggs and beat thoroughly, then beat in about half of the caramel liquid. Fold in the sifted flour alternately with the remaining caramel liquid, mixing lightly to combine. Spoon into two 8-in (20-cm) greased and waxed-paper-lined cake pans.

Bake in an oven preheated to 350°F (180°C) for 25–35 minutes, until springy to the touch. Remove from the oven and let stand for 1–2 minutes before turning out onto fine mesh cake racks to cool.

To make the caramel frosting, place the sugar in a small heavy-based saucepan and heat to form a caramel (as for the cake mixture, above).

Heat the butter and milk until just beginning to boil, then carefully stir into the caramel until the lumps dissolve (as above). Add the vanilla. Pour into a heatproof bowl and let cool. Gradually add the powdered sugar. Beat until the mixture obtains a creamy spreading consistency. Spread over the top and sides of the cooled cake.

Chocolate Fudge Bars

Makes 24: 8 tablespoons (4 oz) butter; ½ cup (4 oz) sugar; 1 egg; 1 teaspoon vanilla; ¼ cup cocoa powder; 1 cup (4 oz) chopped walnuts; 2 tablespoons corn syrup; ½ lb (225 g) graham crackers

Melt the butter in a saucepan, add the sugar, and bring to a boil. Add the well-beaten egg and mix well, then add the vanilla, cocoa powder, walnuts, corn syrup and crackers, broken into small pieces. Mix well and press into a greased jelly roll pan. Frost with chocolate frosting and cut into bars when cold.

Chocolate Fudge Cake

Makes two 9-in (23-cm) layers: 3 oz (75 g) unsweetened chocolate, chopped; 12 tablespoons (6 oz) butter or margarine, softened; 1½ cups (7½ oz) brown sugar; 1 teaspoon vanilla; 3 eggs; 1 cup (8 fl oz) sour cream; 2 tablespoons cocoa; ½ cup (4 fl oz) hot water; 1 tablespoon plum jelly; 2½ cups (10 oz) self-rising flour; 2½ cups (20 fl oz) cream, whipped; Chocolate Caraque (see below)

Melt the chocolate in a bowl over hot — not boiling — water. Allow to cool.

Beat the butter, brown sugar and vanilla until very creamy. Add the eggs one at a time, beating well after each addition, then beat in the sour cream.

Blend the cocoa with the hot water and plum jelly, and add to the butter cream with the melted chocolate. Beat well to combine. Sift the flour over the top and fold in lightly but thoroughly — do not overmix. Spoon into two greased and waxed-paper-lined 9-in (23-cm) pans.

Bake in an oven preheated to 350°F (180°C) for 30–35 minutes before turning out onto cake racks to cool.

Meanwhile, to make the chocolate caraque, melt 3½ oz (80 g) semisweet chocolate over a pan of simmering water. Leave to cool and thicken, then melt again. Spread it very thinly over a marble slab, a laminated countertop, or the back of a flat baking sheet. Leave until just beginning to harden, then, using a sharp flexible knife, curl off splinters of chocolate.

When cold, fill the cake with whipped cream, sandwich together and cover the top and sides with whipped cream, sweetened if desired with a little sugar. Decorate with the chocolate caraque and rosettes of whipped cream and allow to firm before slicing.

Chocolate Praline Pie

Serves 4–6: 6 oz (175 g) Pâte Sucrée (see page 338)
Filling: 3 tablespoons cocoa; ⅓ cup (3 oz) sugar; 2 cups (16 fl oz) water; 1 tablespoon all purpose flour; ¼ cup cornstarch; ½ cup (4 fl oz) milk; 2 egg yolks, lightly beaten; 4 tablespoons (2 oz) butter
Topping: ½ cup (4 fl oz) cream; 1 teaspoon powdered sugar; drops of vanilla
Praline: ⅓ cup whole unblanched almonds; ¼ cup (2 oz) sugar

Roll out the pastry on a lightly floured surface and use to line an 8-in (20-cm) pie plate.

Bake blind in an oven preheated to 375°F (190°C) for 7 minutes. Remove the blind filling and bake for another 15 minutes or until the pastry is crisp and evenly golden. (Do not bake the pastry too dark or it will be bitter.)

To make the filling, place the cocoa and sugar into a saucepan and mix in the water. Bring to a boil and simmer for 10 minutes. Mix the flour and cornstarch with the milk until it forms a smooth paste and add to the chocolate mixture, stirring over the heat until the mixture boils. Pour a little of the hot mixture over the egg yolks, mix in and then pour this into the saucepan. Stir-

Chocolate Praline Pie

367

Cider Honey Cake (see page 370)

ring constantly, gradually add the butter until the butter has melted and the mixture is smooth. Allow it to cool a little and pour into the prepared pie shell. Chill.

Meanwhile, make the topping. Whip the cream with the sugar until it holds its shape, flavoring with a couple of drops of vanilla. Spread over the chilled pie and sprinkle with 3 tablespoons ground praline.

For the praline, place the almonds and sugar into a small heavy-based saucepan. Cook over a very low heat until the sugar begins to caramelize and the nuts begin to toast. Tip the pan from side to side to coat the nuts in the liquid caramel, or use a metal spoon just to prod the nuts into the caramel. Do not stir. When a deep caramel, pour into a greased baking pan. When it is set, crush and store immediately in an airtight jar until ready to use.

Chocolate Prune Cake

Makes one 8 × 6-in (20 × 15-cm) cake: 1 cup whole prunes; 8 tablespoons (4 oz) butter; 1 cup (5 oz) brown sugar; 2 eggs; 2 cups (8 oz) self-rising flour; ½ cup cocoa; ½ teaspoon ground cloves; ½ cup (4 fl oz) prune cooking water

Gently simmer the prunes in 2 cups water for 8 minutes. Cook and drain, saving the liquid. Remove the pits.

Cream the butter and sugar. Add the eggs and beat until well mixed. Sift in the flour, cocoa and ground cloves. Add the prunes and stir in, adding ½ cup of the prune cooking liquid. Pour into a greased 8 × 6-in (20 × 15-cm) pan.

Bake in an oven preheated to 350°F (180°C) for 40 minutes. Allow to cool in the pan. The cake can later be iced with a chocolate icing.

Chocolate Roll

Makes one 12 × 10-in (30 × 35-cm) roll: 2 eggs; butter, sugar and all purpose flour (each to equal the weight of the 2 eggs); 1 teaspoon baking powder; 1 tablespoon cocoa; 1 teaspoon vanilla; 2 tablespoons warm water; sugar and cocoa for rolling and topping
Mock Cream Filling: 1¼ cups (10 fl oz) milk; 2 tablespoons cornstarch; 4 tablespoons (2 oz) butter or margarine; 1 teaspoon vanilla; 2 tablespoons powdered sugar

Separate the eggs. Cream the butter and sugar, add the egg yolks and beat well.

Sift the flour, baking powder and cocoa three times, add to the creamed mixture and fold in. Add the combined vanilla and warm water and fold this in also.

Whisk the egg whites to soft peaks and fold very gently into the cake mixture — do not overmix. Turn into a greased and waxed-paper-lined 12 × 10-in (30 × 25-cm) jelly roll pan. Bake in an oven preheated to 400°F (200°C) 17–20 minutes.

Soak a clean cloth in boiling water, wring it out, and lay it on the work surface. Cover it with waxed paper, then sprinkle sugar over the surface of the paper. Turn the chocolate roll out of the pan and onto the paper and peel away the lining. Carefully roll the cake in the paper, cover it loosely with the hot cloth and allow to cool.

To make the mock cream, blend 3 tablespoons milk with the cornstarch. Heat the remaining milk in a small nonstick saucepan until boiling. Gradually whisk in the cornstarch mixture, whisking until smooth. Lower the heat and simmer for 1–2 minutes, then leave to cool.

Beat the butter, vanilla and sugar until creamy. Gradually add the milk mixture, beating well after each addition.

When cold, unroll the roll and discard the paper. Spread with the mock cream filling, reroll and dust with the combined sugar and cocoa.

Note: To make chocolate mock cream filling, beat 2 tablespoons grated chocolate into the hot milk before cooling.

Chocomallows

Makes 16–18 cakes: 6 tablespoons (3 oz) butter or margarine, softened; ⅓ cup (3 oz) powdered sugar; 2 eggs, beaten; 1½ cups (6 oz) self-rising flour; 2 tablespoons cocoa; ¼ teaspoon salt; ½ teaspoon cinnamon; 2 tablespoons evaporated milk; 2 teaspoons lemon juice
Chocolate Glacé Icing: 1½ cups (7½ oz) powdered sugar; 1–2 tablespoons cocoa; 1 tablespoon butter or margarine; 1–2 tablespoons boiling water
Marshmallow: 1 cup (8 fl oz) orange juice; 1 cup (8 oz) sugar; ¼ teaspoon cream of tartar; 1 tablespoon unflavored gelatin; 2 teaspoons lemon juice; about 1 cup (2½ oz) shredded coconut

Preheat the oven to 400°F (200°C) and heat small muffin cups in the oven.

Beat the butter and sugar until light and fluffy. Add the eggs and beat well. In a sep-

arate bowl, sift the flour, cocoa, salt and cinnamon together. Combine the evaporated milk and lemon juice in a small bowl and set aside for 5 minutes.

Fold the dry ingredients into the butter mixture in alternate amounts with the soured milk.

Quickly grease the well-heated muffin cups and fill two-thirds full with the cake mixture. Bake for 14–16 minutes. Turn out onto the cake racks and let cool.

To make the icing, sift the sugar and cocoa into a bowl and make a well in the center. Melt the butter in about 1½ tablespoons of the boiling water. Add this to the sugar and stir to a smooth consistency, adding the remaining water if necessary. Pour at once onto the cold cakes and smooth with a broad knife or spatula. Allow to set before cutting.

To make the marshmallow, combine the orange juice, sugar, cream of tartar and gelatin in a small heavy-based saucepan, bring slowly to a boil, then allow to boil for 10 minutes. Remove from the heat and allow to cool. Turn into a large bowl and add the lemon juice. When the mixture is about the consistency of unbeaten egg whites, beat with an electric mixer or rotary whisk until the mixture has thickened and increased in volume.

Quickly fill clean, wetted muffin cups and chill until set. Unmold and coat the rounded surface with the coconut, leaving the level tops uncoated.

Place the uncoated side of each marshmallow on top of each chocolate cake.

Chorley Cakes

Makes 4 cakes: double quantity shortcrust pastry (see page 319); ¾ cup (4 oz) currants; powdered sugar

Roll the pastry out ¼ in (6 mm) thick and cut into 4 rounds the size of a dinner plate. Place the currants in the center of the circles, moisten the edges of the pastry with water and bring the edges together in the center, pressing to seal well.

Roll out the cakes until the currants show through, keeping to the round shape.

Place the rounds on baking sheets and bake in an oven preheated to 350°F (180°C) for 30 minutes. When cool, sprinkle with powdered sugar.

Cider Honey Cake

Makes one 9 × 4½-in (23 × 12-cm) cake: 1 cup (4 oz) all purpose flour; 1 cup (4 oz) whole-wheat flour; 1 teaspoon mixed spices (cinnamon, nutmeg, allspice); ¼ teaspoon salt; ¼ teaspoon ground ginger; ½ cup (2 oz) seedless raisins; 2 tablespoons chopped mixed peel; ¼ cup (1½ oz) brown sugar; 8 tablespoons (4 oz) butter or margarine, melted; ⅔ cup (6½ oz) honey; 1 teaspoon baking soda; ⅔ cup (5 fl oz) sparkling cider; 1 egg, beaten

Sift the flours with the spices, salt and ground ginger, returning the whole-grain pieces from the sieve. Combine with the raisins, peel and brown sugar in a bowl, making a well in the center. Pour in the melted butter and honey.

Dissolve the baking soda in the cider and quickly add this and the beaten egg to the bowl. Beat all the ingredients together with a flat egg whisk until mixed thoroughly. Turn into a 9 × 4½-in (23 × 12-cm) loaf pan lined with greased waxed paper.

Bake in an oven preheated to 325°F (160°C) for 55–60 minutes. Remove from the oven and allow to stand for 5–6 minutes before carefully turning out onto a cake rack. When cold, store in an airtight container for 1–2 days before slicing. Spread slices with honey and lemon-flavored butter, if desired.

Cinnamon Shapes ★

Makes 30 cookies: 6 egg whites; pinch of salt; 2½ cups (20 oz) powdered sugar; finely grated peel of 1 lemon; 1 teaspoon cinnamon; 1 lb (500 g) ground almonds

Beat the egg whites and salt until stiff. Gradually add the sugar and continue beating until stiff peaks form. Beat in the lemon peel, then reserve a quarter of the mixture for covering the shapes.

To the larger quantity of mixture, add the cinnamon and ground almonds, mixing well. Sprinkle the work surface with a little additional powdered sugar to minimize sticking and roll the mixture out thinly. Cut into shapes with cookie cutters and spread a small amount of the reserved mixture on the top of each shape. Arrange on well-greased baking sheets.

Bake in an oven preheated to 350°F (180°C) for about 20 minutes or until light brown. Turn onto wire racks to cool.

Cream Horns and Matchsticks (see page 379)

Cream Horns 🇮🇹

Makes 12 pastries: Rough Puff Pastry: 6 tablespoons (3 oz) butter or firm margarine; 6 tablespoons (3 oz) lard; 2 cups (8 oz) all purpose flour; pinch of salt; 3 tablespoons cold water 1 egg white, beaten; ¾ cup (6 fl oz) cream; 2 teaspoons powdered sugar; vanilla; strawberry jelly; pistachio nuts, finely chopped

To make the pastry, mix the butter and lard together on an enamel plate with a round-bladed knife until well blended, then chill until firm.

Sift the flour and salt into a large mixing bowl or into the large bowl of an electric mixer. Cut the fat into even-size pieces the size of a walnut and drop them into the flour, tossing each piece well to coat it. Add the cold water and, using a round-bladed knife, a dough hook, or a pastry blender, mix at low speed for 15 seconds or until a dough forms.

Turn the dough onto a lightly floured board and roll out to an oblong about 10 × 6 in (25 × 15 cm). Fold into thirds and make a half turn so that an open end faces you. Repeat rolling, folding and turning twice more, turning alternately to the right, then to the left. Refrigerate the dough at any stage when it becomes too soft and greasy to handle. Wrap in waxed paper and refrigerate for at least 30 minutes before use.

Roll out the pastry to ¼ in (5 mm) thick, cut into strips 1 in (2.5 cm) long and brush lightly with beaten egg white. Wind the pastry around 12 greased cream horn molds, starting at the point and overlapping each round. Trim the tops, brush again with the egg white and put onto a greased baking sheet.

Bake in an oven preheated to 475°F (240°C) for 7–8 minutes, until crisp and golden brown. Remove the horns.

Whip the cream with the sugar and a few drops of vanilla. When the horns are cold, place ½ teaspoon jam at the bottom of each horn and fill with the whipped cream. Decorate each horn with a sprinkle of pistachio nuts.

Note: The pastry dough stores well for a few days in waxed paper inside a plastic bag in the refrigerator. It also freezes well.

Crumble-Top Coffee Cake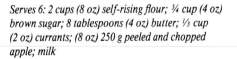

Makes one 8-in (20-cm) cake: 1 egg; ½ cup (4 oz) sugar; ⅓ cup (2½ fl oz) corn oil; 1 teaspoon vanilla; 1½ cups (6 oz) all purpose flour; 1 tablespoon baking powder; ¼ teaspoon salt; ½ cup quick-cooking oats, finely crushed; ½ teaspoon pumpkin pie spice, optional; 1 cup (4 oz) seedless raisins
Topping: ⅓ cup (1½ oz) brown sugar; ½ cup (2 oz) self-rising flour; 1 teaspoon pumpkin pie spice; 4 tablespoons (2 oz) butter or margarine, melted and cooled

Combine the egg, sugar, corn oil and vanilla in a bowl and beat briskly for 2–3 minutes. Sift the flour, baking powder, salt, crushed oats and spice over the egg–oil mixture (including the residue oats from the sifter) and fold in lightly. Do not overmix. Turn into a well-greased 8-in (20-cm) square cake pan and scatter the raisins evenly over the top.

Combine all the topping ingredients and press through the holes of a colander or coarse strainer over the top of the cake mixture.

Bake in an oven preheated to 375°F (190°C) for 15 minutes, then reduce the

oven temperature to 350°F (180°C) and bake for another 30–35 minutes. Remove from the oven and allow to stand for 3–4 minutes before turning out carefully onto a cake rack to cool.

D

Date and Peanut Ragamuffins ★

Makes 10–12 muffins: 4 tablespoons (2 oz) butter or margarine, softened; ¼ cup (2 oz) sugar; 1 egg; 1 cup (4 oz) self-rising flour; ½ cup (2 oz) chopped dates; 2 tablespoons chopped salted peanuts; 1½ tablespoons orange juice; ½ teaspoon baking soda; 1 tablespoon boiling water

Beat the butter and sugar until creamy. Add the egg and mix thoroughly, then fold in the sifted flour.

Combine the dates, peanuts and orange juice in a bowl, and mix well to separate the dates. Add to the butter mixture and fold in.

Dissolve the baking soda in the boiling water. Quickly sprinkle over the mixture and mix in lightly but thoroughly. Spoon the mixture into greased deep muffin tins, filling them two-thirds full.

Bake in an oven preheated to 375°F (190°C) for 17–20 minutes. Turn out onto cake racks to cool and serve while very fresh.

Devonshire Apple Cake 🇬🇧

Serves 6: 2 cups (8 oz) self-rising flour; ¾ cup (4 oz) brown sugar; 8 tablespoons (4 oz) butter; ⅓ cup (2 oz) currants; (8 oz) 250 g peeled and chopped apple; milk

Put the flour and sugar into a bowl and rub the butter in with your fingertips. Add the currants and apple and if the mixture is too dry, add a little milk. Grease an 8-in (20-cm) cake pan and press the mixture in well.

Bake in an oven preheated to 425°F (220°C) for 10 minutes, then reduce the temperature to 275°F (140°C) and bake for 1 hour more. Sprinkle with a little extra brown sugar before serving.

F

Frosted Banana-Cream Cake 🇺🇸

Makes: one 11 × 7-in (28 × 18-cm) cake: 8 tablespoons (4 oz) butter or margarine, softened; 1 cup (8 oz) sugar; 1 teaspoon vanilla; ½ teaspoon cinnamon or nutmeg; 2 eggs, beaten; 1 cup (8 oz) mashed ripe banana; ¼ cup (2 fl oz) milk; 2 cups (8 oz) all purpose flour; 1½ teaspoons baking powder; 1 teaspoon baking soda; ¼ teaspoon salt; ¼ cup (1 oz) chopped walnuts
Cinnamon Cream Frosting: 1 cup (8 fl oz) sour cream; ¼ cup (1¼ oz) brown sugar; ½ to 1 teaspoon cinnamon or nutmeg

Beat the butter, sugar, vanilla extract and cinnamon (or nutmeg) until light and fluffy. Add the eggs, then the mashed banana and milk, beating well after each addition.

Sift the dry ingredients together, then sift over the butter–banana mixture and fold in. Add the walnuts and mix through. Turn into a waxed-paper-lined and greased 11 × 7-in (28 × 18-cm) pan.

Bake in an oven preheated to 350°F (180°C) for 35–40 minutes. Remove from the oven and allow to stand for 5–6 minutes before turning out onto a cake rack to cool.

Combine all the ingredients for the frosting, beating well. Spread over the cake and allow to firm before slicing.

Fruit Tarts

Makes 12 tarts: 1 quantity shortcrust pastry (see page 319)
Vanilla Pastry Cream: 1 cup (8 fl oz) milk; 1 vanilla bean, split lengthwise; 3 large egg yolks; ⅓ cup (2½ oz) sugar; 2 tablespoons flour or cornstarch; 2 teaspoons brandy or liqueur (optional); assorted fresh fruit, such as sliced apricots, sliced banana dipped in lemon juice, blueberries, blackcurrants, blackberries, pitted cherries, sliced kiwi fruit, skinned seedless grapes, ripe gooseberries, melon balls, mandarin orange segments, sliced plums or peaches, raspberries, redcurrants, sliced strawberries; ½ cup apricot jelly; 1 tablespoon water, brandy, liqueur or orange juice

Roll the pastry out thinly on a lightly floured surface to a rectangle. Arrange twelve 3-in (7.5-cm) tart tins close together in rows, three by four. Drape the pastry loosely over the tins, allowing it to fall generously into each one. Press the dough in with the fingers to fit the tins. Roll over the top edge of the tins with the rolling pin to cut off the excess pastry. Press the pastry firmly into each tin with the tops of bent fingers, shaping to an even thickness around the sides. Prick the base of each pastry case with a fine fork, then chill for 20–30 minutes.

Line the pastry cases with waxed paper and baking beans or identical tins. Bake blind in an oven preheated to 400°F (200°C) for 10 minutes, then remove the paper and beans and bake for another 5 minutes or until golden and crisp. Allow to cool on wire racks.

To make the pastry cream, bring the milk and vanilla bean to the boil, cover and keep hot. Whisk the egg yolks and sugar together until thick and falling in a ribbon shape from the whisk. Stir in the flour with a whisk.

Strain the hot milk into the mixture, whisking continuously. Return the mixture to the saucepan and bring to the boil, stirring continuously. Boil for 1 minute to thicken, stirring vigorously. Pour into a bowl and rub the surface with butter to prevent a skin forming while cooling.

Mix the vanilla pastry cream with the brandy. Prepare the fruit accordingly. Heat the jelly, then strain and stir in the water.

To finish the tarts, brush each pastry case with the apricot glaze. Place 1 tablespoon of the pastry cream into each pastry case and top neatly with an attractive arrangement of prepared fresh fruit. Brush the fruit carefully with apricot glaze, making sure that the glaze seals to the edge of the pastry. Serve for afternoon tea or with whipped cream for dessert.

G
Gâteau de Pithiviers Feuilleté

Serves 6–8: Puff Pastry: 24 tablespoons (12 oz) unsalted butter; 3 cups (12 oz) flour; pinch of salt, optional; 1½ teaspoons lemon juice; cold water to mix
Filling: 8 tablespoons (4 oz) butter; ⅓ cup (2½ oz) powdered sugar; 1 whole egg; 1 egg yolk; 1¼ cups (5 oz) ground almonds; 2 teaspoons all purpose flour; 1 teaspoon vanilla; beaten egg for glazing; extra sugar for glazing

To make the pastry, shape the butter into a flat square ¼ in (5 mm) thick and press it between two pieces of cheesecloth to absorb excess moisture. Place it in the refrigerator until cool and firm.

Sift the flour and salt, if used, into a large mixing bowl or the bowl of an electric mixer. Using a round-bladed knife, a dough hook or a pastry blender, mix in the lemon juice and sufficient cold water, at low speed, to form an elastic dough.

Alternatively, mix the flour, lemon juice, and sufficient cold water together in a food processor to form a dough.

Turn the dough onto a floured pastry board or marble slab and knead lightly until it is smooth and elastic and not sticky.

Roll the dough out on a lightly floured surface to a rectangle twice as big as the

butter square. Place the butter on the top half of the dough and fold the bottom half over. Roll it out evenly to a long strip, taking care that the butter does not break through. Fold the strip of pastry into thirds — folding the bottom third up and top third down. Allow to cool in the refrigerator for 10–15 minutes.

Place the pastry on the rolling surface with the folded edge to the right. Roll and fold into thirds twice, placing the folded edge alternately to the left, then return to the refrigerator to cool.

Repeat the rolling and folding processes until the pastry has had seven rolls and folds, chilling whenever necessary. Wrap the dough in waxed paper and chill well before use.

Cream the butter and sugar until pale

Gâteau de Pithiviers Feuilleté

Fruit Tarts

and creamy. Beat in the egg and egg yolk. Stir in the ground almonds, flour and vanilla.

Roll out half the pastry on a lightly floured surface into a round 11 in (28 cm) across. Using a saucepan lid, cut a circle 10 in (25 cm) across, angling the knife away from the lid slightly. Roll out the remaining pastry slightly thicker than for the first and cut into a 10-in (25-cm) round. Place the thinner of the circles onto a baking sheet and mound the filling in the center, leaving a 1-in (2.5-cm) border.

Brush the pastry edge with water and place the second round over the filling. Press the edges together firmly. Scallop the edge of the pie with the back of a knife, pulling it in at intervals. Brush the pie with beaten-egg glaze and, working from the center, score the top in curves like the petals of a flower. Chill for 15 minutes.

Bake in an oven preheated to 425°F (220°C) for 30–35 minutes or until firm and puffed. Sprinkle the top with powdered sugar and place the pie under a hot broiler until the sugar has caramelized and the surface is shiny. Allow to cool on a wire rack.

Note: The pastry dough can be stored overnight in waxed paper inside a plastic bag in the refrigerator. It also freezes well.

Gingerbread

Makes one 8-in (20-cm) cake: 4 cups (1 lb) all purpose flour; 1 tablespoon ground ginger; 1 tablespoon baking powder; 1 teaspoon baking soda; 1 teaspoon salt; 1½ cups (7½ oz) brown sugar; 12 tablespoons (6 oz) butter; ½ cup (5 oz) molasses; ½ cup (5 oz) light corn syrup; 2½ cups (20 fl oz) milk; 1 large egg, beaten

Sift the dry ingredients, except the sugar, into a large bowl.

Warm the sugar, butter, molasses and syrup in a saucepan over low heat until the butter has just melted. Stir this into the dry mixture, together with the milk and beaten egg. Beat thoroughly and pour into a waxed-paper-lined and greased deep 8-in (20-cm) aluminum cake pan.

Bake in the center of an oven preheated to 350°F (180°C) for 1½ hours. Remove from the oven and allow to cool in the pan for 15 minutes, then turn out onto a wire rack. When cold, wrap in aluminum foil without removing the paper. Store for 4–5 days before cutting into squares.

Ginger Coffee Cake ★

Serves 6–8: 6 tablespoons (3 oz) butter or margarine; scant ⅔ cup (4 oz) powdered sugar; 1 large egg; 2 cups (8 oz) self-rising flour; ¼ teaspoon salt; 1 cup (8 fl oz) dry ginger ale; 3 tablespoons (2 oz) seedless raisins; 2 oz (60 g) chopped mixed glacé fruit
Topping: 3 tablespoons (1½ oz) all purpose flour; 2 scant tablespoons (2 oz) brown sugar; 2 tablespoons (1 oz) butter; ¼ teaspoon ground ginger

Beat the butter and sugar until creamy. Add the beaten egg, then the sifted flour and salt alternately with the ginger ale. Lastly add the raisins and glacé fruit and mix well.

Spoon the batter into a 9-in (23-cm) square pan lined with greased waxed paper. Mix the topping ingredients to a crumbly consistency and sprinkle over the batter. Bake in an oven preheated to 350°–375°F (160°–180°C) for 40–45 minutes. Leave in the pan for a few minutes before turning out onto a paper-covered cooling rack, then inverting so that the crumbly topping is uppermost. Serve cut in slices.

Ginger Crunch ★

Makes 24: 8 tablespoons (4 oz) butter; scant ⅔ cup (4 oz) powdered sugar; 1¾ cups (7 oz) all purpose flour; 1 teaspoon baking powder; 1 teaspoon ground ginger
Icing: 2 tablespoons (1 oz) butter; ¼ cup powdered sugar; 2 teaspoons light corn syrup; 1 teaspoon ground ginger

Cream the butter and sugar in a mixing bowl and add the sifted dry ingredients. Mix well and press into a greased 8-in (20-cm) pan. Bake in an oven preheated to 350°–375°F (180°–190°C) for 20–25 minutes.

To make the icing, mix the butter, powdered sugar, corn syrup and ground ginger in a saucepan. Heat over low heat until melted, then pour over base while hot. Cut into slices while still warm.

Golden Ginger Gems ★

Makes 16–18 cupcakes: 4 tablespoons (2 oz) butter or margarine, softened; 1¼ cup (10 oz) sugar; 1 teaspoon ground ginger; 2 tablespoons light corn syrup; 1 egg; 1½ cups all purpose flour; 2 tablespoons chopped crystallized ginger; 1 teaspoon baking soda; ½ cup (4 fl oz) milk

Preheat the oven to 375°F (190°C) and place large muffin tins in the oven to heat them.

Beat the butter and sugar with the ground ginger until light and fluffy. Add the corn syrup, then the egg and beat well. Fold in the sifted flour and chopped ginger. Dissolve the baking soda in the milk and add to the mixture to make a soft dough.

Quickly grease the heated muffin tins and fill two-thirds full. Bake for 12–15 minutes. Turn out onto cake racks and serve warm or cold.

Golden Oat Cake ★

Makes one 9-in (23-cm) cake: 1½ cups (6 oz) self-rising flour; ½ teaspoon salt; ⅔ cup (3½ oz) brown sugar; 2 teaspoons grated orange peel; 1¼ cups quick-cooking oats; 2 eggs; 1 cup (8 fl oz) milk; 1 cup (8 fl oz) corn oil
Topping: ⅓ cup (1½ oz) brown sugar; 2 tablespoons quick-cooking oats; 1 tablespoon corn oil; ½ cup drained crushed pineapple; 2 tablespoons chopped glacé cherries; 2 tablespoons chopped walnuts

Sift the flour and salt into a bowl. Add the brown sugar, orange peel and oats, and toss to mix thoroughly.

Beat the eggs, add the milk and corn oil and mix well. Pour onto the flour–oats mixture and stir to combine all ingredients thoroughly — do not overmix. Turn into cake pan.

Bake in an oven preheated to 350°F (180°C) for 45–50 minutes. Combine the topping ingredients and, briefly removing the cake from the oven, quickly but carefully scatter over the top of the cake. Lower the oven temperature to 325°F (160°C) and bake for another 15–20 minutes. Serve warm.

From left to right: Apricot Nut Loaf (see page 362), Chocolate Roll (see page 369) and Golden Oat Cake

Guinness Cake

Makes one 8-in (20-cm) cake: 8 tablespoons (4 oz) butter; 1½ cups (8 oz) brown sugar; 3 eggs, lightly beaten; 3 cups (12 oz) self-rising flour; pinch of salt; pinch of pumpkin pie spice; 4 oz (125 g) seedless raisins, soaked; 2 oz (60 g) mixed glacé peel, chopped and soaked; 8 oz (250 g) golden raisins, soaked; 2 oz (60 g) glacé cherries; ½ cup (4 fl oz) Guinness stout

Cream the butter and sugar until the sugar has dissolved. Beat in the eggs, then add the flour, salt, spice and the soaked dried fruit. Finally mix in the Guinness. Pour the mixture into a greased 8-in (20-cm) cake pan.

Bake in an oven preheated to 350°F (180°C) for 2 hours. To prevent burning, cover the top with aluminum foil for the last ½–¾ hour of baking. Allow baked cake to cool before removing from the cake pan.

H

Halva

Serves 6: 1 cup (8 fl oz) milk; 1 cup (8 fl oz) water; 1 cup (8 oz) sugar; 1½ teaspoons vanilla; 8 tablespoons (4 oz) unsalted butter; ½ cup (2 oz) pine nuts or unsalted pistachios; 1 cup (5 oz) coarse semolina; 1 teaspoon cinnamon

Gently boil the milk, water and sugar for 15 minutes, then add the vanilla and take off the heat.

Melt the butter in a skillet and lightly sauté the nuts. Add semolina to the pan and cook over low heat for 15 minutes. Do not allow to become too brown. Take off the heat and slowly add the milk mixture. Be careful, as it may spatter. Simmer over a low heat for 5 minutes or until the mixture is very thick and comes away from sides of pan.

Spread the mixture about 1–1½ in (2.5–4 cm) thick in a buttered dish. Cool for 1½ hours. To serve, unmold onto a decorative plate, cut into small squares and sprinkle with cinnamon.

Hazelnut Coffee Cake ★

Makes one 8-in (20-cm) cake: 12 tablespoons (6 oz) butter or margarine, softened; ¾ cup (6 oz) powdered sugar; 1 teaspoon instant coffee powder; 1 tablespoon honey; 4 eggs; 1 tablespoon coffee liqueur; 1¼ cups ground hazelnuts; 1 cup (4 oz) self-rising flour
Coffee Fudge Frosting: ⅔ cup (5 fl oz) evaporated milk; 1 cup (8 oz) sugar; 4 tablespoons (2 oz) butter or margarine; 1 teaspoon coffee extract; 2 teaspoons coffee liqueur

Beat the butter and sugar until creamy. Add the instant coffee powder and the honey, and beat until light and fluffy. Add the eggs one at a time, beating well after each addition. Beat the liqueur in well, and fold in the hazelnuts.

Sift the flour, then sift again over the butter–hazelnut mixture and fold in lightly. Spoon into a greased and floured deep 8-in (20-cm) springform pan.

Bake in an oven preheated to 350°F (180°C) for 45–50 minutes. Remove from the oven and allow to stand for 5–6 minutes before loosening the springform ring. When cold, place the cake on a serving platter.

To make the frosting, place the evaporated milk, sugar, butter and coffee extract in a nonstick saucepan and heat slowly until the sugar has dissolved, stirring gently. Bring to a boil, then boil steadily until it measures 239°F (115°C) on a sugar thermometer or until a teaspoon of mixture dropped into a glass of cold water forms a soft ball.

Take the saucepan from the heat and stand it in a large heatproof bowl of ice water to immediately stop further cooking. Beat constantly with a wooden spoon until the mixture begins to thicken. Remove the saucepan from the bowl.

Add the liqueur and continue beating to a soft whipped-cream consistency. Pour onto the cake, allowing the frosting to drizzle down the sides. Allow to set before cutting.

Note: Cooking to the correct stage and the constant beating are the keys to success in making this creamy frosting.

Hazelnut Coffee Cake

Guinness Cake and Scones (see page 383)

Clockwise from top: Chocolate Prune Cake (see page 369), Orange Blossom Cake (see page 380) and Lemon Yogurt Cake

Healthy Baklava

*Makes 20 pieces: 1 cup (4 oz) chopped walnuts;
1 cup (4 oz) chopped almonds or hazelnuts; 2 oz
(60 g) lecithin granules; 2¼ tablespoons brown
sugar; 2 tablespoons toasted wheat germ;
1 teaspoon cinnamon; pinch of ground cloves;
about 18 sheets filo pastry; 12 tablespoons (6 oz)
unsalted butter, melted
Honey Syrup: 1 cup (8 fl oz) water; ¾ cup (7½ oz)
honey; 1–2 tablespoons lemon juice; piece of
cinnamon stick; 3 whole cloves*

Mix together the walnuts, almonds, lecithin
granules, sugar, wheat germ, cinnamon
and cloves.

Place a sheet of filo pastry into a lightly
buttered large, shallow baking pan, brush
with melted butter and repeat with seven
more sheets, brushing each with butter.
Spread half the nut mixture over this.

Cover with two more sheets of pastry,
brushing each with butter. Spread the
remainder of the nut mixture onto the
pastry. Place seven or eight more sheets of
pastry on top, brushing each with butter,
including the top layer.

Using a very sharp knife, neatly trim
away any pastry overlapping the edges of
the dish. Mark diamond patterns in the
surface, cutting through the top couple of
layers of pastry. Sprinkle with a little cold
water; this creates a crispy, delicious
surface.

Bake on a low shelf in an oven preheated
to 325°F (160°C) for about 30 minutes,
then move the pan up to a higher shelf and
bake for another 30 minutes.

Meanwhile, prepare the honey syrup. In
a saucepan mix together all the ingredients,
bring to a boil, then simmer for another 10
minutes. Strain. Remove the baklava from
the oven and cut it into diamond shapes.
While still hot, spoon the honey syrup over
the top. Allow to stand for at least 4 hours
before serving.

I

Irish Molasses Loaf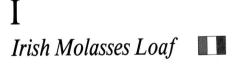

*Makes one 2-lb (1-kg) loaf: ⅓ cup (2½ fl oz) water;
4 tablespoons (2 oz) butter; 2 oz (60 g) dark
molasses; ⅓ cup (2 oz) brown sugar; 1 egg; 2 cups
(8 oz) all purpose flour; ½ teaspoon pumpkin pie
spice; ½ teaspoon ground ginger; 1 teaspoon*

*baking soda; ⅓ cup (2 oz) currants; ⅓ cup (2 oz)
seedless raisins*

Heat the water, add the butter and let stand
until melted. Mix the molasses with the
sugar and egg until creamy. Mix the flour,
spice, ginger and baking soda and add it to
the molasses mixture. Stir in the currants,
raisins and the water–butter mixture. Pour
the dough into a 2-lb (1-kg) bread pan and
bake in an oven preheated to 350°F (180°C)
for 1½–2 hours.

L

Latticed Apple Cake

*Makes one 8-in (20-cm) cake: 12 tablespoons (6 oz)
butter or margarine, softened; ¾ cup (6 oz) sugar;
1 teaspoon grated lemon peel; 4 eggs; 2¼ cups
(9 oz) all purpose flour; 2 teaspoons baking powder
Almond paste: 1 cup (5 oz) powdered sugar; ¾ cup
ground almonds; 1 egg yolk; 1½ teaspoons sweet
sherry; 1½ teaspoons lemon juice
Topping: 1 cup drained cooked (or canned) apples;
1–2 tablespoons sugar (optional); ½ cup apricot
preserve; 1–2 tablespoons powdered sugar*

Beat the butter and sugar with the lemon
peel until creamy. Add the eggs one at a
time, beating well after each addition. Sift
the flour and baking powder over the
cream mixture and fold in. Spread into a
greased and floured 8-in (20-cm)
springform pan and level the surface.

Bake in an oven preheated to 350°F
(180°C) for 35–40 minutes. Remove from
the oven and leave in the pan for 5–6 minutes before adding the topping.

Meanwhile, to make the almond paste,
sift the sugar into a bowl, add the ground
almonds, mix thoroughly and make a well
in the center. Beat the egg yolks, sweet
sherry and lemon juice together. Pour into
the sugar mixture and gradually work into
a firm, smooth paste with one hand, kneading well.

Lightly sprinkle a board or work surface
with a little extra powdered sugar, lift the
mixture onto the board and knead with
both hands to a firm, smooth dough — do
not add too much extra sugar unless the
dough is very soft. Cover tightly until
ready for use, then knead gently before
rolling out.

To make the topping, sweeten the apples
with the sugar, if desired. Roll out the

almond paste to about ¼ in (5 mm) thick
and cut into ¾-in (1.75-cm) strips.

Carefully spread the apples over the
warm cake and arrange a lattice pattern of
almond paste strips on top. Drop a little
apricot preserve between the lattice pieces.

Return to the oven for another 15–20
minutes. Remove from the springform pan
and allow to cool; dust with powdered
sugar before serving.

Lemon Yogurt Cake ★

*Makes one 9 × 5-in (22 × 13-cm) loaf cake:
8 tablespoons (4 oz) butter; ¾ cup (6 oz) powdered
sugar; 3 eggs; finely grated peel of 1 lemon; ¾ cup
(6 fl oz) plain yogurt; 2 cups (8 oz) self-rising flour,
sifted; ½ cup (2 oz) sliced dried apricots*

Cream the butter and sugar until light and
fluffy. Add the eggs one at a time, beating
well after each addition. Gently fold in the
lemon peel, yogurt, sifted flour and dried
apricot slices. Spoon the mixture into a
greased loaf pan.

Bake in an oven preheated to 325°F
(160°C) for 1¼ hours. Turn out onto a wire
rack to cool.

Note: The cake is even more delicious
with yogurt icing. Mix 1 tablespoon plain
yogurt with ½ cup powdered sugar, spread
this over the cake and sprinkle with finely
grated lemon peel.

M

Matchsticks

*Makes 8 cakes: 3 sheets puff pastry, each about
10 × 5 in (25 × 13 cm); 2 tablespoons raspberry
jam; 1 cup (8 fl oz) heavy cream; few drops of
vanilla; water to mix; 1 cup (5 oz) powdered sugar*

Prick each sheet of puff pastry thoroughly
with a fork. Place the three sheets of pastry
on separate baking sheets and bake in an
oven preheated to 350°F (180°C) for 20–30
minutes or until a rich brown color. Allow
to cool on wire cake racks.

Spread one sheet of pastry with the raspberry jam and place a second sheet on top.

Flavor the cream with a few drops of
vanilla and whip until stiff. Spread the
cream down the length of the pastry. Place
the third sheet of pastry on top and press

lightly to spread the encased cream to the edges.

Prepare a spreadable but not oversoft water icing by combining a little water with the powdered sugar. (Color as desired). Spread over the top layer of pastry and allow to set. Using a serrated knife, slice into serving portions.

N

Nut Pumpkin Gems

Makes 18–20 small muffins: 4 tablespoons (2 oz) butter or margarine, softened; ¼ cup (2 oz) powdered sugar; ½ teaspoon cinnamon; ¾ cup pumpkin puree; 1 egg; 2½ cups (10 oz) self-rising flour; ½ cup (2 oz) chopped walnuts; ½ cup (4 fl oz) milk; extra butter or margarine for spreading

Preheat the oven to 425°F (220°C) and heat small muffin tins in the oven.

Cream the butter and sugar until light. Add the cinnamon, pumpkin and egg, and beat thoroughly. Fold in alternate batches of sifted flour, walnuts and milk, about a third of each at a time, to make a soft dough.

Quickly grease the heated muffin tins and fill them two-thirds full with the mixture.

Bake for 12–15 minutes. Turn out onto cake racks and serve warm or cool, split and spread with butter.

O

Orange-Blossom Cake ★

Serves 8: 8 tablespoon (4 oz) butter; 1¼ cups (6½ oz) brown sugar; 1 cup (8 fl oz) milk; 3 egg yolks; 4 teaspoons orange-blossom water; 2 cups (8 oz) whole-wheat flour; 2 teaspoons baking powder; ½ teaspoon salt; ½ teaspoon ground cloves; 1 cup (4 oz) slivered blanched almonds; 1 cup (4 oz) currants; 2 tablespoons coarsely grated orange peel; 3 egg whites, stiffly beaten

Blend the butter and sugar together well. Add the milk, egg yolks and orange-blossom water.

Into a separate bowl, sift together the flour, baking powder, salt and ground cloves, then add this to the mixture and beat well. Add the almonds, currants and

Passionfruit Sponge

Pecan Pie

orange peel and mix well. Fold in the stiffly beaten egg whites. Spread into a large greased loaf pan.

Bake in an oven preheated to 350°F (180°C) for 35–45 minutes. Turn out onto a wire rack.

The cake can be glazed while hot, or after it has cooled it can be coated with a thin icing and sprinkled with finely chopped mixed peel.

P
Passionfruit Sponge

Serves 8-10: 4 eggs; ¾ cup (6 oz) sugar; ¾ cup (3 oz) cornstarch; ¼ cup (1 oz) all purpose flour; 1 teaspoon baking powder; 1¼ cups (10 fl oz) heavy cream
Icing: 1 teaspoon melted butter; 1 cup (5 oz) sifted powdered sugar; 1 small can passionfruit

To make the sponge, separate the eggs and whip the whites until stiff. Add the sugar gradually, beating continuously. Add the egg yolks one at a time and beat again. Sift together the cornstarch, flour and baking powder three times and gently fold into the mixture with a metal spoon.

Divide the mixture evenly between the two 8-in (20-cm) greased and floured pans. Bake in an oven preheated to 350°F (180°C) for 20–25 minutes. Stand in the pans for 2–3 minutes before turning out onto a wire cooling rack, after loosening the sides from the pans with a knife. Cool.

To fill and ice: Place one of the sponges on a serving plate. Spread thickly with whipped cream. Place the second sponge on top. Make the icing by adding the melted butter to the sifted powdered sugar. Add the juice and seeds of the passionfruit until the mixture is of a spreading consistency. Spread over the top of the sponge.

Peanut Butter Cookies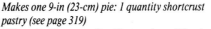

Makes 36: 8 tablespoons (4 oz) butter; ½ cup (4 oz) sugar; ½ cup (3 oz) brown sugar; ½ cup peanut butter; 1 egg; 1¼ cups (5 oz) all purpose flour; ½ teaspoon baking powder; ¾ teaspoon baking soda; ¼ teaspoon salt

Cream the butter, sugars and peanut butter

in a mixing bowl. Add the beaten egg and mix well. Sift and stir in the flour, baking powder, soda and salt. Chill the dough.

Roll the dough into balls the size of large walnuts. Place well apart on greased baking sheets. Flatten with a fork dipped in flour, criss-cross fashion. Bake in an oven preheated to 375°–400°F (190°–200°C) for 10–12 minutes. Cool a few minutes on baking sheets before removing to a cooling rack.

Pecan Pie

Makes one 9-in (23-cm) pie: 1 quantity shortcrust pastry (see page 319)
Filling: 6 tablespoons (3 oz) butter; 1 cup (10 oz) dark corn syrup; ½ teaspoon salt; 1 cup (8 oz) sugar; 4 eggs; 2 cups (8 oz) pecan halves; 1 teaspoon vanilla

Roll out the pastry on a lightly floured surface and use to line a 9-in (23-cm) pie plate. Chill while making the filling.

Melt the butter and stir in the corn syrup, salt, sugar and eggs. Mix well to combine. Add the nuts and vanilla. Pour the filling into the prepared pie crust, arranging the pecans face up.

Bake in an oven preheated to 375°F (190°C) for 35–40 minutes or until the filling is cooked and the pastry golden brown. Serve warm or cold with cream.

Pineapple Ginger Cheesecake ★

Makes one 9-in (23-cm) cake: 8 oz (225 g) coconut-flavored cookies; 2 oz (60 g) whole-wheat cookies; 1 cup (4 oz) drained crushed pineapple; ⅓ cup (1½ oz) chopped preserved ginger; 2 eggs; ½ cup (4 oz) sugar; 1–2 teaspoons lemon juice; 8 oz (225 g) cream cheese, softened; 12 oz (350 g) cottage cheese; 1 cup (8 fl oz) sour cream; ½ teaspoon cinnamon; ½ teaspoon ground ginger

Crush the coconut and whole-wheat cookies, and scatter over the base of a well-greased 9-in (23-cm) springform pan. Cover with the combined crushed pineapple and ginger, pressing firmly into the crumbs. Chill for 30–40 minutes.

Beat the eggs, sugar and lemon juice together until thick and fluffy. Gradually beat in the cream cheese and cottage cheese. Pour into the springform pan on top of the crumb mixture.

Bake in an oven preheated to 325°F (160°C) for 35–40 minutes. Carefully spread the combined sour cream and spices over the surface of the cheesecake and return to the oven for another 7–10 minutes. Open the oven door and allow the cheesecake to cool in the oven for 15–20 minutes. Remove and set in a draft-free area until cold. Chill for several hours or overnight before slicing.

Pumpkin Nut Bread

Serves 6-8: 1½ cups pumpkin puree; ½ cup (5 oz) honey; ½ cup (2½ oz) brown sugar; ½ cup (4 fl oz) vegetable oil; ½ cup (2 oz) chopped dates; ½ cup (2 oz) chopped walnuts; ½ teaspoon salt; ½ teaspoon cinnamon; ½ teaspoon ground cloves; 2 teaspoons baking powder; 1 cup (4 oz) all purpose flour; 1¼ cups (5 oz) whole-wheat flour; 2 tablespoons wheat germ

In a large bowl, combine the pumpkin puree, honey, brown sugar, vegetable oil, dates, walnuts, salt, cinnamon, cloves and baking powder. Mix well.

Stir in the remaining ingredients, then pour the mixture into a greased deep loaf pan.

Bake in an oven preheated to 350°F (180°C) for about 1 hour. Cool in the pan for 20 minutes, then turn out onto a wire rack.

R
Raspberry Peanut Squares ★

Makes one 9-in (23-cm) square slab: 2 cups (8 oz) self-rising flour; ¼ teaspoon salt; 1 cup (8 oz) powdered sugar; 8 tablespoons (4 oz) butter or margarine, chopped; 1 cup (4 oz) chopped peanuts; 3 tablespoons raspberry jam; 2 eggs, beaten; 2 teaspoons lemon juice; ¾ cup (6 fl oz) milk; powdered sugar for topping

Place the flour, salt and sugar in the bowl of a food processor. Using the cutting blade, add the butter and process for a few seconds, then tip the mixture into a bowl. Add the peanuts, raspberry jam, beaten eggs, lemon juice and milk and beat with a flat egg whisk for 1–2 minutes. Pour into the pan.

Pineapple Ginger Cheesecake (see page 381)

Bake in an oven preheated to 350°F (180°C) for 40–45 minutes. Remove from the oven and allow to stand for 3–4 minutes before turning out carefully onto a cake rack to cool.

Sift a little powdered sugar over the top and cut into squares for serving.

Rich Chocolate Butter Cake

Makes one 8-in (20-cm) cake: 2-in (5-cm) strip of vanilla bean; ½ cup (4 fl oz) milk, hot; 5 oz (175 g) unsweetened chocolate, chopped; 12 tablespoons (6 oz) butter, softened; ¾ cup (6 oz) powdered sugar; 4 eggs, separated; 1 cup (4 oz) all purpose flour; ½ cup (20 oz) cornstarch; 1 teaspoon baking powder; ½ teaspoon baking soda
Frosting: 4 squares (4 oz) fruit and nut chocolate; 2 tablespoons (1 oz) butter; ¼ cup (2 fl oz) evaporated milk; ½ cup (2½ oz) powdered sugar, sifted

Soak the vanilla bean in hot milk for 30 minutes. Discard the vanilla bean and add the chocolate to the milk. Over a very low heat, stir in 2 tablespoons of the butter until well blended. Allow to cool.

Beat the remaining butter with the sugar until light and fluffy. Add the cooled chocolate mixture and beat well. Add the egg yolks one at a time and mix in lightly.

Sift the dry ingredients together, then sift them over the butter–chocolate mixture and fold in lightly. Beat the egg whites until they form stiff peaks, then gently fold into the mixture — do not overmix. Turn into a greased deep 8-in (20-cm) cake pan.

Bake in an oven preheated to 350°F (180°C) for 60–80 minutes. Remove from the oven and allow to stand for 5–6 minutes before carefully turning out onto a cake rack to cool.

When cold, wrap a ''collar'' of waxed paper around the cake, allowing the top edge of the paper to stand about 1 in (2.5 cm) above the surface of the cake.

To make the frosting, chop the block of chocolate into small pieces and melt it with the butter in a heatproof bowl placed over hot — not boiling — water. Remove from the heat and stir in the evaporated milk and powdered sugar. Quickly pour onto the top of the cake. Allow the frosting to set before removing the waxed paper. Let stand overnight before cutting into slices.

Rich Chocolate Butter Cake

Rock Cakes

Makes 24–26 small cakes: 2 cups (8 oz) self-rising flour; ¼ teaspoon salt; ½ teaspoon mixed spices (cinnamon, nutmeg, coriander, ginger); 6 tablespoons (3 oz) butter or margarine, chopped; ⅓ cup (2½ oz) powdered sugar; 2 tablespoons mixed dried fruits; 1 tablespoon chopped glacé peel; 1 egg, beaten; 2–3 tablespoons milk; extra butter for spreading

Sift the flour, salt and spices into a bowl, add the butter and rub through with the fingertips until fine. Mix in the sugar.

Combine the dried fruits and peel with the egg and add this to the mixture, with sufficient milk to mix to a stiff consistency. Pile in heaped spoonfuls about 2 in (5 cm) apart on greased cookie sheets.

Bake in an oven preheated to 375°F (190°C) for 15–17 minutes. Turn onto cake racks to cool. Before serving, split each rock cake and spread with butter if desired.

S

Scandinavian Sour Cream Cookies

Makes about 25 cookies: 2 cups (1 lb) powdered sugar; 1 cup (8 fl oz) thick sour cream; 16 tablespoons (8 oz) butter, softened; 2 large eggs, well beaten; 1 teaspoon baking soda; 1½ teaspoons vanilla

Mix together all the ingredients in the order listed to make a dough. Roll the dough out to ¼ in (5 mm) thick, then cut into fancy shapes with a cookie cutter. Arrange on greased baking sheets.

Bake in an oven preheated to 325°F (160°C) for 10–12 minutes. Turn onto wire racks to cool.

Scones

Makes 15 scones: 4 cups (1 lb) self-rising flour; pinch of salt; 8 tablespoons (4 oz) margarine; ⅓ cup (3 oz) sugar; milk; 1 egg yolk mixed with a little cold water

Sift the flour and salt into a bowl, then rub in the margarine with your fingertips. Add the sugar and then the milk, a little at a time, until it is a soft consistency.

Roll out on a floured board to about ¾ in (2 cm) thick. Cut into rounds 2½ in (6 cm) in diameter and place on a lightly greased baking sheet. Paint with the egg yolk and water mixture and bake in an oven preheated to 375°F (190°C) for 20 minutes or until golden brown. Remove from the oven and cool on a wire rack.

Sienna Christmas Cake

Makes one 18 × 15-in (45 × 38-cm) cake: 6½ oz (200 g) blanched almonds; 3½ oz (100 g) hazelnuts, roasted; 3½ oz (100 g) glacé citron; 3½ oz (100 g) glacé pumpkin; 3½ oz (100 g) glacé melon peel; 3½ oz (100 g) dried figs; 5 oz (155 g) walnuts; 1 oz (30 g) sweetened cocoa; 1 teaspoon cinnamon; 1 teaspoon pumpkin pie spice; ⅓ cup (4 oz) honey; 1 cup (5 oz) powdered sugar; 2 sheets rice paper

Finely chop all ingredients up to and including the walnuts. Put them into a bowl and add the cocoa, half of the cinnamon and the pumpkin pie spice. Mix well together.

Put the honey and all but a tablespoon of the powdered sugar into a saucepan. Heat and stir constantly until a drop of the mixture solidifies in contact with cold water. Remove from the heat and add the nut–fruit mixture. Mix together well.

Line the bottom of a shallow 18 × 15-in (45 × 38-cm) baking dish with one of the sheets of rice paper and pour the mixture on top of it. Cover with the other sheet. Bake in an oven preheated to 350°F (180°C) for 30 minutes. Remove from the oven, cool, unmold and sprinkle with the remaining powdered sugar and cinnamon.

Do not serve until the next day. With a sharp knife, cut into bite-size pieces.

Note: If glacé pumpkin and melon peel are not available, use other glacé fruits such as peaches or pineapple.

Snow Cake

Makes two 7-in (18-cm) cakes: 6 tablespoons (3 oz) butter or margarine, softened well; 1 cup (8 oz) powdered sugar; 1 teaspoon vanilla; 1¾ cups all purpose flour; 2 teaspoons baking powder; ¼ teaspoon salt; ½ cup (4 fl oz) milk; 2 egg whites; 2 or 3 ripe passionfruit

Vienna Butter Cream: 4 tablespoons (2 oz) butter or margarine, softened; ½ teaspoon vanilla; 1 tablespoon milk; 1¼ cups (6¼ oz) powdered sugar

Place the butter, sugar and vanilla into a bowl. Sift in the flour, baking powder and salt. Add the milk and whisk for 1–2 minutes.

Whisk the egg whites until soft peaks form, then very gently fold into the cake mixture. Spoon into two waxed-paper-lined and greased 7-in (18-cm) cake pans.

Bake in an oven preheated to 350°F (180°C) for 25–30 minutes or until springy to the touch. Remove from the oven and let stand for 1–2 minutes before turning out onto a cake rack to cool.

To make the butter cream, beat the butter and vanilla in a bowl until creamy. Add the milk and blend in. Gradually add the sifted sugar, beating well after each addition. While still soft, spread onto the top of the cake. Swirl or rough-up into an attractive design. Cut the passionfruit in half and spoon the pulp over. Allow to firm before cutting.

Spice and Sugar Swirls

Makes 10–12 swirls: 2 cups (8 oz) self-rising flour; ½ teaspoon salt; 1 tablespoon sugar; 4 tablespoons (2 oz) butter or margarine; ⅔ cup (5 fl oz) milk; 1 egg, beaten
Filling: 2 tablespoons (1 oz) butter or margarine, melted; 2 tablespoons brown sugar; 1 teaspoon cinnamon; ¾ cup (3 oz) chopped walnuts
Topping: 4 tablespoons (2 oz) butter or margarine, melted; 2 tablespoons brown sugar; 2 tablespoons chopped walnuts

Sift the flour, salt and sugar into a bowl. Melt the butter, add the milk and beaten egg and stir into the flour mixture with a knife blade until mixed to a soft dough. Turn onto a lightly floured board and pat into a 1 in (2.5 cm) thick rectangle .

Combine the filling ingredients and sprinkle over the dough. Roll the rectangle of dough up loosely and cut into 10–12 slices. Into each greased muffin cup, place one slice on its edge so that the swirl is showing. Drizzle the melted butter over and sprinkle with brown sugar and walnuts.

Bake in an oven preheated to 425°F (200°C) for 15–17 minutes.

Sienna Christmas Cake (see page 383)

Spicy Apple Teacake

Makes one 9-in (23-cm) cake: 3 cups (12 oz) self-rising flour; pinch of salt; 1 cup (8 oz) sugar; 6 tablespoons (3 oz) butter or margarine; 1 egg; ½ cup (4 fl oz) milk; 1 cup finely chopped apple; 4 oz (125 g) seedless raisins; 2 teaspoons cinnamon; melted butter

Sift the flour and salt with 6½ oz (185 g) of the sugar. Rub in the butter or margarine and mix to a soft dough with the beaten egg and milk. Turn onto a floured board, knead lightly and cut in two.

Line a greased 9-in (23-cm) loaf pan with half the mixture, spread with apple pulp. Sprinkle with the raisins, half the cinnamon and the remaining sugar. Cover with the remainder of the dough. Glaze with melted butter and sprinkle with the remaining cinnamon. Bake in an oven preheated to 350°–375°F (180°–190°C) for 40–50 minutes.

Strawberry Muffins

Serves 4–6: ½ cup (4 oz) powdered sugar; 1 lb (500 g) strawberries, hulled and sliced; 1¼ cups (10 fl oz) heavy cream, stiffly whipped; 1 lb (500 g) all purpose flour; pinch of salt; 2 teaspoons sugar; 1¼ cups (10 fl oz) warm milk; 2 teaspoons dry yeast; 1 egg, well beaten; 2 tablespoons (1 oz) butter, melted; powdered sugar for garnish

Sprinkle the sugar over the strawberries and refrigerate for 30 minutes. Fold in the cream and return to the refrigerator until ready to use.

To make the muffins, combine the flour and salt. Dissolve the sugar in the milk and add the yeast. Let stand in a warm place for 10 minutes. Add the yeast mixture and the egg to the flour, stir in the melted butter and knead for 10 minutes to a soft dough. Place the dough in an oiled bowl, cover and leave to rest in a warm place until it has doubled in size.

Turn the dough out onto a floured board, punch it down and roll it out to ½-in (1-cm) thickness. Cut into 3-in (7.5-cm) rounds. Place the rounds on a floured board, dust with flour, cover with a tea towel and leave until doubled in size. Lightly grease a hot griddle and cook the muffins about 8 minutes on each side.

To serve, split the muffins in half, toast on both sides, spread one side with butter, heap the strawberries and cream on the bottom half, place the other half on top and sprinkle with powdered sugar.

Swedish Apple Cake

Serves 6: 7 tablespoons (3½ oz) butter; ½ cup (4 oz) sugar; 2 egg yolks, lightly beaten; ¾ cup (3 oz) ground almonds; grated peel and juice of ½ lemon; 3 egg whites, stiffly beaten; 6 apples, peeled and thinly sliced

Cream the butter and the sugar until pale yellow and the sugar has dissolved. Stir in the yolks, almonds, lemon peel and juice, then fold in the egg whites.

Place the apples in a well-buttered shallow baking dish and spread the batter over. Bake in an oven preheated to 400°F (200°C) for 15–20 minutes. Serve warm.

Swedish Christmas Cookies

Makes about 36 cookies: 2 yolks from hard-cooked eggs; 6 tablespoons (3 oz) butter; ⅓ cup (2½ oz) powdered sugar; ⅓ cup (2½ fl oz) thick sour cream; grated peel of ½ lemon; grated peel of ½ orange; 1 raw egg yolk; 1 cup (4 oz) all purpose flour (more if required), sifted; ⅛ teaspoon baking soda; ⅛ teaspoon salt
Topping: 1 egg white, well beaten; 1 tablespoon powdered sugar; 1 tablespoon ground almonds

Mash the hard-cooked egg yolks with the butter until a smooth paste forms. Blend in the sugar, mixing well. Add the sour cream, lemon and orange peel and raw egg yolk.

Sift the flour, baking soda and salt together and add to the other ingredients, mixing well and adding more flour (if necessary) to obtain a firm, rollable dough. Roll out to ¼-in (5-mm) thickness and press out fancy shapes, such as stars or animals. Brush with beaten egg white and sprinkle with sugar–nut mixture.

Bake in an oven preheated to 325°F (160°C) for 15–20 minutes. Turn onto wire racks to cool.

Swedish Tea Ring

Serves 6: 2 cups (8 oz) all purpose flour; ½ teaspoon salt; ¼ oz (7 g) fresh yeast; 1½ teaspoons sugar; ¾ cup (5 fl oz) milk; 2 tablespoons (1 oz) butter or margarine; extra flour or milk, as required
Filling: 4 tablespoons (2 oz) butter; 1 cup (4 oz) seedless raisins or a mixture of dried fruits (larger ones should be coarsely chopped); ½ cup (4 oz) sugar; 2 teaspoons cinnamon; extra 2 tablespoons sugar for glazing

To make the dough, sift flour and salt into a large warm mixing bowl. Make a hollow in the center of the flour. Cream the yeast and sugar. Warm ½ cup of the milk to body temperature and add to the yeast and sugar mixture. Mix well and pour into the hollow. Stir in sufficient flour to make a light, soft batter. Cover the bowl with a cloth and let stand in a warm place. Allow to stand until the batter in the center looks spongy and is full of bubbles.

Melt the butter, add the rest of the milk and warm slightly. Pour the milk and butter mixture over the flour and the "sponge" in the bowl and mix to a soft dough, about the same consistency as a scone dough, using extra flour or warm milk as required.

Knead the dough in the bowl until it is smooth and elastic, leaves the sides of the bowl clean and comes away from the hand. Shape the dough into a ball and press it down in the bottom of the bowl. Sprinkle lightly with flour. Return the bowl to a warm place, cover with a cloth and allow the dough to rise until it doubles in bulk and a finger imprint on the surface disappears quickly. Punch the dough down and knead it lightly again.

Roll the dough into a long narrow rectangle ½ in (1 cm) thick. Brush with melted butter and sprinkle with a mixture of raisins, sugar and cinnamon.

Starting at one of the long edges, roll the dough up tightly. Stretch slightly and shape into a circle. Tuck one end into the other. Make deep slashes on the outer side of the circle about 2 in (5 cm) apart. Open up the cuts a little to show the filling. Cover with a cloth and let rise in a warm place until doubled in size.

Bake in an oven preheated to 400°–450°F (200°–230°C) for 15 minutes, then reduce the temperature to 350°–375°F (180°–190°C) and bake for another 15–20 minutes or until the ring is golden brown top and bottom. While hot, glaze with 2 tablespoons water boiled together for 1 minute with the extra sugar. Serve with butter.

Y

Yorkshire Parkin

Serves 6: ½ cup (2½ oz) brown sugar; 6 tablespoons (3 oz) margarine; 6 oz (185 g) light corn syrup; 1 cup (6 oz) oatmeal; 1½ cups (6 oz) all purpose flour; ½ teaspoon mixed spices; ½ teaspoon ginger; ½ teaspoon baking soda; 1 egg

Melt the sugar, margarine and syrup together. Add the dry ingredients, mix well and beat in the egg. Pour the mixture into a shallow cake pan and bake in an oven preheated to 350°F (180°C) for approximately one hour. When cold, cut into squares.

Note: It is best kept in an airtight tin for at least 2 days before serving.

Glossary

Agar agar: Japanese gelatin made from tengusa seaweed, which has no flavor. Soften 1 tablespoon in small amount of cold water for 5 minutes, then add 4 cups of liquid and heat until dissolved. Allow to cool. Does not need to be refrigerated to set as it jells at 110°F (45°C). It is also available in sticks which, after softening in cold water, add texture to salads and other cold dishes.

Ajowan (ajwain): Delicately flavored seeds, the flavor of which resembles thyme. Crush before using in lentil dishes and batters or for fish and pickles.

Al dente: Term used to refer to pasta cooked until just tender to the bite.

All spice: Dried reddish to brown berry so named because the flavor resembles that of several spices (cinnamon, clove and nutmeg). Often used in fruit or rice dishes, punches and cakes.

Anise: See *star anise*.

Annatto seeds: Seeds used to give a red color to shellfish in Filipino cooking. If unavailable, substitute ¼ teaspoon paprika and ⅛ teaspoon turmeric.

Arrowroot: Starch used as thickening in soups, gravies and sweets. It is derived from the root of the West Indian *salep* or arrowroot plant.

Asafoetida: Dried and ground resin used sparingly in some curries due to its very strong taste and aroma. It is also mainly used to prevent flatulence.

Aspic jelly: Jelly formed by adding gelatin to stock. The term is sometimes used to refer to the arranging of cold meats, vegetables, etc. in molded jelly.

Baking powder: Rising agent, usually sifted into mixtures with all purpose flour. It is important to use only the specified quantity.

Bamboo shoots: Rapid-sprouting edible shoots from certain bamboo plants. The tough outer leaves must be removed before cooking the internal "point." Available fresh in some Chinese food stores but most commonly sold canned in water. Avoid bamboo shoots canned in soy sauce or with spices, unless specifically required for a recipe.

Banana leaves: Large, long flat leaves sometimes used for wrapping ingredients in Malaysian and Indonesian cooking.

Barbecue sauce: Commercially prepared, salty yet very sweet sauce used in dips and barbecue marinades.

Basil: A sweetly scented herb, best used when fresh. It will also keep for a short time in the refrigerator or preserved in olive oil. It can be purchased as a small plant that will produce a regular supply of leaves for several weeks, depending on the degree of use. Best used with tomatoes, bell peppers, eggplant, fish, chicken and pasta. It is also available dried, although the flavor is not as delicate.

Baste: To pour stock, cooking juices, melted fat or marinade over meat, chicken or fish during the cooking period in order to retain moisture, especially if roasting.

Bay leaves: Leaves of the bay or laurel tree, which are slightly bitter when fresh and better used when wilted or dried. Their strong, sweet scent is often included in a bouquet garni.

Bean curd: Soft, jelly-like, cream-colored food made by adding a setting agent to a thin liquid of ground, boiled soybeans and water. Soft bean curd, known as *tofu* in Japan, is the first setting of this liquid, produced by weighting it lightly. It is usually sold in square pieces in water. It can also be purchased in cans packed in water, although the consistency is harder and the flavor stronger than the fresh kind, making it suitable only for braised dishes or soups. Soft bean curd can be stored in cold water covered in plastic wrap for several days in the refrigerator provided the water is changed daily. Dry bean curd can be made by pressing soft bean curd with heavy weights for 30 minutes or so. Shredded dry bean curd is used in sautéed and braised dishes and in salads. Fried bean curd cubes are obtained by deep frying cubes of dried bean curd until the surface is crisp and golden and the inside practically dried up. They store well in an airtight jar.

Beansprouts: Sprouted mung or soy beans, a crisp fresh-flavored vegetable used very much in Chinese cooking. Sold fresh or canned in water, the latter having lost much of its particular taste and crispness in the canning process.

Fresh sprouts will keep at least a week in a sealed plastic bag or box in the refrigerator. They can be sprouted at home using the kits supplied at health food or organic gardening centers. Mung sprouts have a more delicate taste and are smaller in size than soy sprouts, which have large yellow pods.

Bell pepper: Also known as *capsicum* and available in green, red, yellow or black. Paprika is made from special varieties.

Besan: Chick pea or channa flour. It is pale yellow in color and has a very high protein content. Often used as a thickener in sauces and curries.

Beurre manié: Equal quantities of flour and softened butter kneaded together to form a paste. Mixed into stews, soups and casseroles at the end of cooking time to thicken the juices.

Bird's nest: Translucent material produced by Asian swifts or Salagane swallows to line their nests. It is usually ground and sold in cakes. The dangerous method employed in gathering the nests from the ceilings of caves on the coast of Southern China and Thailand, makes them one of the most expensive Chinese ingredients.

Blacan: Also known as *terasi*. This dark brown shrimp paste is made from shrimp fermented with salt and then dried.

Black pudding: Sausage made of pigs' and sometimes other animals' blood mixed with suet.

Bok choy: Dark green leaves on crisp milk-white stems; whole vegetable may be used or only inner heart in recipes requiring vegetable hearts. A crisp-textured, mild tasting vegetable. May also be known as Chinese cabbage.

Bonito flakes (katsuobushi): Dried and fermented bonito shaved into flakes and used as the basis of dashi (stock) or as a garnish. A popular ingredient in Japanese cooking.

Bombay duck: Small, dried, salted fish. These are crisped in the oven or a pan and then crumbled over curries.

Bouquet garni: A bundle of herbs tied together with string or placed in a cheesecloth bag and removed at the end of cooking. Classic combination: 3 stalks parsley, small sprig thyme and a small bay leaf. There are many variations and combinations.

Candlenuts: Hard, oily nuts which may be crushed or ground for use in soups or curries for flavor and thickening. They

are also used as a primitive candle when threaded on the mid rib of a palm leaf.

Cardamom: The seed pods of an Indian plant, which are brown to black in color when opened and somewhat sticky. They have a strong aromatic taste. Used to flavor curries, rice dishes, pickles, punches and spiced wine.

Cellophane noodles: Fine, translucent noodles made from ground mung beans. Used mostly in soups and stews, where they become transparent and almost gelatinous in texture.

Celsius: A scale of temperature in which freezing point of water is 0 degrees and boiling point 100 degrees.

Chilies: There are many different varieties of these slender, red (or green when unripe) members of the capsicum family, including the tiny yet very hot bird's eye chilies. Experts grade their degree of heat from 1 to 120. An ordinary hot chili (perhaps grade 15) should be opened under running water to prevent oils contacting lips or eyes. It is also advisable to remove the seeds (which are the hottest part of a chili) before cooking.

Chili powder: Dried, ground chilies.

Chili sauce: Each Asian country has a version of this sauce made of chilies, onions, garlic, lemon and salt in various combinations.

Chinese bean sauce: A variety of sauces are made using fermented soybeans as the prime ingredient: Hoisin sauce (sweet and hot), Hot Black Bean Sauce (using whole black beans, chilies and garlic) and Yellow Bean Sauce (made using whole yellow soybeans).

Choy sum: Vegetable with thick, round, green stems, sparsely leafed and with small yellow-flowered heads. The taste is very slightly bitter. The stems may be peeled and cooked as a vegetable by themselves, though usually the whole stalk, cut into two or three pieces, is used.

Cinnamon: Native plant of Sri Lanka; thin shavings of bark rolled into quills. May also be purchased in powdered form. Used in curries, sweet dishes and spiced wine.

Cloud ear fungus: Dark brown ear-shaped fungus used to impart its particular musty taste and crunchy texture to some Chinese dishes. Soak to soften, then cut up into small pieces before use. Keeps well in dry conditions.

Cloves: Dried brown bud which should be well formed and

not shriveled. Its potent aroma and taste is also slightly antiseptic. Used in curries, pickles and roast hams.

Coconut cream: Rich layer that forms on surface of coconut flesh after it has been left to soak in water or milk. It may be skimmed off before coconut is squeezed to extract the milk.

Coconut milk: This is not the water found inside a fresh coconut but the creamy milk extracted from squeezing the grated flesh. To make fresh coconut milk, put the peeled flesh into an electric blender with 2 cups water or milk and blend until pulverized. Strain the liquid, then repeat using the same coconut and adding more water. Alternatively, finely grate the flesh by hand, add 1 cup of hot water to 1 cup of flesh, let stand for 10 minutes, then knead to extract the milk. Repeat with more water. Dried coconut can also be used in the same fashion.

Cooking oils: Are usually extracted from seeds such as sunflower or from vegetable sources such as olives or maize.

Coriander (cilantro): Also known as *Chinese parsley.* The lower leaves are flat and fanlike while the upper leaves are feathery, with a strong, fragrant aroma. It is invariably used fresh as it loses flavor when dried. Used in vast quantities in Asia, the Middle East and South America.

Coriander seeds: Have a sweet, aromatic flavor that rapidly declines after grinding. Used in curries, pickles, liqueurs, fish, sausages and sweet dishes.

Cornmeal: Also known as *polenta*; yellow in color and a form of dried, ground corn or maize.

Cornstarch: Powdered corn that has the strongest taste of all the starches. Used as thickening in soups, sauces and gravies.

Court bouillon: An aromatic stock used to poach fish, poultry, meat or vegetables. Basic combination consists of ½ cup oil, 3½ cups water, juice of 2 lemons, a bouquet garni of parsley, celery, fennel, thyme and bay leaf, 12 coriander seeds, 12 peppercorns and salt to taste, boiled together for 20 minutes. Other variations include wine, onions and other herbs or spices.

Cream of tartar: A rising agent added to baking powder and self-rising flour.

Croutons: Diced bread, fried lightly in shallow butter and oil until golden brown. Served sprinkled on soups and salads.

Cumin: Slender seeds with pungent yet aromatic flavor. They are also available ground. Used in curries and can dominate flavor if used excessively.

Curry leaves: Small shiny leaves that have a strong curry aroma when bruised or crushed. When dried they tend to lose their flavor.

Daikon: Long white root with the flavor of radish.

Dashi: Clear stock used in Japanese cooking. Add 1 tablespoon bonito flakes and a 2 × 1-in (5 × 2.5-cm) piece of kombu to 1 cup boiling water and let stand 5 minutes before using. Dashi gives the characteristic Japanese flavor to many dishes. Dashi-no-moto is an instant dashi which is both convenient and reasonably good.

Daun kesom: A pungent dark green leaf, sometimes called Vietnamese mint. Used mainly in Indonesia, Malaysia and Thailand.

Daun salam: Indonesian bay leaves with a flavor similar to curry leaves.

Degorge: To draw out moisture, such as salting eggplant to draw out the bitter juices, or tomatoes to remove excess moisture. Also, to soak food for a period of time in cold water in order to remove any impurities it may contain.

Dhal: Hindi word for grains, legumes and pulses such as lentils, split peas, etc. All dhal should be washed thoroughly and picked over before use. Recipes often specify a period of soaking which reduces the cooking time.

Dill: A flavor long associated with pickled cucumbers. Fresh dill leaves are feathery but lose most of their delicate aroma and flavor if dried or cooked.

Dough: An uncooked mixture of flour, liquid and/or fat, and usually a rising agent such as yeast or baking powder.

Dried fish: Many different varieties of sun-dried fish and shellfish are eaten in Asia, e.g. Bombay Duck. Sometimes they are used to enhance the flavor of other foods during cooking.

Dried shrimp paste: See *Blacan.*

Dried spices: Spices are usually sold in dried form. If possible, purchase as seeds or berries that can be freshly ground before cooking, as most lose some of their flavor after grinding. Store in a cool, dry place in airtight jars. Some spices, especially those to be used in curries, are better dry-roasted in a pan before grinding.

Dropping consistency: Term used to describe the required consistency of a cake or pudding mixture. Test by taking a spoonful of mixture and holding the spoon on its side. The mixture should fall off of its own accord within 5 seconds.

Emulsion: Liquid containing tiny drops of oil or fat in suspension.

En croûte: Term used to describe food which is wrapped and cooked in pastry.

En papillote: Method of cooking in buttered or oiled paper or foil cases to preserve all the flavor and juices during cooking. The food is then served in the parcel.

Escalope: Slices of meat or fish which have been flattened and often coated with egg and crumbs, then fried in fat or oil.

Fahrenheit: A scale of temperature in which the freezing point of water is 32 degrees and boiling point 212 degrees.

Fennel: Vegetable with slight aniseed flavor. The seeds are also used.

Fenugreek: Slightly bitter seeds used whole or ground in curries for flavor and yellow coloring. It is a common ingredient in commercially blended curry powder.

Fines herbes: Combination of three or more delicate herbs used in French cooking; usually parsley, tarragon, chervil and chives.

Fish sauce: Thin sauce made from fermented fish and salt. Use sparingly although its strong odor disappears during cooking.

Five spice powder: A blend of five aromatic spices used as a seasoning and a condiment. Sichuan peppercorns, cinnamon bark, clove, fennel and star anise are the usual components.

Galangal: Aromatic ginger, which is available in two varieties: greater (creamy white flesh) and lesser (orange red flesh). If fresh it is pulped and if dried (usually the case outside Asia) it is ground.

Garam masala: A combination of spices used in Indian cooking. Cardamom, cumin, cloves, cinnamon, coriander seeds and peppercorns may be included.

Gelatin: Colorless powder derived from bones, cartilage and tendons. When dissolved in hot water it forms a thick liquid that turns to jelly when cold. It sometimes needs to be refrigerated to set.

Ghee: Clarified butter (i.e. butter with all the milk solids removed), which can be heated to a higher temperature than butter without burning. If unavailable commercially, heat butter in pan until it froths. Skim foam off top and pour butter into a heatproof dish, discarding the milky sediment in the base of the pan. When butter has solidified, scrape any milk solids off surface, then reheat butter in clean pan. Strain through cheesecloth to remove remaining milk solids. Ghee will keep 3–4 months without refrigeration if prepared properly.

Ginger, fresh: The root of rhizome ginger, with a crinkly grayish-yellow skin and fibrous flesh. Should be peeled before use and may be preserved by infusing in rice wine or dry sherry to produce ginger wine (or it may be grated and the juice extracted to produce ginger juice). Powdered and dried ginger are not suitable substitutes as the flavors differ. Fresh ginger is readily available, but if necessary substitute sweet or salt-pickled ginger, which can be bought at both Chinese and Japanese food stores.

Gingko nuts: Small oval-shaped white nuts sold dried or packed in cans in water. They have a fresh, crisp, nutty flavor which is useful in stuffings, braised dishes and soups.

Guei hwa sauce: Cassia flower wine.

Hoisin sauce: See *Chinese bean sauce.*

Ikan bilis: Tiny fish that have been cooked, then dried. After deep frying they are used as a garnish on food.

Infuse: To steep herbs, tea, etc., in boiling liquid to transfer flavor to the liquid.

Jaggery: Also known as palm sugar (from Nippah palm). It is sold in cakes, which should not be hard. Dark, unrefined and strong in flavor.

Julienne: Method of cutting food, particularly vegetables, in thin, even-sized strips or shreds.

Kamaboko: Loaf or cake of steamed, pureed fish which will keep approximately 1 week in refrigerator. It can be sliced and eaten as it is or used in soup, rice or noodle dishes.

Kombu: Dried kelp (seaweed) usually available in hard sheets. Wash before using in stock (dashi).

Konnyaku: Yam-based hard cake which is often used for texture in Japanese cooking. Blanch with boiling water before use.

Larding: The process of threading thin strips of fat bacon through dry meat, game birds and poultry using a specially designed larding needle.

Lemongrass: Grows profusely in South-east Asia. The lower part of the bulbous stems are used to impart strong, fragrant lemon flavor to dishes, particularly curries.

Lengkuas (laos): Dried and ground root of greater galangal with delicate, woody flavor.

Lentils: The most common varieties are green or split red. Lentils are an excellent source of protein. See *dhal.*

Lime: Fragrant citrus fruit used for its sour flavor in some Asian dishes.

Lotus root: Tubular root of lotus plant, characterized by a series of even-shaped round holes running the length of the root. The flesh is crisp and bland tasting. Used as a vegetable and in certain sweet dishes. Usually available canned in water, but if purchased fresh it must be thoroughly washed and peeled before boiling until tender.

Mint: Many species are available, all with slightly different flavors, e.g. spearmint. It does not blend easily with other herbs due to strong, distinctive flavor. Used fresh or dried in lamb or mutton dishes, salads, fruit drinks and punches.

Mirepoix: Mixture of meat and/or vegetables used to enhance flavor of meat, fish and shellfish dishes. Sauté 2 diced carrots, ½ cup diced onion, ¼ cup diced celery in two tablespoons of butter with a sprig of thyme and ¼ bay leaf until tender.

Mirin: A sweet, low-alcohol rice wine used in Japanese cooking. If unobtainable, substitute 1 teaspoon sugar for 1 tablespoon of mirin.

Miso: Japanese fermented soybean paste available in many different varieties according to the other seasonings and grains added to soybean base. It can take between 6 months and 3 years to ferment to maturity. Used as a basic flavoring in soups and as a topping for grilled foods. After opening, it should be stored in the refrigerator, where it will keep for months.

Mustard, black: Tiny black seeds used after dry roasting as a topping on curries. Their nutty flavor complements vegetarian dishes, in particular.

Noodles: Many different varieties of noodles — some fresh, some dried — are used in Asian cooking. Most are extruded strands of pastes made from water mixed with wheat flour, powdered beans or powdered rice. In some, eggs are added to provide extra flavor and nourishment. Seafood flavorings are sometimes added to those which will be used in soup noodle dishes. Some noodles only need soaking, while others should be cooked in boiling water until just tender. Sometimes deep fried noodles are added to salads or other dishes for texture. Whereas dried noodles will keep indefinitely, fresh will only keep in the refrigerator for a couple of days. Chinese varieties include *cellophane noodles, egg noodles* and *rice vermicelli.* Japanese varieties include *ramen* (egg), *udon* (wheat flour), *soba* (buckwheat) and *shirataki* (konnyaku).

Nori: Dried laver (seaweed) which is used extensively in Japanese cooking. Available in paper-thin sheets which should be broiled or warmed over heat before use, when it will change from a dark green to a more purplish color.

Nutmeg: Dark brown pods which are best purchased whole and then freshly ground before use in both savory and sweet dishes. Sweet, aromatic flavor.

Oyster sauce: Dark brown, viscous and salty sauce used both as a flavoring and a condiment.

Palm sugar: See *jaggery.*

Panada: A paste of flour, bread or toast used for binding minced meat or fish.

Pandan leaf: Long, deep-green leaf of Fragrant Screwpine (a species of the Pandanus family), it has a musky fragrance and adds a bright green color and distinctive flavor to Malay and Indonesian sweets.

Paneer: Fresh crumbly white cheese similar to ricotta. It can be homemade by curdling hot milk with lemon juice and then straining the milk solids through cheesecloth.

Pepper: Black, white and green peppercorns all come from the same vine but are picked at various stages of ripeness. Black peppercorns have been picked while still green, then dried. Used in sauces, marinades, soups and as a condiment. White peppercorns are produced by drying the inner part of the ripe red berry and are the hottest of the peppercorns. Used in fish and white sauces, and in some sweet dishes. Both black and white are also available as ground spices. Green peppercorns are the soft, unripe berries which are usually purchased canned or bottled in water. Used in pâtés and sauces. Unground black and white peppercorns will keep indefinitely in an airtight container. Green peppercorns will keep about six weeks in the refrigerator (in an airtight container) after opening.

Pipe: To decorate with an extruded thin strip of paste or cream, using a piping bag or kit.

Pita bread: Small flat round loaves which can be filled like a pocket (after carefully slicing off a small portion to form an opening) with a variety of sandwich fillings.

Plum sauce: Commercial preparation of mashed plums and seasonings. Used as a sauce dip for roast meats and occasionally as a seasoning in stir-fried dishes. Readily available in jars and small cans.

Pork omentum: Large, lace-like sheet of fat which can be purchased from Chinese or Continental food suppliers. It is sold by weight and will keep 2–3 days in refrigerator or longer in freezer. Used to wrap foods before cooking, to preserve moisture, add oil or simply to hold food together. If coated with flour or batter, it will form a crisp crust rather than simply melting away.

Praline: Melt ½ cup sugar with ½ vanilla bean in pan until a nut brown color. Remove from heat and quickly stir in ¾ cup roasted almonds. Pour into greased baking pan, cool, then pound or grind as finely as possible. Use as directed in individual recipes.

Preserve: To delay decomposition of any foodstuff by canning, pickling, freezing, salting or drying (dehydrating).

Pulses: Edible seeds of legumes, e.g. peas, beans, lentils. Also see *dhal.*

Rice paper: Paper-thin sheets of compressed and dried paste, used as an edible food wrapping. More commonly made with potato flour. Readily available and keeps well in dry conditions.

Rice vermicelli: Thin extruded rice flour noodles. When deep fried they expand into light crisp, white noodles. Also used in stir-fried dishes and soups. May be called rice sticks.

Rice vinegar: Dark vinegar with mild flavor used as a flavoring and condiment. If unobtainable, diluted cider vinegar may be used as a substitute.

Rice wine: See *sake.*

Rose water: Fragrant liquid made by distilling rose petals, usually the pink damask variety. Used to flavor drinks, sprinkled on desserts and added to curries and rice.

Roux: Mixture of butter and flour cooked together in pan before being used as thickening in sauces and gravies. Use equal amounts of butter and flour.

Saffron: Dried stigmas from saffron crocus. It has a strong aroma and honey-like, slightly bitter taste. Only a minute amount is necessary for color and flavor. Used in soups, stews and rice dishes.

Sake: Japanese rice wine often served heated and also used in cooking. Made by fermenting freshly steamed white rice. There are different types of sake but they fall into the two broad categories of sweet and dry. Sweet sake is considered to be the better of the two. Heat sake over hot water and never boil.

Sambal bajak: Red chili paste with dried shrimp and spices added.

Sambal ulek (oelek): Red chili paste. It is sometimes mixed with tamarind water. Used as an accompaniment or in curries.

Sansho: A commercial blend of chili powder, salt and sesame seeds. Used as a condiment with certain Japanese foods.

Salted black beans: Fermented black beans used in Chinese cooking. Drain, rinse and crush before cooking.

Scallion (green onion): Tall dark green leafy onion with a small white bulb. Also known as spring onion. It is used in stir-fries and salads.

Score: To cut lines across pastry, meat, vegetables or fruit using a sharp knife.

Seasoned flour: Flour mixed with seasonings of salt, pepper, herbs or spices.

Semolina: Coarsely ground cereal, usually wheat. Used in soups and puddings.

Serai: See *lemongrass.*

Sesame oil: Dark, strong-flavored cooking and seasoning oil derived from sesame seeds.

Sesame paste: Creamy, thick paste made from ground white sesame seeds. Known in the Middle East as *tahini.* The Chinese version is stronger in taste.

Sesame seeds: Small, flat seeds which may be either black or white. Both have a similar nutty flavor and should be roasted lightly before use as a garnish. Also used in salads, stir-fries and sweets, and as a coating for fried foods.

Shallot: Small member of the onion family with a stronger flavor than the larger onions. Grows in bulbs or clusters of cloves like garlic with a red-brown papery skin covering a pale lavender interior. Commonly used in French cooking, particularly sauces.

Shark's fin: Edible strands of dried cartilage from sharks' fins. Expensive but will keep indefinitely.

Shichimi: A blend of spices used in Japanese cooking and available from Japanese food suppliers. The exact blend varies but usually includes chili, black pepper, dried orange peel, sesame seeds, poppy seeds, slivers of nori and hemp seeds.

Shiitake mushrooms: Japanese dried mushrooms which should be soaked in cold water at least 30 minutes before use.

Shiratake noodles: Transparent noodles made from a tuber called *devil's tongue*. Used extensively in Japanese cooking.

Shrimp paste: If available fresh it is pink in color and must be kept in refrigerator. Dried shrimp paste has been fermented and salted and is usually sold in cakes, slabs or cans. Its strong, somewhat unpleasant aroma disappears during cooking.

Skim: To remove the surface scum of soup, stock, etc., with a spoon or skimmer.

Soybean paste: Known as *miso* in Japanese cooking. A variety of useful, strong-tasting seasoning pastes are made using fermented soybeans as the prime ingredient. Chinese varieties include sweet bean paste, hot bean paste, yellow bean paste.

Soy sauce: There are two main kinds. Light soy sauce is used to add flavor to stir-fried dishes, sauces and stocks, and as a dip, particularly with fried or roasted meats. Dark soy sauce is stronger and saltier in taste and is sometimes thicker. It is used primarily to add color and a salty taste.

Star anise: Eight-pointed star-shaped spice with a strong aniseed flavor.

Stock: Seasoned liquid used as basis for sauces, stews, casseroles, soups, etc.

Suet: Fat of kidneys and loins of sheep and cattle.

Sugar cane juice: The inner sweet liquid of sugar cane.

Sweet bean paste: Soybeans fermented with salt, sugar and seasonings. Used in marinades and dips. Hoisin sauce may be used as a substitute.

Tabasco sauce: Commercially produced thin, hot sauce made from a Mexican variety of chili.

Tahini: See *sesame paste.*

Tamarind: Fruit of the tamarind tree, the pulp of which is used to give a sour taste like lemon juice. If purchased dried, soak slices in warm water for 30 minutes and use only clear liquid after straining. If available fresh, soak 1 tablespoon of pulp in ½ cup (150ml) warm water for 5 minutes before straining.

Tangerine peel, dried: Used for its spicy, citrus flavor. Soak the peel 30 minutes in cold water and remove any pith before using. It is usually cooked whole and removed from dish before serving.

Tofu: See *bean curd.*

Truffle: Wild, pungent underground fungus which is considered to be a great delicacy. There are two main varieties: white, found mainly in Italy, and black (Perigord), found mostly in France.

Unleavened: Term used to refer to bread which has had no rising agent added to the dough.

Wasabi: Powdered green horseradish which is commonly used as an accompaniment to Japanese food, particularly raw fish dishes. It can be purchased ready-made in tubes or as a powder to be mixed up as required.

Water chestnuts: Dark brown-skinned bulbs from a type of water plant. The flesh is crisp, white and has a slightly sweet taste. Usually available canned in water but if fresh they must be peeled before use.

Whisk: To beat eggs, cream, etc., with a whisk to lighten and increase volume.

Wonton wrappers: Thin pastries made from a high-gluten flour and egg paste. If frozen, they must be thawed slowly before use. Keep moist under damp cloth during use as they dry and crack easily.

Yellow bean paste: Bean paste made from whole yellow soybeans.

Yellow beans, salted: Similar to salted black beans but lighter in color.

Index

Abalone Soup, 83
almonds
Almond Fingers, 318
Almond Soup, 83
Apricot and Almond Tart, 320
Austrian Almond Torte, 362
Chocolate Praline Pie, 367
Duck in Almond Sauce, 209
anchovies
Anchovies with Broccoli and Fettuccine, 133
Duck with Wine and Anchovies, 212
Fried Dried Anchovies with Peanuts, 54
Hot Anchovy and Garlic Dip, 56
Spaghetti with Clams, Scallops and Anchovies, 158
Anzac Cookies, 361
apple
Apple Amber, 361
Apple and Ginger Crisp, 318
Apple and Honey Pancake Gâteau, 319
Apple Dumplings, 319
Apple Fritters, 319
Apple Pie, 319
Apple Snow, 320
Apple Soufflé, 320
Apple Strudel, 320
Apples with Bacon, 38
Apples with Fried Calf's Liver, 256
Apple Tart from Alsace, 320
Baked Devonshire Apple Dumplings, 322
Bavarian Apple Strudel, 364
Caramelized Apple Tart, 325
Cheese-Crusted Apple Pudding, 326
Devonshire Apple Cake, 371
German Apple Pancake, 334
Herring and Apple Salad, 117
Latticed Apple Cake, 379
Pear and Apple Pie, 346
Red Cabbage and Apples, 122
Spicy Apple Teacake, 384
Swedish Apple Cake, 385
Toffeed Apple, 356
apricots
Apricot and Almond Tart, 320
Apricot Cheesecake, 321
Apricot Cheese Tart, 321
Apricot Crunchies, 362
Apricot Nut Cream Pie, 321
Apricot Nut Loaf, 362
Apricot Pie, 321
artichokes
Artichoke Heart Salad, 103
Artichoke Hors d'Oeuvre, 38
Pepper Steak with Artichoke Hearts, 280
Stuffed Artichokes, 78
asparagus
Asparagus and Crabmeat Soup, 83
Asparagus Cream Canapés, 38
Asparagus Hollandaise, 38
Asparagus in Butter, 298
Asparagus with Mustard-Flavored Dressing, 38
Asparagus with Tomato-Flavored Tagliatelle, 133
Steamed Asparagus on Egg Custard, 76
avocado
Avocado Mousse Salad, 104
Avocados with Shrimp, 39
Baked Avocados, 39
Chicken, Avocado and Orange Salad, 197
Chicken Livers with Avocado, 43
Orecchiette with Avocado, 61

bacon
Bacon and Broccoli Pasta Pie, 133
Bacon and Date Curls, 39
Fettuccine with Bacon and Mushrooms, 138
Lentils with Bacon, 274
Mushroom and Bacon Topping for Pasta, 150
Spaghetti with Tomatoes, Cheese and Bacon, 159
Bakewell Pudding, 322
Baklava, 362, 379
bamboo shoots
Shredded Beef with Bamboo Shoots, 70
Snow Peas, Mushrooms and Bamboo Shoots, 124
Squid and Bamboo Shoot Salad, 186
banana
Banana Cakes, 322, 362
Banana Cream Pie, 322
Banana Fritters, 320
Frosted Banana-Cream Cake, 371
Frozen Banana Pie, 333
Light Banana Soufflé, 341
Nutmeg Banana Custard, 345
Barley Soup, 83
bean curd
Assorted Vegetables with Bean Curd Skin, 103
Bean Curd Cakes with Fresh Cilantro and Soy Sauce, 104
Bean Curd in Spicy Coconut Milk Gravy, 105
Bean Curd, Mushrooms and Vegetables, 105
Bean Curd Skin "Noodles" with Young Soybeans, 298
Broiled Bean Curd with Miso Topping, 298
Deep Fried Bean Curd, Shrimp and Chicken Fritters, 208
Deep Fried Bean Curd with Sauce, 302
Deep Fried Crab and Bean Curd Balls, 172
Fried Bean Curd, 54
Fried Bean Curd and Scallions, 113
Fried Bean Curd Squares, 113
Hot Bean Curd with Pork, 269
Hotpot of Vegetables and Bean Curd, 305
Ma Po Bean Curd, 274
Minced Bean Curd Cake with Spinach, 118
Pock-Marked Mama's Bean Curd, 121
Smoked Vegetarian "Duck", 312
Spicy Bean Curd Salad, 126
Spinach with Bean Curd Dressing, 126
beans, dried
Broad Beans, Bacon and Sausage, 107
Creamed White Beans, 111
Greek White Beans, 115
Hot Bean Salad, 117
Pasta and Bean Soup, 95
Pistou Soup, 96
Preserved Cucumber and Ginger Stewed Chicken with Beans, 222
Pumpkin and Long Bean Curry, 122
Tuscan Bean Soup, 102
beans, green
Bean and Beet Salad, 104
Green Bean Sambal, 116
Green Beans with Sesame and Miso, 116
Green Beans with Tomatoes, 116
Trenette with Potatoes and Beans, 164
beansprouts
Fried Beansprouts, 113
Stir-Fried Beansprouts with Chicken, 229
beef
Bavarian-Style Sauerbraten, 257
Beef and Broccoli on Ribbon Noodles, 134
Beef and Vegetable Hotpot, 257
Beef in Buddhist Robes, 40
Beef in Coconut Sauce with Cabbage, 258
Beef in Spicy Coconut Gravy, 258
Beef Olives, 258
Beef Samosas, 258
Beef Steak and Kidney Pie, 259
Beef Vindaloo, 259

Beef with Celery and Button Mushrooms, 259
Braised Beef and Eggplant, 260
Burgundy Beef, 261
Cannelloni with Beef Filling, 136
Chinese Beef Steak, 263
Coconut Beef, 264
Consommé with Dumplings, 87
Corned Beef, 264
Fillet of Beef in Filo Pastry, 268
Irish Beef Stew, 270
Korean Barbecue, 218
Korean Hotpot, 271
Lancashire Steak Pie, 273
Malay Beef Stew, 274
Meat Pie — Stage Coach Inn, 276
Mixed Grill, 276
Noodles with Meat and Rich Sauce, 151
Peppered Fillet Steaks, 280
Pepper Steak with Artichoke Hearts, 280
Potato Gnocchi with Beef Sauce, 153
Pot Roast Stuffed Steak, 282
Rainbow Beef in Lettuce Leaves, 65
Roast Beef and Yorkshire Pudding, 284
Rosemary-Smoked Steaks, 287
Sesame Beefballs, 287
Shredded Beef with Bamboo Shoots, 70
Sichuan Beef Stew, 287
Spicy Ground Meat, 288
Steamboat, 228
Steamed Meat and Cabbage Loaf, 289
Stir-Fried Beef with Vegetables, 289
Sukiyaki, 290
Sweet Beef Satay, 292
Teriyaki Steaks, 294
beets
Bean and Beet Salad, 104
Beet and Endive Salad, 105
berries
Frosty Lemon Pie with Berry Sauce, 333
High Hat Berry Cream Pie, 336
Summer Berry Pudding, 356
see also individual berries
Birds' Nest Soup with Quail Eggs, 83
Blackberry Sauce, Floating Islands in, 331
Black-Bottom Pie, 323
Blackcurrants, Honey Ice Cream with a Coulis of, 336
Blueberry Pie, Crustless, 331
Bocuse, Paul, 14
Boeuf Bourguignonne, 261
Borsch, 84
Bouillabaisse, 167
Brazil Nut Stars, 366
breads
Fried Potato Bread, 114
Leavened Bread, 119
Naan, 119
Pumpkin Nut Bread, 381
Puri, 114
Unleavened Bread, 110
Brillat-Savarin, Jean Anthelme, 7, 9–11
British cooking, 28–9
broccoli
Anchovies with Broccoli and Fettuccine, 133
Bacon and Broccoli Pasta Pie, 133
Beef and Broccoli on Ribbon Noodles, 134
Broccoli and Mushroom Lasagne, 135
Broccoli in Foaming Lemon Butter, 107
Broccoli with Sesame Seeds, 107
Chicken Divan, 199
Farfalle with Broccoli Sauce, 138
Sautéed Broccoli, 123
Sliced Roast Duck with Broccoli, 228
Steamed Broccoli with Crabmeat Sauce, 129
Stuffed Dried Mushrooms with Broccoli, 129, 189
Brownies, 366
Brown Sugar Pie, Southern, 352
Brussels Sprouts with Chestnuts, 107

Buco Pie, 324
bulgur *see* cracked wheat
Buttermilk Lemon Pie, 324
Butterscotch Pie, Old-Fashioned, 345

cabbage
    Beef in Coconut Sauce with Cabbage, 258
    Borsch, 84
    Braised and Stuffed Green Cabbage, 260
    Braised Cabbage with Bacon Pieces, 106
    Cabbage in Coconut Milk, 108
    Cabbage Medley, 108
    Cabbage Rolls, 261
    Cabbage Soup, 84
    Chinese Cabbage Rolls, 263
    Chinese Cabbage with Pork or Shrimp, 110
    Coleslaw, 110
    Fried Salted Cabbage, 114
    Hungarian Cabbage Rolls, 270
    Partridges with Chestnuts and Red Cabbage, 243
    Red Cabbage and Apples, 122
    Sour Cabbage with Caraway Seeds, 124
    Sour Cabbage with Walnuts, 125
    Southern Indian Cabbage, 125
    Spaghetti and Cabbage, 313
    Spiced Cabbage, 126
    Steamed Meat and Cabbage Loaf, 289
Caesar Salad, 108
Calamari Provençale, 41
Canard à l'Orange, 219
cannelloni
    Cannelloni with Beef Filling, 136
    Cannelloni with Spinach and Ricotta Stuffing, 299
    Ricotta-Stuffed Cannelloni, 311
caramel
    Caramel Custard, 324
    Caramelized Apple Tart, 325
    Caramelized Oranges, 325
    Caramel Layer Cake, 366
    Caramel Sponge Dessert, 325
Carême, Marie-Antoine, 12–13
Carp, Steamed Golden, 187
carrots
    Carrot and Daikon Salad, 108
    Carrot and Water Chestnut Timbales, 109
    Carrot Soup, 84
    Carrots Vichy, 109
    Steam-Baked Carrot Ring, 352
Cassata, 325
Cassoulet de Castelnaudary, 262
cauliflower
    Cauliflower Cheese, 109
    Cauliflower Masala, 109
    Cauliflower-Stuffed Parathas, 41
    Creamed Cauliflower, 111
    Curried Cauliflower and Zucchini Soup, 89
    French Fried Cauliflower, 113
    Fried Cauliflower, 113
    Fusilli with Cauliflower and Tomato Sauce, 304
Caviar, Tagliolini with, 161
celery
    Braised Celery, 106
    Fresh Celery with Mustard Sauce, 113
Chapati, 110
cheese
    Baked Spinach and Cheese, 40
    Cheese and Cayenne Straws, 41
    Cheese and Macaroni Stuffed Peppers, 136
    Cheese and Tomato Flan, 300
    Cheese Blintzes, 41
    Cheese Fondue, 300
    Cheese Fondue Pie, 300
    Cheese Fritters, 41
    Cheese Mushrooms, 42
    Cheese Pasta in Broth, 84
    Cheese Soufflé, 300
    Fettuccine and Three Cheese Pie, 304

    Macaroni and Cheese, 306
    Macaroni with Cheese and Ham, 148
    Rice and Cheese Balls, 311
    Shrimp and Feta Cheese Casserole, 182
    Spinach Cheese Puffs, 75
    see also ricotta
cheesecakes
    Apricot Cheesecake, 321
    Cheesecake Pie, 325
    Lemon Cheesecake, 339
    Pineapple Ginger Cheesecake, 381
    Refrigerator Cheesecake, 351
cherries
    Black Forest Cherry Cake, 365
    Cherry Clafoutis, 326
    Cherry Pie, 330
    Crumbed Cherry Pie, 330
    Duck with Sour Cherries, 212
    Pigeons with Cherries, 245
    Quails with Cherry Stuffing, 247
    Quick Cherry Strudel, 349
    Roast Turkey with Cherry Stuffing, 226
Chess Pie — Southern Style, 326
chicken
    Balinese Noodles with Chicken in Coconut Sauce, 134
    Black Velvet Chicken, 193
    Broiled Chicken with Wine Sauce, 194
    Broiled Skewered Chicken, 194
    Cantonese Fruit Chicken, 195
    Caucasian Fried Chickens, 196
    Chicken Akbar, 196
    Chicken Amager, 197
    Chicken and Leek Pie, 198
    Chicken and Leek Soup, 85
    Chicken and Orange Kebabs, 198
    Chicken and Seafood Fondue, 198
    Chicken, Avocado and Orange Salad, 197
    Chicken Balls Simmered with Daikon, 199
    Chicken Consommé, 85
    Chicken Cooked with Soy Sauce and Lime Juice, 199
    Chicken Divan, 199
    Chicken in Chilindrón Sauce, 199
    Chicken in Cream Sauce, 200
    Chicken in Honey, 200
    Chicken in Rich Coconut Gravy, 200
    Chicken in Soy Sauce, 200
    Chicken Kashmir, 201
    Chicken Kebabs, 42
    Chicken Kiev Macadamia, 201
    Chicken Liver and Ham Gougère, 201
    Chicken Liver Pâté de Luxe, 42
    Chicken Livers Creole, 42
    Chicken Livers Flambé, 42
    Chicken Livers with Avocado, 43
    Chicken Livers with Green Peppercorns, 43
    Chicken Marengo, 201
    Chicken Mille-Feuille, 202
    Chicken Pie in Filo Pastry, 202
    Chicken Quiche, 203
    Chicken Rice Cake, 137
    Chicken Rolls with Salad, 203
    Chicken Russus, 204
    Chicken Sarma, 204
    Chicken Smothered with Oysters, 204
    Chicken Soup, 86
    Chicken Stew with Peas, Mushrooms and Olives, 204
    Chicken Suprêmes Madeira, 205
    Chicken Vol-au-Vent, 205
    Chicken Walnut Rolls, 43
    Chicken Wings Simmered in Wine, 44
    Chicken Wings with Plum Sauce, 44
    Chicken with Crisp Hot Peppers and Orange Peel, 205
    Chicken with Egg-Lemon Sauce, 205
    Chicken with Mushrooms and Cream, 207
    Chicken with Peppers, 207

    Chicken with Tarragon, 207
    Cock-a-Leekie, 87
    Corn, Chicken and Clam Pie, 169
    Cumin Chicken, 207
    Deep Fried Bean Curd, Shrimp and Chicken Fritters, 208
    Deep Fried Chicken Livers with Spicy Dressing, 208
    Deep Fried Marinated Chicken, 209
    Diced Chicken and Cashew Nuts, 51
    Diced Chicken with Dried Chilies, 209
    Drunken Chicken, 209
    East Indies Barbecued Chicken, 213
    Fried Chicken with Sweet Basil and Chili, 214
    Fried Diced Chicken with Sweet Bean Paste, 214
    Fried Stuffed Chicken Rolls, 54
    Gingered Chicken, 214
    Golden Chicken Casserole, 215
    Honey and Sesame Chicken Wings, 217
    Javanese Fried Chicken, 217
    Korean Barbecue, 218
    Kung Pao Chicken, 218
    Lemon Chicken, 218
    Lemon Chicken Wings, 57
    Mango Chicken, 219
    Mulligatawny Soup, 94
    Noodles with Chicken and Vegetables, 219
    Oyster Sauce Chicken in Parcels, 221
    Pasta and Vegetable Ring with Cream of Chicken
        Filling, 153
    Peking Drumsticks, 221
    Poached Chicken, 221
    Preserved Cucumber and Ginger Stewed Chicken
        with Beans, 222
    Quick Chicken and Mango Curry, 224
    Ravioli in Chicken Broth, 96
    Sake-Steamed Chicken, 226
    Salt-Baked Chicken, 226
    Sambal Chicken, 227
    Saucy Chicken Turnovers, 68
    Skewered Chicken and Pork Adobo, 227
    Skewered Chicken Meatballs with Radishes, 227
    Spicy Barbecued Chicken, 228
    Spit-Roasted Chicken with Piquant Rice, 159
    Steamboat, 228
    Steamed Stuffed Chicken Wings, 76
    Stir-Fried Beansprouts with Chicken, 229
    Tandoori Chicken, 230
    Thai Peppered Chicken, 230
    Threaded Chicken with Peppers, 230
    Tikka Chicken, 231
    Viennese Fried Chicken, 233
    Wine and Chicken Casserole, 233
    Yogurt Chicken, 234
Chickpeas, Spicy, 75
chicory, *see* endive
Chiffon Pie, Black Forest, 323
Chiffon Pie, Paradise, 345
chili
    Chili con Carne, 44
    Chili Eggs, 47
    Chili Pork Spareribs, 262
    Stuffed Chilies, 78
Chinese cooking, 16–17
chocolate
    Black-Bottom Pie, 323
    Chocolate-Coated Pears, 326
    Chocolate Fudge Bars, 367
    Chocolate Fudge Cake, 367
    Chocolate Ice Cream Roll, 328
    Chocolate Mousse, 328
    Chocolate Pie, 328
    Chocolate Praline Pie, 367
    Chocolate Prune Cake, 369
    Chocolate Roll, 369
    Chocomallows, 369
    Frozen Chocolate Velvet Pie, 333
    German Chocolate Tarts, 334

Latticed Chocolate Rum Pie, 338
Rich Chocolate Butter Cake, 382
Sachertorte, 351
Steamed Chocolate Pudding, 354
Chorley Cakes, 369
Choy Sum, Sautéed Fresh, 123
Christmas Cake, Sienna, 383
Christmas Cookies, Swedish, 385
Cider Honey Cake, 370
Cilantro and Soy Sauce, Bean Curd Cakes with, 104
Cinnamon Shapes, 370
clams
 Clams in Yellow Bean Sauce, 47
 Clam Soup, 86
 Clams with Sausage and Ham, 169
 Corn, Chicken and Clam Pie, 169
 Macaroni Shells with Clam Sauce, 150
 Neapolitan Clam Soup, 94
 Noodles with Clams, 150
 Spaghetti with Clams, 156
 Spaghetti with Clams, Scallops and Anchovies, 158
Cock-a-Leekie, 87
coconut
 Balinese Noodles with Chicken in Coconut Sauce, 134
 Bean Curd in Spicy Coconut Milk Gravy, 105
 Cabbage in Coconut Milk, 108
 Chicken in Rich Coconut Gravy, 200
 Chili Shrimp in Coconut Milk, 168
 Coconut Beef, 264
 Coconut Cream Pie, 328
 Coconut Fruit Pie, 328
 Coconut Milk Soup, 87
 Coconut Pancakes, 328
 Coconut Rice, 137
 Fish in Coconut Sauce, 173
 Rice Cooked in Coconut Milk, 154
 Spicy Coconut Pudding, 352
cod
 Cod with Olives and Tomatoes, 169
 Cod with Potatoes, Onions and Black Olives, 169
 Omelet Arnold Bennett, 60
coffee
 Coffee Mousse in Meringue Shell, 330
 Crumble-Top Coffee Cake, 371
 Ginger Coffee Cake, 374
 Hazelnut Coffee Cake, 376
Coleslaw, 110
Coq au Vin, 233
Coquilles Saint Jacques à la Crême, 70
corn
 Corn, Chicken and Clam Pie, 169
 Rich Corn Soup, 99
 Spanish Corn, 126
 Spicy Corn Fritters, 75
Coulibiac, 169
crab
 Asparagus and Crabmeat Soup, 83
 Baked Crab, 166
 Crab Hotpot, 170
 Crab Mornay, 170
 Crab Quiche, 170
 Crab-Stuffed Cucumber, 47
 Crab with Vinegared Dressing, 48
 Deep Fried Crab and Bean Curd Balls, 172
 Deep Fried Crabmeat Balls, 50
 Meeting Street Crab, 176
 Pearls Hiding in a Crab, 63
 Pork, Shrimp and Crab Ball Soup, 96
 Savory Crab Dip, 68
 Singapore Chili Crab, 184
 Steamed Broccoli with Crabmeat Sauce, 129
 Straw Mushrooms in Crab Sauce, 129
 Stuffed Crab Claws, 78
 Stuffed Crab Shells, 79
Crayfish, Fettuccine with, 138
Cream Horns, 370

Crêpes Royale, Strawberry, 355
cucumber
 Burmese Cucumber and Shrimp Salad, 108
 Crab-Stuffed Cucumber, 47
 Cucumber and Wakame Salad, 112
 Cucumber Soup, 89
 Cucumber with Pork Stuffing, 49
 Cucumber with Yogurt, 112
 Cucumber Yogurt Dip, 49
 Portuguese Cucumber, 121
 Preserved Cucumber and Ginger Stewed Chicken with Beans, 222
 Sliced Cucumber Stuffed with Shrimp and Pork, 73
 Spicy Cucumber Dish, 126
curries
 Chicken Kashmir, 201
 Cream Curry of Mushrooms, Peas and Tomato, 302
 Creamed Shrimp Curry, 172
 Dhal Curry with Coconut, 304
 Eggplant Curry, 304
 Ham Curry, 269
 Lamb and Potato Curry, 271
 Lentil and Vegetable Curry, 306
 Mutton and Eggplant Curry, 277
 North Indian Lamb Curry, 278
 Pumpkin and Long Bean Curry, 122
 Quick Chicken and Mango Curry, 224
 Shrimp Curry, 182
 Sour Hot Fish Curry, 186
 Southern Indian Fish Curry, 186
 Vegetable Cutlets in Curry Sauce, 316
Curry Puffs, 50
custards
 Basic Custard Pie, 322
 Caramel Custard, 324
 Lemon Egg Custard, 340
 Nutmeg Banana Custard, 345
 Orange Custard, 345
 Pineapple Custard, 349

daikon
 Carrot and Daikon Salad, 108
 Chicken Balls Simmered with Daikon, 199
dates
 Bacon and Date Curls, 39
 Date and Peanut Ragamuffins, 371
dhal
 Dhal Curry with Coconut, 304
 Simple Dhal Stew, 124
Dhansak, 279
dips
 Eggplant Dip, 52
 Fish Roe Spread, 53
 Hot Anchovy and Garlic Dip, 56
 Savory Crab Dip, 68
 Tahina Cream Dip, 81
Dolmadakia, 66
Doughnuts, Berlin, 364
duck
 Andalusian Duckling with Olives, 193
 Cantonese Roast Duck, 195
 Charcoal-Roasted Duck Stuffed with Lotus Leaves, 196
 Crispy Home-Style Duck, 207
 Duck and Orange Terrine, 52
 Duck in Almond Sauce, 209
 Duckling Stuffed with Apples and Raisins, 213
 Duck Melissa, 210
 Duck Smoked with Camphor Wood and Tea Leaves, 210
 Duck Soup with Water Chestnuts, 89
 Duck with Honey, 210
 Duck with Sour Cherries, 212
 Duck with Wine and Anchovies, 212
 Orange Duck, 219
 Peking Duck, 221
 Roast Duck with Horseradish, 224

 Sliced Roast Duck with Broccoli, 228
 Tangy Braised Game Birds, 252
 Terrine of Duckling with Orange, 82
 Three Courses of Peking Duck, 230
 Wild Duck Casserole, 255
 Wild Duck with Mashed Taro Stuffing and Oyster Sauce, 233
dumplings, 236, 319, 322

eggplant
 Braised Beef and Eggplant, 260
 Braised Eggplant with Onions and Tomatoes, 106
 Crisp Eggplant Slices, 112
 Eggplant Braised with Soybean Paste, 112
 Eggplant Curry, 304
 Eggplant Dip, 52
 Eggplant Sichuan Style, 304
 Eggplant with Dried Shrimp Topping, 112
 Fried Eggplant with Sesame Seed Dressing, 114
 Macaroni and Eggplant Pie, 147
 Mutton and Eggplant Curry, 277
 Stuffed Eggplant, 314
eggs
 Chili Eggs, 47
 Crisp-Fried Egg Rolls, 48
 Egg Flower Soup, 89
 Egg-Lemon Soup, 89
 Egg Masala, 52
 Persian Carpet Eggs, 63
 Piperade, 307
 Sherried Eggs, 63
 Scrambled Eggs Parsi Style, 70
 Stuffed Eggs with Mushrooms, 79
 see also omelets
Empanaditas, 52
Enchiladas, 213
endive
 Beet and Endive Salad, 105
 Belgian Endive with Mornay Sauce, 40
 Braised Belgian Endive, 106
Escoffier, Georges Auguste, 13, 14

Falafels, 50
Farfalle with Broccoli Sauce, 138
fennel
 Braised Fennel, 106
 Fennel Peas, 113
 Onion and Fennel Soup, 95
fettuccine
 Anchovies with Broccoli and Fettuccine, 133
 Fettuccine alla Carbonara, 138
 Fettuccine and Olive Sauce, 138
 Fettuccine and Three Cheese Pie, 304
 Fettuccine with Bacon and Mushrooms, 138
 Fettuccine with Lobster or Crayfish, 138
 Fettuccine with Prosciutto, 139
 Pasta and Vegetable Ring, 153
figs
 Gingered Figs in Brandy, 335
 Stuffed Figs, 356
fish
 Baked Fish with Creamed Tomato Sauce, 166
 Baked Fish with Port, 167
 Baked Stuffed Fish, 167
 Barbecued Whole Fish, 167
 Bouillabaisse, 167
 Cantonese New Year Salad, 168
 Capri Fish Soup, 84
 Deep Fried Fish Fillets with Black Sesame Dressing, 50
 Fish and Fruit Salad Filipina, 173
 Fish Cutlets, 173
 Fish Fritters, 53
 Fish in Coconut Sauce, 173
 Fish in Taucheo Sauce, 174
 Fish Pâté, 53
 Fish Puree, 53

Fish Roe Spread, 53
Fish Soufflé, 174
Fish with Cheese and Tomato Sauce, 174
Fish with Lime and Macadamia Nut Butter, 174
Fish with Tomatoes, Wine and Oregano, 174
Fresh Fish Pie, 174
Fried Fish in Beer Batter, 175
Marinated Fish Appetizer, 58
Pickled Fish, 63
Quenelles of Pike, 179
Ravioli Stuffed with Fish and Ricotta Cheese, 154
Roasted Fish Parcels, 179
Small Fried Fish with Sambal Stuffing, 185
Smoked Fish Salad, 73
Somerset Casserole, 186
Sour Hot Fish Curry, 186
Sour Hot Fish Stew, 186
Southern Indian Fish Curry, 186
Spiced Fish Wrapped in Banana Leaves, 186
Steamed Whole Fish, 188
Sweet and Sour Fish, 190
Treasure Ship Fish, 191
Trenette with Fish Sauce, 163
Whole Baked Fish Served on a Hot Plate, 192
  see also individual fishes
fondues
  Cheese Fondue, 300
  Chicken and Seafood Fondue, 198
French cooking, 8–14, 18–19
fritters
  Apple Fritters, 319
  Banana Fritters, 322
  Cheese Fritters, 41
  Fish Fritters, 53
  Lentil Fritters with Yogurt, 306
  Shrimp Fritters, 72
  Spicy Corn Fritters, 75
  Vine (Grape) Leaf Fritters, 82
  Whitebait Fritters, 82
Fritto Misto di Mare, 53
fruit
  French Fruit Tart with Cream Cheese Crust, 332
  Fried Fruit Pies, 332
  Fruit Basket, 333
  Fruit Tarts, 371
  Fruit Turnovers, 333
  Hot Fruit Salad Flambé, 337
  Tropical Fruit Flambé, 356
  Tropical Fruit Tart, 356
  see also individual fruits
Fusilli with Cauliflower and Tomato Sauce, 304

Gado Gado, 117
Garbanzo Balls, Deep Fried, 50
Garlic Soup, 90
Gâteau de Pithiviers Feuilleté, 372
German cooking, 30–1
ginger
  Gingerbread, 374
  Ginger Coffee Cake, 374
  Ginger Crunch, 374
  Gingered Chicken, 214
  Ginger Rice, 141
  Golden Ginger Gems, 374
  Little Ginger Puddings, 341
  Pineapple Ginger Cheesecake, 381
gnocchi
  Potato Gnocchi with Beef Sauce, 153
  Potato Gnocchi with Tomato Sauce, 308
  Pumpkin Gnocchi, 308
goose
  Austrian Roast Goose, 193
  Garlic Goose, 214
  Goose Brûlée Attunga, 215
  Goose Caprice, 216
  Goose Cassoulet, 216
  Goose Liver Pilaf, 141

Hungarian Goose Loaf, 217
Pomeranian Roast Goose Stuffed with Prunes and Apples, 222
Roast Goose Served with Braised Sauerkraut, 224
Roast Goose with Apricot-Stuffed Apples, 224
Roast Goose with Baked Pears, 225
Stuffed Goose with Applesauce, 229
Goulash, 268
  Székely Goulash, 292
grape leaves
  Grape Leaf Fritters, 82
  Rice-Stuffed Grape Leaves, 66
Gratin Dauphinois, 121
Gravlax, 58
grouper
  Fried Yellow Fish with Garlic Chives, 175
grouse
  Grouse Casserole with Dumplings, 236
  Grouse Liver Dumplings, 236
  Grouse Pie, 239
  Roast Grouse, 248
  Salmis of Grouse, 251
Guérard, Michel, 14
guinea fowl
  Guinea Fowl en Papillote, 239
  Guinea Fowl Royale, 239
  Roast Guinea Fowl Jerez, 248
  Roast Guinea Fowl with Brie, 248
  Salt-Baked Guinea Fowl, 252
Guinness Cake, 376

Haddock, Mousse of Smoked, 59
Halva, 376
ham
  Baked Country Ham with Cumberland Sauce, 256
  Chicken Liver and Ham Gougère, 201
  Clams with Sausage and Ham, 169
  Ham Cornets, 55
  Ham Curry, 269
  Honey Baked Ham, 269
  Honey-Glazed Ham, 56
  Macaroni with Cheese and Ham, 148
  Pea and Ham Soup, 95
  Turkey with Ham and Olives, 233
Hamburgers, Homemade Tasty, 56
hare
  Hare Stew, 239
  Hare with Prune Sauce, 240
  Hare with Sour Cream Sauce, 240
  Hunter's Hare, 241
  Jugged Hare, 241
  Paprika Hare, 242
  Roast Saddle of Hare, 250
Hash, Swedish, 130
Hazelnut Coffee Cake, 376
herrings
  Herring and Apple Salad, 117
  Herrings in Sour Cream, 55
Honey Nut Pastries, 336

ice cream
  Cassata, 325
  Chocolate Ice Cream Roll, 328
  Green Tea Ice Cream, 335
  Honey Ice Cream with a Coulis of Blackcurrants, 336
  Neapolitan Strawberry Ice Cream, 345
  Pumpkin Ice Cream Pie, 349
Indian cooking, 32–3
Indonesian cooking, 26–7
Italian cooking, 7–8, 22–3

Japanese cooking, 20–1
Jewfish, Baked, 167
Junket, Devonshire, 331

kebabs
  chicken, 42, 198, 227
  lamb, 270, 272, 287
kiwi fruit
  Angel Kiwi Tarts, 318
  Kiwi Pie, 338
  Squid and Kiwi Fruit Salad, 76
Kofta, 267
Kugelhupf, 361

Ladies' Fingers, Stuffed, 315
  see also okra
lamb
  Baby Lamb Stew, 256
  Baby Lamb with Herbs and Garlic, 256
  Baked Stuffed Leg of Lamb, Kashmiri Style, 257
  Braised Lamb with Fruit and Nuts, 260
  Crown Roast of Lamb, 264
  Kebabs of Ground Lamb, 270
  Lamb and Potato Curry, 271
  Lamb Biryani, 271
  Lamb in Spinach Puree, 272
  Lamb on Skewers, 272
  Lamb with Olives, 273
  Leg of Lamb Marinated in Wine with Juniper Berries, 273
  Mongolian Lamb, 276
  Moussaka, 276
  North Indian Lamb Curry, 278
  Parsi Meat, Lentil and Vegetable Stew, 279
  Parslied Leg of Lamb, 280
  Roast of Lamb, 285
  Roast Stuffed Loin of Lamb with Marmalade Sauce, 285
  Roast Suckling Lamb, 287
  Shish Kebabs, 287
  Spicy Ground Meat, 288
  Venetian Risotto with Lamb, 297
  see also mutton
la Reynière, Grimod de, 9
lasagne
  Broccoli and Mushroom Lasagne, 135
  Calabrian Lasagne, 135
  Green Lasagne in the Emilia-Romagna Style, 141
  Lasagne Ferrara Style, 143
  Lasagne with Mushroom Sauce, 143
  Lasagne with Veal and Pork, 144
  Vegetable Lasagne, 317
La Varenne, François Pierre de, 8–9
leeks
  Braised Pork and Leek Rolls, 260
  Broiled Leeks with Miso Dressing, 299
  Chicken and Leek Pie, 198
  Chicken and Leek Soup, 85
  Cream of Leek Soup, 87
  Leeks à la Grecque, 57
  Leeks in Tomato and Parsley Sauce, 118
  Northumbrian Leek Pudding, 119
  Venison Sautéed with Leeks, 255
lemon
  Buttermilk Lemon Pie, 324
  Egg-Lemon Soup, 89
  Frosty Lemon Pie with Berry Sauce, 333
  Lemon Cheesecake, 339
  Lemon Cheesecake Pie with Sour Cream Topping, 339
  Lemon Chicken, 218
  Lemon Egg Custard, 340
  Lemon Meringue Pie, 340
  Lemon Soufflé Pie, 340
  Lemon Yogurt Cake, 379
lentils
  Casserole of Rabbit with Lentils, 236
  Cold Lentil Cakes in Yogurt Sauce, 302
  Cream of Lentil Soup, 87
  Deep Fried Lentil Savories, 51
  Lentil and Vegetable Curry, 306

Lentil Fritters with Yogurt, 306
Lentil Soup, 91
Lentils with Bacon, 274
Parsi Meat, Lentil and Vegetable Stew, 279
see also dhal
lettuce
  Green Salad, 116
  Rainbow Beef in Lettuce Leaves, 65
limes
  Fish with Lime and Macadamia Nut Butter, 174
  Strawberry and Lime Tart, 354
linguine
  Linguine with Squid, 145
  Pasta and Vegetable Ring, 153
Linzertorte, 341
liver
  Apples with Fried Calf's Liver, Berlin Style, 256
  Assorted Livers in Coconut Chili Sauce, 256
  see also chicken; grouse
lobster
  American Lobster, 166
  Cornish Lobsters, 169
  Fettuccine with Lobster, 138
  Lobster Thermidor, 176
  Lobster with Mustard Sauce, 57
loganberry
  Chocolate-Coated Pears with Loganberry Sauce, 326
  Loganberry Soufflé, 342
Lotus Rice, 147
Love Letters, Hungarian, 338

macadamia nuts
  Chicken Kiev Macadamia, 201
  Hawaiian Macadamia Nut Pie, 336
macaroni
  Cheese and Macaroni Stuffed Peppers, 136
  Macaroni and Cheese, 306
  Macaroni and Eggplant Pie, 147
  Macaroni and Pork Pie, 148
  Macaroni Shells with Clam Sauce, 150
  Macaroni with Cheese and Ham, 148
Madeira Pudding, 342
Malaysian cooking, 24–5
mango
  Mango Chicken, 219
  Mango Quails, 241
  Quick Chicken and Mango Curry, 224
Matchsticks, 379
meatballs
  Danish Meatballs, 267
  Deep Fried Meatballs, 267
  Greek Meatballs, 269
  Konigsberg Meatballs, 271
  Sesame Beefballs, 287
  Swedish Meatballs with Dill Sauce, 291
Medici, Catherine de, 8
melon
  Frosted Sesame Melon, 333
  Melon in Port, 342
Mexican cooking, 34–5
Mince Pie Alaska, 342
Minestrone, 92
Miso Soup, 94
Molasses Loaf, Irish, 379
Montagné, Prosper, 13
Moules à la Provençale, 59
Moussaka, 276
muffins, 52, 371, 380, 385
Mulligatawny Soup, 94
mushrooms
  Bean Curd, Mushrooms and Vegetables, 105
  Braised Black Mushrooms, 106
  Bróccoli and Mushroom Lasagne, 135
  Cheese Mushrooms, 42
  Clear Soup with Shrimp and Mushroom, 87
  Cream Curry of Mushrooms, Peas and Tomato, 302
  Fettuccine with Bacon and Mushrooms, 138

Fried Savory Pies, 54
Fried Stuffed Mushrooms, 55
Lasagne with Mushroom Sauce, 143
Mushrooms à la Grecque, 59
Mushroom and Bacon Topping for Pasta, 150
Mushrooms with Breadcrumbs and Scallions, 307
Salt Broiled Shiitake Mushrooms, 123
Sautéed Mushrooms, 123
Scallops with Shrimp and Mushrooms, 181
Snow Peas, Mushrooms and Bamboo Shoots, 124
Spaghetti with Tuna and Mushroom Sauce, 159
Straw Mushrooms in Crab Sauce, 129
Stuffed Dried Mushrooms with Broccoli, 129, 189
Stuffed Eggs with Mushrooms, 79
Stuffed Mushroom Caps, 79, 129
Tagliatelle with Prosciutto and Mushrooms, 160
Three Kinds of Mushrooms, 131
mussels
  Mussels Marinière, 177
  Mussel Soup, 94
  Mussels Venetian Style, 177
  Mussels with Garlic, 59
  Spaghetti with Mussels and White Wine, 159
mutton
  Mutton and Eggplant Curry, 277
  Mutton Korma, 277
  Mutton Mysore, 278
  see also lamb

Naan, 119
Nachos, 60
Nasi Goreng, 143
noodles
  Balinese Noodles with Chicken, 134
  Beef and Broccoli on Ribbon Noodles, 134
  Fried Fresh Rice-Flour Noodles, 139
  Fried Hokkien Noodles, 140
  Fried Rice Noodles, 140
  Fried Thai Noodles, 140
  Fried Wheat Noodles, 141
  Hokkien Fried Noodles, 142
  Indian Fried Noodles, 142
  Noodle Baskets, 150
  Noodles in a Pot, 94
  Noodles with Chicken and Vegetables, 219
  Noodles with Clams, 150
  Noodles with Meat and Rich Sauce, 151
  Rich Noodle Soup with Seafood, 154
  Siamese-Style Noodles, 155
  Simple Noodle Dish, 156
  Swabian Noodles, 130
  Vietnamese Noodle Soup, 102
nori
  Nori-Rolled Sushi, 151
  Nori-Wrapped Shrimp, 60
Nut Fudge Pie, 345

Oat Cake, Golden, 374
okra
  Masala Potato with Okra, 118
  Okra Salad, 120
  Stuffed Ladies' Fingers, 315
omelets
  Chinese Vegetable Omelet, 302
  Egyptian Omelet, 213
  Hot Pepper Omelet, 56
  Omelet Arnold Bennett, 60
  Omelet Roll, 120
onions
  French Onion Soup, 90
  Glazed Onions, 114
  Onion and Fennel Soup, 95
  Onion and Tomato Salad, 120
  Onion Pie, 60
  Stuffed Onions, 130
oranges
  California Orange Cake, 366

Caramelized Oranges, 325
Chieken and Orange Kebabs, 198
Chicken, Avocado and Orange Salad, 197
Duck and Orange Terrine, 52
Orange-Blossom Cake, 380
Orange Custard, 345
Orange Duck, 219
Pork-Stuffed Oranges, 65
Roast Woodcocks with Orange Sauce, 251
Strawberries and Oranges with Port, 354
Tagliolini with Orange and Tomato Sauce, 161
Terrine of Duckling with Orange, 82
orecchiette
  Orecchiette with Avocado, 61
  Orecchiette with Olive Pulp, 61
Osso Bucco, 278
Oxtail with Dumplings, English, 267
oysters
  Baked Oysters, 40
  Chicken Smothered with Oysters, 204
  Fried Oysters, 54
  Galway Oyster Soufflé, 55
  Herbed Oysters, 55
  Oysters Mornay, 61
  Oysters Opera, 61
  Russian Oysters, 67
  Spiced Oysters, 74

Paella, 152
pancakes
  Coconut Pancakes, 328
  Cream Cheese Pancakes, 330
  German Apple Pancake, 334
  Layered Pancakes, 339
papaya
  Green Papaya Salad, 116
  Papaya Agar Agar, 345
Parathas, Cauliflower-Stuffed, 41
Parkin, Yorkshire, 385
Parsnips in Orange Sauce, 120
partridge
  Braised Stuffed Partridge with Port Alcantara, 235
  Partridge Pie, 243
  Partridges with Chestnuts and Red Cabbage, 243
  Roast Partridge, 248
passionfruit
  Passionfruit Flummery, 346
  Passionfruit Pavlova, 346
  Passionfruit Sponge, 381
pasta
  Bacon and Broccoli Pasta Pie, 133
  Cheese Pasta in Broth, 84
  Pasta and Bean Soup, 95
  Tuna and Spiral Pasta Casserole, 164
  see also types of pasta
pasta sauces
  Mushroom and Bacon Topping for Pasta, 150
  Quick Seafood Sauce for Pasta, 153
  see also types of pasta
pâté
  Chicken Liver Pâté de Luxe, 42
  Fish Pâté, 53
  Pigeon Pâté with Chinese Herbs, 64
Pavlova, Passionfruit, 346
peaches
  Fresh Peach Pie, 332
  Peaches in Wine, 346
  Pheasant with Peaches, 245
Peanut Butter Cookies, 381
pears
  Chocolate-Coated Pears with Loganberry Sauce, 326
  Golden Pear Pie, 335
  Pear and Apple Pie, 346
  Pear Pie, 347
  Pears in Red Wine, 347
  Pear Tart, 348
  Roast Goose with Baked Pears, 225

peas
   Cream Curry of Mushrooms, Peas and Tomato, 302
   Fennel Peas, 113
   Pea Soup with Sour Cream, 96
   Venetian Rice and Peas, 165
peas, split
   Pea and Ham Soup, 95
   Pea and Pork Rib Soup, 95
   Pease Pudding, 121
Pecan Pie, 348, 381
peppers
   Casserole of Peppers, 109
   Cheese and Macaroni Stuffed Peppers, 136
   Chicken with Crisp Hot Peppers, 205
   Chicken with Peppers, 207
   Hot Pepper Omelet, 56
   Rice with Pork, Tomatoes and Peppers, 154
   Stuffed Red Peppers, 80
   Sweet Pepper Salad, 130
   Threaded Chicken with Peppers, 230
   Tuna and Peppers in Soy Sauce, 191
Persimmon Crunch Pie, 349
pheasant
   Basque Pheasant, 235
   Braised Pheasant with Mushrooms, 235
   Pheasant Ballottine, 243
   Pheasant in a Pot, 244
   Pheasant in Cider, 244
   Pheasant with Bacon and Sour Cream, 244
   Pheasant with Peaches, 245
   Roast Pheasant, 249
   Roast Pheasants with Wild Rice Stuffing, 249
   Sliced Pheasant Sautéed with Bamboo Shoots and
      Mustard Greens, 252
   Tangy Braised Game Birds, 252
Pickled Fish, 63
Pickled Pork, Roast, 285
pigeon
   Pigeon Pâté with Chinese Herbs Steamed in Soup
      Ramekins, 64
   Pigeon Pie, 245
   Pigeons with Cherries, 245
   Roast Pigeons Wonga with Banana Stuffing, 250
Pike, Quenelles of, 179
Pilau, 307
pineapple
   Crusted Pineapple Slices, 331
   Pineapple Boats, 64
   Pineapple Custard, 349
   Pineapple Ginger Cheesecake, 381
   Pineapple Sherbet, 349
   Spiced Pineapple, 126
Piperade, 307
Pistou Soup, 96
pizza
   Pizza Slice, 64
   Neapolitan Pizza, 307
Plum Pie, 349
pork
   Braised Pork and Leek Rolls, 260
   Braised Pork Ribs, 261
   Cassoulet de Castelnaudary, 262
   Chili Pork Spareribs, 262
   Crumbed Pork Slices, 264
   Deep Fried Pork and Shrimp Rolls, 51
   Five Spice and Garlic Spare Ribs, 53
   Hawaiian Pork Chops, 269
   Hot Bean Curd with Pork, 269
   Korean Barbecue, 218
   Lasagne with Veal and Pork, 144
   Macaroni and Pork Pie, 148
   Marinated Roast Pork Fillet, 274
   Pan-Fried Pork in Sweet Ginger Sauce, 279
   Pea and Pork Rib Soup, 95
   "Pearl" Balls, 121
   Pickled Pork with Sauerkraut, 280
   Pork and Veal English Pie, 280

Pork and Vegetable Casserole, 281
Pork Casserole with Herb Scone Top, 281
Pork Chops in Fruit Sauce, 281
Pork in Soy Sauce, 282
Pork Liver Terrine, 64
Pork Pies, 282
Pork Satay, 282
Pork, Shrimp and Crab Ball Soup, 96
Pork-Stuffed Oranges, 65
Pork Vindaloo, 282
Pork Wontons, 65
Red Barbecued Pork, 284
Rice with Pork, Tomatoes and Peppers, 154
Rillettes of Pork, 67
Roast Pickled Pork, 285
Roast Pork with Crackling and Applesauce, 285
Roast Spare Ribs, 285
Shredded Pork in Sesame Pouches, 71
Skewered Chicken and Pork Adobo, 227
Sliced Cucumber Stuffed with Shrimp and Pork, 73
Steamboat, 228
Steamed Meat and Cabbage Loaf, 289
Steamed Pork and Yam Slices, 289
Sweet and Sour Pork Vietnam Style, 292
Székely Goulash, 292
Vegetable Pork Rolls, 82
Vindaloo, 297
Potage "la Mer", 178
potatoes
   Baked Chive Potatoes, 104
   Baked Stuffed Potatoes, 298
   Bavarian Potato Salad, 104
   Cardamom Glazed Sweet Potatoes, 108
   Creamed, Scalloped Potatoes with Rosemary, 111
   Fried Potato Bread, 114
   Game Chips, 114
   Indonesian Salad, 117
   Irish Potato Soup, 91
   Jacket Baked Potatoes, 117
   Lamb and Potato Curry, 271
   Masala Potato with Okra, 118
   Miso Potatoes, 119
   Potato Cakes, 121
   Potato Cheese Puff, 121
   Potato Cutlets, 122
   Potatoes and Cheese au Gratin, 121
   Potatoes Sautéed with Onions, 122
   Potato Gnocchi with Beef Sauce, 153
   Potato Gnocchi with Tomato Sauce, 308
   Puréed Potatoes and Apples with Black Pudding,
      122
   Swedish Hash, 130
   Swiss Fried Potatoes, 131
   Trenette with Potatoes and Beans, 164
   Trieste Potato Cake, 131
prunes
   Chocolate Prune Cake, 369
   Prune Parfait Pie, 349
   Rabbit with Prunes in Cider Sauce, 248
   Raisin Prune Pie, 350
pumpkin
   Braised Pumpkin, 106
   Golden Pumpkin Pie, 335
   Nut Pumpkin Gems, 380
   Pumpkin and Long Bean Curry, 122
   Pumpkin Gnocchi, 308
   Pumpkin Ice Cream Pie, 349
   Pumpkin Nut Bread, 381
   Pumpkin Soup, 96
Puri, 114

quail
   Birds' Nest Soup with Quail Eggs, 83
   Broiled Quails, 236
   Mango Quails, 241
   Marinated Roast Quails, 242
   Quails Poached in Port, 246

Quails with Cherry Stuffing, 247
Quails with Herb Sauce, 247
Roast Quails and Juniper Berry Sauce, 250
Roast Quails with Rice, 250
Wrapped Quails with Grapes, 255
quiches
   Chicken Quiche, 203
   Crab Quiche, 170
   Quiche Lorraine, 65

rabbit
   Casserole of Rabbit with Lentils, 236
   Creole Rabbit, 236
   Farmer's Rabbit Pie, 236
   Honeyed Rabbit, 241
   Rabbit with Maple Sauce, 247
   Rabbit with Prunes in Cider Sauce, 248
   Tamarillo Rabbit, 252
radishes
   Radish Balls with Scallops, 122
   Skewered Chicken Meatballs with Radishes, 227
   White Radish with Sweet Miso Filling, 359
   see also daikon
raisins
   Raisin Prune Pie, 350
   Sour Cream Raisin Pie, 352
raspberries
   Chilled Raspberry Whip, 326
   Macaroon Raspberry Torte, 342
   Peil Wyke Raspberry Syllabub, 348
   Raspberry Fool, 350
   Raspberry Peanut Squares, 381
Ratatouille, Sicilian, 124
ravioli
   Ravioli in Chicken Broth, 96
   Ravioli Stuffed with Fish and Ricotta Cheese, 154
Red Fruit Dessert, 351
rhubarb
   Country Rhubarb Tart, 330
   Fluffy Rhubarb Pie, 332
rice
   Black Risotto, 135
   Buttered Saffron Rice with Cashew Nuts, 135
   Chicken Rice Cake, 137
   Coconut Rice, 137
   Cold Turkey Pilaf, 137
   Compressed Rice Cakes, 137
   Fried Rice, 140
   Ginger Rice, 141
   Goose Liver Pilaf, 141
   Herbed Rice Moulds, 142
   Indonesian Fried Rice, 143
   Lotus Rice, 147
   Paella, 152
   Pilau, 307
   Rice and Cheese Balls, 311
   Rice Cooked in Coconut Milk, 154
   Rice with Pork, Tomatoes and Peppers, 154
   Seafood Risotto, 181
   Sevillian Salad, 124
   Shrimp Pilaf, 155
   Shrimp Rice, 155
   Spit-Roasted Chicken with Piquant Rice, 159
   Sushi Rice Cakes, 159
   Tomato Pilaf, 163
   Turmeric Rice, 165
   Vanilla Creamed Rice Pudding, 359
   Venetian Rice and Peas, 165
   Venetian Risotto with Lamb, 297
   Vinegared Rice Salad, 165
   see also sushi
ricotta
   Cannelloni with Spinach and Ricotta Stuffing, 299
   Fried Ricotta, 333
   Ravioli Stuffed with Fish and Ricotta Cheese, 154
   Ricotta-Stuffed Cannelloni with Tomato Sauce, 311
Rigatoni, Tomatoes and Tuna Fish with, 163

Ritz, César, 13, 14
Rock Cakes, 383
Rollmop Salad, 67
Rösti, 131
Roti Paratha, 122

Sacchi, Bartolomeo de, 7
Sachertorte, 351
St. James, Tart of, 356
Salade Niçoise, 123
salmon
    Coulibiac, 169
    Marinated Salmon, 58
    One-Pot Salmon, 177
    Salmon Pie with Dill Sauce, 179
    Salmon Sautéed with Lemon, 179
    Salmon with Horseradish Cream, 67
    Smoked Salmon Feuilletés, 73
    Steamed Salmon with Roe, 188
Samosas, 67
    Beef Samosas, 258
    Vegetable Samosas, 317
sardines
    Sardine Hors d'Oeuvre, 67
    Sardines with Tomatoes, 180
Sauerbraten, Bavarian Style, 257
Sauerkraut, Swabian, 130
scallops
    Radish Balls with Scallops in Cream Sauce, 122
    Satay Scallops, 68
    Scallop Puffs, 69
    Scallops Indienne, 180
    Scallops in Garlic Oyster Sauce, 181
    Scallops in Pernod, 68
    Scallops with Cream, 70
    Scallops with Shrimp and Mushrooms, 181
    Spaghetti with Clams, Scallops and Anchovies, 158
    Whiting Fillets Sandwiched with Scallop Mousseline, 192
Schnitzel, Wiener, 297
Scones, 383
seafood
    Chicken and Seafood Fondue, 198
    Deep Fried Battered Seafood and Vegetables, 172
    Italian Seafood Marinara, 176
    Mixed Seafood Hotpot, 176
    Potage "la Mer", 178
    Quick Seafood Sauce for Pasta, 153
    Rich Noodle Soup with Seafood, 154
    Seafood Chowder, 99
    Seafood Cocktail, 70
    Seafood Risotto, 181
    Seafood Tartlets, 181
    Steamboat, 228
    Trenette with Seafood Sauce, 164
    see also fish; individual fishes and other seafoods
Semolina Crisps, 70
Shoo-Fly Pie, 352
shrimp
    Burmese Cucumber and Shrimp Salad, 108
    Chili-Fried Shrimp, 168
    Chili Shrimp in Coconut Milk, 168
    Clear Soup with Shrimp and Mushroom, 87
    Creamed Shrimp Curry, 172
    Crisp-Fried Shrimp with Garlic and Chili, 49
    Curled Shrimp Steamed with Five Shreds, 49
    Deep Fried Bean Curd, Shrimp and Chicken Fritters, 208
    Deep Fried Pork and Shrimp Rolls, 51
    Deep Fried Shrimp Puffs, 51
    Fried Shrimp Balls, 54
    Herb Marinated Shrimp, 175
    Honey-Glazed Shrimp, 56
    Masala Shrimp, 58
    Nori-Wrapped Shrimp, 60
    Pork, Shrimp and Crab Ball Soup, 96
    Scallops with Shrimp and Mushrooms, 181

Shrimp and Feta Cheese Casserole, 182
Shrimp Biriyani, 182
Shrimp Brochettes with Dill Mayonnaise, 71
Shrimp Curry, 182
Shrimp Fritters, 72
Shrimp in Black Bean Sauce, 182
Shrimp in Garlic Butter, 72
Shrimp in Wine and Chili Sauce, 184
Shrimp Pie, 184
Shrimp Pilaf, 155
Shrimp Rice, 155
Shrimp Satay, 184
Shrimp Toast, 72
Shrimp with Yogurt Dressing, 72
Sichuan Shrimp in Chili Oil Sauce, 72
Sliced Cucumber Stuffed with Shrimp and Pork, 73
Sour Shrimp Soup, 100
Steamed Shrimp Canton, 76
Sugar Cane Sticks Coated with Shrimp, 190
Tagliolini with Baby Shrimp, 161
Tamarind Flavored Shrimp, 191
Singaporean cooking, 24–5
Snails in Burgundy Sauce, 74
Snapper Fillets with Herbed Butter, Poached, 178
Snipe with Juniper Butter, Broiled, 236
Snow Cake, 383
Snow Peas, Mushrooms and Bamboo Shoots, 124
Sole
    Sole Normande, 185
    Sole Véronique, 185
    Stuffed Fillets of Sole, 189
soufflés
    Apple Soufflé, 320
    Cheese Soufflé, 300
    Fish Soufflé, 174
    Galway Oyster Soufflé, 55
    Light Banana Soufflé, 341
    Loganberry Soufflé, 342
soups, 83–102
    seafood, 154, 167
Soup Under a Hat, 99
Sour Cream Cookies, Scandinavian, 383
Sour Soup, Hot, 90, 99
Souvlákia, 272
Soyer, Alexis, 13
spaghetti
    Oven-Baked Thin Spaghetti with Spinach, 152
    Spaghetti alla Bolognese, 156
    Spaghetti alla Pizzaiola, 312
    Spaghetti and Cabbage, 313
    Spaghetti and Spinach Frittata, 313
    Spaghetti Sabatini-Style, 156
    Spaghetti Salad, 125
    Spaghetti with Clams, 156
    Spaghetti with Clams, Scallops and Anchovies, 158
    Spaghetti with Mussels and White Wine, 159
    Spaghetti with Tomatoes, Cheese and Bacon, 159
    Spaghetti with Tuna and Mushroom Sauce, 159
Spanakopita, 313
Spätzle, 130
Spice and Sugar Swirls, 383
spinach
    Baked Spinach and Cheese, 40
    Belgique Spinach Bowl, 105
    Cannelloni with Spinach and Ricotta Stuffing, 299
    Creamed Spinach, 111
    Gold Coast Salad, 115
    Lamb on Spinach Purée, 272
    Minced Bean Curd Cake with Spinach, 118
    Oven-Baked Thin Spaghetti with Spinach, 152
    Spaghetti and Spinach Frittata, 313
    Spinach Cheese Puffs, 75
    Spinach Egg Puffs, 126
    Spinach Pie, 313
    Spinach with Bean Curd Dressing, 126
    Spinach with Cottage Cheese, 128
Spring Rolls, 76

Malaysian-Style Spring Rolls, 57
squid
    Fried Squid Rings, 175
    Hot and Spicy Squid, 176
    Linguine with Squid, 145
    Squid and Bamboo Shoot Salad, 186
    Squid and Kiwi Fruit Salad, 76
    Squid in Tamarind Sauce, 187
    Squid Stuffed with Nuts and Rice, 187
    Squid with Spicy Stuffing, 187
    Stuffed Baby Squid in its Ink, 188
steak see beef
Steamboat, 228, 288
strawberries
    Bavarian Strawberry Pie, 323
    Neapolitan Strawberry Ice Cream, 345
    Strawberries à la Romanoff, 354
    Strawberries and Oranges with Port, 354
    Strawberry and Lime Tart, 354
    Strawberry Crêpes Royale, 355
    Strawberry Muffins, 385
    Strawberry Pastries, 355
strudel
    Apple Strudel, 320
    Bavarian Apple Strudel, 364
    Quick Cherry Strudel, 349
Sugar Cane Sticks Coated with Shrimp, 190
Sukiyaki, 290
sushi
    Nori-Rolled Sushi, 151
    Sushi Rice Cakes, 159
    Vinegared Rice Salad, 165

Tabbouleh, 110
tagliatelle
    Asparagus with Tomato-Flavored Tagliatelle, 133
    Tagliatelle with Gorgonzola, 160
    Tagliatelle with Prosciutto and Mushrooms, 160
tagliolini
    Tagliolini with Baby Shrimp, 161
    Tagliolini with Caviar, 161
    Tagliolini with Orange and Tomato Sauce, 161
Tahina Cream Dip, 81
Tamale Pie, 294
Taramosaláta, 53
Tarator Soup, 100
Taro Stuffing, Wild Duck with, 233
Teacake, Spicy Apple, 384
Tea Ring, Swedish, 385
Tempura, 81, 172
Teppanyaki, 276
Teriyaki, 260
    Teriyaki Steaks, 294
terrines, 52, 64, 82
Tirel, Guillaume, 7
tomatoes
    Cheese and Tomato Flan, 300
    Cream Curry of Mushrooms, Peas and Tomato, 302
    Greek Salad, 115
    Green Tomato Pie, 336
    Onion and Tomato Salad, 120
    Sicilian Stuffed Tomatoes, 312
    Stuffed Tomatoes, 130
    Tomatoes in Cream Sauce, 131
    Tomato Pilaf, 163
    Tomato Soup, 100
Tortellini in Broth, 101
Treacle Tart, English, 331
trenette
    Trenette with Fish Sauce, 163
    Trenette with Fresh Tomato, Garlic, Basil and Oil Sauce, 164
    Trenette with Pesto Sauce, 315
    Trenette with Potatoes and Beans, 164
    Trenette with Seafood Sauce, 164
trout
    Fried Trout with Almonds, 175

Fried Yellow Fish with Garlic Chives, 175
Sea Trout Baked in Butter with Sorrel Sauce, 181
Smoked Trout, 74
tuna
Spaghetti with Tuna and Mushroom Sauce, 159
Tomatoes and Tuna Fish with Rigatoni, 163
Tuna and Chili Sambal, 191
Tuna and Peppers in Soy Sauce, 191
Tuna and Spiral Pasta Casserole, 164
Tuna Steak with Wine and Bacon, 192
Turbot with Red Butter Sauce, Fillet of, 173
turkey
Castilian Turkey, 195
Cold Turkey Pilaf, 137
Herb-Roasted Turkey, 216
Roast Turkey with Cherry Stuffing, 226
Stuffed Roast Turkey, 229
Turkey Cobbler, 231
Turkey Fillets in Sour Cream, 232
Turkey Paprikash, 232
Turkey Provençale, 232
Turkey with Ham and Olives, 233
Turnips, Glazed, 114
Tzatziki, 49

Upside-Down Pudding, 359

Vatel, Henri, 9
veal
Emmentaler Schnitzel, 267
Fricassée of Veal with Mushrooms, 268
Goulash, 268
Lasagne with Veal and Pork, 144
Marinated Roast Veal, 274
Osso Bucco, 278
Pork and Veal English Pie, 280
Stuffed Shoulder or Breast of Veal, 290
Stuffed Veal Olives, 290
Swedish Meatballs with Dill Sauce, 291
Veal Escalopes with Chicken Liver Croutons, 294
Veal Pizzaiola, 294
Wiener Schnitzel, 297
vegetables
Assorted Sautéed Vegetables in Cream Sauce, 103
Assorted Vegetables with Bean Curd Skin, 103
Batter-Dipped Vegetables, 104
Bean Curd, Mushrooms and Vegetables, 105
Broiled Vegetables, 107
Chinese Mixed Vegetables, 301
Chinese-Style Vegetable Platter, 110
Chinese Vegetable Omelet, 302
Crustless Vegetable Pie, 302
Hearty Vegetable Soup, 90
Hotpot of Vegetables and Bean Curd, 305
Iced Vegetable Soup, 90
Lentil and Vegetable Curry, 306
Malay Vegetable Salad, 307
Mixed Vegetable Dish, 119
Vegetable Caraway Pie, 316
Vegetable Cutlets in Curry Sauce, 316
Vegetable Kugel, 316
Vegetable Lasagne, 317
Vegetable Pork Rolls, 82
Vegetable Salad Rolls, 294
Vegetable Samosas, 317
Vegetables in Coconut Milk, 316
see also individual vegetables
venison
Australian Roast Venison, 235
Roast Venison, 250
Thirlmere Forest Casserole of Venison, 253
Venison Braise, 253
Venison Pepper Stew, 253
Venison Rolls, 253
Venison Sautéed with Leeks, 255
Venison Stew, 255
Vergé, Roger, 14
Vermicelli with Green Sauce, 317
Vine Leaf Fritters, 82
Vol-au-Vent, Chicken, 205

Wakame Salad, Cucumber and, 112
Waldorf Salad, 317
water chestnuts
"Pearl" Balls, 121
Watercress Soup, 102
wheat, cracked
Cracked Wheat and Parsley Salad, 110
Cracked Wheat Pilaf, 138
Whitebait Fritters, 82
Whiting Fillets Sandwiched with Scallop Mousseline, 192
Wontons, Pork, 65
Won Ton Soup, 102
woodcocks
Roast Woodcocks with Orange Sauce, 251
Woodcock Casserole, 255

Yakitori, 194
Yam Slices, Steamed Pork and, 289
Yeast Cake, Alsatian, 361
Yogurt Balls, 82

Zabaglione Pie, 360
Zabaione, 360
zucchini
Crisp Zucchini Slices, 112
Curried Cauliflower and Zucchini Soup, 89
Marinated Zucchini, 118
Stuffed Zucchini, 80
Zucchini Pie, 317

Dep. Leg. B-1694-88